MANAGERIAL ECONOMICS
WITH APPLICATIONS

Marilu Hurt McCarty
Georgia Institute of Technology

Scott, Foresman and Company
Glenview, Illinois   London, England

Library of Congress Cataloging-in-Publication Data

McCarty, Marilu Hurt.
  Managerial economics with applications.

  Includes bibliographical references and index.
  1. Managerial economics.   I. Title.
HD30.22.M395   1986   338.5'024658   85-22206
ISBN 0-673-18190-1

Preface

For many business managers of the coming generation, a course in managerial economics can be the capstone that integrates and actualizes the substance of their business education. Few of the texts now in use achieve this objective. Their theoretical sophistication places them beyond the interests and abilities of many students and their focus on mathematical derivations reduces their practicality. At the same time, the increasing computational capabilities of business managers make the concepts and procedures of managerial economics even more essential and more accessible than ever before.

This text is intended to bridge the gap between academic procedures and managerial practice. It places microeconomic theory and tools in a setting of accounting, statistics, and finance to illustrate the combined use of these techniques in real-world situations. The writing style is low-key. Calculus is used on occasion, but is thoroughly explained by a parallel stress on economic intuition. (Also, there is an appendix to Chapter 1 that covers the basic techniques and notation of the necessary calculus.) Theoretical explanations are clear, and essential mathematical procedures are developed carefully and simply. The final chapters draw together concepts and procedures from throughout the text into an integrated decision-making process.

This text stresses, perhaps more than other texts in this field:

1. An abundance of real-world boxed examples and numerical case studies,
2. In-depth coverage of core topics such as production costs and product market theory,
3. Complete chapter coverage of topics such as business uncertainty, international business, location theory, and non-profit firms,
4. Research examples throughout, providing examples of the most recent findings and their application to managerial economics, and
5. Several end-of-chapter appendices, providing either optional review material or extensive technical coverage of a topic.

The student should be aware that there is an inexpensive, accompanying IBM microcomputer simulation game in managerial economics and a problems-oriented student workbook, both authored by John Conant of Indiana State University.

This text has benefited from an extensive review process, during which the author responded to all reviewer suggestions consistent with the book's fundamental objective and emphasis. The objective is to integrate economic theory with business practice in such a way that theory is seen to be a useful guide to thinking. The emphasis is on decisions: the development of scientific patterns of thought, including the use of mathematical procedures for modelling significant business relationships and planning strategic policy.

The organization of topics is clear and well developed, with a unifying theme throughout and with easy transitions from chapter to chapter and from topic to topic within chapters. The unifying theme involves the inevitability of technical, human, and/or organizational changes, which call for new business strategy and require scientific analysis of business conditions.

Chapter 1 introduces students to the goals of the text, significant definitions, and procedures for building economic models. The appendix to Chapter 1 reviews differential and integral calculus and the use of LaGrangian multipliers. Chapters 2–4 develop the theory of consumer demand, including the determinants of demand, regression analysis to estimate demand, and econometric forecasting to project demand. Chapters 5–9 explore the core of production functions and cost curves, the use of break-even analysis and isoquants for making production decisions, consideration of long-run economies of scale and industry structure, and a demonstration of linear and geometric programming.

Chapters 10 and 11 concentrate on price policy as it relates to industry structure, including the significance of demand elasticity, firm interdependence, multi-product firms, and advertising. Chapters 12–14 develop topics related to long-term capital investment, including the time value of money and internal rate of return, the cost of capital, and risk and uncertainty in planning investments.

Chapters 15–18 include material new to many courses in managerial economics: the relevance of government regulation for managerial decisions, production decisions in not-for-profit firms, the economic theory of location, and managerial decisions in international business. Each of these final chapters reviews concepts and procedures explained in previous chapters and serves as final evidence of the useful integration of theory and practice.

Text chapters include examples, case studies, and exercises illustrating concrete and significant managerial problems. Some examples of these applications are: ''Competition Comes to the Airlines,'' ''Kaiser Aluminum Deals with Risk and Uncertainty,'' ''The Rise of the Sunbelt,'' ''Breaking Even in Farming,'' ''Measuring Elasticity of Demand for Electricity,'' ''Extracting Chemicals from Vegetable Oil,'' ''Linear Programming for Managing a Bank's Portfolio,'' ''Market Strategy in Inflation,'' ''Scale Economies and Concentration in U.S. Industries,'' ''Choosing Between Investments with Different Economic Lives,'' ''Corporate Contributions,'' ''Changing Costs with Changes in Plant Utilization,'' and ''Choosing Technology for a Foreign Enterprise.''

The positioning of examples and case studies within each chapter is in keeping with the author's belief that students of complex material need to pause occasionally to reflect on, to apply, and to evaluate material they have read. Nevertheless, these sections are set off so that they can be omitted. Both examples and case studies include thought-provoking questions and exercises, which appear also at the end of each chapter. Suggested answers to selected questions are provided at the end of the text.

The ideas presented in the numerous pedagogical aids help ensure that the reader does not lose track of the book's base in economic theory. The accompanying instructor's manual includes a variety of problem sets, providing ample opportunity for practice in the use of mathematical procedures explained in the text.

This textbook is relatively comprehensive and, therefore, lengthy. The decision to include significant amounts of new material was made with the expectation that instructors may be selective in their coverage. For a basic course, the appropriate chapters to cover would be Chapters 1–14, with the possible omission of Chapter 9 (Linear and Geometric Programming) and the possible addition of Chapter 15 (Government and Business). For students with extensive background in finance and statistics, the appropriate chapters would be Chapters 1–11 and Chapters 15–18.

In summary, the text represents a judicious blend of current mainstream thinking with a dash of the new. The base in economic theory is obvious throughout, but the clear intention is to apply the theory in the making of routine and periodical managerial decisions. The approach is contemporary, informative, and interesting and will motivate students to explore the ideas presented further in the business press.

Marilu Hurt McCarty

Table of Contents

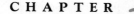
An Introduction to Managerial Economics

Defining the role of a manager is both difficult and quite easy—*difficult* in the sense that a manager's responsibilities range over many varied and complex activities and *easy* in that the important activities can be summed up in one simple phrase. Simply stated, the role of a manager is to make decisions.

Far more than giving orders, evaluating performance, and distributing rewards, the manager's job is to answer important questions. What is to be produced, in what quantities, styles, and models, and for what markets? How should production be carried out, with what resources and technologies, and under what cost conditions? How can the company meet future challenges most effectively, allocating its human and material resources to satisfy immediate and long-range goals?

The manager's role is significant for one important reason: *change*. If circumstances remained the same year after year, managerial decisions might be made once and then implemented again and again without re-examination. In an unchanging business environment, organizations could run themselves, and managers would not be needed. By the same token, unless managers anticipate and plan for change, they are of little value to an organization. Change requires management and, in fact, justifies its existence.

The sources of business change may be classified in three ways: **technical**, **human** or **organizational**, and **financial** or **economic**.

Technical change. Changes in the techniques of production are the most obvious sources of change. A technological breakthrough in a particular indus-

1

try brings changes in industrial processes. For example, the development of industrial robots brought significant changes to the U.S. automobile industry. Substituting robots for high-cost labor helped U.S. auto manufacturers cut production costs and compete more effectively with low-cost auto makers abroad. Changes in the availability and costs of raw materials force changes in methods of production. For example, the recent scarcity of petroleum forced changes in the way many firms use energy. Many manufacturing firms in the United States responded to the high price of purchased energy by arranging to "co-generate" their own power.

Human or **organizational change**. Even more complex than technical changes are changes in the human or organizational environment for production and exchange. Changing consumer markets force changes in the kinds of goods produced for sale. Moreover, as the quality and composition of the workforce change, methods of production must change. Today's better educated workers respond to different sorts of incentives than did workers of the past. They are more concerned about the quality of work life and more eager to participate in business decisions. Many firms have found that using human resources most effectively requires new concepts in business organization, such as quality circles, participatory management, and profit sharing.

Financial or **economic change**. Finally, an important source of change is the financial or economic characteristics of the markets in which firms operate. The availability of financial capital critically affects a firm's ability to function, as construction firms learned to their dismay in 1980. The high cost of funds for home mortgages that year forced many small home builders out of business. Other manufacturing firms found themselves with unsold inventory, financed at ever-rising short-term interest rates. In addition, consumer markets are notoriously fickle, yielding welcome profits (as was true for Levi Strauss and Company in 1980) or embarrassing losses (as was true for Del Taco, a regional corporation, in the same year).

To deal effectively with change emanating from only one of the sources described above requires extensive management training and experience. Few managers are fortunate enough, however, to encounter only one area of change at a time! In general, managers are constantly bombarded with new circumstances requiring careful thought and decisive action. (Some managers see new circumstances as "problems"; others view them as "opportunities.")

Making decisions is especially difficult because there is generally no *absolutely* right or wrong answer. Most decisions involve trade-offs among alternative goals. In this respect, the final answer might be described as "optimum": the best course of action given all the contradictory circumstances facing the decision maker. Suppose, for example, a necessary raw material used in a firm's operation rises in price. Production costs increase and profits fall. Managers must decide on an appropriate strategy for dealing with the change. What would you do?

1. *Would you raise the price the firm charges for its product?* Raising your product's price might cause such a drop in sales that revenue from sales falls. Also, producing a smaller volume could mean that the firm's plant and equip-

ment would be under-utilized and that each item sold would have to bear a larger share of overhead costs. You may find that deciding to increase price causes an even sharper drop in profits and a more severe decrease in the firm's share of the market.

2. *Would you substitute a similar material available at a lower cost?* In many manufacturing processes, adapting a firm's existing equipment to use a substitute material would cost more than the material itself. Also, if the managers of other firms respond as you do, the increase in demand for the substitute material may cause its price to rise. Before choosing this strategy, you also should consider the effect of the substitute material on the quality of your product. Using a substitute material could damage beyond repair your firm's hard-won reputation for quality.

3. *Would you discontinue all production requiring the costly material?* In this case, you would be painfully aware that charges for plant use, equipment, and salaried personnel already in place or contracted for will continue, regardless of whether a salable product is being produced. Until all fixed contracts have run out, you may be forced to carry on production at a loss. You can use sales revenue to cover your direct costs of labor, materials, and utilities, and as much of your fixed overhead as possible. Then, when all of your fixed contracts have run out, you will have to decide whether to continue in this area of business.

4. *Would you adjust your firm's methods of production to use the costly material more efficiently?* Most manufacturing processes can be improved to the point at which further efforts at improving efficiency cost more than they save. You might use the cost increase as the basis for a company-wide campaign to increase productivity. A cost-cutting campaign should ensure that all resources contribute a value to production at least as great as their cost.

A creative manager could probably suggest other possible solutions to this question. The point is that no single decision is absolutely correct. Every decision involves some balancing of costs and benefits. Furthermore, each different course of action raises new questions that must also be evaluated and answered. Your ultimate decision is likely to include a combination of tactics whose relative importance is dependent on the trade-offs implied by your firm's ⁻hoice of goals, whether the goals are short-range profits or long-range market share, a reputation as a technological pace-setter or a reputation for consistent good quality. As a manager, you must weigh all the alternatives in the context of your firm's goals and choose a strategy that comes closest to satisfying those goals.

WHAT IS MANAGERIAL ECONOMICS?

A course in managerial economics is designed to help a manager deal with change. As the name implies, the course combines management with economics. The objective is to analyze management problems in the context of economics—to integrate theory and practice, you might say. Thus, managerial

CASE STUDY 1.1 "Box Stores": Responding to Change in Food Retailing

To illustrate business response to change, let us consider recent trends in the United States that have called for new strategies in the way a particular business is conducted. You will notice that the sources of change in this case are *technical, human or organizational,* and *financial or economic.* Choosing a strategy to deal with change requires managers to evaluate many possible courses of action, consider the benefits of each relative to costs, and arrive at a combination of tactics that yields optimum results.

Not too many years ago, American consumers could call the neighborhood grocer and have the week's food supply delivered to their doorsteps. Some families even had a standing order to be filled regularly, and some grocers sold on credit, running a tab on good customers until payday. Often, such establishments were "Mom and Pop" operations, with "Sonny" driving the delivery truck and Cousin Ed serving at the meat counter. Aunt Edna, who enjoyed figures, kept the books. The store's customers came to know the proprietors and trust the quality of the merchandise.

Change drove most of these establishments out of business, however. The rising prosperity of the 1950s led many families to want a wider variety of food and non-food items than could be carried by small, independent grocers. Cheap gasoline spurred the growth of suburbs, and suburban shopping centers sprang up to serve consumers' every need. The focal point of many shopping centers was the supermarket, perhaps the most fundamental innovation in retailing of this century. Giant chain stores introduced spectacular marketing techniques, with all sorts of razzle-dazzle to capture the affluent shopper's eye.

Supermarkets enjoyed many of the advantages typically associated with production on a large scale. They could buy a wide variety of goods in large quantities, frequently at lower prices than smaller grocers. They could satisfy more customers with proportionally fewer employees, employees whose skills ranged from those of the professional manager to those of the teenager who bagged the groceries. Membership in a nationwide chain brought modern marketing techniques and upbeat advertising to individual stores at low cost. As "Moms" and "Pops" around the country grew old and retired from business, "Sonny" often went to work for the supermarket.

The story doesn't end here, of course. (In economics, stories never do.) New changes are continuously causing new adjustments and still newer strategies in food retailing. Price inflation throughout the 1970s made consumers more conscious of value for their money. Many cost-conscious shoppers refused to pay higher food prices for the sake of fancy store displays, national advertising campaigns, and name-brand products. At the same time, rising food costs and the skyrocketing costs of utilities, land, and labor reduced supermarket profits to less than one cent for each dollar of sales. Hiring qualified personnel became more and more difficult as higher-paying jobs in industry began to attract a better-educated workforce. Supermarket managers had to adapt their strategies to deal with continuing change.

All of these technical, human, and financial changes have called for a strong new marketing technique, not only in retail grocery markets but also in the markets for clothing, household items, and automotive accessories. In the latter markets, the new technique is called discounting; in food retailing it is often referred to as "box stores."

"Box stores" don't have any of the frills that were once thought to be necessary to attract customers. Box stores stock only a limited selection of staple food items, usually stacked in their original shipping boxes. Many feature generic, or "no-brand," household items. Store layout is designed for easy shopping, and hand-lettered signs provide information about prices and special sales. There are few salespeople, and customers bag their own purchases. At the check-out counter, newly developed computerized equipment reads prices, computes total charge, and records inventory information for re-stocking shelves and ordering stock. Low labor and material costs keep prices low and ensure acceptable profits.

Perhaps even more changes are in store for food retailing—changes in consumer markets, in the technology of shopping, and in the costs of doing business. More wives are working today, and there are more single-parent families. For such households, conventional shopping is becoming increasingly difficult. Also, today's higher gasoline prices discourage casual shopping trips, so many consumers are deciding to shop by mail. Large, centrally located mail order houses specialize in goods targeted to the tastes of particular groups of consumers. For mail order houses, low operating costs keep profits high. Some shopping now is even being done electronically. Soon, we may all be able to shop for groceries by using computer connections between retailers and our television sets!

MANAGERIAL THINKING

If you study the previous case carefully, you can find examples of all of the kinds of change we have identified: technical, human and organizational, and financial and economic. Discuss each source of change and describe the benefits and costs of the strategies selected for dealing with these changes.

---

economics is the application of economic theory to business situations requiring decisions.

That is the goal of this text: to apply the tools and procedures of economics to real business problems. An understanding of economic theory is essential, first of all, for analyzing the real circumstances affecting a business firm. Economic theory helps the decision maker strip away non-essential details and identify the most critical elements of a business problem. In practical terms, economic theory helps the decision maker focus on the benefits and the costs that may be caused by alternative courses of action. And, finally, given the goals of a particular firm, economic theory helps the decision maker choose the optimum strategy for satisfying those goals.

Managerial Economics and Microeconomic Theory

Making the decisions mandated by change is the subject of managerial economics. Managerial decision making has an important characteristic in common with the study of economics: that is, awareness of the scarcity of resources. Material resources, physical capital, and human skills are limited. Optimum business decisions require that scarce resources be allocated in a way that comes closest to satisfying a firm's goals. Information is also limited, as is the time for considering alternatives and selecting a strategy. Scarcity of decision-making resources makes the job of managers especially exacting.

The important economic theory for managerial decision making is microeconomics. **Microeconomics** is the study of individual consuming and producing units and is distinguished from **macroeconomics**, which is concerned with the workings of the economic system as a whole. The growth and prosperity of the economic system is, of course, essential to the growth and prosperity of the individual firm and will be considered in this course of study. Our major emphasis, however, will be on microeconomics.

Microeconomics involves the decisions of individual consumers and producers. Individual consumers base their buying decisions on their incomes and accumulated wealth and on the quality and prices of goods and services available in the market. Consumers communicate their preferences to producers through their willingness to purchase particular goods and services at particular prices. Producers base their production decisions on the strength of consumer demand and on the costs and nature of production.

The interaction between consumers and producers takes place in markets and establishes a market price. For this reason our economic system is called the market system. Market prices serve as a *signal to producers* to supply more or less of a particular good or service and a *signal to consumers* to purchase more or less. The importance of price in the market system is the reason why the market system is sometimes called the price system.

Managerial economics is concerned with how producers respond to changes in consumer preferences and changes in the costs and nature of production. The nature of a producer's response depends strongly on the goals of the particular firm. For many firms, the most important goal is to maximize the firm's profit. **Profit** is the difference between the total revenue and the total cost of operating the firm.

In economic theory, a distinction is made between *normal* profit and *economic* profit. **Normal profit** is a necessary payment to the entrepreneur or owner of a business. In the terminology of economics, normal profit is the entrepreneur's ''opportunity cost.'' Unless business operations provide sufficient normal profit, the entrepreneur or owner may allocate his or her resources to some other enterprise. Beyond normal profit, however, some firms may enjoy **economic profit**: payment over and above that necessary to keep existing resources in the business. Economic profit may result from the use of an exceptionally low-cost technology, from the sale of an exceptionally desired good or service, or from an exceptional ability to exclude competing firms from the market. In general, economic profit is expected to be temporary, since the passage of time normally acts to reduce a particular firm's advantage in the market.

Economists consider normal profit a true cost of doing business, along with the costs of materials, labor, electric power, and so forth. If total revenue from operations is greater than all costs (including normal profit), the firm earns positive economic profit. If total revenue is less than full costs, economic profit is negative, and the firm suffers a loss. A firm may be able to sustain a loss for a short period of time, but if losses are expected to continue or worsen, a manager must make the decision of whether to change the firm's fundamental policies or even whether to go out of business entirely.

Scientific Decision Making

Modern managers employ scientific procedures for analyzing market conditions and choosing an optimum strategy. Making decisions scientifically requires a series of definite steps:

Step 1—Define the problem. Managers of business firms receive a continuous flow of information about market conditions: product prices and quantities, materials costs and sources, sales revenues and profits. Managers must organize and interpret incoming data in order to anticipate and define business problems. The relevant data then become the basis for making a business decision.

Step 2—State the objective. Certainly, before the decision-making process is very far along, there should be a clear understanding of the desired results. In general, a firm's objective is assumed to be maximum profit, but this objective is not always so straightforward. The conditions required for maximum profit from current operations may not be consistent with those required for maximum profit over the long run. Other objectives might include minimizing unit production costs in order to become competitive in new markets, producing a mix of products that enables the firm to retain its work force even in recession, satisfying stockholder-owners while maintaining healthy production standards, or meeting community environmental standards most efficiently.

Step 3—Propose alternative solutions and choose the optimum strategy. Step 3 calls for the manager to analyze the factors affecting the market environment and to identify the cause-and-effect relationships among them. Then, the manager can propose alternative strategies and project the expected results of each in terms of the stated objective. Finally, the manager will select the one strategy most likely to satisfy the firm's objective.

Step 4—Implement and evaluate the selected strategy. Once the selected alternative is put into effect, the manager must monitor its results, collecting new information and taking note of further changes in the business environment. Feedback from the current strategy provides some of the data for making the next decision.

Look at the flow diagram in Figure 1.1 for an illustration of scientific decision making. In each step of the decision-making process the manager receives information and decides whether to proceed to the next step. Frequent feedback and constant re-evaluation help ensure decisions that satisfy the firm's objectives. Failure to follow the scientific process outlined in the diagram can mean that decisions are contrary to the firm's objectives, poorly grounded in evidence, and/or logically unsound. Unwise decisions may make the difference between prosperous growth and dismal decline—or even bankruptcy. There is no clear and certain route to correct decisions. However, the improved flow of information to managers and the refinement of analytical tools can add precision to the decision-making process.

Our primary concern in this text is with Step 3: proposing and analyzing alternatives for selecting strategy consistent with a firm's objectives. Analysis

FIGURE 1.1   Scientific Decision Making

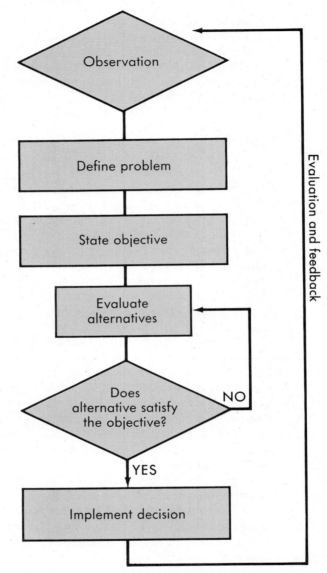

consists of taking apart and explaining a business problem. It requires experimentation in which conditions have been controlled so that the effects of systematic changes can be accurately measured.

Scientific analysis frequently occurs in laboratories in which environmental conditions can be precisely duplicated, examined, and controlled by the researcher. Economic analysis requires experimentation of a different sort, however. Changes in the economic environment affect the lives and behavior of *people,* and people usually are not readily available to participate in laboratory experiments. Therefore, analysis of economic events must be based on *hypothetical* changes whose results can be predicted on the basis of an economic model. Whereas a physical scientist makes a change in a controlled laboratory environment, an economist must "assume" changes in real-world conditions and deduce the results from the behavior of an economic model. Economic models are important tools of managerial economics.

Economic Models

An **economic model** is a method of analyzing and explaining circumstances in the economic environment. It is a simplified view of reality, stated verbally, mathematically, and often graphically.

Managers use economic models to simulate business conditions and to test hypothetical changes associated with alternative business strategies. Results obtained from an economic model can then be compared with a firm's objectives so that an optimum strategy can be selected. We will make much use of models in this text. Therefore, it is appropriate to describe in detail the essential components of an economic model and show how a simple model can guide decision makers.

Some definitions are essential at this point:

Variables. Variables are the kinds of data in the economic environment that are to be included in the model: such things as material costs, consumer incomes, and prices and quantities of particular goods and services. In any economic model variables may be labeled *independent* or *dependent* variables. **Independent variables** are those that are subject to change, either by the decision maker (**endogenous independent variables**) or by some outside force (**exogenous independent variables**). An example of an independent variable is the number of units of a good or service a firm may produce during a particular period of time (endogenous). Another is average family income in the local market (exogenous).

Dependent variables are those whose value *depends on* the value of the independent variables included in the model. Total production cost is a dependent variable that depends on a firm's total production. The firm's sales of a particular consumer good or service is a dependent variable that depends on average family income.

Functions. The relationship between an independent variable (or variables) and the dependent variable is expressed in mathematical form as a function. Thus, total production cost for a particular period of time is a function of the total quantity of output produced, or TC = function $(Quantity)$ = $f(Q)$. Sales are a function of local family income, or S = function $(Income)$ = $f(Y)$. When actual values are included in the functional relationship, the result is an equation that measures the precise relationship among the variables. For instance, with constant costs of $100 per week and material costs of $5 for each unit produced, an equation for the total cost function might be

$$TC = f(Q) = 100 + 5(Q).$$

The use of mathematical shorthand helps decision makers examine many aspects of the business environment and the relationships among them. When this type of model is used, the resulting business decision is more likely to take into consideration all significant information and yield the desired results.

Assumptions. Whether the actual results of a business decision conform to those of a model may depend on the validity of the analyst's assumptions. **Assumptions** are the analyst's beliefs concerning certain fundamental characteristics of the environment, including the relationships among the independent and dependent variables. Thus, assumptions involve the *form* of the equation used to represent functional relationships. The form of the total cost equation above depends on assumptions about the actual behavior of costs at various levels of production. What are the assumptions behind a sales equation of the form $S = f(Y) = Y^2 - 400$?[1]

Parameters. Some values in every equation remain the same, while systematic changes occur in the values of the independent and dependent variables. The unchanging values in an equation are called the **parameters**. Parameters include **constants, coefficients** applied to the independent variables, and **exponents** of the independent variables. The parameters define the precise relationship among the independent and dependent variables. Thus, they reflect the analyst's assumptions. The parameters of the total cost and sales equations above are the constants 100 and 400, the coefficients 5 and 1, and the exponent 2.

Ceteris Paribus. We have noted that a model is a simplified view of reality that omits many of the complexities that exist in the real economic environment. A model describes the relationships among certain significant variables in the environment and assumes that circumstances outside the model remain briefly unchanged. Holding outside circumstances unchanged in a model is expressed in the form of a Latin phrase, **ceteris paribus**. While the condition ceteris paribus reduces the realism of a model, it is a necessary condition for observing the variables of special interest to the analyst.

Models can be presented verbally, algebraically, and graphically[2] as well as in tabular form. A verbal presentation may be a rather broad statement of the assumed relationship among the variables such as the statement that food prices affect the volume of food sales. Algebraic and graphical presentations require more precise parameters that measure the precise effect of a change in one variable on the behavior of another. Thus, food sales $= S_f = f(p_f) = 5$

---

1. The assumptions are that sales would be -400 if income (Y) should fall to zero and that sales increase exponentially as income increases.

2. Graphical presentation is not possible if the number of variables exceeds the dimensions of the space for graphing.

TABLE 1.1 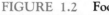 Demand for Food

Price per bushel (p_f)	Sales in millions (S_f)
.50	10
1.00	5
1.50	3.3
2.00	2.5

FIGURE 1.2 Food Sales

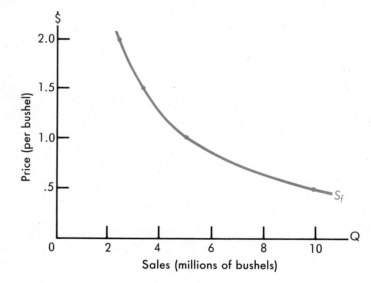

Sales (millions of bushels)

million/p_f, where p_f represents the price of food. When the parameters of a model are known, the variables may also be presented in tabular form and plotted on a graph as is done here.

A graph helps the analyst estimate the effect on the dependent variable of a small change in the independent variable. For example, can you use the graph in Figure 1.2 to estimate the effect on food sales of a price increase from $1.00 to $1.25 per bushel?[3]

---

3. Find the point on the line that corresponds to a price of $1.25 and measure the difference in quantity from the point corresponding to a price of $1.00.

EXAMPLE 1.1   Constructing an Economic Model

One example of an economic model is the model of economic profit. A profit model includes equations representing a firm's **total revenue** from sales (TR) and **total cost** of production (TC). The independent variable in both equations is the quantity of the product (Q) to be produced. The functional relationship among the variables describes the behavior of total sales revenue and total cost when various quantities of output are produced, ceteris paribus. When the revenue and cost functions are combined, the result is a model of economic profit.

To illustrate, suppose a grocery sells farm produce in a competitive market at a price of $p = \$8$ per bushel. Total revenue per day is a function of quantity sold at the market price:

$$\text{Total revenue} = (TR) = f(Q) = (p)(Q) = 8(Q).$$

Total cost includes the firm's constant cost of $50 per day for labor and utilities plus an additional cost of $6 for each bushel of farm produce sold:

$$\text{Total cost} = (TC) = f(Q) = 50 + 6(Q).$$

Economic profit per day is the difference between total revenue and total cost:

$$\text{Economic profit} (\pi) = TR - TC = 8(Q) - [50 + 6(Q)].$$

Thus, economic profit is also a function of volume of sales:

$$\text{Economic profit} (\pi) = f(Q) = 2(Q) - 50.$$

The constant 50 and the coefficients 8 and 6 are the parameters of the total revenue and total cost equations. The parameters and the relationships among the variables are the assumptions on which the profit model is based. The model of economic profit enables the analyst to estimate the amount of the dependent variable, profit, associated with any quantity of the independent variable, sales. Thus, the sale of 50 bushels per day would yield an estimated economic profit determined by the equation:

$$\text{Economic profit} (\pi) = 2(50) - 50 = \$50 \text{ per day.}$$

Sale of only 20 bushels would yield a **negative profit,** or estimated **loss** of $-\$10$ per day because:

$$\text{Economic profit} (\pi) = 2(20) - 50 = -\$10 \text{ per day.}$$

This model of economic profit can be shown graphically as well as algebraically. In Figure A, volume of sales per day (Q) is measured along the horizontal axis and revenue and costs are measured along the vertical axis. The total revenue equation is drawn as a straight line rising from the origin where $Q = 0$ and $TR = 8(0) = 0$. The slope of the TR line depends on price. With a price of $8, its slope is 8/1, indicating an increase in TR of $8 for each unit increase in Q. At $Q = 20$ and $Q = 50$, total revenue per day is read in Figure A by following the dashed lines to the total revenue line and reading the corresponding amount on the vertical axis.

Total cost includes a constant cost of $50 per day and an additional $6 for each unit increase in Q. Thus, the line representing total cost begins at a value of $50 on the vertical axis, where $Q = 0$, and rises with a slope of 6/1.

Economic profit per day is the difference between total revenue and total cost. In Figure A, economic profit is the vertical distance between the TR line and the TC line. At $Q = 20$, the vertical distance is $-\$10$, and at $Q = 50$ the vertical distance is $50. Economic profit per day is represented graphically in Figure B. For quantities of Q less than $Q = 25$, economic profit per day is negative. For quantities of Q greater than 25, economic profit increases $2 for each bushel of farm produce sold.

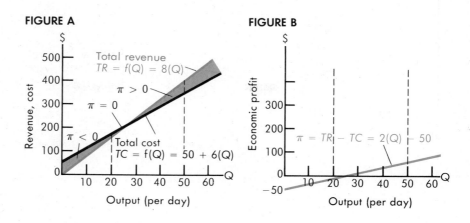

FIGURE A

FIGURE B

APPLYING THE MODEL

The model illustrated in Figures A and B is useful for business planning. Its validity for decision making, however, depends on the validity of the assumptions on which it is based. A change in any of the parameters in the model or a change in the relationship among the variables would change the results.

Suppose, for example, the grocery described previously normally sells Q = 30 bushels of farm produce per day for economic profit of $\pi = 2(30) - 50 = \$10$. The firm has an opportunity to increase its hours of operation and change its method of sales. Longer hours of operation will increase the firm's constant charges for labor and utilities by \$10 per day, but new selling technology will reduce unit costs by \$1 per bushel. Managers can use this economic model to estimate the effect of the proposed change on economic profit. Changing the parameters changes the economic profit equation to:

$$\text{Economic profit } (\pi) = TR - TC = 8(Q) - [60 + 5(Q)] = 3(Q) - 60.$$

What is economic profit using these parameters when 30 bushels are sold daily? Substituting for this value yields:

$$\pi = 3(30) - 60 = \$30 \text{ per day.}$$

The proposed change in the parameters of the model has a favorable effect on the firm's objective, economic profit. By changing the underlying assumptions of the model, the decision maker can make a more informed judgment about the proposed change in sales techniques.

Now let us consider another question that involves objectives other than economic profit. Suppose the grocery wishes to expand its share of the local consumer market by aggressive price cutting. Managers are willing to reduce selling price and accept negative profit of up to \$10 a day temporarily in order to attract new customers. With a selling price of only $p = \$7$, how many bushels of produce must the firm sell if daily losses are to be held to \$10?

Remember the original economic profit equation:

$$\text{Economic profit } (\pi) = 8(Q) - [50 + 6(Q)] = 2(Q) - 50.$$

Now substitute the proposed values for π and price:

$$-10 = 7(Q) - [50 + 6(Q)] = 1(Q) - 50$$

and solve:

$$-10 = 1(Q) - 50$$
$$= 40 = 1(Q).$$

Therefore, Q = 40 units. Producing and selling only 10 additional bushels per day would enable the firm to achieve its profit (loss) objective at the lower selling price.

MANAGERIAL THINKING

Write an equation that describes the cost of leasing a copy machine for three years when the lease charge diminishes by 5 percent each year and maintenance and equipment costs increase by 10 percent each year.

In this text, we will use all four forms of presentation and state assumptions about the relationships among the independent and dependent variables. We will begin with simple assumptions, leaving out many of the variables that affect economic behavior (ceteris paribus) so that we can concentrate on a significant few.

MARGINAL ANALYSIS AND MARGINAL CHANGES

The circumstances described in Example 1.1 involve decisions at the *margin* of the problem. **Marginal decisions** are incremental changes in current operations. Decisions to produce 10 additional units per week, to employ 5 additional units of labor, or to reduce price by 10 percent are incremental or marginal decisions. Marginal decisions differ from absolute decisions, such as decisions to produce a total of 50,000 units per week, to employ a total of 100 workers, and to set a unit price of $10. Thus, the economic model in Example 1.1 projects the expected outcome of a marginal decision to alter the firm's sales techniques or to change product price.

Look again at the equations represented in Figures A and B of Example 1.1. The total revenue, total cost, and economic profit equations in Example 1.1 can be described as **linear equations**. Linear equations have constant slopes over their entire length. In a linear equation, the dependent variable changes by the same amount for each unit change in the independent variable. The change in the dependent variable is identified by the coefficient of the independent variable. Thus, in our example, total revenue and total cost change by 8 and 6 dollars, respectively, with each unit increase in bushels of farm produce sold.

With constant changes in total revenue and total cost, we say that marginal revenue and marginal cost are constant. **Marginal revenue** and **marginal cost** are defined as the *change in* total revenue and total cost associated with a *change in* total output. Constant marginal revenue and marginal cost are shown by the constant slopes of the total revenue and total cost lines.

FIGURE 1.3   Non-Linear Total Revenue, Total Cost, and Economic Profit

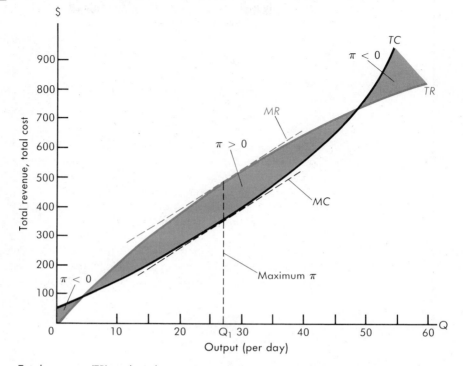

Total revenue (*TR*) and total cost (*TC*) are non-linear functions of volume of sales (Q). Economic profit (π) is the difference between total revenue and total cost. For quantities less than 5 or greater than 50 bushels, economic profit is negative.

Such conditions are not likely to persist in a real business environment. In fact, linear changes in total revenue and total cost would mean that increasing sales *ad infinitum* would yield continuing increases in the firm's profits!

We know this does not happen in the real world. In real markets, increasing sales *ad infinitum* could take place only if price were to be reduced. Likewise, producing additional goods for sale would ultimately create scarcities in resource markets and higher production costs. Lower prices for additional sales will mean smaller changes in total revenue. Higher costs for additional production will mean greater increases in total costs. Both these circumstances will call for changes in the slopes of the total revenue and total cost lines.

These more realistic business conditions are shown in Figure 1.3. In this situation, the change in total revenue decreases with volume of sales. Smaller increases in total revenue cause the total revenue line to rise with a decreasing slope. In this case, we say that marginal revenue decreases. Similarly, additions to total cost increase with volume. These larger changes in total costs cause the total cost line to rise with an increasing slope. Here, we say that marginal cost increases. In general, marginal revenue and marginal cost are shown as the slopes of total revenue and total cost.

When the total revenue and total cost lines have changing slopes, the behavior of profit varies with quantity of output. Again, economic profit is defined as the difference between *TR* and *TC*:

$$\pi = TR - TC.$$

The graph of economic profit in Figure 1.4 measures the vertical distance between the total revenue and total cost lines in Figure 1.3. Note that profit in Figure 1.4 does not continue to increase *ad infinitum* with increased volume of sales. Because marginal revenue falls and marginal cost increases, economic profit reaches a maximum amount and then falls back to zero. In fact, given the behavior of marginal revenue and marginal cost, beyond a certain volume of sales, economic profit would be negative. That is, the firm would suffer a loss.

The equations graphed in Figures 1.3 and 1.4 are described as non-linear or curvilinear. Curvilinear equations like these are expressed algebraically as quadratic equations. Quadratic equations have the form

$$Y = a + b(X) + c(X)^2,$$

where *Y* and *X* represent the values of the dependent and independent variables, respectively.

The quadratic equation for total revenue in this case is

$$\text{Total revenue } (TR) = f(Q) = 0 + 20(Q) - .1(Q)^2.$$

The constant $a = 0$ indicates that for sales of $Q = 0$, total revenue would also be zero. The coefficients $b = 20$ and $c = -.1$ and the exponent 2 measure the initial upward slope of the *TR* line and its diminishing slope as *Q* increases.

The quadratic equation for total cost is

$$\text{Total cost } (TC) = f(Q) = 50 + 9(Q) + .1(Q)^2.$$

The constant $a = 50$ indicates constant costs of $50 even if $Q = 0$ units are produced. The coefficients $b = 9$ and $c = .1$ and the exponent 2 measure the initial upward slope of the *TC* line and its increasing slope as *Q* increases.

Economic profit is also described by a quadratic equation:

$$\text{Economic profit } (\pi) = f(Q) = TR - TC = -50 + 11(Q) - .2(Q)^2.$$

The constant $a = -50$ indicates negative profit when $Q = 0$. The coefficients $b = 11$ and $c = -.2$ and the exponent 2 measure the initial upward slope of the π line and its diminishing slope as *Q* increases.

FIGURE 1.4 **Non-Linear Economic Profit**

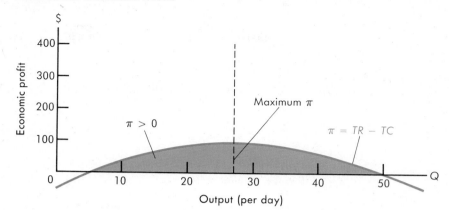

Determining the Zero-Profit Quantity of Output

There are some simple algebraic tools for identifying specific values in a quadratic equation like the profit equation graphed in Figure 1.4. For example, managers are interested in determining the quantity of output (Q) at which economic profit (π) would be zero. The zero-profit quantity of output is the value of Q at which the profit line crosses the horizontal axis and the firm "breaks even." For quadratic equations, the value of the independent variable at which the graph crosses the horizontal axis can be determined by using the quadratic formula:

$$X = \frac{-b \pm \sqrt{b^2 - 4ac}}{2c}$$

where X represents the value of the independent variable and a, b, and c are the parameters of the equation. The quadratic formula identifies the value of the independent variable (X) at which a quadratic equation has a value of zero.

Substitute the values of the parameters, a, b, and c, from the economic profit equation in our previous example and solve for the independent variable, quantity of output (Q). Substituting for these values yields:

$$Q = \frac{-11 \pm \sqrt{121 - 40}}{-.4} = 5 \text{ and } 50.$$

Thus, the sale of fewer than 5 or more than 50 bushels of produce per day would yield negative economic profit. The firm will "break even" with sales of 5 bushels but will suffer economic losses with sales of more than 50 bushels. Refer to Figure 1.4 to confirm these results.

Determining the Profit-Maximizing Quantity of Output

Another piece of useful information to managers is the quantity of output (Q) at which the firm would collect maximum economic profit. **Maximum economic profit** occurs at the quantity of output at which the vertical distance between total revenue and total cost on a graph is greatest. On a graph of TR and TC, the maximum vertical distance occurs where the slopes of the two curves are equal. Since the slopes of TR and TC represent marginal revenue and marginal cost, maximum economic profit occurs where marginal revenue is equal to marginal cost: $MR = MC$ yields maximum economic profit.

To understand this, compare the relationships shown in Figures 1.3 and 1.4. Production begins to be profitable with a daily output of $Q = 5$ units. This is the point at which TR rises above TC. The steeper slope of MR at this range indicates that increases in output add more to revenue than to costs so that economic profit increases. Gradually, however, further increases in sales require price reductions and yield smaller additions to revenue. Likewise, increases in production create higher costs. Additions to economic profit become smaller until at $Q = 27.5$ units additions to revenue are precisely equal to additions to costs. When the slopes of TR and TC are equal, the distance between them is greatest and economic profit is maximum. Beyond the profit-maximizing quantity of output, additions to revenue are smaller than additions to costs, and economic profit falls with increases in output. At $Q = 50$, TR once again falls below TC, and economic profit becomes negative.

The dashed lines measuring the slopes of TR and TC in Figure 1.3 are parallel at the value of Q at which the slopes of the two curves are equal. This is also the point of maximum profit, as shown in Figures 1.3 and 1.4 at $Q = 27.5$.

A LOOK BACK

We might summarize the content of a course in managerial economics as "the application of scientific analysis to business decisions." Scientific analysis of the economic environment can help managers evaluate alternative strategies in order to select the optimum strategy, the strategy that comes closest to satisfying a firm's objectives.

We illustrated modern circumstances for managerial decision making in the case study on "Box Stores." Very likely, chain store managers followed a step-by-step process similar to the one outlined in this chapter for deciding on their new marketing strategy.

Step 1 was to recognize the environmental changes that were cutting into the profits of retail grocers, that is, the technical, human, and financial changes that were creating new problems and opening new opportunities in food retailing.

Step 2 was to define the firm's objectives, including profit, market share, and long-range efficiency in the use of scarce resources.

Step 3 was to propose alternative marketing strategies and compare their expected results by using the tools of managerial economics.

Remember that the fundamental tool of managerial economics is the economic model. We have seen that an economic model includes variables, functions, assumptions, and parameters. Let's consider the significant elements in food retailing that should be included in a model for deciding an optimum strategy.

Variables. Managers of retail groceries have certain immediately controllable variables: number and skill level of employees, number of food and non-food items, number of brands to stock, days and hours of store operation, and so forth. Other variables are controllable over longer periods of time, such as location and size of stores, installation of technical equipment, and introduction of new marketing techniques. All these things constitute the independent variables whose values are determined by the decision maker. Dependent variables are the results of managerial decisions. Dependent variables include such things as total costs, revenue from sales, economic profit, and market share. In a sense, the dependent variable represents a firm's objective. The value of the dependent variable reflects managers' expectations concerning the effect of proposed changes in the independent variables on a firm's objective.

Functions. A function states the relationship between independent and dependent variables in an economic model. It is based on actual data collected over time and on a manager's informed judgment regarding such things as:

1. The volume of total sales associated with various store sizes and locations, consumer demand for particular food and non-food items, and the amount of advertising expenditures.
2. The amount of total costs associated with particular sizes and locations of stores, number of employees, use of technical equipment, and stocks of goods for sale.

Assumptions. Observation and experience help managers draw up specific assumptions about the relationships among all of the pertinent variables.

Parameters. Finally, parameters defining specific relationships are included in the revenue and cost equations. Alternative strategies are proposed, and the equations are solved for the value of the dependent variable associated with each strategy.

At this point in our example, chain store managers would have compared the results of the economic model with the objectives stated in Step 2. The strategy that came the closest to satisfying the firm's objectives would have been considered the optimum choice and would have been implemented in Step 4. Throughout the process of analyzing the market environment and implementing business strategy, managers frequently would have referred to Steps 1 and 2 to decide whether the problem and the objective had been defined correctly.

Finally, competent managers would have remembered the ceteris paribus limitations of their model and would have looked for circumstances that might change the fundamental relationships involved. They would have looked for new information that might improve the realism of the decision model, and they would have been aware that the technical, human, and financial conditions that made box stores profitable might change again, making them obsolete and calling for newer strategies.

The use of the scientific method as described in this chapter has greatly advanced microeconomic theory. Mathematical analysis has brought a significant degree of precision to managerial decision making, enabling managers to compare hypothetical results of alternative strategies and subsequently choose an optimum strategy. Subjective judgment on the part of the manager is still necessary, however. No mathematical tool can ever take into account all the minute bits of information that are routinely processed by a creative manager. No algebraic equation can correctly predict future conditions and guarantee favorable results for managerial decisions.

In short, the mathematical tools of managerial economics are just that: *tools,* designed to help managers understand fundamental economic principles, judge alternative solutions to business problems, and estimate the effects of changes in the business environment. Mathematical tools force managers to organize their thinking scientifically. In this sense, these tools help managers learn *how* to make decisions, but they cannot actually make the decisions. *They cannot dictate exactly what should be done.* Like any other tools, the tools of managerial economics must be used carefully by managers who understand the tools' limitations and who contribute their own judgment to the decision-making process.

A LOOK AHEAD

The objective of this text is to help future managers learn to make optimum decisions. Toward that purpose, we will develop and use economic models to describe the environment in which a firm operates and to project the results of alternative policy decisions. We will begin by discussing the use of economic models appropriate for describing, analyzing, and projecting consumer demand. Then we will focus on the supply side of markets, examining the effect on production costs of a firm's response to consumer demand. We will contrast short-run policy decisions with long-term decisions in which the supply of capital resources can be altered to suit changing market conditions and changing objectives of a firm. We will show how a firm's capital resources can be financed efficiently, and how firms can meet new market circumstances effectively. Finally, we will consider in detail the significance for managers of the actions of the federal government regarding business and the increasing international involvement of U.S. businesses.

In exploring these areas, this text will employ four methods of description and analysis: verbal, mathematical, graphical, and tabular. Increasing familiarity with the combined use of these techniques will help students describe more precisely underlying economic conditions and will provide more scientific bases for making optimum business decisions.

CASE STUDY 1.2   The "Graying" of America

Major changes are in store for American business firms in the 1980s and 1990s—not only as a result of changing technology, but as a result of an aging population.

During the Great Depression of the 1930s, hard times restricted family formation in the United States, and population growth slowed. Then, during World War II and its aftermath, prosperity encouraged population growth, and the United States experienced a historic "baby boom." By the mid 1960s, however, "boom" had turned to "bust," with lower than normal population growth for the United States once again.

Changes in the rate of population growth make for changes in the age distribution of the population and corresponding changes in markets for consumer goods and services. When the "baby boom" generation entered the teen years, for example, recording studios, fast-food restaurants, recreational businesses, and firms producing school supplies became especially profitable. When the "baby boom" generation reached adulthood, apartments, consumer electronics, and automobiles garnered much of its spending. Around the turn of this century, "baby boomers" will become retirees, with an entirely new set of wants to be satisfied in consumer markets.

Over the next half-century, the median age of the U.S. population is expected to increase to about 38 years of age (from about 30 years of age in 1980). Improved health and medical care is enabling older people to live longer and is keeping middle-aged people in the job market longer. With fewer dependent children to care for, more wives will also enter the labor force. Families will have more money to spend on discretionary items. Many analysts predict that the popularity of junk food, popular music, and faddish clothing will fade and that the most popular forms of recreation and entertainment will become more sedate. Generally higher levels of education among "baby boom" adults will make for greater sophistication in tastes and cultural interests. A higher level of consumer sophistication will make these shoppers more conscious of quality in the things they buy. Housing patterns may also change to accommodate the living patterns of childless adults.

When the "baby boom" generation reaches middle and old age, further changes may be expected. The nation will require greater emphasis on health and medical care, more volunteer work opportunities for old people, and cheap food and personal care items for the low-income elderly.

MANAGERIAL THINKING

Consult the business section of your local paper or *The Wall Street Journal* for information about particular manufacturing firms whose sales are likely to be affected by the changing age structure of the U.S. population. What strategies would you propose for adjusting to new patterns of consumer demand in the coming decades?

Source: "The End of the Youth Culture," *U.S. News & World Report*, October 3, 1977, pp. 54–58.

SUMMARY

Changing business conditions call for managers who can evaluate new information and decide new strategy. Microeconomic theory can provide the framework for scientific decision making. The four steps in making informed decisions are: (1) define the problem, (2) state the objective,

(3) propose alternatives and select the optimum strategy, and (4) implement and evaluate the decision.

Analysis of alternatives involves the use of economic models, simplified views of reality in which managers test hypothetical changes associated with alternative business strategies. Algebraic models using calculus can be employed to decide the profit-maximizing quantity of output, at which marginal revenue is equal to marginal cost. For quadratic equations, the quadratic formula can be employed to identify the zero-profit quantities of output.

The usefulness of economic models depends on the validity of their assumptions and on correct estimates of their parameters.

KEY TERMS

technical change

organizational change

economic change

microeconomics

macroeconomics

profit

normal profit

economic profit

economic model

independent variable

dependent variable

endogenous independent variable

exogenous independent variable

function

constant

coefficient

exponent

assumption

parameter

ceteris paribus

negative profit

marginal decision

linear equation

total revenue

total cost

marginal revenue

marginal cost

maximum economic profit

QUESTIONS AND PROBLEMS

1. Consult recent issues of *Business Week* or *The Wall Street Journal* for examples of *technical* changes that call for new strategies in particular industries. Imagine yourself in the role of a decision maker and list the alternative strategies available to your firm. What independent variables can you control (endogenous) and what independent variables are beyond your control (exogenous)?

2. A major *human* change affecting the U.S. economy is the increase of single-parent households. What industries are most strongly affected by this change, and how might particular industries adapt their strategies to profit from it?

3. A critical economic factor for any firm is the degree of competition in its relevant market. What are some ways of adapting business strategies to deal with an increase in competition?

4. "Your Place" Tune-Up Service performs auto tune-ups in the parking lots of business firms while the owners are at work. In this way, the firm minimizes fixed overhead charges and is able to charge only $50 per tune-up. The firm has three employees, each earning $700 a month, and leases a van for $500 a month. Gas and maintenance expenses average $100 a month, and materials for each tune-up are $20. Write equations for total revenue, total cost, and economic profit. How many tune-ups must the firm perform each month to cover all its costs and begin to earn a profit?

5. Construct a graph of the model described in Question 4. Label the horizontal axis "Units of Service" and the vertical axis "Dollars." Graph lines representing total revenue and total cost. Label positive and negative economic profit. Use your graph to estimate profit at a production level of 120 tune-ups per month.

6. The van leasing firm mentioned in Question 4 has offered to sell "Your Place" its leased van in return for five monthly payments of $600 and 15 free tune-ups per month over this five-month period. Write a new economic profit equation that will help in making this decision. How will the profit equation change after five months? What additional information is needed before a decision can be made on this offer? What factors would influence a manager's decision?

7. Examine the hypothetical cost equation that follows. Identify the independent and dependent variables. What has the writer of this equation assumed about the effect of the variable K on total cost? How is the effect of R different from that of L. Can this equation be shown graphically?

$$TC = f(L, R, K) = 700 + 5L + 6R - .5R^2 + .1K.$$

8. During the 1960s and 1970s demand for electric power in the northeastern United States grew at a rate approaching 7 percent annually. In anticipation of increased demand, power companies increased substantially their investment in new productive facilities, incurring high levels of debt. Can you speculate on some of the problems for power producers in the 1980s? How had the tools of economics been misused in this case?

9. Ferrell Shipping Company has been unprofitable for several years. Currently, management has two alternative proposals for dealing with this problem: (1) Selling some of the firm's assets would reduce fixed monthly costs from $4,500 to $3,500 and raise unit costs per ton-mile from $150 to $175. (2) Borrowing $20 million to purchase more modern equipment would raise monthly fixed costs to $4,750 but reduce unit costs to $125 per ton-mile. Market demand is expected to remain at about 3,700 ton-miles a month. Which alternative should the firm choose?

10. Study each of the following situations and describe the technical, human/organizational, and financial/economic changes that require decisive

action. Imagine yourself as the manager of a firm that is affected by these changes and discuss alternative methods of solving the problem (or dealing with the "challenge"). What additional information should you seek before selecting a strategy? Can you anticipate other significant changes that may call for further consideration in the future?

a. U.S. refiners of gasoline are faced with slow growth in consumer demand as autombiles become more fuel-efficient. At the same time, world oil producers have shifted toward greater production of "sour" crude, low-quality petroleum with high sulfur content. De-regulation of oil prices in the United States has caused a substantial rise in "sour" crude prices at the same time that substantial funds are needed to equip refineries to accept the lower-quality crude.

b. Between 1940 and 1980 an estimated 10 million U.S. workers were exposed to asbestos. Ten to twenty years after exposure, workers exposed to asbestos can develop lung disease, including cancer. Estimates of the proportion of lung cancer fatalities associated with asbestos exposure are between 20 and 25 percent. Benzene, vinyl chloride, diethylstilbestrol, and other substances in work environments have also been linked to cancer in humans. Thousands of lawsuits demanding compensation for disabled workers are filed every year. Settlements have resulted in the distribution of millions of dollars to affected workers.

c. A tennis racket manufacturer bought the right to the design of an innovative tennis racket which had been used with astonishing success in tennis tournaments. Called the "spaghetti" racket, the equipment contains only six horizontal strings and fourteen vertical strings held together by narrow plastic guides. Kits for re-stringing existing rackets were produced, but sales collapsed following a judge's ruling that the rackets are unacceptable for tournament play.

A Review of Differential and Integral Calculus

A powerful mathematical tool used in managerial economics is differential calculus. **Differentiation** provides ways to measure the change in a dependent variable associated with a small change in an independent variable. Thus, calculus enables us to measure "marginal" values associated with a one-unit change in an independent variable. The marginal revenue from an increase in sales is

$$\Delta TR/\Delta Q = MR.$$

The marginal cost of an increase in output is

$$\Delta TC/\Delta Q = MC.$$

And, the marginal profit from increased production is

$$\Delta \pi/\Delta Q = M\pi.$$

Consider again the revenue and cost functions discussed in Chapter 1:

$$TR = f(Q) = 0 + 20(Q) - 0.1(Q)^2$$

and

$$TC = f(Q) = 50 + 9(Q) + 0.1(Q)^2.$$

With differential calculus we can use the revenue and cost functions to write *marginal* revenue and *marginal* cost functions for determining the profit-maximizing quantity of output.

The function for a *change in* value of another function is called a *derivative*. Thus, the change in any of the dependent variables in this example (*TR, TC,* or π) can be determined by computing the derivative of the appropriate equation. A derivative is the "limit" of a function, formally defined as the change in the dependent variable (*Y*) when the change in the independent variable (*X*) approaches zero. It is expressed in this way:

$$\text{The derivative of } Y = f(X) \text{ is the } \lim_{\Delta X \to 0} \frac{\Delta Y}{\Delta X} = \frac{dY}{dX}.$$

A "limit" is a value which is approached but never quite achieved.

Marginal values are reflected in the slope of the curve drawn from a particular equation. Thus, calculus enables us to measure the slopes of various equations and determine the value of the independent variable at which the slopes are equal.

Figure 1A.1 illustrates the change in total revenue (*TR*) associated with small changes in output (*Q*). Figure 1A.1b is an enlargement of a segment of the total revenue curve over a small change in output. Marginal revenue is the change in the value of the *TR* function as the change in quantity (*Q*) approaches zero, as measured on the horizontal axis.

FIGURE 1A.1   **Marginal Revenue**

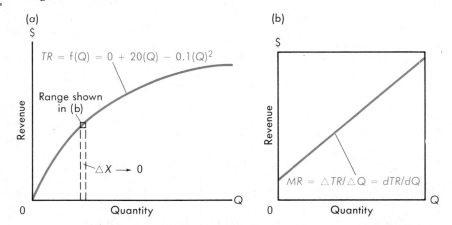

A derivative describes the change in the value of the dependent variable (a) as the change in the independent variable approaches zero (b). On a graph of total revenue, the derivative of the function measures the marginal revenue associated with changes in quantity (Q).

FIGURE 1A.2   **The Graph of a Constant**

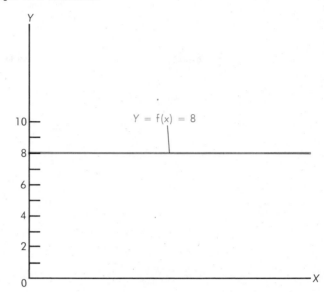

The graph of a constant has a slope of zero. Therefore, the derivative of a constant is zero.

THE RULES OF DIFFERENTIAL CALCULUS

The use of differential calculus requires the understanding of a few simple rules that we will now discuss.

Rule 1. The derivative of a constant. A constant does not change in value whatever the value of the independent variable may be. Therefore, the marginal value of a constant is zero:

The derivative of $Y = f(X) = n$ is $dY/dX = 0$.

This is easy to see on the graph of a constant. Graph any number, say 8, as is done in Figure 1A.2 and measure the slope of the curve associated with a small change in the independent variable. The slope of the curve is zero, and the derivative is zero.

Rule 2. The derivative of a term containing the independent variable (X). The derivative of a term containing the independent variable (X) is computed by multiplying the coefficient of X by the exponent of X and reducing the exponent by *one:*

The derivative of $Y = f(X) = aX^b$ is $dY/dX = (ba)(X)^{(b-1)}$.

The derivatives of the following terms are as shown:

The derivative of $Y = f(X) = 5X$ is $\dfrac{dY}{dX} = (1 \cdot 5)(X)^{(1-1)} = 5(X)^0 = 5$.

The derivative of $Y = f(X) = 3X^2$ is $\dfrac{dY}{dX} = (2 \cdot 3)(X)^{(2-1)} = 6(X)^1 = 6X$.

The derivative of $Y = f(X) = .8X^3$ is $\dfrac{dY}{dX} = (3 \cdot .8)(X)^{(3-1)} = 2.4X^2$.

The derivative of $Y = f(X) = 1.5X^{-2}$ is $\dfrac{dY}{dX} = (-2 \cdot 1.5)(X)^{(-2-1)} = -3X^{-3}$.

Each of these functions is graphed in Figure 1A.3. Note that the slope of the curve $Y = 5X$ in Figure 1A.3a remains constant at 5 units all along the curve. The slope of the curve $Y = 3X^2$ in Figure 1A.3b increases from 6 where $X = 1$ to 12 where $X = 2$, to 27 where $X = 3$, and so forth. The slope of the curve $Y = .8X^3$ in Figure 1A.3c increases by 2.4 times the square of X. And in Figure 1A.3d the slope is negative and diminishes by 3 times the reciprocal of X to the third power.

Rule 3. The derivative of a sum (or difference). The derivative of a sum (or difference) is the sum of (or difference between) the derivatives of the terms. Thus, the derivative of the function

$$Y = f(X) = 8 + 5X + 3X^2 - .8X^3$$

is

$$\frac{dY}{dX} = 5 + 6X - 2.4X^2.$$

Using Derivatives to Locate the Profit-Maximizing Quantity of Output

In Chapter 1 we observed how marginal values determine the profit-maximizing quantity of output (Q). We reasoned that maximum profit occurs where the slopes of total revenue (TR) and total cost (TC) are equal (and, therefore, where the positive difference between the curves is greatest).

Using calculus, we can write equations for the slopes (or marginal values) of the revenue and cost functions. Thus, for

$$TR = f(Q) = 0 + 20Q - 0.1Q^2$$

and

$$TC = f(Q) = 50 + 9Q + 0.1Q^2,$$

marginal revenue and marginal cost are

FIGURE 1A.3   Graphing the Derivative of Various Terms

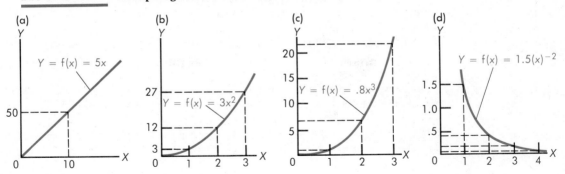

$$MR = \frac{dTR}{dQ} = 20 - 0.2Q$$

and

$$MC = \frac{dTC}{dQ} = 9 + 0.2Q.$$

The slopes of *TR* and *TC* are equal where *MR* = *MC*:

$$MR = 20 - 0.2Q = 9 + 0.2Q = MC.$$

Solving for these values yields:

$$20 - 9 = 0.2Q + 0.2Q$$

and

$$Q = 27.5.$$

Maximum profit occurs with total output of $Q = 27.5$. This is the same answer we obtained through observation in Chapter 1.

Optimization

Calculus provides another means for determining the value of the independent variable associated with certain maximum (or minimum) values of the independent variables. The process is called **optimization**, and it identifies the *optimum* value of *X* for achieving some objective relative to *Y* such as the *optimum* level of output for achieving maximum economic profit, the *optimum* level of output for achieving minimum total cost, or the *optimum* level of resource use for achieving maximum total output.

Optimization enables the analyst to locate the highest peak (or lowest trough) of a function. The highest peak (or lowest trough) occurs where the graph of the function has stopped moving in one direction and has leveled off before moving in the other direction. Thus, the peak or trough occurs where the slope of a graph is zero. The value of the independent variable at the peak or trough is the value at which the derivative of the function is zero.

To illustrate optimization, consider again the total revenue, total cost, and economic profit functions from Chapter 1 in which

$$TR = f(Q) = 20Q + 0.1Q^2,$$
$$TC = f(Q) = 50 + 9Q + 0.1Q^2,$$

and

$$\pi = TR - TC = -50 + 11Q - 0.2Q^2.$$

Maximum economic profit occurs where the derivative of the profit function is equal to zero. The derivative of the profit function is

$$M\pi = \frac{d\pi}{dQ} = 11 - 0.4Q.$$

Setting $M\pi$ equal to zero yields $11 = 0.4Q$ and $Q = 27.5$. This is the same answer we achieved by observation and by setting MR equal to MC.

The Second Derivative

Optimization requires one further step. The process we have described identifies the value of the independent variable at which the slope of the curve is zero. Setting the derivative of the function equal to zero, however, identifies the highest peak *or the lowest trough* of the curve. To ensure that the point we have identified is actually the point of maximum (not minimum) profit, we must compute the **second derivative** of the profit function.

The second derivative is computed similarly to the first derivative. It is the derivative of the derivative and is expressed in this manner:

The second derivative of $Y = f(X)$ is $\dfrac{d^2Y}{dX^2}$.

In our example, the second derivative of the profit equation is

FIGURE 1A.4   **Profit and Marginal Profit**

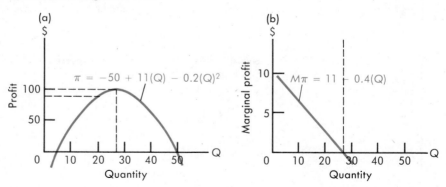

The negative slope of the marginal profit function (b) indicates a peak in the profit function (a). Maximum profit occurs where the marginal profit function is equal to zero.

$$\frac{d^2\pi}{dQ^2} = -0.4.$$

The second derivative measures the slope of the derivative. Thus, the second derivative in our example measures the slope of the marginal profit curve.

In Figure 1A.4 we have graphed the profit and marginal profit curves. The negative value of the second derivative indicates a negative slope for the marginal profit curve. That is, the value of marginal profit is at first positive, becomes zero where $Q = 27.5$, and then is negative. This tells us that changes in economic profit are at first positive as Q increases. The positive changes in economic profit become smaller as Q approaches 27.5 units, at which point the addition to economic profit is zero. Here, the profit function reaches a peak. Beyond $Q = 27.5$, changes in economic profit are negative, such that economic profit diminishes with further increases in Q.

In general, we can say that a negative value for the second derivative of a function indicates a peak in the function, and a positive value indicates a trough.

Partial Differentiation

Frequently, the analyst may be called upon to evaluate a function with two independent variables. For example, total product (Q) may be expressed as a function of two resource inputs, labor (L) and capital equipment (K):

$$Q = f(L,K) = 40L - 0.8L^2 + 50K - 4.9K^2.$$

In this case, maximum (or minimum) output occurs where the **partial derivatives** with respect to the two independent variables are equal to zero.

A partial derivative is written $\frac{\partial Y}{\partial X}$ and is computed separately with respect to each of the independent variables. Thus, the partial derivative of the total product function above with respect to labor is

$$\frac{\partial Q}{\partial L} = 40 - 1.6L$$

and with respect to capital is

$$\frac{\partial Q}{\partial K} = 50 - 9.8K.$$

Following the optimization procedures we have discussed enables us to identify the values of L and K at which total product output (Q) is maximum (or minimum).

To begin, set both partial derivatives equal to zero and solve simultaneously:

$$\frac{\partial Q}{\partial L} = 40 - 1.6L = 0$$

$$\frac{\partial Q}{\partial K} = 50 - 9.8K = 0.$$

Thus, $L = 25$ and $K = 5.10$. To verify that the values $L = 25$ and $K = 5.10$ will yield *maximum Q*, compute the second partial derivatives:

$$\frac{\partial^2 Q}{\partial L^2} = -1.6$$

and

$$\frac{\partial^2 Q}{\partial K^2} = -9.8.$$

Negative second derivatives indicate that the total product function does indeed reach a peak where $L = 25$ and $K = 5.10$.

To determine the actual quantity of output at the maximum point, substitute the values of L and K in the total product function:

$$Q = f(L, K) = 40(25) - 0.8(25)^2 + 50(5.1) - 4.9(5.1)^2$$
$$= 1,000 - 500 + 255 - 127.45 = 627.55.$$

This is the value of the total product function at its highest point.

Constrained Optimization Using LaGrangian Multipliers

Managers are frequently called upon to identify the value of some independent variable (X) that will achieve the maximum (or minimum) value for a dependent variable (Y). Occasionally, the problem involves a constraint that must also be satisfied. Solving a "constrained optimization" problem requires the use of a **LaGrangian multiplier.**

To understand LaGrangian multipliers, consider again the total product function with two resource inputs, labor and capital:

$$Q = f(L, K) = 40L - 0.8L^2 + 50K - 4.9K^2.$$

Suppose the manager must identify the quantities of L and K that yield maximum output (Q) given the constraint that the quantity of labor must be twice the quantity of capital or

$$L = 2K.$$

Rearranging the constraint equation to bring all the terms to one side of the equality yields:

$$L - 2K = 0.$$

To solve the problem, first multiply the constraint equation by the LaGrangian multiplier (expressed as λ) and add the constraint equation to the equation to be maximized (or minimized). Thus,

$$Q = f(L, K, \lambda) = 40L - 0.8L^2 + 50K - 4.9K^2 + \lambda (L - 2K).$$

Then calculate the partial derivatives of the total product function with respect to each of the three independent variables:

$$\frac{\partial Q}{\partial L} = 40 - 1.6L + \lambda,$$

$$\frac{\partial Q}{\partial K} = 50 - 9.8K - 2\lambda,$$

and

$$\frac{\partial Q}{\partial \lambda} = L - 2K.$$

To maximize the function, set the three partial derivatives equal to zero. The result is a system of three equations with three unknowns, which can be solved simultaneously:

(1) $40 - 1.6L + \lambda = 0$
(2) $50 - 9.8K - 2\lambda = 0$
(3) $\qquad\quad L - 2K = 0.$

Solving equation (3) for L yields $L = 2K$. Substituting this value in equation (1) yields:

(1) $40 - 1.6(2K) + \lambda = 0$
(1) $40 - 3.2K + \lambda = 0$
(2) $50 - 9.8K - 2\lambda = .$

Multiplying equation (1) by 2 gives us:

(1) $80 - 6.4K + 2\lambda = 0$
(2) $50 - 9.8K - 2\lambda = 0,$

and adding equations (1) and (2) produces:

$130 - 16.2K = 0$

so that $K = 8.02$. Substituting the value of K in equation (3) yields:

(3) $L = 2(8.02) = 16.04.$

With the constraint that the quantity of labor must be twice the quantity of capital, the optimum resource inputs are $L = 16.04$ and $K = 8.2$.

We can verify that these are indeed the output-maximizing quantities of labor and capital (including the constraint) by taking the second partial derivatives of the total product function:

$$\frac{\partial^2 Q}{\partial L^2} = -1.6$$

and

$$\frac{\partial^2 Q}{\partial K^2} = -9.8.$$

The negative values for the second derivatives ensure a maximum in the total product output function.

The quantity of output with the constraint is determined by substituting the appropriate values of L and K in the total product function:

$$Q = f(L, K) = 40(16.04) - 0.8(16.04)^2 + 50(8.02) - 4.9(8.02)^2$$
$$= 641.6 - 205.825 + 401 - 315.17 = 521.60.$$

Note that the effect of the constraint (in this example) is to reduce the maximum quantity of output.

Interpreting the LaGrangian Multiplier

Using the LaGrangian multiplier provides further information to a manager in this situation. Solve the preceding system of equations for the value of λ. Substituting $L = 16.04$ and $K = 8.02$ in equations (1) and (2), we find that $\lambda = -14.3$. The value of λ is interpreted as follows: λ *is the change in the maximum value of the original function associated with a one-unit change in the constraint equation.* In our example, $\lambda = -14.3$ denotes the increase in quantity of output (Q) generated by allowing the quantity of labor (L) to exceed twice the quantity of capital (K) by one unit.

To prove this is so, compare the quantity of output produced by the optimum quantities of labor and capital with the quantity of output produced when $K = 8.02$ and $L = 17.04$:

$$Q = 40(17.04) - 0.8(17.04)^2 + 50(8.02) - 4.9(8.02)^2$$
$$= 681.6 - 232.29 + 401 - 315.17 = 535.14.$$

This is almost precisely 14.3 units greater than the quantity of output under the constraint. Actually, however, λ indicates the average rate of change associated with very small increments of the independent variable and will not exactly equal the change in output. (The sign of λ is immaterial. Note that the sign of λ will depend on whether the constraint equation is stated as $L - 2K = 0$ or $2K - L = 0$.)

INTEGRAL CALCULUS

Until now, we have described processes by which managers can use differential calculus to solve optimization problems in order to maximize or minimize a function within a fixed constraint. Understanding differential calculus also enables a manager to perform an additional mathematical process that is helpful in solving other types of managerial problems. This procedure is the reverse of differentiation and is called **integration.**

Recall that differentiation yields an equation describing the slope of a function and that the derivative measures the *change in* the dependent variable associated with a small change in the independent variable. Integration yields the opposite results. The integral measures the aggregate of *all changes* in the dependent variable associated with any number of very small changes in the independent variable.

Integration is useful because it enables a manager to estimate total values when only expected *changes in* values are known. For example, by using integrals a manager can find:

1. *total revenue* associated with some quantity of output, given that revenue changes by a known amount with small changes in output;

2. *total cost* associated with some quantity of output, given that costs change by a known amount with small changes in output;
3. *total output* associated with some quantity of resources, given that output increases by a known amount with small changes in resource employment.

The integral of a function is denoted by

$$\int f(X) \, dX,$$

which is read as "the integral of the function f(X) with respect to X."

The rules for integration are the opposite of the rules for differentiation.

Rule 1. The integral of a term containing the independent variable. The integral of a term containing the independent variable is computed by first raising the exponent of X by *one* and dividing the coefficient of X by the new exponent. With f(X) = aX the integral is

$$\int f(X) \, dX = \frac{a}{1+1} X^{(1+1)} = \frac{1}{2} a X^2 \, dX.$$

Then, since the integral may include a constant, which does not appear in the derivative, a constant is added to complete the integral. Thus with f(X) = aX, the complete integral is

$$\int f(X) \, dX = C + \frac{1}{2} a X^2 \, dX.$$

Rule 2. The integral of a constant. To find the integral of a constant, first state the constant as a coefficient of X to the power of zero. Thus,

$$b = bX^0.$$

Then apply Rule 1 for computing the integral of a term containing the independent variable. Raise the exponent by *one* and divide the coefficient by the new exponent. For f(X) = bX^0, the integral is

$$f(X) \, dX = \frac{b}{0+1} X^{0+1} = bX \, dX.$$

Again, add a constant to complete the integral:

$$f(X) \, dX = C + bX \, dX.$$

Rule 3. The integral of a sum (or difference). The integral of a sum (or difference) is the sum of (or difference between) the integrals of the separate terms. For $f(X) = aX + b$, the integral is

$$f(X) \, dX = C + \frac{1}{2} a X^2 + bX \, dX.$$

Graphing the Integral

We used the derivative of a function to measure the marginal change in the dependent variable. The derivative measures the increase or decrease in the dependent variable associated with an infinitely small change in the independent variable. (In economics, the derivative measures the slope of a total cost or total revenue function and is the equation for marginal cost or marginal revenue.)

The integral of a function, on the other hand, is the accumulated total of all the minute changes in the dependent variable associated with some number of changes in the independent variable. (The integral may be viewed as the sum of all the "slopes"—marginal revenues or costs—which, taken together, yield the function for total revenue or total costs.)

The integral of a function may be shown on a graph in either of two ways. One way is simply to graph the total function that is produced by integrating the original function (or derivative). Look first at the marginal revenue curve shown in Figure 1A.5.

FIGURE 1A.5   **The Derivative**

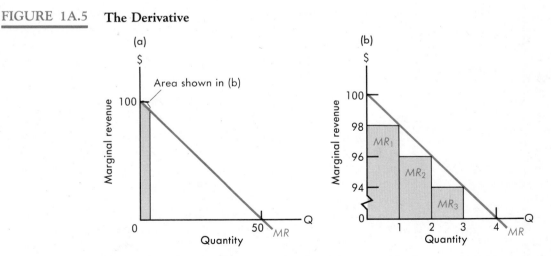

The derivative is the change in the dependent variable associated with minute changes (b) in the independent variable.

The graph in Figure 1A.5 shows the change in revenue associated with various levels of sales. A portion of the marginal revenue curve has been magnified in Figure 1A.5b to show the marginal revenues associated with the first, second, and third units. The first unit is sold at a price of $p_1 = \$100$, for $MR_1 = 100$. Selling a total of two units requires a price reduction to $p_2 = \$99$ for both units. The change in revenue is

$$TR_2 - TR_1 = 2(99) - 1(100) = 198 - 100 = 98 = MR_2.$$

Selling three units requires a further price reduction to $p_3 = \$98$ for a change in revenue of

$$TR_3 - TR_2 = 3(98) - 2(99) = 294 - 198 = 96 = MR_3.$$

The integral of the MR function in Figure 1A.5 yields total revenue, determined by applying the rules for integration: $\int f(X)\ dX$. Total revenue is graphed in Figure 1A.6, beginning at $TR = 0$ where $Q = 0$ and rising with a slope defined by the equation for marginal revenue. The total revenue function reaches a peak where $Q = 50$ and falls to zero where $Q = 100$.

The second way to show the integral graphically entails graphing an area rather than a line. Remember that the integral is the accumulated total of all the minute changes in the dependent variable. Each single change is measured by the space beneath the derivative associated with the corresponding unit of the independent variable. Thus, the accumulated total of all the changes up to some quantity of the independent variable is the sum of the spaces beneath the derivative for that quantity.

In Figure 1A.5, the marginal revenues associated with sales of the first, second, and third units, respectively, are 100, 98, and 96. The accumulated total of the revenue changes is shown in Figure 1A.6, as $100 + 98 + 96 = 294$, which is the total revenue associated with sales of 3 units at a price of $p = \$98$. $TR = 294$ is also the area of the space beneath the MR curve between $Q = 0$ and $Q = 3$. Again, a portion of the curve has been magnified to show the accumulation of marginal revenue that constitutes total revenue.

Maximum total revenue occurs with sales of $Q = 50$, where TR is represented by the entire area beneath the MR curve. At values greater than $Q = 50$, MR falls below zero. For negative changes in total revenue, the TR function slopes downward, as shown on Figure 1A.6. For sales greater than $Q = 50$, the negative space below the horizontal axis must be subtracted from the positive space above the axis to yield an area that equals total revenue. Thus, beyond $Q = 50$ total revenue begins to decline.

Either of the two graphing procedures can be used to illustrate economic profit. In the first case, economic profit is illustrated by graphing a total cost curve with the graph of total revenue and measuring the (positive) vertical distance between total revenue and total cost. In Figure 1A.7a, economic profit begins with the production and sale of $Q = 4$ units, reaches a maximum at $Q = 20$ units, and becomes negative beyond $Q = 32$ units. The process of

FIGURE 1A.6

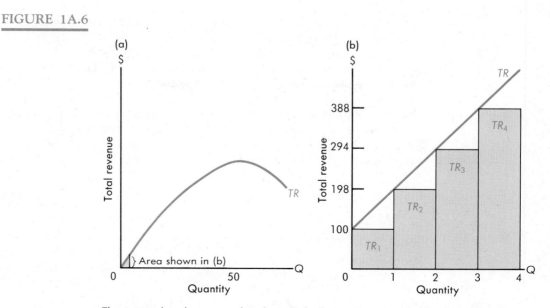

The integral is the accumulated total of all changes in the dependent variable associated with minute changes (b) in the independent variable.

FIGURE 1A.7 **Economic Profit Determined by Total and Marginal Values**

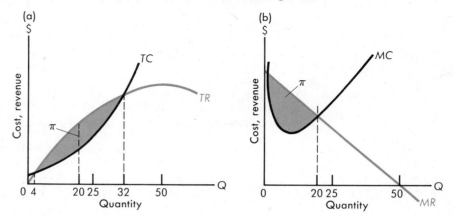

Economic profit (π) can be illustrated by the (positive) vertical distance between the total revenue and total cost curves (a) or by the (positive) area between the marginal revenue and marginal cost curves (b).

optimization explained earlier in this appendix can be used to identify the precise profit-maximizing level of Q.

In the second case, economic profit is illustrated by including a marginal cost curve on the graph of marginal revenue and measuring the (positive) area between the curves. In Figure 1A.7b, the area beneath MR is total revenue and the area beneath MC is total cost. The area between MR and MC is economic profit. Note that economic profit becomes positive in both graphs at $Q = 4$ units and reaches a maximum at $Q = 20$ units. The process of profit-maximizing explained earlier in this appendix can be used to identify the precise points in Figure 1A.7b where $MR = MC$.

KEY TERMS

derivative   LaGrangian multiplier
optimization   integration
second derivative   differentiation
partial derivative

QUESTIONS AND PROBLEMS

1. Dan's Dairy sells ice cream at $8 a gallon. Daily costs of production have been estimated at $TC = 50 - 6(Q) + 0.5(Q)^2$, where Q represents hundreds of gallons produced per day. What level of production per day would yield maximum profit?

2. What will Dan's economic profit be on the interval between 1,000 and 1,200 units sold per day?

3. Bob's Bearings has estimated total cost at $TC = \sqrt[4]{75(Q)} + 120$ over the range of Q between 10 thousand and 20 thousand units per day. Find the marginal cost and determine whether it increases or decreases over this range.

4. A truck leasing firm leases trucks for an annual fee that includes the cost of maintenance and repairs. Expected annual maintenance and repair costs are estimated to increase with the life of the trucks according to the formula

$$MC = f(t) = 500 + 20(t) - 2.4(t)^2,$$

where t represents time in years. If the expected life of the average truck is 5 years and if the leasing firm wants to charge the same leasing fee each year, how much should be included in the lease payment to cover annual maintenance and repair costs?

5. Rusty's Diner sells Blue Plate Specials for $5.98. The diner's costs include

constant weekly costs of $500 and food and labor costs that increase with the number of meals served according to the following equation:

Average cost of meals $= 2.50 + .003(Q)$,

where Q represents the number of meals. What is the minimum number of meals that must be served per week if Rusty is going to cover his costs?

6. What quantity of meals would earn Rusty maximum economic profit?

7. The Robin's Nest sells toys and gifts for children by mail order. Catalogues are sent to households in three mid-western states. Management estimates that annual orders depend on the number of catalogues sent according to the equation $S = 5(N) - .1(N)^2$, where $S =$ annual orders and $N =$ thousands of catalogues. One order brings in an average revenue of $7.50 and incurs average costs of $6.75. How many catalogues should the firm mail for maximum profit? What is the largest number of catalogues the firm should send? Explain your answer.

The Theory of Consumer Demand

No action can occur in the consumer market without first a decision by a buyer. This makes buyer intentions of special concern to managers. Changes in buying patterns can lead to years of exciting profit growth or to dismal losses. Managers must anticipate and plan for such changes, altering their firms' product lines, expanding or contracting production facilities, or seeking new markets to ensure sales growth.

Several years ago, the managers of Kentucky Fried Chicken, Inc. (KFC) discovered the unhappy consequences of ignoring changes in consumer buying patterns. From healthy sales growth in the 1960s, KFC settled down to slowing growth in the 1970s, with declining profits and low morale among franchise holders and employees. KFC managers looked for the sources of *technical, human,* and *economic* change in the market environment and sought a strategy that would increase sales and profits.

In their decision-making process, KFC's managers would have followed the steps toward scientific decision making outlined in Chapter 1. Step 1 would have been to *define the problem:* changes in consumer preferences had reduced KFC's share of the fast-food market. Specifically, concern about nutrition had driven many old customers away, and others were attracted to the chicken dishes served by competing restaurant chains. Step 2 was to *state the firm's objective:* that is, to regain KFC's standing as a leader in the fast-food market. Step 3 was to *propose alternative strategies, evaluate their expected results,* and *select the optimum strategy.* As a part of Step 3, KFC scientists tested a variety of recipes for improving their product's nutritional quality and taste. When managers were satisfied with test results, they introduced their new recipe to KFC restaurants, newly redesigned to appeal to today's discriminating consumers. Then, they mounted a bold, new advertising campaign to convince consumers of their product's consistent superiority over other fast-food products.

Feedback from KFC's new strategy must have pleased the decision makers. In 1980, profits from their restaurants in the United States leaped 65 percent, and the firm's managers began planning new strategies to adapt to continuing changes in consumer habits and attitudes.

Analyzing buyer behavior in this manner is the subject of this chapter. We will use microeconomic theory to explain how buyers decide what combination of goods and services they will purchase with a limited budget. In the following chapter, we will use mathematical techniques to show how the theory of consumer demand can be applied to real managerial decisions.

PURCHASING DECISIONS

Demand for a good or service depends on certain characteristics or **attributes** of the good or service. Attributes are those characteristics of a thing that distinguish it from another. The attributes associated with Kentucky Fried Chicken, for example, are different from those of McDonald's or Taco Bell. The first step in any buyer's decision is to obtain information about the attributes of various goods and services such as taste and nutritional value in the case of food items and speed, reliability, and convenience in the case of, say, auto repair services. Certain attributes of a good or service yield benefits to buyers. In general, a buyer seeks to acquire the combination of goods and services that provides the maximum total benefits.

Another attribute of a good or service is its cost. Because the buyer's budget is limited, he or she must allocate available funds toward those goods and services that provide the greatest benefits per dollar of cost.

Most buyers are **consumers**, purchasing goods and services for their own use. Consumers compare the attributes of various goods and services, including their expected benefits and costs, before deciding to purchase precise quantities of each. Other buyers are **business firms**, purchasing goods and services for use in producing items for sale. Like consumers, business firms decide what purchases to make on the basis of the attributes of the industrial materials and services available in the market. They must consider the benefits gained from each relative to its cost. Finally, **governments** purchase goods and services for use in government programs. Aircraft, concrete, penicillin, and the services of pilots, construction workers, and public-health nurses are all examples of goods and services purchased by governments.

The basis for choosing a preferred combination of goods and services is similar for all of these buyers. In each case, choice is limited by the budget available for spending. All buyers want to make their decisions efficiently: that is, to purchase the combination of goods and services that yields the greatest benefits per dollar of cost paid.

Total and Marginal Utility

Purchasing decisions are incremental or **marginal decisions**: whether to purchase one additional restaurant meal during the week, whether to stock an additional order of radial tires for satisfying this month's customers, or whether to commission an additional order of military aircraft.

Economists describe the benefits from acquiring a good or service in terms of *utility*. **Total utility** is the sum of all the benefits a buyer enjoys from the entire array of goods and services acquired. **Marginal utility** is the *change in* benefits a buyer enjoys from acquiring an additional unit of a particular good or service. Acquiring more of a good or service typically causes total utility to increase. But, in general, the added utility gained by acquiring additional units of a particular good or service tends to diminish as more units are acquired. Thus, we say that marginal utility decreases. Decreasing marginal utility is the result of the relatively smaller gain in benefits associated with the purchase of *one more* restaurant meal, *one more* radial tire, or *one more* military aircraft during a particular period of time.

Buyers seek to acquire a combination of goods that yields maximum total utility. To do this, they compare the utility gained per dollar paid for each of the available goods and services: that is, the marginal utility per dollar of purchase price. To illustrate this process of comparison, suppose the marginal utility of all goods a through z can be measured and shown as

$$MU_a, MU_b, MU_c, \ldots, MU_z.$$

Each MU is in fact a declining schedule showing the utility associated with the first, second, third, and nth purchase of goods a through z. When marginal utility declines, acquiring the nth unit of a good adds less to total utility than acquiring the first, second, or third unit.

For goods with constant prices, the marginal utility per dollar of purchase price is

$$MU_a/p_a, MU_b/p_b, MU_c/p_c, \ldots, MU_z/p_z.$$

A buyer achieves maximum total utility by acquiring quantities of goods for which the marginal utility per dollar of purchase price is equal. Thus,

$$MU_a/p_a = MU_b/p_b = MU_c/p_c \ldots = MU_z/p_z$$

yields maximum total utility. If the marginal utility per dollar associated with acquiring more of good a were to be greater than that associated with good b, the buyer would reallocate his or her budget to purchase more of good *a*. By acquiring goods with equal *MU* per dollar of cost, the buyer ensures that each dollar spent contributes the greatest possible benefits to total utility.

Another way of expressing this is to say that the marginal utilities of all purchases should be proportional to their prices. Goods with high prices will be purchased in small quantities, such that their marginal utilities are high. Goods with low prices will be purchased in large quantities, such that marginal utility is low.

Benefit/cost comparisons are useful for explaining the buying decisions of consumers, business firms, and governments. In this chapter, we will be most concerned with the buying decisions of consumers. In later chapters we will find that many of the analytical tools used in the theory of consumer demand are also applicable to the analysis of other business decisions.

AN "ORDINAL" THEORY OF DEMAND: INDIFFERENCE CURVES[1]

The marginal utility theory of demand suffers from a major weakness: the need to measure utility. While buyers cannot precisely measure utility, they may be able to *rank* goods and services according to their expected contributions to utility. A theory of consumer demand that focuses on the rank order of buyer preferences is described as an "ordinal" theory (as opposed to a "cardinal" theory, like the marginal utility theory, which requires measurement of utility).

Buyers' rankings of goods and services differ according to their attributes and according to the quantities of goods and services already owned in a particular time period. A consumer may say, "I would prefer to purchase a jacket rather than a sweater, but I would prefer a *second* sweater to a *second* jacket if I have already acquired one of each." Ranking goods enables a buyer to compare particular combinations of goods that provide equal satisfaction or utility. Thus, a consumer may obtain the same level of utility from any of the following combinations of jackets and sweaters:

TABLE 2.1   Combinations Yielding the Same Level of Utility

Jackets (Y)	Sweaters (X)
4	1
2	2
1	4

We say the buyer is "indifferent" concerning the combinations yielding th level of utility represented in the table.

---

1. The sections on indifference curves may be omitted without significant loss of continuity in the text.

The same buyer would obtain a higher level of total satisfaction or utility from combinations containing larger quantities of the two goods. For example:

TABLE 2.2   **Combinations Yielding a Higher Level of Utility**

Jackets (Y)	Sweaters (X)
10	1
6	2
3	5

Likewise, the buyer could identify other combinations that would yield still higher levels of utility.

Combinations yielding the same level of utility are graphed in Figure 2.1. The curve labeled U_1 represents all combinations of the two goods yielding some level of utility (1).[2] Higher levels of total utility are represented by the curves labeled U_2, U_3, . . . U_n. The curves in Figure 2.1 are called **indifference curves** because the buyer is indifferent in choosing among any of the combinations on a single curve.

Indifference curves have the following characteristics:

1. *Indifference curves slope downward from left to right.* This is because a buyer must sacrifice some quantity of one good to obtain some quantity of another if total utility is to remain unchanged. In our example, the buyer must sacrifice some quantity of jackets when gaining some quantity of sweaters if total utility is to remain the same. The slope of an indifference curve is defined as the **marginal rate of substitution** of good Y (jackets) for good X (sweaters) and is expressed algebraically as

$$MRS_{YX} = -\Delta Q_Y / + \Delta Q_X = \text{slope.}[3]$$

2. *The slope of an indifference curve becomes more horizontal as it approaches the horizontal axis.* This is because a buyer's willingness to sacrifice a good declines as combinations include less of that good. Thus, the ratio $-\Delta Q_Y / + \Delta Q_X$ decreases as combinations include fewer units of good Y (jackets) and more of good X (sweaters). Therefore, we may say that the marginal rate of substitution of Y for X (jackets for sweaters) decreases. The reason for this is the principle of decreasing marginal utility, which implies lower utility for a good owned in larger quantities.

3. *Indifference curves representing higher levels of utility are drawn higher and farther to the right.* The reason for this is that combinations must

---

2. The points listed in the table are connected to form a smooth curve. The continuous curve suggests that the consumer would receive comparable utility from purchasing, say, 2½ jackets and 7½ sweaters. Such combinations would be relevant for goods that are divisible into smaller increments than in our example.

3. Our explanation has focused on the marginal rate of substitution of Y for X, reflected by movements down an indifference curve. The marginal rate of substitution of X for Y is the reverse, reflected by movements up the indifference curve. The characteristics of indifference curves remain true regardless of the arrangement of the goods on the axes.

FIGURE 2.1 An Array of Indifference Curves

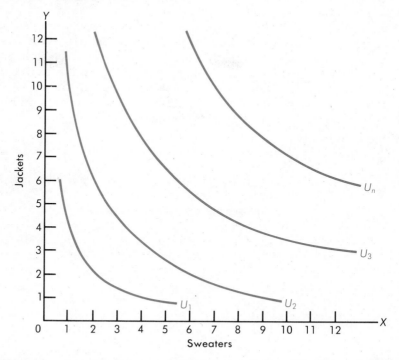

Indifference curves slope downward from left to right according to consumers' marginal rate of substitution of one good for another. The slope becomes more horizontal because the marginal rate of substitution decreases. Indifference curves representing higher levels of utility are drawn higher up and to the right. Indifference curves representing equal increments of utility are drawn farther and farther apart because of the principle of diminishing marginal utility.

include more of one good (the other remaining constant) or more of both goods if total utility is to increase. Thus, points representing higher levels of utility must lie higher and/or to the right of points representing lower levels of utility.

4. *Indifference curves cannot intersect.* Intersecting indifference curves would imply that higher levels of utility could be achieved with a constant or decreasing quantity of both goods. Larger (or smaller) quantities of *both* jackets and sweaters would yield the same level of utility.

5. *Indifference curves representing equal increments of utility are graphed farther and farther apart.* Again, the reason is the principle of decreasing marginal utility. Because additional units of goods provide decreasing marginal utility, the additional quantities of goods must be increasingly larger if combinations are to provide equal increments of utility.

The Budget Line

Indifference curves represent buyer preferences: combinations of goods that satisfy the buyer's preferences at successively higher levels of utility. Normally, a buyer will attempt to purchase a combination of goods on the highest possible indifference curve. The highest indifference curve available to a particular buyer depends on the prices of the goods and on the buyer's total budget. Available quantities of particular goods and services are determined by the budget equation, or **budget line**:

$$B = Q_Y(p_Y) + Q_X(p_X),$$

where Q represents quantities, p represents prices and B represents the buyer's total budget.

A budget line representing a budget of $B = \$50$ has been drawn in Figure 2.2.

The line is drawn with $p_Y = \$5$ and $p_X = \$10$. Its position is determined as follows. First, suppose the total budget is allocated to purchases of Q_Y:

$$Q_Y(p_Y) + Q_X(p_X) = 50,$$

and

$$Q_Y (5) + 0(10) = 50,$$

so that

$$Q_Y = 10.$$

Then, suppose the total budget is allocated to Q_X, so that

$$0(5) + Q_X(10) = 50,$$

and

$$Q_X = 5.$$

The values $Q_Y = 10$ and $Q_X = 5$ are the intercepts of the budget line, as shown in Figure 2.2. The slope of the budget line is Q_Y/Q_X, the ratio of the intercepts of the vertical and horizontal axes. However, because the budget line has a constant slope, its slope can be expressed as $-\Delta Q_Y/+\Delta Q_X$ all along its length. Thus,

$$Q_Y/Q_X = -\Delta Q_Y/+\Delta Q_X = \text{the slope of the budget line.}$$

The slope of the budget line also is determined by prices. For any budget

FIGURE 2.2 A Budget Line

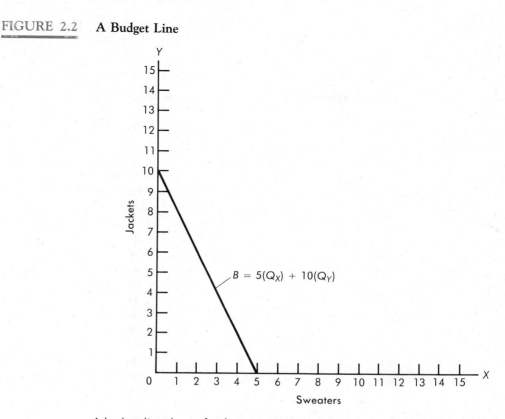

A budget line drawn for the equation $B = Q_Y(p_Y) + Q_X(p_X)$ has as its slope $p_X/p_Y = Q_Y/Q_X$. The position of the budget line is determined by the size of the budget.

line drawn to represent a fixed budget, the negative change in units of Y relative to a positive change in units of X produces no change in the total budget. This means that $\Delta Q_Y (p_Y) + \Delta Q_X (p_X) = 0$, or, rearranging terms:

$$-\Delta Q_Y (p_Y) = \Delta Q_X (p_X).$$

Dividing both sides of this equation by $(p_Y \times p_X)$ and rearranging terms yields

$$p_X/p_Y = -\Delta Q_Y/\Delta Q_X,$$

the slope of the budget line. To summarize:

1. The slope of the budget line is defined by the relative quantities of the two goods available within the buyer's budget.
2. The slope of the budget line also is defined by the prices of the two goods, with the good on the horizontal axis providing the numerator of the price ratio.

3. The position of the budget line is defined by the maximum quantities of the two goods permitted within the buyer's budget.

The "Maximum-Utility" Combination of Goods

The budget line represents a buyer's capacity, that is, the permitted quantity of goods available within the buyer's budget at the given prices of the goods. Combining a budget line with a buyer's indifference curves identifies the "maximum-utility" combination of goods: the combination available within the buyer's budget that satisfies buyer preferences at the highest level of utility.

In Figure 2.3, the maximum-utility combination of goods is shown at Z, the point at which the budget line is tangent to the highest possible indifference curve.

For a very brief segment where the curves are tangent, their slopes are equal. Thus, the slope of the budget line equals

$$\frac{Q_Y}{Q_X} = \frac{p_X}{p_Y} = MRS_{YX}$$

which equals the slope of the indifference curve. Note that any position other than Z on the buyer's budget line would yield a lower level of total utility than that achieved at Z. Moreover, any position other than Z on this particular indifference curve is not available within the buyer's budget.

The tangency of the buyer's indifference curve with the budget line is significant for another reason. We have noted that slope MRS_{YX} reflects the buyer's willingness to sacrifice one good for another: $-\Delta Q_Y / +\Delta Q_X$. Along a single indifference curve, the buyer's willingness to sacrifice a particular good depends on its marginal utility. Since total utility is constant along a single indifference curve, it must be true that the sacrifice of utility associated with $-\Delta Q_Y$ is equal to the gain in utility associated with $+\Delta Q_X$. Thus,

$$-\Delta Q_Y(MU_Y) = +\Delta Q_X(MU_X).$$

This allows us to say that

$$-\Delta Q_Y / +\Delta Q_X = MU_X / MU_Y = MRS_{YX}$$

which equals the slope of the indifference curve.

Furthermore, since the slope of the indifference curve is equal to the slope of the budget line at the point of tangency, the slope of the indifference curve equals

$$\frac{MU_X}{MU_Y} = \frac{p_X}{p_Y}$$

FIGURE 2.3   **Tangency of the Budget Line with the Highest Possible Indifference Curve**

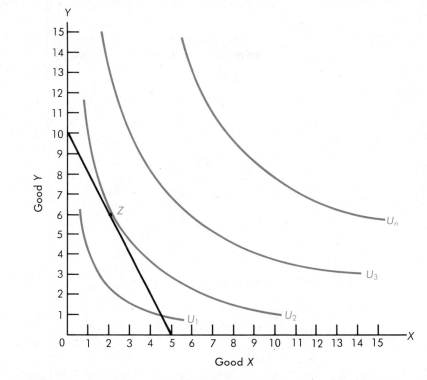

The "maximum-utility" combination of goods is shown at Z, where the buyer's budget line is tangent to the highest possible indifference curve. Where the curves are tangent, their slopes are equal. Thus, $MRS_{YX} = MU_X/MU_Y = p_X/p_Y$, or $MU_X/p_X = MU_Y/p_Y$. At this point, the marginal utilities of the goods are proportional to their prices.

which equals the slope of the budget line. Subsequently, rearranging terms yields:

$$\frac{MU_X}{p_X} = \frac{MU_Y}{p_Y}$$

at the point of tangency. Thus, at the point of tangency the *MU* per dollar spent on the two goods is equal.[4] The buyer could achieve no further gain in utility

---

4. Another way of stating this is to say that at the point of tangency the marginal utilities of all goods are proportional to their prices.

by increasing purchases of either good. This is the same objective we sought in using a "cardinal" measure of utility in the marginal utility theory of consumer demand.

Now look at a portion of the budget line in Figure 2.3 above the point of tangency with an indifference curve. At any point above the point of tangency the slope of the budget line is less than the slope of the indifference curve:

$$p_X/p_Y < MU_X/MU_Y.$$

In this case,

$$MU_Y/p_Y < MU_X/p_X,$$

and the buyer would move down the indifference curve to purchase more of X and less of Y. Below the point of tangency,

$$p_X/p_Y > MU_X/MU_Y,$$

and the reverse is true. Only at the point of tangency is the buyer purchasing both goods in quantities that maximize total utility.

Changes in the Budget Line

Changes in a buyer's budget or in the prices of goods will cause shifts in the budget line and changes in the "maximum-utility" combination of goods. An increase in a buyer's budget will increase the maximum quantity of goods permitted within the budget and shift the budget line to the right. A budget increase is illustrated in Figure 2.4. Note that the new budget line is tangent to a higher indifference curve, so the buyer is able to enjoy a higher level of total utility. A decrease in a buyer's budget would be shown by a leftward shift in the budget line and a lower level of total utility.

As long as relative prices remain unchanged, the slope of the budget line will remain the same. A buyer will purchase the combination of goods that yields equal marginal utility per dollar of expenditure. Another way of stating this is to say that goods will be purchased so that their marginal utilities will continue to be proportional to their prices.

A change in price will cause a change in the slope of the budget line. A decrease in p_X will decrease the price ratio p_X/p_Y and make the budget line more horizontal, as shown in Figure 2.5 on page 54. This flatter budget line is tangent to a higher indifference curve along a more horizontal segment. At the point of tangency, the quantity of the lower-priced good is greater. Since the maximum-utility combination is one in which marginal utilities are equally proportional to prices, the larger quantity of the cheaper good ensures that its marginal utility will be lower.

FIGURE 2.4 An Increase in the Buyer's Budget

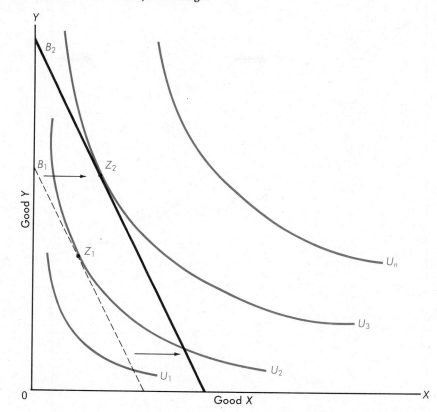

An increase in the buyer's budget shifts the budget line to the right. The budget line is now tangent to a higher indifference curve. The buyer purchases a larger combination of goods such that their marginal utilities remain proportional to their prices.

The Income-Expansion Path: Superior and Inferior Goods

We have seen how changes in the position or slope of the budget line affect the quantity of various goods that can be purchased. In this section, we will examine in detail the effects of changes in **income**. In the section that follows, we will examine the effects of changes in **price**.

As income increases, purchases of most goods increase. Goods whose purchases increase with income are called superior goods. Purchases of **strongly superior goods** increase at a greater rate than the rise in income and include

FIGURE 2.5   A Decrease in Price

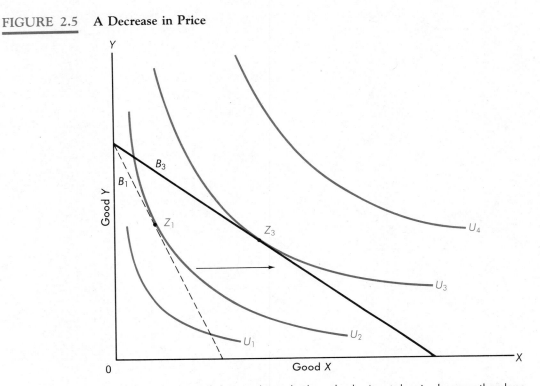

A decrease in price of the good graphed on the horizontal axis changes the slope of the budget line. The new budget line becomes tangent to a higher indifference curve. The buyer purchases a new combination of goods in which marginal utilities are proportional to prices. Because the price of X is lower, the buyer may purchase a larger quantity of good X, such that its marginal utility per dollar is equal to the MU/p of other goods purchased.

luxury goods like pleasure boats, fine wines, antique furniture, and tickets to cultural events. Strongly superior goods tend to be purchased only by consumers with incomes greater than some minimum level necessary to provide the basic needs of life.

Purchases of **mildly superior goods** increase at a lesser rate than the rise in income and include necessities like basic food products and staple clothing, ordinary home furnishings, basic transportation, and certain kinds of entertainment. Mildly superior goods are purchased at all levels of income but do not become especially attractive at higher incomes.

For a few goods, purchases tend to decline as income increases. Such goods are classified as **inferior goods**: inferior goods are necessary to sustain life at low income levels but become unattractive as incomes rise. Cheap food items like dried beans, luncheon meat, and some soft drinks are purchased in large quantities by low income families. As income increases, however, many families prefer fresh vegetables and meat, milk, and fruit. Public transportation and certain types of sporting events are also popular at low income levels and less popular as income rises.

Figure 2.6 illustrates changes in purchases of strongly superior and mildly superior goods associated with changes in income. As the budget line shifts from B_1 to B_2 to B_3, the points of tangency are X, Y, and Z. Connecting the points of tangency yields an **income-expansion path** showing the quantities of the two goods purchased at successively higher levels of income.

Compare the magnitude of the increases in purchases of the two goods associated with an increase in income. As income doubles from B_1 to B_2, purchases of strongly superior goods more than double, rising from $0a$ to $0b$. On the other hand, purchases of mildly superior goods increase only from $0x$ to $0y$. Again, as income doubles from B_2 to B_3, purchases of the strongly superior

FIGURE 2.6 The Income-Expansion Path

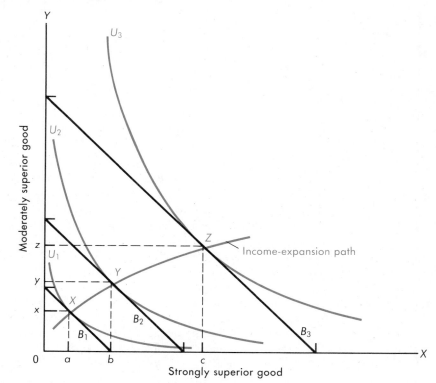

The income-expansion path curves toward the axis of the strongly superior good, whose purchases increase more than proportionally to income.

FIGURE 2.7   **The Income-Expansion Path When Certain Goods Are Inferior**

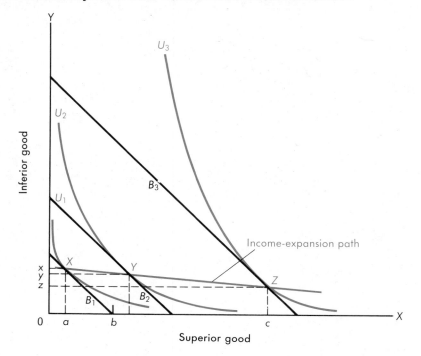

The income-expansion path curves strongly away from the axis representing the inferior good, showing that purchases of this good decline with increases in income.

good increase more than proportionally to the rise in income, and purchases of the mildly superior good increase less than proportionally. The character of the two goods is reflected in the slope of the income-expansion path. The income-expansion path curves toward the horizontal axis, which represents the strongly superior good, and away from the vertical axis, which represents the mildly superior good.

In Figure 2.7, the income-expansion path curves strongly away from the axis representing the inferior good, illustrating that the quantity purchased actually declines. In Figure 2.7, goods such as dried beans and bus tickets would be measured on the vertical axis and goods such as steaks and sports cars would be measured on the horizontal axis.

Purchases for some goods may increase at a rate equal to increases in income. In this case, the income-expansion path rises at a constant slope from the origin. Other goods may be strongly superior as income rises from zero to the middle-income range, mildly superior for income increases in the middle-income range, and inferior at high levels of income. This situation is illustrated

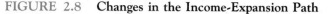

FIGURE 2.8   Changes in the Income-Expansion Path

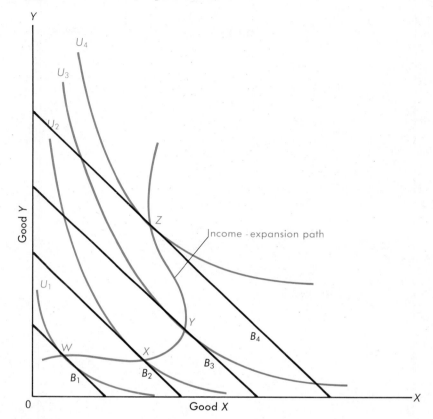

Some goods are strongly superior at low income levels, neutral with respect to income at moderate levels, and inferior at high income levels.

in Figure 2.8, in which the income-expansion path curves toward the horizontal axis at low-income levels, gradually away from the horizontal axis at the middle-income ranges, and strongly away from the horizontal axis at high income levels.

The Price-Expansion Path

Price changes are reflected in the *slope* of the budget line. This is because price changes affect the *relative* quantities of the various goods that can be purchased with a fixed budget.

FIGURE 2.9   The Price-Expansion Path

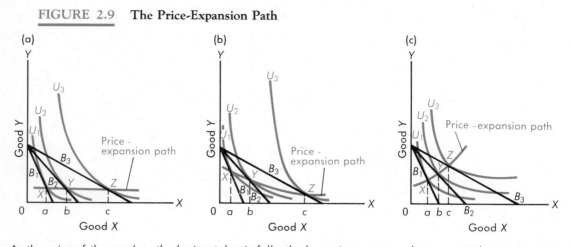

As the price of the good on the horizontal axis falls, the buyer increases purchases precisely in proportion to the decrease in price (a). The portion of income spent on the good remains the same. As the price of the good on the horizontal axis falls in (b), the buyer increases purchases in greater proportion to the decrease in price. The portion of income spent on this good increases. Finally, as the price of the good on the horizontal axis falls in (c), the buyer increases purchases at a rate less than the decrease in price. The portion of income spent on this good falls.

In Figure 2.9, the price of the good on the horizontal axis is cut in half between B_1 and B_2 and between B_2 and B_3. In other words, the maximum quantity of the good available within the buyer's budget doubles. As price falls for the good on the horizontal axis, the maximum-utility combination changes from X to Y to Z, as shown by the **price-expansion path**. In Figure 2.9a, the buyer continues to spend the same portion of income on this good, increasing the quantity purchased precisely in proportion to the decrease in price. In Figure 2.9b, however, the buyer increases purchases of this good in greater proportion than the decrease in price. In fact, the buyer increases the portion of income spent on this good and decreases the quantity purchased of the good on the vertical axis (whose price has not fallen). Finally, in Figure 2.9c the buyer increases purchases of this good at a rate less than the rate of the price reduction, reducing the portion of income spent on the good and increasing purchases of the good on the vertical axis.

All of these quantity adjustments are reflected in the slope of the price-expansion path. The price-expansion path curves toward the axis of the good whose purchases change at a rate greater than the change in price, indicating a higher proportion of income spent for this good.

OTHER FACTORS THAT INFLUENCE CONSUMER PURCHASES

Changes in Tastes

The "ordinal" theory of consumer demand also is useful for describing the effects of changes in consumer tastes. Buyers' preferences or tastes are shown by the shape of indifference curves. The slope of an indifference curve reflects a buyer's marginal rate of substitution of one good for another. We have seen that a steep slope reflects a buyer's willingness to sacrifice a relatively large quantity of the good on the vertical axis for a relatively small quantity of the good on the horizontal axis. Indifference curves normally have a steep slope along the portion of the curve where combinations include a relatively large quantity of the good on the vertical axis, indicating that its marginal utility is low.

A change in buyer preferences away from the good on the vertical axis can cause the indifference curve to become steeper along its entire length. A steeper indifference curve will become tangent to the buyer's budget line at a lower point on that line, as shown in Figure 2.10 on page 60. Along the upper portion of the indifference curve, the slope

$$MRS_{YX} = -\Delta Q_Y / + \Delta Q_X = MU_X / MU_Y$$

is greater than the price ratio p_X / p_Y. For

$$-\Delta Q_Y / + \Delta Q_X > p_X / p_y,$$

it is also true that

$$MU_X / p_X > MU_Y / p_Y.$$

As long as good X is yielding greater marginal utility per dollar of purchase price, the buyer will tend to increase purchases, moving down the indifference curve until

$$MU_Y / p_Y = MU_X / p_X$$

at the point of tangency with the budget line.

Changes in Availability of Other Goods: Substitutes and Complements

In addition to the situations we have already discussed, the theory of consumer demand can be used to explain buyer behavior with respect to **substitutes** and **complements**. **Substitute goods** are goods that can be used in place of each other. Such goods have similar attributes and include items like meat and fish,

FIGURE 2.10   A Change in Tastes

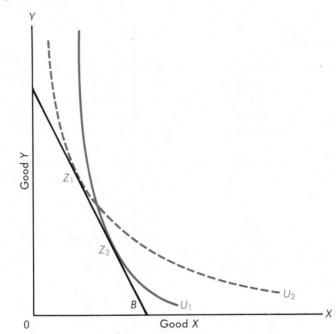

A change in taste alters the shape of the indifference curve according to the buyer's MRS_{YX}. The buyer moves along the budget line to a point on a new indifference curve at which the marginal utilities of both goods are proportional to their prices.

coats and sweaters. If goods have identical attributes, they are described as **perfect substitutes** and they are interchangeable with another good in every respect. **Complementary goods** are goods whose attributes "complete" those of other goods—for example, meat and potatoes, coats and slacks. **Perfect complements** are complements that must be used in some precise proportion, such as cars and tires.

Indifference curves are different for substitutes and complements. When goods are easily substitutable, the MRS_{YX} is roughly constant all along the indifference curve, indicating a relatively constant slope. In such cases, the buyer's willingness to sacrifice one good for the other changes very little, regardless of the quantity of either good in the relevant combination. In the case of substitute goods, a change in price can cause a buyer to shift greatly from one good to another, as shown in Figure 2.11a. In this graph, the price of X is halved, and the buyer shifts from purchasing $0a$ of Y to $0b$ of X. (If Y and X

FIGURE 2.11 **Substitute and Complementary Goods**

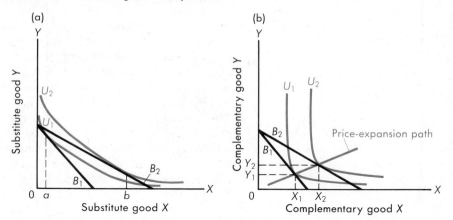

When goods are perfect substitutes, a change in the price of one can cause a total re-allocation of the buyer's budget from one good to the other (a). When goods are complementary, a change in the price of one will cause buyers to continue to purchase the goods in the same proportion necessary for their use (b).

were *perfect* substitutes, how would you describe a buyer's indifference curves? What would be the effect of a price change?[5])

When goods are complements, they typically are purchased in some roughly constant proportion. Their indifference curves bow sharply at a point that represents the necessary quantities of the two goods, as shown in Figure 2.11b. When the price of X is halved in this example, the buyer moves to a point on a higher indifference curve that represents the same proportion of the two goods purchased at the lower price. (How would you describe indifference curves for *perfect* complements?[6])

A CONSUMER DEMAND CURVE

Consumers' responsiveness to changes in incomes, prices, and tastes can be shown more simply than by using indifference curves. The fundamental economic model for observing consumer behavior is the **demand curve**. A demand curve shows the quantities of a particular good or service that will be

---

5. The indifference curves would have a constant slope. A price change would cause a total shift from purchases of one good to purchases of the other.

6. The indifference curves would bend at a point on the graph at which quantities of the two items are in proper proportion.

purchased at various prices for a particular period of time during which other factors in the economic environment do not change.

Remember that an economic model includes assumptions about relationships among market variables. Some of the variables that affect consumer demand are the price of the good in question, consumer incomes and tastes, and the prices and availability of related goods and services. In order to draw a demand curve, we will set aside, ceteris paribus, uncontrollable variables—tastes, incomes, and the availability and prices of other goods—and consider only the relationship between the price of a particular good and the quantity of that good that will be purchased. We also will assume that all other variables remain constant, ceteris paribus, while we construct our model.

Excluding all other factors from our analysis allows us to express consumer demand for a particular good as a function of its price:

Quantity demanded (Q_d) = f(p).

In this demand function, quantity demanded is the dependent variable whose behavior depends on changes in the independent variable, price. The precise form of a consumer demand function depends on the relationship between price and the quantity desired by a particular consumer. This relationship depends, in turn, on the benefits (or utility) the consumer gains from purchasing the good.

Most consumer demand functions follow the **law of demand**. The law of demand states that larger quantities will be purchased only at lower prices. Thus, there is normally an inverse relationship between price and quantity demanded. This inverse relationship is based on benefit/cost comparisons for all goods and on the assumption of diminishing marginal utility for particular goods. (Because additional units of a particular good yield smaller gains in total utility, additional purchases will be made only at lower prices. Lower prices ensure that the marginal utility per dollar associated with an additional purchase of one good is equal to that of all other goods.) The inverse relationship between price and quantity demanded is frequently indicated by a minus sign for the price variable in the demand equation.

Many consumer demand functions have the form of a linear equation. Linear equations are written:

$Y = a + b(X)$,

where Y represents the dependent variable and X the independent variable, and a and b are the parameters of the equation.

The linear equation for a demand function is written

$Q_d = a - b(p)$,

where Q_d is quantity demanded, and p is the price of the good. The parameters of the demand equation are the constant a and the coefficient b. The negative sign for *b* reflects the inverse relationship between price and quantity demanded.

Graphing a consumer's demand equation produces a demand curve. A typical consumer demand curve is shown in Figure 2.12. Price is measured on the vertical axis and quantity on the horizontal axis. The downward slope of the demand curve indicates an inverse relationship between price and quantity demanded in keeping with the law of demand.

The arrangement of the axes in Figure 2.12 is the conventional one for depicting a demand curve. However, the student should note a difference between the typical demand curve and curves drawn from equations describing other market phenomena. In graphing most economic models, the independent variable is measured on the horizontal axis and the dependent variable on the vertical axis. When graphing demand, however, the dependent variable, quantity, appears on the horizontal axis and the independent variable, price, appears on the vertical axis.

A single consumer's demand function combines with the demand functions of all other consumers to constitute the **market demand function** for a particular good or service. The market demand function depicts the *total* quantities

FIGURE 2.12   **A Typical Demand Curve**

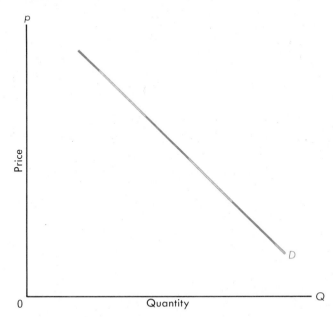

Quantity demanded is inversely related to price. When drawing a demand curve, the independent variable (price) is normally measured on the vertical axis, and the dependent variable (quantity) is measured on the horizontal axis.

EXAMPLE 2.1   Using Least-Squares Regression to Estimate the Parameters of a Linear Demand Equation

An important role of managers is to project the effect on sales of changes in the price of a firm's product. By using **least-squares regression**, a manager can estimate the parameters of the demand equation and draw a demand curve for the firm's product. This model of demand can help project sales and total revenue for alternative market strategies.

No estimated equation can correctly describe the quantity that will be demanded at every price. Some actual values typically will fall above or below the demand curve drawn from an estimated demand equation. Still, least-squares regression analysis enables the analyst to write an equation that represents the closest approximation to observed market data. *The equation that comes closest to approximating observed market data is the one for which the squared differences between actual observations and values determined from the regression equation are at a minimum.*

To illustrate least-squares regression, suppose a firm supplies a product to a number of similar markets at various prices. The quantity the firm sells to each market is listed in the following table as Column (1).

TABLE A   Price and Quantity Data for Estimating a Linear Demand Equation

(1) Quantity demanded (Q)	(2) Market price (p)	(3) $p(Q)$	(4) p^2	(5) Q_e	(6) $(Q - Q_e)$	(7) $(Q - Q_e)^2$	(8) $(Q - \bar{Q})$	(9) $(Q - \bar{Q})^2$	(10) $(Q_e - \bar{Q})$	(11) $(Q_e - \bar{Q})^2$
11	3.5	38.5	12.25	10.55	.45	.20	4.79	22.92	4.34	18.81
9.2	4.5	41.4	20.25	8.81	.39	.15	2.99	8.93	2.6	6.75
8	5	40	25	7.94	.06	.0036	1.79	3.2	1.73	2.98
6.5	5.8	37.7	33.64	6.55	−.05	.0025	.29	.08	.34	.11
5.5	6	33	36	6.20	−.70	.49	−.71	.51	− .01	.0001
4.5	7.1	31.95	50.41	4.29	.21	.04	−1.71	2.93	−1.92	3.7
3	7	21	49	4.46	−1.46	2.13	−3.21	10.32	−1.75	3.07
2	9	18	81	.98	1.02	1.04	−4.21	17.75	−5.23	27.38
Σ = 49.7	Σ = 47.9	Σ = 261.55	Σ = 307.55			Σ = 4.06		Σ = 66.64		Σ = 62.80

The various prices for selling these quantities are listed in Column (2), and these data points are plotted in Figure A. Notice that the arrangement of the points suggests the typical inverse relationship between price and quantity demanded. Nevertheless, the observations do not constitute a smooth demand curve. The use of least-squares regression will enable us to write an equation and draw a line that comes closest to all the data points.

We will assume that the demand function has the form of a linear equation,

$$Q_d = a - b(p).$$

Linear least-squares regression enables us to estimate the values of the parameters, a and b. For this purpose it is necessary to solve "normal" equations:

$$(1)\ \Sigma Q = n(a) + b\Sigma p$$

and

$$(2)\ \Sigma p(Q) = a\Sigma p + b\Sigma p^2,$$

where ΣQ, Σp, $\Sigma p(Q)$, and Σp^2 are the sums of the indicated values and n is the total number of observations. The values for substituting in the normal equations are calculated in columns (1) through (4) in Table A.

FIGURE A

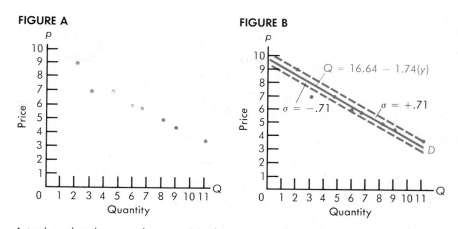

FIGURE B

Actual market data are shown in (a). The projected demand curve is shown in (b).

Substituting these in the normal equations yields:

$$(1)\ 49.7 = 8a + 47.9b$$

and

$$(2)\ 261.55 = 47.9a + 307.55b.$$

Solving (1) for a gives us

$$a = 6.21 - 5.99b.$$

Using this value, we can compute the value of b:

$$261.55 = 47.9(6.21 - 5.99b) + 307.55b$$
$$= 297.46 - 286.92b + 307.55b.$$

Thus, $-35.91 = 20.63b$ and $b = -1.74$. Now, we can substitute to determine a:

$$a = 6.21 - 5.99(-1.74) = 16.64.$$

The preceding computations allow us to write a demand equation describing the observed market conditions. For $a = 16.64$ and $b = -1.74$, the demand equation is

$$Q = 16.64 - 1.74(p).$$

The negative value of the price variable indicates an inverse relationship between price and quantity demanded, in keeping with the law of demand. A line describing $Q = 16.64 - 1.74(p)$ has been added to our previous graph in Figure B to illustrate the functional relationship between price and quantity demanded that is reflected in the observed data.

THE STANDARD ERROR OF THE ESTIMATE

We have indicated that least-squares regression yields the equation that comes closest to fitting the observed data. The difference between the values computed from the regression equation and the actual values determines the **standard error of the estimate.** The standard error of the estimate is a measure of how closely the regression equation fits the data and is an indication of the equation's usefulness for managerial decision making.

The formula for the standard error is:

$$\text{Standard error } (\sigma) = \sqrt{\Sigma(Q - Q_e)^2/n},$$

where Q represents actual values, Q_e represents values estimated from the regression equation, and n is the number of observations.

Thus, the standard error of the estimate is determined by first computing the regression values of Q for all observed values of p, subtracting the regression values from the actual values of Q and squaring the differences, and then determining the average of the squared differences. (Squaring the differences is necessary because unless the differences are squared, positive differences above the regression equation values would be cancelled out by the negative differences below. The sum of the differences would be zero.) The standard error is the square root of the average of the squared differences.

Look again at Table A. Column (5) lists values for Q_e, the estimated values of Q using the regression equation, and Column (6) lists the differences between observed and estimated values. The differences are squared in Column (7) for computation in the formula. Thus,

$$\text{Standard error } (\sigma) = \sqrt{(4.06)/18} = \sqrt{.51} = \pm.71.$$

The value $\sigma = .71$ is interpreted as follows. Over the range for which the linear regression equation is appropriate, $\frac{2}{3}$ of the actual values of Q will lie within a range extending one standard error above and below the estimated value. Now, refer back to Figure B and the line representing the linear demand equation. Parallel lines drawn $\sigma = .71$ units above and below the linear equation would, in fact, include $\frac{2}{3}$ of the data points. Thus, an analyst might conclude that a price of, say, $6.50 would yield monthly sales of $Q = 16.64 - 1.74(6.50) \pm .71 =$ between 4.62 and 6.04 units of output at least $\frac{2}{3}$ of the time.

Further, we can say that actual values will lie within two standard errors of the estimate at least 95 percent of the time. This allows us to note that a price of $6.50 would yield monthly sales of $Q = 16.64 - 1.74(6.50) \pm 2(.71) =$ between 3.91 and 6.75 units of output at least 95 percent of the time.

THE COEFFICIENT OF DETERMINATION

Another useful statistic allows the analyst to measure the portion of the variation of observed data that is, in fact, explained by the regression equation. The **coefficient of determination** is the ratio of explained variation to the total variation of the data:

$$\text{Coefficient of determination } (R^2) = \frac{\text{explained variation}}{\text{total variation}}.$$

The **total variation** of the observations is determined by first computing the average of the observations. The average of the observations in Table A is

$$\bar{Q} = 49.7/8 = 6.21.$$

Next, we must compute the difference between the actual observations and the average, or $(Q - \bar{Q})$. As before, the differences should be squared and summed to determine total variation:

$$\text{Total variation} = \Sigma(Q - \bar{Q})^2.$$

The differences between the actual observations and the average are shown in Column (8) of Table A, and their squares are shown in Column (9).

The **explained variation** of the observations is determined by computing the difference between the estimated values and the average, squaring the differences and summing. Thus,

$$\text{Explained variation} = \Sigma(Q_e - \bar{Q})^2,$$

where Q_e represents values computed using the regression equation. These values are listed in Columns (10) and (11) of Table A. Finally, the coefficient of determination is computed by substituting the sums from Table A into the formula:

$$\text{Coefficient of determination } (R^2) = \frac{\text{explained variation}}{\text{total variation}} = \frac{\Sigma(Q_e - \overline{Q})^2}{\Sigma(Q - \overline{Q})^2}$$

$$= 62.80/66.64 = .94.$$

The coefficient of determination tells us that .94 or 94 percent of the variation of the data is explained by our regression equation.

---

that would be purchased at every price during a period of time when consumers' incomes and tastes and the prices and availability of related goods remain unchanged. Graphing the market demand function yields a market demand curve. The position of the market demand curve depends on the number of consumers in the market, their incomes and tastes during the period of time in question, and the prices and availability of related goods. The shape of the demand curve depends on the shape of individual consumer demand curves, which depend in turn on consumers' responsiveness to changes in price, ceteris paribus.

CHANGES IN QUANTITY DEMANDED

The demand curve in Figure 2.12 describes demand over a short period of time during which factors other than price remain constant. During the period of time the demand curve represents, changes in price lead to movements along the curve. Movements along the demand curve are described as changes in "quantity demanded."

The magnitude of a change in quantity demanded depends on two effects: the **income effect** and the **substitution effect**.

The income effect results from the fact that a single price change alters the buying power of the consumer's total budget and the total quantity of goods he or she can buy. Lower prices mean greater buying power and increased purchases of most goods and services. Higher prices mean the reverse. Therefore, we can say that the income effect produces opposite changes in price and quantity for most goods and services.

The substitution effect also results from a change in price, which alters the MU/p for the affected good and calls for a re-allocation of the consumer's budget according to benefit/cost comparisons with other goods. Lower prices increase the marginal utility per dollar of a particular good. The consumer would be expected to increase purchases of that good until the MU/p's of all goods are once again equal.

Thus, movements down a consumer's demand curve reflect two circumstances—greater total spending power and higher MU/p—both of which call for larger purchases of a particular good or service.

For most goods and services, the income and substitution effects work together, producing a demand curve that slopes downward. In other words, consumers buy more at lower prices because lower prices mean greater buying power and also because lower prices increase the *MU/p* of a particular good. There are exceptions to this rule, however. As we discussed earlier, some goods are less highly valued as consumers' buying power increases. Examples are cheap food items such as dried beans. Lower prices for such staple food items enable consumers to substitute higher-priced foods and purchase a smaller quantity of beans. For some consumers, the quantity demanded for these goods may change in the same direction as price.

When changes in consumers' incomes cause purchases to change in the opposite direction, the income effect works in the opposite direction from the substitution effect. A lower price for an inferior good, for example, increases the consumer's buying power, but with increased buying power the consumer wants *less* of the inferior good. A strongly negative income effect may affect purchases so strongly as to offset completely the substitution effect. Stated differently, if a price decrease causes a consumer to reduce his or her desire for a particular good or service significantly, lower prices may mean fewer total quantities. In this extreme case, a demand curve might slope back to the left as price approaches zero. A backward-bending demand curve is so rare that we will not consider it further in this analysis. We will assume that quantity demanded changes in the opposite direction from price and that demand curves obey the law of demand.

CHANGES IN DEMAND

Economists distinguish between changes in "quantity demanded" and changes in "demand." Changes in demand originate with changes in factors in the economic environment other than price: changes in incomes, tastes, and the prices and availability of other related goods and services. (Remember that these were the factors we held constant when drawing our demand curve.) Changes in "demand" are shown as shifts in the entire demand curve. Rightward shifts reflect larger quantities at every price and are described as increases in demand. Leftward shifts reflect smaller total quantities and are termed decreases in demand.

Figure 2.13a illustrates an increase in demand for automobiles associated with an increase in consumers' incomes. The rightward shift in the demand curve indicates that automobiles are a superior good. Figure 2.13b illustrates a decrease in demand for bus tickets, also associated with an increase in consumers' incomes. The leftward shift in the demand curve indicates that bus tickets are an inferior good.

You might think of changes in demand as changes in the "ceteris paribus" conditions we held constant when we drew a demand curve. (When conditions in the economic environment change, "ceteris" are no longer "paribus," and we must draw a new curve.) New economic conditions call for new informa-

FIGURE 2.13   **Demand Curves for Superior and Inferior Goods**

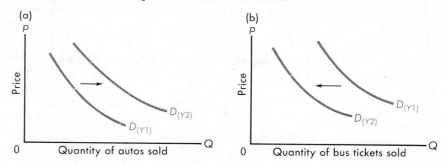

Demand for superior goods increases as income increases (a). Demand for inferior goods decreases as income increases (b).

tion, which becomes the basis for making a new business decision. Managers must be aware of these and other changes in the economic environment and plan strategies to deal with them.

KFC REVISITED

Probably without actually using all of the decision-making tools we have just talked about—indifference curves, marginal utility, and demand curves—the managers of Kentucky Fried Chicken came to understand and put to use some important facts about the theory of consumer demand:

1. Consumers' incomes were increasing, so budget lines were shifting to the right. Moreover, many families regarded meals prepared away from home as superior goods, so purchases tended to increase at higher income levels. In general, demand curves for restaurant meals were shifting to the right.

2. At the same time, however, other restaurants were competing for the consumer's food dollar, so there were more substitute goods for consumers to choose among. In fact, many consumers' preferences had begun to shift from fried chicken to other varieties of fast foods. The marginal utility of KFC's product declined relative to products of other suppliers, and KFC demand curves shifted to the left.

3. Following KFC's analysis of the problem, the firm's strong marketing effort helped increase the attractiveness of the firm's product and increased its marginal utility. As their indifference curves changed shape again, consumers began to purchase more fried chicken. KFC's demand curves shifted to the right again, and the portion of income spent in KFC's restaurants began to increase.

4. As for the future, KFC's managers must continue to be alert to market changes that may affect sales of their product. Smaller average family size and

more families with two bread-winners will tend to increase consumers' demand for meals prepared away from home. On the other hand, a rising average age for the consumer population will tend to reduce sales of what many adults may regard as an "unsophisticated" food. Also, denser concentrations of population will tend to increase the profitability of existing fast-food enterprises even though rising transportation costs may discourage trips away from home for meals.

Perhaps you can suggest other trends that may affect fast-food sales in the future. The theory of consumer demand will help managers visualize the processes by which changes in the economic environment affect purchases of particular goods and services. Then, using these models can help managers plan marketing strategy for maximizing a firm's profit.

SUMMARY

Buyers compare the attributes of particular goods and services—their benefits and costs—and choose a combination that achieves equal marginal utility per dollar of price for each good. The tangency of an indifference curve with a buyer's budget line identifies the maximum-utility combination of goods. At the maximum-utility combination, the marginal rate of substitution of one good for another is equal to a ratio of their prices.

Substitute goods have indifference curves with a fairly constant slope, and complements have indifference curves that curve where quantities of the two goods are in the proper proportion. Shifts in the buyer's budget line signify changes in price or income and result in changes in the maximum-utility combination of goods. Lower prices cause purchases of larger quantities of superior goods because of the substitution and income effects. Lower prices may also mean smaller quantities of inferior goods are purchased because a negative income effect fully offsets the substitution effect.

An economic model of demand can be constructed to show the relationship between quantity demanded and other variables, including the price of the particular good or service, buyers' incomes, prices of related goods and services, and buyers' tastes and preferences. A linear demand curve can be estimated using least-squares regression. Changes in price cause movements along the demand curve. Changes in buyers' incomes, tastes, and prices of related goods cause shifts in the demand curve.

KEY TERMS

attribute	marginal utility
consumer	indifference curve
business firm	marginal rate of substitution
government	budget line
total utility	strongly superior good

mildly superior good	**law of demand**
inferior good	**market demand function**
income-expansion path	**least-squares regression**
price-expansion path	**standard error of the estimate**
substitute goods	**coefficient of determination**
perfect substitutes	**total variation**
complementary goods	**explained variation**
perfect complements	**income effect**
demand curve	**substitution effect**

QUESTIONS AND PROBLEMS

1. Explain clearly why the following budget allocation is not an optimum position for the consumer: $MU_a/p_a > MU_b/p_b$.

2. Discuss the significance of the slope of an indifference curve. How does slope reveal marginal utilities for the goods graphed on the curve? What is significant about the tangency of an indifference curve to the budget line?

3. Describe and explain the changes in shape of indifference curves at higher levels of utility when superior goods are measured along the vertical axis and inferior goods along the horizontal axis. What are the consequences of such changes for a consumer's income-expansion path?

4. Explain the consequence of a strong negative income effect for purchases of a good whose price has increased. Give examples of goods that might fall in this category.

5. Distinguish between cardinal and ordinal theories of consumer demand and explain their advantages and/or disadvantages.

6. Consider two goods that are close substitutes. Explain the basis for the slope of their indifference curves.

7. The theory of consumer demand explains how consumers make choices. How might this theory be adapted to explain a *business firm's* choice of materials for use in production? In the corresponding theory of business demand, what variables would be used in place of utility, total utility, and marginal utility? Rewrite the expression of a consumer's benefit/cost comparisons so that it appies to a business's decision to purchase industrial materials.

8. Distinguish between a consumer's preferred *proportions* of goods and services and the consumer's preferred *quantities*. How do benefit/cost comparisons help determine both?

9. After vigorous growth at the start of the decade, Atari Inc. suffered a loss of $500 million in 1983. Sales for the video-game industry as a whole fell

also. What events in the economic environment may have occurred over this period to change Atari's sales? What strategies would have been considered for dealing with the problem?

10. Rising rates for electric power have caused significant cut-backs in aluminum production in the 1980s, with a resulting drop in employment in the industry. Discuss the substitute/complement relationships between: electric power and aluminum ore, aluminum ore and labor, and finished aluminum and tin. Draw a series of graphs showing indifference curves and a budget line for (a) electric power and aluminum ore, (b) aluminum and labor, and (c) aluminum and tin.

11. Suppose a consumer is equalizing benefit/cost ratios by purchasing 12 restaurant meals with $MU_r/p_r = 15/3$ and 12 gallons of gasoline with $MU_g/p_g = 10/2$ on a budget of $60. What other possible combinations are possible within this consumer's budget? What additional information is needed for drawing a demand curve for restaurant meals? Explain the expected result of an increase in the consumer's total budget.

12. Graph a consumer's demand curve for restaurant meals showing $p_r = \$5$ and $Q_r = 8$ for a particular month. Now assume a $1 increase in price and show the effect on monthly purchases on your graph. Explain how the higher price can be said to produce an income effect and a substitution effect.

13. Between 1970 and 1973 an index of gasoline prices rose from 105.6 to 118.1, yet total gasoline consumption increased by 13 percent. Use a graph to illustrate the market for gasoline over the period. Explain the basis for your drawing.

14. As the average age of the U.S. population increases, bicycle manufacturers expect sales growth to slow. Illustrate changing tastes for bicycles by using indifference curves. Then suggest strategies bicycle manufacturers might employ to regain their market.

15. Draw a diagram that illustrates the expected effect of the Surgeon General's warning on cigarette packages on consumer demand for cigarettes.

16. HMOs are organizations that provide health care to their members for a regular monthly fee. What is the likely effect of the growth of HMOs on consumer demand for medical services? Support your answer.

3

Estimating Demand and Constructing a Demand Curve

The theory of consumer demand provides a framework for explaining why buyers behave the way they do. In this chapter, we will demonstrate mathematical techniques through which managers can apply the theory of consumer demand to decisions regarding business strategy.

A REVIEW OF THE FACTORS THAT DETERMINE DEMAND

Purchases of certain goods are strongly affected by particular factors in the economic environment that managers can identify and monitor. Then, managerial decisions can be based on expected buyer response to expected changes in these factors.

We have identified four important factors that affect consumer purchases: *price, income, tastes,* and the *prices and availability of related goods and services.*

1. *Price.* Changes in manufacturers' costs of production may cause price changes that strongly affect sales. Higher raw material costs may mean that some products are no longer profitable at current prices. Managers may be forced either to raise the product's price or to seek new production processes or new product designs. Even lower costs can create problems for manufacturers whose production processes are not equipped to take advantage of new, less costly production techniques. In the past few years, many manufacturers of electronic equipment have adjusted well to new technologies and thus have

reduced their production costs significantly. Others, however, retained old techniques too long and fell prey to competition from new, more innovative manufacturers.

2. *Incomes*. Changes in income affect purchases in different ways depending on whether the income change is part of a long-term trend or simply a short-term fluctuation above or below a trend. Long-term growth of income can ensure sales growth for producers of strongly superior goods, but income growth may mean decreasing markets for producers of goods that are only mildly superior. Manufacturers of denim jeans have discovered this fact in recent years and have taken steps to expand their product lines to include goods that are more strongly superior.

Short-term fluctuations of income can mean instability in sales and production for manufacturers of durable goods. The recession of the early 1980s produced losses and layoffs for many firms producing motor vehicles, appliances, and furniture. Managers learned to cut costs by cutting inventory stocks, reducing bank borrowing, and increasing productivity.

3. *Tastes*. Changes in consumer tastes can render existing productive capacity obsolete, making the extensive use of capital equipment impractical in highly changeable markets. For this reason, managers in the clothing industry tend to recommend a greater use of labor than capital in their manufacturing processes. The same is true in the electronics industry, where rapid changes in products on the market could wipe out a manufacturer's entire investment.

4. *Prices and availability of related goods and services*. Finally, managers must be alert to changes in prices and availability of related goods and services. If automobile manufacturers had anticipated and planned for higher gasoline prices, they might not have been caught with unsold inventories of large, gas-guzzling automobiles. If U.S. producers of livestock feed had anticipated and planned for competition from soybeans grown in Latin America, the United States might not have experienced heavy build-ups of grain surpluses and increases in farm bankruptcies.

Consumers' responsiveness to changes in all of these factors is described in terms of **elasticity of demand**. Elasticity of demand is measured as the percentage change in sales associated with a percentage change in any of the important determinants of consumer purchases. Thus, *price* elasticity of demand is measured as:

$$\text{Price elasticity } (\epsilon_p) = \frac{\text{percentage change in quantity demanded}}{\text{percentage change in price}}.$$

The following sections will explain the computation and uses of demand elasticity with respect to each of the major factors that affect demand. In each case, we will compute consumers' responsiveness to changes in one of the factors with *the others remaining constant*. Finally, we will show how each of the factors affecting demand can be incorporated in a demand function for use in evaluating alternative business strategies.

FIGURE 3.1   Elasticity for Various Segments of a Linear Demand Curve

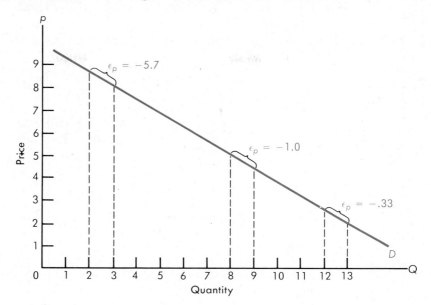

PRICE ELASTICITY OF DEMAND[1]

Changes in quantity demanded are measured in terms of **price elasticity of demand**. Price elasticity of demand can be shown on a demand curve like the one introduced in Chapter 2 and shown again in Figure 3.1. Movements along the demand curve reflect the responsiveness of consumers to changes in price. For example, in Figure 3.1 an increase in price from $2.09 per unit to $2.67 per unit causes quantity demanded to fall from 13 units to 12 units per month. The increase in price is shown mathematically as

$$\Delta p = p_2 - p_1 = \$0.58,$$

and the decrease in quantity is expressed as

$$\Delta Q = Q_2 - Q_1 = -1.$$

---

1. Elasticity computations in this explanation are computed by conventional means, using averages. This procedure differs somewhat from the procedures for computing "arc" elasticity (elasticity over a range of the demand curve) and "point" elasticity (elasticity at a specific point on the demand curve). However, the shorter the range over which elasticity is measured, the more nearly the three procedures will yield the same answer.

The absolute changes in price and quantity demanded are less significant to managers than the percentage changes in these values. This is because price levels and units of product differ widely among goods. For this reason *price elasticity* of demand is defined in terms of percentages:

$$\epsilon_p = \frac{\text{percentage change in quantity demanded}}{\text{percentage change in price}} = \frac{\% \Delta Q_d}{\% \Delta_p}.$$

To determine the percentage change in both variables, it is necessary to compare absolute changes with a base figure. Thus, percent change in quantity demanded is

$$\% \Delta Q_d = \Delta Q/Q,$$

and percent change in price is

$$\% \Delta p = \Delta p/p,$$

where Q and p are a base level of quantity and price. Percentage change will differ depending on whether the base used is the value before or after the price change. Therefore, it is customary to select an average of the two values as the base of the percentage. Thus:

$$\% \Delta Q_d = \frac{(Q_2 - Q_1)}{1/2(Q_2 + Q_1)} = \frac{-1}{12.5},$$

and

$$\% \Delta p = \frac{(p_2 - p_1)}{1/2(p_2 + p_1)} = \frac{0.58}{2.38}.$$

In our example, price elasticity of demand for a price increase from \$2.09 to \$2.67 is

$$\epsilon_p = \frac{\% \Delta Q_d}{\% \Delta p} = \frac{-1/12.5}{.58/2.38} = -.33.$$

Note that the value for price elasticity in our example has a negative sign. Price elasticity of demand is almost always negative since we have assumed an inverse relationship between price and quantity demanded for most goods. (Higher prices generally mean smaller purchases, ceteris paribus.) Because we are primarily interested in the magnitude of buyer response, however, we will generally omit the minus sign and refer only to the absolute value of elasticity.

In our example, a 1-percent change in price produces less than a 1-percent change in quantity purchased. For an absolute value of ϵ_p less than one, we say that demand is relatively **price inelastic**.

On linear demand curves, price elasticity of demand differs at various prices. Look again at Figure 3.1. For a price increase from $7.84 to $8.41 per unit, quantity demanded falls from 3 units to 2 units per month. In this case, price elasticity is

$$\epsilon_p = \frac{\%\Delta Q_d}{\%\Delta p} = \frac{-1/2.5}{.57/8.12} = -5.7.$$

At this price, a 1-percent change in price produces more than a 1-percent change in quantity purchased. For an absolute value of ϵ_p greater than one, we say that demand is relatively **price elastic**.

Let us look at one more example of a price change and compute elasticity. In Figure 3.1, a price increase from $4.39 to $4.97 causes quantity demanded to fall from 9 to 8 units per month. Price elasticity in this case is

$$\epsilon_P = \frac{\%\Delta Q_d}{\%\Delta p} = \frac{-1/8.5}{.58/4.68} = -1.0.$$

A 1-percent change in price in this example produces an equal percentage of change in quantity purchased. In such cases we say that price elasticity of demand is **unitary**.

The three measures of price elasticity are marked in Figure 3.1. A linear demand curve like the one in Figure 3.1 will always have inelastic demand at low prices, elastic demand at high prices, and unitary elasticity at the precise midpoint of the demand curve. This is always true of a downward-sloping linear demand curve, regardless of the angle of slope. Demand curves with steeper slopes will have unitary elasticity at higher prices, since the midpoint of the curve occurs at a higher price. More horizontal curves will have unitary elasticity at lower prices.

Elasticity values computed according to the process we have just described are relevant for price reductions as well as for price increases. In the case of price reductions, the denominator of the elasticity ratio will have a negative sign, and the sign of elasticity will also be negative. (Lower prices will mean larger purchases, ceteris paribus.)

Price Elasticity and Total Revenue

Price elasticity of demand is useful for predicting the behavior of total revenue at various price levels. The behavior of total revenue depends on the magnitude of the change in sales relative to the change in price. To understand this, look again at Figure 3.1. The demand curve in Figure 3.1 was shown to have high (absolute) elasticity at high prices, low (absolute) elasticity at low prices, and unitary (absolute) elasticity at the midpoint of the curve. In practical terms, this means:

1. For high (absolute) elasticity, quantity demanded changes in a *greater percentage* than price.
2. For low (absolute) elasticity, quantity demanded changes in a *smaller percentage* than price.
3. For unitary (absolute) elasticity, quantity demanded changes in the *same percentage* as price.

If quantity demanded changes by a greater percentage than price, a price *reduction* will yield an increase in total revenue. This is because a lower price will attract enough new orders to more than offset the reduction in revenue per unit sold. On the other hand, if quantity demanded changes by a smaller percentage than price, a price *increase* will yield an increase in total revenue. The higher price will reduce sales, but not enough to offset the effect on revenue produced by the higher price per unit.

Figure 3.2 has the same horizontal axis, quantity, as Figure 3.1. The vertical axis of Figure 3.2 measures total revenue associated with quantity demanded at the prices shown in Figure 3.1. Total revenue is calculated by multiplying price by quantity at each point on the demand curve. Notice that high prices and small quantities are associated with low total revenue. This is the range of high (absolute) price elasticity in which price *reductions* would cause total revenue to increase. Low prices and large quantities are also associated with low total revenue. This is the range of low (absolute) price elasticity in which price *increases* would cause total revenue to increase. At some level of price and quantity on the curve, small price changes cause equal percentage changes in quantity demanded and total revenue remains the same. This is the point of maximum total revenue, and it is also the point at which price elasticity of demand is unitary.

Using Calculus to Locate the Point of Maximum Revenue

For any linear demand curve, total revenue reaches a peak at the point of unitary elasticity. We can use the process called "optimization" (explained in Appendix 1A) to identify the quantity of output at which a firm's sales will yield maximum total revenue.

Consider again the demand curve graphed in Figure 3.1. The equation for this curve is $Q = 16.64 - 1.74(p)$. Total revenue is computed by multiplying price times quantity:

$$TR = (p)(Q) = p(16.64 - 1.74p) = 16.64p - 1.74p^2.$$

Note that the total revenue function has the form of a quadratic equation. (The constant that typically appears in a quadratic equation is equal to zero in this example, since at a price of $p = 0$, *TR* also would have a value of zero.)

FIGURE 3.2 **Total Revenue and Price Elasticity of Demand**

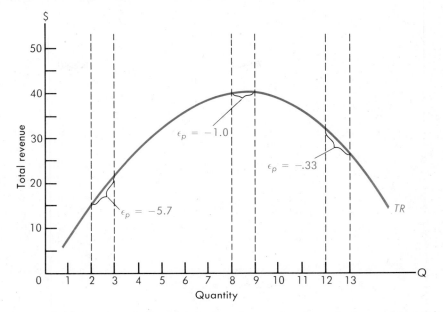

For an absolute value of elasticity greater than one, price reductions cause total revenue to increase. For an absolute value of price elasticity less than one, price increases cause total revenue to increase. For an absolute value of price elasticity equal to one, total revenue is at a maximum.

The first step in the process of optimization is to compute the derivative of the function to be optimized:

The derivative of $TR = 16.64p - 1.74p^2 = \dfrac{dTR}{dp} = 16.64 - 3.48p.$

The maximum (or minimum) value of the function occurs where the curve levels off and the slope (or derivative) is equal to zero. Thus,

$16.64 - 3.48p = 0$ and $p = \$4.78.$ [2]

For $p = \$4.78$, quantity sold is determined by using this value in the demand function:

$Q = 16.64 - 1.74(4.78) = 8.32.$

---

2. We know this is the maximum value of the function because the second derivative of the function is $d^2TR/dp^2 = -3.48$, a negative number.

Thus, total revenue at the revenue-maximizing quantity of output is

$$TR = (p)(Q) = \$4.78 \cdot 8.32 = \$39.7696.$$

Now look again at Figures 3.1 and 3.2 and verify that maximum total revenue occurs when $p = \$4.78$ and $Q = 8.32$, and that total revenue is equal to \$39.76.

Some Factors That Determine Price Elasticity of Demand

Price elasticity of demand is affected by four attributes of the product relative to the consumer's total market basket of goods. One significant attribute is *whether the good is a **luxury** or a **necessity***. Necessities tend to have low price elasticities, since they must be bought regardless of price. Staple food items, electric power, certain health services, and medicinal drugs are examples of necessities. Luxuries tend to be more price elastic, since consumers decide whether to buy a luxury item depending on its price. As consumers' budgets increase, however, some luxury goods may become practical necessities. Power lawn mowers may be an example of a good that was once a luxury but is now becoming a practical necessity for suburban home owners.

Other luxury goods can be made to seem like necessities through clever advertising. Cosmetics and personal care products are examples of this. One goal of advertising is to add positive attributes to a product, making the good appear to be a necessity and causing price elasticity to decrease.

Closely related to this first attribute is the *existence of acceptable substitutes*. If acceptable substitutes are available, consumers will respond to a price change by freely re-allocating their budgets. Price elasticity in such a case will be relatively high. Indeed, continuing price increases for beef have led many consumers to substitute lower-priced meats, poultry, or cheese for this item. On the other hand, for many consumers fuel oil has no substitute as a source of heat (at least in the short run), so the quantity of fuel oil purchased has scarcely been affected by substantial price increases. Another objective of advertising is to convince consumers that a particular product has no substitute and to keep price elasticity of demand low.

A third attribute of goods and services involves *the necessary expenditure* for a certain good relative to a consumer's total budget. Goods that require a small expenditure relative to the consumer's total budget may be unaffected by price changes. For example, the price of restaurant coffee has increased substantially without significantly affecting consumer purchases. On the other hand, rising costs of housing during the 1980s forced many families to postpone purchases or to purchase smaller houses.

The fourth attribute that affects price elasticity may be of greatest interest to managers. This is the factor of *time*. Time can work to make consumers either more or less responsive to price change. Over time, new substitute products can be developed such that price elasticity of demand for existing goods increases. Or, time can reduce price elasticity through advertising that convinces consumers of a good's necessity. Over time, changes in consumers' budgets may also affect elasticity. Increases in consumers' budgets can reduce price elasticity of demand for many goods. When budgets increase, consumers will continue to buy, but with less regard for price. If consumers' budgets decline, however, buyers may become more sensitive to price so that price elasticity of demand increases.

Computing Price Elasticity

There are several problems with actually measuring price elasticity of demand. To compute price elasticity, the analyst must be able to set several different prices and measure sales at each price level. Experiments like this must be made at different points in time and at different geographical locations. Since many factors other than price may be affecting sales over the intervals of distance and time, the resulting data may not reflect responsiveness to price alone. (Economics is quite different from chemistry, in which experiments can be conducted under controlled laboratory conditions without uncontrollable influences on the results.) Nevertheless, the researcher should conduct several sales experiments under market conditions as nearly identical as possible, with only differences in price allowed to influence sales.

The hypothetical data in Table 3.1 represent market testing in cities of similar population, per capita income, climate, employment, and consumption patterns. The figures show a pharmaceutical firm's sales at various prices during a representative week. In general, the data follow the expected inverse relationship between price and quantity sold. However, sales at the highest selling price are not substantially less than those at lower prices, reflecting some buyer loyalty even at high prices. Furthermore, the limited substitutability

TABLE 3.1 **Pharmaceutical Sales and Revenue Data**

(1) Price (p)	(2) Quantity in thousands (Q)	(3) Total revenue in thousands (p × Q)	(4) ϵ_p
$5.50	7.95	43.73	
5.25	8.25	43.31	−2.33
5.00	9.01	45.05	−1.81
4.75	9.13	43.37	−.26
4.50	10.35	46.58	−2.32
4.25	10.97	46.62	−1.02
4.00	11.54	46.16	.84
3.75	11.70	43.88	.21
3.50	13.00(X)	45.50(X)	−.58
3.25	12.67	41.18	
3.00	12.80	38.40	.13

of pharmaceutical products makes them poorly suited for a wide range of applications. As a result, a lower selling price does not increase sales appreciably.

The inverse relationship between price and quantity sold affects total sales revenue in the expected manner. Total sales revenue is expressed algebraically as $TR = p \times Q$, where p is the price per unit of sales and Q is the number of units sold. Thus, in our example total sales revenue at a price of $5 is $5 \times 9,010 = \$45,050$. Total sales revenue at each price is shown in Column (3) of Table 3.1. You will notice in Column (3) that high prices and low volume are associated with low total revenue. Low prices and high volume likewise produce low total revenue. Over some mid-range of price, however, volume is high enough that total sales revenue is a maximum.

In order to visualize the data in Table 3.1, it is helpful to graph price-quantity values in a scatter diagram such as Figure 3.3 In this graph, price is measured along the vertical axis and quantity sold in thousands of units is measured along the horizontal axis. In general, the scatter diagram confirms the expected inverse relationship between price and quantity sold. The point

FIGURE 3.3   **Results of Marketing Research Testing of Demand**

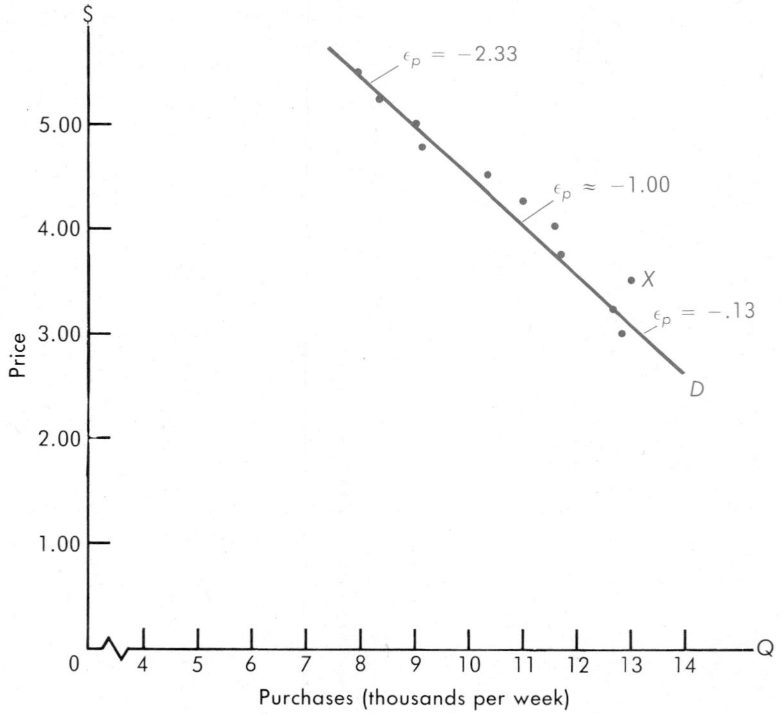

FIGURE 3.4   **Total Revenue for Various Levels of Price and Quantity Demanded**

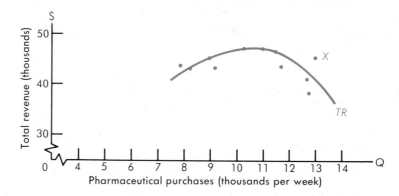

labeled X lies outside the expected pattern, suggesting that some factors other than price may have caused abnormally high sales in this market. Figure 3.4 has the same horizontal axis as Figure 3.3, but its vertical axis measures total sales revenue in thousands of dollars. The pattern of points in this graph confirms the behavior of total revenue at low, medium, and high volumes. Again, the point marked X lies outside the expected pattern as a result of some unspecified random influence on sales.

CHANGES IN DEMAND

To this point, we have considered demand over a short period of time during which factors other than price remain the same. Consumers' responsiveness to price changes have been shown as movements along a single demand curve. Factors other than price might be expected to affect demand over a longer period of time. Changes in consumer tastes might be expected to cause demand curves to shift to the right (an increase in demand) or to the left (a decrease in demand). Changes in income would have the same effect, increasing consumer demand for the types of goods that are preferred at the new income level. Changes in the prices and quantities of other goods may also affect demand curves, as consumers buy larger or smaller quantities of goods related to other goods available in the market.

In the sections that follow, we will look at the other factors that affect consumer purchases: incomes, tastes, and the prices and availability of related goods and services. All these factors are held constant in the ceteris paribus conditions for drawing a single demand curve. Relaxing any of these conditions, however, could cause a change in demand.

FIGURE 3.5   **Demand Curves for Various Levels of Income**

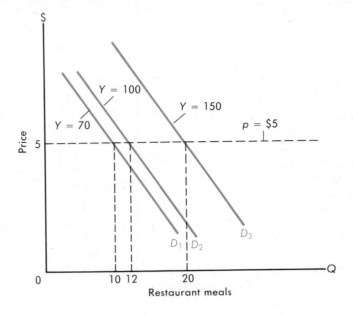

Income Changes and Changes in Demand

The effect of a change in income (Y) is especially significant in decisions involving a firm's product line, productive capacity, and intended market.

One consumer good that is relatively responsive to income changes is meals eaten away from home. Figure 3.5 shows demand curves for restaurant meals at three different weekly income levels: $70, $100, and $150. Holding price constant at $p = \$5$, we can define income elasticity of demand similarly to price elasticity. That is,

Income elasticity of demand $= \epsilon_Y$

$$= \frac{\text{percent change in quantity demanded}}{\text{percent change in income}} = \frac{\%\Delta Q_d}{\%\Delta Y}.$$

The base value for computing the percentage change is an average of the beginning and ending values. From Figure 3.5, we see that

$$\%\Delta Q_d = \frac{(Q_2 - Q_1)}{1/2(Q_2 + Q_1)} = \frac{2}{11},$$

and

$$\%\Delta Y = \frac{(Y_2 - Y_1)}{1/2(Y_2 + Y_1)} = \frac{30}{85}.$$

Therefore, income elasticity of demand in this case is

$$\epsilon_Y = \frac{2/11}{30/85} = .52.$$

Note that here income elasticity of demand is positive. For most goods income elasticity will be positive, since changes in income produce quantity changes in the same direction. Only in the case of certain goods will income changes cause opposite changes in quantity demanded, producing negative income elasticity. In these cases, rising incomes would cause leftward shifts in demand curves such that $\%\Delta Q_d$ would have a negative value.

In this example, $\epsilon_Y = .52$. For $\epsilon_Y < 1$, the percentage change in quantity demanded is less than the percentage change in income. In this case we say that demand is relatively income **inelastic** over the range $Y = \$70$ through $Y = \$100$. Over the income range $Y = \$100$ to $Y = \$150$, income elasticity of demand is

$$\epsilon_Y = \frac{8/14}{50/125} = 1.43.$$

For $\epsilon_Y > 1$, percentage change in quantity demanded is greater than percentage change in income, and we say that demand is relatively income **elastic**.

Superior and Inferior Goods

For the good shown in Figure 3.5, income elasticity of demand is positive. That is, an increase in income causes an increase in purchases. Most goods have positive income elasticity like this one and are classified as *superior* goods. Superior and inferior goods were discussed earlier in Chapter 2. For certain goods, purchases increase at a greater rate than increase in income, and income elasticity is greater than one. Such goods are described as luxuries, or *strongly superior goods*.

Purchases of other goods increase at a lesser rate than increases in income and have income elasticity of between zero and one. Such goods are described as necessities, or *mildly superior goods*.

For a few goods, purchases tend to decline as income increases, and income elasticity is negative. Goods with negative income elasticity are classified as *inferior goods*. Demand curves for inferior goods shift to the left as income increases.

Table 3.2 summarizes the usual relationship between classes of products and income elasticity of demand:

TABLE 3.2   **Income Elasticity for Various Classes of Goods**

Class of product	Income elasticity of demand
Luxuries (strongly superior)	$\epsilon_Y > 1.00$
Necessities (mildly superior)	$0 \leq \epsilon_Y \leq 1.00$
Less preferred goods (inferior)	$\epsilon_Y < 0$

The responsiveness of consumer purchases to income was first recognized by Ernst Engel, a German statistician of the nineteenth century. The differing pattern of expenditures for luxuries and necessities is thus called Engel's law, and curves drawn to relate expenditures to income are called Engel's curves.

Managers of a business firm will probably have a fairly clear idea of the classification of its chief product as either luxury, necessity, or inferior good. They will seek to diversify output in order to ensure a mix of output for which total sales increase at least as fast as consumers' incomes. For forecasting purposes, managers will want to compute more precise values for measuring the responsiveness of sales to income. Using historical data, the manager may determine the responsiveness of sales to income changes in the past and predict a similar percentage change for the future (based on projections of future income).

Computing Income Elasticity Using Cross-Sectional Data

When income elasticity is computed over a period of time, the results reflect changes other than income: technological changes, changes in tastes and lifestyles, changes in the age distribution of a population, population shifts from country to city to suburbs, and many others. Such changes distort consumer response to income changes and make interpretation of elasticity figures uncertain.

One way to eliminate effects of these long-term changes is to use cross-sectional data gathered in a single period of time. Purchases are measured relative to family income during a particular period, and changes in purchases indicate differences between families at various income levels.

To illustrate, we have used Department of Commerce data for average annual expenditures for new and used autos in 1974. Table 3.3 lists expenditures for several broad income brackets. We have used the midpoint of each bracket for making our computations. Income elasticity of expenditures for autos is

$$\epsilon_Y = \frac{(Q_2 - Q_1)/[1/2(Q_2 + Q_1)]}{(Y_2 - Y_1)/[1/2(Y_2 + Y_1)]},$$

where Y represents the midpoint of a particular income bracket.

TABLE 3.3 Income Elasticity for Autos Using Cross-Sectional Data

(1)	(2)	(3)	(4)	(5)	(6)
Income bracket	Midpoint Y	Average annual expenditures for new autos	ϵ_Y (new autos)	Average annual expenditures for used autos	ϵ_Y (used autos)
Less than $3,000	$ 1,500	$103		$ 76	
$ 3,000– 5,000	4,500	164	.46	160	.71
$ 5,000– 7,500	6,250	228	1.00	209	.82
$ 7,500–10,000	8,750	322	1.02	258	.63
$10,000–15,000	12,500	465	1.03	297	.40
$15,000–20,000	17,500	640	.95	303	.06
$20,000–25,000	22,500	832	1.04	324	.26

Source: Department of Commerce, A Guide to Consumer Markets, 1974.

Several specific characteristics of elasticity are revealed in Table 3.3. First, both new and used autos are definitely superior goods. New autos are more strongly superior, although not clearly luxury goods—rather on the borderline between luxury and necessity. Income elasticity of demand for new autos is fairly high, at least for incomes of less than $25,000. Higher elasticity in the $15,000 to $25,000 range suggests that income elasticity may rise at very high incomes. Income elasticity of demand for used autos falls with increased income, as higher-income families shift to new car purchases. The rise in elasticity for incomes ranging from $20,000 to $25,000 probably reflects purchases of second cars.

Managers in the auto manufacturing and retailing industry should be aware of the possible implications of these results. A general shift to higher family incomes may mean proportionally greater sales growth for new cars and proportionally lower sales growth for used autos. Appropriate long-range policy might call for diversification into production of vehicles whose sales respond more strongly at higher incomes, that is, luxury cars, recreational vehicles, and the like.

The food service industry is already experiencing some modifications as a result of the different income elasticities at high incomes. Table 3.4 on page 88 provides data on the income elasticity of expenditures for food eaten at home and away from home. Notice how food purchases respond strongly and positively to income increases at low income levels but become only mildly superior goods at high incomes. Higher income families increase their spending for food by a smaller percentage when income increases. This is true even for food eaten away from home, a strongly superior good up to incomes of $20,000.

There are several possible explanations for the changing income elasticity of demand for food. Higher income families are likely to be smaller, including middle-aged executives whose children have grown up and moved away, single professionals and couples without children, and some elderly individuals.

TABLE 3.4 Income Elasticity for Food Using Cross-Sectional Data

(1) Income bracket	(2) Midpoint Y	(3) Average annual expenditures for food at home	(4) ϵ_Y (food at home)	(5) Average annual expenditures for food away from home	(6) ϵ_Y (food away from home)
Less than $5,000	$ 2,500	$ 262.50		$ 150.00	
			1.56		1.71
$ 5,000–10,000	7,500	1,237.50		900.00	
			1.15		1.62
$10,000–15,000	12,500	2,250.00		2,125.00	
			.92		1.17
$15,000–20,000	17,500	3,062.50		3,150.00	
			.39		.66
$20,000–25,000	22,500	3,375.00		3,712.50	
			1.27		.59
$25,000–30,000	27,500	2,612.50		3,300.00	
			3.39		3.57
$30,000–35,000	32,500	1,462.50		1,787.50	

Source: The Conference Board, 1977.

In any case, managers in this industry should plan their product lines to guard against sales declines as incomes rise. Food retailers might attempt to capture some of the demand for food away from home by providing more processed and carry-out foods, more luxury and delicatessen items, and even catering services. Restaurants should develop their product to appeal to families for which income elasticity of demand is high. This would require market research into the food preferences and dining habits of families in the middle to high income range.

Income Elasticity During a Recession

Our discussion thus far has focused on changes in sales as incomes rise. Using this analysis, managers were advised to plan a product-mix that would allow for rising sales as average incomes rise. Of course, incomes don't always rise. The 1980s have brought at least two years of falling income, or **recession.**

In periods of falling incomes, goods with high income elasticity will suffer the greatest *decline* in sales. The result of high income elasticity may be widely fluctuating levels of employment and production with the risk of business losses in some years. For these reasons, managers might be advised to avoid concentrating production on goods that respond very strongly to income changes. A balance of products for which income elasticity is approximately *one* is probably preferable. A firm that follows this strategy may not enjoy enormous profits in boom years, but, then, it will probably avoid extreme losses during recession.

Including Income in the Demand Function

In Chapter 2 we wrote a demand function using price (p) as the independent variable that determines quantity sold (Q_d). When income is included with price as an independent variable in the demand function, the equation for the

CASE STUDY 3.1   Income Elasticities for Selected Goods

Managers of business firms are interested in the responsiveness of sales of particular consumer goods to changes in consumers' incomes. The following table provides elasticity computations for selected consumer goods. Disposable personal income per capita in current dollars was used for the income computations. Unit sales per capita were used for quantity computations. The data were obtained from the *Economic Report of the President, A Guide to Consumer Markets,* and the *Statistical Abstract of the United States.*

	Wine	Power mowers	Cigarettes	Wringer washing machines	Overalls
1950	−.39		.27		−1.2
1955	16.25		3.24		−7.51
1960	5.19		.16		2.02
1965	1.51	1.26	−.51	−.51	3.36
1970	3.86	1.07	.35	.12	3.86
1972	1.03	3.26	.41	−.04	−.59
1973	1.11	−.77	0	.08	
1974			−.65		
1975			.15		
1976					
1977					

From the table, we see that generally high income elasticities for wine identify it as a strongly superior good. Power mowers are also somewhat strongly superior. Purchases of luxuries like these will probably continue to increase faster than income—at least until ownership becomes so commonplace that consumers begin to regard these items as necessities. Cigarettes appear to be only mildly superior. Sales depend on factors other than per capita income, and they are considered a necessity by many consumers. Old-fashioned wringer-style washing machines are probably inferior, as indicated by the frequency of negative signs for income elasticity. Purchases of this item probably continue to decline proportionately as income increases. The pattern of demand for overalls is quite interesting. It appears to reflect changing life-styles during the 1960s and early 1970s, when overalls ceased being an inferior good and became strongly superior!

CASE STUDY 3.2   Demand Elasticities Nationwide

To illustrate the relationship between consumer purchases of particular goods and the prices of these goods, consumer incomes, and prices of related goods, it is interesting to examine data on these variables nationwide. The *Economic Report of the President,* published in January or February of each year, provides data for a number of past years. The sections that follow will demonstrate the use of these data for calculating income and price elasticity.

INCOME ELASTICITY OF DEMAND FOR FOOD

Food is a necessary commodity whose purchases remain relatively constant regardless of family income. To prove this, it is helpful to observe family food purchases over short periods of time during which food prices were roughly constant but fam-

TABLE A

	Consumer price index: food	Median family income ($1982)	Food expenditures per family	$\frac{\%\Delta Q_d}{\%\Delta Y}$	ϵ_Y
1961	89.1	$18,504	$1,793	1.22	
1962	89.9	19,005	1,815	2.67	.457
1966	99.1	22,402	2,167	0.96	
1967	100.0	22,934	2,188	2.35	.411

ily incomes changed. There were two periods in the 1960s when these conditions were true, as shown in Table A.

Note that consumer food prices were relatively constant during the first period in the table, and family income rose almost 3 percent. Still, food expenditures per family rose only 1.2 percent, for an income elasticity of $\epsilon_Y = \dfrac{1.22\%}{2.67\%} = .457$. The sign of income elasticity is positive, since both income and food expenditures increased. But because the percentage change in purchases was less than the percentage change in income, income elasticity of demand is less than one. Since $\epsilon_Y < 1$, the portion of total income spent for food declined during this period from 24.8 percent of income in 1961 to 24.1 percent of income in 1962.

Similar results occurred in the second period, in which the portion of income spent on food dropped again from 22.9 percent to 22.4 percent. These results confirm our expectation that food is a superior good, but only slightly superior. In fact, if the data were separated according to types of foods, it would be possible to classify particular foods according to their relative superiority (or inferiority) with respect to changes in income. (The characteristics of food described in this section were illustrated in Chapter 2 in which we showed that the income-expansion path bends toward the axis of strongly superior goods and away from the axis representing mildly superior goods.)

PRICE ELASTICITY OF DEMAND FOR DURABLE GOODS

As Americans have come to satisfy their basic needs for food using smaller portions of income, more income has been made available for purchases of other goods. Over the years, purchases of durable consumer goods have grown to absorb an increasing portion of family incomes. Still, because few durable goods are actually essential for life, these purchases tend to fluctuate with changes in incomes and prices. For our purposes, we will be concerned only with the effect of price changes

TABLE B

	Disposable personal income per capita ($1972)	Consumer price index: durable goods (1967 = 100)	Consumer expenditures for durable goods per family ($1972)	$\frac{\%\Delta Q_d}{\%\Delta p}$	ϵ_p
1973	$4,080	121.9	$2,201		
1974	4,009	130.6	2,016	−9.32	
1975	4,051	145.5	2,005	17.65	−.53
1981	4,587	227.1	2,315	−1.66	
1982	4,567	241.1	2,277	5.98	−.28

on family expenditures for durable goods. Two periods during which per capita income changed very little are shown in Table B.

In both periods, disposable personal income per capita was relatively constant, but durable goods prices rose 17.7 percent and 6.0 percent, respectively. Family expenditures for durable goods decreased 9.3 percent in the first period and 1.7 percent in the second. In this case, price elasticity of demand is negative, indicating the inverse relationship between price and quantity demanded. However, because the absolute value of elasticity is between zero and one, we would describe demand for durable goods as relatively inelastic. (The circumstances described in Table B were also illustrated in Chapter 2. Because purchases decrease by a smaller percentage than the price increase, the price-expansion path curves away from the axis representing durable goods. The portion of family income spent for durable consumer goods fell from 15.2 percent in 1973 to 12.3 percent in 1982.)

---

function is written $Q_d = f(p,Y)$. The precise form of the demand function depends on conditions in individual markets for goods and services. However, we have seen that for most goods changes in price (p) cause opposite changes in quantity demanded, such that the sign of the price variable is generally negative. We also know that changes in income (Y) cause changes in the same direction for superior goods and in the opposite direction for inferior goods. Thus, the income variable will be positive for superior goods and negative for inferior goods.

Including income in the demand function produces a linear equation with two independent variables:

$$Q_d = a - b(p) \pm c(Y),$$

where the coefficient c is the change in quantity demanded associated with a change in income. The sign of the income variable is positive for superior goods and negative for inferior goods.

Regression techniques similar to the technique demonstrated in Chapter 2 can be used to estimate the parameters of the expended demand equation. Then, the equation can be used to project sales at various price and income levels. We will demonstrate the process later in this chapter. But first, let us consider the effects on demand caused by the other factors that affect consumer purchases.

Changes in Tastes and Changes in Demand

The third factor that affects consumer purchases is consumer tastes or preferences. Changes in consumer tastes produce changes in the utility associated with purchases of particular goods and services. Increasing preference for a particular good should have two results: Larger quantities will be purchased at all prices, and larger quantities will be purchased in each consumer budget.

As consumers re-allocate their expenditures, demand curves will shift to

FIGURE 3.6   **Changes in Taste**

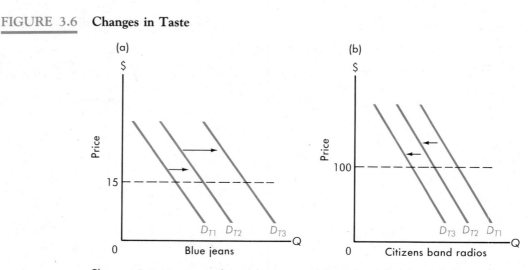

Changes in tastes cause demand curves to shift to the right (a) or left (b).

the right to reflect greater purchases of preferred goods and to the left to reflect decreased purchases of less preferred goods. Figure 3.6 shows hypothetical demand curves illustrating recent changes in consumer tastes. In Figure 3.6a, changing tastes dictate larger purchases of blue jeans at every price and income level. In Figure 3.6b, changing tastes indicate fewer purchases of citizens band radios, ceteris paribus.

You may be familiar with other examples of how changing tastes have affected other U.S. markets. A shift in consumer preferences away from large luxury cars has reduced demand for U.S.-made cars. A decline in the popularity of professional soccer has reduced ticket sales for many of the nation's soccer teams. On the other hand, the increasing popularity of Mexican food has caused rising demand and has prompted a boom for many Mexican restaurants. An increased preference for roller skating has caused rising sales for roller skating equipment.

A demand function that includes tastes as an independent variable would be expressed as $Q_d = f(p, Y, T)$. The definition of the taste variable would depend on the circumstances that determine tastes. Some examples of taste variables include the median age of the population, the rate of family formation, ethnic background of the population, educational level, and amount of advertising expenditures.

Adding taste to the demand function produces a linear equation with three independent variables:

$$Q_d = a - b(p) \pm c(Y) \pm d(T),$$

where the coefficient d measures the change in quantity demanded associated with a change in the taste variable.

The sign of the taste variable depends on the analyst's assumptions regarding the effect of the taste variable on quantity demanded. For example, an increase in the rate of family formation would tend to increase demand for home furnishings. On the other hand, an increase in the median age of the population would tend to reduce demand for toys and school supplies. An increase in advertising expenditure is generally expected to increase demand, but this is not always the case. Managers are interested in the likely effect of advertising expenditures before they undertake costly advertising campaigns.

Changes in Prices and Availability of Other Goods and Services

Consumer purchases of any particular good are affected by the attributes of other goods because of the interrelationships among similar goods. We have called consumer goods that must be used together *complementary goods* and those that can be used in place of each other *substitute goods*. The *effect* of changes in prices and availability of other goods and services on purchases of a particular good or service depends on whether they are substitutes or complements.

First, consider a pair of complementary goods: automobiles and gasoline. If the price of gasoline rises, less fuel will be bought. When less gasoline is purchased, the utility of automobiles falls, and fewer automobiles will be purchased. Thus, for complements, a change in the price of one good affects the quantity demanded of the other in the *opposite direction*.

There are many obvious complementary goods in a consumer's total market basket: beer and pretzels, shirts and ties, tables and chairs. Other complements are not so obvious, such as gasoline and hotel rooms. Why are these items complements? Because many vacation trips depend on automobile transportation, rising gasoline prices may discourage travel and reduce demand for hotel rooms.

Now consider a pair of substitutes: gasoline and bus tickets. For substitute goods, a rise in the price of one causes quantity demanded for this good to fall. However, the absence of this particular good in the consumer's market basket enhances the utility of its substitute, and purchases of the substitute good will increase. Thus, for substitutes, a change in the price of one good affects demand for the other in the *same direction*.

Many consumers substitute freely between food items—such as beef and pork—and between recreation activities—such as movies and bowling. Even a consumer's choice of residence is based on substitution according to price: houses versus condominiums, city neighborhoods versus suburban neighborhoods, even "snowbelt" locations versus "sunbelt" locations. The U. S. pop-

FIGURE 3.7   **Changes in Demand**

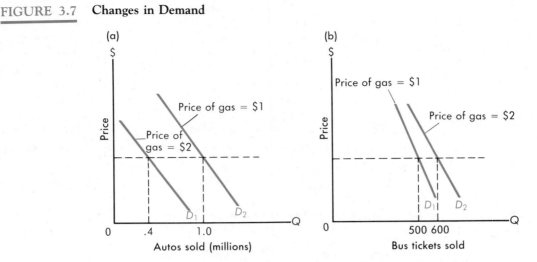

Changes in demand for a good when the price of its complement changes are shown in (a). Changes in demand when the price of the good's substitute changes are shown in (b).

ulation has been undergoing major shifts in living patterns in response to changing home costs in various regions.

Because of these interrelationships, when goods are related in use, the demand function of one includes the price of the other:

$$Q_d = f(p, Y, T, p_o),$$

where p_o represents the price of another good. A change in the independent variable p_o should produce opposite changes in Q_d for complements and changes in the same direction in Q_d for substitutes. Figure 3.7 illustrates this difference. Figure 3.7a shows demand curves for automobiles when the price of gasoline is $p_g = \$1$ and $p_g = \$2$. Autos and gasoline are complementary goods. Figure 3.7b shows demand curves for bus tickets when the price of gasoline is $p_g = \$1$ and $p_g = \$2$. Gasoline and bus tickets are substitutes.

Including other prices in the demand function produces a linear equation with four independent variables:

$$Q_d = a - b(p) \pm c(Y) \pm d(T) \pm e(p_o),$$

where the coefficient e measures the change in quantity demanded associated with a change in price of the other good. The sign of the "other price" variable is positive for substitute goods and negative for complements.

Cross Price Elasticity of Demand

The relationship between interrelated goods can be measured by **cross price elasticity of demand**. Cross price elasticity is the percentage change in quantity demanded of one good relative to a percentage change in price of another:

$$\epsilon_c = \frac{\text{percentage change in quantity of good } a}{\text{percentage change in price of good } b} = \frac{\%\Delta Q_a}{\%\Delta p_b}.$$

If quantity demanded and price move in the same direction, cross price elasticity is positive, and the two goods are substitutes. If quantity demanded and price change in opposite directions, cross price elasticity is negative, and the two goods are complements. The magnitude of the value of cross price elasticity depends on the strength of the relationship between goods. Easily substitutable goods have high positive cross price elasticity, and complements that must be used in precise proportions have high negative cross price elasticity. Goods with more tenuous substitutability or complementarity have cross price elasticities nearer zero.

Automobiles and gasoline are complementary goods with a strong price-quantity relationship. Look again at Figure 3.7a. The percentage change in quantity demanded for autos is

$$\%\Delta Q_a = \frac{(Q_2 - Q_1)}{1/2(Q_2 + Q_1)} = \frac{-.6}{.7}.$$

The percent change in the price of gasoline is

$$\%\Delta p_g = \frac{(p_2 - p_1)}{1/2(p_2 + p_1)} = \frac{1}{1.50}.$$

Cross price elasticity of demand for autos relative to gasoline prices is

$$\epsilon_c = \frac{-.6/.7}{1/1.50} = -1.29.$$

Figure 3.7b suggests the opposite relationship between gas prices and bus tickets. Since bus tickets can be substituted for purchases of gasoline, these items are classified as substitutes. Cross price elasticity of demand is determined as before:

$$\epsilon_c = \frac{\%\Delta Q_b}{\%\Delta p_g} = \frac{100/550}{1/1.50} = .27.$$

Note the appropriate sign of elasticity in both cases. As expected, the sign of elasticity for complements is negative, and the sign for substitutes is posi-

CASE STUDY 3.3 Cross Price Elasticity of Demand for Motor Vehicles Relative to the Price of Motor Fuel

In addition to data from specific local markets, nationwide data are also helpful in examining cross price elasticity of demand. The data in the following table illustrate a strong relationship between purchases of motor vehicles and prices of motor fuel. (Again, these periods were selected because per capita incomes remained relatively constant during them.)

	Disposable personal income per capita ($1972)	Family expenditures for motor vehicles and parts	Consumer price index: motor fuel	$\frac{\%\Delta Q_m}{\%\Delta p_f}$	ϵ_c
1973	$4,080	$1,036	118.1	$\dfrac{-.135}{.301}$	$-.449$
1974	4,009	905	159.1		
1981	4,587	1,666	410.9	$\dfrac{.072}{-.054}$	-1.34
1982	4,567	1,790	389.4		

During the first period in the table, fuel prices rose by 30.1 percent, and motor vehicle purchases dropped 13.5 percent, for a cross price elasticity of −.449. During the second period, prices dropped by 5.4 percent and purchases increased by 7.2 percent, for a cross price elasticity of −1.34. The negative signs in both cases indicate that the two items are indeed complements.

These changes in magnitude of cross price elasticity can be interpreted in several ways. The fact that cross price elasticity increased from one period to the next suggests that between the two periods consumers were able to adjust their purchasing habits so as to respond more easily to motor fuel price changes. Changes in modes of transportation, driving habits, and so forth were partly responsible for this. Also, there may be differences in cross price elasticity, depending on the direction of price change. Finally, remember the other factors in the environment that cannot be controlled or measured when observing the results of a single change. Thus, one or both of the two periods cited may be aberrations from a normal value of cross price elasticity that falls somewhere between these extremes.

tive. Also note the absolute values of elasticity. According to the hypothetical relationship in Figure 3.7, the complementary relationship between autos and gasoline is stronger than the substitutability of bus tickets for gasoline.

APPLYING THE MODEL OF CONSUMER DEMAND TO MANAGERIAL DECISION MAKING

The model of consumer demand is easily stated in terms of fundamental assumptions, clearly defined variables, and predictable consumer behavior. Applying the theory to managerial decisions requires information about real economic conditions, including empirical data for describing conditions in particular markets. Using empirical data, the analyst can write equations describing consumer demand over a range of values for the independent variables involved. The form of the demand function depends on the underlying circumstances that govern consumer decisions relative to a particular good.

We have described one form of demand function in which the variables are *additive:*

$$Q = a - b(p) + c(Y) + d(T) \pm e(p_o) \pm z,$$

where Q is the dependent variable quantity, and the independent variables are price (p), income (Y), tastes (T), as reflected in some characteristic of the relevant market, and prices of other goods (p_o). The parameters of the demand equation are a, b, c, d, and e: a is a constant, $-b$ denotes the typical negative response of quantity demanded to price change, c indicates the change in Q associated with a unit change in income, d measures the effect on Q of changes in tastes, and e reflects the responsiveness of Q to changes in the prices of substitute or complementary goods. The last term, $\pm z$, is an error term. It measures the average difference between observed values of demand and those that would have resulted from applying the regression equation. In effect, $\pm z$ measures all the other factors that affect demand but are not included in a simple demand equation.

Using regression procedures, a manager can estimate values for the parameters and write an additive demand equation that describes the behavior of demand in a particular market for a particular period of time. For example, an estimated equation

$$Q = 150 - 2(p) + .75(Y) + .5(T) - 2(p_o) \pm 3$$

could be used to predict demand during a period in which $p = 5$, $Y = 200$, $T = 50$, and $p_o = 4$. Substituting these values in the demand equation yields:

$$Q = 150 - 2(5) + .75(200) + .5(50) - 2(4) \pm e = 307 \pm 3.$$

A linear demand equation can be used to estimate elasticities over a narrow range of the independent variables. A simple computation of **price elasticity** in this case is

$$\epsilon_p = b(p/Q) = -2(5/307) = -.033.$$

With relatively inelastic demand in this region of price, price increases bring proportionally smaller decreases in quantity demanded so that volume of sales changes very little. Similarly, a simple computation of **income elasticity** in this case is

$$\epsilon_Y = c(Y/Q) = .75(200/307) = .489,$$

indicating that this good is only mildly superior. Increases in consumers' incomes will cause less than proportionate increases in quantity demanded. And, finally, a simple computation of **cross price elasticity** in this example is

$$\epsilon_c = c(p_o/Q) = -2(4/307) = -0.026,$$

indicating very low complimentarity with the other good.

A Multiplicative Demand Function

A linear equation is appropriate for estimating quantity demanded only when the influence of each of the variables in the equation is independent of that of other variables. Frequently, empirical data suggest that the variables are not, in fact, independent of each other. In these cases, a multiplicative form of the demand function reflects more accurately the actual behavior of the dependent variable. A multiplicative demand function allows for a greater degree of interaction among the independent variables.

A **multiplicative demand function** has the form

$$Q = ap^b Y^c T^d p_o^e(z),$$

where a is a constant as before, and the exponents b, c, d, and e measure the *percentage change* in the dependent variable relative to percentage changes in the respective independent variables. Multiplicative demand functions have several advantages over additive demand functions. These include the fact that their parameters may be easier to estimate, multiplication implies some interaction among the independent variables, and elasticity is shown directly by the exponents. There is also a disadvantage. Constant exponents for the independent variables imply constant elasticities. The assumption of constant elasticities may only be correct over a limited range of the independent variables.

Consider the multiplicative demand function

$$Q = 150p^{-2} Y^{.75} T^{.5} p_o^{-2}.$$

In this equation, price elasticity of demand is $\epsilon_p = -2$, income elasticity is $\epsilon_Y = .75$, and cross price elasticity is $\epsilon_c = -2$. The signs of the exponents indicate that this is a normal consumer good, it is mildly superior, and it is a complement for the good whose price is p_o. For $p = 5$, $Y = 200$, $T = 50$, and $p_o = 4$ as before,

$$Q = 150(5^{-2})(200^{.75})(50^{.5})(4^{-2}) = 141.02.$$

How can this demand function be utilized? Let us look at each of the independent variables in turn. First, suppose management expects an increase in productivity, such that unit costs of production fall and price can be reduced by 5 percent. For $\epsilon_p = -2$, a 5-percent decrease in price might be expected to increase sales by 2(5 percent) = 10 percent, so that Q = 1.10(141.02) = 155.12. How does the price reduction affect the firm's revenue? Consider revenue from sales before and after the price change:

$$TR = (p)(Q) = \$5 \times 141.02 = \$705.10 \text{ (before)}$$

and

$$TR = (p)(Q) = \$4.75 \times 155.12 = \$736.82 \text{ (after)}.$$

Reducing price would increase quantity demanded more than proportionally, so that revenue from sales would increase.

Now, let us suppose a recession in this region's principal industry is expected to reduce consumer incomes by 10 percent over the period relevant to the demand function. For ϵ_Y = .75, quantity demanded will fall by .75(10 percent) = 7.5 percent to Q = (1 − .075)(141.02) = 130.44 and revenue will fall to $5 × 130.44 = \$652.20.

Similarly, a change in tastes might be expected to result from a vigorous advertising campaign. Let us define the taste variable (T) as advertising expenditures over a particular period of time. A 50-percent increase in advertising expenditures (from $50 to $75) might yield an increase in quantity demanded of .5(50 percent) = 25 percent, for sales volume of

$$Q = (.125)(141.02) = 176.28,$$

and revenue of

$$TR = (p)(Q) = (5)(176.28) = \$881.38.$$

With an increased expenditure of only $25 for additional advertising, there is a gain in revenue of $881.38 − 705.10 = \$176.28, making this a worthwhile strategy.

Finally, suppose the price of the complementary good shown as $p_o^e = 4^{-2}$ falls by 10 percent. For ϵ_c = −2, the result should be a −2(−10 percent) = +20 percent increase in quantity demanded, for total sales volume of

$$Q = (1.20)(141.02) = 169.22,$$

and revenue of

$$TR = (p)(Q) = (5)(169.22) = \$846.12.$$

The actual results of all of these changes probably would not turn out to be precisely as estimated here. Remember the standard error term, z, representing all the other conditions assumed to be unchanged, ceteris paribus. Changes in any of the conditions not explicitly included in the model may

CASE STUDY 3.4   Measuring Elasticity of Demand for Electricity

A linear demand function may be expanded far beyond the simple model discussed in this chapter. Economists Robert B. Archibald, David H. Finifter, and Carlisle E. Moody, Jr., used survey data on electric power consumption to write a demand equation containing 105 independent variables! They used a computer program to estimate parameters for separate demand equations for each of the twelve months of the year. Then, they computed the elasticity of demand for electricity associated with each of the independent variables for each of the twelve months.

Some of the significant variables that affect consumer demand for electricity are price, family income, family characteristics (including number of family members and number of wage-earners in the family), ownership of household appliances, number of heating or cooling days in the month, and characteristics of the home (including number of stories and use of storm windows). Their regression equation had the form

$$KWH = a + b(p) + c(Y) + d(FAM) \ldots + n(STORM).$$

Most of the results were as might have been expected. Price elasticity of demand varied from $-.12$ to $-.60$ over the year, being highest (in absolute value) during the months of peak demand, June, December, and January. (Can you explain why?) Income elasticity dropped as low as .03 and had no general seasonal pattern. The researchers suggest that income elasticity might be greater in the long run because of the relatively high income elasticity of demand for home appliances. (Can you suggest a reason for this?) The response of electricity demand to number of people in the family was large and positive, a credible result. On the other hand, demand responded negatively to number of wage earners in the family, a result of the fact that fewer occupants would be using the home during the day.

One surprising result of these computations was the response of electricity demand to improved home insulation. A positive sign for this variable indicates that improved insulation actually *increases* the demand for electric power. The researchers suggest that this reflects a relatively higher desire for "comfort" and a greater willingness to purchase electricity among persons who also purchase insulation. (These results cast doubt on the notion that tax incentives to improve home insulation will encourage energy conservation.) And, finally, researchers found no significant relationship between the level of education of consumers and electricity demand.

MANAGERIAL THINKING

On the basis of information in this case study, would you characterize electric power and home insulation as substitutes or complements? Explain your answer.

Source: Robert B. Archibald, David H. Finifter, and Carlisle E. Moody, Jr., "Seasonal Variations in Residential Electricity Demand: Evidence from Survey Data," *Applied Economics*, 1982, vol. 14, pp. 167–181.

CASE STUDY 3.5   A Real-World Problem in Consumer Demand

Economist A. D. Owen, writing in 1979 in *The Economic Record*, reported on his study of wine sales in Australia between the years 1955–1977. Per capita sales of winemakers provided the data for Q. In order to remove the effects of inflation over the period, wine prices (*p*) were expressed in the form of a price index with a base year of 1967. The taste variable (*T*) was defined as an index of immigration into

Australia from Europe. The reason for this was the analyst's expectation that European immigrants would ordinarily have a higher preference for wine than native-born Australians.

The other price variable in the demand function was an index of the price of beer (p_o), which was assumed to be a substitute for wine for many consumers. The analyst added two other independent variables that he believed would reflect consumer tastes: wine consumption in the previous period (Q_{t-1}) and advertising expenditures (A). The reason for including advertising was to determine the responsiveness of consumer demand to efforts of the wine industry to influence consumer tastes in favor of their product.

The multiplicative form was chosen for the demand function because it was believed that the forces working on demand were not independent of each other. Thus, the form of the demand function was

$$A = ap^b Y^c T^d p_o^e A^f Q_{t-1}^g.$$

The first attempt at regression analysis produced the following estimated equation:

$$Q = .012 p^{-.8} Y^{.18} T^{1.9} p_o^{-.5} A^{-.1} Q_{t-1}^{.8}.$$

Note the signs of the exponents: $b = -.8$ indicates negative price elasticity, $c = .18$ indicates a superior good, $d = 1.9$ has the expected sign, $f = -.1$ indicates a negative response by consumers to advertising expenditures, and $Q_{t-1}^{.8}$ suggests an upward trend in wine consumption over time. However, $e = -.5$ indicates that beer and wine are complementary goods, contradicting our initial assumption.

In addition to incorrect signs, the analyst found such large standard errors from the use of the above equation that he selected another form. The final form of the equation was

$$Q = .0131 \left(\frac{p}{p_o}\right)^{-.28} Y^{.55} T^{.88} Q_{t-1}^{.55}.$$

Changing the price variable to (p/p_o) to indicate *relative* prices now gives its exponent the appropriate sign. Thus, a 1-percent increase in the price of wine relative to the price of beer would reduce quantity demanded by 0.28 percent. Income elasticity of $\epsilon_Y = .55$ indicates that wine is a moderately superior good. The independent variable with the greatest effect on demand for wine sales is consumer tastes, as reflected in the percentage of European immigrants in total population.

This analysis was useful first for revealing the poor results of advertising expenditures. Australian wine makers would be advised that past efforts to stimulate sales through advertising had little (or negative) effect, so plans for future advertising campaigns should be reconsidered. The low absolute value of price elasticity suggests that price reductions will not add significantly to sales volume. In fact, since price increases would reduce quantity demanded by smaller percentages, a price *increase* would lead to higher total sales revenue. The positive response of demand to income and the generally upward trend indicated by the positive exponent for Q_{t-1} suggest increasing demand for the industry and relative stability of demand during short-run declines in income. Finally, the apparent taste of European immigrants for wine suggests that promotional efforts, if any, should be directed toward this segment of the population.

Analyses of this kind should be used with caution. Their conclusions are based on historical data that reflect past circumstances. New circumstances might be expected to alter old relationships, rendering the estimated equation irrelevant. Changing circumstances make it necessary to revise estimates frequently and include the good judgment of the analyst in assessing the estimates' validity.

MANAGERIAL THINKING

Use the model in this example and the following hypothetical data to construct a typical consumer's short-run demand curve for wine. Use intervals of 5 percent above and below the current price index.

Q_{t-1} = 8 gallons per capita.
Y = 7,000 average per capita disposable income.
T = 1.8 cumulative index of European immigration.
p = 1.15 index of wine prices (1967 = 100).
p_o = 1.20 index of beer prices (1967 = 100).

Now assume that all factors remain constant and estimate average wine consumption for the next three years.

Source: A. D. Owen, "The Demand for Wine in Australia, 1955–1977," *The Economic Record*, September 1979, vol. 55, no. 150, pp. 230–35.

affect the actual level of quantity demanded and the actual level of revenue. Still, including the most significant independent variables allows managers to organize their thinking about market conditions and helps them plan scientifically.

SUMMARY

Elasticity of demand is a means of measuring the responsiveness of buyers to changes in (1) the price of a good or service, (2) their own incomes, (3) prices of related goods or services, and (4) buyers' tastes, as reflected in such things as age, exposure to advertising, ethnic background, and other characteristics. A linear demand curve has high price elasticity of demand at high prices, low price elasticity at low prices, and unitary elasticity at the precise midpoint of the demand curve. Changes in price elasticity along a linear demand curve cause changes in total revenue to occur as price changes, with maximum total revenue occurring where price elasticity is equal to one. Among goods and services, price elasticity of demand varies depending on whether the item is a necessity or a luxury, whether there are acceptable substitutes, the price of the good or service relative to the buyer's budget, and the time over which quantity adjustments can be made.

Changes in factors other than price can cause changes in demand, shown as shifts in the demand curve. Income elasticity of demand depends on whether a good or service is strongly superior, mildly superior, or inferior. The relationship between income and quantity demanded can be shown by including an income term in the demand equation. Quantity demanded responds positively to income changes for superior goods and negatively for inferior goods.

Changes in tastes cause changes in demand, in either a positive or negative direction. Price changes for related goods and services also cause changes in demand, in the same direction as price when the items are substitutes and in the opposite direction from price when they are complements. The effects of consumer tastes and the prices of other goods can also be included in the demand equation, with appropriate signs (positive or negative) indicating the direction of the change. A typical linear demand function can be expressed mathematically as

$$Q = a - b(p) \pm c(Y) \pm d(T) \pm e(p_o) \pm z.$$

Multiple linear regression can be used to estimate the parameters of the demand equation. Furthermore, demand elasticities can be estimated as follows:

Price elasticity of demand $= \epsilon_p = b(p)/Q,$
Income elasticity of demand $= \epsilon_Y = c(Y)/Q,$
Cross price elasticity of demand $= \epsilon_e = e(p_o)/Q.$

KEY TERMS

elasticity of demand	recession
price elasticity of demand	cross price elasticity
price elastic	additive demand function
price inelastic	price elasticity
luxury	income elasticity
necessity	multiplicative demand function

QUESTIONS AND PROBLEMS

1. Between 1973 and 1976, an index of gasoline prices increased from 118.1 to 177.9 and per capita consumption decreased by 6 percent. Compute price elasticity of demand for this period. Draw a series of short-run demand curves to illustrate your results.

2. Use demand curves to illustrate the effect of a recession on sales of particular goods and services: for example, luxury automobiles and fur coats, on the one hand, and gasoline and sport shirts, on the other. How do the results depend on the distribution of recession unemployment among the population? What is the effect of extended unemployment compensation on sales of particular goods?

3. Rising interest rates and the rising value of the dollar in international exchange were blamed for a sharp drop in the price of copper mined in the United States in 1984. What complementary and substitution relationships were responsible for this result? (Hint: A higher dollar makes imports cheaper and exports more expensive.)

4. The extended Iran-Iraq war of the 1980s has raised the threat of a shortage of oil and an increase in oil prices. Discuss the probable effects of an oil shortage on consumer demand in the immediate period and over the longer term. What does your answer suggest about price elasticity of demand in the short and long run?

5. A drought in the Soviet Union reduced Soviet grain production in 1984 by 10 percent and caused wheat prices to rise by 3 percent. Discuss the probable effects of this event on world prices, livestock production, fertilizer sales, and the economy of Argentina.

6. The use of supermarket coupons is a way of reducing prices for particular goods. What do supermarket managers believe about price elasticity of demand for items whose price is reduced by the use of coupons? What expectations do they have about sales of other, non-reduced items during a coupon promotion campaign? Discuss this in terms of price elasticity of demand.

7. During the late 1970s and early 1980s, the cost of owning an automobile increased fairly regularly, but purchases decreased only slightly. Explain this result in terms of price elasticity.

8. Most American families seem to progress through three states of income: first, rising income in which housing is a strongly superior good, followed by rising income in which housing is a mildly superior good, and, finally a period in which housing is an inferior good. How would you describe income elasticity of demand for housing?

9. The nation's third-largest steel manufacturer attributes 88 percent of its revenue to steel and related steel products. The recession of 1982–83 prompted a move toward diversification, but the firm's losses in the recession reduced the funds available for acquiring other firms. Likely acquisitions include firms involved in financial services, insurance, petroleum, and plastics. What considerations should enter into decisions to acquire particular firms?

10. Use the following market information to write a demand equation for coffee. Quantity is the dependent variable and price the independent variable.

Price per pound	Millions of pounds
$3.00	71
2.67	75
2.15	82
2.00	84
1.50	92

Compute elasticity at all points along the curve. On the basis of this information alone, what would you expect to be the price trend for coffee? How will price elasticity in the long run differ from short-run price elasticity? Use your demand equation to estimate the revenue-maximizing price for coffee.

11. The following cross-sectional data describe family expenditures for alcoholic beverages and tobacco at various income levels in 1973. Draw an Engel curve describing consumer expenditures, plotting expenditures on the vertical axis and income on the horizontal axis. How would you describe the behavior of the curves?

Consumer Good	Income Groups (thousands of $)					
	0–5	5–10	10–15	15–20	20–25	25–100
Alcoholic beverages	32	59	81	106	117	177
Tobacco	77	119	150	172	172	149

Calculate income elasticity for both goods along the range of incomes and comment on your results. Discuss the significance of this information for firms producing and selling these goods. Include such considerations as type of advertising and location of retail outlets.

12. Use regression analysis to write a demand equation using the data in Table 3.1. Then write an equation for total revenue. Finally, use optimization to determine the values of p and Q at which TR reaches a maximum.

13. What is the highest price the pharmaceutical firm in Question 12 could charge before it would lose all of its sales?

14. Between 1975 and 1978 the consumer price index for cola drinks fell from 132.8 and 127.2, while most fruit prices did not change. Per capita disposable income was also relatively stable. Over the same period, the index of per capita consumption of fruit increased from 111 to 112.8. On the basis of this information alone, compute cross price elasticity for the two products. How would you interpret your results?

15. Scott's Shirtery sells T-shirts for $5 each and estimates the demand curve for T-shirts according to $Q = 55 - 5(p)$, where Q represents daily sales and p represents unit price. Scott has an opportunity to place an advertisement in a high school paper that is expected to increase demand and reduce price elasticity. After placing the advertisement, demand is estimated according to $Q = 75 - 2(p)$. Was the advertisement successful? Explain your answer. What strategy should Scott follow to increase daily revenue? What is the highest price Scott can charge without reducing sales to zero?

16. The Pizza Palace operates fast-food restaurants in three neighborhoods with weekly per capita incomes of $100, $200, and $300, respectively. The neighborhoods are similar in ethnic composition, median age, level of

education, and other socioeconomic characteristics. Pizza Palace has used a variety of pricing schemes to promote pizza sales in the three communities, the results of which are shown below:

	Income (thousands)	Price	Quantity (thousands)
Community A:	$100	$2.00	5
		2.50	3.5
		4.00	3
		5.00	2
Community B:	200	6.00	3
		5.00	4
		4.00	5.5
		2.00	6
		1.00	7.4
Community C:	300	5.80	5
		4.70	7
		3.50	7
		2.50	9

Use multiple-linear regression to write a demand curve for Pizza Palace. Then determine price and income elasticity of demand in the three communities for a current price of $5.00. Interpret your results.

3A

Multiple-Linear Regression Using Least-Squares

When two or more independent variables are believed to influence consumer demand, estimating the parameters of the demand equation is more time-consuming. For two independent variables, there are three "normal equations":

(1) $\Sigma Q = na + b\Sigma p + c\ \Sigma Y$
(2) $\Sigma p(Q) = a\Sigma p + b\Sigma p^2 + c\Sigma p(Y)$
(3) $\Sigma Y(Q) = a\Sigma Y + b\Sigma p(Y) + c\Sigma (Y)^2.$

As before, the terms represent the sums of the observations, but the equations must now be solved for the parameters a, b, and c. The coefficient b represents the net relationship between price and quantity demanded when income is constant. The coefficient c measures the effect of income when price is constant. (For regression analysis with three independent variables, it would be necessary to add a fourth term to each of the equations above and construct a fourth equation using the values of the fourth variable in combination with the values above.)

In order to illustrate multiple-linear regression, Table 3A.1 provides observations of product demand in markets similar in all respects except price and income.

Estimate the parameters for the analysis by substituting the values from Table 3A.1 in the normal equations:

(1) $\ \ 41 = 5a + 30b + 45c$
(2) $218 = 30a + 190b + 269c$
(3) $372 = 45a + 269b + 407c.$

TABLE 3A.1   Price, Income, and Quantity Data for Estimating a Multiple-Linear Demand Function

(1) Quantity demanded (Q)	(2) Market price (p)	(3) Income (Y)	(4) p(Q)	(5) p^2	(6) p(Y)	(7) Y^2	(8) Y(Q)
3	8	9	24	64	72	81	27
5	7	8	35	49	56	64	40
8	6	10	48	36	60	100	80
11	5	9	55	25	45	81	99
14	4	9	56	16	36	81	126
$\Sigma = 41$	$\Sigma = 30$	$\Sigma = 45$	$\Sigma = 218$	$\Sigma = 190$	$\Sigma = 269$	$\Sigma = 407$	$\Sigma = 372$

(9) Q_e	(10) $(Q - Q_e)$	(11) $(Q - Q_e)^2$	(12) $(Q - \bar{Q})$	(13) $(Q - \bar{Q})^2$	(14) $(Q_e - \bar{Q})$	(15) $(Q_e - \bar{Q})^2$
2.63	.37	.14	5.2	27.04	5.57	31.02
5.42	.42	.18	3.2	10.24	2.78	7.73
8.23	.23	.05	.2	.0004	.03	.0009
11.03	.03	.0009	2.8	7.84	2.83	8.01
13.83	.17	.03	5.8	33.64	5.63	31.70
		$\Sigma = .40$		$\Sigma = 78.76$		$\Sigma = 78.46$

From (1), determine that $a = 8.2 - 6b - 9c$ amd substitute this value in (2) and (3).

(2) $218 = 30(8.2 - 6b - 9c) + 190b + 269c$
(3) $372 = 45(8.3 - 6b - 9c) + 269b + 407c.$

Now, solving for b gives us

(2) $-28 = 10b - 1c$
(3) $3 = -1b + 65c$

and

$b = 65c - 3.$

By substituting the value for b into (2), we obtain

(2) $-28 = 10(65c - 3) - 1c$
     $= -28 = 650c - 30 - 1c$
     $= 2 = 649c$

and $c = .0003$. Now, we can solve for b:

$$b = 65(.0003) - 3 = -2.8.$$

And, computing for a:

$$a = 8.2 - 6(-2.8) - 9(.0003) = 25.$$

Thus, the demand equation is

$$Q = 25 - 2.8p + .0003Y.$$

The negative sign for the price coefficient indicates that this is a normal good for which quantity demanded declines with an increase in price. The positive sign for the income coefficient indicates that this is a slightly superior good, but that quantity demanded increases only slightly with an increase in income.

Computations for determining the standard error and coefficient of determination for this equation are shown in Columns (9) through (15) in Table 3A.1. The formula for standard error requires the sum of the squared deviations of observations from the regression estimates:

$$\text{Standard error } (\sigma) = \sqrt{(Q - Q_e)^2/n} = \sqrt{.40/5} = \sqrt{.08} = .28.$$

The standard error tells us the average deviation of quantity demanded from the regression estimate. The coefficient of determination states the portion of variation of observed data that is explained by the regression equation:

$$\text{Coefficient of determination } (R^2) = \frac{\text{explained variation}}{\text{total variation}} = \frac{(Q_e - \overline{Q})^2}{(Q - \overline{Q})^2}.$$

Substituting the values from Table 3A.1 gives us:

$$\frac{(Q_e - \overline{Q})^2}{(Q - \overline{Q})^2} = \frac{78.46}{78.76} = .996 = 99.6 \text{ percent.}$$

Thus, 99.6 percent of the variation is explained by the regression equation.

3B

Least-Squares Regression for Estimating a Multiplicative Function

Interaction among the independent variables in a demand function yields a function of the form

$$Q = a p^b Y^c T^d p_o{}^e,$$

where a is a constant, and the exponents b, c, d, and e measure the *percentage change* in the dependent variable associated with *percentage changes* in the independent variables: price, income, tastes, and prices of other goods. Converting the values in a multiplicative equation to logarithmic form permits the use of least-squares regression for estimating the parameters. The logarithmic form of the multiplicative demand function in this case is

$$\log Q = \log a + b(\log p) + c(\log Y) + d(\log T) + e(\log p_o).$$

Note that the logarithmic equation is a linear equation with four independent variables representing the logs of price, income, tastes, and other prices. This equation can be estimated using multiple-linear regression. For simplicity, in this example we will consider only the first two independent variables and use the normal equations for estimating the values of a, b, and c.

Table 3B.1 gives observed values of consumer demand (Q) in various markets in which price (p) and income (Y) differ. These observed values have been converted to logarithms and summed.

<u>TABLE 3B.1</u> **Quantity and Price Data for Estimating a Multiplicative Equation**

Q	log Q	p	log p	Y	log Y	log p^2	log Y^2	(log p) × (log Q)	(log p) × (log Y)	(log Y) × (log Q)
275	2.4393	25	1.3979	700	2.8451	1.9541	8.0946	3.4099	3.9772	6.9401
300	2.4771	21	1.3222	725	2.8603	1.7482	8.1813	3.2752	3.7832	7.0852
325	2.5119	18	1.2553	730	2.8633	1.5758	8.1985	3.1532	3.5943	7.1923
355	2.5502	16	1.2041	750	2.8751	1.4499	8.2662	3.0707	3.4619	7.3321
360	2.5563	15	1.1761	740	2.8692	1.3832	8.2323	3.0065	3.3745	7.3345
	Σ = 12.5348		Σ = 6.3556		Σ = 14.3130	Σ = 8.1112	Σ = 40.9729	Σ = 15.9155	Σ = 18.1911	Σ = 35.8842

The normal equations for multiple-linear regression are:

(1) $\quad \Sigma Q = na + b\Sigma p + c\Sigma Y$
(2) $\quad \Sigma p(Q) = a\Sigma p + b\Sigma p^2 + c\Sigma p(Y)$
(3) $\quad \Sigma Y(Q) = a\Sigma Y + b\Sigma p(Y) + c\Sigma Y^2.$

To use the normal equations for estimating a multiplicative equation, we must convert the variables to logarithms:

(1) $\quad \Sigma\log Q = n(\log a) + b\Sigma\log p + c\Sigma\log Y$
(2) $\quad \Sigma(\log p)(\log Q) = \log a\Sigma\log p + b\Sigma\log p^2 + c\Sigma(\log p)(\log Y)$
(3) $\quad \Sigma(\log Y)(\log Q) = \log a\Sigma\log Y + b\Sigma(\log p)(\log Y) + c\Sigma\log Y^2.$

The values from Table 3B.1 have been substituted in the normal equations as follows:

(1) $\quad 12.5348 = 5(\log a) + 6.3556b + 14.3130c$
(2) $\quad 15.9155 = 6.3556(\log a) + 8.1112b + 18.1911c$
(3) $\quad 35.8842 = 14.3130(\log a) + 18.1911b + 40.9729c.$

The equations can now be solved by determining the value of log a from equation (1) and substituting this value in equations (2) and (3). These values were found to be log $a = 1.5469$, $b = -.48$, and $c = .55$. Now, the revised equation is:

$$\log Q = \log a - .48(\log p) + .55(\log Y).$$

Converting this form back to a multiplicative equation yields:

$$\text{Quantity demanded } (Q) = 35.23\ p^{-.48}\ Y^{.55}.$$

The value of coefficient a is determined by raising 10 to the log a power. The exponent $b = -.48$ is negative, indicating that this is a normal good with an inverse relationship between price and quantity demanded. Price elasticity of demand is constant at $\epsilon_d = -.48$ over this range of prices. The exponent c

= .55 is positive, indicating that this is a superior good for which purchases increase with income. Income elasticity of demand is constant at $\epsilon_Y = .55$ over this range of income.

QUESTIONS AND PROBLEMS

1. Write a hypothetical demand equation for an inferior good that is also a nearly perfect substitute for another good. How does your equation differ from one for a good that is only slightly substitutable?

4

Forecasting Sales

Early in 1979 the nation's home builders began cutting back their production plans for the coming year. Managers of construction firms had been listening to economic forecasts predicting, at best, slow growth in home purchases and, at worst, a moderate recession. Builders remembered only too well the collapse of the housing market during the 1974–75 recession and didn't want to be caught again with unsold housing inventories.

The 1970s were characterized by wide swings in economic activity called **business cycles**. Rapid growth early in the decade prompted a great surge in new construction, with surplus building of homes, apartment buildings, and office parks in many parts of the country. By 1974, however, rising prices for consumer goods and industrial materials had caused the Federal Reserve Bank to cut back growth of the nation's money supply. Home mortgage credit dried up, and interest rates on construction loans soared. The plight of builders worsened as they were unable to sell or rent their properties. Many declared bankruptcy, losing the fruits of years of hard work.

Experiences like these make managers very cautious. The construction firms that did survive the 1974–75 recession learned a valuable lesson about the close relationship between the health of the national economy and consumer demand for their product. This is true not only for the firms that actually clear land, design new buildings, pour concrete, add roofs, and install plumbing and wiring. It is true also for those firms that manufacture draperies and carpets, build furniture and appliances, and install driveways and lawns. When all related activities are included, building construction represents the largest single industry in the United States. Fluctuations in the economy as a whole are felt quickly by firms in the construction industry. In turn, changes in the construction industry are quickly transmitted to the economy as a whole.

While emphasizing the close relationship between the construction industry and the economy, we mustn't forget the many other industries that are strongly affected by cycles in business activity. Production and sales of most goods and services rise and fall with changing levels of spending in the national economy. Few, if any, manufacturing industries are unaffected by general business conditions, and only one, red ink, is said to move in the opposite direction from the economy as a whole! For this reason, it is important that managers be alert to changes in the economic climate nationwide, assessing the behavior of their own industry relative to the national economy and planning their firm's strategies so as to benefit most (or suffer least) from nationwide business cycles.

The study of business cycles falls under the heading of *macroeconomics*. Although our emphasis in this text is on microeconomics, the prosperity of a single firm is so strongly influenced by the national economic environment that a careful consideration of macroeconomics is essential. This chapter will explore the determinants of economic activity in the nation as a whole, showing how interrelationships among spending groups affect the general business climate. Then we will show how economists use their understanding of macroeconomics to forecast business activity. Few managers will actually attempt to implement all the forecasting procedures described here. However, an awareness of these procedures should help managers develop a sense of the general business conditions that affect their own firm's prosperity and growth. Finally, we will show how a firm's past experiences can help identify historical patterns of sales for use in projecting future market activity.

MACROECONOMIC MODELS

Over the years, total production in the United States has increased significantly along with our nation's growing productive capacity. Our **labor** force has grown in numbers as well as quality—through improved health, better education, and greater skill development. The productivity of existing **land** has increased also through the application of new scientific techniques in agriculture. Finally, many years of **capital** accumulation have added greatly to our industrial capacity, and advances in industrial **technology** have further enhanced productivity.

Growth in real production has averaged more than 3 percent annually over the last thirty years. However, like most averages, this 3-percent growth figure conceals substantial deviations above and below the long-term trend. In 1974 and 1975 business activity actually declined by almost 2 percent. The new recession feared by homebuilders in 1979 finally arrived in 1980, with another drop in real production in that year and 1982. It is these short-term deviations from steady growth that must concern the managers of business firms.

Economists forecast macroeconomic activity through the use of **macroeco-**

nomic models. The most common form of macroeconomic model examines the spending behavior of four groups of spenders during a typical year: consumers, business firms, governments, and foreigners. Combining the spending behavior of all of these groups yields the value known as **gross national product** (GNP) and is a measure of economic activity for the nation. Forecasts of spending behavior among these groups enable an analyst to forecast the level of business activity for the coming year.

Forecasting Business Activity

Macroeconomic models include algebraic equations reflecting spending in each of the four major components of total spending: **private consumption spending**; **business investment** for buildings, equipment, and inventories; **government purchases** of goods and services; and **net foreign investment**. Each of the four fundamental equations breaks down one of the major spending categories into particular sub-categories and identifies the significant variables that affect each of these. For example, total consumption might be expressed as a function of income: $C = f(income)$. Within the general equation for consumption there would be more specific equations describing consumer purchases of, for example, automobiles, other durable goods, non-durable goods, and services.

Economists have compared data on private **consumption spending** (C) and income and have discovered a fairly close correlation between changes in income and changes in consumer spending. Of course, perfect correlation in the income-consumption relationship would make forecasting quite simple. Actually, other factors enter into consumers' decisions to purchase goods and services. The stock of consumer goods already owned, the amount of consumer savings and interest charges on consumer loans, expectations about future prices, and expectations about income and job security also affect consumer spending. More correctly, private consumption spending should be considered a function of all these factors and more: $C = f(income, stock of goods, credit conditions, expectations, and other factors)$.

Some of these other factors enter significantly into consumers' decisions to purchase particular consumer goods, such as autos. The analyst considers all of these factors and writes separate equations describing consumer spending for automobiles and other durable goods, food and other non-durable goods, and consumer services. Taken together, projections for all these consumer expenditures describe the expected behavior of consumption for some future time period.

Investment spending (I) is more difficult to forecast, since business firms must consider many diverse factors in making an investment decision, including the supply of retained earnings in the firm or the interest costs of borrowed money, technological and environmental factors that may affect the profitability of new investment, changing raw material costs and price trends for finished goods, expected competition in product markets, and the stock of existing plant space and equipment and its rate of utilization. All of these factors influence the expected profitability of a new investment and should be included in the equation for forecasting purchases of business plant, equipment, and inventory. In addition to plant, equipment and inventory investment, the analyst must project spending for new housing construction. Credit conditions for home mortgages, the stock of existing housing, average family income, and demographic conditions such as the average age of the population are significant determinants of investment in new housing. Thus, private domestic investment can be expressed as: $I =$ f (*retained earnings, interest rates, technological and environmental factors, prices of raw materials and finished goods, expected competition, existing plant and equipment, and demographic conditions*). Obviously, estimating the investment equation is a tedious and uncertain exercise at best.

Government spending (G) is easier to estimate, however, since the federal budget is planned in advance and state and local spending can be estimated from past trends. And, finally, **net foreign spending** (F_n) can be estimated on the basis of outstanding orders and trends in foreign purchases and sales.

Combining estimates and forecasts for all of these classes of spending yields an expression of expected total spending or gross national product (GNP):

$$GNP = C + I + G + F_n.$$

The analyst must provide values for all of the variables that affect each component of total spending. Interactions among these variables are included also. Solving the equation for GNP yields a forecast of business activity for the coming year.

The case studies that follow illustrate the use of regression techniques (explained in Chapter 3) to estimate equations that predict automobile sales and housing construction. These equations constitute important parts of the consumption and investment components of total spending and have great influence on the level of total economic activity.

INDICATORS OF ECONOMIC ACTIVITY

It is impossible to know in advance the behavior of the various components of total spending and the implications of spending changes for sales of a particular business firm. However, as changes in spending begin to take place, they are reflected in data collected regularly by the U.S. Department of Commerce. The National Bureau of Economic Research analyzes the Commerce Department data describing sales and production activity in various sectors of the economy and makes the results of its research available for use by business managers.

Changes in spending in any one of the data series will eventually affect economic activity in others, often triggering a similar movement in business revenues and GNP. As spending in one sector increases (or decreases), orders

CASE STUDY 4.1   **Projecting Automobile Sales**

Automobile sales affect such a broad sector of the total U.S. economy that accurate forecasting in this area is especially important. Consumer purchases of automobiles fluctuated widely during the 1970s, dropping sharply in 1974 and 1975 in response to the foreign oil embargo and energy crisis but increasing once again in 1976 as Americans renewed their love affairs with large cars. By 1979 a new energy crisis raised questions about the direction of U.S. automobile industry in the 1980s.

In 1980, Rodney Carlson and Michael Umble reported on their forecasting studies for autos of various size classifications in *The Journal of Business*. The two analysts used quarterly sales data for the years 1967–1978 to estimate market demand equations for subcompacts, compacts, intermediate, standard, and luxury cars. The demand equations had the following form:

$$D = a + bY + cp + dG + eZ_E + fZ_L + u,$$

where a is a constant, Y is disposable income adjusted for inflation and population size, p is the average selling price in each size classification adjusted for inflation, and G is the average price of gas adjusted for inflation. The variables Z_E and Z_L are called "dummy" variables and take on values of zero or one only: $Z_E = 1$ if there is a gas shortage and $Z_L = 1$ if there is a strike of the United Auto Workers union.

This analysis confirmed some expected relationships. The independent variable with the greatest impact on auto sales was disposable income, and auto selling price also had a significant effect. The signs of these variables indicated positive income elasticity and negative price elasticity for all classes of autos.

The gas price variable affected demand differently for different automobiles. The sign of the variable was positive for subcompacts and compacts, negative for standard-sized autos, and not significant for luxury and intermediate-sized autos. (What does this tell us about the relationship between gasoline and various types of autos?) When the dummy variable Z_E is set to equal one, sales of subcompacts will increase, sales of compacts will remain the same, and all others will decline. (What does this result reveal?)

The estimated equations in this example are:

Subcompacts: $Q = -709,170 - 275\,p + 2,570Y + 3,470G + 101,000Z_E,$

Compacts: $Q = 209,010 - 158p + 760Y + 2,575G,$

Intermediate: $Q = 289,400 - 161p + 1,136Y - 170,100Z_E - 82,700Z_L,$

Standard:[1] $Q = 3,565,600 - 342p - 28,030G - 171,500Z_E - 230,100Z_L$
$\qquad\qquad - 42,370T + 636T^2,$

and

Luxury: $Q = 234,600 - 53.1p + 694Y - 56,010Z_E - 61,900Z_L.$

After estimating the above relationships, the analysts projected auto sales up to 1983 using alternative assumptions about the behavior of the independent variables. Disposable income was assumed to increase either 1 percent or 2.7 percent annually. The retail price for small cars was assumed either to remain constant or to increase by 2 percent, and the price of large gas guzzlers was assumed either to remain constant or increase 10 percent. Gas prices were assumed to reach $1.25 or $2.00 per gallon by 1983. The value of Z_E was set at both zero and one.

Two alternative values for each of four significant variables produced a total of sixteen equations for each auto. The result was a range of projected sales for each.

---

1. The general form of the equation proved to be inappropriate for this class, so trend variables T and T^2 were used in place of the income variable Y.

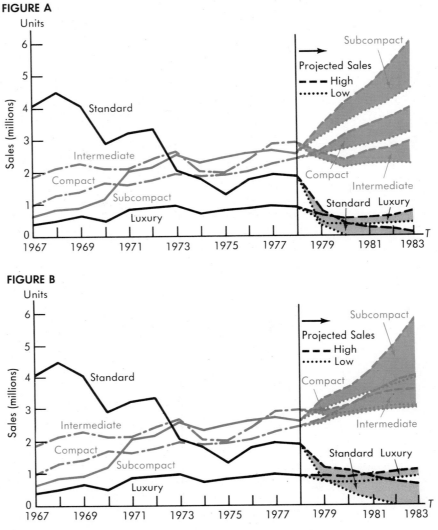

FIGURE A

FIGURE B

Projections are made under the assumption of a gasoline shortage in Figure A and under the assumption of no gasoline shortage in Figure B.

Figures A and B show actual auto sales to 1978 followed by the projected range of future sales with or without a gasoline shortage.

Many of the results of the analysis are those that would be expected. According to the analysis, subcompacts will dominate future demand, garnering between 35 percent and 45 percent of total sales by 1983, compared with less than 25 percent in 1978. Together, subcompacts and compacts are projected to constitute 75 percent of demand. Demand for large cars is projected to be unstable, responding to changes in gas prices and shortages. Luxury car sales have been stable since the 1950s at between 7.5 percent and 9 percent; sales are projected to continue at this rate unless there is an extreme fuel shortage. Standard-sized cars are projected to disappear gradually from the market.

In summary, the analysis projected that total annual sales will depend primarily on the health of the national economy, dropping to 9.4 million units sold in years of gasoline shortage but regaining 1978's peak sales of 10.9 million units by 1983. In addition, exceptionally high income growth could push sales to 13 or 14 million. These forecasts, however, are substantially below those foreseen by auto manufacturers as recently as 1979.

Source: Rodney L. Carlson and M. Michael Umble, "Statistical Demand Functions and Their Use for Forecasting in an Energy Crisis," *The Journal of Business*, April 1980, vol. 53, no. 2, pp. 193–204.

CASE STUDY 4.2   An Analytical Model of the Housing Industry

Between World War II and 1979, residential construction in the United States underwent seven cycles lasting an average of three-and-a-half years. The percentage change in housing starts averaged about 40 percent from peak to trough. Cyclical declines in home building are generally attributed to periodic scarcity of mortgage credit and the resulting high interest charges on mortgage loans.

A normal business cycle low was expected to hit the housing industry in late 1978 and early 1979, but housing starts remained surprisingly high. Some possible explanations included the maturing of the "baby boom" generation and an increasing demand for housing as investment property. Other explanations involved the development of new savings opportunities in banks and thrift institutions, which were helping to increase the flow of funds available for mortgage loans.

Dwight M. Jaffee and Kenneth T. Rosen set out to measure the impact of various economic and demographic factors on the U.S. housing industry. They developed a model of the housing industry based on historical data extending as far back as 1960. The model included the following five equations.

1. The *supply of new housing* was estimated as a function of the following independent variables: (a) the change in the number of owner-occupied housing units ($\Delta HOWN$)—this variable was included as a measure of tendencies to buy homes rather than rent; (b) the number of housing units already in existence (KSF_{-1})—this is a lagged variable, measured for a previous period; (c) the interest rate on single-family home mortgages (RM); (d) the flow of deposits into thrift institutions, adjusted for inflation in housing prices ($\Delta DEP/PH$); (e) the availability of mortgage credit from federal home lending agencies, also adjusted for inflation in housing prices ($\Delta FAC/PH$). The dependent variable was the number of single-family housing starts (SSF). The regression equation for this function was found to be:

$$SSF = a + .25\,\Delta HOWN + 0.2KSF_{-1} - .001\,(RM)(KSF_{-1})$$
$$+ 1.35(\Delta DEP/PH)(KSF_{-1}) + 1.16(\Delta FAC/PH)(KSF_{-1}).$$

The standard error of the estimate was only 7.37 percent, reflecting a close approximation of historical data. The coefficient of determination was .80.

Notice the signs of each of the coefficients. Positive signs for the first two variables suggest an increasing tendency toward home ownership. The negative sign for the interest-rate coefficient is to be expected, as are the positive signs for new funds flows into lending institutions.

Other equations were written to estimate the following:

2. The *demand for new homes* was estimated as a function of the rate of household formation and the availability of mortgage credit (positive effects), and the relative cost of owning versus renting, the unemployment rate, and mortgage interest rates (negative effects).

3. The *supply of multifamily housing* was estimated as a function of profit margins

and the availability of mortgage credit (positive effects), and interest rates, vacancy rates in existing multifamily housing, and the outstanding stock of multifamily units (negative effects).

4. The *cost of mortgage credit* was estimated as a function of the interest rates on government and corporate securities (positive effects), and deposits and deposit inflows in thrift institutions and the relative availability of federal agency credit for housing (negative effects).

5. *Deposit flow into thrift institutions* was estimated as a function of personal savings and interest rates in savings and loan associations (positive effects), and the interest rate on government securities (negative effect).

Some of the variables appear in more than one equation and link the equations together in the model. Interest rates are an example of this. A higher interest rate on securities tends both to increase mortgage interest rates (equation 4) and to reduce the flow of funds to thrift institutions (equation 5). In both cases, the effect is to reduce housing starts. On the other hand, an increase in interest rates paid to depositors tends to increase deposit flow but also to increase mortgage interest rates. The effect on housing starts of increased deposits may be partly offset by the effect of higher mortgage rates.

The five regression equations in this model were combined with four identities specifying the outstanding housing stock and vacancy rates in existing housing. When the equations were solved simultaneously, estimated values for all of the dependent variables over the relevant period were determined. A comparison of the estimated values with actual values yielded a very low amount of errors—with one exception. This was the first quarter of 1979, when extremely cold and snowy weather reduced actual single-family housing starts substantially below the level predicted by the model.

The model revealed some additional information about the housing industry in 1979. The period prior to 1979 was strongly influenced by the flow of savings into high-yielding Money Market Certificates (MMCs) in banks and savings and loan associations. By 1979, funds going into MMCs were primarily a transfer of funds from other savings instruments, thus representing a smaller net increase in deposits available for mortgage lending in 1979. Still, the model identified a significant impact of MMCs on housing starts, particularly multifamily units that are more strongly influenced by business cycles. Without MMCs, single-family housing starts would have fallen by about twice the actual decline in 1979.

Federal agency credit was also increased during 1978 before being cut back to normal levels in 1979. The effect of increased federal mortgage credit was to reduce mortgage interest rates and increase housing starts by about 40,000 units.

The analysts concluded that cycles in home building are most strongly affected by the pattern of deposit flows to savings institutions. As interest rates on competing securities rise and rates paid on MMCs are held below other available interest rates, a withdrawal of savings deposits will cause a sharp cyclical drop in housing starts.

Source: Dwight M. Jaffee and Kenneth T. Rosen, "Mortgage Credit Availability and Residential Construction," *Brookings Papers on Economic Activity,* 1979, vol. 2, pp. 333–376.

for new productive equipment will be placed (or cancelled), workers will be asked to work longer (or shorter) hours, supplies of inventory will be depleted (or will accumulate), the prices of corporate stocks will increase (or decrease), and business firms will increase (or reduce) their borrowing for new investment. The effect of the initial change in spending will gradually work its way through various industries, increasing or decreasing profits and calling for new business strategies.

Certain series of data would be of particular interest to managers in particular industries. For instance, firms in the construction industry would be interested in data measuring the number of contracts and orders for business plant and equipment. Firms using or supplying basic industrial materials would be interested in changes in sensitive prices for industrial commodities. Producers of durable consumer goods would be interested in changes in the average workweek for production workers in manufacturing. Changes in any of these data reflect changing conditions in various markets which may have potential consequences for a firm's own profits.

Series of economic data can be divided into three groups.

1. Series that measure initial changes in spending are called **leading indicators**. Leading indicators begin to move upward or downward before major changes in economic activity take place. They signal the beginning of a new business cycle. For this reason, leading indicators are useful for projecting future sales.

2. Other series move upward or downward according to changes in sales and production. These are called **coincident indicators** and include the kinds of basic employment and production data that define the business cycle.

3. A third group of series reflects changes in economic activity only after they have taken place. These so-called **lagging indicators** measure the reactions to changes that persist after a major swing in economic activity has ended. Lagging indicators include outstanding consumer debt, investment expenditures, and unit labor costs, all of which reach a peak or trough after a business cycle has ended. The major economic indicators are as follows.

Leading indicators:

1. Average workweek for production workers in manufacturing
2. Layoff rate per 100 employees in manufacturing
3. New orders for consumer goods and materials
4. Net business formation
5. Stock prices for 500 common stocks
6. Contracts and orders for plant and equipment
7. New building permits for private housing
8. Vendor performance (firms reporting slow deliveries)
9. Change in inventories on hand and on order
10. Change in sensitive commodity prices
11. Change in total liquid assets
12. Money supply (M1)

Coincident indicators:

1. Employees on nonagricultural payrolls
2. Industrial production
3. Personal income minus transfer payments
4. Manufacturing and trade sales

Lagging indicators:

1. Labor cost per unit of output in manufacturing
2. Manufacturing and trade inventories
3. Commercial and industrial loans outstanding in large commercial banks
4. Average duration of unemployment intervals
5. Ratio of consumer installment debt to personal income
6. Average prime rate charged by banks

Business Conditions Digest combines leading, coincident, and lagging indicators into three separate **composite indexes** that signal or reflect changes in business conditions.[1] The composite **index of leading indicators** is especially useful for managers in planning business strategy. In general, a change in direction of the leading index that persists for two or three months is considered a valid signal of underlying strength or weakness in the economy as a whole. The leading index has been fairly consistent in its projections of business cycle upturns, usually projecting changes in direction from two to eight months before business conditions begin to improve. Downturns, on the other hand, have been predicted as far as twenty-seven months before the trough actually occurred, giving somewhat less credibility to the index's predictions of recessions.

Projections also can be improved through the use of **diffusion indexes**. A diffusion index measures the percentage of indicators that are moving upward. Thus, it tells how widespread an expansion or contraction is and how fast it is spreading. An increase in the leading index that involves less than 50 percent of the indicators cannot be considered a strong signal of major economic change. On the other hand, a large diffusion index suggests that all data are contributing to fundamental strength or weakness in the business environment. A change in the diffusion index generally precedes a change in the composite index, making this a particularly useful forecasting tool.

TIME SERIES ANALYSIS

The preceding sections explored the macroeconomic environment in which business firms operate and described various tools for projecting total spending, production, and business sales. In this section we will consider another method of forecasting that may be used instead of or in addition to macroeconomic models and indicators. This method is **time series analysis**. Because time series analysis is a purely mechanical extension of the past onto the future, it is sometimes described as "naive." Naive forecasting ignores the complex relationships among variables in the economic environment except for the assump-

---

[1]Indicators are adjusted to account for wide differences in amplitude among the various indicators and are weighted according to their reliability for prediction.

CASE STUDY 4.3   An Indicator of Consumer Sentiment

One important indicator of business trends in the United States is the Index of Consumer Sentiment (ICS). The University of Michigan's Survey Research Center produces the Index of Consumer Sentiment based on surveys of consumer responses to certain questions. Researchers ask consumers questions like:

Are you financially better or worse off today than you were a year ago?

Do you expect better or worse conditions over the coming year?

Do you expect better or worse conditions for the country as a whole for the coming year?

Do you expect better or worse conditions for the country as a whole over the coming five years?

Is this a good time to buy major household items?

Results of the survey are combined to yield an index with base 100 in 1969–70. The index reached its lowest point in late 1974 during the gasoline crisis (less than 40) and has exceeded 100 only in mid-1972 and 1977. By the beginning of 1984, the index had risen to 91.5 after recovering from a low of 48 at the end of 1979.

The ICS has been a useful variable for predicting consumer expenditures, especially expenditures for durable consumer goods. The index itself reflects a wide range of circumstances in the economic environment. In particular, the ICS is strongly affected by consumers' certainty or uncertainty about their own future financial conditions. The existence of consumer debt tends to increase uncertainty about the future, and consumer holdings of financial assets contribute to greater consumer certainty.

A number of economists have measured the relationship between the ICS, consumer debt (DEBT), and financial assets (FIN) and have developed the following regression equation:

$$ICS = 74.57 - 38.15(DEBT) + 11.55(FIN) + .07732(u_{-1}).$$

The last term is an error term measuring average deviations of the ICS from regression estimates. The equation has a coefficient of determination of $R^2 = .8778$ and a standard error of 3.57. Note the strong negative influence of debt on the index and the relatively weak positive effect of holdings of financial assets.

Expectations of future income, price inflation, and unexpected events like an oil embargo also affect consumer certainty. Including these variables in the analysis yields the following regression equation:

$$ICS = 42.20 + 136.10(INCOME) - 93.68(PRICE) - 11.79(EVENT) -$$
$$26.36(DEBT) + 7.35(FIN) + .7705(u_{-1}).$$

This equation has a standard error of 2.89 and a coefficient of determination of $R^2 = .9225$. The DEBT and FIN variables remain significant factors, but income and price expectations clearly dominate consumer sentiment.

Frederic S. Mishkin suggests that the ICS is actually a proxy for the other economic factors and proposes including all of these determinants in an equation describing consumer expenditures. He used expenditure data for consumer durables between the years 1954 and 1976 and performed regression analysis relating consumer expenditures to temporary income (Y_T), permanent income (Y_P), a measure of current interest rates (i), existing stock of consumer durable goods (K), household debt (DEBT), total financial assets (FIN), and the ICS for the preceding period. The resulting regression equation is:

$$C_d = -.5431 + .1663(Y_T) + .4883(Y_P) - .3794(i \times Y_P) - .1937(K)$$
$$- .2077(DEBT) + .0408(FIN) + .007(ICS_{-1}).$$

The standard error for this equation was only .0103 and the coefficient of determination was $R^2 = .992$.

The independent variables with the strongest influence on purchases of consumer durables continue to be those that reflect the status of consumers' balance sheets: that is, their debt and financial assets. Income and interest rate variables are also significant. The least effect is represented by the ICS variable, given that the influence of debt and financial assets have already been taken into account. If debt and financial assets are excluded from the analysis, the ICS variable becomes a much more significant determinant of expenditures.

When expenditures for automobiles were analyzed using this method, the regression equation was:

$$C_a = -.3135 + .0469\ (Y_T) + .2329(Y_P) - .1692(i \times Y_P) - .3407(K)$$
$$- .1103(DEBT) + .0305(FIN) + .0007(ICS_{-1}).$$

The standard error in this case was .0105, and the coefficient of determination was $R^2 = .95$. Note that purchases of autos are much less affected by temporary income and more strongly affected by current holdings of consumer durables.

Source: Frederic S. Mishkin, "Consumer Sentiment and Spending on Durable Goods," Brookings Papers on Economic Activity, 1978, issue 1, pp. 217–232.

tion that past relationships will affect sales in somewhat similar ways in the future. Often, this assumption is correct, or, if not, changing relationships that move the data "off course" in one direction will be offset by equal changes in the opposite direction. A forecaster who relies on naive forecasting techniques should examine these underlying assumptions to ensure that they are valid, at least for the immediate future.

Time series analysis can be used to explain the pattern of change in a wide variety of data. Most series of data experience **trends**: that is, general increases or decreases in the values of data. **Cycles** above and below a trend may occur over various time spans. For example, our four-year political schedule is sometimes associated with cycles-in certain time series. **Seasonal changes** produce other short-run cycles in time series during a single year. And, finally, all series experience **random fluctuations** that are unexplained by trend, cyclical, and seasonal factors. The typical result of combining these tendencies is a pattern of behavior somewhat like that shown in Figure 4.1. The dashed line represents an upward trend, the dashed blue line represents cyclical fluctuations above and below the trend, and the solid line represents actual data including trend, cyclical, seasonal, and occasional random factors.

For a business manager, the most obvious application of time series analysis is total sales. Analysis of past sales data should help identify the underlying trend, cyclical, and seasonal factors in a firm's own sales record. Then, these past tendencies can be used to forecast future sales, even though the manager must recognize that unexpected events may occur to push sales above or below the forecast. Like other economic models, time series analysis depends on the assumption of ceteris paribus.

In time series analysis, sales data must be collected in the recent past. The period in which the data are collected must be long enough to provide sufficient data but not so long as to include periods sharply different in technological or

FIGURE 4.1   **Trend, Cycle, and Season**

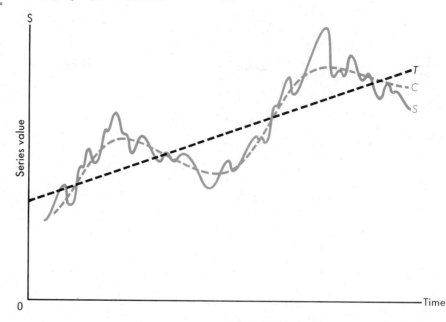

Most economic series exhibit a long-term upward or downward trend (*T*) interrupted by periodic cycles (*C*) and influenced by seasonal (*S*) and random (*I*) fluctuations.

market conditions from those expected in the forecasting period. Monthly data for a period of three or four years would satisfy these requirements for most types of production.

In general, time series data appear to be affected by four sets of environmental factors:

1. **Secular trends** (*T*) affect sales over very long periods of time. Many series of sales data show long-range increases that result from such factors as population growth, technological progress, and rising material standards of living. More people need more furniture, automobiles, clothing, recreation and travel services. Firms producing these goods and services expand production and sales, as do their suppliers. They develop new technologies to reduce costs and provide new products for a growing consumer market.

2. **Cyclical fluctuations** (*C*) in sales appear somewhat regularly and may last from two to twenty years depending on production characteristics of particular industries. Cyclical swings in housing, for example, occur on an average of every eighteen years, while swings in pork production average about three years. The length of the cycle is often related to the time required to produce the good in question and the time required to consume it. It appears that con-

sumers tend to replace their durable household goods, and manufacturers their inventory, at fairly regular and consistent intervals.

3. **Seasonal fluctuations** (S) occur throughout a single year as such variables as weather, holidays, and school schedules affect buying patterns. Some industries are strongly affected by seasonal factors, while the sales of others remain constant year-round. Ice cream and turkeys, swim suits and school shoes, fuel oil and building materials all have fairly regular seasonal cycles.

4. Finally, time series data experience some **irregular swings** (I) that result from particular events such as strikes, major disasters, and so forth. Random events like these cause "blips" in time series that may never be repeated and cannot be predicted.

The total value of sales for any period of time may be summarized by the equation

$$Q = T + C + S + I,$$

and sales growth may be expressed as

$$\Delta Q = \Delta T + \Delta C + \Delta S + \Delta I.$$

Sales equations are additive as shown only if the analyst believes there is no interaction among the various forces of change. An expected long-term trend of 3-percent annual growth with a seasonal factor for the forecast month of $+1$ percent and a cyclical downswing of -2 percent would yield forecasted growth of

$$\begin{aligned} \Delta Q &= \Delta T + \Delta C + \Delta S + \Delta I \\ &= (.03/12) - .02 + .01 + (?) = -.0075 \end{aligned}$$

equals $-.75$ percent below the current month.

Most time series are assumed to be multiplicative, however, since there is believed to be some interaction among the variables. In this case, the equation describing sales would be

$$Q = (T)\,(C)\,(S)\,(I),$$

where $T =$ the trend value of sales in thousands, and C, S, and I, are sales factors based on cyclical, seasonal, and irregular market changes. For long-term trend sales of 100 thousand units, expected cyclical change of -3 percent and seasonal change of $+8$ percent, for example, the best forecast of sales for the next period is

$$Q = (100)\,(.97)\,(1.08)\,(I) = 104.76 \text{ thousand units,}$$

with I being unknown.

TABLE 4.1 Health-Glo Sporting Goods Company Monthly Sales Analysis

		(1) Sales (thousands) (T)(C)(S)(I)	(2) M.A. (12 mos.)	(3) Seasonal factor = (1)/(2)	(4) Average seasonal factor (S)	(5) Average seasonal factor(S) (adjusted)	(6) $\frac{(T)(C)(S)(I)}{S}$ = (1)/(5)	(7) Trend: T = 11.34 + .36t	(8) (C)(I) = $\frac{(1)}{(5)(7)}$	(9) C Adjusted
1979	Jan.	11					11.46	11.70	.98	
	Feb.	10					10.99	12.06	.91	1.00
	Mar.	12					13.79	12.42	1.11	1.00
	Apr.	12					12.37	12.78	.97	1.06
	May	14					14.29	13.14	1.09	1.09
	June	17					16.35	13.50	1.21	1.13
	July	16	15.08	1.06	1.06	1.05	15.24	13.86	1.10	1.15
	Aug.	16	15.5	1.03	1.00	.99	16.16	14.22	1.14	1.12
	Sept.	18	15.92	1.13	1.11	1.09	16.51	14.58	1.13	1.14
	Oct.	18	16.17	1.11	1.06	1.05	17.14	14.94	1.15	1.15
	Nov.	17	16.58	1.03	.97	.96	17.71	15.30	1.16	1.15
	Dec.	20	16.50	1.21	1.14	1.13	17.70	15.66	1.13	1.11
1980	Jan.	16	17.17	.93	.97	.96	16.67	16.02	1.04	1.06
	Feb.	15	17.42	.86	.92	.91	16.48	16.38	1.01	1.03
	Mar.	15	17.58	.85	.88	.87	17.24	16.74	1.03	1.02
	Apr.	17	17.67	.96	.98	.97	17.53	17.10	1.03	1.04
	May	18	17.75	1.01	.99	.98	18.37	17.46	1.05	1.05
	June	20	17.67	1.13	1.08	1.04	19.23	17.82	1.08	1.04
	July	19	17.67	1.08	Total	Total	18.10	18.18	1.00	1.02
	Aug.	18	17.83	1.01	12.16	12.00	18.18	18.54	.98	.98
	Sept.	20	18.09	1.11			18.35	18.90	.97	.95
	Oct.	18	18.25	.99		(5')	17.14	19.26	.89	.90
	Nov.	16	18.42	.87		% of	16.67	19.62	.85	.88
	Dec.	20	18.59	1.08		sales occurring in month	17.70	19.98	.89	.89
1981	Jan.	18	18.66	.96		8.75	18.75	20.34	.92	.92
	Feb.	18	18.92	.95		9.25	19.78	20.70	.96	.94
	Mar.	17	19.25	.88		9.08	19.54	21.06	.93	.93
	Apr.	19	19.58	.97		8.75	19.59	21.42	.91	.93
	May	20	20.17	.99		8.00	20.41	21.78	.94	.94
	June	22	20.80	1.06		9.42	21.15	22.14	.96	.94
	July	22	21.42	1.03		8.00	20.95	22.50	.93	.94
	Aug.	21	22.00	.95		7.58	21.21	22.86	.93	.94
	Sept.	24	22.50	1.07		7.25	22.02	23.22	.95	.96
	Oct.	25	23.08	1.08		8.08	23.81	23.58	1.01	1.00
	Nov.	24	23.67	1.01		8.17	25.	23.94	1.04	1.01
	Dec.	27	24.17	1.12		8.67	23.89	24.30	.98	1.04
1982	Jan.	25	24.66	1.01			26.04	24.66	1.06	1.03
	Feb.	24	25.00	.96			26.09	25.02	1.04	1.05
	Mar.	23	25.25	.91			26.44	25.38	1.04	1.04
	Apr.	26	25.59	1.02			26.80	25.74	1.04	1.03
	May	25	25.83	.97			25.51	25.10	1.02	1.03
	June	27	26.08	1.04			25.96	25.46	1.02	1.01
	July	27	26.42	.95			25.71	25.82	1.00	1.01
	Aug.	26					26.26	26.18	1.00	.99
	Sept.	28					25.69	26.54	.97	.99
	Oct.	28					26.67	26.90	.99	1.00
	Nov.	27					28.13	27.26	1.03	1.00
	Dec.	31					27.19	27.62	.98	

To illustrate time series analysis, we will look at an example using a hypothetical firm. Table 4.1 on page 127 provides data for Health-Glo Sporting Goods Company. Health-Glo's managers believe that the forces that have governed sales in the past will continue to operate similarly in the future. They want to break down sales data into their regular and irregular components by using time series analysis. Then, Health-Glo's managers will project regular past sales behavior into the future, taking into account an allowance for the occurrence of irregular factors.

Estimating the Seasonal Factor

The first step in time series analysis is to separate out the seasonal factor. This is done by first calculating a moving average in order to smooth out sales variations that result from seasonal changes during the year. We compute a twelve-month moving average by averaging sales data for six preceding and five succeeding months together with data for the current month. Moving averages for months 7 through 43 are shown in Column (2) of Table 4.1.

The seasonal factor is determined by dividing actual sales for each month by the moving average. Thus, the result is the percent of average monthly sales normally occurring in a particular month. These values are shown in Column (3). For July 1979, sales are $16/15.08 = 1.06 = 106$ percent of the moving average. For July 1980, sales are $19/17.67 = 1.08 = 108$ percent. And, for July 1981 sales are $22/21.42 = 1.03 = 103$ percent of the moving average. The values 106 percent, 108 percent, and 103 percent are seasonal factors governing July sales. Because these values are all greater than one, we can assume that Health-Glo Sporting Goods Company experiences higher than average sales during a typical July. Note also that higher than average sales occur throughout the summer months and in December, a big gift-buying month. Sales appear to fall below average during the winter months and early spring when participation in sports is less popular.

Monthly seasonal factors for the three years of data must now be averaged to yield a single seasonal factor for each of the twelve months of the year. This has been done in Column (4). For July, the seasonal factor is $1.06 + 1.08 + 1.03/3 = 1.06 = 106$ percent. Notice that the monthly seasonal factors do follow the pattern we found for the period as a whole, rising above 1.00 in the summer and December and falling below 1.00 during the winter months.

The average of the twelve seasonal factors for the year must be 1.00. In our data, rounding produced total seasonal factors of 12.16, which yields a monthly average greater than 1.00. Since the average cannot be greater than one, we have subtracted 16 percentage points from each computed figure. The distribution of these deductions was on the basis of the forecaster's judgment, but deductions might also be distributed equally. Column (5) supplies adjusted seasonal factors whose monthly average is precisely 1.00.

Dividing actual monthly sales data by the seasonal factor for that particular month has the effect of removing seasonal fluctuations from the data series:

FIGURE 4.2   **Monthly Sales—Health-Glo Sporting Goods Company**

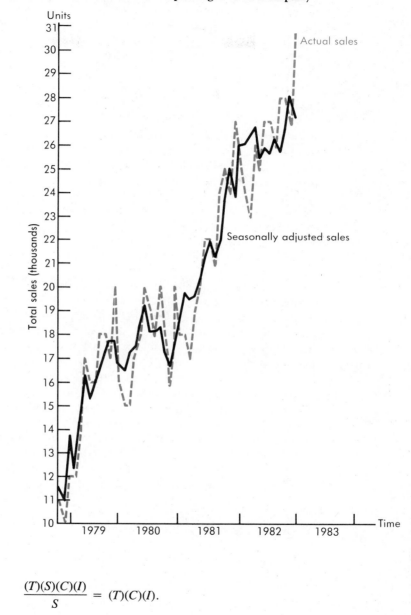

$$\frac{(T)(S)(C)(I)}{S} = (T)(C)(I).$$

The adjusted data now are influenced only by trend, cyclical, and irregular variation. Seasonally adjusted sales data are shown in Column (6).

Actual and seasonally adjusted data have been graphed in Figure 4.2. Much of the seasonal variation has been removed, leaving a somewhat smoother curve. However, there is still evidence of cyclical fluctuations deviating from a generally upward long-term trend. The next step will be to eliminate the trend factor to reveal the influence of cyclical factors alone.

Estimating Trend

The second step in time series analysis is the computation of the long-term secular trend. For most sales data, the long-term trend is upward, in keeping with national population growth, advances in productivity, and development of new resource supplies. While some series might experience rather long periods of accelerated growth followed by periods of relatively slower growth, a straight line or **linear growth** projection yields reasonably good estimates of growth for many industries. A series that experiences linear growth can be described by the linear equation

$$T = a + b(t),$$

where T is the trend value of sales for a particular month. In the equation, the constant a is the first trend value in the series and determines the height of the trend line. The coefficient b is the slope of the trend line. In other words, b is the change in the trend data associated with a unit change in t, where t represents time, or number of months from the origin. For a trend line with an upward slope, b has a positive sign.

Calculating values for the parameters of a linear projection requires the use of an odd number of data points. This is because it is necessary to work with the midpoint of the data, and a unique midpoint is possible only when an odd number of data points is used. For Health-Glo's sales, it would be appropriate to drop the first data point and work with the remaining forty-seven. The unique midpoint of the forty-seven months is the twenty-fifth month, January 1981.

The value of a is calculated by first determining the average of the monthly sales data, $\Sigma\, y/t$, where y represents monthly sales. Thus,

Average monthly sales $= \Sigma\, y/t = 956/47 = 20.34$.

The value of b is found by using the following formula:

$$b = \Sigma xy/\, \Sigma x^2,$$

where x is the number of months from the midpoint, January 1981, and y is monthly sales. All numbers occurring before the midpoint have a negative sign. The value of b in our example is

$$\Sigma\, xy/\Sigma x^2 = (-4{,}045 + 7{,}173)/8{,}648 = 3{,}128/8{,}648 = .36.$$

These computations produce a trend equation of $T = 20.34 + .36(t)$. However, the equation is centered on the midpoint of the data, January 1981. To shift the origin back to the beginning of the series ($t = 0$) it is necessary to subtract twenty-five months from the constant $a = 20.34$. Moving backward 0.36 in sales for each month yields

$$a = 20.34 - .36(25) = 20.34 - 9.0 = 11.34.$$

This changes the equation for secular trend to:

$$T = 11.34 + .36(t),$$

where $t = 0$ is January 1979.

Using the trend equation, the trend value of sales has been computed for each of the forty-eight months and entered in Column (7) of Table 4.1. These figures represent what sales would be if they were unaffected by seasonal or cyclical fluctuations. This trend represents sales resulting only from secular increases in such things as population, technology, and income.

Isolating Cyclical Variation

Remember that removing seasonal fluctuations (in cases where variations are multiplicative) requires dividing actual data by the seasonal factor:

$$\frac{(T)(S)(C)(I)}{S} = (T)(C)(I).$$

Eliminating trend is accomplished similarly:

$$\frac{(T)(C)(I)}{T} = (C)(I).$$

The remaining variation is a result of cyclical and irregular variation only. The results of these computations for our example have been entered in Column (8) of Table 4.1.

Seasonal and trend variation also can be removed simultaneously. To do this, first compute the normal expected sales for each month that result from trend and seasonal variation: $(T)(S)$. For January 1979, total sales resulting from trend would be

$$11.34 + .36(1) = 11.70.$$

Seasonal factors affecting January sales make them only 96 percent of average monthly sales. Therefore, January 1979 sales should be

$$(11.70)(.96) = 11.23.$$

With actual sales of 11, the $(C)(I)$ component of sales would be

$$\frac{(T)(S)(C)(I)}{(T)(S)} = \frac{11}{11.23} = .98.$$

The data in Column (8) of the table reflect only cyclical and irregular fluctuations in sales. These values are the ratio of each month's actual sales to the sales that result from normal seasonal variation and the long-term secular trend. The series still includes irregular fluctuations which can be eliminated in part by a process of "smoothing." In this case, a three-month moving average was used to produce the smoother cycles shown in Column (9). Values less than one indicate low periods in the business cycle, and values greater than one indicate high periods.

The series in Column (9) begins with a period of expansion reaching a peak late in 1979. This high level of sales is sustained throughout the first half of 1980, followed by a mild recession in sales having a low point in November of the same year. Fifteen months of moderate expansion then follow, with sustained high sales for the remaining period for which we have data.

Figure 4.3 includes a graph of trend sales for Health-Glo Sporting Goods Company. The trend line begins with sales of $a = 11.34$ for $t = 0$ and increases $b = 0.36$ (thousand) each month. The curve labeled $(T)(C)(S)$ represents predicted sales based on our analysis of trend, seasonal, and cyclical variation in sales. Compare this sales curve with the curve of actual data in Figure 4.2. Deviations of actual from predicted sales may be assumed to be the result of irregular or random events.

Forecasting Sales

The analyst's prediction for January of the next year should incorporate seasonal, trend, and cyclical factors. The trend value for January 1983 would be

$$T = a + b(t) = 11.34 + .36(49) = 11.34 + 17.64 = 28.98.$$

Since only .96 of average monthly sales normally occur in January, including the seasonal factor yields:

$$(T)(S) = (28.98)(.96) = 27.82.$$

The best estimate for the cyclical factor would be that of the previous month, 1.00, but a range of values might be used based on the judgment of the analyst. Thus, an alternative value for C might be $C = 0.99$. Including the cyclical factor yields sales of $(T)(S)(C) = (27.82)(1.00) = 27.82$ for January 1983.

FIGURE 4.3   **Trend and Predicted Sales for Health-Glo Sporting Goods**

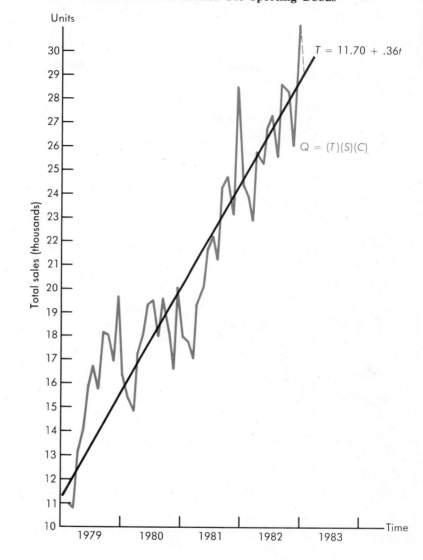

Other months could be forecast similarly, varying the cyclical factor according to the analyst's judgment with respect to the business cycle. Projected sales for any month i would be

$$(T)(S)(C) = (11.34 + .36t_i)(S_i)(C_i).$$

As actual sales data come in, the forecaster should re-evaluate the cyclical factor and update forecasts. Periodically, it will be helpful to compute new seasonal factors and a new trend line that reflects any fundamental changes in market conditions.

Yearly sales also can be predicted on the basis of monthly sales. First determine the percentage of annual sales normally occurring in a particular month (January in our example). On the basis of our seasonal factor for January (Column (5)), we would expect .96 of one month's sales or .96 of $\frac{1}{12}$ of annual sales to occur in January: $.96(\frac{1}{12}) = .08$ or 8 percent of yearly sales. If, as in our example, next January's sales are projected at 27.82 thousand, then estimated sales for the year would be:

$$\left[\frac{\text{monthly sales}}{\frac{1}{12}\ \text{monthly seasonal factor}}\right] = \frac{27.82}{.08}$$

$$= 347.75 \text{ thousand} = 347{,}750 \text{ units.}$$

The processes we have described in this section are primarily mechanical, leaving little room for the analyst's judgment. However, the results obtained from these calculations may become the basis for judgment. Many years of experience with such data should enable the analyst to relate cyclical variation of the economy to that of the firm. Accumulated information about the average length and amplitude of cycles can also be used to modify projections. A range of values of the cycle (C) for any forecast period might also be identified, with one range set to reflect the apparent direction and strength of the cycle. Generally, the analyst should retain a measure of skepticism when using such projections, relying heavily on his or her own perceptions of the business conditions that affect sales and modifying his or her projections accordingly.

EXPONENTIAL SMOOTHING

Some managers forecast sales by using a simple moving average. In a moving average, all past sales data are weighted equally to estimate a trend value, which is then updated each period according to the actual performance of the data. A more reasonable method of weighting past observations is to apply greater weights to more recent values and to allow the weights to diminish for less recent observations. This procedure is called **exponential smoothing.**

In exponential smoothing, a forecast value is the sum of all previous observations, weighted so that the sum of the weights is equal to *one*. The mathematical procedure for determining such weights is called a geometric progression. The first step in such a weighting procedure is to choose the weight for the current period, for example, $a = .30$. Weights for earlier observations are then determined according to the following formula:

Weight $(n) = a(1 - a)^n,$

CASE STUDY 4.4   Forecasting Sales of Productive Equipment

Ajax Industrial Equipment Company produces conveyor belts for use in the forestry industry. The firm's sales are strongly affected by the production of lumber, which is affected in turn by such economic variables as *population* growth, existing stock of *housing, credit* conditions for home mortgages, *weather,* and international *trade.* Forecasts of sales for this product might be based on these parameters, with $Q = f(p, h, c, w, t, z)$ where $p, h, c, w,$ and t represent the previously mentioned independent variables. On the other hand, the analyst might assume that whatever structural variables have affected lumber production in the past will continue to affect production in much the same way in the future. This assumption allows the analyst to use the more mechanical forecasting technique of **time series analysis.**

Using time-series data the analyst can isolate the secular trend, seasonal, and cyclical factors affecting lumber production and project their past behavior onto coming months. The U.S. Department of Commerce's *Survey of Current Business* provides data on materials production for a number of past years. According to the survey, lumber production ranged from 2,072 million board feet per month in January 1975, to 2,631 million board feet per month in December 1979. Over those five years, monthly production rose as high as 3,412 million board feet in October 1979, when the economy was approaching a business cycle peak. However, production was below its long-term trend throughout 1979. The solid blue line in Figure A on page 136 is a graph of actual monthly production over this period.

Adjusted seasonal factors for lumber production were computed as follows:

January	.93	May	1.02	September	1.06
February	.94	June	1.02	October	1.07
March	1.06	July	.95	November	.94
April	1.03	August	1.06	December	.92

Note that lumber production is heavily concentrated during the late spring and fall months, with substantial cut-backs during the winter. The dashed line in Figure A is a graph of lumber production adjusted for this seasonal behavior. Notice that the curve for seasonally adjusted production demonstrates less variability during the year but still shows an upward trend modified by a cyclical downturn in 1979. The long-term trend is represented by the solid black line drawn from $Q = 2,765.4$ in January 1975 to $Q = 3,278.4$ in December 1979. Its equation is $T = 2,765.4 + 8.55\ t$, where t is months after the origin, January 1975.

Figure B shows a ratio of seasonally adjusted production to trend values based on the previous equation. Thus, it takes into account the effect of the business cycle (irregular fluctuations have been removed through the use of a three-month moving average). From a cyclical trough early in 1975, lumber production rose to a peak in mid-1977, fluctuated around the long-term trend throughout 1978, and declined sharply during 1979.

Since $C = .93$ in November 1979, the cyclical factor for January 1980, should fall between $C = .90$ and $C = .96$. Under these assumptions, lumber production would be between

$$Q = (T)(S)(C)(I) = [2,765.4 + 8.55(61)](.92)(.90) = 2,721.6$$

and

$$[2,765.4 + 8.55(61)](.92)(.96) = 2,903 \text{ million board feet.}$$

Since January production is typically .92(1/12) of annual production, production for the coming year should be between $2,721.6/.92(1/12) = 35,499.13$ and $2,903/.92(1/12) = 37,865.22$ million board feet.

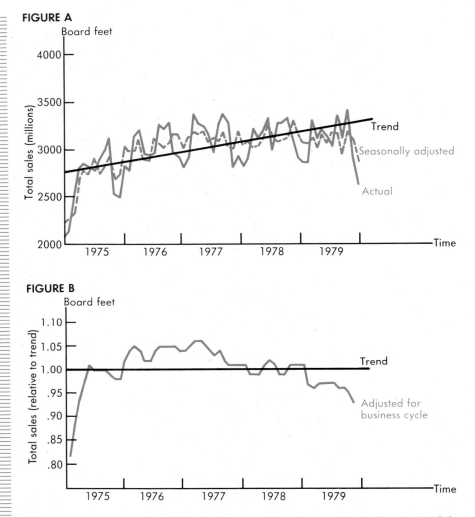

FIGURE A

FIGURE B

Actual total and seasonally adjusted sales and trend are shown in Figure A, while total sales adjusted for seasonal and business cycles and irregular fluctuations are shown in Figure B.

MANAGERIAL THINKING

Suppose policy makers at Ajax Equipment Company have noticed a strong correlation between annual lumber production and sales volume of industrial belting such that for every million board feet of lumber produced annually Ajax sells .15 units of belting. Thus, $Q_B = .15Q_L$, where Q_B = demand for belting and Q_L = millions of board feet of lumber produced annually. The sales price of industrial belting is $2,700 per unit. Production costs include overhead of $500,000 per year and $1,900 per unit of belting produced. Write an economic profit equation for Ajax and forecast Ajax's profit for the coming year.

CASE STUDY 4.5   Time Series Analysis of Profit Trends Since World War II

During the 1970s, many businesspeople complained about a decline in profits in proportion to national income. Business decision-makers blamed falling profits for a drop in new investment and declining productivity growth nationwide. Economist Michael C. Lovell used time series analysis to examine the behavior of profits since World War II and thereby either support or contradict the claim of falling profits.

It is difficult to measure total profits for the nation as a whole because of the many different ways of defining and recording profits among business firms. This is particularly true during periods of inflation, when accounting measures of depreciation fall short of actual replacement costs of business equipment (with the result that profit data are overstated). In order to allow for various definitions of profit, Professor Lovell used a variety of profit measures (14 in all) to describe trends for the nation as a whole. Whatever the measure used, the share of profit as a fraction of total income was found to decline since World War II, with an especially sharp drop during the Vietnam War period and a weak recovery in the 1970s.

The form of the regression equation used in this analysis was multiplicative:

$$\text{Profit } (\pi) = a(TREN47)^b(TREN65)^c(TREN70)^d(GAP)^e.$$

Translated into logarithmic form the equation becomes:

$$\log \pi = \log a + b(\log TREN47) + c(\log TREN65) + d(\log TREN70) + e(\log GAP).$$

The dependent variable, π, is profit as a percent of total income in the nation. The *TREN* variables represent economic growth in the nation immediately after World War II (*TREN47*), during the Vietnam War (*TREN65*), and throughout the 1970s (*TREN70*). *GAP* is the percentage shortfall between *actual* gross national product and estimates of potential GNP that appear in the annual *Economic Report of the President*. Thus, *GAP* is a measure of cyclical forces that affect profits. The coefficient of the *GAP* variable will generally be negative, since a decline in economic activity for the nation as a whole generally means a decline in profits. The absolute value of the *GAP* coefficient reflects the sensitivity of profits to the business cycle.

One of Professor Lovell's profit equations measures the share of profits of all nonfinancial corporations, adjusted for variations in accounting procedures and with depreciation expenses adjusted to reflect replacement costs of equipment as opposed to purchase price. The regression result for this equation is as follows

$$\pi_1 = 3.196(TREN47)^{-.0121}(TREN65)^{-.0647}(TREN70)^{+.0943}(GAP)^{-.0364}$$

The coefficient of determination for this equation is $R^2 = .832$. Other profit equations have produced similarly close approximations of the actual data.

Notice that the regression parameter (b) for the first *TREN* variable is slightly negative, indicating a slight downward trend of the profit share immediately following World War II. The parameter (c) was more sharply negative for the period that corresponds to the Vietnam War. The third parameter (d) was strongly positive, indicating a revival of the profit share during the 1970s. The combined change in profit share over the three trend periods turned out to be a net increase in the profit share of $b + c + d = 1.7$ percent. Only one of the fourteen equations Lovell used showed a continuing decline in profit in the 1970s. A few of the equations did not show a profit squeeze during the Vietnam War, generally because the data series used were not adjusted for the effects of inflation.

In order to measure the effect on profits of other changes in the economic environment, Professor Lovell added the annual rates of productivity change and price inflation to the original equations. If increases in productivity were passed on to consumers in the form of price reductions, there would be no effect on profit shares. The same would be true of inflation. If price increases for finished goods reflected only higher production costs, profit share would not be affected.

Including changes in labor productivity (ΔALP) and price inflation (Δp) produced a second equation for π_1:

$$\pi_1 = 3.050(TREN47)^{-.0093}(TREN65)^{-.0558}(TREN70)^{.0628}(GAP)^{-.0257}(\Delta ALP)^{2.42}(\Delta p)^{.67}.$$

The coefficient of determination in this case was $R^2 = .898$. The positive regression parameters for (ΔALP) and (Δp) reveal that increases in labor productivity and in price inflation have tended to increase profit share. The most significant result of including productivity and inflation variables in the regression equation was the fact that the TREN variables continued to play a major role in explaining profits. Although productivity growth and price inflation do have an impact, they do not explain the downward trend in profits prior to 1970 and the recovery after 1970.

Professor Lovell concluded by recognizing that the bunching of investment expenditures affects profits in ways that cannot be explained by the TREN variables. He recommends a structural approach relating finished goods prices to labor and energy costs for a more complete analysis of profits.

Source: Michael C. Lovell, "The Profit Picture: Trends and Cycles," *Brookings Papers on Economic Activity,* 1978, issue 3 pp. 769–789.

where n represents the number of periods distant in the past. The weights in this case are:

$$a(1 - a)^1 = .30(.70)^1 = .2100$$

for the first period in the past,

$$a(1 - a)^2 = .30(.70)^2 = .1470$$

for the second period in the past,

$$a(1 - a)^3 = .30(.70)^3 = .1029$$

for the next period, and so on until we reach:

$$a(1 - a)^n = .30(.70)^n.$$

As the number of past observations increases, the sum of the weights approaches 1.

Summing all the weighted observations each time a forecast is made would be difficult and time consuming. Fortunately, a simple formula is available for computing the exponentially smoothed estimate. The formula is:

$$F_{t+1} = a(X_t) + (1 - a)F_t,$$

where F_t is the forecasted value for the current period and X_t is the actual value.

TABLE 4.2 Exponential Smoothing for Durable Auto Parts Company

	Jan.	Feb.	Mar.	Apr.	May	June	July	Aug.	Sept.	Oct.	Nov.	Dec.	σ	F_t	F_{t+1}
(1) Actual (X_t)	98	100	115	113	109	97	99	103	110	108	110	100			
(2) $a(1-a)^n = .2(.8)^n$	.017	.021	.027	.034	.042	.052	.066	.082	.102	.128	.160	.200		97.96	98.37
(3) Forecasted values		104	103	105	107	105	104	104	105	106	106	105	5.94		
(4) $a(1-a)^n = .3(.7)^n$	.006	.008	.012	.017	.025	.035	.050	.072	.103	.147	.210	.300		100.97	100.68
(5) Forecasted values		103	102	106	108	108	105	103	105	106	107	105	6.38		

The forecast value (F_{t+1}) is the weighted sum of the actual value in the current period and the forecasted value for the current period.[2]

The behavior of an exponentially smoothed series depends strongly on the values of a and $(1 - a)$ used to weight past observations. A relatively large value of a will put more emphasis on recent observations, and a smaller value will distribute weights further in the past. If observations fluctuate widely, a large value of a will accentuate the fluctuations. If actual data are stable, a small a will reduce the effects of random fluctuations. If the data are increasing or decreasing, a large a will reflect the trend that is more correct. One way to estimate a is to apply the following formula:

$$a = \frac{2}{n + 1},$$

where n is the number of past observations. In general, a value less than $a = .3$ provides estimates closer to the actual performance of the series.

To illustrate exponential smoothing, let us look at hypothetical sales data for Durable Auto Parts Company. In the past, monthly sales have fluctuated fairly widely, with no apparent seasonal pattern and a slight growth trend. The data are shown in Row (1) of Table 4.2. Rows (2) and (4) show the values of the weights $a(1 - a)^n$ for $a = .2$ and $a = .3$. The exponent n represents the number of months in the past. Thus, for the current month (December), $n = 0$ and $a(1 - a)^0 = a$. For November, $a(1 - a)^1 = a(1 - a)$ and so forth. Notice that $a = .3$ gives substantially greater weight to recent data, and the weights decrease more rapidly than for $a = .2$.

Before proceeding further, it may be useful to apply the two weighting

---

2. Since the forecasted value for the current period (F_t) is based on the weighted sum of all past observations, the second term in the formula is actually

$$(1 - a)F_t = (1 - a)[a(X_{t-1}) + (1 - a)F_{t-1}].$$

In turn, the term $(1 - a)F_{t-1}$ is also a weighted sum of past observations, so that the simple formula above includes all past observations, weighted according to $a(1 - a)^n$.

FIGURE 4.4   **Exponential Smoothing**

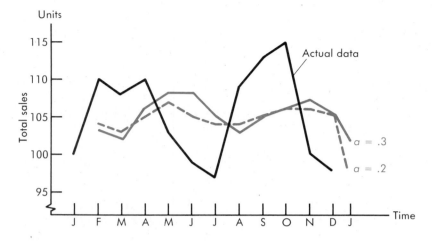

systems to past data and measure the deviation of forecasted values from actual values. Using the formula

$$F_{t+1} = a(X_t) + (1 - a)F_t$$

requires an initial forecast value F_t for beginning the series. Therefore, we have used a simple average as a forecast for January. (The selection of an initial starting forecast is not especially critical, since its value is far in the past and has little significance for recent forecasts.) With a simple average $\bar{X} = 105.17$ the forecast values were calculated for the eleven subsequent months according to both $a = .2$ and $a = .3$. The forecasted values appear in Rows (3) and (5) in the table. The standard deviation of forecasted values from actual values also was computed and appears in the indicated column. The smaller standard deviation for $a = .2$ suggests that this is the appropriate weighting system in this case to use for exponential forecasting.

The next step is to apply weights to all past observations and compute their sum. The resulting sum is the value F_t to be used in forecasting. Applying the formula $F_{t+1} = a(X_t) + (1 - a)F_t$ yields the forecast for January of the following year. The result of applying this formula is shown in the indicated column.

Actual data are plotted as a solid line in Figure 4.4. The solid and dashed blue lines represent series using the two weighting systems and beginning with a simple average. Some characteristics of the smoothed series should be noted. The smaller value of a neutralizes fluctuations better but does not capture the effects of growth as well as the larger value. Both series lag behind changes in the actual data, with peaks and troughs occurring at least one month later.

A Closing Note

No one can correctly predict the future. Understanding even the most sophisticated forecasting techniques cannot guarantee the selection of strategies consistent with future business activity. However, like other tools of managerial economics, macroeconomic forecasting tools do play a vital role in managerial decision-making. They force decision makers to consider the many factors that affect a firm's sales. We have defined the first step in strategic planning as observation: the gathering of data for making a decision. Macroeconomic forecasting tools expand the range of observation from the immediate environment to the national (and even international) market. They ensure that current information about significant market trends is included when evaluating alternative strategies. Then, they constitute a basis for evaluating feedback from events as they occur. By using these tools, managers can constantly re-assess their forecasts in the light of developing events and modify their strategies to conform to new information.

SUMMARY

Cycles in economic activity nationwide strongly affect the sales of individual business firms. Macroeconomic models describe the behavior of consumer, business, government, and foreign spending in the United States and project gross national product for the coming year. Consumer spending is described as a function of income, stock of goods owned, credit conditions, expectations regarding prices and employment, and other factors. Business spending on plant, equipment, and inventories is a function of retained earnings, interest rates, technological and environmental factors, prices of raw materials and finished goods, expected competition, existing plant and equipment, demographic conditions, and other factors. Government spending is determined by government budgets, and foreign spending can be estimated from outstanding orders and recent trends. Projections of spending for particular goods and services may be based on data describing particular factors that strongly influence those types of spending.

Economic indicators are series of data describing selling and production activity in various sectors of the economy. Leading indicators are series that indicate change before changes in economic activity as a whole actually become evident and are useful for projecting sales. Coincident indicators define the cycle, and lagging indicators change direction after changes in economic activity as a whole have occurred.

Time series analysis is a mechanical procedure for projecting data describing past economic activity into the future. In time series analysis, the analyst first removes seasonal fluctuations from the data and then estimates the secular trend. Movements above and below the trend are characterized as business cycles. The length of a cycle in sales of a particular industry may depend on the time required to produce the good in question and the time required to consume it. Time series equations may be additive or multiplicative.

Exponential smoothing applies diminishing weights to past data in order to forecast the future. All forecasting techniques require the good judgment of the analyst if they are to produce useful results.

KEY TERMS

business cycle	coincident indicator
labor	lagging indicator
land	index of leading indicators
capital	diffusion index
technology	trend
macroeconomic model	cycle
gross national product	seasonal change
private consumption spending	random fluctuation
business investment	linear growth
government purchases	time series analysis
foreign investment	exponential smoothing

QUESTIONS AND PROBLEMS

1. Use the following hypothetical information to make a macroeconomic forecast of GNP. All figures are in billions of dollars.

$$GNP_t = C + I + G + F_n,$$
$$C = 90 + .6(GNP_t),$$
$$I = 400,$$

and

$$G = 600.$$

Sales to foreign buyers = 400.

Purchases from foreign sellers = 375.

2. Use the data in Problem 1 to determine the effect on next year's GNP of a $50 billion increase in government spending and a $50 billion increase in purchases from foreign sellers.

3. What economic and social conditions probably determined the value of the constant $90 billion included in the consumption function in Problem 1?

4. Define "indicators" and explain how an index of leading indicators can provide useful information for business planning. What is the significance of the "diffusion index"?

5. What potential dangers are associated with the use of economic indicators?

6. Explain why the use of macroeconomic models is a more accurate method of business forecasting than simple extrapolation from recent GNP trends. What are the weaknesses of macroeconomic forecasting?

7. Distinguish between "naive" forecasting techniques and those involving structural relationships. Under what conditions are these methods either appropriate or inappropriate?

8. Consult recent issues of the *Survey of Current Business* for production data in various industries. Scan the data to determine the direction of trends and evidence of seasonality. How might the length of the business cycle differ among the industries examined?

9. Select an industry from a recent issue of *Survey of Current Business* and determine a seasonal factor for it. On the basis of your information, project total sales over the next eleven months.

10. Number One Auto Parts estimates sales on the basis of trend, $T = 57,500 + .05t$, where T is the dollar value of monthly sales and t is months from origin (December 1982 = 36). Auto parts sales tend to move opposite to the business cycle with a high of $C = 1.10$ expected in January 1983, declining to .86 in December 1983. Project the total dollar value of sales for 1983.

11. Consider each of the following goods and discuss the pattern of demand in terms of trend, cyclical, seasonal, and random factors. What news items would be significant to a manager of a firm producing any of these items? What indicators or surveys would be of additional help in making production plans?

unfinished furniture	auto parts
generic food products	trucks
instant photographic equipment	home entertainment equipment

12. Use the following hypothetical data on monthly purchases of bicycles (in thousands) in the United States to determine seasonal factors for bicycle sales.

January	50	May	85	September	100
February	55	June	90	October	80
March	60	July	90	November	100
April	75	August	100	December	100

Suppose sales are 65,000 for the following January. On the basis of the information given, what would be your projection for annual sales?

13. Consult *Business Conditions Digest* or *Business Week* for information about the recent behavior of significant economic indicators. Speculate on the implications for producers of: mobile homes, office equipment, management consulting, and cargo transportation. Select a major local industry and comment on its immediate prospects.

14. *Business Week* publishes a summary of macroeconomic forecasts for the coming year every January. Consult your library for January issues of the current year and report on macroeconomic forecasts. What considerations influenced particular forecasts? What industries are expected to be particularly affected by changes in economic activity in the coming year?

Recent Results of Macroeconomic Forecasts

In January 1985, macroeconomic forecasters faced a more stable outlook than the nation had experienced in several years. In fact, the early 1980s had brought extreme volatility in total production, including two years of decline in gross national product (1980 and 1982) and one year (1984) in which quarterly economic growth bounced around from a low of 1.6 percent to a high of 10.1 percent.

In order to get a better idea of the formidable task faced by macroeconomic forecasters even in a relatively "stable" year, we will summarize some of the more important assumptions and expectations formulated by analysts at the beginning of 1985. In addition, several actual forecasts of economic activity in 1985 have been listed in Table 4A.1 so that you can compare the actual data for the year with these predictions and see how well the analysts did.

Consumption. Consumers were heavily stocked with consumer durables in 1985 as a result of a buying binge in 1984. Therefore, consumer spending was expected to slow moderately. Prices were expected to rise less than 5 percent during the year. Unemployment was expected to remain at about 7.4 percent, with the result that certain depressed industries or regions of the country might hold down consumer spending nationwide.

Investment. After a major surge of investment spending in 1984, business firms had accumulated new stocks of productive equipment. Investment expenditures were expected to continue at a moderate pace, however, at least as long as the costs of borrowing remained stable. Housing starts were expected to remain steady, too, after a growth spurt early in the year. Still, all kinds of

TABLE 4A.1   1985 GNP Predictions

	Real growth in GNP	Price increases	Average unemployment
Townsend-Greenspan	3.8%	4.7%	7.0%
RSQE, University of Michigan	4.3	4.2	7.0
Data Resources	1.8	3.7	7.7
Georgia State University	2.8	4.6	7.2
Wharton Econometrics	3.9	3.9	6.8
University of California at Los Angeles	4.4	4.0	7.2
Chase Econometrics	2.5	4.7	7.6
Merrill Lynch	3.0	4.6	7.2
Average	2.9	4.3	7.4

Source: *Business Week* publishes a summary of macroeconomic forecasts for the coming year every January.

investment spending were expected to react strongly if interest rates should begin to rise.

Government spending. Government spending has exceeded tax revenues significantly throughout the 1980s and the federal government deficit was expected to be nearly $200 billion again in 1985. Most economic forecasters were hoping that Congress would take steps in 1985 to reduce the budget deficit. Otherwise, it was feared that interest rates would rise, having negative effects on sales of consumer durables and business investment.

Foreign spending. Net foreign spending was expected to continue to decline, as the strong dollar kept U.S. goods more expensive for foreign buyers and made foreign goods remain cheaper for U.S. consumers. The increasing trade deficit (more than $100 billion in 1984) represented a substantial loss of revenue for U.S. manufacturing firms, a drag on employment, and a deterrent to investment. Most analysts blamed the strong dollar on high U.S. interest rates (relative to U.S. inflation) which, in turn, were believed to be a result of the high government deficit.

On balance, forecasters predicted real growth in GNP of almost 3 percent for 1985, making total output about $3,767.5 billion. Inflation was predicted at about 4.3 percent, and unemployment at 7.4 percent. The major forecasters and their predictions are listed in Table 4A.1.

Detailed projections of individual sectors can be obtained from the individual forecasters. For example, Georgia State University's forecast for 1985 included auto and parts sales of $158.6 billion,[1] an increase of about 6.2 percent; residential construction of $165 billion,[1] an increase of 6.9 percent; farm income of $24.1 billion,[1] a decrease of almost 15 percent; federal defense purchases of $248.9 billion,[1] an increase of 12.4 percent; a small decrease in housing starts; and a 2-percent increase in building prices.

---

[1]Not adjusted for inflation.

Production Theory

The United States is the richest nation on earth. We possess greater total wealth than any other nation in history, and each year American business firms produce more new goods and services for a larger number of people than in any other nation. Yet even with this great wealth we cannot produce everything we want. In every industry, production is limited by the existing technology and by the quantities of resources available.

In recent years, growth of production in the United States has slowed. A few years of *negative* growth have raised concerns about our potential for increasing production in the future. Policymakers in the federal government have looked for the sources of the growth slowdown and for new policies to offset it. Many new policy proposals have emphasized the "supply side" of economic activity. Supply-side policies consist primarily of inducements to increase productivity. Tax incentives for saving and investing, removal of certain regulatory restraints on business, and a reduction in marginal income tax rates are some examples of these inducements.

Business firms play a major role in these efforts to increase productivity. By using productive resources more efficiently, business firms can increase output, reduce costs, and satisfy their customers more effectively. Moreover, successfully satisfying consumer demand at lower costs provides increased profits that can be used to expand a firm's productive capabilities in the future.

This chapter is the first of a series of chapters devoted to the behavior of production and production costs. Understanding production is essential to an understanding of costs and is, therefore, a necessary part of managerial economics. This is due to **opportunity costs**. Whenever a business firm allocates resources to one kind of production it must expect to sacrifice other goods and services that might have been produced with those resources. Thus, each unit of materials and equipment used and each unit of labor hired incurs an opportunity cost. For production to be efficient, the total value of a firm's production must be at least as great as the sum of all opportunity costs.

Production decisions may involve the short run, during which production can vary over a fairly limited range, or a much longer period, during which production options are much greater. In this chapter, we will examine the theory behind production decisions, with particular emphasis on decisions involving the short run. Chapter 6 will describe the relationship between quantity of production and costs in the short run. Subsequent chapters will describe production planning, including practical applications of production theory to long-run business decisions.

RESOURCES FOR THE SHORT RUN AND THE LONG RUN

Let us consider first the relationship between production in the current period and production in the future. Circumstances of production vary because of differences in the resources available to a firm over the short and the long run.

Over any given production period, some resources may be described as **fixed resources**: that is, their quantities are firmly established and their purposes are rather clearly defined. Fixed resources include buildings and equipment owned or leased by the firm as well as specialized managerial or technical personnel under contract for a certain time. Other resources may be described as **variable resources**. Variable resources include materials, energy, component parts, and workers employable for variable amounts of time. Managers may decide to use larger or smaller quantities of variable resources in order to utilize the firm's fixed resources more or less intensively.

Decisions to employ variable resources along with existing fixed resources are called short-run decisions. The **short run** is the period of time over which certain resources are indeed fixed: purchase, lease, or contract arrangements firmly establish their quantities. Managers must decide the most efficient quantities of variable resources to use with existing fixed resources during the short run: that is, the proper number and amount of technicians and electric power to operate machines, drivers and fuel to operate vehicles, and clerks and supplies to equip offices and showrooms.

The actual length of the short run differs among firms according to the character of each firm's fixed equipment and specialized personnel. The short run for a taxicab company may be only the amount of time required to purchase (or sell) additional cabs and sign (or allow to expire) a contract with an additional dispatcher. The short run for a subway system would be much longer, since years are required to purchase land and design and construct subway facilities. Whatever the length of the short run, managers must decide the appropriate allocation of variable resources to satisfy a firm's objectives.

The **long run** requires another kind of decision. The long run is defined as the period over which the quantities of *all* resources can be varied. Buildings and equipment can be bought, sold, or abandoned. Specialized personnel can be hired or dismissed. In fact, no resource is so fixed in quantity and function that it cannot be added to or subtracted from a firm's available resources. Over the long run, managers must decide the appropriate quantities of all resources necessary to satisfy a firm's objectives.

The existence of both fixed and variable resources in the short run imposes certain limits on a firm's total production. With available fixed resources (buildings, equipment, and specialized personnel), there is likely to be some maximum quantity of output that can be produced, regardless of the quantity of variable resources employed. A single taxicab cannot carry a million passengers a day, regardless of the number of drivers employed! Moreover, in the short run there may be a fairly limited range of resource employment that will yield maximum efficiency (greatest total output per unit of resources employed). To choose a level of production outside this range would utilize an inefficient quantity of variable resources causing higher production costs than would occur at maximum efficiency. Higher production costs can be justified only if demand for a product is greater than demand for any other product that could have been produced: in other words, *only if the value of production is greater than the product's opportunity costs.*

PRODUCTION FUNCTIONS

The quantity of goods and services that may be produced is described by a firm's **production function**. A production function states the relationship between resources used in production and total quantity of output. A short-run production function measures the quantity of output that can be produced when various quantities of variable resources are added to the firm's stock of fixed resources. It is expressed algebraically as

Total product $(Q) = \mathrm{f}(VR)$,

where VR represents the quantities of variable resources—labor, materials, and so forth—that may be employed along with existing fixed resources. (The analysis of production assumes no difference in the quality of a particular resource as its quantity is changed.)

Some Characteristics of Production Functions

The form of a particular firm's production function depends on unique technological and organizational factors, but some characteristics are common to all production functions. The dependent variable (Q) represents total output when various quantities of variable resources (VR) are employed. The **average prod-**

uct of a particular variable resource is determined by dividing total product by the quantity of that resource. Thus,

$$\text{Average product of labor } (AP_L) = \frac{\text{quantity of output}}{\text{units of labor}} = \frac{Q}{L}.$$

Average product is a measure of a resource's **productivity** and is useful for making productivity comparisons among resources.

Resource productivity depends on the nature of the resource and on the other resources with which it is used. Because labor is an important variable resource in many production processes, managers must be especially concerned about the productivity of labor. Labor productivity in the United States is relatively high because of high labor motivation and generally high standards of health and education. Moreover, technologically advanced capital equipment and (until recently) inexpensive energy have enhanced worker productivity. Since World War II, average worker productivity in the private business sector of the United States has increased about 2.5 percent annually. During the 1970s, productivity growth slowed to 1.5 percent, in part a result of rising energy costs (that reduced workers' capacity for production) and recurrent recessions (that reduced investments in new equipment and new technology). If high levels of worker productivity are to continue, managers must employ skilled and motivated workers and provide productive capital with which to work.

A production function also reveals a firm's **marginal product**, another useful measure for making short-run decisions. Marginal product is defined as the *change in* total product associated with a one-unit *change in* variable resources employed:

$$\text{Marginal product of labor } (MP_L) = \frac{\text{change in total product}}{\text{change in quantity of labor}} = \frac{\Delta Q}{\Delta L}.$$

Marginal product may be thought of as the *slope* of the total product function. Marginal product can be computed by using calculus[1] or by computing total product at two consecutive levels of resource employment and finding the difference of these values.

Managers use marginal product data to compare the cost of additional resources with the value of additional production. We will find that increasing the use of a variable resource when other resources remain fixed will ultimately cause marginal product to decline. It is important not to increase the use of any resource to the point that its cost exceeds the value of its marginal product.

---

1. Marginal product is the first derivative of the total product function, determined through the use of calculus. Computation of first derivatives was demonstrated in Appendix 1A and will be used again later in this chapter.

The Form of a Production Function

Production functions can take various forms depending on fundamental assumptions concerning the behavior of total product, average product, and marginal product. We will look at three forms of production functions, each of which describes a different pattern of behavior and is appropriate for use under different technical conditions.

Linear Production Functions

Linear production functions involve simple assumptions and are simple to calculate and use. To illustrate a linear production function, let us suppose that a firm owns buildings and equipment and employs managerial personnel to operate an employment agency. Clerical workers are hired to schedule interviews, mail job information, and so forth. Employing two clerical workers a week yields total output of 40 units of service over the week.

The equation for a linear production function is:

Total product (Q) = f(VR) = $a + b(L)$.

The independent variable in this production function is L, the number of workers employed during the week. The constant a is the quantity of output that would be produced without the use of any variable resource. In this example, the value of a is zero since without workers no output would be produced. The coefficient b measures the contribution of a single unit of labor to total output. This coefficient represents the marginal product of labor when all other resources—buildings, equipment, and managerial personnel—are fixed in quantity. A constant coefficient for L implies that the marginal product of L is constant. That is, successive additions of workers to the production process while all other resources remain constant continue to add b units of output to the total. Solving the production function for observed data yields:

Total product (Q) = $a + b(2)$ = 40 units.

For $a = 0$,

$Q = 0 + b(2) = 40$.

Therefore, $b = 20$, making the production function

Q = f(VR) = $0 + 20(L)$.

The linear production function is illustrated graphically in Figure 5.1a. Quantity of labor employed (L) is measured on the horizontal axis and quantity

FIGURE 5.1   **Linear Production Functions**

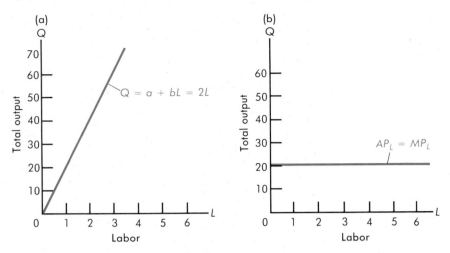

A linear production function of one variable resource, $Q = a + bL = 2L$, is shown in (a). For any linear production function with $a = 0$, average and marginal product are constant and equal (b).

of output (Q) is measured on the vertical axis. The production function is a line rising from the origin with a constant slope. The value of the coefficient b tells us that additional units of labor increase total product by a constant quantity, $b = 20$. Therefore, the slope of the production function is $+20$. Total product at any level of resource use can be determined by checking the vertical coordinate of the line at a particular quantity (L).

Linear production functions are appropriate for describing specific technical processes. To see why, calculate values of total, average, and marginal product at various levels of resource use. This has been done in Table 5.1.

Total product is determined by substituting values of L in the production function and solving the equation for Q. Once again, average product of labor is total product divided by units of labor:

$$AP_L = Q/L.$$

Marginal product of labor is the *change in* total product associated with each additional unit of labor employed:

$$MP_L = \Delta Q/\Delta L = dQ/dL.$$

For a linear production function, the marginal product of any resource is shown by the coefficient of that resource variable. Thus, $MP_L = b$. Since marginal

TABLE 5.1   **Production Data for the Short Run**

Units of labor (L)	Product in units of service (Q)	Marginal product (MP_L)	Average product (AP_L)
0	0		0
1	20	20	20
2	40	20	20
3	60	20	20
4	80	20	20

product occurs in the process of adding units, the value is shown between rows in Table 5.1.

Note that total product increases by constant amounts when the quantity of labor is increased. Therefore, marginal product is constant at $b = 20$. Moreover, for $a = 0$, average product is also constant and equal to marginal product, indicating that resource productivity is unaffected by the number of clerical workers employed over the range shown. Average and marginal product are graphed in Figure 5.1b.

Linear production functions are easy to use, but they are precisely correct only for production processes with constant and equal average and marginal product. In fact, many production processes exhibit constant and equal average and marginal product over a certain range of resource use. An employment agency, for example, may be operated for longer hours, using additional workers, supplies and electric power with little or no change in worker productivity. Many factories may also operate additional shifts, using fixed resources more intensively but not changing workers' average and marginal product. In situations when additional units of variable resources add a constant quantity to total production, linear production functions are useful for deciding resource employment.

Quadratic Production Functions

Linear production functions are appropriate only for a range of resource utilization in which average and marginal product are constant and equal. Other types of functions more accurately describe the behavior of total product over a broader range of variable resources. **Quadratic production functions** are examples of this type of equation. Quadratic production functions can take any of the forms shown in Figure 5.2 on page 154. As in Figure 5.1, quantity of resource (L) is measured on the horizontal axis and quantity of output (Q) is measured on the vertical axis.

The form of the equation that produces the line in Figure 5.2a is

$$Q = a + bL + cL^2,$$

where the constant a is zero. The coefficient $+b$ represents the upward slope of the production function as it leaves the origin, and the coefficient $+c$ rep-

FIGURE 5.2   **Quadratic Production Functions**

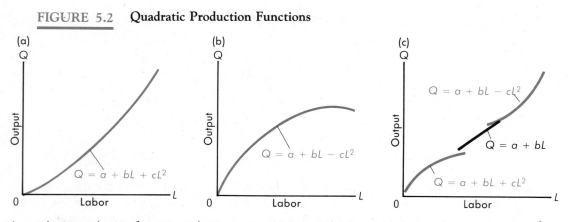

A quadratic production function with increasing average and marginal product, $Q = a + bL + cL^2$, is shown in (a). A quadratic production function with decreasing average and marginal product, $Q = a + bL - cL^2$, is shown in (b). Three production functions combined to illustrate increasing, constant, and diminishing average and marginal product are shown in (c).

resents the additions that give the function an increasingly steeper slope. In Figure 5.2b, the equation is

$$Q = a + bL - cL^2,$$

and the coefficient $-c$ represents the reductions that give the function an increasingly horizontal slope.

As before, average product is total product divided by the quantity of the variable resource employed. For any resource, average product is a measure of the productivity of that resource. Thus, in Figure 5.2a

$$AP_L = Q/L = (bL + cL^2)/L = b + cL,$$

and in Figure 5.2b

$$AP_L = Q/L = (bL - cL^2)/L = b - cL.$$

The sign of the coefficient c indicates whether labor productivity increases or decreases as more labor is used along with a firm's fixed resources. In Figure 5.2a, employing more labor enables the firm to use its fixed resources more efficiently. In other words, labor productivity increases. In Figure 5.2b, fixed resources limit increases in average product as more workers are added, and labor productivity declines.

Marginal product is the change in total product associated with additional units of the variable resource. Look again at the total product functions. The total product function in Figure 5.2a has an increasing slope, indicating increasing marginal product. Each additional worker contributes more to total product than the one before. The production function in Figure 5.2b, however, has a decreasing slope, indicating decreasing marginal product. Each additional worker contributes less than the previous worker, and, in fact, at some level of employment, hiring additional workers causes total product to decline.

Marginal product is the first derivative of the total product equation, determined through the use of calculus. In Appendix 1A we demonstrated the computation of the first derivative of a quadratic equation. Through calculus, the marginal product equations for the quadratic production functions in Figures 5.2a and 5.2b are found to be:

$$MP_L = \Delta Q/\Delta L = dQ/dL = (1)\ (b)\ (L)^{1-1} + (2)\ (c)\ (L)^{2-1} = b + 2cL$$

in Figure 5.2a, and

$$MP_L = \Delta Q/\Delta L = dQ/dL = (1)\ (b)\ (L)^{1-1} - (2)\ (c)\ (L)^{2-1} = b - 2cL$$

in Figure 5.2b.

Remember that marginal product is also the slope of the total product function, which becomes steeper for higher values of L in Figure 5.2a and becomes flatter in Figure 5.2b. The steeper slope in Figure 5.2a indicates *increasing* marginal product, shown also by the positive coefficient for $2cL$. The more horizontal slope in Figure 5.2b indicates *decreasing* marginal product, as shown by the negative coefficient for $2cL$. Note that for equation 5.2b, marginal product could become zero or negative when L becomes very large.

In Figure 5.2c, quadratic equations 5.2a and 5.2b have been combined with a linear equation to produce a more typical production function. Figure 5.2c describes a production process for which low levels of resource use are associated with **increasing marginal product**, moderate levels of resource use with **constant marginal product**, and high levels of resource use with **decreasing marginal product**. Increasing, constant, and decreasing marginal product characterize most production processes in which certain resources are fixed. In the next section, we will demonstrate the use of a production function that embodies all of these characteristics in a single equation.

Cubic Production Functions

The **cubic production function** in Figure 5.2c describes the behavior of production more accurately than any of the other production functions taken separately. The reason for this has to do with proportions of fixed and variable resources. When various quantities of some resources are combined with a certain quantity of fixed resources, there is some quantity of variable resources that is technically correct and, therefore, yields maximum marginal product. As the use of variable resources approaches this quantity, total product rises more steeply and marginal product increases. At the technically correct level (or range) of employment of variable resources, total product rises at a constant rate and, thus, marginal product is constant. Finally, as the use of variable resources exceeds the technically correct proportion relative to fixed resources, total product rises less steeply and marginal product declines. At some very high level of resource use, total product may reach a peak. If additional resources are employed beyond this point, total product will begin to fall and marginal product will become negative.

Variations in the behavior of marginal product also affect average product, causing average product to increase over some range of employment of variable resources and eventually to decrease when the employment of variable resources exceeds the technical capacity of existing fixed resources.

Processes experiencing increasing and decreasing marginal and average product may be correctly described by a cubic production function. To illustrate, consider a food service company that owns a building and equipment and has contracted managerial personnel to organize its day-to-day operation. Variable quantities of labor may be employed and various food items may be purchased, changing the number of meals that can be produced each day. The behavior of total product in this example is illustrated in Figure 5.3. Units on the horizontal axis represent composite units of the variable resources, labor and food (L), and units on the vertical axis represent total number of meals served (Q).

Study carefully the behavior of total product as the quantity of variable resources increases. Over some range of employment, increasing composite units of food and labor will cause total product to rise at an increasing rate. In this case, marginal product is increasing. This is the range of employment over which the proportion of variable to fixed resources is approaching the level for which the building and equipment are designed. Over this range, additional cafeteria employees can divide responsibility to improve worker productivity, and additional food materials can be used more efficiently to reduce waste. When additional units of food and labor add successively larger amounts to total product, the total number of meals rises at an increasing rate, and marginal product increases. Average product also increases, since successively larger additions to total product increase the average productivity of workers.

The range of increasing average and marginal product is shown in Figure 5.3a as Stage 1, in which the quantity of food and labor units varies from $L = 0$ to $L = L_1$ and Q rises from zero to Q_1. Over Stage 1, marginal product is greater than average product, pulling average product up.

Within some range in Stage 1, additional composite units of food and labor increase meal production by smaller and smaller amounts, so that Q rises at a decreasing rate. In this range, marginal product is decreasing. At some point, marginal product falls below average product and begins to pull average product down. Beyond this point, average worker productivity and efficiency of food preparation begin to fall. Again, this has to do with the ratio of variable to fixed resources. Most buildings and equipment are designed for use with a certain quantity of labor and material resources. Exceeding this quantity yields

FIGURE 5.3   A Cubic Production Function

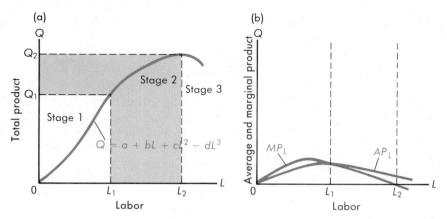

A cubic production function with increasing, constant, and diminishing average and marginal product is shown in (a). Average and marginal product are shown in (b).

decreasing average product. The range of decreasing average product (with positive marginal product) is shown between $L = L_1$ and $L = L_2$ in Figure 5.3a and labeled as Stage 2. During Stage 2, total product rises from Q_1 to reach a peak at Q_2.

Note especially the relationship between average and marginal product over the entire range of resource employment, as shown in Figure 5.3b. When marginal product is above average product, the effect is to increase average product. When marginal product is below average product, the effect is to reduce average product. At some level of employment, marginal product is precisely equal to average product, and there is no tendency for average product to increase or decrease. (Remember that we found this to be true over the entire range of employment when a linear production function is used.)

Finally, beyond some level of employment (L_2 in our example), using additional composite units of food and labor may cause meal production to decline. When certain resources are fixed, excessive quantities of variable resources interfere with production and reduce efficiency. (You might say that beyond this point too many cooks spoil the soup.) This extreme level of employment is shown in Figure 5.3a as Stage 3, where total product is decreasing and marginal product becomes negative. Average product is still positive but decreasing in Stage 3.

We would not expect managers to choose a level of resource employment in the range of Stage 3, in which total product is decreasing. Neither would we expect employment in the range of Stage 1, since deciding to employ additional resource units in this range would increase the average productivity of all units. This means that production decisions will normally involve Stage 2, the range of employment over which average and marginal product are falling, but marginal product is still positive.

A production function that describes these circumstances is a cubic equation and has the form:

$$\text{Total product} = (Q) = f(VR) = a + bL + cL^2 - dL^3.$$

In our example, the constant a is zero and the coefficient b defines the slope of the production function as it leaves the origin. The positive term $+cL^2$ influences the increasing slope over the range of increasing marginal product. The negative term $-dL^3$ influences the slope such that production eventually experiences decreasing marginal product. At some level of resource use, the negative term $-dL^3$ becomes large enough to cause total product to decline.

The average product associated with a cubic production function is determined by dividing total product by quantity of the resource. Thus, when $a = 0$,

$$AP_L = \frac{bL + cL^2 - dL^3}{L} = b + cL - dL^2.$$

This is a quadratic equation and can be solved for any value of L by substitution. Thus, the productivity of labor when ten workers are employed is

$$AP_L = b + 10(c) - 100(d).$$

Marginal product is the first derivative of the total product equation, determined through the use of calculus. Following the procedure described in Appendix 1A, the marginal product of a cubic production function is found to be:

$$\begin{aligned}
\text{Marginal product of labor} = (MP_L) &= \Delta Q/\Delta L = dQ/dL \\
&= (1)\,(b)\,(L)^{1-1} + (2)\,(c)\,(L)^{2-1} \\
&\quad - (3)\,(d)\,(L)^{3-1} \\
&= b + 2cL - 3dL^2.
\end{aligned}$$

This is also a quadratic equation. It tells us that the marginal product of the tenth worker is

$$MP_L = b + 20(c) - 300(d).$$

The actual values of marginal and average product when ten workers are employed depend on the values of the parameters, b, c, and d. To illustrate, suppose the values of the parameters are estimated to be $b = 100$, $c = 10$, and $d = .1$. Substituting for average and marginal product when ten workers are employed yields:

$$AP_L = b + 10(c) - 100(d) = (100) + 10(10) - 100(.1) = 190$$

and

$$MP_L = b + 20(c) - 300(d) = (100) + 20(10) - 300(.1) = 270.$$

In this situation, marginal product is greater than average product and is causing average product to increase. Production must be occurring in the range of Stage 1. On the other hand, suppose the parameters are estimated as $b = 50$, $c = 5$, and $d = .5$. Substituting for these values, again with $L = 10$, yields:

$$AP_L = b + 10(c) - 100(d) = (50) + 10(5) - 100(.5) = 50$$

and

$$MP_L = b + 20(c) - 300(d) = (50) + 20(5) - 300(.5) = 0.$$

In this case, marginal product is less than average product and is causing average product to decrease. Moreover, since marginal product of labor is zero in this case, production is occurring at the border between Stages 2 and 3. To continue to employ additional labor would have the effect of reducing total product; marginal product would be negative.

Look again at the values for the parameters in these two examples. See if you can determine the characteristics of the parameters that distinguish the second production function from the first.[2]

Power Production Functions

Cubic production functions come closest to describing the typical behavior of production when variable resources are applied to a fixed quantity of other resources. However, estimating the parameters of a cubic equation is difficult and time consuming. This makes cubic equations less useful for describing production than a fourth form of equation, the power function. **Power production functions** can be used to describe the behavior of production over a limited range of resource employment. Their parameters are simpler to estimate, and they are easier to use than the functions we have previously described. Examples of power production functions are shown in Figures 5.4a, 5.4b, and 5.4c.

The equation for a power production function has the form

$$Q = aL^b.$$

The constant a represents the quantity of output associated with the first unit of L and is the same for the curves in Figure 5.4. The exponent b measures the *percentage change* in total product as more resources are added. A value of b

---

2. The second equation's initial upward slope is less, the slope increases by smaller amounts, and the reduction in slope is greater.

FIGURE 5.4   **Production and Marginal Product**

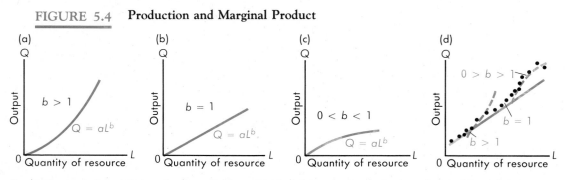

Production experiences increasing marginal product in (a), constant marginal product in (b), and decreasing marginal product in (c). Increasing, constant, and decreasing marginal product are shown in (d).

greater than one indicates a greater percentage change in total product than in resource quantity. The graph of a power production function when $b > 1$ is illustrated in Figure 5.4a. A value of *b equal to one* indicates an equal amount of change in total product for each percentage increase in resources. The graph of the equation when $b = 1$ is illustrated in Figure 5.4b. A value of *b between zero and one* indicates smaller percentage increases in total product than in resource quantity. The graph of the function when $0 < b < 1$ is illustrated in Figure 5.4c. What would $b < 0$ signify?[3]

The average product of a power production function is determined by dividing the total product equation by units of resource:

$$\text{Average product of labor} = (AP_L) = Q/L = aL^b/L = aL^{b-1} = a/L^{1-b}.$$

When b is greater than one, average product increases, indicating increasing productivity of labor. When b is less than one, average product is constant at a.

The marginal product of a power production function is determined through the use of calculus. Determining the first derivative of the average product yields:

$$\text{Marginal product of labor } (MP_L) = \Delta Q/\Delta L = dQ/dL = (b)(aL)^{b-1}$$
$$= baL^{b-1} = ba/L^{1-b}.$$

Compare the equations for marginal and average product. Note that for values of b greater than one, marginal product will be greater than average product

---

3. A negative value for b indicates a negative slope for the production function. If b is between zero and *minus one,* the curve declines by that percentage, with the result that the downward slope becomes smaller with each increase in L and, in fact, never reaches the horizontal axis.

over the entire range of resource employment. Thus, marginal product will cause average product to increase, as was true in Stage 1 of Figure 5.3a. A value of b less than one indicates a marginal product less than the average product over this range of employment. Marginal product will cause average product to decrease in this case, as was true in Stage 2 of Figure 5.3a. If b is equal to one, marginal and average product are identical. This would be true on the border between Stage 1 and Stage 2 of Figure 5.3a, where $MP = AP$ at its highest point.

A disadvantage of the power function as a decision-making tool is that it never reaches a maximum. It continues to increase (or to decrease, if $b < 0$) by larger (or smaller) amounts without ever leveling off. Under these circumstances, marginal and average product continue to move in the same direction. Since this contradicts observations of real production, power functions are useful only over a fairly limited range of resource employment. Fortunately, managerial decisions usually involve choices within the immediate range of current production, and power functions may be easily adapted for this purpose.

Whereas the use of a cubic equation enables the analyst to apply constant parameters over the entire range of resource employment, the use of power equations requires different values of a and b over different ranges of employment. Thus $b > 1$ would be appropriate for the range of increasing marginal product, $b = 1$ would be appropriate for the range of constant marginal product, and $0 < b < 1$ would be appropriate for decreasing marginal product. Values of $b < 0$ would be appropriate for the range of decreasing total product. Of these possibilities, the most frequently used values of b would be in the range $0 < b < 1$, corresponding to Stage 2 in Figure 5.3a.

Figure 5.4d combines three power functions over three segments of a total product function. In the first segment, the exponent b is greater then one, indicating increasing marginal product. In the second segment, b is equal to one, indicating constant marginal product.[4] In the third segment, b is between zero and one, indicating decreasing marginal product.

PRODUCTION FUNCTIONS WITH TWO VARIABLE RESOURCES

All of the production functions we have described thus far can be expanded to include more than one variable resource. When production follows the form of a linear equation, the appropriate equation might be

$$Q = f(VR) = a + b(L) + c(M),$$

where L represents units of labor and M represents units of materials. The coefficients b and c are the marginal products of labor and materials.

A production function of two variable resources must be represented in

---

4. A power equation with exponent $b = 1$ is a linear equation.

EXAMPLE 5.1   **Estimating the Parameters of Linear and Curvilinear Production Functions**

The process of least-squares regression can be used to estimate the parameters of a production function. Remember that least-squares regression uses all observed data to produce an equation that represents the closest approximation to the actual observations.

Linear production functions.   In Chapter 2 we used least-squares regression to estimate the parameters of a linear demand equation of the form

$$Q = a - b\,(p).$$

The normal equations for estimating the parameters are useful for writing a production function of the form $Q = a + b(L)$. In a production function, Q represents quantity of output, a is a constant, and b measures the change in output (Q) associated with a unit change in the use of labor (L). The normal equations for estimating a linear equation are :

$$(1)\ \ \Sigma Q = na + b\Sigma L$$

$$(2)\ \ \Sigma L(Q) = a\Sigma L + b\Sigma L^2,$$

where ΣQ, ΣL, $\Sigma L(Q)$, and ΣL^2 are the sums of the indicated values and n is the total number of observations.

Quadratic production functions.   A quadratic production function has the form

$$Q = a + bL + cL^2.$$

A quadratic function differs from a linear function in that it exhibits increasing or decreasing average and marginal product, depending on the sign of c. The following normal equations are useful for estimating the parameters of a quadratic equation:

$$(1)\ \ \Sigma Q = na + b\Sigma L + c\Sigma L^2$$

$$(2)\ \ \Sigma L(Q) = a\Sigma L + b\Sigma L^2 + c\Sigma L^3$$

$$(3)\ \ \Sigma L^2(Q) = a\Sigma L^2 + b\Sigma L^3 + c\Sigma L^4.$$

Cubic production functions.   Cubic production functions can be estimated by adding a fourth normal equation. To estimate a cubic production function it is necessary to add a fourth term to each equation ($d\Sigma L$ raised to a higher power) and include a fourth equation. Thus,

$$(1)\ \ \Sigma Q = na + b\Sigma L + c\Sigma L^2 + d\Sigma L^3$$

$$(2)\ \ \Sigma L(Q) = a\Sigma L + b\Sigma L^2 + c\Sigma L^3 + d\Sigma L^4$$

$$(3)\ \ \Sigma L^2(Q) = a\Sigma L^2 + b\Sigma L^3 + c\Sigma L^4 + d\Sigma L^5$$

$$(4)\ \ \Sigma L^3(Q) = a\Sigma L^3 + b\Sigma L^4 + c\Sigma L^5 + d\Sigma L^6.$$

The standard error of the estimate for these functions is computed as before:

$$\text{Standard error of the estimate } (\sigma) = \sqrt{\Sigma(Q - Q_e)^2/n}.$$

Computing the parameters of quadratic and cubic equations is tedious even when a pocket calculator is used. Computations of these values are much more useful when done by computer because computers can also find the equation's standard error and coefficient of determination. These statistics enable the analyst to compare production functions of various forms and choose the equation with the smallest error to use in making decisions.

Power functions.   The process of estimating regression equations for quadratic and cubic production functions is long and tedious. Over ranges of observations that follow the shape of a power curve, however, an analyst may use a power function of the form

$$Q = aL^b.$$

The parameters of a power function can be estimated using logarithms. The logarithmic equivalent of the production function of the form $Q = aL^b$ is

$$\log Q = \log a + b(\log L).$$

Note that this is a simple linear equation that can be estimated by linear regression. To do this, the observed values of Q and L should first be expressed as logarithms. Then the logarithmic values can be substituted in the normal equations for linear regression and solved.

This process is illustrated using the values in Table A and is shown graphically in the following figure.

TABLE A

Q	log Q	L	log L	(log Q) (log L)	(log L)²
3.5	.5441	1.5	.1761	.0958	.0310
4.2	.6232	2.5	.3979	.2480	.1583
5.5	.7404	4	.6021	.4458	.3625
6.5	.8129	5.5	.7404	.6019	.5582
7.2	.8573	7	.8451	.7245	.7142
	3.5779		2.7656	2.1160	1.8242

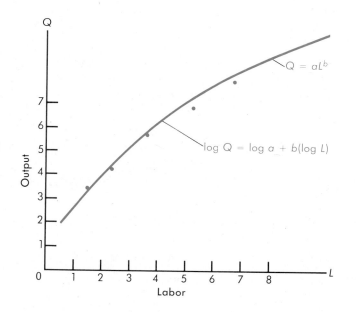

Thus, to solve for equations (1) and (2),

(1) $3.5779 = 5\log a + 2.7656b$

(2) $2.1160 = 2.7656(\log a) + 1.8242b$

we multiply (2) by $\dfrac{5}{2.7656}$ = 1.81, producing

(2) $3.8256 = 5\log a + 3.2980b$.

Now, subtracting (1) from (2) gives us:

$.2477 = 0 + .5324b$ and $b = .4653$.

Substituting this value in (1) yields:

$3.5779 = 5\log a + 2.7656(.4653)$

$2.2912 = 5\log a$.

Hence, $\log a = .4582$. Thus,

$$\log Q = .4582 + .4653(\log L)$$

and

$$Q = (10^{.4582})(L^{.4653}) = 2.87L^{.4653}.$$

The standard error of the estimate is

$$\sigma = \sqrt{\Sigma(Q - Q_e)^2/n} = \sqrt{.0774/5} = .12,$$

and the coefficient of determination is

$$R^2 = \frac{\Sigma(Q_e - \overline{Q})^2}{\Sigma(Q - \overline{Q})^2} = .89 = 89 \text{ percent}.$$

The result of the calculation in Table A is a production function with a value of $Q = 2.87L^{.4653}$. The coefficient $a = 2.87$ represents total product when L is equal to one. The exponent $b = +.4653$ indicates positive but decreasing marginal product. Thus, production in this case is occurring in Stage 2 of our model in Figure 5. 3.

Under these conditions, the use of, say, 10 units of labor should result in total output of $Q = 2.87(10)^{.4653} = 8.38$ units of output. Similarly, the quantity of labor required to produce 10 units of output can be determined by rearranging the production function to solve for L when $Q = 10$:

$$L = (Q/a)^{1/b} = L = (10/2.87)^{2.15} = 14.64 \text{ units of labor}.$$

Thus, to produce 10 units of output would require 14.64 units of labor.

Average product of labor is determined by dividing the total product function by L:

$$AP_L = Q/L = (2.87L^{.4653})/L = 2.87L^{.4653-1} = 2.87L^{-.53} \text{ or } 2.87/L^{.53}.$$

Marginal product, therefore, is

$$MP_L = dQ/dL = (.4653)2.87L^{.4653-1} = 1.34L^{-.53} \text{ or } 1.34/L^{.53}.$$

As expected, marginal product is less than average product, whatever the value of L.

Power functions such as this can be solved easily on many pocket calculators, which also provide a measure of the accuracy of approximation of estimated to actual values.

FIGURE 5.5   A Linear Production Function of Two Variable Resources

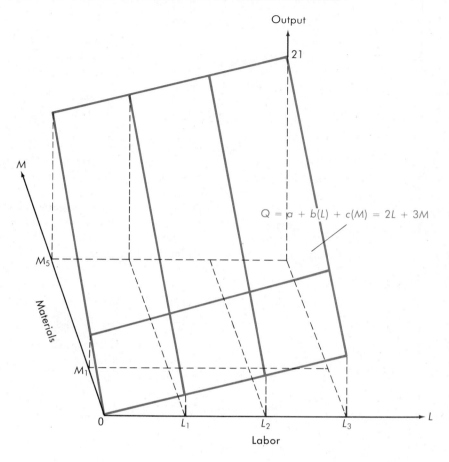

three-dimensional space, as shown in Figure 5.5.[5] The equation for the production function shown is

$$Q = 2L + 3M.$$

The coefficients $b = 2$ and $c = 3$ reveal the marginal products of labor and materials as 2 and 3, respectively.

A production function for two variable resources is not a line but a surface.

---

5. It is not possible to illustrate production processes using three or more resources graphically because four or more dimensions would be required.

Points along the surface represent quantity of output when various combinations of labor and materials are used. Thus, using 3 units of L and 5 of M produces $Q = 2(3) + 3(5) = 21$ units of output. In Figure 5.5, measure 3 units along the L axis to line L_3 then proceed 5 units to line M_5. Now follow the line up to the production surface and measure quantity of output on the scale at the corner. The output from any other combination of L and M also can be determined in this way.

Note that the quantity of output from the use of L alone is measured along the L axis, where the quantity of materials employed is zero. Some points along the nearer edge are $L = 1$ and $Q = 2$; $L = 2$ and $Q = 4$; $L = 3$ and $Q = 6$. The slope of the production surface is labor's marginal product, $b = 2$. Likewise, the output from M alone is measured along the M axis, with a slope equal to the marginal product of materials, $c = 3$.

For any fixed quantity of materials ($M = 0$, $M = 1$, or $M = n$), the quantity of output produced using various quantities of labor can be found by imagining a vertical plane intersecting the production surface. For example, for $M = 5$ a plane would be drawn parallel to the labor axis at $M = 5$ on the materials axis. Some points at which the production surface intersects plane $M = 5$ are $L = 1$ and $Q = 17$; $L = 2$ and $Q = 19$; $L = 3$ and $Q = 21$.

If a plane drawn at some value of M indicates the quantity of output associated with various quantities of L when M remains constant, what is the significance of a plane drawn *horizontally* through the production surface at some total quantity of output, say $Q = 20$? Such a plane would represent all possible combinations of labor and materials that could be used to produce 20 units of output. We will have more to say about this concept later.

When two resources are used together in a linear production function, the average product of each is determined by dividing the production function by the number of units of that resource. Thus,

$$AP_L = \frac{a + bL + cM}{L} = b + \frac{a + cM}{L} = 2 + \frac{3M}{L},$$

and

$$AP_M = \frac{a + bL + cM}{M} = c + \frac{a + bL}{M} = 3 + \frac{2L}{M}.$$

This equation for average product indicates rising productivity for one resource as the quantity of the other resource is increased and the quantity of the first resource does not change. Increasing both resources proportionally yields constant average product.

Quadratric production functions also can be expanded to include other variables:

$$Q = a + b(L) \pm c(L)^2 + d(M) \pm e(M)^2 \pm g(LM).$$

The term $g(LM)$ reflects the interaction between the two variable resources. A cubic production function of more than one variable resource would be written

$$Q = a + b(L) + c(L)^2 - d(L)^3 + e(M) + f(M)^2 - g(M)^3.$$

Power Functions of More than One Variable Resource

Power production functions of more than one variable resource are written

$$Q = aL^b M^c,$$

where a is a constant, and the exponents b and c represent the contributions of labor (L) and materials (M) to total output. The exponent b indicates the percentage change in Q associated with a percentage change in L when M is constant.

The shape of the production surface for power functions depends on the exponents associated with the two resources. Over the range of decreasing marginal product ($0 < b < 1$ and $0 < c < 1$), the production surface curves upward by smaller amounts. A vertical plane drawn through the production surface at any given level of one resource indicates decreasing marginal product for the other. Thus, with labor (L) fixed at some quantity, total product would increase by $c < 1$ percent for each one percent increase in materials (M).

When both resources are increased proportionately, the combined effect on total product is measured by the sum of the exponents, $b + c$. The sum indicates the percentage increase in total product associated with a percentage increase in both resources. Thus, a sum less than one indicates a less-than-proportionate increase in Q, a sum equal to one indicates an equal proportionate increase in Q, and a sum greater than one indicates a greater-than-proportionate increase in Q.

To estimate a power function with two variable resources, first convert the equation to its logarithmic form. For a power function of the form

$$Q = aL^b M^c,$$

the logarithmic equivalent is

$$\log Q = \log a + b (\log L) + c (\log M).$$

Note that the logarithmic equation is linear and can be estimated through the use of normal equations for multiple linear regression (as demonstrated in Chapter 3). The exponents b and c in this case measure elasticity of production, that is, the percentage change in output for each percentage increase in a particular resource, the other resource being held constant.

The Elasticity of Production

A useful characteristic of power functions is the ease of calculating the elasticity of production. **Elasticity of production** is the percentage change in total product associated with a small percentage change in use of a variable resource:

$$\text{Elasticity of production of labor } (\epsilon_{QL}) = \frac{\%\Delta Q}{\%\Delta L}.$$

The most familiar use of cubic production functions was developed by economists Paul H. Douglas and C. W. Cobb. The form of the Cobb-Douglas function is

$$Q = aL^b K^c,$$

where L represents units of labor and K represents units of capital resources. The elasticities of production of labor and capital are b and c, respectively. Thus, a one-percent increase in labor would increase total production by b percent, and a one percent increase in capital would increase production by c percent. Increasing the use of labor and capital by the same percentage would increase total product by the sum of their elasticities, or $b + c$.

Professors Douglas and Cobb used national production data to estimate the parameters of a national production function and found that

$$A = 1.01 L^{.75} K^{.25}.$$

Thus, when $b = .75$ and $c = .25$, a one-percent increase in labor and capital would increase total product by 0.75 percent and 0.25 percent, respectively, for a total increase of 1.00 percent.

The fact that the sum of the elasticities of production equals *one* has particular significance in the Cobb-Douglas model. This means that equal percentage increases in both resources will yield equal percentage increases in total product for the nation. The distribution of the added output can then be shared between labor and capital in proportion to their contribution to total product. Thus, the income share of labor would be .75 and the income share of capital would be .25.

CASE STUDY 5.1   **Extracting Chemicals from Vegetable Oil**

Jojoba oil is useful for producing amides used in many chemical processes. To produce amides, the oil must first be refined and purified. Then, other chemicals are added and the mixture is heated for several hours. The result is a cake-like material that yields amides. Researchers have tested various procedures for extracting amide cake, including changing the temperature and the time duration of the heating process. The results of these tests are shown in the following table. The amide yield is shown in Column (3) as percent by weight of the oil processed. Temperature in degrees centigrade (C) is shown in Column (1). The time of the test is shown as hours (H) in Column (2).

(1) Temperature (degrees Centigrade) (C)	(2) Duration of test in hours (H)	(3) Amide yield as percentage of oil weight (Q)
60	24	28
90	48	44
130	12	32
150	24	44
150	48	56
190	24	49
190	13	40
190	9	34
190	4	26

Examine the data carefully. Note that increasing the temperature of the solution appears to increase the amide yield, as does increasing the duration of the cooking process. However, the gains in yield diminish with higher values of the independent variables. Thus, the relationship follows the form of a power function of two independent variables, or

$$Q = aC^bH^c,$$

where Q = amide yield in percent of input weight, a is a constant, C is temperature in degrees centigrade, and H is duration of the extraction process in hours. The sum of the exponents b and c must be less than one, since gains in Q occur at a diminishing rate.

Regression analysis was performed to estimate the parameters of the production function. First, all values were converted to logarithms. Then, the process of multilinear regression was used as illustrated in Chapter 2. The resulting equation was

$$Q = 1.3C^{.48}H^{.35}.$$

The parameters of this equation can be interpreted as follows: The constant a = 1.3 indicates initial output if C and H equal one. Since the sum of the coefficients b = .48 and c = .35 is less than one, we would conclude that equal percentage increases in the independent variables yield smaller percentage increases in total product. Therefore, increasing both the temperature and time of the cooking process by the same percentage would increase amide yield by a smaller percentage. This result is understandable, in particular because of the physical limit of Q = 100 percent in this production process.

A production function of the form $A = 1.3C^{.48}H^{.35}$ is graphed in the figure on page 170. Degrees centigrade are measured on the axis labelled C and time in hours is measured on the axis labelled H. Production as a percentage of input weight is shown as a production surface rising from the origin, with percentage of yield measured along the vertical scale. Both increasing the temperature of the solution and increasing the duration of the heating process increase the percentage yield but by smaller percentage amounts with each increase.

The production function illustrated here is useful for planning production within the range of values represented. To extrapolate far beyond the range actually dealt with in the test would not be appropriate since there is no clear evidence that these relationships would continue to hold. However, within this range decision-makers can use the production function to plan lowest-cost production.

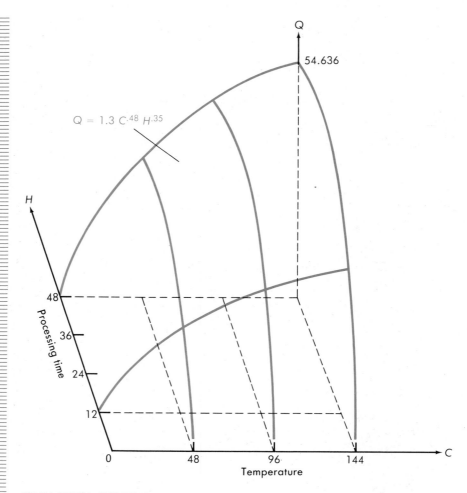

MANAGERIAL THINKING

Holding temperature constant at 190 degrees, determine the marginal yield associated with increasing the time of processing from 4 to 9 hours, from 9 to 13 hours, and from 13 to 24 hours. Then, hold time constant at 24 hours and determine the marginal yield associated with raising temperature from 60 to 150 to 190 degrees. Interpret your results.

Source: Adapted from A. Shani, P. Lurie, J. Wisniak, "Synthesis of Jojobamide and Homojojobamide," *Journal of the American Oil Chemists' Society*, March 1980, pp. 112–14.

CASE STUDY 5.2   **A Production Function for the Nation**

Productivity is generally defined as output per unit of resource input. Economists refer most frequently to **labor productivity** (output per unit of labor employed), since labor costs represent a major part of the total cost of production. Moreover, rising output per worker is necessary to improve per capita living standards.

The productivity of labor in manufacturing rose substantially in the United States throughout the 1960s but has increased more slowly in the 1970s and 1980s (2.9 percent and 1.6 percent, respectively). Some possible explanations for the slowdown in growth include: (1) the greater frequency of recessions during the latter period, (2) a decrease in the rate of capital formation and inefficient allocation of capital, (3) a decline in the rate of technological change, (4) a shift in the composition of the labor force toward less-skilled workers, and (5) increases in energy prices.

Economists Robert H. Rasche and John A. Tatom analyzed the effect of energy prices on industry output and reached the following conclusion. Higher energy costs caused business firms to substitute other resources for energy, with the result that the growth rate of labor productivity fell to only 1.3 percent annually over the years 1973–78. Lower productivity growth reduced the demand for other resources, including capital equipment, which in turn reduced the capital-labor ratio in manufacturing. The estimated equation used in this model is

$$Q = 1.426(h^{.524})(k^{.476})(p^{-.128}),$$

where Q represents manufacturing output, h represents number of labor hours employed, k represents net capital stock times the utilization rate of capital, and p represents the relative price of energy in each manufacturing sector.

The first two exponents in the equation reflect the elasticity of production associated with labor resources (h) and capital resources (k). Thus, a one-percent increase in labor hours increases total manufacturing output by 0.524 percent. Since the sum of the exponents associated with h and k equals one, we would expect that equal percentage changes in both resources would increase manufacturing output by the same percentage, ceteris paribus. The exponent associated with the price of energy is negative, which means that a percentage change in energy prices would cause an opposite change in manufacturing output of 0.128 percent.

In the decade between 1972 and 1982, the Organization of Petroleum Exporting Countries (OPEC) acted repeatedly to increase the relative price of energy. Rasche and Tatom compared productivity growth rates before and after 1973 for eleven industrial countries. Productivity growth slowed substantially in Sweden, the United Kingdom, Italy, and Japan and fell moderately in the United States, Canada, Denmark, and France. West Germany suffered only a small decline in productivity. Most of the nations studied also experienced a significant decrease in real investment expenditures over the period.

MANAGERIAL THINKING

Using the information in Case Study 5.2, write equations for the average and marginal products of labor.

Source: John A. Tatom, "The Productivity Problem," *Federal Reserve Bank of St. Louis Review*, September 1979, vol. 61, no. 9, pp. 3–16.

SUMMARY

Production theory differs in the short run and the long run because of the existence of fixed resources in the short run. In the short run, variable resources are applied to fixed resources to produce some quantity of output. A linear production function describes the behavior of total product when marginal product is constant. A quadratic production function describes total product when marginal product is increasing or decreasing as variable resources are added. A cubic production function describes total product when marginal product increases with the first increases in variable resources, becomes constant at some quantity of variable resources, and decreases as variable resources are added beyond some technically efficient quantity. Production normally takes place within the range of variable resources in which marginal product is decreasing.

In any production function, the behavior of marginal product affects the average product of the variable resource, pulling average product up when marginal product is above average product, pulling average product down when marginal product is below average product, and being equal to average product when average product reaches its maximum value.

Power production functions are commonly used to describe the behavior of total product over a limited range of resource employment in which marginal product is falling. These functions' parameters are simple to estimate, and the elasticity of production of one of their resources is shown by the variable's exponent. Power production functions, however, have the disadvantage of never reaching a maximum or minimum.

A production function can be estimated for any number of variable resources. When a power function is used, the effect on total product of increasing all variable resources in the same proportion is shown by the sum of their exponents.

KEY TERMS

opportunity cost

fixed resource

variable resource

short run

long run

production function

average product

productivity

linear production function

quadratic production function

increasing marginal product

constant marginal product

decreasing marginal product

cubic production function

power production function

elasticity of production

labor productivity

QUESTIONS AND PROBLEMS

1. Write a hypothetical production function for a process that uses two variable resources, one yielding constant marginal product and one yielding decreasing marginal product.

2. Write an equation for the average and marginal products of labor and materials for each of the following production functions:

   a. $Q = 3L + 7M$.

b. $Q = 4 + 2L - .8L^2$.

c. $Q = 7L + 2M + 5M^2 - .1M^3$.

3. Refer to the production functions listed in Question 2. Suppose the quantities of labor and materials are, respectively, $L = 5$ and $M = 10$. Calculate total, average, and marginal product for each equation. What do your results reveal about the characteristics of the three production processes? How realistic are your conclusions?

4. Define productivity. What real economic circumstances affect productivity. Suggest an empirical research project for aid in deciding policy to promote productivity growth.

5. What is the ultimate effect on total output of the increased use of a resource that experiences decreasing marginal product, ceteris paribus? What other circumstances might modify these results?

6. Discuss the advantages and disadvantages of linear, quadratic, cubic, and power production functions for describing a production process.

7. List as many pieces of information as you can learn from the following production function:

$$Q = 3.9L^{.82}M^{.5}.$$

8. Use the production function in Question 7 in answering this question. Suppose the quantity of material in this equation is fixed at $M = 750$ and a firm's desired total output is 50,000 units per month. How many units of labor must be employed?

9. Suppose past production data for a certain firm suggest a linear production function for values of L between 8 and 15 and a power function for values of L between 15 and 25. These equations are, respectively $Q = -3.14 + 1.14L$ and $Q = 2.77L^{.6}$. How would you describe the behavior of marginal product in this case? Graph production over the range between 8 and 25 units of L. Use your graph and the two equations to determine the necessary quantity of labor for producing 16.5 units of output.

10. Greystone Farms produces eggs for local retail grocers and baby chicks for sale to poultry producers. Existing equipment and personnel limit monthly production to the following combinations:

Eggs	Chicks
3,500	0
3,000	1,000
1,500	3,000
600	4,000
0	4,400

Compute the opportunity cost of producing the first 1,000 chicks (in terms of eggs per chick). Similarly, compute the cost per chick of producing larger quantities of chicks throughout the firm's range of possible production. What are some possible explanations of the behavior of opportunity costs over this range? What circumstances might increase capacity for producing both products?

11. Refer again to Problem 10. Suppose eggs sell for 5¢ each and chicks sell for 7¢ each. What product mix would yield maximum revenue for the firm? Given that chicks sell for a higher price, why would the firm produce any eggs at all?

12. Cole Mountain Sand Company delivers 37 tons of sand a day to customers throughout a 50-square-mile area. The firm owns 5 trucks and employs 8 workers. The company owner believes that hiring an additional worker could increase deliveries to 40 tons a day. What is the owner's assumption about average and marginal product of labor? Why does the owner hold this to be true?

13. Four Star Equipment Company estimates that weekly production follows a cubic function of the form $Q = 3L + 6L^2 - .5L^3$, where L represents labor over the range of 2.5 thousand to 6.5 thousand hours. The firm employs a fixed quantity of capital equipment. Current employment is 4.9 thousand labor hours a week. Calculate the marginal product of an additional 100 hours of labor. What is average product per 100 labor hours at the current employment level? On the basis of these figures alone, what can you conclude about the behavior (rising, constant, or falling) of average product in the range of current employment? Why?

   Draw a graph of values for the equation over the relevant range. Identify the level of employment at which marginal product begins to diminish. Is the firm likely to employ fewer hours than this? Why?

   Write an equation for the firm's average product.

14. Economists at the St. Louis Federal Reserve Bank have estimated the production function for the nation to be:

$$GNP = 1.464h^{.705}k^{.295}p^{-.093},$$

where h represents total hours of employment, k represents utilized capital stock, and p represents technological change and the relative price of energy. Calculate the effect of the 40-percent increase in energy prices which occurred between October 1978 and April 1980 on potential output.

6

Costs of Production and Supply in the Short Run

Much of what students read in textbooks is looked upon as "just theory—not like the real world." It isn't often that students can look around them and see the graphs, charts, and equations of economic theory actually come to life. But beginning in 1978, changing conditions in the air travel industry became obvious even to those unfamiliar with economic theory. For students of economics, the changes provided a valuable lesson in market behavior. For managers of airline firms, the changes called for new business strategies to respond to changes in the economic environment.

PRODUCTION FUNCTIONS AND ECONOMIC COSTS

The preceding chapter explored production functions, that is, the relationship between resource inputs and quantity of output. We described the behavior of total output in the short run when certain resources are fixed and various quantities of other resources are added. We found that adding variable resources causes total output to increase first at an increasing rate, then at a constant rate, and finally at a decreasing rate. We referred to these ranges of output as the range of *increasing marginal product, constant marginal product,* and *decreasing marginal product*. At some level of employment of variable resources, the limitations imposed by fixed resources may even cause total output to decline, so that *marginal product is negative*.

CASE STUDY 6.1   Competition Comes to the Airlines

Prior to the Airline Deregulation Act of 1978, interstate air travel was regulated by the Civil Aeronautics Board (CAB). Routes and fares were subject to approval by the board, one of whose objectives was to guarantee air service to as many U.S. cities and towns as practical.

There are three kinds of airlines in the United States: (1) *trunk lines* have routes from coast to coast; (2) *regional lines* serve particular regions or states;[1] and (3) *commuter lines* provide "feeder" service to major transportation centers. Most trunk lines operate on the "hub and spoke" principle. The *hub* is a major population center. *Short spokes* are routes that come in to feed the *long spokes* leaving the hub. Maintaining terminal facilities in a hub entails high fixed costs, generally making short-spoke flights money losers. However, retaining short-spoke passengers for long-spoke journeys on trunk lines helps make up for this loss.

Under regulation, airline fares were regulated so that profits on long hauls would help defray the costs of short hauls. Using profits in one market to offset losses in another is called **cross subsidization.** Cross subsidies are common in industries in which consumers can be clearly separated and charged a price based not on the cost of a service but on what they are willing to pay for that service. Cross subsidies are possible only in situations in which there is no competition. With competition, other firms would be able to undercut prices in the low-cost market and eliminate the profits used for subsidies. The CAB tended to award routes so as to give particular airlines a protected market in particular hubs. Moreover, high terminal costs made the entry of new firms in a particular market difficult and preserved long-haul profits for trunk lines.

Regulation had another effect on total capacity in the air travel industry. In an effort to guarantee service to more markets and to protect small airlines from dominance by the giants, the CAB held average fares above the minimum costs of the service. The result was to protect inefficient firms and to maintain excess capacity in operation far beyond the time when competition would have forced modernization and consolidation.

Slowing overall productivity growth in the 1970s increased public clamor for improved efficiency throughout the airline industry and, particularly, for the removal of unnecessary government regulation. It was expected that competition would force the airlines to streamline their operations, cut costs, eliminate excess capacity, and match service to the kinds of capital resources held by particular firms.

Deregulation in 1978 established competition in the air travel industry.[2] Deregulation meant that firms could decide routes and fares on the basis of their own costs and according to market demand. Major changes took place almost immediately because most firms reacted precisely as economic theory would have predicted.

The first noticeable effect of deregulation involved routes. Many trunk lines quickly abandoned their money-losing short hauls and rushed to exploit the profitable coast-to-coast routes. Competition was keen, and fare discounts on the most popular routes slashed airline revenues. Losses soared, but high fixed-terminal costs forced some firms to continue providing coast-to-coast service. In the meantime, sharply escalating fuel costs and a recessionary decline in passenger traffic produced total losses in the hundreds of millions of dollars in 1980.

On the other hand, deregulation brought some advantages to regional and commuter airlines. Unlike the trunk carriers, regional firms are generally non-unionized, with lower labor costs, higher labor productivity, and fewer costly "frills" to attract passengers. Flying only one type of plane more hours each day helped hold down maintenance and fuel costs. High traffic density on short commuter routes kept ter-

---

1. Intrastate air service is not regulated by the CAB.
2. Some minor regulations remained in effect, but the CAB was to be eliminated entirely by 1985.

minal facilities fully used, so that each passenger's contribution to total profit was relatively high. Many new commuter lines sprang up—some resembling the "Mom and Pop" enterprises of the early days of aviation. Starting a new commuter business was fairly easy, since trunk lines had many excess planes to sell cheaply. Some small firms made agreements to coordinate ticketing and baggage handling with other commuter lines or trunk lines, in order to improve the flow of traffic.

As you read this chapter, keep in mind the sources of change in the economic environment and the basis for decisions made by the managers of airline firms. Consider the following questions: What is the character of the short-run production function in air transportation? How does the shape of the production function affect air transportation costs? What are the important considerations for deciding the amount of transport service in the short run?

You might also consider the following broader questions concerning regulation: What technical, human, and organizational factors seemed to call for airline regulation in the first place? What were the economic costs of regulation? What are likely to be the costs of deregulation?

Understanding production is important to the discussion in this chapter because of the inverse relationship between production and costs. We will find that the behavior of production produces an opposite effect in the behavior of cost. In the short run, for example, increasing marginal product implies decreasing marginal cost. This is because greater output from each additional unit of variable resource means lower additional cost. On the other hand decreasing marginal product implies increasing marginal cost, for the opposite reason. The behavior of marginal product also influences average product, with corresponding effects on average cost.

In Chapter 5, we divided a production function into three stages according to the behavior of marginal and average product. We identified Stage 2 as the relevant stage for making production decisions. Stage 2 was characterized by falling average and marginal product and, hence, rising average and marginal costs.

In the sections that follow, we will examine average and marginal costs in detail and show how understanding the behavior of costs can help managers plan production. First, we will consider the firm in the context of the economic model of perfect competition. Competitive firms are assumed to pursue the goal of maximum profit and to make their production decisions on this basis.

After developing the economic model of production for the theoretical firm, we will look more specifically at decision-making tools for actual firms. The fundamental concepts will be the same as for a theoretical firm, but actual firms may make their production decisions under circumstances that differ from those assumed in the model.

Production Costs in the Short Run

Short-run production decisions depend on *marginal costs*. This is due to the existence of fixed resources. A firm's current holdings of buildings and equipment and its salaried personnel are fixed in the short run. These costs must be paid regardless of the level of current production. What matters in the production decision is the cost of *additional* variable resources for producing *additional* output.

Consider the airline firms again. Each firm's existing terminal facilities, planes, and management personnel cannot be changed readily, but pilots can be asked to work varying hours (within limits) to meet differences in service demand. Additional terminal workers may be hired or laid off, and varying quantities of fuel may be purchased. Average and marginal costs will vary with changes in the proportion of variable to fixed resources as the level of passenger service varies. The question managers must answer is: What quantity of service should the firm provide, given current market conditions?

Answering this question requires an understanding of the elements that constitute economic costs. Economic costs can be described in two ways: as **explicit** or **implicit costs** and as **fixed** or **variable costs**.

Explicit or Implicit Costs

Explicit costs are the out-of-pocket and accrued costs of producing goods or services over a particular period of time. They appear on a firm's records and tax returns as specific amounts associated with specific resources used in production. The most obvious explicit costs are wages, salaries, rent, royalties, costs of materials and utilities, and interest on debt. These costs represent the opportunity costs of productive resources. They must be paid regularly as the resources are used in production.

Other explicit costs are *accrued* continuously but paid only after a stated time. Amounts are set aside during each production period and allowed to accumulate until payment is due. An important accrued expense is taxes. Tax liability accrues weekly or monthly until the quarterly return is paid. Another accrued expense is depreciation of capital equipment. Buildings and equipment are gradually depreciated in the course of production, but the expenditure for replacement takes place only after a period of several years. Firms are allowed to deduct from taxable income a portion of the value of their capital equipment during each production period, increasing their after-tax profits and enhancing their potential for re-investment.

Explicit costs are sometimes called **accounting costs**. They are calculated regularly as a measure of the costs of a firm's production and are included in regular accounting statements.

Certain other costs also represent the value of resources used in production but are not typically included in business accounts. Such costs are called implicit costs. Although implicit costs are real costs of production, they represent neither an out-of-pocket payment nor an accrued allowance for payment in the future.

The most common examples of implicit costs occur in single proprietorships. When an individual owner uses his or her personal resource holdings in production, certain implicit costs may not actually be paid out. A proprietor's salary, interest on a proprietor's own funds used in a business, and rent or royalties on properties owned by a proprietor are examples of implicit costs. To disregard such costs understates a firm's true costs of production and may overstate the firm's profit. Other implicit costs might include dividend payments to stockholders. Dividends are not included in accounting costs of production, but unless they are paid with some regularity, future stock issues may be impossible. Thus, there is some basis for considering dividends when computing a firm's costs of production.

A part of a firm's profit is also considered an implicit cost. An acceptable level of profit is a necessary payment to entrepreneurs who conceive ideas, plan policy, and organize resources for production. If such creative activity is to continue, entrepreneurs must be rewarded through receipt of profit. In Chapter 1, we stated that the necessary payment to entrepreneurs is called *normal profit*. Normal profit is distinguished from *economic profit,* which may result when business firms are slow to adjust to changing market conditions. Failure to adjust to market conditions may result from technical factors, from the use of market power, or, as we have seen, from government regulation. In any case, for firms that have successfully adjusted to change market price may include economic profit in addition to full production costs. For less successful firms, market price may fall below full costs, so that economic profit is negative and a firm experiences losses.

In this discussion, we will include all explicit and implicit costs, including normal profit, in our calculations of production costs. Whenever market price differs from full unit costs including normal profit, we will indicate that economic profit (or loss) has occurred.

Fixed or Variable Costs

In the short run, full costs of production include all of the opportunity costs of fixed resources (plant, equipment, and salaried personnel) and variable resources (labor, materials, fuel, and electric power). The graphs in Figures 6.1 through 6.5 illustrate the typical behavior of fixed and variable costs for a hypothetical commuter airline. These graphs are drawn for the short run, defined in this example as one month. Costs are measured along the vertical axes, and quantities of output (Q) are measured on the horizontal axes in millions of passenger miles.

Fixed costs (FC) are defined as those costs that are constant over the short run, regardless of the number of passenger miles flown. Fixed costs include the regular monthly cost of terminal facilities, transportation equipment, and salaried managers. Their contribution to total costs is represented as a constant (FC) equal to their contractual amount for the month. Figure 6.1 on page 180 shows fixed costs as a horizontal line drawn at the value (FC) on the vertical axis and unvarying with respect to the firm's level of production. Figure 6.2 on page 180 is a graph of average fixed costs (AFC). Average fixed costs are defined mathematically as

$$AFC = FC/Q,$$

FIGURE 6.1   **Monthly Fixed Cost**

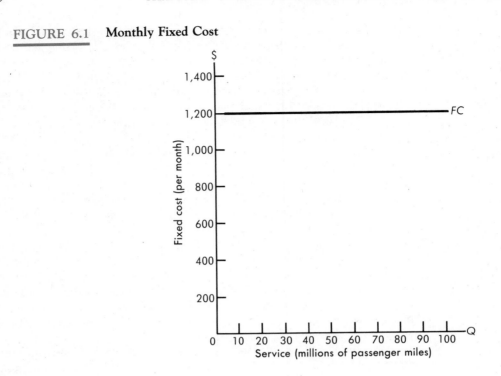

FIGURE 6.2   **Average Fixed Cost**

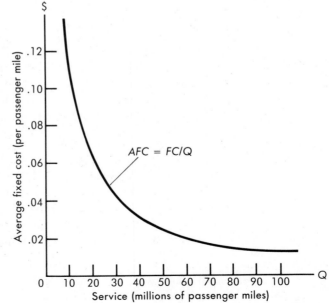

FIGURE 6.3   Average Variable Cost

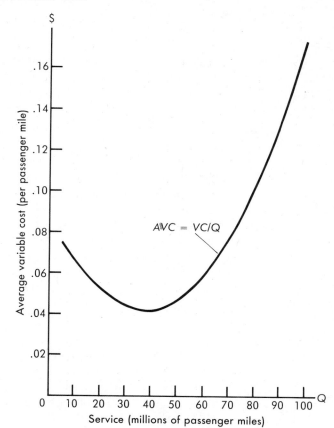

Service (millions of passenger miles)

where Q is quantity of output. The graph of average fixed costs is a *rectangular hyperbola:* a curve that decreases for higher values of Q and approaches, but does not touch, the horizontal axis.

Variable costs (VC) are the costs of resources whose quantity varies with the number of passenger miles flown. For our hypothetical airline, variable costs include the cost of variable labor and fuel required to produce varying quantities of passenger service during the month. Figure 6.3 illustrates the typical behavior of variable costs per unit of service: that is, decreasing for one range of passenger miles, remaining constant for another range of passenger miles, and finally increasing for a very large range of passenger miles. (Remember that the behavior of average variable cost depends on the behavior of average product when variable resources are added to a certain quantity of fixed resources. Because average product tends to increase at low levels of resource employment, variable cost per unit of service tends to decrease. Over some range of resource employment, average product may be constant, making variable cost per unit of service constant. At very high levels of resource employ-

FIGURE 6.4   **Total Cost**

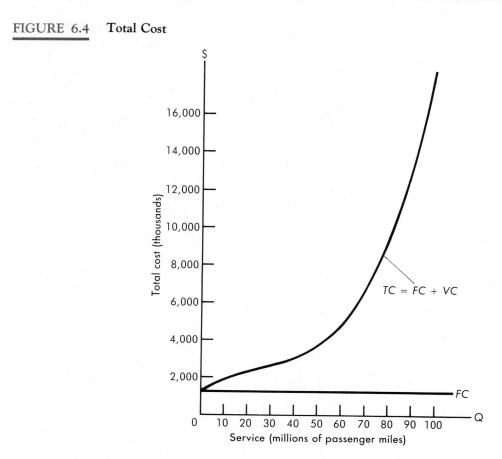

ment in the short run, average product tends to decrease and unit variable cost tends to increase.)

The data represented by Figures 6.1 through 6.5 appear in Table 6.1. Column (1) of the table lists quantity of output in millions of passenger miles. Column (2) lists the constant amount of fixed cost for the short run. Column (3) lists average fixed cost associated with the production of ten million through one hundred million passenger miles. Unit or average fixed cost is computed by dividing total fixed cost by Q. Thus,

$$AFC = FC/Q.$$

Columns (4) and (5) list variable cost and average variable cost. Column (6) is the sum of average fixed cost and average variable cost for all quantities of passenger service that might be produced during the month.

Figures 6.4 and 6.5 show total cost (TC) and average total cost (ATC). Total cost is computed by adding fixed and variable cost at every level of passenger service,

TABLE 6.1   Cost Data for Dependable Airlines

(1) Quantity of service in millions of passenger miles (Q)	(2) Fixed cost per month (FC)	(3) Average fixed cost per passenger mile (AFC)	(4) Variable cost (VC)	(5) Average variable cost per passenger mile (AVC)	(6) Total cost (TC)	(7) Average total cost per passenger mile (ATC)	(8) Marginal cost ($\Delta TC/\Delta Q$)
0	$1,200,000	∞	0	0	$1,200,000	∞	
10	$1,200,000	.12	$ 675,000	.0675	1,875,000	.1875	.0675
20	$1,200,000	.06	1,050,000	.0525	· 2,250,000	.1125	.0375
30	$1,200,000	.04	1,325,000	.0442	2,525,000	.0842	.0275
40	$1,200,000	.03	1,700,000	.0425	2,900,000	.0725	.0375
50	$1,200,000	.024	2,375,000	.0475	3,575,000	.0715	.0675
60	$1,200,000	.02	3,550,000	.0592	4,750,000	.0792	.1175
70	$1,200,000	.0172	5,425,000	.0775	6,625,000	.0946	.1875
80	$1,200,000	.015	8,200,000	.1025	9,400,000	.1175	.2775
90	$1,200,000	.0134	12,075,000	.1342	13,275,000	.1475	.3875
100	$1,200,000	.012	17,250,000	.1725	18,450,000	.1845	.5175

FIGURE 6.5   Average Total Cost

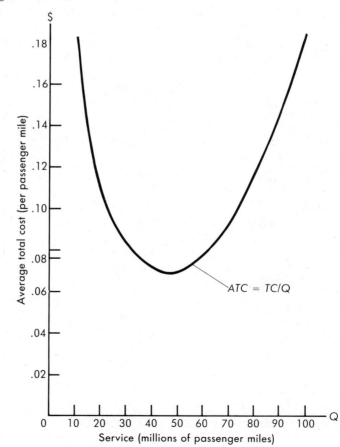

$$TC = FC + VC,$$

as is done in Column (6) of Table 6.1. Average total cost can be computed in either of two ways:

$$ATC = TC/Q$$

or

$$ATC = AFC + AVC = FC/Q + VC/Q.$$

ATC is listed in Column (7).

Notice the behavior of average total cost and total cost in the short run. Average total cost is represented by a saucer-shaped curve. This reflects two circumstances: first, the decrease in average fixed cost as passenger service expands, and second, the eventual increase in average variable cost as production approaches the maximum quantity of passenger miles possible with existing fixed resources. The ATC curve reaches a minimum at production of fifty million passenger miles and increases as production goes beyond this point.

The behavior of variable cost also is reflected in the total cost curve. Notice that in Figure 6.4, total costs originate at a fixed cost of $1,200,000, where production is zero. As the quantity of service increases from zero to forty million passenger miles, average variable cost decreases. This is the range of increasing marginal product, in which each additional unit of service requires fewer additional variable resources (and, thus, lower costs) than the previous one. As production expands beyond forty million passenger miles in the short run, average variable cost increases. This is the range of decreasing marginal product, in which each additional unit of service requires more additional variable resources (and, thus, higher costs) than the previous one.

Marginal Cost

We have seen that average total cost depends on the quantity of service produced over the short run. Now we will find that the quantity of service produced depends, in turn, on marginal cost.

Marginal cost is the *change in* total cost associated with producing an additional unit of output during the short run. (Because fixed cost does not change in the short run, marginal cost includes only changes in variable cost.) Marginal cost is computed as the difference in total cost at various levels of production divided by the difference in quantity:

$$MC = \Delta TC/\Delta Q.$$

The values for this computation are listed in Column (8). Values are written between the lines because marginal cost is incurred in the process of movement

FIGURE 6.6   Marginal Cost

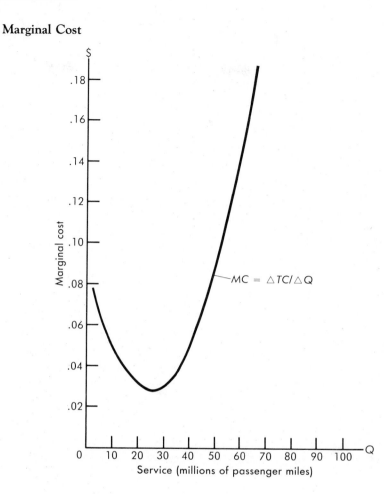

from, for example, $Q = 10$ million to $Q = 20$ million passenger miles. Marginal cost data are plotted in Figure 6.6.

An interesting feature of marginal cost is its relationship to average cost. When marginal cost is plotted on the same graph as average variable and average total cost, as in Figure 6.7 on page 186, the marginal cost curve will intersect both average cost curves at their lowest points. This is because marginal cost that is lower than average cost tends to pull the average down. In other words, lower additional cost for additional passenger miles reduces the average cost of all other passenger miles. Similarly, marginal cost that is greater than average cost pulls the average up. That is, higher additional cost for additional passenger miles increases the average cost of all other passenger miles. In addition, when marginal cost is equal to average cost, average cost is constant. The same additional cost for additional passenger miles leaves the average cost of all other passenger miles unchanged. This statement is true of

FIGURE 6.7   **Average and Marginal Costs**

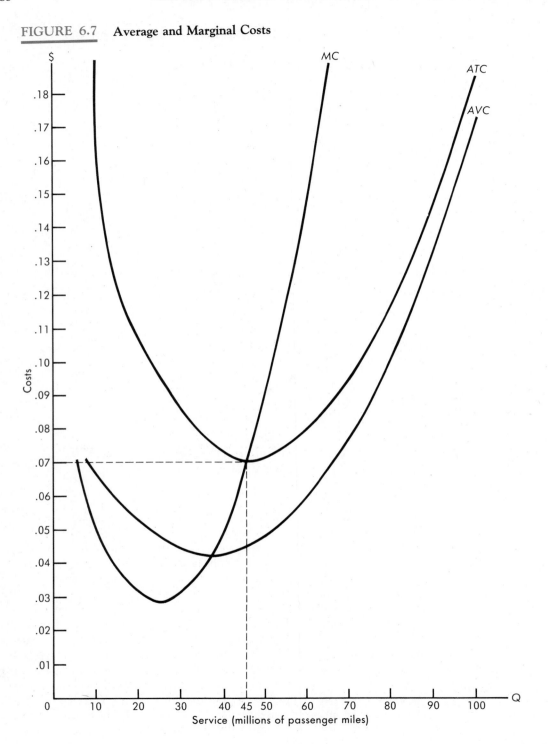

the average cost curve at the point at which it has stopped decreasing and has yet to increase.

The marginal cost of passenger service for Dependable Airlines reaches a minimum at $Q = 25$ million passenger miles. However, low marginal cost continues to pull the average cost of service down until marginal cost rises above average total cost at $Q = 45$ million passenger miles. This is the lowest-cost level of operation for Dependable Airlines.

In most manufacturing processes, the behavior of marginal and average cost conforms to the behavior we have described here:

1. *At low levels of output in the short run, increasing production will cause total cost to rise at a decreasing rate.* Marginal cost decreases, pulling the average cost of each unit down.

2. *At some level of ouput in the short run, marginal product is at a maximum, and, alternatively, marginal cost is at a minimum.* When marginal cost is less than average total cost, the effect is to pull average total cost down until $MC = ATC$ and ATC is at a minimum. We call this level of output the lowest-cost level of plant operation in the short run. The lowest-cost level of operation is that at which variable resources are used in the technically correct proportion to fixed resources with the result that production is most efficient.[1]

3. *Finally, at high levels of output in the short run, continuing to increase production will cause total cost to rise at an increasing rate.* Over this range, marginal cost will rise, pulling the average cost of each unit up.

The Relevant Range of Plant Operation in the Short Run

We have described three ranges of production in the short run over which average cost tends to fall, to rise, or to remain constant at some lowest-cost level or range of production. The profit-maximizing level of production for a particular firm may not be in the lowest-cost range. The profit-maximizing level of production depends on the relationship between the marginal cost and the selling price of a good or service, a topic which will be explored later in detail. At this point, however, it is possible to locate a minimum quantity (other than zero) that should be produced in the short run.

Consider first the range of decreasing marginal cost. Competitive firms will not normally choose to produce in this range since producing additional units adds less to total cost for each additional unit and pulls average cost per unit down. Producing and selling additional units increases a firm's profit. This makes any quantity of output less than $Q = 25$ million passenger miles in our example irrelevant for production decisions.

---

1. In fact, there may be a range of quantities for which any increase in unit variable cost is precisely offset by a decrease in unit fixed cost so that average total cost remains constant (and marginal cost is equal to average total cost). In this case, there would be a range of output over which the proportion of variable to fixed resources can be described as "technically correct."

Similarly, competitive firms will not choose to produce in the range of decreasing average variable cost. As long as market price is high enough to cover average variable cost, a firm would normally continue to increase production during the short run. Additional units of output can be sold for a price that covers variable cost and adds some amount toward the payment of fixed costs. This makes any quantity of output less than $Q = 40$ million passenger miles irrelevant for production decisions in the short run. Refer to Table 6.1 to confirm these figures. (The range of decreasing marginal and average costs corresponds to Stage 1 of production.)

Given these considerations, the relevant range of operation in our example begins at $Q = 40$, where average variable cost is at a minimum. Beyond $Q = 40$, marginal cost is greater than average variable cost, pulling average variable cost up. However, because average fixed cost decreases with greater quantity, the sum of average variable and average fixed costs continues to decrease. This is true until $Q = 45$, where MC rises above ATC and begins to pull ATC up.

The relevant range of MC and AVC has been reproduced in Figure 6.8. This graph shows the significant cost curves for choosing the profit-maximizing quantity of output in the short run.

Note that the curves are practically linear and can be approximated by a linear cost equation. The use of a linear equation simplifies computations considerably and is a reasonable means for estimating costs over a limited range of production. In the sections to follow we will use linear equations in examples of decisions concerning the profit-maximizing quantity of production in the short run.

DETERMINING PROFIT-MAXIMIZING QUANTITY IN THE SHORT RUN

We have identified the range of a firm's cost curves that is relevant for making production decisions in the short run. Many firms are guided in their short-run production decisions by the goal of maximum economic profit. To achieve maximum economic profit in the short run, a firm's managers must select the level of output for which the difference between total revenue and total cost is greatest. Note that for most firms, maximum revenue is *not* an important goal, nor is minimum average cost. The absolute level of total revenue and total cost is less important than the *difference* between them.

A firm's economic profit can be expressed algebraically as

Economic profit (π) = total revenue − total cost = $TR - TC$,

where TC includes all explicit and implicit costs of production. Every additional unit of output affects economic profit in two ways: (1) its selling price affects total revenue, and (2) its marginal cost affects total cost. If a firm is to achieve its maximum-profit goal, it must produce a quantity of output that adds at least as much to total revenue as to total cost.

Notice that we have been speaking in terms of *marginal* relationships: that is, *additions to* total revenue and *additions to* total cost. Marginal relationships

FIGURE 6.8   **The Relevant Range of Operation**

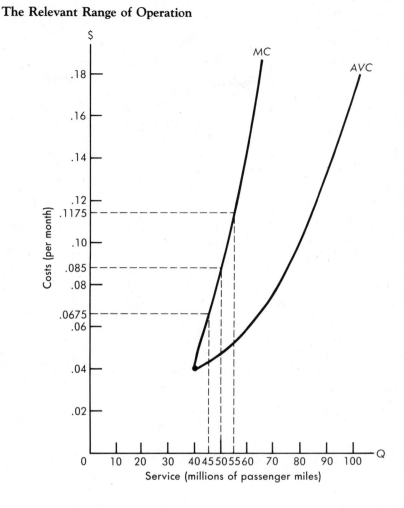

are important in production decisions because they measure the effect on total profit of producing an additional unit of output. **Marginal revenue** measures the effect of an additional unit on total revenue, and **marginal cost** measures the effect of an additional unit on total cost.

Let us illustrate the production decision with another look at our hypothetical example. Suppose the airline firm described previously sells air service in a competitive market at a price of $0.085 per passenger mile. Under these circumstances, each additional unit of service adds $0.085 to total revenue. Thus, marginal revenue is constant at $p = MR = \$0.085$. Suppose the current level of production is thirty million passenger miles per month, so that total revenue is

$$TR = (p)(Q) = (\$0.085)(30) = \$2.55 \text{ million.}$$

According to Table 6.1, total cost is

$$TC = FC + VC = \$2.525 \text{ million},$$

for economic profit of

$$\pi = TR - TC = \$2.55 - \$2.525 = \$.025 \text{ million} = \$25,000.$$

A manager of this firm must ask, "Is this the maximum economic profit possible in the short run?" To answer this question, we must compare marginal revenue (or price) with marginal cost, that is, the *added* effects of producing additional units of service. Look again at Column (8) of Table 6.1. According to Column (8), increasing production from thirty million to forty million passenger miles would add $MC = .0375$ to total cost for each passenger mile of service. With $MR = p = \$0.085$, total revenue would increase by $\$0.085$ per passenger mile. Each additional unit of service would add more to total revenue than to total cost. In fact, since $MR > MC$, production and sale of an additional 10 million passenger miles would increase economic profit by the difference between MR and MC for each additional unit.

These relationships are shown again in Table 6.2. Total cost, shown in Column (2) of the table, increases as output increases. Marginal cost, in Column (3), is the change in total cost for each additional unit of output. Again, marginal cost is shown between rows because each change in cost results from a change in quantity of output. Since price per unit remains unchanged for whatever number of units are sold, marginal revenue is market price or $\$0.085$ per passenger mile. Marginal revenue, in Column (4), is also shown between rows. Total revenue, in Column (5), is market price times quantity. Finally, economic profit, in Column (6), is the difference between total revenue and

TABLE 6.2   **Additional Cost Data for Dependable Airlines**

(1) Total output in millions of passenger miles (Q)	(2) Total cost (TC)	(3) Marginal cost (MC)	(4) Price, marginal revenue (p = MR)	(5) Total revenue (p)(Q)	(6) Economic profit (π = TR − TC)
0	$1,200,000			0	− $1,200,000
10	1,875,000	$.0675	$0.085	$ 850,000	− 1,025,000
20	2,250,000	.0375	.085	1,700,000	− 550,000
30	2,525,000	.0275	.085	2,550,000	25,000
40	2,900,000	.0375	.085	3,400,000	500,000
50	3,575,000	.0675	.085	4,250,000	675,000
60	4,750,000	.1175	.085	5,100,000	350,000
70	6,625,000	.1875	.085	5,950,000	− 675,000
80	9,400,000	.2775	.085	6,800,000	− 2,600,000
90	13,275,000	.3875	.085	7,650,000	− 5,625,000
100	18,450,000	.5175	.085	8,500,000	− 9,950,000

total cost at various levels of production *(Q)*. At the current level of production, $Q = 30$ million passenger miles, economic profit is $25,000.

Continuing to produce thirty million passenger miles each month would yield continuing economic profit of $25,000. Producing an additional ten million passenger miles each month would add $850,000 to revenue, however, and only $375,000 to cost. Since $MR > MC$, a profit-maximizing firm would normally choose to produce the additional ten million passenger miles, causing economic profit for the period to increase to

$$\pi = 40(.085) - 2.9 = 3.4 - 2.9 = .5 \text{ million} = \$500,000.$$

Production of fifty million passenger miles would present further opportunities for increasing economic profit. In fact, producing fifty million passenger miles would finally add just enough revenue to offset all additional production costs. The profit-maximizing level of output in this case is fifty million passenger miles.[2]

The process we have described can be stated generally as an important principle of production planning in the short run: *The profit-maximizing quantity of output is the quantity for which marginal revenue is equal to marginal cost: (MR = MC)*. If marginal revenue is greater than marginal cost, the profit-maximizing firm should expand output, as in our hypothetical example above. The result of this decision is an increase in economic profit for the month. If marginal revenue is less than marginal cost, the firm should reduce output. Refer to the data for the sixtieth unit of service in Table 6.2. Verify that production of sixty million passenger miles would yield less than maximum economic profit. When $MR < MC$, the correct production decision would be to reduce output.

The principle of the profit-maximizing quantity of output can be applied to the graph of costs in Figure 6.8 on page 189. We have shown that only the rising portion of the firm's MC curve (above AVC) is relevant for making production decisions in the short run. Now we can see that the value of MC for any quantity of output determines the quantity actually produced at any given market price. Together with marginal revenue, the MC curve identifies the profit-maximizing quantity in the short run. The firm in our example sells its service in a competitive market for a price of $0.085. Thus, $MR = \$0.085$. To determine the profit-maximizing quantity of output, use the MC curve in Figure 6.8 to read the quantity at which $MR = \$0.085 = MC$. Verify that fifty million passenger miles is the profit-maximizing quantity, as shown in Table 6.2.

Now suppose that market price falls to $0.0675. Move down the MC curve and locate the profit-maximizing quantity at $MR = p = \$0.0675 = MC$, for production of forty-five million passenger miles. Similarly, an increase in mar-

---

2. Because marginal changes occur as quantity increases, the profit-maximizing quantity is between forty and fifty million units. The precise profit-maximizing quantity is 48.98 million passenger miles, as will be demonstrated shortly.

ket price to $p = \$0.1175$ would call for a movement up the *MC* curve to a profit-maximizing quantity of fifty-five million passenger miles. For any price, the profit-maximizing quantity for the month is determined by locating the point on the *MC* curve where $MC = MR = p$. Points on the firm's short-run *MC* curve constitute the firm's short-run **supply curve**. More precisely, the *MC* curve above the lowest point on the *AVC* curve is the firm's short-run supply curve, since prices lower than *AVC* will not normally lead a firm to produce anything at all. The relevant portion of the *MC* curve has been reproduced in Figure 6.9 and is labeled *supply*.

Determining Economic Profit in the Short Run

Economic profit for the month is calculated in Table 6.2 as the difference between total revenue (for the quantity determined by the MC curve) and total cost:

$$\pi = TR - TC.$$

FIGURE 6.9   **Supply**

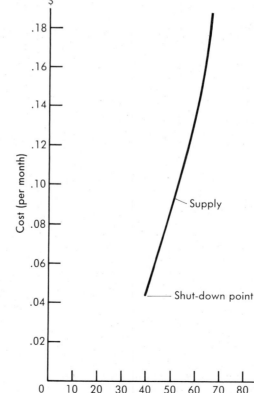

Economic profit per unit is the difference between price and average total cost:

$$\pi/Q = p - ATC.$$

In Figure 6.10, average or unit economic profit at $p = \$0.085$ is the vertical distance between price (read from the MC curve) and the average total cost curve. For any price, economic profit is average or unit profit $(p - ATC)$ times the number of units produced (Q). Since Q is measured horizontally to this point and since the area of a rectangle is its base times its height, the rectangle formed between p and ATC at any value of Q has as its area economic profit.

Any rectangle drawn between $MC = $ price and ATC in this way has its maximum area at the value of Q that is identified as the profit-maximizing quantity. Profit rectangles drawn for any other value of Q will be smaller than the maximum-profit rectangle. Move down the supply curve in Figure 6.10 to a price equal to average total cost at its lowest point. When price is equal to

FIGURE 6.10   Profit

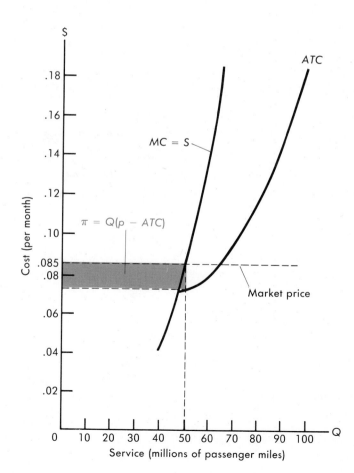

minimum *ATC,* price is just sufficient to cover all explicit and implicit costs of production. Thus, at the lowest-cost level of production in the short-run, economic profit is zero.

The Shut-Down Point in the Short Run

Our example thus far has illustrated the production decision for a profit-maximizing firm. However, when a firm's total revenue falls below total cost for the month, a profit-maximizing firm becomes instead a "loss-minimizing" firm. Deciding on the level of output for minimum loss involves analysis similar to that for maximum profit.

Consider an airline firm whose fixed cost is $1,200,000 per month. If total production (and total revenue) were to fall to zero, fixed cost would still have to be paid. Negative economic profit or loss for the month would be −$1,200,000. The firm might have to sell certain assets to acquire the necessary funds to pay fixed cost. On the other hand, any quantity of service that yields revenue for paying part of monthly fixed cost reduces loss and should be produced. In fact, any quantity of service that adds at least as much as its variable cost of production reduces the burden of a firm's fixed cost and helps minimize loss in the short run.

Look again at Figure 6.8. Average variable cost reaches its lowest point at $0.0425, where $Q = 40$ million passenger miles. Suppose price falls as low as $0.0425 and the firm moves down its $MC =$ supply curve to production of 40 million units. Producing forty million passenger miles at a unit price of $0.0425 would yield total revenue of $40(.0425) = 1.7$ million $= \$1,700,000$ to cover variable cost of $1,700,000. This level of production would leave fixed cost unpaid, however, for negative economic profit or loss of $TR − TC = −\$1,200.000$. Producing more than forty million passenger miles for any price greater than $0.0425 (as shown on the supply curve) would cover all variable cost and pay a portion of fixed cost. Follow the supply curve up to a price of $0.0675 at production of forty-five million passenger miles. Note that $p = \$0.0675$ is greater than average variable cost for forty-five million units, yielding

$$(p − AVC)(Q) = (.0675 − .0450)\,(45) = 1.01 \text{ million} = \$1,012,500$$

to apply toward payment of fixed cost. The excess of price over average variable cost reduces loss to

$$−\$1,200,000 + \$1,012,500 = \$187,500$$

for the month. Any revenue above total variable cost that can be applied to fixed cost reduces the firm's negative economic profit or loss.

We would call a price of $0.0425 per passenger mile the **shut-down price** for this firm. Since any price less than $0.0425 fails to cover average variable

CASE STUDY 6.2   Reducing Quantity of Output When Demand Declines

High interest rates and a decline in new home building during 1980 reduced the demand for lumber, forcing many forest-product companies to lay-off workers, cut days of operation, and even close some plants. Cascade Lumber Company had been maximizing profits by producing 15 thousand board feet a week. Fixed costs were $5,000 per week. The firm's managers used the following cost data for making production decisions during the period of declining demand and falling prices:

Q (thousands of board feet)	AVC (per thousand board feet)	TVC	MC
10	1,280	12,800	
11	1,270	13,970	1,170
12	1,275	15,300	1,330
13	1,295	16,835	1,535
14	1,325	18,550	1,715
15	1,355	20,325	1,775
16	1,400	22,400	2,075

If Cascade is currently maximizing profits, it must be true that $MC = MR$. A profit-maximizing output of $Q = 15,000$ board feet implies a price of $p = MR = \$1,775$, as shown on the table. With the drop in demand, however, price dropped 25 percent to $1,330. The firm moved down its MC curve to production of 12,000 board feet, a reduction of 20 percent. Economic profit had been averaging $\pi = TR - TC = 15(1,775) - (20,325 + 5,000) = \$1,300$ per week. Following the drop in demand, positive economic profit turned to negative economic profit or loss of $12(1,330) - (15,300 + 5,000) = -\$4,340$. However, since price was greater than average variable cost, the firm continued to operate, applying revenue over variable cost to fixed charges.

Cascade operated seven plants, each with a different status regarding fixed contracts. As fixed contracts began to expire in various locations, Cascade's managers ordered plants closed and in this way gradually reduced weekly fixed charges. With this kind of flexibility, managers hoped to be able to respond readily to an eventual increase in demand.

MANAGERIAL THINKING

Use graph paper to illustrate a firm's decision to reduce output when price falls. How would your graph change as a firm's plants are shut down?

EXAMPLE 6.1   Using Quadratic Equations to Plan Production

The marginal and average cost curves in Figures 6.8 and 6.10 can be estimated using curvilinear regression. To illustrate the use of curvilinear cost equations, consider again Dependable Airlines' cost data as shown in Table 6.1. We will use the procedure described in Chapter 5 to write a quadratic equation for supply originating at the lowest point on Dependable's average variable cost curve. In our equation the dependent variable is marginal cost, and the independent variable is quantity of output. Thus, the form of the marginal cost equation is

$$\text{Supply } (MC) = a + b(Q) + c(Q)^2.$$

Least-squares regression yields the following parameters: $a = .09$, $b = -.005$, and $c = .0001$. Therefore, the equation for marginal cost is

$$MC = .09 - .005(Q) + .0001(Q)^2.$$

Using an equation for marginal cost, it is possible to write equations for total cost, average total cost, and average variable cost. Remember that integral calculus enables us to write equations for *total* values from an equation for the *change in* a particular value. Using the procedure demonstrated in Appendix 1A, the integral of the marginal cost equation is:

$$\int MC\, dQ = C + .09(Q) - .0025(Q)^2 + .000033(Q)^3\, dQ.$$

We know that the constant to be added to this equation is the value of fixed cost for the month, so the complete equation for total cost is:

$$TC = \int MC\, dQ = 1.2 + .09(Q) - .0025(Q)^2 + .000033(Q)^3\, dQ.$$

Notice that the total cost equation is a cubic equation whose graph begins at $TC = 1.2$, $Q = 0$ and rises with an initial upward slope of $b = .09$. Then, the slope diminishes over a certain range until it once again begins to increase for higher values of Q.

It is easy to write equations for average total cost and average variable cost:

$$ATC = TC/Q = 1.2/Q + .09 - .0025(Q) + .000033(Q)^2$$

Average variable cost is determined by omitting the fixed cost variable from the ATC equation:

$$AVC = .09 - .0025(Q) + .000033(Q)^2.$$

With this information, it is possible to locate the firm's shut-down point. We know that the shut-down point occurs where AVC is at its minimum point. The minimum value of a function is determined by taking the derivative, setting it equal to zero, and solving. Thus

$$\frac{dAVC}{dQ} = -.0025 + .000066(Q) = 0 \qquad \text{and } Q = 37.88.$$

To ensure that $Q = 37.88$ is actually a minimum, take the second derivative:

$$\frac{d^2AVC}{dQ^2} = .000066.$$

The positive sign of the second derivative indicates that $Q = 37.88$ is the minimum of the function.

The value of AVC at its minimum point is now determined by substituting for this value:

$$AVC = .09 - .0025(37.88) + .000033(37.88)^2 = .0427.$$

Thus, we know that the firm's supply curve can be written

$$\text{Supply } (MC) = .09 - .005(Q) + .0001(Q)^2,$$

for values of $Q \geq 37.88$.

The equation for supply allows us to determine the profit-maximizing quantity of output associated with any price. For example, with a price of $0.075 per passenger mile and $p = MR$, quantity supplied would be determined by setting MC equal to MR. Thus,

$$MC = .09 - .005(Q) + .0001(Q)^2 = .075 = MR.$$

To solve for Q, set the equation equal to zero and use the quadratic formula (demonstrated in Chapter 1) or a pocket calculator. Thus,

$$.015 - .005(Q) + .0001(Q)^2 = 0,$$

and

$$Q = \frac{-b \pm \sqrt{b^2 - 4ac}}{2c}$$

$$= \frac{-(-.005) \pm \sqrt{.000025 - .000006}}{.02}$$

which equals 46.79 million and 3.21 million passenger miles. Since Q must be greater than the shut-down quantity Q = 37.88, we know that Q = 46.79 is the profit-maximizing quantity for price p = $0.075.

A price of $0.075 is above the firm's shut-down price, so service should be continued. The actual level of economic profit depends on total cost for production of Q = 46.79 million passenger miles. For

$$TC = 1.2 + .09(Q) - .0025(Q)^2 + .000033(Q)^3,$$

economic profit is

$$\pi = TR - TC = .075(Q) - [1.2 + .09(Q) - .0025(Q)^2 + .000033(Q)^3]$$
$$= -1.2 - .015(Q) + .0025(Q)^2 - .000033(Q)^3.$$

Substituting the profit-maximizing quantity yields:

$$\pi = -1.2 - .015(46.79) + .0025(46.79)^2 - .000033(46.79)^3$$
$$= .191 \text{ million} = \$191,000.$$

Now let us consider the possibility of a decrease in market price to p = .05. With p = MR = .05, the profit-maximizing (or loss minimizing) quantity is determined by the equation:

$$MC = .09 - .005(Q) + .0001(Q)^2 = .05 = MR.$$

Solving for Q by using the quadratic formula gives us:

$$Q = \frac{-(-.005) \pm \sqrt{.000025 - .000016}}{.0002} = 40 \text{ and } 10.$$

Q = 40 million passenger miles is above the shut-down point, so production should be continued. Economic profit in this case is:

$$\pi = .05(Q) - [1.2 + .09(Q) - .0025(Q)^2 + .000033(Q)^3]$$
$$= -1.2 - .04(Q) + .0025(Q)^2 - .000033(Q)^3.$$

Substituting for the profit-maximizing value yields:

$$\pi = -1.2 - .04(40) + .0025(40)^2 - .000033(40)^3$$
$$= -.912 \text{ million} = -\$912,000.$$

Whereas production with p = .05 yields economic loss for Dependable Airlines, continuing to provide service at a price greater than average variable cost contributes some revenue toward the payment of fixed costs and holds loss below the maximum of FC = $1,200,000. At the end of Dependable's short run, it would be wise to re-evaluate the firm's contractual obligations with a view toward eliminating this route.

MANAGERIAL THINKING

1. Determine Dependable Airlines' average profit per passenger mile at a competitive price of $0.065 per passenger mile.
2. How would you determine the level of service at which Dependable simply breaks even, that is, pays for all fixed and variable costs with no economic profit? ("Break-even" analysis is the subject of the following sections.)

---

cost, no service should be provided. At a price of precisely $0.0425 per passenger mile, the firm would suffer negative economic profit or loss equal to the entire amount of fixed cost for the month.

For a competitive firm, the shut-down point is the quantity and price at which $p = MR = MC$ is just sufficient to cover AVC. No quantity less than the shut-down quantity should be produced, and no price less than the shut-down price should be accepted. A lower price and quantity would increase negative economic profit by the difference between price and average variable cost for each unit produced.

The shut-down point identifies the minimum price and quantity (other than zero) in the short run. It is the extreme minimum of the firm's short-run supply curve. Whereas a competitive firm may produce at this point in the short run, production cannot continue indefinitely in the face of such losses. When short-run contracts expire, a firm is free to re-allocate resources toward more profitable production. At the end of the short run, resources are no longer fixed, and new long-run decisions can be made. Operations that have yielded short-run economic profit may be expanded, while operations that have yielded losses may be abandoned. These kinds of decisions will be discussed further in Chapter 8.

BREAK-EVEN ANALYSIS

Our discussion thus far has considered a hypothetical firm in the context of the economist's market model. An actual firm must consider the same cost factors and pursue the same profit-maximizing goals as the theoretical firm. There are certain techniques for applying theoretical principles to actual decision-making. Many of these techniques involve the subject of this discussion, break-even analysis.

Break-even analysis enables managers to calculate the level of output in the short run that will allow all fixed and variable costs to be paid. The break-even quantity is valid over any period of time in which certain costs are fixed. Selling any quantity of output greater than the break-even quantity yields economic profit.

Determining a firm's break-even level of output requires information about total cost and total revenue. To illustrate, we will examine a simple case in which costs are known and predictable. We will assume a linear total cost equation of the form $TC = FC + (AVC)(Q)$. The linear total cost equation assumes fixed costs *(FC)* that do not change during the short run and constant average variable costs *(AVC)* for any quantity of output *(Q)*. A linear cost equation implies that marginal cost is constant and equal to average variable cost: that is, the firm is operating in the range of production over which marginal cost is equal to average variable cost at its lowest point.

Over the range of production for which these conditions are true, total cost rises by a constant amount for each increase in quantity. Therefore, the total cost equation for the month can be shown graphically as a straight line that rises from a point on the vertical axis equal to fixed cost and that has a slope equal to average variable cost. A linear cost equation of this type has been graphed in Figure 6.11.

Fixed cost is $600,000 per month and variable cost increases $55.00 with each unit of product sold: Thus,

$$TC = FC + (AVC)(Q) = \$600,000 + 55\ (Q).$$

FIGURE 6.11   **The Break-Even Point**

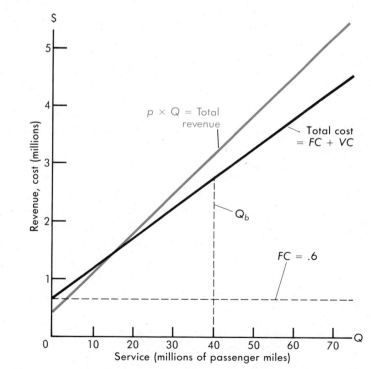

The break-even point (Q_b) occurs where $TR = TC$ or $(p)(Q) = FC + VC$.

Total revenue is price times quantity or $TR = (p)(Q)$. For this example, we will assume that price is $p = \$70.00$ per unit. Thus, total revenue is

$$TR = (p)(Q) = (70)(Q),$$

shown in Figure 6.11 as a straight line starting at the origin with a slope equal to a price of $70.00. Look at the relationship between TC and TR. For quantities less than $Q = 40,000$, TC is greater than TR and the firm experiences negative economic profit or loss. The amount of loss is equal to the vertical distance between TC and TR at the appropriate quantity. Producing quantities greater than $Q = 40,000$ units will yield positive economic profit equal to the vertical distance between TR and TC. Producing exactly $Q = 40,000$ units will enable the firm to pay all costs, including normal profit, but economic profit will be zero. This is the firm's break-even quantity (Q_b).

A firm's break-even quantity can be determined algebraically. For a fixed cost of $600,000 per month, constant average variable cost of $55 per unit, and a market price of $70, the break-even quantity is the value of Q at which total revenue is equal to total cost. Thus,

$$TR = (70)(Q_b) = 600,000 + 55(Q_b) = TC.$$

Solving for Q_b yields:

$$(70 - 55)(Q_b) = 600,000 \text{ and } Q_b = 40,000 \text{ units.}$$

In Figure 6.11, $Q_b = 40,000$ is the quantity of output at which TR crosses TC and economic profit is zero.

Profit Contribution, Operating Leverage, and Margin of Profitability

The break-even quantity of output can be determined another way. Notice that the unit selling price of $70 is used to cover the average variable cost of $55 per unit. The remaining $15 is each unit's contribution to fixed cost and profit: $p - AVC = contribution$ to fixed cost and profit per unit of service. The break-even quantity of output is the quantity at which the sum of all unit contributions yield fixed cost for the month or:

$$Q_b(p - AVC) = FC.$$

Stated differently,

$$\frac{FC}{p - AVC} = Q_b.$$

The numerator of the ratio is fixed cost, and the denominator is unit contribution to fixed cost and profit. With fixed cost of $600,000 and unit contribution of $15 per unit, 40,000 units must be sold for the firm to break even:

$$\frac{600,000}{70 - 55} = 40,000 \text{ units} = Q_b.$$

Now suppose the firm's managers set a target level of economic profit that they hope to achieve during the month. Each unit sold must pay its variable cost of $55 and its contribution to fixed cost *plus* target economic profit. For example, for target economic profit of $300,000, the total quantity sold must be at least

$$Q_b' = \frac{FC + \pi}{p - AVC} = \frac{900,000}{70 - 55} = 60,000 \text{ units per month.}$$

Q_b' is referred to as the **target-profit break-even point**. This is the quantity of output that yields revenue above variable cost sufficient to pay fixed cost *plus* the target level of profit.

The target-profit break-even point would be shown in Figure 6.11 by adding a line $(FC + \pi)$ drawn parallel to and (π) units above the line representing fixed cost. Intersection of the $(FC + \pi)$ line with the total revenue line identifies the target-profit break-even point.

The break-even quantity of output differs among various firms primarily because of differences in the ratio of fixed to variable costs. In general, the higher the level of fixed cost, the greater the quantity of output needed to break even. (More unit contributions are necessary to cover fixed cost.) Once the break-even quantity is passed, however, a firm with relatively high fixed cost may enjoy substantial profits. For such firms, relatively low average variable cost beyond the break-even point absorbs substantially less of product price, making unit profit greater.

The effect on profit of various combinations of fixed and variable cost also is reflected in a firm's **operating leverage**. The degree of operating leverage measures the percentage change in profit associated with a percentage change in sales:

$$\text{Degree of operating leverage } (DOL) = \frac{\text{percent change in profit}}{\text{percent change in sales}} = \frac{\%\Delta\pi}{\%\Delta Q}.$$

Degree of operating leverage is sometimes called **elasticity of profit**. *DOL* or elasticity of profit differs at different levels of sales, being greatest at levels of sales just beyond the break-even point since percentage change in profit is greater in this range.

The absolute value of *DOL* can be useful for deciding the character of production: that is determining the most efficient relationship between fixed and variable resources and, hence, the most profitable relationship between fixed and variable cost. If managers expect a level of sales high enough to break even using a high proportion of fixed resources, *DOL* just beyond the break-even point will be quite high. Production with a relatively high proportion of fixed resources would be especially profitable. If the expected level of sales is lower, a firm must use a smaller proportion of fixed resources if it is to break even. In this case, *DOL* just beyond the break-even point will be lower, and profit will increase more slowly beyond the break-even point.

The degree of operating leverage changes with output if average variable cost changes. However, over a range for which average variable cost is expected to be constant, degree of operating leverage can be calculated by using a simple ratio:

$$\text{Degree of operating leverage } (DOL) = \frac{Q(p - AVC)}{Q(p - AVC) - FC}.$$

The numerator of the fraction is the contribution to fixed cost and profit of all units, and the denominator is economic profit.

Look at Figure 6.12 for a graphical representation of operating leverage. The vertical distance between *TR* and *TC* measures the economic profit associated with any level of *Q* (negative economic profit for quantities to the left of the intersection at Q_b and positive economic profit to the right). Increasing economic profit at any level of output, say Q_1, requires using one of the following options:

Option 1. Change the proportion of fixed to variable resources, so that average variable cost falls. A reduction of average variable cost is shown in Figure 6.12a as a reduction in the slope of *TC* relative to *TR*.

Option 2. Change the proportion of fixed to variable resources so that fixed

FIGURE 6.12   Managerial Options

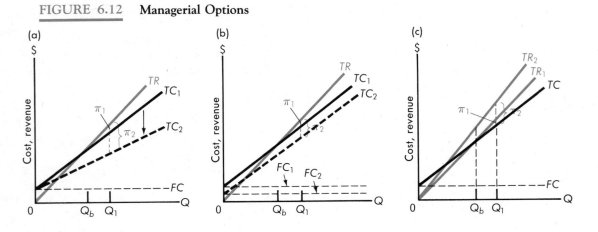

Option one is to reduce average variable cost as shown in (a). Option two is to reduce fixed cost as shown in (b). Option three is to increase price as shown in (c).

cost falls. A reduction of fixed cost is shown in Figure 6.12b as a downward shift in *TC*.

Option 3. Raise product price, shown in Figure 6.12c as an increase in the slope of *TR*.

In each of these options, the increase in economic profit for $Q = Q_1$ is shown as a dashed line at the vertical measure of profit for that quantity of output. The percentage increase in economic profit depends on the relative values of fixed and variable cost for any cost or price change.

A third measure of current profitability is a firm's margin of profitability. The **margin of profitability** is the ratio of economic profit to fixed cost. This is a measure of a firm's ability to satisfy its fixed obligations. The margin of profitability (*MOP*) is defined as the amount of profit as a percentage of fixed cost.

$$MOP = \frac{\pi}{FC}.$$

Or, margin of profitability can be calculated as

$$MOP = \frac{Q - Q_b}{Q_b}.$$

In this sense, margin of profitability is a measure of the amount of production in excess of the break-even (zero profit) quantity.

Margin of profitability is a significant tool for decision-making because it measures how close a firm is to falling below its break-even quantity. With a comfortable margin of profitability, a firm can be assured sufficient sales to cover fixed cost.

In Figure 6.12, Q_1 is 33 percent beyond Q_b for a margin of profitability of

$$MOP = \frac{Q_1 - Q_b}{Q_b} = .33.$$

Employing any of the three options stated previously reduces Q_b and increases the firm's *MOP*, thus increasing the firm's cushion against unfavorable changes in market conditions.

BREAK-EVEN ANALYSIS FOR NONLINEAR COSTS

The assumption of constant average and marginal costs has until now allowed us to use a linear equation for total cost. However, as we have seen, many production processes experience rising average variable costs in the short run. When average variable costs rise with output, break-even analysis requires the use of a quadratic cost equation.

To illustrate, let us assume that average variable costs increase with output

EXAMPLE 6.2   Evaluating a Firm's Profit Position

To illustrate the use of unit contribution, degrees of operating leverage, and margin of profitability, suppose that Tuff Tire Company is producing 50,000 tires per month for economic profit of

$$\pi = (70)(50,000) - [600,000 + (55)(50,000)] = \$150,000 \text{ per month.}$$

Unit contribution to fixed cost and profit is:

$$\text{Unit contribution} = p - AVC = 70 - 55 = \$15.$$

Because 50,000 tires exceeds the firm's break-even level of service, the entire unit contribution of $15 goes toward economic profit for each additional tire produced and sold. As a result, Tuff Tire Company's operating leverage is relatively high:

$$\text{Degree of operating leverage} = (DOL) = \frac{Q(p - AVC)}{Q(p - AVC) - FC} = \frac{750,000}{150,000} = 5.$$

With $DOL = 5$, Tuff's profit will increase 5 percent for each percentage increase in service. For example, a one-percent increase in production to $50,000(1.01) = 50,500$ tires will yield economic profit of

$$\pi = (70)(50,500) - [600,000 + (55)(50,500)] = \$157,500 \text{ per month.}$$

This is an increase of 5 percent: $157,500/150,000 = 1.05$. Finally, for $Q = 50,000$, Tuff's margin of profitability is

$$MOP = \frac{\pi}{FC} = \frac{150,000}{600,000} = .25.$$

The firm now is producing .25 beyond its break-even quantity.

Now let us suppose that changes in the market for tires are threatening Tuff's profitable position. Competition is reducing Tuff's freedom to set price, and rising energy costs are threatening to raise average variable cost. Managers must decide on a new strategy for the changing conditions. With options 1 and 3 from the previous section closed to Tuff's managers, consideration must be given to option 2, a reduction in fixed cost. One possibility in option 2 might be a reduction in production facilities, causing a downward shift in *TC*. If Tuff can reduce the fixed cost of production to $500,000 per month, what would be the consequences for profit, degree of operating leverage, and margin of profitability?

Reducing fixed cost would have no effect on unit contribution: $P - AVC = 15$. However, lower fixed cost would reduce the break-even quantity to

$$Q_b = \frac{FC}{P - AVC} = \frac{500,000}{15} = 33,333 \text{ units per month.}$$

For $Q = 50,000$, profit (π) would be

$$Q(p - AVC) - FC = \$250,000.$$

Operating leverage (*DOL*) would fall to

$$\frac{Q(p - AVC)}{Q(p - AVC) - FC} = \frac{75,000}{25,000} = 3,$$

and margin of profitability (*MOP*) would increase to

$$\frac{250,000}{500,000} = .50.$$

The changes in these measures are a result of the fact that current production of $Q = 50,000$ would be substantially beyond Tuff's break-even point in option 2.

Note that a lower operating leverage is not necessarily a disadvantage. We have discussed operating leverage in terms of an expected *increase* in profit resulting from an *increase* in service. In fact, if quantity of service *declines*, a low operating leverage would mean a smaller percentage *decrease* in profit. Suppose Tuff's managers expect a 5-percent decrease in sales as a result of increased competition. What would be the effect on profit at a lower level of production, given that option 2 is put into effect? For Q = .95(50,000) = 47,500, economic profit would fall to

$$\pi = 47,500(15) - 500,000 = \$212,500,$$

a drop of 5 times 3 = 15 percent:

$$\frac{212,500}{250,000} = .85.$$

Without using option 2, the 5-percent drop in sales would cause a 5 times 5 = 25 percent drop in profit:

$$\pi = 47,500(15) - 600,000 = \$112,500.$$

Thus, 112,500/150,000 = .75. A higher margin of profitability is also a favorable measure for the firm. Under option 2, economic profit is half the level of fixed cost, giving Tuff substantial protection against loss.

CASE STUDY 6.3   Breaking Even in Farming

The relationship between fixed and variable costs is especially critical for farmers. Farming is highly capital-intensive: land, machinery, buildings, and storage facilities constitute a substantial portion of farming resources. With relatively low variable costs, the shut-down price for farm commodities can be very low. Thus, many farmers continue to produce farm commodities for extended periods while losses accumulate. Short-run losses must be offset by selling farm assets or by engaging in non-farming activities.

Certain characteristics of demand and supply curves also create problems for farmers. Record harvests increase food supplies and push down food prices. For many manufactured goods lower prices increase quantity demanded and reduce quantity supplied until price is equal to production costs for surviving firms. Not so for farm commodities. When prices fall, consumers will not purchase substantially more food, and farmers cannot produce substantially less. This means continued low prices and hard times on the farm.

Low farm prices reduce the unit contribution of farm commodities and increase the break-even quantity necessary for covering fixed cost. Many farmers operate with a low margin of profitability, such that abrupt changes in prices or costs can mean bankruptcy. In addition, operating leverage is relatively high, causing wide swings in profit and "feast-or-famine" conditions for farmers.

These factors affect farmers' responsiveness to profits in good years as well as bad. When food supplies are scarce and prices rise, farming is profitable. New farmers enter the market, and existing farmers expand their operations. For farmers, investment in productive capacity generally means hefty bank loans. Rising land values are collateral for the purchase of more land and machinery. However, financing new bank debt raises the fixed cost of farming further and forces farmers to increase crop production in spite of short-term losses. During the late 1970s, inflated land values enabled farmers to increase their borrowings and cover their losses, but the recession of 1981–1982 reduced land values causing farm bankruptcies to increase.

Early in 1983, the problems of farmers prompted Congress to initiate a program called "payment-in-kind" (PIK). Under PIK, U.S. farmers agreed not to cultivate almost a third of the nation's arable land. In return farmers received payment in the form of surplus farm commodities. The program was expected to cause a decrease in supplies and boost farm prices and incomes. However, bumper harvests and a decline in farm exports kept food supplies high and prices low.

MANAGERIAL THINKING

1. Discuss the statements in this case study regarding farming in terms of degree of operating leverage, profit contribution, and margin of profitability.
2. What circumstances in farming make short-run supply highly inelastic? Are there any implicit costs in farming? Explain.

Source: "Farmers Are Swamped by Grain and Debt," *Business Week*, August 30, 1982, pp. 20–21, and "Long U.S. Dominance in World Grain Trade Is Slowly Diminishing," *The Wall Street Journal*, May 19, 1983, p. 1.

CASE STUDY 6.4   **Break-Even as a Percent of Plant Capacity**

A Carolina furniture company has been experiencing short-run losses averaging $5.5 million in each of the last three years. In 1979, sales fell by 30 percent to $153.75 million. Production in 1980 was only 75 percent of plant capacity, and the firm's managers now must decide whether to go out of business altogether or to attempt a new marketing strategy for increasing sales. One proposal is to change the firm's marketing strategy to favor small retailers and higher-priced furniture products. The higher selling costs of serving small retailers will raise average total costs by 11 percent, but price increases are expected to average 13 percent. Currently, fixed cost is $19 million annually, and marginal and average variable costs are constant within the expected range of plant utilization.

This is a break-even problem in which Q is measured in terms of percent of plant capacity. At the current level of operation, 75 percent of capacity, total revenue is $153.75 million, or 153.75/75 = 2.05 million for each one percent of plant utilization. Total costs are 153.75 + 5.5 = 159.25 million, for average variable cost of (159.25 − 19)/75 = 1.87 million for each one percent of capacity. With current revenue and costs, the break-even level of plant operation occurs where

$$TR = TC = Q_b(2.05) = 19 + Q_b(1.87),$$

so that Q_b = 105.6 percent of plant capacity.

A Q_b of greater than 100 percent of capacity indicates that the firm's costs are too high and market prices are too low for the firm ever to be profitable under existing revenue and cost conditions. The proposed new marketing strategy should raise average variable cost by 11 percent to 1.11(1.87) = 2.08 million for each one percent of plant capacity. Revenue should increase by 13 percent to 1.13(2.05) = 2.28 million for each percentage of capacity. The new break-even quantity is the level of Q at which

$$TR = TC = Q_b(2.28) = 19 + Q_b(2.08)$$

so that Q_b = 95 percent of capacity.

In order to achieve profitability under the new marketing strategy, the firm must increase its total production by 95/75 = 1.27 = 127 percent, for an increase of 27 percent. Unless managers are confident that sales will increase to this extent, the plant should close down.

MANAGERIAL THINKING

Use a graph to illustrate the firm's break-even conditions under current revenue and cost conditions and under the proposed new marketing strategy. Show how changing the revenue and cost functions produce a lower break-even point.

EXAMPLE 6.3

Degree of Operating Leverage and Production of Joint Products

Many firms produce several products using the same fixed equipment but varying labor and material resources according to the requirements of each product. The decision to allocate a firm's productive resources to one product or another may depend on the degree of operating leverage, or elasticity of profit, of each product. Automobile manufacturers are examples of firms that produce several different products under similar technical arrangements. By comparing operating leverages of alternative products, managers can determine the most profitable combination of products.

Suppose an automobile manufacturer is paying all fixed and variable costs for the production of two separate products, luxury cars and compact cars. At current production of 1,500 luxury cars and 3,700 compact cars per month, operating leverages are 1.2 and .6 respectively. Current profits are $8,000,000 a month. Within a limited range of quantities, total profit may be estimated by a power function of the form

$$\pi = aL^b C^c,$$

where L and C are quantities of the two products and b and c are their operating leverages, or profit elasticities. The value of a is determined by substituting production values:

$$8,000,000 = a(1,500)^{1.2}(3,700)^{.6},$$

and $a = 8.93$.

Thus, the profit equation is

$$\pi = 8.93L^{1.2}C^{.6}.$$

Now suppose additional orders for compacts are received, such that production rises to $C = 4,000$ per month. Each percentage increase in compact car production will increase profit by less than 1 percent. Therefore, if total profit is to remain $8,000,000, luxury car production must not fall substantially. What level of production is necessary to maintain current profits?

Substituting for the new production value yields:

$$8,000,000 = 8.93(L)^{1.2}(4,000)^{.6},$$

and $L = 1,443$. Unless fixed equipment is capable of producing a total of 4,000 compacts and 1,443 luxury cars, the order should be rejected.

This procedure can be expanded to determine the combination of luxury cars and compact cars that would yield maximum profit when total productive capacity is limited. Given that only 100 percent of capacity can be used at any time, the quantities L and C can be expressed in percentage terms such that L = percentage of output represented by luxury cars and $C = 100 - L$ or the percentage of output represented by compacts. Under these assumptions, the profit-maximizing combination of products is the one for which quantities are proportional to operating leverages, or profit elasticities:

$$\frac{L}{C} = \frac{b}{c} \text{ or } \frac{L}{100 - L} = \frac{b}{c}.$$

Using these profit elasticities, the maximum-profit combination of products is determined as follows:

$$\frac{L}{100 - L} = \frac{1.2}{.6}.$$

Thus, $L = 66.67$ percent and $C = 33.33$ percent. Note that the order for production of $L = 1{,}443$ and $C = 4{,}000$ (from our previous example) is significantly different from the maximum-profit product mix.

MANAGERIAL THINKING

Assume that the automobile firm's productive equipment is equally capable of producing luxury or compact cars and that the quantities determined in the last example constitute 100 percent of capacity. Determine the level of profit at the maximum-profit product mix.

according to $AVC = a + b(Q) = .04 + .0001(Q)$ over the short run. With $AVC = .04 + .0001(Q)$, total costs are determined by

$$\begin{aligned} TC = FC + VC &= .6 + [.04 + .0001(Q)]Q \\ &= .6 + .04(Q) + .0001(Q)^2, \end{aligned}$$

a quadratic equation. The break-even level of service is that at which $TR = TC$. Thus, with a price of \$.07 per passenger mile,

$$TR = TC,$$

or

$$.07(Q_b) = .6 + .04(Q_b) + .0001(Q_b)^2.$$

This is also a quadratic equation. To solve a quadratic equation, set the equation equal to zero and use the quadratic formula

$$(Q_b = \frac{b \pm \sqrt{b^2 - 4ac}}{2c}).^3$$

For $0 = .6 - .03(Q_b) + .0001(Q_b)^2$,

$$Q_b = \frac{-(-.03) \pm \sqrt{(-.03)^2 - 4(.6)(.0001)}}{2(.0001)} = \frac{.03 \pm .0257}{.0002}.$$

---

3. Or use a pocket calculator.

Thus,

$$Q_{b1} = .0043/.0002 = 21.5,$$

and

$$Q_{b2} = .0557/.0002 = 278.5.$$

A quadratic equation can have two solutions. Two positive values for Q_b indicate two break-even levels of service. To see why, look at the graph of total revenue and total costs shown in Figure 6.13. Total revenue is drawn with a constant slope indicating constant marginal revenue at a market price of $.07 per passenger mile. Total cost has the form of a quadratic equation beginning with fixed cost of $.6 million and increasing with an average variable cost of

FIGURE 6.13   **Break-Even for Non-Linear Costs**

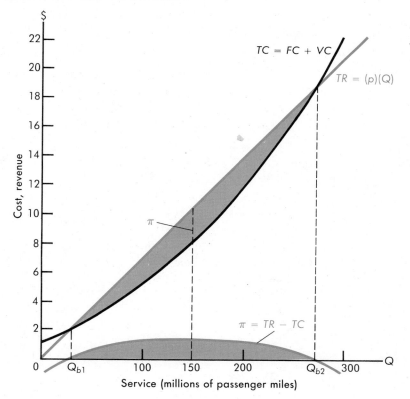

A non-linear cost function produces two break-even points. Profit is maximum where $MR = MC$, shown at $Q = 150$.

AVC = $.04 + .0001(Q)$ per passenger mile. Total cost exceeds revenue up to Q_{b1} = 21.5 million passenger miles. Over the range Q_{b1} = 21.5 to Q_{b2} = 278.5, total revenue exceeds total cost, yielding positive economic profit, as shown by the vertical distance between TR and TC for any level of service. At Q_{b2} = 278.5 million passenger miles, TC again rises above TR. Beyond this level of service in the short run, the firm's fixed resources are inadequate for providing service without incurring a loss.

A profit equation for the firm is also graphed in Figure 6.13. Economic profit associated with any level of service is determined by substitution in the profit equation. Thus, with production of 50 million passenger miles, economic profit is

$$\pi = TR - TC = .07(Q) - [.6 + .04(Q) + .0001(Q)^2]$$
$$= -.6 + .03(Q) - .0001(Q)^2$$
$$= -.6 + .03(50) - .0001(50)^2 = .65 = \$650,000.$$

Is a monthly profit of $650,000 the maximum profit possible for this firm? Remember that the maximum profit level of output is that at which marginal revenue is equal to marginal cost. We have assumed a constant market price of $.07, implying constant marginal revenue $(MR) = p = .07$. Marginal cost is the change in total cost, which we have said is the first derivative of the total cost function (determined through calculus). The marginal cost equation in our example is

$$\text{Marginal cost } (MC) = (1)(.04)(Q)^{1-1} + (2)(.0001)(Q)^{2-1}$$
$$= .04 + .0002(Q).$$

Maximum profit occurs where $MR = MC$, so that

$$MR = .07 = .04 + .0002(Q) = MC,$$

and Q = 150 million passenger miles. Note that in Figure 6.13 the total profit function reaches a peak at Q = 150. Given the current market price and the firm's existing fixed resources, Q = 150 is the most profitable level of service in the short run. Maximum economic profit is:

$$\pi = TR - TC = .07(150) - [.6 + .04(150) + .0001(150)^2]$$
$$= 1.65 = \$1,650,000.$$

SUMMARY

The behavior of production costs is the opposite of the behavior of production. In the short run, increasing marginal product is associated with decreasing marginal cost, decreasing marginal product is associated with increasing marginal cost, and constant marginal product is associated with constant marginal cost.

The behavior of marginal cost determines the behavior of average cost. Production typically occurs in the range of resource employment in which marginal cost is above average cost and average cost is rising.

Explicit costs are amounts that are paid out to suppliers of resources used in production. Implicit costs measure the value in production of resources owned by the firm and include normal profit. Fixed costs are contracted by the firm for the short run and must be paid regardless of quantity of output. Variable costs are the costs of variable resources that vary with quantity of output.

The profit-maximizing quantity of output in the short run occurs where marginal revenue from sales is equal to marginal cost of production. In competition, marginal revenue is equal to price. Therefore, the profit-maximizing quantity of output can be read from the firm's marginal cost curve where $p = MC$. Total economic profit in the short run is the difference between $p = MC$ and average total cost times quantity at the profit-maximizing quantity. In the long run, competition may be expected to push price down so that $p = MC = ATC$ at its lowest point. If $p = MC$ falls below ATC, the firm experiences negative economic profit or loss. However, production will continue in the short run as long as $p = MC$ is at least as high as average variable cost. By producing with $p = MC \geq AVC$, the firm minimizes the loss resulting from the necessary payment of fixed costs in the short run.

Quadratic equations can be used to estimate marginal cost, average variable cost, and average total cost and to locate a firm's shut-down point, profit-maximizing quantity, and total profit or loss.

Break-even analysis determines the quantity of output at which all fixed and variable costs will be paid. Degree of operating leverage can be used to project the effect on profit of changes in the proportion of fixed and variable resources and changes in product price.

KEY TERMS

cross subsidization	supply curve
explicit cost	shut-down price
implicit cost	break-even analysis
fixed cost	target-profit break-even point
variable cost	operating leverage
accounting cost	elasticity of profit
profit-maximizing quantity of output	margin of profitability

QUESTIONS AND PROBLEMS

1. Maple syrup is made by boiling sap from maple trees. Three to four gallons of fuel oil are needed to boil enough sap to produce one gallon of syrup. Over the period between 1977 and 1980, rising fuel costs increased the average total cost of producing syrup 35 percent, from $8.50 to $11.50 a gallon. Explain·this result in terms of short-run average costs and illustrate this data graphically.

2. Over the same period, the selling price of maple syrup rose only 25 percent, from $12.40 to $15.50. How did the cost increase affect unit profit? How would you account for this result?

3. In the meantime, some small syrup producers have turned to wood for fuel, reducing production costs to $11.10 a gallon. Producers who chop firewood on their own land experience production costs of only $8.54 a gallon. Interpret this information in terms of explicit and implicit costs.

4. Large syrup producers reduce fuel consumption through installation of reverse osmosis equipment which filters excess liquid from the maple sap before heating. The equipment leases for $4,000 and reduces variable production costs to $9.75 a gallon. How large must a producer be (in terms of gallons produced per year) to break even on this equipment?

5. The purchase price of reverse osmosis equipment is $32,000. This process has been shown to reduce production costs by 15 percent. If the selling price of syrup is $15.50 a gallon for output of 700 gallons annually, how many years must pass before the equipment would pay for itself?

6. Pre-heaters use the steam from boiling maple sap to warm incoming cold sap and can be purchased for $600. The result is a 15-percent savings in fuel consumption. If the cost of fuel represents $\frac{3}{4}$ of the average total cost of $11.50, determine the economic profit on annual production of 700 gallons with and without the use of a pre-heater.

7. Metropolitan Delivery Company estimates the terminal costs of handling its Number 3 packages at $1.30 each and costs per mile at 17¢. Currently, the firm's delivery charges for Number 3 packages are 35¢ per mile. What is the shortest distance the firm can carry Number 3 packages without losing money? If the average trip distance is 9 miles, what is the degree of operating leverage for Number 3 packages? Explain the significance of this measure for management decision making.

8. Reliable Battery Company's Red River plant was built to produce 1,350 units per hour at lowest cost and regularly operates at 20 percent above this level, with unit costs at 5 percent above the minimum. Price is $50.00 per unit, of which $7.50 is economic profit. Fixed cost is $2,000 an hour. What is the firm's shutdown price?

9. Continental Corn Company has fixed investments in plant and equipment costing $575 thousand a year. It produces soybeans for $5.25 a bushel on land yielding 110 bushels per acre per year. Cost per acre cultivated averages $5,300 annually. How many acres must the firm plant to break even?

10. Refer again to the data in Problem 9. Suppose the firm contracts for the necessary break-even acreage, and during the growing season soybean price falls to $5.00 a bushel. Calculate the firm's losses.

11. Refer once more to the data in Problem 9. Suppose unusually good weather increases yield per acre by 20 percent. Calculate the firm's profit at a price of $5.00 a bushel.

12. Value-Plus Discount Mart has fixed costs of $575 per hour and variable costs of $415 for the first 8 hours of operation. Remaining open beyond 8 hours raises variable costs by 20 percent while hourly sales fall from $535 to $450 an hour. How many hours must the store remain open to break even?

13. Refer to the data in Problem 12. What is the maximum number of hours the store can remain open profitably?

14. a. Western Farm Equipment Company is producing 94 fertilizer spreaders monthly at its most efficient level of plant operation and is experiencing monthly losses of $115,000. Revenues are $705,000, and fixed costs are $250,000 a month. Management wants to determine the lowest price for which the firm could continue to operate in the short run.
b. What is actual price in this case? Why should this firm continue to operate under circumstances of loss?
c. Western Company's marketing department proposes a campaign to identify potential users of the equipment and promote a wider market. The campaign would increase monthly sales by an estimated 37 units and would cost $50,000 a month. Should the campaign be undertaken?
d. What price would be necessary for the firm to break even following the marketing campaign?

15. a. Luxury Carpet Company has observed the following cost relationships over a series of weeks. Complete the table below using the information given. Then, using the techniques described in Chapter 2, write linear equations for AVC and MC. (Associate MC figures with the unit that is added.)
b. Use your equations from (a) to predict the total cost of producing 18 units. Modify your AVC equation to one that measures total cost. How would you describe your TC equation?
c. Graph the data in the table and verify that the TC, AVC, MC, and ATC curves have the typical shapes.
d. Suppose the market price of output is $65. Determine the profit-maximizing output and compute profit.
e. Suppose price falls to $55. What advice would you give the firm's management? Would your advice differ in the short versus the long run?

Q	FC	TC	AVC	MC	ATC
10	250	605			
11	250	640			
12	250	685			
13	250	740			
14	250	805			
15	250	880			

16. Avion Aircraft Corporation had been earning economic profit of $.08 million monthly until management decided to take out a $2 million long-term loan which added $.031 million to monthly fixed costs, which were previously $.43 million. Sales are expected to remain at about 112 units and revenues at about $21.67 million. How will the new loan obligation affect the firm's break-even point? What is elasticity of profit under the old and new conditions? Interpret your results.

17. Space Electronics has monthly fixed cost of $9,890 and variable cost averaging $87 per unit up to 1,000 units and $90 per unit beyond monthly production of 1,000 units. (1) At a price of $95, how many units must the firm produce each month to break even? (2) Sales for the coming month are estimated at $1,510. Compute expected economic profit for the month. (3) What is the degree of operating leverage at the projected level of production? How is this information useful to management?

18. Dependable Airlines has the opportunity to purchase a second-hand aircraft for $5 million or a new one for $20 million. The new plane is more fuel-efficient, such that variable cost per mile flown would be only $2.00, compared to $3.50 in the second-hand plane. Seating capacity is identical, so revenue per mile is expected to be $7.50. How many miles would both planes have to be flown to be economical?

19. Durable Engine Parts Company is operating with monthly fixed cost of $5,000 and a margin of profit of .20. Normal production is 57,000 units, a level of production the firm expects to continue. Production requires the use of 2 fittings for every unit of output, which the firm purchases for $1.55 each. Company engineers estimate that the fittings could be produced within the firm for only $1.45, but using the firm's own equipment for this purpose would add $3,500 to monthly maintenance charges. Calculate the potential effect on the firm's margin of profit, total profit, and break-even quantity of producing the fittings within the firm.

20. Hometown Brewery is considering entering the market for low-calorie beer, which is currently about 50 million barrels annually. The venture would require additional annual fixed costs of $84 million and variable costs of $3.70 per barrel. The company requires a 5-percent profit margin on the product, which would sell for $7.90. What share of the market must Hometown have if it is to break even on this venture?

Planning Production in the Long Run

To this point, we have been describing the behavior of production over the short run, when certain resources are fixed. We showed how changing the quantity of variable resources would affect total product according to linear, quadratic, cubic, or power production functions. In the short run, managers of business firms must decide how many variable resources to employ to produce a quantity of output consistent with a firm's objectives. In general, we have assumed that a firm's primary objective is maximum profit.

In the long run, production decisions are more complex, but the fundamental principles are the same. In long-run planning, managers must first decide the quantity of total production for some future period and then decide the quantities of *all* resources required to produce that quantity.

During the 1970s, some managers of electric power companies made long-run decisions that they later came to regret. Early in the decade, hefty annual increases in consumer and industrial demand for electric power convinced strategic planners of the need for increasing generating capacity. New plants were designed and construction was started. When completed, it was expected that the new power plants would use various quantities of oil, coal, or natural gas to produce electricity for their service areas.

Economic circumstances began to change in the mid-1970s, however. Rising fuel costs and a push to conserve energy instigated by the federal government slowed growth in demand for electric power. Some power companies found themselves with greater generating capacity than they could utilize efficiently. High construction costs, as well as increasing fuel costs, began to cut into profits, and many power companies were forced to scale down their expansion plans.

In this chapter, we will look at long-run production relationships when *all* resources can be varied. Initially, we will show how the short-run production functions developed in Chapter 5 can be adapted to describe the long run. Then we will use algebraic and graphical techniques to show how managers can arrive at long-run production decisions.

THE PRODUCTION SURFACE

Long-run production functions differ from short-run production functions in that all resources are variable. Thus, the production function $Q = f(VR)$ includes not only labor, materials, and so forth (which were considered variable in the short run), but also buildings, equipment, and contracted personnel (which were considered fixed in the short run).

Over the long run, the use of *all* resources can be varied, and managers must decide the appropriate combination of *all* resources for achieving a firm's objectives. However, once managers have decided on the quantities of buildings, equipment, and contracted personnel, these resources again become fixed. Once a decision has been made, the firm is back in its short run, with established quantities of certain resources. Total production may be expected to behave according to the short-run production functions described in Chapter 5, with additional quantities of labor, materials, and other variable resources yielding *increasing, constant,* or *decreasing* marginal product.

The relationship between the short and long run can be shown in a model of production using two resources, labor and capital. In Figure 7.1a, the quantity of labor (L) is measured along one horizontal axis and the quantity of capital (K) is measured along the other. Total product (Q) is measured upward on the vertical axis.

Total production is shown as a surface, rising from a quantity of zero at the origin and forming a "hill" as larger quantities of both resources are used. The shape of the hill depends in part on the behavior of total product when one resource is held constant and the other is increased. Figure 7.1 is drawn with the assumption that holding one resource constant and varying the quantity of the other produces first *increasing,* then *constant,* and finally *decreasing* marginal product.

To understand this, move along the capital axis to $K = 5$ and imagine a vertical cross section passing through the production hill parallel to the labor axis. This is shown in Figure 7.1b. The cross section in Figure 7.1b represents total production for various quantities of labor with capital held constant at $K = 5$ units. Move up the surface of the cross section to the quantity of output associated with $K = 5$ and $L = 11$ and follow the dashed line to the vertical axis. The vertical axis tells us that 5 units of capital and 11 units of labor produce total output of $Q = 80$ units.

Note that the cross section of the production surface displays the typical

FIGURE 7.1   A Production Function of Two Variables

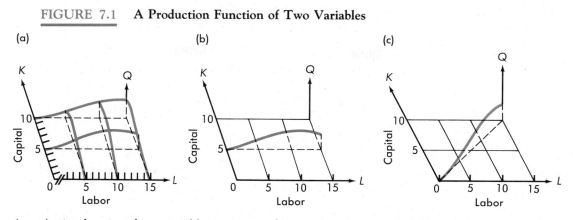

A production function of two variable resources with increasing, constant, and diminishing marginal product (a). To find total output for any combination of resources L and K, follow the appropriate coordinates along the surface of the hill. Total production when various quantities of labor are used with a fixed quantity of capital K = 5 is shown in (b). A straight line drawn from the origin identifies equal proportional quantities of K and L in (c). The effect of changes in scale is first to produce increasing returns, then to produce constant returns, and finally to produce diminishing returns.

behavior of marginal product when larger quantities of labor are added to a fixed quantity of capital: Marginal product first increases, then remains constant, and finally decreases. Similar cross sections cut through the production surface for any quantity of capital parallel to the labor axis would represent production when capital is held constant at that quantity. Likewise, cross sections parallel to the capital axis for any fixed quantity of labor would display the behavior of total product when various quantities of capital are added to a fixed quantity of labor.

Scale Effects in the Long Run

The shape of the production "hill" also depends on the effects of increasing and decreasing returns to scale in the long run. Scale effects are the result of equal percentage increases in all resources, labor and capital in particular.

Look again at the production surface in Figure 7.1. Begin at the origin and move diagonally across plane *LK* such that quantities of *L* and *K* increase in the same proportion. Points on such a line would represent a series of combinations such as 1 unit of capital and 10 units of labor, 2 units of capital and 20 units of labor, 3 units of capital and 30 units of labor, and so forth. Another diagonal would include a series of combinations such as 1 *K* and 5 *L*, 2 *K* and 10 *L*, 3 *K* and 15 *L*. Now imagine a cross section passing through the production surface whose base lies on such a diagonal. The behavior of total product along this cross section reflects the effects of scale.

Economists identify three possible scale effects:

1. **Increasing returns to scale** occur when equal percentage changes in all resources yield larger percentage changes in total output.
2. **Constant returns to scale** occur when equal percentage changes in all resources yield the same percentage change in total output.
3. **Decreasing returns to scale** occur when equal percentage changes in all resources yield smaller percentage changes in total output.

The cross section shown in Figure 7.1c suggests that equal percentage increases in labor and capital first yield greater percentage increases in total product, then smaller percentage increases, and, finally, decreases in total product. The implication for managers is that over some range, increasing labor and capital proportionately may yield gains in productivity. (That is, the average product of all resources will increase.) However, beyond some level of fixed and variable resources, further proportionate increases in labor and capital may cause resource productivity to decline.

Restaurant chains are a common example of scale effects. We are all familiar with restaurants whose menu, decor, and atmosphere (the popular term is "ambience") suddenly catch on with the public. Demand is so great and economic profit so high that the firm's managers decide to duplicate the original operation in another location—and another and another. At first, increasing all capital and labor resources in some constant proportion may enable the firm to use all its resources more efficiently: consolidating storage in a central location, taking advantage of quantity discounts for large purchases, producing staple food items in large quantities, and providing restaurant managers with market information for planning and evaluating current operations. When such scale effects cause greater increases in production, unit cost will be lower and economic profit per unit of sales will be higher. However, at some point, expanding restaurant chains may find that further additions become difficult to manage efficiently. If efficiency drops enough to cause total product to increase by smaller amounts with further increases in restaurant facilities, unit cost will rise and economic profit per unit of sales will fall.

Some Explanations for the Effects of Scale

Increasing, constant, and decreasing returns to scale may result from the technical or the financial aspects of the business.

Technical returns to scale occur in most production processes up to some minimum quantities of all resources. One reason is the fact that certain resources cannot be divided into small quantities for employment at low levels of production. Thus, it is said that some resources are not "divisible" and therefore cannot be combined in precise proportions with other resources. Certain pieces of equipment, skilled personnel, and physical facilities are examples of resources that must be available if production is to be carried on at all, but cannot be broken down into very small quantities. Often such resources need not be increased proportionately at higher levels of production. While they may be under-utilized at low levels of production, they can be used more intensively when production expands. When certain resources are essential for any production at all but are not divisible into small quantities, expanding the use of other resources may yield increasing returns to scale.

One resource with these characteristics is high-level management. At low levels of resource use, high-level managers' skills may be under-utilized. Expanding the use of other resources can take place without expanding managerial resources, but simply by using existing managers more intensively. At some level of resource use, however, existing managers may become over-utilized. It may become increasingly difficult to gather and process the information needed for making decisions and to coordinate production according to the firm's goals. On the other hand, duplicating existing management in the precise amounts needed to expand production may be impossible. At this level of resource use, production may begin to experience decreasing returns to scale.

We may conclude that technical returns to scale result from the particular character of certain resources at some level of employment. The indivisibility of certain resources—particularly managerial resources—and the difficulty of duplicating existing resources make it difficult to ensure that *all* resources are, in fact, increased proportionately. When there are resources whose quantities cannot be increased in precise percentage amounts, the result may be increasing or decreasing returns to scale.

Financial returns to scale result from imperfections in the flow of funds within the firms. A large business firm may be able to use its funds more efficiently by shifting surplus funds from one division to another when needed. In addition, a large firm may have greater opportunities to purchase necessary goods and materials at discounted prices. Still, there are limits to the increasing returns that result from more efficient use of funds.

Over some range of plant size, the tendency toward increasing returns to scale probably will be precisely offset by decreasing returns, causing production to experience constant returns. Over this range, increasing resource employment yields an equal percentage increase in total output. Look once again at the production function in Figure 7.1c and, in particular, at the cross section beginning at the origin. Returns to scale are shown as the slope of the cross section for which values of L and K remain in constant proportion to each other. Thus, a movement from (K_2, L_4) to (K_4, L_8) indicates a doubling of scale. The effect on total output depends on whether increases in scale experience increasing, constant, or decreasing returns. In fact, the cross section in Figure 7.1c initially has an increasing slope, indicating increasing returns to scale over some range of L and K, then has a constant slope, indicating constant returns over some range, and finally has a decreasing slope, indicating decreasing returns.

Scale Effects and Marginal Product

The concept of *scale* differs from the concept of *marginal product* in an important way. In the case of marginal product, resources within the short-run production function are classified as fixed or variable. In the short run, the quantity of variable resources can be varied over an infinite range of quantities. The behavior of total product depends on marginal product of the variable resource when other resources are fixed. In the case of scale, all resources can be varied, and the behavior of total product depends on the effects of scale. Scale effects vary because of the characteristics of a particular resource—its indivisibility into smaller units or the inability to expand indefinitely into larger units—and the more efficient use of the firm's funds.

ISOQUANTS

In this section we will illustrate the production relationships shown in Figure 7.1 in a more convenient form for use by business managers. We will begin by assuming that managers have decided on a quantity of output to be produced during the coming production period. The question now is: What quantity of labor and capital should be employed for producing the desired quantity of output? More precisely, given the current prices of resources, what is the least costly, most efficient combination of labor and capital resources for producing that quantity of output?

Imagine a horizontal cross section through the production surface at a particular quantity of output Q. A horizontal cross section through the production surface at $Q = 80$ is shown in Figure 7.2a. The cross section shows all combinations of labor and capital that will produce 80 units of output. Two possible combinations are: (K_5, L_{11}) and (K_{12}, L_5). The horizontal cross section in Figure 7.2a is shown again in 7.2b. Since the cross section is horizontal, only the axes representing labor and capital are shown in this graph. The cross section takes the shape of a curve drawn convex to the origin. Points on the curve represent quantities of labor and capital that will produce $Q = 80$ units of output.[1] Other curves have been drawn in Figure 7.2c representing various cross sections from $Q = 30$ to $Q = 90$ units of output. Similar curves could be drawn representing cross sections from the production surface for every possible value of Q. Each cross section would form an outline of the production function in Figure 7.1a at a constant altitude (constant value of Q).

The curves shown in Figure 7.2c are called **isoquants.** An isoquant is a curve that represents combinations of resources required to produce a particular quantity of output. Values on the curve are determined by choosing a constant value for Q, then substituting various quantities of K in the relevant production function and solving for a corresponding value of L. We will demonstrate this process and show how isoquants can help managers make production decisions shortly.

Some characteristics of isoquants should be noted:

1. *On a graph representing two resources, isoquants slope downward from left to right.* This is because a decrease in the allocation of one

---

1. Drawing the cross section would actually produce a circle. However, we will disregard the dashed portion of the circle, since it calls for larger than necessary quantities of both resources to produce any given quantity of output.

FIGURE 7.2   Isoquants

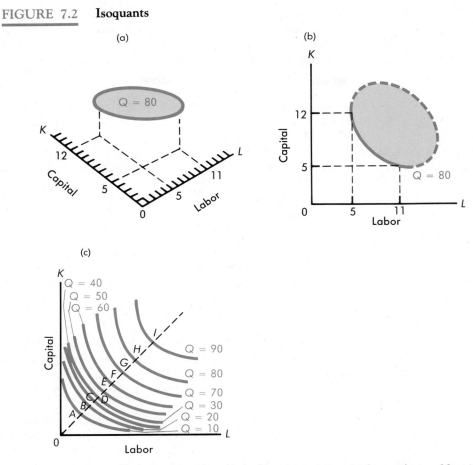

A horizontal cross section at Q = 80 identifies all combinations of K and L for producing 80 units of output (a). The isoquant for Q = 80 is shown in (b). The dashed portion of the cross section is not relevant for decision making since points on the dashed portion include larger quantities of both K and L than are necessary for producing 80 units of output. Isoquants for Q = 10 through Q = 90 at 10-unit intervals are shown in (c). From Q = 10 through Q = 40, production experiences increasing returns to scale. From Q = 40 through Q = 60, production experiences constant returns. From Q = 60 through Q = 90, production experiences decreasing returns to scale.

resource must be offset by an increase in the other if total product is to remain the same. (This is true for all resources with marginal product greater than zero.)

2. *Isoquants are convex to the origin because of the principle of decreasing marginal product for each of the resources used in any combination.* If a relatively large quantity of one resource is used, its marginal product will be low relative to that of the resource used in smaller quantity. A large quantity of the first resource might be exchanged for

a small quantity of the second to achieve a combination yielding the same total product. (This is true for all resources that experience decreasing marginal product.)

3. *Isoquants representing larger quantities of output are graphed higher and farther to the right.* This is because larger quantities of resources are required to produce greater total output.

4. *Isoquants cannot touch or intersect.* Intersecting isoquants would imply that larger quantities of output could be produced with the same or smaller quantities of resources.

5. *Isoquants may or may not intersect an axis.* If an isoquant touches an axis, it means that a particular quantity of output can be produced without using the resource graphed on the other axis.

Isoquants and the Effects of Scale

Note the position of the isoquants in Figure 7.2c. For equal changes in total output, isoquant F (representing $Q = 90$) lies substantially farther to the right of isoquant I ($Q = 80$) than isoquant D ($Q = 40$) lies to the right of isoquant C ($Q = 30$). This is because of the effect of scale. The closeness of isoquants C and D indicates increasing returns to scale. Increasing returns to scale make it possible to produce a given increase in output with smaller percentage increases in resources employed. The larger distance between isoquants H and I indicates decreasing returns to scale. Decreasing returns to scale make it necessary to employ proportionately more units of resources to produce a given increase in output.

Increasing and decreasing returns are illustrated by the ray drawn from the origin in Figure 7.2c. Points on the ray represent combinations of capital and labor used in constant proportions. Intersections with the isoquants define quantity of output in increments of 10. The intersections become closer together over the range $Q = 10$ to $Q = 40$ indicating smaller proportional increases in capital and labor to produce 10 additional units. This is the range of increasing returns to scale. Beyond $Q = 40$, the intersections lie farther apart, indicating larger proportional increases in capital and labor to produce 10 additional units. This is the range of decreasing returns.

Constructing an Isoquant

Now let us look at isoquants drawn for a particular production function whose parameters can be estimated from available production data. We will assume that production can be described by a power function of the form

$$Q = aL^bK^c,$$

where a is a constant close to one and L and K represent quantities of labor and capital. The exponents b and c measure the percentage change in total product associated with a percentage change in the respective resource.

Remember that the percentage change in total product associated with a percentage change in resource use is called the **elasticity of production** (ϵ). In our example, elasticity of production is determined by:

$$\epsilon_{QL} = \frac{\%\Delta Q}{\%\Delta L} = b$$

and

$$\epsilon_{QK} = \frac{\%\Delta Q}{\%\Delta K} = c.$$

A useful feature of power functions is the ease of determining the effects of scale. Scale effects are represented by the sum of the exponents of the resource variables. A sum of *one* indicates constant returns to scale. Thus, in this case, increasing the quantity of variable resources increases total product in equal proportion. A sum greater than *one* indicates increasing returns to scale. In this case, increasing variable resources increases total product in greater proportion. A sum less than *one* indicates decreasing returns to scale. In this case, increasing variable resources increases total product at a rate less than the increase in resources.

In our example, we will assume that managers have estimated the parameters of the production function and have found the elasticities of production to be $\epsilon_{QL} = 0.3$ and $\epsilon_{QK} = 0.7$. Thus, a percentage increase in labor resources will increase total product by $b = \epsilon_{QL} = 0.3$ percent and capital resources by $c = \epsilon_{QK} = 0.7$ percent. This information tells us that, over this range of total product, production is occurring with constant returns to scale. Substituting the estimated values in $Q = aL^bK^c$ along with known values for Q, L, and K yields an estimate for a. Including estimated values for all the parameters yields the production function $Q = .7L^{.3}K^{.7}$ for the range of output covered by available production data.

An isoquant includes values of L and K necessary for producing a given quantity of Q. The values for drawing the isoquants in Figure 7.3a on page 224 were determined by first selecting a value for Q, then substituting various values for L, and solving for corresponding values of K. To illustrate, let us select $Q = 40$. The values of L and K necessary for producing $Q = 40$ are determined by substituting $L = 20, 25, 50$, and so forth and solving for K. Computing for a value of $L = 10$ yields:

$$40 = .7(10)^{.3}K^{.7} = \frac{40}{1.4} = K^{.7}.$$

Raising both sides of the equation to the power $1/.7 = 1.43$ gives us

$$28.64^{1.43} = K^{.7(1.43)} = K = 120.61.$$

FIGURE 7.3　Isoquants and the Isocost Line

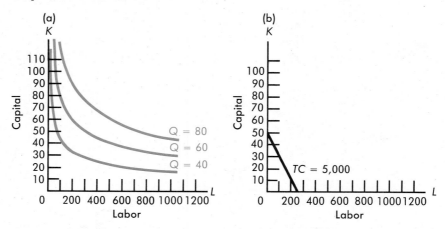

Isoquants for the production function $Q = .7L^{.3}K^{.7}$ are shown in (a). The slope of the isoquants is $MP_L/MP_K = .3K/.7L$. An isocost line is shown in (b). The line has a slope of p_L/p_K and is drawn for a total budget of $TC = 5,000$.

Thus, 40 units of output may be produced by a combination including 10 units of labor and 120.61 units of capital resources.

Similarly, substituting for a value of $L = 25$ yields:

$$40 = .7(25)^{.3}K^{.7} = \frac{40}{1.84} = K^{.7}.$$

Raising both sides of the equation to the power $1/.7 = 1.43$ gives us

$$21.76^{1.43} = K^{.7(1.43)},$$

and $K = 81.41$. The first row in Table 7.1 lists values of K associated with various quantities of L that produce 40 units of output. Values for the second row are computed similarly. Thus, for $Q = 60$ and $L = 10$:

$$60 = .7(10)^{.3}K^{.7} = 42.96 = K^{.7},$$

and $K = 215.25$.

Isoquants are determined in the same manner for production functions whose equations are linear, quadratic, or cubic. Once again, to solve such an equation, select the desired quantity for Q, substitute various quantities of one variable resource, and solve for the corresponding quantities of the other resource.

TABLE 7.1   Combinations of Labor and Capital Resources for Drawing Isoquants

Cells in the table are values of K.

When Q =	L = 10	25	50	100	200	400	600	800	1,000
40	120.61	81.44	60.50	44.96	33.40	24.82	20.86	18.44	16.76
60	215.25	145.34	107.99	80.23	59.61	44.29	37.23	32.91	29.91
80	324.65	219.22	162.88	121.02	89.92	66.81	56.15	49.64	45.11

USING ISOQUANTS TO PLAN LOWEST-COST PRODUCTION

Isoquants are useful to managers in deciding the most efficient resource combination for producing a desired quantity of output. The most efficient combination of resources is also the lowest-cost combination. Economic theory tells us that the lowest-cost combination of resources is the one for which the marginal products per dollar of resource cost are equal:

$$\frac{MP_K}{p_K} = \frac{MP_L}{p_L} = \frac{MP_M}{p_M},$$

and so forth. Thus, for lowest-cost production, the marginal products per dollar of capital, labor, and materials must be equal. This principle is called the **equal marginal product principle** and is valid for any number of resources.[2]

The equal marginal product equation can be rearranged so that

$$\frac{MP_L}{MP_K} = \frac{p_L}{p_K}.$$

Thus, for lowest-cost production the marginal products of any two resources must be proportional to their prices. In the following two sections we will demonstrate, first, the procedure for determining MP_L/MP_K and, second, the procedure for determining p_L/p_K. Then we will set the two ratios equal to determine the lowest-cost combination of the two resources.

The Ratio of Marginal Products

Marginal product is the change in total product that results from a change in one resource, all others held constant. The marginal products of two resources are shown graphically as the slope of the isoquant derived from their production

---

2. The equal marginal product principle is similar to the marginal utility comparisons used in Chapter 2 to explain a consumer's choice of goods and services. The equal marginal product principle is simple to understand intuitively. If one resource costs twice as much as another, for instance, its marginal product should also be twice as much. If a resource costs one-tenth as much as another, its marginal product should also be one-tenth as much as the other.

function for any quantity of output: slope $= MP_L/MP_K$, where the resource on the horizontal axis provides the numerator. We know this because for any small segment along a given isoquant, its slope is $\Delta K/\Delta L$. Moreover, by definition

$$MP_K = \frac{\Delta Q}{\Delta K}$$

and

$$MP_L = \frac{\Delta Q}{\Delta L}.$$

Rearranging terms yields:

$$MP_K(\Delta K) = \Delta Q$$

and

$$MP_L(\Delta L) = \Delta Q.$$

Since along any isoquant ΔQ is zero, it must be true that

$$MP_K(\Delta K) - MP_L(\Delta L) = 0.$$

Therefore,

$$MP_K(\Delta K) = MP_L(\Delta L)$$

and

$$\frac{MP_L}{MP_K} = \frac{\Delta K}{\Delta L} = \text{the slope of the isoquant.}$$

The ratio of marginal products associated with a particular isoquant is called the **marginal rate of technical substitution** (*MRTS*):

$$MRTS \text{ of capital for labor } (MRTS_{KL}) = \frac{MP_L}{MP_K}.$$

The $MRTS_{KL}$ measures the substitutability of capital for labor to produce a given quantity of output. The *MRTS* of any one resource for another tends to be greater the larger the quantity of that resource. Larger quantities of that resource may be removed from any resource combination in return for smaller quantities of the other, scarcer, resource.

Look again at the isoquants in Figure 7.3a. Note that the slope MP_L/MP_K differs along different segments of the isoquant, decreasing as larger quantities of labor are combined with smaller quantities of capital. This is due to the principle of decreasing marginal rate of technical substitution. When resource combinations include relatively small amounts of labor, labor's marginal product is relatively high and the slope of the isoquant is more vertical. On the other hand, larger amounts of labor generally mean that labor's marginal product is relatively low (according to the principle of decreasing marginal product) and the isoquant is more horizontal.

The marginal rate of technical substitution associated with a particular isoquant can be derived from the production function used to graph the curve. First, calculate the marginal products of both resources. Mathematically, marginal product is the first derivative of the total product function and is determined through the use of calculus. For a power function of the form $Q = aL^bK^c$, the marginal product of labor is the partial derivative of the function with respect to the variable resource labor. Thus,

$$\text{Marginal product of labor} = \frac{\partial Q}{\partial L} = MP_L = (b)(a)(L)^{b-1}K^c = baL^{b-1}K^c.$$

Similarly, the marginal product of capital is the partial derivative of the function with respect to capital:

$$\text{Marginal product of capital} = \frac{\partial Q}{\partial K} = MP_K$$
$$= (c)(a)(L)^b(K)^{c-1} = caL^bK^{c-1}.$$

The ratio of marginal products is

$$\frac{MP_L}{MP_K} = \frac{baL^{b-1}K^c}{caL^bK^{c-1}} = \frac{bK}{cL}.$$

That is, the ratio of marginal products is the ratio of the elasticities of production for the two resources, each multiplied by the quantity of the other resource.

Using the above ratio, we find that at point A on the isoquant representing $Q = 60$, the marginal rate of substitution of capital for labor is

$$MRTS_{KL} = \frac{bK}{cL} = \frac{.3(80)}{.7(100)} = .34.$$

For this combination of resources, the marginal product of labor is .34 times the marginal product of capital. The $MRTS_{KL}$ at point B is smaller ($bK/cL = .3(40)/.7(500) = .03$), since the larger quantity of labor and smaller quantity of capital implies a smaller marginal product of labor. What is the $MRTS_{KL}$ at point C?[3]

---

3. $.3(50)/.7(300) = .07$.

The Ratio of Resource Costs

Selecting the most efficient combination of resources requires a consideration of resource costs: p_L/p_K. Resource costs are represented on a graph by a line drawn with slope p_L/p_K for any given level of total cost. The numerator is the cost of the resource plotted on the horizontal axis, and the line is called an **isocost line.**

An isocost line has been drawn in Figure 7.3b. The isocost line shows all combinations of L and K that would require a given level of total cost. Thus,

$$K(p_K) + L(p_L) = TC.$$

Since, TC, p_K, and p_L are constant at all points along the isocost line, it must be true that

$$\Delta L(p_L) - \Delta K(p_K) = \Delta TC = 0.$$

Rearranging terms yields:

$$\Delta L(p_L) = \Delta K(p_K) \text{ and } \frac{p_L}{p_K} = \frac{\Delta K}{\Delta L} = \text{the slope of the isocost line.}$$

The isocost line in Figure 7.3b is drawn for total cost of $TC = 5,000$. The cost of capital resources is $p_K = 100$ and the cost of labor resources is $p_L = 20$. Therefore, the isocost line has a slope of $p_L/p_K = 20/100 = 1/5$. The line is drawn between points on the horizontal and vertical axes representing the maximum quantities of both resources that would exhaust the entire budget by themselves. Thus, for $TC = 5,000$ the maximum quantity of capital resources is $TC/p_K = 5,000/100 = 50$ and the maximum quantity of labor resources is $TC/p_L = 5,000/20 = 250$. Isocost lines for larger total budgets would be drawn farther to the right, but they would have the same slope as the isocost line drawn in Figure 7.3b: that is, $p_L/p_K = 1/5$.

The Lowest-Cost Combination

The lowest-cost combination of resources for producing a given quantity of output is represented by a point on that isoquant at which the slope of the isoquant (MP_L/MP_K) is equal to the slope of the isocost line (p_L/p_K) (where both numerators refer to the resource on the horizontal axis). Hence, setting the price ratio equal to the ratio of marginal products yields:

$$\frac{MP_L}{MP_K} = \frac{bK}{cL} = \frac{.3K}{.7L} = \frac{20}{100} = \frac{p_L}{p_K}.$$

Computing for L yields:

$$\frac{.3K}{.7L} = \frac{1}{5}$$

and

$$L = 2.14(K).$$

That is, the lowest-cost combination of capital and labor should be that combination in which the ratio of their quantities is $L/K = 2.14$. Stated differently, the quantity of labor should be 2.14 times the quantity of capital.

The quantities of labor and capital for producing 60 units of output now can be determined by substituting $L = 2.14(K)$ and $Q = 60$ in the production function:

$$Q = aL^bK^c = .7(2.14K)^{.3}K^{.7} = 60.$$
$$= (.88)(K^{.3})(K^{.7}) = 60 = K = 68.22.$$

Solving for L gives us

$$L = 2.14(68.22) = 146.$$

The combination $L = 146$ and $K = 68.22$ is the lowest-cost combination of resources for producing 60 units of output. It is the point on the isoquant for $Q = 60$ at which $MP_L/MP_K = p_L/p_K$. The total cost of production at this point is determined by substituting quantities of L and K in the total cost equation. Thus,

$$TC = L(p_L) + K(p_K) = (146)(20) + (68.22)(100) = \$9,741.93.$$

This solution can be interpreted in terms of Figure 7.4 on page 230. First, select the isoquant for the desired quantity of output, $Q = 60$. At every possible combination of resources, the slope of the isoquant is equal to the ratio of marginal products MP_L/MP_K, where the marginal product of the resource on the horizontal axis provides the numerator. Relative prices are shown by an isocost line with slope p_L/p_K, where the price of the resource on the horizontal axis provides the numerator. The lowest-cost combination of labor and capital for producing $Q = 60$ is identified at a point on the isoquant at which its slope is equal to the slope of an isocost line with slope $p_L/p_K = 1/5$. The isocost line that touches the isoquant for $Q = 60$ is the one for a budget of $9,741.93.

When resource prices and elasticities of production are known, it is easy to express the most efficient combination of resources in terms of a ratio and substitute this value in the production function for any desired quantity of total output. Once the quantity of one resource is determined, the quantity of the other can be determined through substitution in the original ratio. These equa-

FIGURE 7.4   The Lowest-Cost Combination of Resources

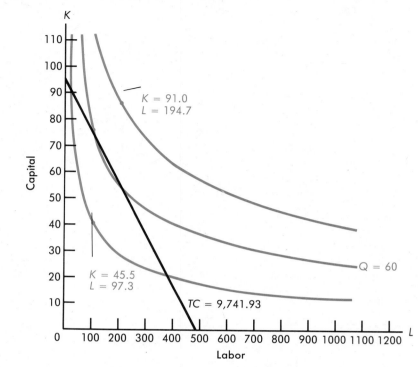

The lowest-cost combination of K and L for producing 60 units of output occurs where the slope of the isoquant for $Q = 60$ is equal to the slope of the budget line. The necessary budget for producing 60 units is $TC = 9{,}741.93$.

tions are easy to use and are appropriate for production functions demonstrating increasing, constant, or decreasing returns to scale. The points labeled in Figure 7.4 indicate the most efficient combinations of resources for producing 40, and 80 units, given a price ratio of 20/100 = 1/5 for labor and capital.

Changing the Parameters

Now let us change the circumstances in our example to conform to technical or financial changes in the business environment. A change involving the technical character of production would affect the elasticities of production associated with the various resources. A change involving financial circumstances would be a change in resource prices.

Suppose a technical advancement increases the elasticity of production of capital by 5 percent. Thus, $\epsilon_K = .7(1.05) = .735$. The production function becomes $Q = .7L^{.3}K^{.735}$. Changing a parameter of the production function changes the marginal rate of technical substitution to

$$MRTS_{KL} = \frac{MP_L}{MP_K} = \frac{bK}{cL} = \frac{.3K}{.735L}.$$

On a graph of the production function, the isoquants would become more horizontal. That is, smaller quantities of capital could be exchanged for larger quantities of labor without affecting total product.

Next assume a corresponding 5-percent increase in the cost of capital resources: $p_K = 100(1.05) = 105$. This price change alters the slope of the isocost line according to $p_L/p_K = 20/105$. With a higher cost for capital resources, the isocost line also becomes more horizontal.

Now let us determine the lowest-cost combination of resources for producing $Q = 60$ units. As we have demonstrated, the slope of the isoquant for $Q = 60$ must be equal to the slope of the isocost line. The slopes are equal when

$$MRTS_{KL} = \frac{MP_L}{MP_K} = \frac{p_L}{p_K} = \frac{.3K}{.735L} = \frac{20}{105}.$$

Cross multiplying yields:

$31.5K = 14.7L$ and $K = .47L$.

For $Q = 60$, the production function now becomes

$60 = .7L^{.3}(.47L)^{.735}$.

Combining terms yields:

$60 = .7(.57)L^{.3}L^{.735} = 150.08 = L^{1.035}$.

Thus, $L = 126.69$. Now, substituting this value to determine K gives us

$K = .47(126.69) = 59.54$.

The increased elasticity of production for capital reduces the resource requirements for both resources.

What is the effect of this change on total costs? For $p_L = 20$ and $p_K = 105$, total costs become

$TC = L(p_L) + K(p_K) = 633.45 + 6{,}251.70 = \$6{,}885.15$.

The cost savings is $\$9{,}741.93 - 6{,}885.15 = \$2{,}856.78$.

Note also the effect of improved capital resources on average costs. Before the technical advance, for $Q = 60$ and $TC = \$9,741.93$, average cost was $ATC = TC/Q = \$162.37$. After the technical advance, $ATC = \$6,885.15/60 = \$114.75$.

DETERMINING MAXIMUM OUTPUT WITH A COST CONSTRAINT

Let us change the circumstances in our example once again and assume that our objective is to maximize the quantity of output produced within the constraint of a fixed budget. Suppose we have established a budget of $10,000 for the coming production period, and we seek to determine the appropriate quantities of labor and capital resources for achieving maximum total output. For this purpose we will be concerned with the total production function:

$$Q = aL^bK^c = .7L^{.3}K^{.7}$$

and total costs:

$$TC = L(p_L) + K(p_K) = 20L + 100K = 10,000.$$

We know that lowest-cost production occurs where

$$\frac{MP_L}{MP_K} = \frac{p_L}{p_K}$$

or

$$\frac{bK}{cL} = \frac{p_L}{p_K}.$$

Therefore, $.3K/.7L = 20/100$. Solving for K in terms of L yields $.3K = 1/5(.7L)$ and $K = .47L$. Thus, lowest-cost production requires that the quantity of capital be .47 times the quantity of labor. Substituting this value in the total cost function for a budget of $10,000 yields:

$$TC = 20L + 100(.47L) = 10,000$$

so that $67L = 10,000$ and $L = 149.25$ units. Since $L = 149.25$, $K = .47L = 70.15$ units. The use of 149.25 units of labor and 70.15 units of capital would exhaust the entire budget for the coming production period:

$$TC = 149.25(20) + 70.15(100) = 10,000.$$

Total production for the period would be:

$$Q = .7(149.25^{.3})(70.15^{.7}) = 61.59 \text{ units of output.}$$

FIGURE 7.5 **Maximum Output**

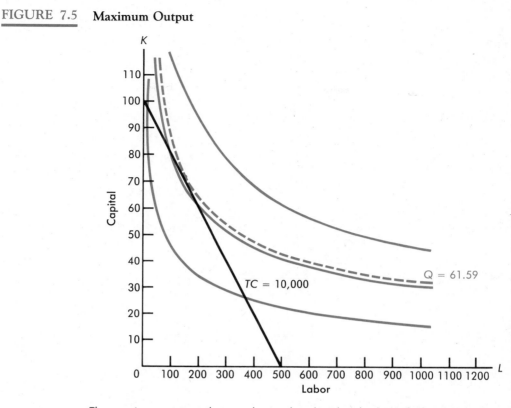

The maximum output that can be produced with a budget of $TC = 10,000$ occurs where the budget line for 10,000 is tangent to an isoquant. The highest isoquant tangent to the budget line is the one for $Q = 61.59$.

This result can be interpreted in terms of Figure 7.5. In this case, the first step is to draw an isocost line at the level of resource use that would exhaust the fixed budget. With a budget constraint of $10,000, total resource employment could be $TC/p_K = 10,000/100 = 100$ units of capital and zero units of labor, or $TC/p_L = 10,000/20 = 500$ units of labor and zero units of capital. In other words, total resource employment could range along a line connecting these values on the vertical and horizontal axes. Such a line has been drawn in Figure 7.5. The point of tangency between this isocost line and an isoquant is the point at which their slopes are equal:

$$\frac{p_L}{p_K} = \frac{MP_L}{MP_K}.$$

The quantity of output (Q) for the isoquant is the greatest output possible within the budget constraint, in this case $Q = 61.59$.

EXAMPLE 7.1   *Making Production Decisions Using a LaGrangian Multiplier*

Maximum output with a cost constraint also can be determined by using the La-Grangian multiplier. To illustrate, consider a firm with a quadratic production function of the form

$$Q = a + b(L) - c(L)^2 + d(K) - e(K)^2,$$

where L and K represent units of labor and capital. The firm's managers have estimated the parameters of the production function, such that

$$Q = 100(L) - .025(L)^2 + 35(K) - .04(K)^2.$$

Prices are $p_L = 3.5$ and $p_K = 1.6$, and the budget is \$5,000, for a budget constraint of:

$$5,000 = 3.5(L) + 1.6(K).$$

In this case, the first step in computing maximum output is to multiply the budget constraint by the LaGrangian multiplier, then add this value to the function to be maximized:

$$Q = 100(L) - .025(L)^2 + 35(K) - .04(K)^2 + \lambda [3.5(L) + 1.6(K) - 5,000].$$

Now take the partial derivatives of the expanded production function with respect to each of the three independent variables:

(1) $\partial Q/\partial L = 100 - .05 (L) + 3.5(\lambda)$
(2) $\partial Q/\partial K = 35 - .08(K) + 1.6(\lambda)$
(3) $\partial Q/\partial \lambda = 3.5(L) + 1.6(K) - 5,000.$

Now set the three partial derivatives equal to zero and solve the system of equations simultaneously. Solving equation (1) for λ yields:

$$0 = 100 - .05(L) + 3.5(\lambda) = -28.57 + .0143(L) = \lambda.$$

Substituting this value in equation (2) yields:

(2) $0 = 3.5 - .08(K) + 1.6(-28.57 + .0143L)$
$= -10.73 - .08(K) + .0229(L).$

Now, multiplying equation (2) by 20 and summing equations (2) and (3) yields:

(2) $0 = -214.60 - 1.6(K) + .458(L)$
(3) $\underline{0 = -5,000 + 1.6(K)\quad + 3.5(L)}$
$0 = -5,214.6 \qquad\qquad + 3.96L$

Hence, $L = 1,316.82$. Substituting the value of L in equation (3) gives us:

(3) $0 = 5,000 + 1.6(K) + 3.5(1,316.82)$

and $K = 244.46$. The optimum combination of labor and capital for maximizing output with the cost constraint is 1,316.82 units of labor and 244.46 units of capital. The cost of this combination is

$$3.5(1,316.82) + 1.6(244.46) = \$5,000,$$

which satisfies the budget constraint.

The maximum quantity of output with the cost constraint is determined by substituting these values in the original production function:

$$Q = 100(1,316.82) - .025(1,316.82)^2 + 35(244.46) - .04(244.46)^2$$
$$= 94,497.24.$$

MANAGERIAL THINKING

Compute the ratio of labor to capital in this production process. Explain how the ratio of labor to capital would change if the price of labor were to rise to 5. How do you account for this result?

A FIRM'S LONG-RUN EXPANSION PATH

Understanding the theory of resource allocation enables managers to plan a firm's growth path for the long run. Examples of typical long-run planning models are shown in Figure 7.6. The isoquants indicate (a) decreasing, (b) constant, and (c) increasing returns to scale. The isocost line indicates a relatively high cost of capital resources: $p_L/p_K = 1/5$. The tangency of the isocost line with the isoquant for Q_1 in each graph represents the level of current production using K_1 units of capital and L_1 units of labor.

Over time, expected growth in demand for the firm's product would move the firm to higher isoquants with larger combinations of capital and labor. This process of growth is shown by the firm's **long-run expansion path**. The long-run expansion path connects points of tangency between all isoquants and isocost lines. Successive tangencies determine the quantities of labor and capital resources that will produce $Q_2, Q_3, \ldots, Q_n$ units of output. The slope of the long-run expansion path reflects the ratio between labor and capital resources and depends on the ratios between the marginal products and the costs of the two resources.

FIGURE 7.6   **Long-Run Expansion Paths**

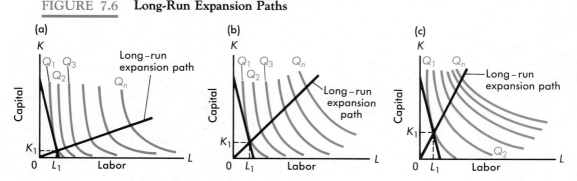

Long-run expansion paths having a labor-intensive production function (a), equal quantities of labor and capital (b), and a capital-intensive production function (c).

RETURNS TO SCALE AND COSTS OF PRODUCTION IN THE LONG RUN

Managers are concerned about scale effects because of the effect of scale on costs of production. Typically, expanding scale to some minimum plant size causes average or unit total cost to fall. Then, increasing scale beyond some level causes average total cost to rise. Over some range of plant size, average total cost may remain constant at the lowest possible level. We might call this range of constant returns to scale the **optimum scale** of plant. Operating a plant of optimum scale at the lowest-cost level of plant operation yields the most efficient production in the long run.

Data on the behavior of costs at various levels of scale may be obtained from trade association journals, or a firm may operate several plants of varying size, using internal cost data to make scale decisions. Long-run average cost data differ from short-run data in that there is no distinction between fixed and variable costs for the long run. Plant, equipment, and salaried personnel that are fixed in the short run can be increased or decreased in the long run. In fact, a firm may confront an entire array of cost data for plants of an infinite range of sizes. Since a firm may choose any one of the corresponding cost curves in the long run, no costs are regarded as fixed. Managers must decide the appropriate level of plant size for satisfying the firm's own profit and market-share goals. (Once this decision is made, however, the firm is back in the short run, with contractual commitments to pay certain fixed costs.)

Graphs of short-run marginal and average costs for plants of various sizes would look like those in Figure 7.7. As the size of plant increases, the higher plant and equipment costs would be shown by beginning the average cost curve at a higher point on the vertical axis. Then, because of the greater productive capacity of larger plants, the average cost curves would decrease over a wider range of quantities. For all plants, the eventual pressure on productive capacity would be shown by increasing marginal and average total cost curves in the short run.

Plant A in Figure 7.7 is designed to produce 250 units per production period. Plant B is designed to produce 500 units, and plant C is designed to produce 1,000. For each plant, average total cost reaches a minimum at the level of production for which the plant was designed. In each case, production at the lowest-cost level of operation involves the most efficient combination of variable labor, materials, and power with the equipment and managerial personnel at that plant.

The cost curves in Figure 7.7 illustrate the effects of increasing and decreasing returns to scale. Compare the short-run cost curves for Plant B with those of Plant A and note that the average total cost for $Q = 500$ is lower than the average total cost for $Q = 250$. This is the range of increasing returns to scale. Further, note that the average total cost for $Q = 1,000$ is higher than average total cost for $Q = 500$. Over this range, decreasing returns to scale appear to offset any further gains from increasing plant size. The optimum scale of plant appears to be the plant designed to produce $Q = 500$ units per production period.

FIGURE 7.7   Increasing and Decreasing Returns to Scale

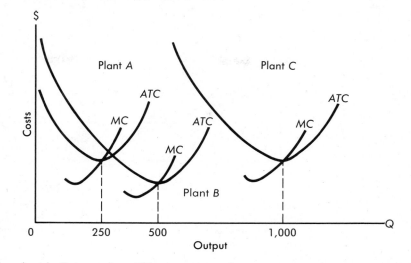

The plant built to produce 500 units per production period experiences increasing returns to scale. The plant built to produce 1,000 units experiences decreasing returns to scale.

Many manufacturing processes display the cost behavior shown in Figure 7.8 on page 238. Figure 7.8 shows that plants beyond a certain minimum size achieve all possible cost advantages. In this case, average cost curves become roughly identical, such that a wide variety of plant size is consistent with lowest-cost production. Figure 7.8 also implies that very large size is possible without experiencing decreasing returns to scale. Thus, optimum scale may vary over a wide range of plant size. This seems to be true for most industries operating in the United States.

LONG-RUN AVERAGE COSTS

Plants of sizes A, B, and C in Figure 7.7 are not the only options for long-run production decisions. In fact, short-run curves such as those in Figure 7.7 could be drawn for plants designed to produce at every quantity shown on the horizontal axis. The result would be a solid array of curves, each typically saucer-shaped and each reaching a minimum at a different level of Q. Every short-run average cost curve would intersect a typical, corresponding marginal cost curve at its lowest point.

An array of average total cost curves is shown in Figure 7.9. Firms with plants designed to produce from $Q = 90$ to $Q = 500$ units per production period experience increasing returns to scale. Plants designed to produce more than $Q = 1,000$ units experience decreasing returns. Between production of Q

FIGURE 7.8   **Constant Returns to Scale**

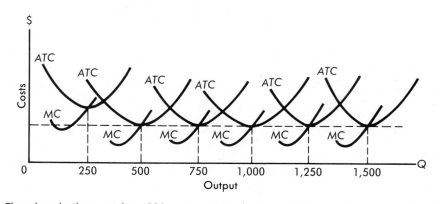

The plant built to produce 500 units per production period experiences increasing returns to scale. The plant built to produce 1,000 units experiences decreasing returns to scale. Plants built to produce quantities greater than 500 units per production period experience constant returns to scale.

$= 500$ and $Q = 1,000$, increasing returns are precisely offset by decreasing returns, and average total cost at the lowest-cost level of plant operation is constant.

Notice an interesting feature of the average cost curves in the range of increasing and decreasing returns to scale. In the range of increasing returns, for example, plants designed to produce $Q = 110$ units can produce $Q = 90$

FIGURE 7.9   **Lowest-Cost Plants**

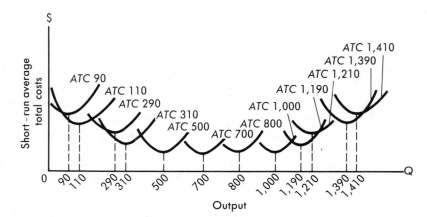

The lowest-cost plant for producing a given quantity of output may not be the plant designed to produce precisely that quantity.

units more cheaply than plants designed precisely for production of 90 units. This is true also of plants designed to produce 310 units. Underutilizing a plant designed to produce 310 units can result in lower average total cost for producing 290 units than would result in using a plant designed to produce precisely 290 units. In the range of decreasing returns, on the other hand, plants designed to produce 1,190 units can produce 1,210 units more cheaply than those designed to produce precisely 1,210 units. And, finally, plants designed to produce 1,390 units can produce 1,410 units more cheaply than plants designed to produce precisely 1,410.

This suggests that lowest-cost production in the short run does not necessarily mean that plants are built at optimum scale and are producing at their lowest-cost level of operation. A firm may achieve maximum profit by operating its fixed plant and equipment at less than or greater than the level of production for which it was designed and charging a price high enough to compensate for higher-cost operation. A firm might choose to operate under these conditions in the short run, in the absence of competition. However, the long run brings the opportunity for new firms to enter the industry and for existing firms to construct new plants. Competition will lead new firms to construct plants of optimum scale: in our example, between $Q = 500$ and $Q = 1,000$ units per production period. *Operating optimum-scale plants at their lowest-cost level yields minimum average total cost in the long run.*

Long-run average cost (*LRAC*) is defined as total cost per unit of output when the quantity of plant, equipment, and salaried personnel can be varied along with other typical variable resources. A firm's *LRAC* curve is the series of points showing the lowest average total cost for producing any given quantity of output during a given production period.[4] Refer to Figure 7.9 and note the lowest average total cost for producing $Q = 90, 290, 500, 1,000, 1,210$, and 1,410 units. These points, together with relevant points for all other quantities of output, have been transferred to Figure 7.10. The points form a smooth curve, labeled *LRAC*. The curve is saucer-shaped, indicating falling average total cost for plants producing larger outputs up to a production level of 500 units per production period. Decreasing average total cost reflects increasing returns to scale between $Q = 90$ and $Q = 500$. Between production of $Q = 500$ and $Q = 1,000$, average total cost is constant, and average total cost increases for plants producing larger quantities. Increasing average total cost reflects decreasing returns to scale for plants producing more than $Q = 1,000$ units per production period.

Long-Run Average Cost and the Scale of Plant

There is a significant relationship between the short-run cost curves in the array in Figure 7.9 and the *LRAC* curve in Figure 7.10 on page 240. Only between $Q = 500$ and $Q = 1,000$ are the points transferred from Figure 7.9 associated

---

4. A curve defined in this way is called an "envelope" curve.

FIGURE 7.10   **Short-Run and Long-Run Average Total Costs**

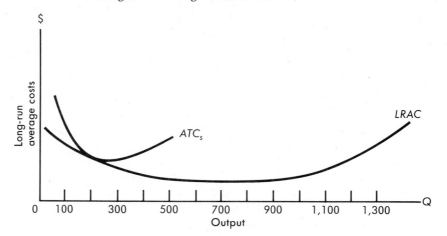

with lowest-cost level of operation for the plant. Only for plants designed to produce at optimum scale is the lowest-cost quantity in the short run relevant for long-run production decisions. In practical terms this means that:

1. *When a very small quantity is to be produced, plants should be built to produce a larger quantity and operated at less than the lowest-cost level of output.* Look again at Figure 7.9 and the short-run average cost curve associated with $Q = 90$ units per production period. If the market for this good or service is so small as to require only 90 units, production can never achieve maximum efficiency. The market is too small to build a single plant of optimum scale and operate that plant at the lowest-cost level. However, given these circumstances, the most efficient choice would be to build a plant designed to produce $Q = 110$ units and operate it at less than the lowest-cost level of operation. This would yield increasing returns to scale and is more efficient than building a plant of smaller size and operating it at its lowest-cost level.

2. *When a very large quantity is to be produced, plants should be built to produce a smaller quantity and operated at more than the lowest-cost level of output.* For a market that requires 1,410 units per production period, for example, a single plant cannot achieve lowest-cost operation. However, given these circumstances, the most efficient choice would be to build a plant designed to produce $Q = 1,390$ units and operate it at greater than the lowest-cost level of operation. This avoids decreasing returns to scale and is more efficient than building a larger plant and operating it at its lowest-cost level.

3. *There is some moderate range of output for which plants designed to produce within that range should be operated precisely at the lowest-cost level of output.* Within this range, plants may be built at any scale, achieving lowest average total cost and maximum efficiency.

EXAMPLE 7.2 Using Production Data to Describe the Effects of Scale

Table A lists production data for Zeta Company's three plants. Plant A is the smallest, with fixed plant, equipment, and salaried personnel costing $500 per week. Plant B has twice the fixed resources of Plant A and Plant C has three times the fixed resources of Plant A. Labor is hired in increments of 25 labor-days per week, and total production is listed in the table.

TABLE A

Units of capital	Units of labor (labor-days/week) 25	50	75	100	125
Plant A: 1	95	200	285	350	400
Plant B: 2	100	210	360	450	525
Plant C: 3	105	225	375	530	675

MANAGERIAL THINKING

1. Holding the quantity of capital constant and varying the quantity of labor, plot points for production in each plant and connect the points to form a short-run production function. How would you describe these functions? Which of the following forms would the production equations take: $Q = a + bL$, $Q = a + bL + cL^2$, $Q = a + bL - cL^2$, $Q = a + bL + cL^2 - dL^3$, or $Q = aL^b$?
2. Consider Plant B alone. Compute average and marginal product associated with various quantities of labor for this plant. Describe the relationship between average and marginal product at various levels of employment. Plot average and marginal product.
3. Assume that the production relationships shown here are correct for this industry. How would you describe scale effects for the industry?
4. At a cost of $50 per labor day, draw short-run and long-run average total cost curves for this industry.

Solutions

1. Each of the production functions demonstrates first increasing marginal product, then (briefly) constant marginal product, and finally diminishing marginal product. The form of the production function is $Q = a + bL + cL^2 - dL^3$.

TABLE B

Units of labor	Average product	Marginal product
0	0	
25	4	4
50	4.2	4.4
75	4.8	6
100	4.5	3.6
125	4.2	3

2. Marginal product reaches a peak before average product, decreases and intersects the average product curve at its highest point, $L = 75$.
3. To answer this question, it is necessary to read Table A diagonally from the

upper left-hand corner to the lower right-hand corner. Doubling both capital and labor (from $C = 1$ and $L = 25$ to $C = 2$ and $L = 50$) produces a proportionally larger increase in output (from $Q = 95$ to $Q = 210$). Thus, this industry experiences increasing returns to scale over the range shown in the table.

4. Short-run cost curves are calculated according to $TC/Q = [500(K) + 50(L)]/Q$. After plotting SRAC curves, select the lowest cost for each level of output in order to draw the LRAC curve.

EXAMPLE 7.3   **Using Short-Run Data for Making Long-Run Plans**

Prestige Motor Courts operates highway motor hotels in 15 Southeastern states. Hotel capacity varies from 45 units to 215 units, with fixed and variable costs as shown in the following table.

Number of hotels	Capacity (units)	Fixed costs per day	Variable costs per day w/occupancy:		
			60%	80%	100%
5	45	$ 275	$100	$120	$ 220
3	75	410	160	195	350
8	110	548	205	264	475
5	190	944	265	275	850
6	215	1,233	477	585	1,100

MANAGERIAL THINKING

1. Determine average total costs per day per unit occupied for hotels of every size. For example, in the smallest hotel with 60-percent occupancy unit cost per day is $ATC = (FC + VC)/Q = (275 + 100)/27 = 13.89$. With 80-percent occupancy, unit cost is $(275 + 120)/36 = 10.97$. With 100-percent occupancy, unit cost is $(275 + 220)/45 = 11.00$. Plot short-run cost curves for all of the motor hotels on a single graph. What additional information would be needed to draw a long-run supply curve?
2. What range of motor hotel capacity appears to represent optimum scale? At what level of operation are average total costs lowest?
3. Suppose management is planning to expand to a new market with expected market quantity of 200 units per day. What advice would you provide?

EXAMPLE 7.4   **Deriving a Long-Run Cost Curve**

Once the long-run production function is known, it is a simple matter to measure production costs and construct a long-run cost curve. To illustrate, let us assume that an apparel firm has established its production function in the form of a power function:

$$Q = aL^{1.5}K^{.8},$$

where Q is thousands of units of output per week, L is labor hours in thousands, and K is units of capital resources in thousands per week. The coefficient a is approximately one.

The first step in arriving at a solution is to use the relationship described by the production function to construct isoquants. Recall that an isoquant identifies combinations of resources necessary for producing a certain quantity of output. The production function in this case tells us that 10,000 units of apparel per week can be produced using any of the combinations of L and K in Table A.

TABLE A

With $Q = (1)L^{1.5}K^{.8}$ and $Q = 10$.	Units of K	Units of L
	1	4.6
	2	3.2
	3	2.6
	4	2.22
	5	2
	6	1.8
	7	1.6
	8	1.5
	9	1.44
	10	1.4

These combinations have been plotted and connected to form the isoquant for $Q = 10$ in Figure A. Similar procedures were used to determine the combinations for

FIGURE A

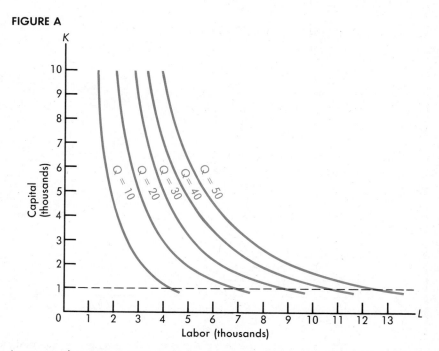

Isoquants showing quantities of labor and capital for producing various quantities of output.

producing 20, 30, 40, and 50 thousand units, and these isoquants also appear in the figure.

Note that isoquants for producing 10,000 more units per week lie closer and closer together on the graph, indicating increasing returns to scale over the relevant range of values of K. Increasing returns to scale are indicated also by the sum of the exponents: $b + c = 1.5 + .8 = 2.3$ which is greater than one.

To show the effect of scale on costs, it is necessary to know the prices of resources. Let us assume that the price of 1,000 labor-hours per week is $p_L = \$5,000$ and the weekly price of capital resources is $p_K = \$10,000$. Short-run cost curves can now be drawn for plants combining various quantities of labor with a fixed quantity of capital. Begin with $K = 1$ in Figure A. The horizontal line at $K = 1$ shows the quantities of labor which, together with one unit of K, are required to produce 10, 20, 30, 40, and 50 units of apparel per week. For $Q = 10$, 4.6 thousand hours of labor are required. For $Q = 20$, $L = 7.4$. For $Q = 30$, $L = 9.7$, and so forth.

Table B shows various plant sizes ranging from $K = 1$ to $K = 4$ and the quantities of labor required to produce from 10 to 150 units of output per week at lowest cost. Total costs for each combination have been calculated according to

$$TC = (L)(p_L) + (K)(p_K),$$

with $p_L = 5,000$ and $p_K = 10,000$. Short-run average costs are calculated by dividing total costs by quantity of output: $ATC = TC/Q$.

TABLE B

	Q	L	TC	ATC	Q	L	TC	ATC	Q	L	TC	ATC	Q	L	TC	ATC
$K = 1$	10	4.6	$33,000	$3,300												
$K = 2$	20	5.1	45,500	2,275	30	6.7	$53,500	$1,780	40	8.1	$60,500	$1,513	50	9.4	$670,000	$1,340
$K = 3$	60	8.5	72,650	1,211	70	9.45	77,250	1,104	80	10.3	81,650	1,021	90	11.2	85,800	954
	100	11.99	89,950	900	110	12.8	93,890	854	120	13.5	97,706	814	130	14.3	101,417	780
$K = 4$	140	12.9	104,361	745	150	13.5	107,400	716								

Larger plants experience higher total costs but diminishing average total costs over the range of economies of scale.

Note that all plants experience decreasing average total costs in the short run as the cost of fixed capital is spread over larger quantities of output. Ten units of output can be produced most efficiently by a plant of size $K = 1$. Quantities ranging from

about 18 units to about 55 units can be produced most efficiently by a plant of size
$K = 2$. Quantities ranging from about 60 units to about 130 units can be produced
most efficiently by a plant of size $K = 3$, and so forth.

Short-run average cost curves for plants of various sizes are shown in Figure B.
Increasing returns to scale are shown where the *SRAC* curve for a larger plant drops
below the *SRAC* curve of a smaller plant. Plant size is determined by the lowest
SRAC for any desired level of output per time period. The long-run average cost
curve is the envelope curve drawn at the minimum total cost for producing each
quantity. The envelope curve includes a portion of short-run average cost curves
from plants $K = 1$, $K = 2$, $K = 3$, and so forth. If K could be varied infinitely (so
that $K = 1.01$, 1.02, 1.03, and so forth), the envelope curve drawn from short-run
average cost curves would be a perfectly smooth curve.

FIGURE B

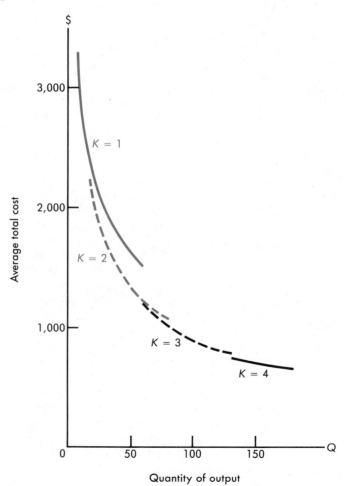

Short-run average total cost curves for plants of various sizes. Average costs are
computed as $TC/Q = [p_L(L) + p_K(K)]/Q$, where $Q = L^{1.5}K^{.8}$.

MANAGERIAL THINKING

Suppose the firm we have just described plans to construct a plant for producing 180 units of output per week. Assume that the relationships defined in the production function remain as given and determine the most efficient plant size: that is, the value of K at which $SRAC$ is lowest for $Q = 180$.

Solution

Solve $180 = L^{1.5}K^{.8}$ for various values of K as shown in Table C and determine average costs according to $ATC = (L)(p_L) + (K)(p_K)/Q$.

TABLE C

K	L	TC	ATC
1	31.88	169,399	941.10
2	22.03	120,137.6	667.43
3	17.74	118,719.8	659.55
4	15.22	116,100.3	645.00*
5	13.51	117,561.77	653.12

Increasing returns to scale favor larger values of K up to $K = 4$ for the production of 180 units per week. However, $Q = 180$ is not sufficient to justify the higher fixed costs of plants larger than $K = 4$, and average total costs are greater.

SUMMARY

In the long run, production decisions may involve changes in resources that are considered fixed in the short run. Changes in all resources may be accompanied by increasing returns to scale, constant returns to scale, or decreasing returns to scale. Scale effects may result from technical circumstances: the indivisibility of certain resources, particularly managerial resources, and the difficulty of precisely duplicating existing resources. Scale effects can also result from financial circumstances such as the possibility of more efficient use of funds in large firms.

The behavior of production can be shown on a graph of isoquants drawn for linear, quadratic, cubic, or power production functions. The most efficient combination of resources for producing any quantity of output is the one at which the marginal products of the resources are proportional to their prices, shown on a graph as the tangency between the isoquant for that quantity and the lowest possible isocost curve. Similarly, the maximum quantity of output within any cost constraint is shown as the tangency between the isocost curve for that budget and the highest possible isoquant. The same information can be gathered through the use of a LaGrangian multiplier. A firm's long-run expansion path connects points of tangency between isoquants and isocost curves; its slope depends on the ratio between the marginal products and the costs of resources.

Long-run cost curves are envelope curves, derived from points on short-run curves drawn for plants of various size. For most industries, increasing and decreasing returns to scale produce saucer-shaped *LRAC* curves. For some industries, constant returns to scale yield minimum average total cost over a wide range of plant size.

When lowest-cost plant size is larger than the size of the market, plants should be built to produce more than the desired quantity and operated at less than the efficient quantity of output. When lowest-cost plant size is smaller than the size of the market, plants should be built to produce less than the desired quantity and operated at greater than the most efficient quantity of output.

KEY TERMS

increasing returns to scale	**elasticity of production**
constant returns to scale	**equal marginal product principle**
decreasing returns to scale	**marginal rate of technical substitution**
technical returns to scale	**isocost line**
financial returns to scale	**long-run expansion path**
isoquant	**long-run average cost**

QUESTIONS AND PROBLEMS

1. Distinguish clearly between decreasing marginal product and decreasing returns to scale. Explain why the two concepts are represented differently on the production "hill" shown in Figure 7.1.

2. List necessary productive resources that are not "divisible" in small-scale production.

3. Write a precise definition for "isoquant." Then, list distinguishing features of isoquants.

4. Compute values for isoquants at $Q = 100$ and $Q = 200$ for the following production functions:
   a. $Q = 2L + 3K$
   b. $Q = 20L - .5L^2 + 3K$.

5. Graph the isoquants computed in Question 4. What are the distinguishing features of each?

6. Vibrant Color Corporation produces dyes for use in the textile industry. Each color is rated on a tone-scale from zero to ten according to its intensity. Higher values indicate richer colors. The firm's chemists have calculated that color intensity depends on the use of two ingredients according to

the following formula: $Y = .5C_1^{.3}C_2^{.4}$, where C_1 is units of the first chemical per 100 gallons of dye and C_2 is units of the second per 100 gallons of dye, both in the range 0 to 70 units. Y is color intensity.

  a. What is the elasticity of production of C_1? Explain the significance of this value. How would you describe scale effects in this production process? Explain your answer.

  b. Suppose the available quantity of C_2 is fixed at 25 units. What is the marginal product of a change in C_1 from 15 to 16 units? Reverse these conditions and determine the marginal product of a change in C_2. Explain the difference in results.

  c. Write an equation for the average product per unit of C_1 and per unit of C_2.

  d. Suppose the price of C_1 is twice that of C_2. What is the least-cost combination of chemicals to yield a color intensity rating of 5?

7. The Standard Chemical Company can produce a unit of its Standard floor cleaning fluid using the following combinations of materials:

Combination	Chemical 1	Chemical 2
A	.9 litres	.32 litres
B	.8	.35
C	.5	.5
D	.3	.65
E	.1	.85

  a. Construct an isoquant describing this relationship. Verify that it has the characteristics typically associated with isoquants.

  b. What is the slope of the isoquant between combinations A and B?

  c. Suppose Chemical 1 sells for $1.00 per unit and Chemical 2 sells for $2.50 per unit. What is the least-cost combination for producing the fluid? Demonstrate computation of the least-cost combination graphically.

  d. Would you expect this process to involve increasing, constant, or decreasing returns to scale?

8. Texas Power and Light Company uses oil and natural gas to produce electricity. Current production is 3.25 billion KWH per week sold at a price of 5¢ per KWH. Power production can be described by the production function $Q = .09Z^{.58}G^{.1021}$, where Q = quantity in KWH, Z = thousands of barrels of oil, and G = thousands of cubic feet of natural gas. Oil had been selling at $13.50 a barrel and gas had been selling at $3.50 per thousand cubic feet until 1980 when Mexican suppliers of natural gas raised their price from $3.50 to $4.50. Determine the least-cost combination of fuels for supplying the market with electric power before and after the price change.

9. Refer again to the data in Question 8. Compute total costs of producing

3.25 billion KWH per week before and after the price change. What is TPL's economic profit under both cost conditions?

10. Case study 5.1 uses the production function $Q = 1.3C^{.48}H^{.35}$ to describe percentage production of amide, where C = degrees centigrade and H = hours of processing. The costs of processing are p_C = \$3.80 and p_H = \$21.00. Suppose the firm has set a budget of \$750 and determine the percentage of amide yield within the budget constraint. Explain the basis for your answer.

11. Heavy rain and hot weather for AgriCorp's soybean acreage has promoted the growth of insects and fungus. AgriCorp has budgeted \$3,000 per acre to treat its fields against further infestation. Farm Chemical Co. has agreed to supply products C150 and F40 at prices of \$17.50 and \$21.90 per hundred pounds. The effectiveness rate of the two chemicals is described in terms of quadratic equations in which the independent variable is 100 pounds applied per field:

$$\text{Effectiveness rate of C150} = 50(C150) - .03(C150)^2$$

and

$$\text{Effectiveness rate of F40} = 75(F40) - .05(F40)^2.$$

Determine the lowest-cost combination of the products to use.

12. Dakota Grain Corporation estimates production per acre according to a power function $Q = 1.15 \, N^{.75}P^{.37}$, where Q is hundreds of bushels of wheat and N and P represent hundreds of pounds of nitrogen and phosphorous applied per cultivated acre. Nitrogen and phosphorous sell for \$12.15 and \$13.50 per 100 pounds, respectively, and Dakota has established a \$50 budget per acre. Determine the lowest-cost combination of fertilizers and the corresponding output per acre.

13. Vego-Products, Inc. estimates that each percentage increase in labor-hours per week increases crop production by 0.6 percent and each percentage increase in farm equipment increases production by 0.5 percent. Last season, the use of 3.7 thousand labor-hours and 2.1 thousand equipment hours yielded 210 bushels per acre. Assume production follows the form of a power production function and write an equation for Vego-Products' total output. Current labor and equipment costs are \$7.50 and \$13.50 an hour, respectively. Calculate the cost per bushel and the lowest-cost combination of resources for producing 210 bushels.

14. HiHo Beverage Company uses sugar and corn sweetener in its soda pop. High world demand pushed sugar prices to \$2.60 per 5-pound bag in 1985, making corn sweetener at \$7.30 a gallon more economical for some purposes. Company chemists describe the sweetness of their cola with the

equation $I = S^{.27}C^{1.9}$, where I is the sweetness factor, S is pounds of sugar per 100 parts liquid, and C is gallons of corn sweetener per 100 parts liquid. The minimum sweetness factor acceptable to consumer tastes is $I = 10$. What is the lowest-cost use of S and C to accomplish this requirement?

15. Trufine Products estimates its production function according to the following equation:

$$Q = 5(L) + .2(L)^2 - .02(L)^3 + 2(K) + .5(K)^2,$$

where Q = units of output per week, and L and K thousands of units of labor and capital respectively employed per week. The prices of labor and capital are $p_L = 800$ and $p_K = 1,000$ per week. Draw short-run average cost curves for plants of sizes $K = 1$, $K = 2$, and $K = 3$, using $L = 5$ through $L = 13$. What conclusions can you draw about returns to scale in this industry? Draw a long-run average cost curve. What size plant should be built to produce $Q = 45$, $Q = 50$, $Q = 55$, $Q = 60$, and $Q = 65$ units per week?

16. First Class Auto Maintenance Company is planning to construct new facilities to meet expected demand of 265 auto service jobs per month. Plants of two sizes are being considered, varying in quantity of capital. Total costs are estimated according to a power function of the form $TC = 1.37L^{.7}K^{1.1}$ for the smaller plant and $TC = 2.58L^{.4}K^{1.3}$ for the larger plant. If each service job requires an average of 3.5 units of labor and 5.0 units of capital, determine the optimum plant size.

8

Long-Run Competitive Equilibrium and Long-Run Supply

Economic theory for the short run is essentially static. It takes as given the fundamental pattern of consumer demand, the productive capacity of existing firms, and the existing supplies of fixed resources. In the short run, managers of business firms make marginal changes in quantity of output, with the objective of maximizing profit (or minimizing loss) with their existing productive capacity.

In the short run, production may yield positive or negative economic profit for a firm. Continuing economic profit, however, depends on the "structure" of the industry in which the firm operates. Industry structure refers to the number and size of firms and, consequently, the degree of competition or **market power.** When there is competition, positive economic profit serves as a signal for existing firms to expand productive capacity and for new firms to enter the industry. Negative economic profit (or loss) is a signal to reduce productive capacity or leave the industry. Through adjustments like these, a competitive industry moves toward long-run competitive equilibrium.

Long-run competitive equilibrium is a condition in which the following circumstances are true:

1. There are precisely enough firms in a particular industry to satisfy market demand at prices that precisely offset full unit costs of production, including normal profit. Changes in productive capacity in the industry affect industry supply, so that market price rises or falls, finally coming to equal average total cost. In long-run competitive equilibrium, economic profit is zero.

2. Firms build plants large enough to achieve all technical and financial returns to scale but not so large as to experience decreasing returns. Thus, industry output is produced with the least sacrifice of scarce resources.

We would describe these results as *efficient*. **Efficiency** occurs when the maximum quantities of desired goods and services are produced at the lowest possible average total cost.

Competition forces firms to make these kinds of adjustments in the long run. Without competition, a firm may enjoy the power to set price and continue to collect economic profit. Power to set price may be achieved through a firm's manipulation of market forces or through government policies that regulate a firm's pricing and output policy. Whatever its source, market power can interfere with movement toward long-run competitive equilibrium and reduce the efficiency of production.

In this chapter we will describe the process by which firms in a competitive industry move toward long-run competitive equilibrium. Then we will discuss competitive industry supply in the long run. Long-run industry supply curves vary among industries according to long-term trends in costs of production. We will begin our discussion with a further look at the airline industry.

The airline industry was opened to competition in 1978 when it was deregulated by the federal government. Long-run adjustments in the industry illustrate the typical response of competitive firms to short-run economic profit or loss.[1]

In the chapters that follow, we will explore the process of determining price and output policy in markets characterized by various degrees of market power.

FROM THE SHORT RUN TO THE LONG RUN IN COMPETITION

Our emphasis thus far in this text has been on the responses of competitive firms to changes in the economic environment. We have identified the significant cost variables for making production decisions in the short run. We showed that the profit-maximizing firm chooses the quantity of output for which marginal cost is equal to marginal revenue (or price). This means that a part of a competitive firm's marginal cost curve becomes its supply curve in the short run. In fact, the competitive firm's supply curve is the increasing portion of marginal cost (MC) above average variable cost (AVC).

The sum of individual supply curves for all firms in an industry is industry

---

1. In microeconomic theory, all firms in a competitive industry have identical technologies and identical cost curves. These characteristics are not true of the air travel industry, as will be pointed out in Case Study 8.1 and the sections of Chapter 8 that follow it. The case study is presented to illustrate the more realistic circumstances in which firms actually make production decisions and the diversity of scale that may result in the long run.

CASE STUDY 8.1   The Air Travel Industry Approaches Long-Run Competitive Equilibrium

Developments in the air travel industry since deregulation have been a nearly classic example of movement toward long-run competitive equilibrium. Like most periods of adjustment, this one has produced both pleasure and pain for managers of affected firms. Deregulation has probably made airline service *more efficient* in the sense that the service is produced only if the benefits it provides its customers justify its cost. However, deregulation has probably made airline service *less convenient* in the sense that many services are no longer profitable in the newly competitive environment and, therefore, are not provided.

When airline deregulation was first proposed, opponents worried about the effect of deregulation on air service to small towns. Naturally, small towns enjoyed the prestige of being on an airline's trunk route, but there were also economic benefits. Travel stopovers meant increased business for local merchants and service workers. Moreover, the assurance of dependable air service encouraged business firms to invest locally, providing jobs in the community and increasing local tax revenues. Some air travelers worried that competition would force the airlines to focus their attention more fully on "bottom line" profits and withdraw service from unprofitable routes.

"Not to worry," replied economists. "Allow the market to operate," they said, "and the result will be a level of service in each community at which the benefits are sufficient to justify the costs. What's more," they said, "in the long run, firms will adjust their capital and labor resources to provide the desired service at minimum cost. Competition will ensure that prices fall to the lowest level possible to cover costs, including the payment of normal profit to stockholder/owners of airline firms."

Long-run competitive equilibrium may be achieved quickly in the air travel industry. This is due to the ease of reducing, or re-allocating, productive capacity for air travel firms. Terminal buildings are stationary, of course, but wide-bodied jets can be routed to serve any major airport. Mid-sized jets and surplus equipment can be sold easily to smaller airlines or refitted for cargo transport in other countries.

Expanding air transport capacity, however, may be more difficult. Replacing old, fuel-inefficient planes with modern, efficient ones requires billions of dollars of new capital investment. New investment expenditures depend on earnings. Earnings are needed to pay interest and principal on new bank loans, to pay dividends to new stockholders, or to provide funds for new purchases. In a highly competitive environment, earnings may be scarce. Some airlines may find leasing planes a more practical means of expansion that avoids the large outlay associated with a major capital investment. Other airlines, though, may be forced to reduce capacity and cut service to all but the most profitable routes.

Ultimately, the structure of the air travel industry will most likely adjust to accommodate consumer demand for various types of service. Some firms can be expected to concentrate on commuter routes and adapt their capital and labor resources to flying short distances efficiently. With low fixed costs, small-scale commuter lines will be able to adjust supply quickly to changes in service demand.

Other firms can be expected to concentrate on medium or large-scale operations, flying regional or cross-country routes. The larger quantities of fixed resources inherent in these operations will be costly and will require intensive utilization to keep average total cost down. Competition throughout the market will probably rule out the emergence (or survival) of giant firms that provide all types of air service. Without the benefits of cross-subsidization, such firms will not be able to compete with commuter lines on short-haul routes. On trunk routes, intense competition for passengers will force price below the level of average total costs for highly capital-intensive firms. Finally, many giant firms will find coordinating policy and adapting to change increasingly difficult, causing their operations to lose efficiency.

Each of these different types of firms will have different production functions and different short-run cost curves. Each will adjust its level of service to maximize profits—with marginal cost equal to marginal revenue—in the short run. Wherever existing firms collect economic profit, competitors may be expected to enter the industry, pushing price down to the level of long-run average total cost. Many airline firms will use **multi-tiered pricing** to increase earnings: that is, regularly scheduled fares for prearranged travel and discounts for stand-by passengers. Within limits imposed by antitrust legislation, small and medium-sized firms may be allowed to coordinate ticketing and baggage handling in order to improve efficiency. In this way, smaller firms working together can compete successfully with the large trunk lines.

As you read this chapter, think about the kinds of decisions managers of airline firms were forced to make because of deregulation. Consider the effect of competition on economic profit in the short run, and imagine how firms will begin to adjust their fixed resources to achieve minimum average total cost in the long run. Try to evaluate particular firms in the context of the microeconomic model of long-run competitive equilibrium. Then ask yourself the following questions:

1. How typical is the airline case as an example of the ways industries respond to change?

2. What circumstances outside the airline firms themselves may be operating to shift long-run average cost curves and upset even the most careful plans of managers?

3. Finally, consider the question of airline deregulation more fundamentally. To what extent are the advantages of a deregulated air travel industry offset by the disadvantages?

To answer this third question, regulated airlines provided the nation with certain services that may not be produced by competitive firms. Cross-subsidization enabled regulated airline firms to provide low-priced service to small communities using the profits earned in larger, protected markets. Not all of the benefits of safe, dependable transportation to small communities are measurable, however. This means that they may not be included in managers' decisions about airline policy. The costs resulting from a loss of airline service can be devastating for business firms, governments, and individuals in communities isolated by the loss of air transportation.

Another disadvantage of deregulation involves the competitive position of U.S. airlines in relation to foreign airline firms. Many foreign airlines are subsidized and protected by their governments. Government subsidies help protect foreign firms from declines in service demand and help the firms remain in business through economic crises. Often, government subsidies enable firms to provide services at prices below full costs. Without government support, U.S. airlines are more subject to economic crises and more vulnerable to foreign competition.

---

supply in the short run. In a model of competition, all firms are assumed to have identical technologies and identical cost curves. Therefore, the lowest point of the supply curve will be the common shut-down point for all firms, and larger quantities will be supplied for higher prices.

The market for a good or service in the short run is shown graphically in Figure 8.1. Market supply is determined by finding the sum of the quantities supplied by all firms and plotting the total quantity associated with each price. Likewise, market demand is determined by finding the sum of quantities demanded at all prices. Equilibrium quantity and price are determined by the intersection of market supply and demand at Q_m and p_m.

FIGURE 8.1   Demand and Supply

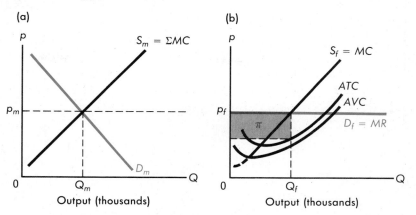

Market supply is the sum of individual firms' short-run supply curves (a). A firm's short-run supply curve is its marginal cost curve above minimum average variable cost (b). Economic profit depends on the difference between marginal cost and average total cost for the quantity of output in the short run.

The quantity of output produced by each firm depends on the relationship between MC = supply for the firm and the market price p = MR. Figure 8.1b is a graph of an individual firm's MC = supply curve. The firm's profit-maximizing quantity is Q_f, and economic profit is the area of the shaded rectangle. If all firms in the industry have identical cost curves, each would be in **short-run equilibrium** at this level of output, Q_f.

Equilibrium in the short run may involve positive or negative economic profit. In fact, for any price greater than ATC at its minimum, as shown in Figure 8.1b, economic profit (π) is the area of a rectangle with sides (p − ATC) and (Q). Thus,

$$\pi = Q(p - ATC).$$

For any price less than minimum ATC, continued production in the short run depends on the relationship between p and AVC. Price greater than average variable cost will provide some revenue to apply to fixed cost, ensuring minimum loss in the short run.

The existence of positive economic profit has long-run implications for a competitive industry. Economic profit offers incentives to new firms to enter the industry, adding their quantities supplied to total industry supply and shifting the market supply curve to the right. An increase in industry supply is shown in Figure 8.2a on page 256. The rightward shift of market supply pushes the competitive price down, causing existing firms to move down their MC = supply curves and reducing their economic profits. As long as there is economic profit, competing firms will continue to enter a particular industry. Price

FIGURE 8.2   **An Increase in Market Supply**

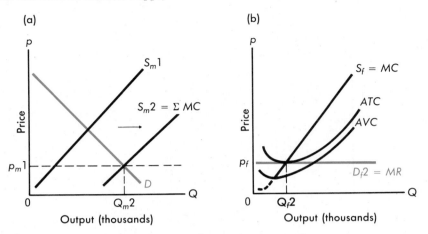

An increase in market supply (a) forces price down until price is equal to average total cost at its minimum point (b). Economic profit is zero.

will continue to fall until economic profit is zero and market price is equal to lowest average total cost. Thus, at this point, p = minimum ATC and $\pi = 0$, as shown in Figure 8.2b. Each firm will be operating at the most efficient level of production, producing Q' units of output.

The opposite adjustments will take place if competitive firms are experiencing negative economic profit or loss. In this event, firms will leave the industry until a leftward shift of market supply raises competitive price to the zero-profit level. With $p = ATC$ at the lowest level of ATC, firms will be operating at maximum efficiency in the short run.

Scale Adjustments in the Long Run

When new firms enter or leave an industry or existing firms make changes in their productive capacity, an important consideration is the appropriate scale of plant. Competitive firms seek to construct plants of optimum scale, given current conditions in the industry. Then, once the scale decision is made, the firm is once again in its short run, with fixed costs that must be paid and a short-run marginal cost curve that serves as the firm's short-run supply curve. The level of plant operation will depend on the current market price, and economic profit (or loss) will depend on the difference between price and average total cost. The shut-down price in the short run is the price that precisely offsets average variable cost.

As short-run contracts expire, existing firms adjust their productive capacity toward a plant size closer to the optimum level. Competition pushes the industry toward long-run competitive equilibrium, with price precisely offset-

FIGURE 8.3   Effects of Competition in the Long Run

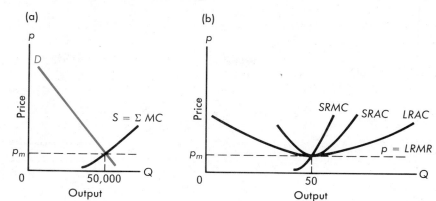

With competition in the long run, the entry of new firms pushes price down to minimum average cost in the short run (a). Moreover, plants will be built of optimum scale, so that price is also equal to long-run average cost and long-run marginal cost.

ting average total costs for all firms and with all firms operating plants of optimum scale. There are no economic profits to encourage new entry into the industry and no short-run losses to push firms out of the industry. In long-run competitive equilibrium, price is equal to long-run average total cost at its minimum point, and the industry is using resources with maximum efficiency to produce the quantity of output consumers want to buy at price $= p$.

Figure 8.3 shows long-run competitive equilibrium in an industry in which $p = MR = MC =$ minimum $SRAC$ (short run average cost) for all firms. Average total cost is at a minimum, not only in the short run but also in the long run. That is, plants have been constructed at *optimum scale* and are operated at the *lowest-cost level of production*. The profit-maximizing quantity of output for each firm is also the most efficient quantity.

The industry represented in Figure 8.4 on page 258 is also in long-run competitive equilibrium, but because constant returns to scale exist over a wide range of plant size, firms need not be of uniform size to be efficient. Firms operating relatively small plants can operate profitably alongside large ones, each in particular markets requiring particular levels of service. This characteristic seems to be true of the air travel industry in the United States.

Long-run competitive equilibrium is not likely to be achieved in a particular industry or, if achieved, to remain stable very long. This is because consumer demand curves shift frequently, and resource prices fluctuate. In addition, advances in technology change the nature of consumer goods and industrial processes. Disturbances in market conditions cause changes in price which, in turn, cause economic profit or loss. For all of these reasons, equilibrium is said to be a *tendency* of free markets rather than a state that actually exists.

FIGURE 8.4   **Effects of Constant Returns to Scale in the Long Run**

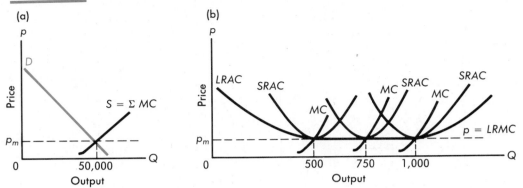

Over the range of output in which production experiences constant returns to scale, long-run average cost curves become horizontal (b). Plants may be built of various sizes, with production at minimum short-run average cost (a).

Scale Effects and Industry Structure

We began this chapter by distinguishing among industries on the basis of their degrees of competition or market power. In this section, we will see that technical factors yielding increasing, constant, or decreasing returns to scale may influence the structure of an industry. In fact, the degree of competition or market power in an industry depends strongly on the relationship between market demand and optimum scale.

Consider first an industry in which demand for its good or service is small relative to the optimum scale. If market demand is too small for firms to achieve the optimum scale, a single firm could produce the entire industry output. This single firm would constitute a **monopoly**, and the price and output decisions of monopoly would apply. If only a few large firms supply the entire industry output, the firms would constitute an **oligopoly**, and oligopoly pricing policies would apply. In both cases, one or a few large firms could operate large plants and produce at lower average total cost than several small firms, each operating small plants to serve small shares of a small market. Industries with very large optimum scale relative to market demand might be made subject to government regulation in order to preclude the exercise of market power.

Figure 8.5 illustrates a market in which the optimum scale is very large relative to market demand. Because of increasing returns to scale over a wide range of plant sizes, many small firms cannot operate efficiently. Indeed, with relatively small market demand, not even a single giant firm can operate with maximum efficiency. In this case, a single firm should build a plant at less than optimum scale and operate it at less than the lowest-cost level of production. Such industries are **natural monopolies**: industries in which resource allocation

FIGURE 8.5   **Number of Plants for Increasing Returns to Scale**

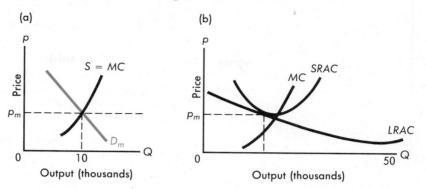

When production experiences increasing returns to scale over a wide range of output, a single plant can supply the market more efficiently than many smaller plants.

is most efficient when there is only one firm in the industry. Natural monopolies in the United States are often subject to government regulation, since there is no competition to ensure maximum output at minimum cost.

Now consider an industry in which market demand is sufficient for many firms to operate plants of optimum scale, but price is higher than minimum long run average cost (*LRAC*) so that the existing firms earn economic profit. Under these conditions, we would expect new firms to enter the market and build plants of the optimum scale to be operated at their lowest-cost level of production. Then price would be forced down to the level of minimum *LRAC*, and economic profit would disappear.

Figure 8.6 illustrates a market in which high *LRAC*, high price, and posi-

FIGURE 8.6   **Number of Plants for Decreasing Returns to Scale**

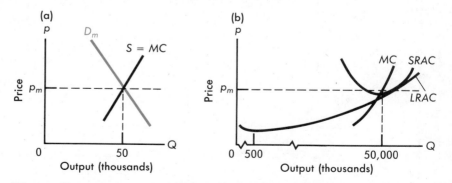

When production experiences decreasing returns to scale, many small plants can supply the market more efficiently than a single large plant.

CASE STUDY 8.2   Returns to Scale and Competition in U.S. Industry

The existence of increasing, constant, and decreasing returns to scale is significant for the structure of U.S. industries. **Industry structure** refers to whether a market is divided among many small firms or a few large firms, or dominated by a single giant firm. Whenever there are significant returns to scale relative to the size of the market, the most efficient level of production can be supplied by a single firm. In this case, competition would disappear. On the other hand, if an industry experiences constant returns to scale, efficient production can be carried out by many firms ranging from small to large, and competition can be vigorous. Finally, if decreasing returns are likely, firms can not be larger than a certain size if they are to be efficient.

Economist John Moroney used Commerce Department data from manufacturing industries in the United States to estimate production functions in each major industrial classification. The regression equation he developed has the form:

$$Q = aL_1^{\,b}L_2^{\,c}K^d,$$

where Q is value added[1] in production by the firm, L_1 and L_2 are production workers and non-production workers (in man-hours and man-years, respectively), and K is the firm's stock of depreciable or depletable assets. The exponents b, c, and d, represent elasticity of production associated with each of the resource inputs.

The sum of the exponents represents the percentage change in total output associated with equal percentage changes in all resource inputs. Thus, a sum of one indicates constant returns to scale. Indeed, Moroney found the sum of the exponents remarkably close to one in all of the industries he examined. Table A summarizes his results:

TABLE A	Elasticity of production for production workers:	Elasticity of production for non-production workers:	Elasticity of production for capital:	Evidence of scale effects:
	b	c	d	b + c + d
Food and beverages	.43882	.07610	.55529	1.07021
Textiles	.54881	.33462	.12065	1.00407
Apparel	.43705	.47654	.12762	1.04121
Lumber	.50391	.14533	.39170	1.04094
Furniture	.80154	.10263	.20458	1.10875
Paper and wood pulp	.42054	.36666	.19723	.98443
Printing	.45900	.04543	.57413	1.07856
Chemicals	.55345	.33626	.20025	1.08996
Petroleum	.54621	.09309	.30783	.94713
Rubber and plastics	.48071	1.03317	.45754	1.05634
Leather	.07597	.44124	.52273	1.03994
Stone, clay, and glass	.63167	.03165	.36592	1.02924
Primary metals	.07734	.50881	.37146	.95761
Fabricated metals	.15110	.51172	.36457	1.02739
Non-electric machinery	.40382	.22784	.38870	1.02036•
Electric machinery	.36796	.42908	.22905	1.02609
Transportation equipment	.74885	.04103	.23353	1.02341
Instruments	.20557	.81865	.01978	1.04420

---

1. Value-added is the difference between the value of a firm's output and the value of inputs purchased from other firms. Thus, value-added is a firm's or an industry's total contribution to national output.

Standard errors were small in each industry, and the coefficients of determination ranged from .95 to .99.

This evidence suggests that scale economies are not significant in U.S. manufacturing industries, and that small firms would be able to operate efficiently in most industries. Only five industries showed significant increasing returns to scale: food and beverages, furniture, printing, chemicals, and rubber and plastics.

Professor Moroney then examined the actual sizes of firms to determine the size variation within each industry. The results appeared to confirm his primary conclusion. Table B compares firms in each industry in terms of value added. Column (1) lists the production of the smallest firms in each industry, and Column (2) lists the production of the largest. Column (3) lists average firm size. The wide differences between columns (1) and (2) indicate substantial opportunities for firms of a wide range of sizes. Thus, there appears to be no single minimum-cost level of scale for most manufacturing industries in the United States.

TABLE B	(1) Value-added in smallest firm (thousands of $)	(2) Value-added in largest firm (thousands of $)	(3) Value-added in average firm (thousands of $)
Food and beverages	191.5	774.6	361.9
Textiles	203.4	2,277.9	827.1
Apparel	88.6	1,013.9	367.2
Lumber	40.6	201.1	85.8
Furniture	85.1	726.9	281.3
Paper and wood pulp	360.7	5,156.9	1,693.3
Printing	134.7	321.5	214.1
Chemicals	365.7	6,414.3	1,410.00
Petroleum	299.1	5,046.7	1,986.4
Rubber and plastics	203.7	6,452.7	1,304.1
Leather	202.0	1,475.9	725.0
Stone, clay, and glass	156.2	575.5	335.8
Primary metals	344.3	9,349.2	2,239.0
Fabricated metals	167.1	645	387.5
Non-electrical machinery	NA	NA	NA
Electrical machinery	NA	NA	NA
Transportation equipment	194.0	5,196.4	2,286.8
Instruments	148	1,528.5	840.3

MANAGERIAL THINKING

Now consider the various markets in which air travel firms operate and the capital requirements of each. What are the implications of this study for the air travel industry?

Source: John R. Moroney, "Cobb-Douglas Production Functions and Returns to Scale in U.S. Manufacturing Industries," *Western Economic Journal*, 1967, vol. 6, pp 39–51.

CASE STUDY 8.3   Scale Effects in the Life Insurance Industry

Life insurance is a major industry in modern, highly developed economies, with annual income representing about 5 percent of Gross National Product in the United States. The importance of the industry to the economy and to the nation's financial sector make efficiency of operations especially critical. Efficiency requires that firms be of optimum scale and operate at lowest cost. Achieving both conditions may depend on vigorous competition in the industry. Healthy competition depends, in turn, on the behavior of long-run average cost for firms of various size or scale.

There may be many opportunities for increasing returns to scale in firms providing financial services such as insurance. Large firms can make greater use of computers for financial analysis and can carry on many management and marketing functions more efficiently than can smaller firms. However, there is still some efficient size beyond which there are fewer opportunities for returns to scale, so insurance firms should not grow to giant size.

Economist D. W. Colenutt analyzed returns to scale in Great Britain's insurance industry to determine the optimum plant size for achieving minimum average costs. Using a cross section of firms in one year, he measured commissions and costs of management as a fraction of total premium income. He called the average cost variable the **expense ratio** and estimated the cost function according to the following equation:

$$ER = a + bX_1 + cX_2 + dX_3 . . . , + 1X_{11},$$

where ER is expense ratio and reflects average cost, a is a constant, X_1 is company size in terms of total annual premium income, and X_2–X_{11} are other company characteristics.

Using regression analysis, Colenutt estimated coefficients for each of the independent variables. He found the strongest negative effects on average cost associated with the following factors: the firm's emphasis on investing premium revenues profitably, the portion of group insurance in the firm's total insurance business, and the firm's size in terms of total annual premium income. A strong positive effect on average cost was associated with having a large portion of overseas business in a firm's total insurance business. Average policy size and the proportion of new business annually had no significant effect on average cost.

Colenutt graphed the equations for average cost and came up with some interesting conclusions:

1. All increasing returns to scale appeared to be achieved at a size of between £20 million and £40 million in annual premiums.[1]

2. Firms of only £5 million annual premiums had only slightly higher average costs than firms of optimum size.

3. There appeared to be no decreasing returns associated with very large size. Figure A is a graph of Colenutt's average cost equation.

With total industry income of £1,224 billion annually, Colenutt reasoned that minimum efficient size could be reached with only 20/1,224 = 1.6 percent of the total life insurance market. This means that many small firms could operate efficiently and that competition could prevail. Two-thirds of the firms in Colenutt's study were smaller than £20 million, but the remaining one-third together earned more than 75 percent of total premium income. This suggests a wide range of optimum plant size in the insurance industry. Thus, restructuring the industry to achieve optimum efficiency would produce only a slight cost reduction.

MANAGERIAL THINKING

1. There are about 1,824 life insurance companies in the United States (1978) providing almost $3 trillion in life insurance and receiving annual income of about

---

1. At the time of Colenutt's study, £1 was equivalent to about $2.40, making the comparable amount in the United States between $48 million and $96 million in annual premium income.

FIGURE A

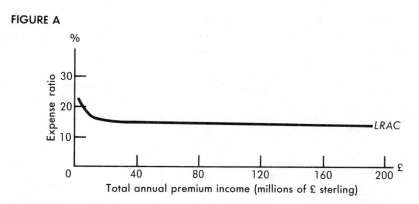

In the life insurance industry, the advantages of large scale appear to end with annual premium income of approximately 20 million pounds sterling.

$108.2 billion. The 50 largest companies provide more than $2 trillion in life insurance annually, and the 10 largest provide almost $1.5 trillion annually. How would you describe the structure of this industry in the United States?

2. Since 1960, the share of the 50 largest companies in total life insurance service has fallen from 83 percent to 70 percent, and the share of the 10 largest has fallen from 59 percent to 47 percent. What are the possible effects of this change on efficiency in this industry? In addition, since 1960 the number of life insurance firms has increased by about 400. Would you expect average costs to rise or fall as the number of insurance firms increases? Why?

Source: D. W. Colenutt, "Economies of Scale in the United Kingdom Ordinary Life Assurance Industry," *Applied Economics*, 1977, vol. 9, pp. 219–25.

tive economic profit serve as a signal for new firms to enter. With market demand of 50,000 units and optimum scale of 500 units, precisely 100 firms could operate plants in this market. Competition would force price down until each firm would be paying all explicit and implicit costs and collecting zero economic profit. Each plant would be large enough to experience all available increasing returns to scale but not so large as to experience decreasing returns.

THE LONG-RUN INDUSTRY SUPPLY CURVE IN COMPETITION

We have considered competitive firms' adjustments to change in the short run, during which certain resources are fixed. In the short run, industry supply is the sum of quantities supplied by all firms in the industry. Market price is established by market supply and demand, and quantity supplied by the individual firm is determined by the firm's marginal cost curve. In the long run, competition causes firms to build plants of optimum scale and operate them at the lowest-cost level of operation. In long-run competitive equilibrium, competition forces price down to the level of average total cost, so that economic profit is zero.

Long-run industry supply includes quantities supplied by all firms after all these long-run adjustments have been made. Long-run industry supply curves have certain characteristics that are determined by the effect of changes in the number of firms in the industry on costs. In many industries, an increase or decrease in the number of firms has no effect on production costs. Movement of new firms into or out of the industry or expansion or contraction of existing firms can be accomplished without causing average total costs to rise or fall. Thus, larger or smaller quantities can be produced at a constant market price. In such industries, the long-run industry supply curve is parallel to the horizontal axis at the price at which $MC = LRAC$.

In other industries, however, an increase or decrease in the number of firms can cause production costs to rise or fall. Changes in production costs shift the position of short- and long-run cost curves and change the quantity that can be produced at each price level. The result is that the industry supply curve slopes up or down. When changes in the number of firms bring changes in average total costs, the industry experiences **external economies** or **external diseconomies of growth.**

External Economies and Diseconomies

Increasing the number of firms in a particular industry can affect production costs for individual firms in either of two ways. Increasing demand for resources used in the industry may cause their prices to rise. Suppliers of materials and component parts may be unable to increase production sufficiently to meet rising demand at constant costs. Their higher production costs cause higher resource prices for firms producing the finished product. The effect of rising resource prices is to cause all of the firms' cost curves to shift upward, raising the firms' shut-down prices and increasing average costs and prices at long-run competitive equilibrium. When this happens, the industry is said to experience **external diseconomies of growth.**

Under other circumstances, increasing demand for resources used in a particular industry may cause the resources' prices to fall. This is true for materials and component parts whose production involves increasing returns to scale. Producing for a larger market enables suppliers of such resources to expand their productive capacity to a size closer to the optimum level, causing their own costs to fall. Greater resource demand might also lead to technical improvements that would contribute to further cost reductions in the production of necessary resources. For firms producing finished goods, the effect of falling resource prices is to shift cost curves downward, reducing the shut-down price and reducing the long-run competitive equilibrium price. When this happens, we say the industry experiences external economies of growth.

FIGURE 8.7   An Increasing-Cost Industry

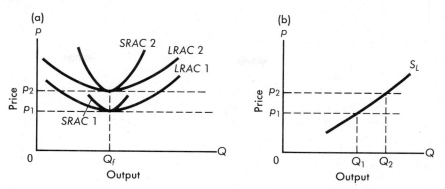

The firm's average cost curves are shown in (a) and long-run market supply is shown in (b). Because increasing the number of firms increases industry production costs (a), larger quantities can be supplied only at higher prices (b).

Industries that experience rising average total costs when growth occurs are called **increasing-cost industries**. Industries that experience falling average total costs are called **decreasing-cost industries**. If a particular industry's tendencies toward rising resource costs are precisely offset by tendencies toward falling resource costs, the industry is called a **constant-cost industry**.

Figures 8.7 through 8.9 illustrate how industry growth can lead to higher average costs, lower average costs, and constant average costs. Summing the minimum-cost quantities for all firms represented in Figures 8.7a, 8.8a, and 8.9a produces an industry supply curve for the long run during which changes

FIGURE 8.8   A Decreasing-Cost Industry

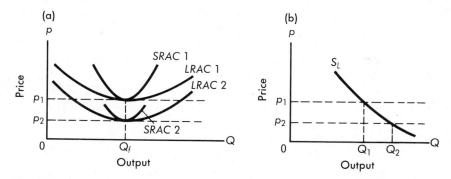

The firm's average cost curves are shown in (a) and long-run market supply is shown in (b). Because increasing the number of firms reduces industry production costs (a), larger quantities can be supplied at lower prices (b).

FIGURE 8.9   A Constant-Cost Industry

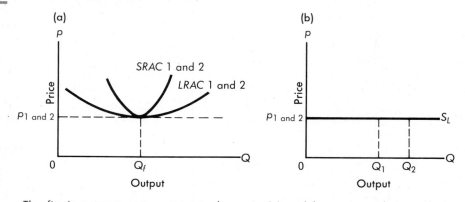

The firm's average cost curves are shown in (a) and long-run market supply is shown in (b). Increasing the number of firms has no effect on industry production costs (a), so larger quantities can be supplied at a constant price (b).

in the number of firms affect production costs for all firms in the industry (these are shown in Figures 8.7b, 8.8b, and 8.9b). In each case, Q_f is the level of production for firms with plants of optimum scale, Q_1 is industry supply at a particular point in time, and Q_2 is a larger quantity that will be supplied after industry growth. In long-run competitive equilibrium, the larger supply is produced by a larger number of firms, each producing the optimum quantity, Q_f, and each subject to higher, lower, or constant average total costs.

An increase in industry supply in the long run is shown as a rightward shift of short-run industry supply curves. When rising resource costs limit the shift in industry supply curves as in Figure 8.7b, the slope of the long-run supply curve rises. When falling costs cause industry supply curves to shift by larger amounts as in Figure 8.8b, the slope of the long-run supply curve moves downward. When industry growth yields no changes in resource costs or technology, the long-run supply curve is horizontal, as is shown in Figure 8.9b.

Elasticity of Supply

These observations enable us to make some useful generalizations about the behavior of industry supply over time. Recall that in competition a firm's supply curve is that portion of its short-run marginal cost curve that is greater than AVC. Market supply in a competitive industry is the sum of all supply curves in the industry, as we showed in Figure 8.1a.[2] Compare the short-run industry supply curves with the long-run industry supply curves in Figures 8.7, 8.8, and

---

2. Long-run supply curves can also be determined by finding the sum of the industry's marginal cost curves, since the lowest point on the long-run total cost curve is also the point of intersection with long-run marginal cost.

8.9. Note especially the responsiveness of quantity supplied to changes in market price. We have referred to the responsiveness of buyers to price changes as price elasticity of demand. The corresponding responsiveness of sellers to price change is called **price elasticity of supply**. Price elasticity of supply is calculated as:

$$\epsilon_S = \frac{\text{percent change in quantity supplied}}{\text{percent change in price}} = \frac{\%\Delta Q_S}{\%\Delta p}.$$

In general, quantity supplied may be expected to change in the same direction as a change in price, making the sign of the elasticity ratio positive.

Elasticity of supply depends strongly on the time frame for which market data apply. In the short run, industry response to price changes is limited by the productive capacity of the plants operated by existing firms. Marginal costs tend to increase as production approaches the technical capacity of fixed plant and equipment. Rising marginal costs cause average costs to increase and lead to rising prices. In such cases, the percentage change in quantity supplied is small relative to the percentage change in price, and supply is said to be relatively inelastic.

In the long run, industry response to price changes is greater, since total productive capacity in the industry can be expanded or cut back in response to short-run economic profit or loss. The responsiveness of producing firms depends on their ability to acquire (or to abandon) fixed resources. When plant and equipment, technical and managerial personnel, and technical licenses are freely available, long-run supply may be relatively elastic. This result is favorable to consumers, since the prices of finished goods in such cases tend to remain fairly stable.

Results are especially favorable when demand increases for the products of a decreasing cost industry. In this case—if production costs decrease with improved technology and increased resource supplies—larger quantities may eventually be supplied at lower prices. The sign of the elasticity ratio is negative when this occurs. An example of negative supply elasticity is U.S. agricultural production, in which the dissemination of scientific knowledge and the development of new equipment have enabled farmers to produce greater total output at lower average cost.

LEARNING CURVES

The behavior of long-run industry supply in a growing industry is often described in terms of a **learning curve**. This name arises from the fact that increasing the level of production in an industry often increases the ability to apply improved techniques throughout the industry. As workers, technicians, and managers "learn" to do their jobs better, productivity tends to increase and average total costs tend to fall.

Learning curves typically take the form of power functions, in which long-run average total cost is a function of the total quantity produced in the indus-

FIGURE 8.10 **Learning Curves**

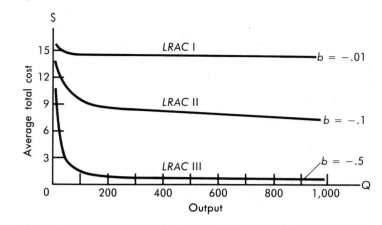

As industry output grows, average total cost declines according to a learning curve :
$LRAC = aQ^{-b}$.

try. A learning curve for a decreasing cost industry would have the form $LRAC = aQ^{-b}$, where a is a constant and b is the percentage change in average total cost associated with a percentage increase in total production for the industry. The exponent b is negative because a learning curve assumes that average total costs decline as an industry grows. When a learning curve is shown graphically, a is the theoretical cost of the very first unit produced and $-b$ reflects the percentage decrease in average total cost associated with percentage increases in production for the industry.

Figure 8.10 shows learning curves for a process in which the cost of the first unit is $a = \$15$. Curves I, II, and III are drawn for percentage cost changes of $b = -0.01$, $b = -0.1$, and $b = -0.5$ respectively. Greater negative values of b imply greater capacity for learning and greater cost reductions as the industry grows.

Learning curves are compared in terms of the **percentage of learning**. Percentage of learning is defined as the percentage cost change that results from a doubling of industry output. Look again at the learning curves in Figure 8.10, specifically at the average costs associated with industry output of $Q = 100$ and $Q = 50$ units. For each curve, the percentage of learning is calculated as:

$$\text{Percentage of learning} = \frac{LRAC\ 100}{LRAC\ 50}.$$

Thus,

$$\text{Percentage of learning I} = \frac{14.32}{14.42} = .99 = 99 \text{ percent},$$

FIGURE 8.11   **Long-Run Industry Growth**

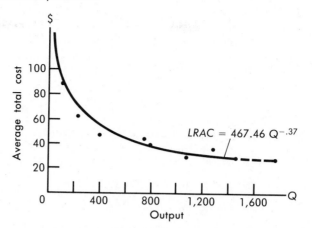

Average total costs for a firm associated with industry growth.

$$\text{Percentage of learning II} = \frac{9.46}{10.14} = .93 = 93 \text{ percent},$$

and

$$\text{Percentage of learning III} = \frac{1.50}{2.12} = .71 = 71 \text{ percent}.$$

The greater the absolute value of b, the smaller the percentage of learning and the greater the decrease in average total cost.

For each of the three learning curves, the greatest absolute cost reduction occurs early in industry growth, where production costs tend to be highest and quantity lowest. As output increases and production costs decline, the absolute cost reduction associated with a doubling of industry output is lower, even though the percentage reduction is the same.

The parameters of a learning curve can be estimated by using a pocket calculator or logarithmic regression techniques (see Chapter 5). To illustrate their usefulness in decision making, let us suppose that a firm is considering entering a new industry whose average production costs have been declining with industry growth as shown in Figure 8.11. Decreasing costs in this case have been the result of newly developed technology, reduced costs of materials and component parts, and increased labor productivity. The greatest gains have occurred in the earliest stages of industry growth, but the percentage of learning is expected to remain roughly the same, and average total costs are expected to continue to decline according to the learning curve. Total production to date is 1,500.

The equation for the cost data in Figure 8.11 is $LRAC = 467.46 \ (Q)^{-.37}$. In theory, the first unit produced would cost $467.46, and average total costs would decline by 0.37 percent for each 1-percent increase in industry output. If the hypothetical firm in our example enters the industry and produces 300 additional units of output, average total costs for the industry can be estimated as:

$$LRAC = 467.46(1,800)^{-.37} = \$29.19.$$

This cost figure has been added to the series in Figure 8.11. To illustrate the use of the learning curve, compute the level of industry output that must occur before production can be carried on at an $LRAC$ of $25.

For $LRAC = \$25$,

$$25 = 467.46(Q)^{-.37}.$$

To solve, raise both sides of the equation to a power of $1/-.37$:

$$25^{1/-.37} = (467.46(Q)^{.37})^{1/-.37}$$
$$= .000166 = .00000006088(Q)$$
$$= 2,737.22 = Q.$$

Thus, total industry output must grow to 2,737 units before production can be carried on with $LRAC = \$25.00$.

CASE STUDY 8.4   Economies of Scale in the Automobile Industry

Over the past several decades, the U.S. auto manufacturing industry has become more and more concentrated. By 1970, three large firms supplied more than 90 percent of the domestic market. Because the auto industry is highly capital-intensive, consolidation was necessary to achieve all the advantages of scale in each individual plant. (A capital-intensive industry is one with a large quantity of capital resources relative to labor resources.) Small auto manufacturing firms merged into giant firms both horizontally and vertically: *horizontally*, when similar firms joined, and *vertically*, when a supplying firm joined with its customer firm. An example of a vertical merger is the merger of a manufacturer of auto transmissions with an auto assembly firm.

Large-scale auto manufacturers were able to distribute the fixed costs of plant, equipment, designers, specialized managers, marketing, and distribution facilities over a larger volume of output, enjoying lower average total costs and higher profits than smaller firms. By 1970, however, the following changes also required a new structure for the U.S. auto industry:

1. *Technological changes* such as the rising price of gasoline caused the need for new fuel-efficient cars. Re-designing plants and equipment to produce these new models cost auto manufacturers billions of dollars.

2. In addition to the demand for fuel efficiency, there were other *human and organizational changes* in the automobile market. Concern for air quality led the federal government to require improved emissions standards in new cars. The decreasing popularity of luxury automobiles also caused many car buyers to purchase foreign-made cars, which were characterized by simpler designs and lower cost.

3. These changes came at a time when the U.S. auto industry was suffering severe *financial problems*. Declining sales meant declining earnings for re-invest-

ment. Inflation and cost-of-living escalator clauses in labor contracts led to skyrocketing labor costs. High interest rates on borrowed funds discouraged new car buyers and increased the cost of capital investment. How could managers justify the enormous sums of "front-end money" needed to make the changes necessary to remain competitive in the face of uncertain markets for U.S. cars?

The three major U.S. auto firms tackled their technical, human, and financial problems by implementing a new global strategy. By expanding production worldwide, the firms expected to achieve greater economies of scale and to serve consumer and industrial markets in more nations. The growth of U.S. auto sales had been slowing in recent years. From sales growth of greater than 10 percent annually during much of the 1950s and 1960s, sales growth had slowed to 2 or 3 percent in the 1970s. The same was true for industrialized nations in Europe. However, U.S. auto makers saw a potentially profitable market in many newly developing nations. Building new plants in these nations meant that a firm could ensure easy, duty-free access to a growing market, increasing sales volume and reducing average total costs. Selling their products around the world made U.S. auto manufacturing firms less vulnerable to domestic recessions and declining sales in any single nation. Global manufacturing also helps create a world-wide pool of technical expertise for servicing automobiles and further improving product design.

Other advantages associated with world-wide production include lower wage rates and the opportunities to exploit resource advantages for producing particular component parts in various nations. Thus, industry expansion caused external economies of scale as well. Many foreign governments expect to enjoy external benefits from industry growth and have offered tax advantages to new auto manufacturing firms. All of these advantages have enabled U.S. auto manufacturers to adjust to the technological, financial, human, and organizational changes they encountered during the 1970s and show healthy profits throughout the early 1980s.

MANAGERIAL THINKING

1. What does this case study imply about the shape of the *LRAC* curve for automobile production?
2. Is the *LRAC* curve likely to change over time? Illustrate graphically the theoretical changes that occur in elasticity of supply for the auto industry as the industry moves toward world-wide production of autos in the long run.
3. What does this case study suggest about the future of small firms in the auto industry? What circumstances are necessary if such firms are to survive in the changing economic environment?

Source: Robert B. Cohen, "Brave New World of the Global Car," and Marina V. N. Whitman, "Automobiles: Turning Around on a Dime?" *Challenge*, May/June 1981, pp. 28–44.

SUMMARY

In long-run competitive equilibrium there are precisely enough firms in the industry to satisfy market demand at prices that precisely offset full unit costs. Furthermore, firms build plants large enough to achieve all technical and financial returns to scale but not so large as to experience decreasing returns. This result occurs as firms enter or leave the industry, increasing or decreasing industry supply, and adjusting plant scale to achieve lowest average total cost.

If market demand is too small for firms to achieve optimum scale, the industry is called a natural monopoly, and production may be subject to government regulation. If market demand is large enough for many firms to achieve optimum scale, competition may be expected to push the industry toward long-run competitive equilibrium. Many U.S. industries can accommodate a large number of firms of differing scale, all with the lowest-cost level of operation.

In competition, the long-run industry supply curve may slope upward or downward depending on whether the industry experiences external economies or external diseconomies of growth. External economies and diseconomies result from changes in resource prices as the number of firms in the industry grows. Elasticity of supply tends to be greater in the long run than in the short run because of changes in productive capacity in the long run. Although elasticity of supply is generally positive, significant external economies can make elasticity of supply negative, so that the long-run industry supply curve slopes downward. A downward-sloping long-run industry supply curve can be estimated through use of a learning curve.

KEY TERMS

market power	expense ratio
long-run competitive equilibrium	external economies of growth
efficiency	external diseconomies of growth
multi-tiered pricing	increasing-cost industries
short-run equilibrium	decreasing-cost industries
optimum scale	constant-cost industries
monopoly	elasticity of supply
oligopoly	learning curve
natural monopoly	percentage of learning
industry structure	

QUESTIONS AND PROBLEMS

1. Mavis Specialty Products Company has the following short-run cost schedule for its deluxe gift packages as shown in the table at the top of page 273.

   Plot Mavis' short-run average and marginal cost curves. Determine the profit-maximizing quantity and economic profit. Then explain the process by which this industry would move toward zero-profit equilibrium in the long run.

2. Refer to the information in Question 1. Suppose production is subject to economies of scale. Show how scale economies would affect the cost data above. What would be the effect on size and output of individual producers in the long run?

3. Use the data in Question 1 to determine short-run price elasticity of supply at the current price. How would you expect long-run price elasticity to be different?

Q_f	FC	VC	TC	ATC	AVC	MC	p = MR
0	100	0	100	∞	0		
						50	75
1	100	50	150	150	50		
						40	75
2	100	90	190	95	45		
						30	75
3	100	120	220	73	40		
						40	75
4	100	160	260	65	40		
						65	75
5	100	225	325	65	45		
						75	75
6	100	300	400	67	50		
						85	75
7	100	385	485	69	55		

4. Explain the significance of scale economies for the level of competition in the nation's industries.

5. Under what circumstances should a plant be built at (a) *less than* or (b) *greater than* optimum scale?

6. The oil crisis of the 1970s increased the use of coal as a source of energy in many parts of the United States, putting payload pressure on coal-transportation facilities. Railroad companies have been merging, and federal regulation of railroads has been relaxed in order to encourage competition. What are some of the possible consequences of these changes in terms of external economies for the coal industry, which moves much of its product by rail? What are some possible consequences for U.S. consumers in markets other than coal?

7. Krypton Electronics is a competitive firm. In 1975, Krypton sold 15,000 Model J-11 calculators at a price of $325. In 1980 the firm sold 35,000 at a price of $195. On the basis of the information given, determine Krypton's long-run elasticity of supply. How do your results differ from results expected in a short-run analysis? What circumstances within the firm and throughout the industry have helped achieve this result?

8. American Home Products Company operates plants in three locations which had cost data during the past year as listed in the following table.

	1st Quarter		2nd Quarter		3rd Quarter		4th Quarter	
	Q (units)	TC (thousands)	Q (units)	TC (thousands)	Q (units)	TC (thousands)	Q (units)	TC (thousands)
A	530	$28.6	570	$29.1	510	$28.0	585	$32.2
B	550	29.2	580	28.4	620	30.4	640	32.6
C	620	31.6	635	33.7	610	31.7	650	35.8

Draw the firm's long-run average total cost curve. Suppose a new plant must be built to produce 570 units per quarter. What size plant should be built? What size plant should be built to produce 630 units? Explain your answers. What long-run adjustments would you predict for this industry?

9. Medical Products Corporation has produced 10 measuring devices at a current unit cost of $80. The firm expects the percentage of learning to be about 60 percent. The theoretical cost of the first unit produced was $500. Write a "learning curve" equation for Medical Products' long-run average cost.

Linear and Geometric Programming

There is one characteristic that most management decisions have in common: scarcity. Materials and labor are scarce, as are machines and the financial capital for acquiring any of these. Solving management problems involves using scarce resources efficiently to accomplish a firm's goals. In general, decisions involve allocating available resources to produce the *most* output at the *least* cost.

Making production decisions efficiently is complicated by the fact that most firms produce more than one product and use more than one resource. Managers must choose the *combination* of products or the *combination* of resources that will yield maximum profit or minimum cost.

Solutions to these kinds of problems depend first on the character of a firm's production function. We have shown that production functions differ in their form (linear, quadratic, cubic, or power) and on whether increasing all resources at the same time yields increasing, constant, or decreasing returns to scale. The tools that we will develop in this chapter are appropriate for *linear* production functions that exhibit *constant* returns to scale: that is, increases in *particular* resources yield constant marginal product, and equal percentage increases in *all* resources yield equal percentage increases in total product.

While few production functions are linear over their entire length, many are linear within a range close to current production. This makes linear analysis appropriate for many planning problems in the short run. The technique that we will describe is called **linear programming**. Linear programming can help managers decide the product or process that will come closest to satisfying a firm's maximum-profit or minimum-cost objectives.

Linear programming is appropriate for production planning when there are several products or processes involved in the decision. Managers must choose the optimum *product-mix* for maximum profit or the optimum *resource-mix* for minimum costs. In both cases, the choice is limited by certain **constraints**. Here are some typical examples of linear programming problems:

1. A bakery has ingredients in stock that can be combined in various ways to produce different foods: Flour can be used for cakes or rolls, nuts can be used for cookies or pies, and fruit can be used for tarts or pies. Given current prices the manager must choose the combination of baked goods that will yield maximum profit.
2. A manufacturer of electronic equipment allocates a portion of its total budget to an expanded marketing effort that includes market research, new product design, advertising, and sales. The manager must decide how the fixed marketing budget should be used to achieve maximum profit.
3. A chemical firm supplies cleaning materials to industrial users throughout the state. Trucks make regular deliveries to the firm's customers. Managers must determine which routes the trucks should follow to serve all of the firm's customers promptly and at lowest cost.
4. A manufacturer of robotics equipment sub-contracts production of certain parts among a variety of small machine shops. Other parts are produced in the firm's own plants where the final product is assembled. Managers must determine the most efficient, lowest-cost method for producing the equipment.

CHOOSING THE OPTIMUM PRODUCT-MIX FOR ACHIEVING MAXIMUM PROFIT

In the following sections we will illustrate the use of linear programming through a simple example: choosing the optimum product-mix for producing maximum profit. First, we will show how a simple linear programming problem can be solved graphically. Then we will demonstrate an algebraic solution for problems with too many variables for a graphical solution. Complex linear programming problems must be solved by computer. Computers are often used by managers because they can perform computations quickly, set aside solutions that are not optimum, and provide other useful information for making more efficient production decisions.

Defining the Problem

The Vita-Pep Drug Company produces a variety of vitamin supplements for a chain of retail drug stores. The products are similar in their use of direct labor and capital, making their overhead costs identical. However, each product uses a different combination of ingredients to meet customers' different health needs. Each day's production depends on currently held supplies of ingredients.

TABLE 9.1

	Necessary ingredients per unit of output		
	A	B	Iron
Multivitamin	2	3	0
Iron booster	1	5	4
	Available quantities of ingredients		
	A	B	Iron
	60	150	80

Thus, the firm's available supplies of particular ingredients limit the quantities of finished goods that can be produced. The goal of production each day is to produce the combination of products that will yield maximum profit for the firm.

Vita-Pep's problem includes the necessary circumstances for solution by linear programming:

1. Production functions are *linear*. Since the formula for each vitamin supplement remains the same regardless of the quantity produced, marginal product and returns to scale are constant.
2. Limited quantities of certain ingredients impose *constraints* on production.
3. The firm's objective is to *maximize profit* within the existing constraints.

Vita-Pep's products are "Multivitamin" capsules and vitamin capsules containing an "Iron Booster." Ingredients on hand include vitamins A and B and iron. The formulas for the two products are as shown in Table 9.1. Production can be carried on only so long as the use of vitamin A $\leq$ 60 units, the use of vitamin B $\leq$ 150 units, and the use of iron $\leq$ 80 units.

The constraints on production can be expressed algebraically, letting X represent units of Multivitamins and Y represent units of the Iron Booster product. Thus, the vitamin A constraint states that 2 times the quantity of X plus one times the quantity of Y cannot be greater than 60 units of vitamin A. The constraint equations are:

$$2X + 1Y \leq 60$$

for vitamin A,

$$3X + 5Y \leq 150$$

for vitamin B, and

$$4Y \leq 80$$

for iron.

Note that the constraints are **inequalities**: total use of an ingredient must be *equal to or less than* available supplies. There is no algebraic technique for solving inequalities simultaneously, but each inequality can be converted to an equality by adding a **slack variable.** In our example, a slack variable is the quantity of the ingredient that would *not* be used when the maximum-profit product-mix is produced. We will use S_A, S_B, and S_i as slack variables for vitamins A and B and iron, respectively. Including the slack variables produces the equalities:

$$2X + 1Y + S_A = 60 \text{ (vitamin A)},$$
$$3X + 5Y + S_B = 150 \text{ (vitamin B)},$$

and

$$4Y + S_i = 80 \text{ (iron)}.$$

The three constraint equations include five unknown variables: two resource variables and three slack variables. There is no unique solution for a series of three equations with five unknowns. In fact, there are many possible values of X, Y, S_A, S_B, and S_i that would satisfy all the equations. Our objective is to identify the one set of values for the five variables that would yield maximum profit.

Graphing the Constraints

The constraint equations we have identified can be illustrated graphically. Figure 9.1 is a graph of the vitamin A constraint in which the two products are plotted on the x and y axes. The constraint line for vitamin A shows all possible combinations of the two products using existing stocks of vitamin A. With 60 units of vitamin A available, the possible product combinations are 30 units of Multivitamins, 60 units of Iron Booster, or any combination of the two products shown by the constraint line.[1] Along the constraint line, all available supplies of vitamin A are used, and the slack variable S_A is zero. Between the constraint line and the axes, smaller quantities of both products might be produced, and the slack variable would be greater than zero.

Figure 9.2 combines the constraint line from Figure 9.1 with the constraints for vitamin B and iron. The vitamin B constraint permits production of 50 units of Multivitamins, and 30 units of Iron Booster, or any combination in between. Since iron is used only in the Booster product, the iron constraint does not limit Multivitamin production. Available supplies of iron permit 20 units of Booster and any otherwise feasible quantity of Multivitamins.

---

1. The equation for drawing the constraint line is determined by solving the constraint inequality for Y. Thus, $2X + 1Y \leq 60$ is graphed as $Y = 60 - 2X$.

FIGURE 9.1 The Vitamin A Constraint

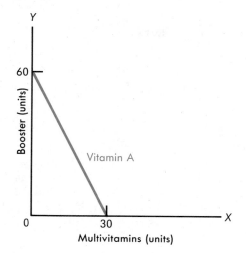

The constraint lines in Figure 9.2 identify all maximum combinations of the two products that can be produced. Where maximum quantities shown on one constraint lie outside other constraints, the quantities shown are not relevant for decision making. This means that only combinations within the shaded area are possible. In fact, only combinations on the heavy border of the shaded space will be considered. This is because a profit-maximizing firm will choose to produce the maximum possible quantities of both products.

You may have noticed that the area of possible production for the vitamin firm resembles production possibilities curves used in introductory economics

FIGURE 9.2 All Possible Combinations of Booster and Multivitamins

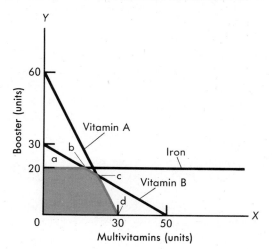

textbooks to describe a nation's total capacity for producing goods and services. Production possibilities for an individual firm depend on the same circumstances that determine production possibilities for a nation: current technology and available resources. Like nations, firms seek to produce the maximum quantities of goods and services possible with their available resources and technology.

A firm's production possibilities curve may differ from the production possibilities curve of a nation in that the curve for the firm may not be smooth, as it often is for nations as a whole. This is due to the assumption of linear production functions for the firm. Production of each of the firm's products requires precise quantities of each of the resources involved. This means that movements along the curve involve abrupt changes in resource trade-offs. The result is a set of "corners." Each angle represents maximum quantities of Multivitamins and Iron Booster producible with the available stock of materials. The following section will show how producing at one of the corners of the firm's production possibilities curve will yield maximum profit.

The Objective Function

In order to select the maximum-profit corner for production, a manager must first state the amount of economic profit associated with units of each of the firm's products. This statement of profit is called the firm's **objective function**, and the manager's goal is to *maximize* the objective function. The objective function for maximizing economic profit in this case is written:

(maximize) $\pi = aX + bY,$

where the coefficients a and b represent economic profit associated with units of Multivitamins and Iron Booster produced, respectively. Unit profit of 25 and 50 for the two products respectively would yield an objective function of:

(maximize) $\pi = 25X = 50Y.$

The objective function for economic profit of $\pi = 1,000$ is shown graphically as the blue line in Figure 9.3. The slope of this profit line is the ratio of economic profit associated with the two products: slope $= a/b$, where the numerator is the unit profit associated with the product on the horizontal axis and the denominator is associated with the vertical axis. (The slope of any straight line between the axes is $\Delta Y/\Delta X$. Since total economic profit is constant at all points on the objective function, any movement along the line produces no change in π. Thus, $(\Delta Y)(b) = (\Delta X)(a)$. Rearranging terms yields: $a/b = \Delta Y/\Delta X =$ slope of the line.)

Profit of 1,000 can be earned through production of $\pi/a = 1,000/25 = 40$ units of X alone, or $\pi/b = 1,000/50 = 20$ units of Y alone, or any combination of X and Y on the black line. Other objective functions could be drawn

FIGURE 9.3 Economic Profit

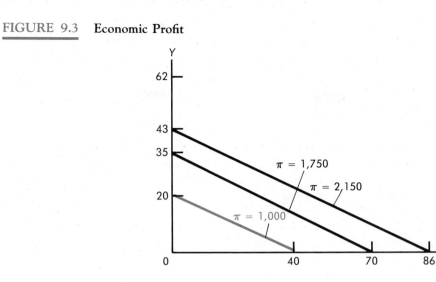

for any other profit level. The goal of the linear programming problem is to locate the corner of the production possibilities space that touches the highest possible objective function.

The Corners

We have established production possibilities within the firm's resource constraints, and we have written an objective function for the goal of maximum economic profit. Now we want to determine the maximum-profit combination of products that can be produced within the firm's resource constraints. Solving the linear programming problem requires a mathematical procedure that grows more complex when the number of products and the number of constraints increase. Most linear programming problems require a computer to solve constraint equations that involve many product variables and slack variables. Our simple example, however, can be solved without this type of help to illustrate the process. Recall that our example includes two products and three constraints that are written algebraically as:

$$2X + 1Y + S_A = 60 \text{ (Vitamin A constraint)},$$
$$3X + 5Y + S_B = 150 \text{ (Vitamin B constraint)},$$

and

$$4Y + S_i = 80 \text{ (Iron constraint)}.$$

The series of three constraint equations has five variables: X, Y, S_A, S_B, and S_i. There are not enough equations to yield unique values for all five variables. In fact, as Figure 9.2 illustrates, the shaded area represents an infinite number of possible values for X and Y (with corresponding values for the slack variables). We will confine our attention only to those values at the corners of the shaded area and select the one corner that yields maximum profit according to our objective function:

(maximize) $\pi = 25X + 50Y$.

These corners have been labeled a, b, c, and d in Figure 9.2. Beginning with corner a, we know that the quantities of X and Y at this point are determined by the iron constraint $0X + 4Y + S_i = 80$ only. Since both the first and third terms are equal to zero at a, the value of Y at this point is easy to determine: $4Y = 80$ and $Y = 20$. This value has been listed as a first possible solution in Table 9.2.

At corner b the quantities of X and Y are determined by both the vitamin B and iron constraints:

$$3X + 5Y + S_B = 150$$

and

$$0X + 4Y + S_i = 80.$$

Since the slack variables S_B and S_i equal zero at corner b, the constraint equations can be solved simultaneously:

$$3X + 5Y = 150 \text{ (vitamin B constraint)}$$
$$4Y = 80 \text{ (iron constraint).}$$

Multiply the iron constraint by 5/4 and subtract from the vitamin B constraint:

$$3X + 5Y = 150$$
$$\underline{5Y = 100}$$
$$3X = 50 \text{ (and } X = 16.7).$$

Now, substituting this value into the vitamin B constraint produces:

$$3(16.7) + 5Y = 150$$
$$50 + 5Y = 150$$
$$5Y = 100 \text{ and } Y = 20.$$

This solution is also shown in Table 9.2.

The solution at corner c also is determined by both vitamin constraints. Again, since both slack variables are zero at this corner, the equations can be solved simultaneously:

$$2X + 1Y = 60 \text{ (vitamin A constraint)}$$
$$3X + 5Y = 150 \text{ (vitamin B constraint).}$$

TABLE 9.2   **Profit-Maximizing Values**

Corner	X	Y	Total profit
a	0	20	1,000
b	16.67	20	1,416.67*
c	21.43	17.14	1,392.75
d	30	0	750

Multiply the vitamin A constraint by 5 and subtract the vitamin B constraint:

$$10X + 5Y = 300$$
$$\underline{3X + 5Y = 150}$$
$$7X = 150 \text{ (and } X = 21.43).$$

Once again, substituting this value in the constraint equation allows us to find a value for the variable in question:

$$2(21.43) + 1Y = 60$$
$$42.86 + 1Y = 60 \text{ and } Y = 17.14.$$

This solution is also shown in Table 9.2.

Finally, the solution at corner d is determined using only the vitamin A constraint. Since Y and S_A are zero at d, the solution is $2X + 0 + 0 = 60$ and $X = 30$. Again, this value is shown in Table 9.2.

Total Profit

The next step is to compute total economic profit according to the objective function and select the corner with maximum profit. Using the profit equation

$$\pi = 25X + 50Y,$$

total economic profit has been calculated for all four corners and is listed as shown in Table 9.2. Maximum profit occurs at corner b, with production of 16.7 units of Multivitamins and 20 units of Iron Booster. Total economic profit at this point is $\pi = 25(16.7) + 50(20) = \$1,416.67$. This is also represented graphically in Figure 9.2, since corner b is tangent to the highest objective function.

Interpreting the Slack Variables

It is often useful to measure the slack resources not used in producing the maximum-profit quantities of X and Y. If the maximum-profit product-mix uses all available supplies of a particular ingredient, the value of the slack variable is zero. A value of zero indicates that this ingredient imposes a significant constraint on production decisions. A value greater than zero indicates ample supplies of the ingredient.[2] This makes the value of slack variables a useful guide to purchasing agents when ordering supplies for future production.

Recall the ratio of ingredients in X and Y and the available stocks of vitamins A and B, and iron shown in Table 9.1. According to the constraint equation, production of 16.7 units of X and 20 units of Y would use

$$2(16.7) + 1(20) = 53.4$$

units of vitamin A, leaving unused slack of $S_A = 60 - 53.4 = 6.6$. Similarly, unused quantities of vitamin B and iron would be:

$$S_B = 150 - 3(16.7) - 5(20) = 150 - 150 = 0$$

and

$$S_i = 80 - 0(16.7) - 4(20) = 80 - 80 = 0.$$

Limited quantities of vitamin B and iron impose the most severe constraints on production. They are **bottle-neck resources**, resources that should be ordered in larger quantities. $S_A = 6.6$ indicates that there are ample stocks of vitamin A.

Most linear programming problems involve substantially more computation than our simple example and are solved with the aid of a computer. The computer will follow the procedures we have just outlined for a larger set of information. It will identify the value at the corners, compute total economic profit at each corner, and measure the slack at the most profitable corner. Even in problems with a large number of products and many constraints, the computer can quickly identify the one solution that satisfies a firm's maximum-profit objective.

CHOOSING THE LOWEST-COST COMBINATION OF RESOURCES

We have demonstrated the use of linear programming for maximizing a firm's objective function, but linear programming techniques also are useful in cost-minimizing situations. In this case, a firm's objective might be to minimize costs when there is more than one way to produce a desired quantity of output. When a firm can choose among several resources for production, the constraint equations measure the expected production from alternative resource combinations, and the objective function measures total resource cost. The solution

---

2. A negative sign for a slack variable would be impossible, since a negative value would fail to satisfy the inequality constraint. In fact, a negative value would imply that the corresponding corner lies outside the shaded space relevant for decision making.

EXAMPLE 9.1   Maximizing Profit at a Publishing Company

The New World Publishing Company produces both hard-cover and paperback books at its Fall River plant. Production processes differ in the amount of machine time and labor time required, with hard-cover books requiring .4 hours of machine time and .25 hours of labor time, and paperbacks requiring .25 hours of machine time and .1 hours of labor. Hard-cover books sell for $20 and cost $12 to make, while paperbacks sell for $8 and cost only $5. Total production is limited by available labor time of 400 hours per week and available machine time of 800 hours per week. A limited supply of a special type of paper necessary for paperback production restricts paperback publication to 3,000 books per week.

First, let us establish the firm's constraints on weekly production. The constraint equations are:

$$.25X + .10Y + S_L = 400 \text{ (labor)},$$

$$.40X + .25Y + S_M = 800 \text{ (machine)},$$

and

$$1Y + S_P = 3,000 \text{ (paper)}.$$

The manager's objective is to maximize the economic profit function:

$$(\text{maximize}) \; \pi = (20 - 12)X + (8 - 5)Y.$$

The constraints are graphed in Figure A and the feasible corners are labelled a, b, c, and d. Possible solutions are listed in the table on page 286 along with the total economic profit for each. Maximum profit occurs at d, where X = 1,600 and Y = 0 units per week.

Let us find the value of the slack variables at the maximum profit. Substituting the values X = 1,600 and Y = 0 in the constraint equations yields:

$$.25(1600) + .1(0) + S_L = 400 \text{ and } S_L = 0,$$
$$.40(1600) + .25(0) + S_M = 800 \text{ and } S_M = 160,$$

and

$$1(0) + S_P = 3,000 \text{ and } S_P = 3,000.$$

FIGURE A

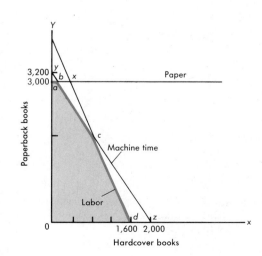

	X	Y	π
a	0	3,000	9,000
b	125	3,000	10,000
c	800	2,000	12,400
d	1,600	0	12,800

For $S_L = 0$, labor is the constraint limiting more profitable production. Machine-time is ample, and the limited paper needed to print paperbacks is not used at all.

Graphing the conditions of a problem such as this aids in its solution, since the feasible corners are easy to see. When graphing is not possible, computation is more lengthy. In such cases it is necessary to evaluate every corner and discard those that lie outside the feasible space. Look again at Figure A. Note that corners w, x, y, and z lie outside one or more of the constraints and are irrelevant to the linear programming decision. What characteristic is common to all of these corners? Because they lie outside the feasible space, it must be true that certain slack variables at these corners are negative. To illustrate this point, let us solve for X and Y at the corner labeled x.

$$.25X + .1Y = \quad 400 \text{ (labor constraint)}$$
$$1Y = 3,000 \text{ (paper constraint)}$$

Multiply the paper constraint by .1 and subtract from the labor constraint:

$$.25X + .1Y = 400$$
$$\underline{.1Y = 300}$$
$$.25X \quad\quad = 100 \text{ (and } X = 400).$$

Substituting the value of x in the equation yields:

$$.25(400) + .1Y = 400$$
$$100 + .1Y = 400$$
$$Y = 3,000.$$

Now let us find the value of the slack variables at this corner. Substituting the values for x and y in the original constraint equations yields:

$$.25(400) + .1(3,000) + S_L \quad = 400$$
$$400 + S_L = 400$$
$$S_L = 0$$

for the labor constraint,

$$.4(400) + .25(3,000) + S_M = 800$$
$$910 + S_M = 800$$
$$= S_M = -110$$

for the machine constraint, and

$$1(3,000) + S_P = 3,000$$
$$3,000 + S_P = 3,000$$
$$S_P = 0$$

for the paper constraint. Since machine time would be over-used at x, this cannot be a feasible solution.

The remaining corners could be evaluated similarly and discarded if other slack variables are determined to be negative. Evaluating corners for a host of variables and constraints is tedious and time consuming, but the process is performed easily by computer.

MANAGERIAL THINKING

Compute values for all of the variables at the corners labeled *w, y,* and *z* in Figure A. Interpret your results.

___

identifies the combination of resources that accomplishes production goals at the lowest resource cost.

This difference is also evident in the graph of a cost-minimizing problem. In the graph of a minimizing problem, the area containing all possible solutions is the area that lies upward and to the right of the restraint equations. That is, possible solutions are equal to or *greater than* the minimum solution. The objective of a cost-minimization problem is to locate the corner of the constraint space that is tangent to the *lowest* total cost function.

We will now use a simple example to illustrate cost-minimization through linear programming. As before, solving the problem requires solution of the equations and measuring the cost at the corners of the restraint equations. In cost-minimization problems, however, there are no slack variables, since the minimum value of the constraints must be achieved. Rather, *overproducing* the necessary quantity of output results in "surplus" variables.

Defining the Problem

National Meat Products Company feeds livestock a combination of fish meal and soybean cake at costs of $10.00 and $7.50 per 100 pounds, respectively. Dressed weight of animals is estimated to increase under the feeding program according to the values in Table 9.3 on page 288.

Thus, each 100 pounds of fish meal adds 50 pounds to the dressed weight of hogs and 75 pounds to the dressed weight of cattle. The firm wants to achieve a dressed weight of at least 500 pounds for hogs and 1,000 pounds for cattle. The managers of National Meat Products must determine the lowest-cost feeding program for the animals.

The objective in this problem is to minimize the cost of the feeding program. The objective function can be stated:

(minimize) Total cost = (TC) = $10X + 7.5Y$,

where X and Y represent 100 pounds of fish meal and soybean cake, respectively. The constraints in this case are *minimum* amounts that must be satisfied. Thus, the constraint for hogs is written

$50X + 30Y \geq 500$,

TABLE 9.3   **Feeding Program Results**

	Fish meal (Per 100 lbs.)	Soybean cake (Per 100 lbs.)
Dressed weight: hogs	50	30
Dressed weight: cattle	75	70

to indicate a minimum acceptable weight of 500 pounds, and the constraint for cattle is written

$$75X + 70Y \geq 1{,}000.$$

Including surplus variables changes the inequalities to equalities so that:

$$50X + 30Y - S_H = 500$$

becomes the hog constraint and

$$75X + 70Y - S_C = 1{,}000$$

becomes the cattle constraint. The surplus variables measure any weight gain in excess of 500 pounds and 1,000 pounds, the acceptable weights. Notice that cost minimization problems require negative surplus variables. Since the constraint inequalities are equal to or greater than the stated minimum, an unknown amount must be *subtracted* to bring the equation into balance.

The Solution

The constraint equations for this example have been plotted in Figure 9.4. Since the firm will be choosing between resources in this problem (rather than products, as before), the axes of the graph represent the two resources. The corners are labeled a, b, and c. Once again, in cost minimization problems, the possible solution area is the shaded space above and to the right of the bold line, and the objective is to find the corner that minimizes total costs. The minimum-cost corner will be tangent to a budget line drawn between the two axes whose slope is equal to a ratio of the resource prices:

$$\text{Slope} = p_X/p_Y,$$

where the resource on the horizontal axis provides the numerator.

First solve the constraint equations separately according to Figure 9.4. At corner a, the values of X and S_H are zero. At corner c, Y and S_C are zero. At corner b, S_H and S_C are zero. Thus, the solutions are $X = 0$ and $Y = 16.67$ at

FIGURE 9.4   Total Costs Associated with Use of Fish Meal and Soybean Cake

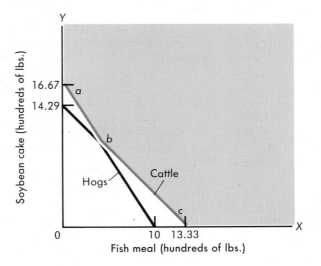

corner a, $X = 4$ and $Y = 10$ at corner b, and $X = 13.33$ and $Y = 0$ at corner c. Total costs associated with each corner solution are

$$TC = 0(10) + 16.67(7.5) = 125.00$$

for corner a,

$$TC = 4(10) + 10\,(7.5) = 115.00$$

for corner b, and

$$TC = 13.33(10) + 0(7.5) = 133.33$$

for corner c. Thus, the lowest cost feeding program occurs at corner b using 400 pounds of fish meal and 1,000 pounds of soybean cake, for an average total cost of \$115.00 for each animal.

Now calculate the surplus variables by substituting the recommended quantities of X and Y in the constraint equations and solving. For the hog constraint,

$$50(4) + 30(10) - S_H = 500 = S_H = 0.$$

Similarly, for the cattle constraint,

$$75(4) + 70(10) - S_C = 1{,}000 = S_C = 0.$$

In this problem the value of both surplus variables is zero at the optimum solution.

The value of the surplus variable at any solution of a cost minimization problem has a definite meaning. It is the amount by which production at that point exceeds the minimum required under the constraint equations. Thus, at corner c 13.33 hundred pounds of fish meal alone would produce dressed weight of 50(13.33) = 666.67 pounds for hogs and 75(13.33) = 1,000 for cattle for total weight of 666.67 − 500 = 166.67 greater than the minimum acceptable weight. At corner a, Y = 16.67 hundred pounds of soybean cake would produce a weight of 30(16.67) = 500 pounds for hogs and 70(16.67) = 1,166.67 for cattle. Thus, total weight exceeds the objective by S_H = 166.67 and increases the cost of the feeding program. With S_H = 0 and S_C = 0 at corner b, production precisely equals the minimum stated in the constraints.[3]

SHADOW PRICES AND THE DUAL

In both of the preceding linear programming examples, we discovered one or more "bottleneck" constraints: in these cases, a limited supply of resources that constrained profit-maximizing efforts and rigid product specifications that constrained efforts to minimize costs. The "bottleneck" variables in both cases are those whose slack (or surplus) values were zero.

Managers are concerned about the limitations imposed by "bottleneck" constraints and are interested in the effect on the objective function of relaxing them. In profit-maximizing problems, it is helpful to know the effect on profit of acquiring additional units of a bottleneck resource. In cost-minimizing problems, it is helpful for managers to know the effect on costs of reducing product specifications.

The individual contribution of each unit of resource (or product specification) to the objective function is called its **shadow price**. The sum of all shadow prices associated with all resources (or product specifications) is the total value of the objective function. Shadow prices are calculated by solving the **dual** associated with a linear programming problem. Every original or **primal** linear programming problem has a corresponding dual. In profit-maximizing problems, the objective of the dual is to *minimize* the sum of the shadow prices, or the value to the firm of resources used in production. In cost-minimizing problems, the objective of the dual is to *maximize* the contribution of all resources toward achieving product specifications.

To illustrate the dual solution and the use of shadow prices, let us return to the Vita-Pep example. The equations for Vita-Pep's primal problem are:

(maximize) Economic profit $= \pi = 25X + 50Y$,

subject to constraints

---

3. A negative value for the surplus variable would cause the absolute value of the variable to be positive and would indicate a corner lying between the area of feasible solutions and the two axes.

$$2X + 1Y \leq 60 \text{ (vitamin A)},$$
$$3X + 5Y \leq 150 \text{ (vitamin B)},$$

and

$$4Y \leq 80 \text{ (iron)}.$$

Recall that we also added slack variables S_A, S_B, and S_i to change the inequalities into equalities.

The dual objective function in a profit-maximizing problem is to minimize the sum of all shadow prices involved in production. This is because minimizing the sacrifice associated with resources used is equivalent to maximizing profit actually earned. The total shadow price is the sum of the shadow prices of all resources multiplied by their quantities. For 60 units of vitamin A, 150 units of vitamin B, and 80 units of iron, the objective function is:

$$\text{(minimize) Shadow prices} = 60p'_A + 150p'_B + 80p'_i,$$

where p' represents the shadow prices of the individual resources.

The constraints in a dual problem are different as well. The constraints state that the shadow prices included in each unit of output must be at least as great as the profit from the sale of one unit. Thus, one unit of Multivitamins (X) requires 2 units of vitamin A, 3 units of vitamin B, and zero units of iron, for a shadow price of

$$2p'_A + 3p'_B + 0p'_i.$$

Since the profit per unit of X is 25, the Multivitamin constraint is

$$2p'_A + 3p'_B + 0p'_i \geq 25.$$

Likewise, the Iron Booster constraint measures the value of the resources included in Y:

$$1p'_A + 5p'_B + 4p'_i \geq 20.$$

Because these are "greater than" constraints, we will subtract surplus variables to change the inequalities to equalities:

$$2p'_A + 3p'_B + 0p'_i - S_X = 25$$

for the Multivitamin constraint and

$$1p'_A + 5p'_B + 4p'_i - S_Y = 50$$

for the Iron Booster constraint.

TABLE 9.4   Zero Values of Constraint Equation Solutions

Solutions	P'_A	P'_B	P'_i	S_X	S_Y
(1)	0	0	0		
(2)	0	0		0	
(3)	0	0			0
(4)	0		0	0	
(5)	0		0		0
(6)	0			0	0
(7)		0	0	0	
(8)		0		0	0
(9)		0	0		0
(10)			0	0	0

SOLVING THE DUAL

An advantage of the dual of a linear programming problem is that it is frequently easier to solve than the initial or primal problem. To solve this example, let us first remember that we found a number of zero values when we solved the constraint equations in the primal problem. Zero values occur when constraint lines intersect each other or one of the axes on the graph. In fact, for any set of constraint equations there will be only as many non-zero values as there are constraints. For the set of two constraints above, we would expect to find two non-zero values. Recognizing this, we can set up a table such as Table 9.4 to show the zero values of every possible solution of the two constraint equations. Each row in the table represents the values of all variables for a particular solution of the two constraint equations. For each solution, three of the variables are assumed to be zero. Zeros occur at intersections of the constraint lines with each other or with one of the axes. To complete the rows of the table it is necessary to set the indicated variables in the constraints equal to zero and solve simultaneously. Thus, for solution (1),

$$2(0) + 3(0) + 0(0) - S_X = 25,$$

and

$$1(0) + 5(0) + 4(0) - S_Y = 50,$$

so that $S_X = -25$ and $S_Y = -50$. For solution (2),

$$2(0) + 3(0) + 0p'_i - 0 = 25,$$

and

$$1(0) + 5(0) + 4p'_i - S_Y = 50,$$

TABLE 9.5   Objective Function Values

Solution	p_A'	p_B'	p_i'	S_X	S_Y		Value of objective function
(1)	0	0	0	−25	−50	*	
(2)	0	0	**	0	**		
(3)	0	0	12.5	−25	0	*	
(4)	0	8.33	0	0	−8.33	*	
(5)	0	10	0	5	0		1,500.00
(6)	0	8.33	2.09	0	0		1,416.70
(7)	12.5	0	0	0	−37.5	*	
(8)	12.5	0	9.38	0	0		1,500.40
(9)	50	0	0	75	0		3,000.00
(10)	−3.57	10.71	0	0	0	*	

so that p_i' and S_Y are indeterminate (there is no intersection). For solution (3),

$$2(0) + 3(0) + 0(p_i') - S_X = 25,$$

and

$$1(0) + 5(0) + 4(p_i') - 0 = 50,$$

so that $p_i' = 12.5$ and $S_X = -25$. Solutions have been calculated for all ten combinations in the table and are shown in Table 9.5.

Certain solutions in the table must be discarded because the values of the surplus variables in these cases are negative. Negative values for the surplus variables fail to satisfy the "greater than" requirement of the constraints. Solutions with negative surplus variables are signified by an * and disregarded in further computations.

The relevant results in Table 9.5 have been used to calculate the value of the objective function: $60p_A' + 150p_B' + 80p_i'$. This is the sum of the shadow prices involved in production and, thus, the value to the firm of the resources used. These values are also shown in the table.

Remember that the objective in this dual problem is to minimize the value of the objective function: that is, to minimize the use of resources required to earn the firm's profits. The lowest value of the objective function occurs for solution (6) with resource value of $1,416.70 Note that this is the same solution we reached when we previously solved the primal problem. This solution differs from the primal solution, however, in that the values of the variables are the "shadow prices" of the resources used in production. Knowing that the shadow prices are $p_B' = 8.33$ and $p_i' = 2.09$, we know the effect on profit caused by increasing supplies of vitamin B and iron by one unit, respectively. Vitamin A has a shadow price of zero, indicating ample supplies of this resource.

Shadow prices indicate the change in the objective function caused by relaxing one of the constraints. A change in a constraint can be shown graphically by changing the slope of the relevant constraint line. A change in the slope alters the quantities of both products that can be produced and changes the point of tangency with the objective function. The shadow price continues to be relevant for changes in resource supplies up to the point at which production encounters another constraint.

The dual surplus variables compare the profit contribution of each product with the value to the firm of the resources used to produce it. A zero value for a surplus variable indicates that the profit contribution is equal to the value of the resources. Thus, resources in this case are used to their best advantage. A positive value for a surplus variable indicates that the resources used to produce a particular item are worth more than the profit contribution of the resources for producing another item. A negative value is not acceptable since it implies that the resources would be worth more in some other kind of production than their profit contribution for this particular product.

As we have said, the dual solution can be used to solve the primal problem: that is, the quantities of Multivitamins and Iron Boosters that should be produced. The existence of shadow prices for vitamin B and iron indicates that these resources are fully used in production. This means that their slack variables are equal to zero. With S_B and S_i equal to zero, two of the original constraint inequalities become equalities and can be solved simultaneously:

$$3X + 5Y = 150 \text{ (vitamin B)},$$

and

$$4Y = 80,$$

so that $Y = 20$ and $X = 16.67$. This is the result we achieved when solving the primal problem.

CASE STUDY 9.1   **Linear Programming for Managing a Bank's Portfolio**

The Federal Reserve Bank of Richmond instructs commercial banks in the use of linear programming so that they may allocate bank funds to achieve maximum total income. Banks have three sources of funds: demand (D) and savings or time deposits (T) from customers and capital accounts (C) contributed by bank stockholders. Banks use their funds in two ways, loans (L) and investments (I).

Banks are constrained in their selection of loans and investments by three considerations: risk, liquidity, and yield.

1. *Risk* refers to the probability that loans or investments may decrease in value. Losses on loans or investments may threaten a bank's ability to satisfy its customers' need for cash. Loans tend to be more risky than investments, but many bank customers depend on a ready source of bank loans in order to meet business and personal obligations.

2. *Liquidity* refers to the availability of funds to satisfy depositors' needs. Since demand deposits may be withdrawn at any time, it is important to maintain an

adequate level of liquidity in the bank's use of funds. Investments tend to be more liquid than loans.

3. *Yield* refers to the income earnings from loans and investments. In general, the highest yields are associated with loans and investments with the greatest risk and lowest liquidity.

Banks attempt to use their funds in a way that will balance the effects of these three considerations. In other words, banks want to achieve the highest possible yield while maintaining a reasonable level of liquidity and an acceptable level of risk.

A model of these circumstances can be created using linear programming. Suppose a bank has $500 million available for purchasing loans and investments. The available funds constraint for this bank is

$$L + I \leq 500 \text{ million.}$$

Furthermore, the bank wants to maintain loans equal to at least $200 million. Thus, the loans constraint is

$$L \geq 200 \text{ million.}$$

Also, in order to achieve a reasonable level of liquidity, the bank wants to maintain a level of investments equal to at least 20 percent of the total of loans and investments. Thus, the investments constraint is

$$I \geq .20(L + I).$$

Converting the previous constraint into a form similar to the other constraints gives us:

$$-.25L + I \geq 0.$$

The constraint equations are graphed in Figure A. Note that one of the equations is a "less than" constraint, binding the firm's choices on the outside. Two constraints are "greater than" constraints, binding the firm's choices from the inside. The feasible space is the area inside the "less than" constraint and outside the two "greater than" constraints.

FIGURE A

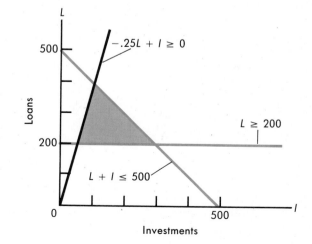

The objective function for the bank's managers is to maximize income from the purchase of loans and investments. If loans earn 15 percent and investments earn 10 percent, the objective function is:

$$\text{(maximize) Income} = .15(L) + .10(I).$$

The constraints are

$$L + I + S_F = 500$$

for funds,

$$L - S_L = 200$$

for loans, and

$$-.25L + I - S_I = 0$$

for investments. Notice especially the signs of the slack and surplus variables. For the $\leq$ constraint, the sign of the slack variable must be positive to yield an equality. For the $\geq$ constraints, the sign of the surplus variable must be negative.

To solve the problem, we will set up a table that will help us evaluate all of the possible solutions to simultaneous equations. For each solution there will be two zero values (identifying the intersection). These values are shown in the following table. A —— represents values that are indeterminate (because there is no intersection).

Equations	L	I	S_F	S_L	S_I		Income
(1)	0	0	500	−200	0	*	
(2)	0	500	0	−200	500	*	
(3)	0	——	——	0	——	*	
(4)	0	0	500	−200	0	*	
(5)	500	0	0	300	−125	*	
(6)	200	0	300	0	−50	*	
(7)	200	300	0	0	250		60
(8)	400	100	0	200	0		75
(9)	200	50	250	0	0		35

Any solution with a negative value for a slack variable is unacceptable, since negative values fail to satisfy the inequality constraints. Therefore, solutions with negative values for the slack variables are indicated by an asterisk (*) and discarded. The remaining solutions have been used to calculate earnings according to the objective function, and the results of these calculations appear in the table. Maximum earnings occur when the bank purchases $400 million in loans and $100 million in investments. Selecting this combination will leave slack of $S_L = 200$; that is, the bank will be over-fulfilling by $S_L = 200$ its intention to keep at least $200 million in loans. The optimum combination of loans and investments will yield total income of

$$.15(400) + .10(100) = \$75 \text{ million}.$$

Source: Alfred Broaddus, "Linear Programming: A New Approach to Bank Portfolio Management," Federal Reserve Bank of Richmond Monthly Review, November 1972.

CASE STUDY 9.2   Solving a Non-Linear Problem

A machine tool company sells lapping machines and tap-sharpening machines to manufacturing firms. It uses advertising and personal selling to stimulate sales and allocates $22,600 and 6,000 man-hours respectively to these promotional activities.

Advertising is expected to yield profits of $6 and $10 per dollar spent. However, the firm's managers believe that the effectiveness of personal selling diminishes as more hours are allocated to this activity. For lapping machines, the return on the first 2,000 man-hours of personal selling is expected to generate profits of $24 per hour, but the return on additional hours is only $18 per hour. Likewise, for tap-sharpening machines, the first 1,500 hours of selling are expected to generate profits of $40 per hour, but the return on additional hours is is expected to be $20 per hour. Managers agree to spend at least $5,000 and no more than $18,000 for advertising. Personal selling will consume at least 2,200 hours but no more than 4,500 hours for each product.

The firm's managers want to allocate the available advertising budget and selling time to the two products in a way that will maximize profit. However, they realize that not all the relationships in the problem are linear. With changing profit levels associated with hours of personal selling, the usual linear programming solution is not possible. In fact, the managers have decided to treat hours of selling time as four separate quantities:

1. an initial maximum of 2,000 hours for selling lapping machines followed by
2. up to 4,000 additional hours (the total of 6,000 hours less the initial 2,000 hours);
3. an initial maximum of 1,500 hours for selling tap-sharpening machines followed by
4. up to 4,500 additional hours (the total of 6,000 hours less the initial 1,500).

Allowing S_{11} and S_{12} to represent initial and additional hours for selling lapping machines and S_{21} and S_{22} to represent initial and additional hours for selling tap-sharpening machines, the time constraints are:

$$S_{11} \leq 2,000,$$
$$S_{12} \leq 4,000,$$
$$S_{21} \leq 1,500,$$

and

$$S_{22} \leq 4,500.$$

Allowing A_1 and A_2 to represent advertising dollars for selling the two machines, the advertising constraint is:

$$A_1 + A_2 \leq 22,600.$$

The policy decisions of the firm's managers dictate the following additional constraints:

$$A_1 + A_2 \geq 5,000,$$
$$A_1 + A_2 \leq 18,000,$$
$$S_{11} + S_{12} \geq 2,200,$$
$$S_{21} + S_{22} \geq 2,200,$$
$$S_{11} + S_{12} \leq 4,500,$$

and

$$S_{21} + S_{22} \leq 4,500.$$

The objective is to maximize economic profit. Thus, the objective function is:

$$(\text{maximize}) \ \pi = 6A_1 + 10A_2 + 24S_{11} + 18S_{12} + 40S_{21} + 20S_{22}.$$

The problem has a total of eleven constraints: three "greater than" constraints that require negative slack variables and eight "less than" constraints that require positive surplus variables. Including slack and surplus variables, there are seventeen variables.

Solving the equations manually would be difficult and time-consuming. However, a simple computer program yields the following values for variables in the objective function:

$$A_1 = \quad\quad 0,$$
$$A_2 = 18,000,$$
$$S_{11} = \quad 2,000,$$
$$S_{12} = \quad 2,500,$$
$$S_{21} = \quad 1,500,$$

and

$$S_{22} = 3,000.$$

The maximum value of the objective function is $\pi = \$393,000$.

By spending the maximum agreed portion of the advertising budget on tap-sharpening machines and dividing personal selling time as shown, the firm expects to earn profit of $393,000. The slack variables are zero or positive at the optimum solution.

MANAGERIAL THINKING

Calculate the value of the slack variables at the optimum solution.

Source: Arthur Meidap, "Deterministic Techniques and Their Marketing Uses," Marketing Applications of Operational Research Techniques, Management Decisions, 1981, vol. 19, No. 4–5, pp. 13–35.

EXAMPLE 9.2   Linear Programming Problems in Transportation

One of the many uses of linear programming techniques is solving transportation problems. Linear programming can be used to minimize the total cost of shipping goods from plant to market while satisfying market demand and remaining within available plant capacity. When a problem involves a large number of routes, a linear programming model can get very large. Step-by-step computation such as the example that follows is more convenient for simple problems.

To illustrate the transportation problem, let us assume that a manufacturing firm operates three plants producing 8,000, 10,000, and 20,000 units of output per week. The firm serves four major distribution centers that require 6,000, 9,000, 10,000, and 13,000 units per week. Notice that total plant capacity is just sufficient to satisfy market demand, so there is no cost associated with shortages or storage of surpluses. We will assume also that unit production costs are identical in the various plants, so that nothing can be gained by operating one plant more or less intensively. The firm's managers know the transportation cost per unit associated with each route and want to choose the allocation of products that will yield minimum costs.

Table A shows transportation costs from each plant to each distribution center.

One possible solution would be to begin with plant 1 and allocate 6 units of plant 1's capacity to market 1. The remaining 2 units from plant 1 could be shipped to market 2, which requires a total of 9 units. The remaining 7 units for market 2

TABLE A

Plants	Distribution centers				Plant capacity (thousands)
	1	2	3	4	
1	15	25	40	10	8
2	60	25	30	50	10
3	30	12	80	15	20
Market requirement (thousands)	6	9	10	13	

would then be supplied by plant 2. Plant 2 would have 3 remaining units to supply to market 3, and market 3's final 7 units would come from plant 3. Finally, plant 3 would have 13 units to supply to market 4. Total transportation costs associated with this solution would be

$$6(15) + 2(25) + 7(25) + 3(30) + 7(80) + 13(15) = 1,160 \text{ or } \$1,160,000.$$

Is this the lowest-cost transportation plan? A more efficient plan would be to use the lowest-cost routes in the table first. To do this, managers would begin by shipping all 8 units from plant 1 to market 4 at a cost of $10 per unit. They would supply the remaining 5 units for market 4 from plant 3 at a unit cost of $15. Plant 3 has 15 units remaining, of which 9 units can be shipped to market 2 for a unit cost of $12 and 6 can be shipped to market 1 for a unit cost of $30. At this point, the only relevant part of the table is the part that relates 10 units of production from plant 1 to market 3 at a unit cost of $30. Total transportation costs for this plan would be:

$$8(10) + 5(15) + 9(12) + 6(30) + 10(30) = 743 = \$743,000.$$

Total cost has been reduced, but it is possible to reduce costs even further. The procedure for doing this involves selecting parts of the table that yield the greatest cost "savings" for the firm: that is, the parts at which the loss from *not* selecting the lowest-cost route is greatest.

Table B shows an additional row and column measuring the cost "savings" associated with that row or column. The "savings" for the firm is the difference between the lowest cost in that row or column and the second-lowest cost.

TABLE B

Plants	Distribution centers				Plant capacity (thousands)	Savings
	1	2	3	4		
1	15	25	40	10	8	5
2	60	25	30	50	10	5
3	30	12	80	15	20	3
Market requirements (thousands)	6	9	10	13		
Savings	15	13	10	5		

The managers must now begin with the cell having the largest savings: that is, the plant and market for which an efficient transportation choice represents the greatest savings. The cell with the largest savings in Table C is (1, 1), with a cost of 15 and a savings of 15. Managers now allocate as much of plant 1's capacity as possible in order to satisfy market 1. The managers eliminate column 1 from the table. New figures are now computed for plant capacity and cost saving and are shown in Table C.

TABLE C

Plants	Distribution centers				Plant capacity (thousands)	Savings
	1	2	3	4		
1		25	40	10	2	15
2		25	30	50	10	5
3		12	80	15	20	3
Market requirements (thousands)		9	10	13		
Savings		13	10	5		

Again managers choose the cell with the largest savings (1, 4). They allocate the 2 remaining units from plant 1 to market 4. They must now eliminate row 1 from Table D and recompute the values as before.

TABLE D

Plants	Distribution centers				Plant capacity (thousands)	Savings
	1	2	3	4		
1						
2		25	30	50	10	5
3		12	80	15	20	3
Market requirements (thousands)		9	10	11		
Savings		13	50	35		

Once again, managers choose the cell with the largest savings (2,3) and allocate all of plant 2's 10 units to market 3. They now eliminate row 2 and column 3, since neither is relevant to further decisions. The new cost table is shown as Table E.

TABLE E

Plants	Distribution centers				Plant capacity (thousands)	Savings
	1	2	3	4		
1						
2						
3		12		15	20	3
Market requirements (thousands)		9		11		

Finally, nine of plant 3's 20 units may be shipped to market 2 and the remaining 11 units may be shipped to market 4. The managers have now found the minimum total cost, which is

$$6(15) + 2(10) + 10(30) + 9(12) + 11(15) = 683 = \$683,000.$$

MANAGERIAL THINKING

How would you construct a linear programming problem to solve the transportation problem in this example?

Solution

The objective is to minimize total transportation costs. Therefore, the objective function is:

(minimum) Total costs $= 15(1,1) + 25(1,2) + 40(1,3) \ldots + 80(3,3) + 15(3,4),$

where the parentheses indicate the quantities shipped via each of the routes indicated in the table. The constraints indicate the minimum required in each distribution center and the maximum available from each plant:

$$(1,1) + (2,1) + (3,1) \geq 6 \text{ (requirement for market 1)}$$
$$(1,2) + (2,2) + (3,2) \geq 9 \text{ (requirement for market 2)}$$

$$(1,1) + (1,2) + (1,3) + (1,4) \leq 8 \text{ (capacity of plant 1)}$$
$$(3,1) + (3,2) + (3,3) + (3,4) \leq 20 \text{ (capacity of plant 3)}$$

The terms in the first set of constraints indicate quantities shipped from each of the three plants to markets 1, 2, 3, and 4, respectively. The terms in the second set of constraints indicate quantities shipped to each of the four markets from plants 1, 2, 3, and 4, respectively.

Source: Russell L. Ackoff and Maurice W. Sasieni, Fundamentals of Operations Research, (New York: John Wiley and Sons, 1968), pp. 123–30.

A MORE ADVANCED DECISION MODEL: GEOMETRIC PROGRAMMING

Linear programming is appropriate only when the relationships among the variables in the programming problem are linear. When relationships are non-linear, **geometric programming** may be used to determine a value or a range of values for the controllable variable. To illustrate, let us look at a simple problem that can be solved by geometric programming.

A manufacturing firm incurs **set-up costs** every time it begins a production run. Therefore, it is to the firm's advantage to minimize the number of production runs necessary to fill consumer demand during the year. On the other hand, goods held in inventory incur **storage and insurance costs,** making it desirable to run the production line more frequently and to produce fewer units of output each time. The question facing managers is: What is the number of production runs that will minimize the total of set-up and inventory costs?

For simplicity, let us assume that our firm does not produce until all our inventory is depleted. Let us suppose that annual demand is $Q = 1,000$ units, set-up costs are $S = \$100$ per set-up, and inventory costs are $I = \$5$ for each unit held in inventory. In addition, suppose the number of production runs is X and the quantity produced in each run is $Q/X = 1,000/X$. The costs to be controlled, then, are the sum of set-up and inventory costs:

$$TC = S(X) + I(Q/2X) = 100(X) + 2,500/X.[4]$$

The objective is to find the value of X that minimizes the value of the controllable cost equation.

This problem can be solved by calculus through the use of derivatives. However, geometric programming lets us solve the problem without all the trouble. This is accomplished by using a mathematical principle called the **algebraic-geometric mean inequality** or A-G. The algebraic-geometric mean inequality states that a weighted sum of values must be at least as great as their products, when the corresponding weights are used as exponents.[5] Thus,

$$1/2(X) + 1/2(Y) \geq (X^{1/2})\,(Y^{1/2})$$

or

$$1/3(X) + 2/3(Y) \geq (X^{1/3})\,(Y^{2/3}),$$

or

$$1/2(X) + 1/4(Y) + 1/4(Z) \geq (X^{1/2})\,(Y^{1/4})\,(Z^{1/4}),$$

and so forth.[6] To apply the A-G mean inequality to the controllable cost equation mentioned previously, let us first note the following:

$$TC = 1/2[2(TC)] = 1/2(2)(100X) + 1/2(2)(2,500/X) = 1/2(200X) + 1/2(5,000/X).$$

Now, applying the A-G mean inequality to controllable costs and using 1/2 as both weights, we have:

$$TC = 1/2(200X) + 1/2(5,000/X) \geq (200X)^{1/2}\,(5,000/X)^{1/2}.$$

Cancelling the X's from the right side of the inequality, we see that:

$$TC \geq (1,000,000)^{1/2} = 1,000 = \$1,000.$$

Thus, the minimum level of controllable costs must be at least \$1,000. This is

---

4. The number of units in inventory is determined as an average of units held. Thus, inventory is the number produced initially and held for inventory plus the number remaining at the end of the period divided by two. In our example, inventory is $[Q/X + 0]/2 = Q/2X$.

5. The algebraic-geometric mean inequality can be proved algebraically. However, such a proof is beyond the scope of this text.

6. For computing any mean, the weights must be positive and must total *one*.

a lower limit for the firm's set-up and inventory cost. In fact, we will soon show that this lower boundary of controllable costs is actually achieved when the terms in the equation to be minimized have certain characteristics. In our example, there is equality in the inequality (that is, $TC = \$1,000$) only when the terms in the equation are equal. Thus, we achieve minimum costs when $200X = 5,000/X$ or when $X = 5$. The lowest-cost number of production runs is $X = 5$, with $1,000/5 = 200$ units produced in each run. For $X = 5$, total controllable costs are

$$TC = 100(5) + 5(200/2) = 1,000,$$

the minimum possible level of costs.

This fact has an important economic consequence for the original cost equation. Each term in that equation contributed an equal amount to the minimum of $TC = \$1,000$. This result is not unexpected, since the A-G mean inequality principle also states that at the minimum, each term in the original equation contributes the amount represented by its weight. In the previous example, each weight is $\frac{1}{2}$. Therefore, each term contributes $\frac{1}{2}$ of minimum controllable costs at the optimum value of X. Later, we will show how the weights were chosen to be $\frac{1}{2}$ in order to achieve the optimum (minimum) value of controllable costs.

Choosing the Weights

The preceding procedure can be generalized into a procedure for solving a variety of management problems. The first step is to choose the weights so as to eliminate the unknown (X) from the right side of the inequality, leaving a single number. For X^1 and X^{-1} in the two terms above, the weights must be chosen such that

$$t_1 w_1 + t_2 w_2 = 0,$$

where the t's are the exponents of the unknown in the equation to be minimized and the w's are the weights to be applied in the A-G mean inequality. For the cost equation above,

$$(+1)w_1 + (-1)w_2 = 0$$

eliminates the unknown X from the right side of the equation. For any mean, the sum of the weights must total one. Therefore, we can also say that

$$w_1 + w_2 = 1.$$

Now we have two equations that can be solved simultaneously:

$$w_1 - w_2 = 0,$$

and

$$w_1 + w_2 = 1.$$

Solving for w_1 gives us

$$w_1 = w_2,$$

and substituting this value into the second equation yields:

$$w_2 + w_2 = 1 = 2w_2 = 1$$

or simply,

$$w_2 = 1/2.$$

Again, substituting, we get

$$w_1 = w_2 = 1/2.$$

Using weights $w_1 = 1/2$ and $w_2 = 1/2$ enabled us to cancel the X's from the right side of the algebraic-geometric mean inequality, leaving a single number to solve for in the cost equation.

Solving a Problem with Three Terms

Let us now look at a more complex problem in which the cost equation has three terms:

$$TC = (100X) + \frac{2,500}{X} + 30\,X^2.$$

In this problem, the first term is *set-up cost,* the second *inventory cost,* and the third *shipping cost.* In order to cancel the X's from the right side of the equation, the weights in the A-G mean inequality must satisfy the equation

$$t_1w_1 + t_2w_2 + t_3w_3 = 0.$$

Therefore,

$$(+1)w_1 + (-1)w_2 + (+2)w_3 = 0.$$

Since we know that the sum of the weights in any mean must equal 1, we can also say that

$$w_1 + w_2 + w_3 = 1.$$

We now have two equations, but we also have three unknowns. Therefore, there is no unique value for the weights that can be determined by solving simultaneously. However, we may determine a range of values for them. Look again at the two equations:

(1) $w_1 - w_2 + 2w_3 = 0$

and

(2) $w_1 + w_2 + w_3 = 1$.

Use equation (1) to identify a value for w_1 and substitute this value in equation (2). Since

$$w_1 = w_2 - 2w_3,$$

equation (2) becomes

$$w_2 - 2w_3 + w_2 + w_3 = 1,$$

or simply

$$2w_2 - w_3 = 1.$$

Therefore,

$$w_3 = 2w_2 - 1.$$

All the weights in an A-G mean inequality must be positive and less than 1. Therefore, we can say that

$$0 < 2w_2 - 1 < 1.$$

Now, solving for w_2 yields:

$$1/2 < w_2 < 1.$$

This tells us that the weight for the second term must be between 1/2 and 1. Similarly, solving equation (1) for w_3, we learn that

$$w_3 = 1/2w_2 - 1/2w_1$$

and substituting for this value yields:

(2) $w_1 + w_2 + 1/2w_2 - 1/2w_1 = 1$,

or, simply,

$$1/2w_1 + 3/2w_2 = 1.$$

Therefore,

$$w_1 = 2 - 3w_2.$$

Again, we know that the value of w_1 is between 0 and 1. Therefore,

$$0 < 2 - 3w_2 < 1,$$

and, subtracting 2:

$$-2 < -3w_2 < -1.$$

Now, multiplying by -1 and reversing the signs to solve for w_2:

$$2 > 3w_2 > 1$$

and

$$2/3 > w_2 > 1/3.$$

The value of w_2 must be between 1/3 and 2/3. Through our previous calculations, we learned that w_2 must be at least 1/2. Now we know that w_2 cannot be greater than 2/3. This information tells us that the weight for the second term, inventory costs, must be at least 1/2 and no greater than 2/3. Accordingly, we know that the total cost function is minimized when inventory costs are held to no more than 2/3 but no less than 1/2 of total costs.

This procedure can be followed in estimating a range of values for all the weights in the A-G mean inequality. The results are as follows:

1. *Set-up costs* must be between zero and ½ of total controllable costs.
2. *Inventory costs* must be between ½ and ⅔ of controllable costs.
3. *Shipping costs* must be between zero and ⅓ of controllable costs.

Solving for a range of values is not as intellectually satisfying as solving for a precise value. However, analysts have found remarkably small differences in costs associated with typical deviations from the precise minimum values. Also, managers frequently lack precise data for identifying the unique minimum point of a total cost function. Therefore, such ranges or controls are very useful in the actual decision processes of a firm. In addition, conditions of demand, costs, and so forth may change, such that a unique value under one set of circumstances may not be the correct value in another. Therefore, the procedure outlined here is useful in many different decisions.

A significant feature of geometric programming is that the lowest-cost value for a variable is independent of the costs actually associated with either of the terms in the total cost function. The lowest-cost relationship between set-up costs, inventory costs, and shipping costs is the same, regardless of the absolute value of the costs. Lowest cost depends only on the exponent of the variable in the equation to be minimized.

One further point should be noted. The two problems we have described differ in that a unique value was determined in the first problem and a range of values was determined in the second. The reason for this difference is the number of equations and the number of variables involved. When there are an equal number of variables and equations, we say the problem has zero **degrees of difficulty**. In such cases, unique values can be determined by solving the system of equations simultaneously. When there are fewer equations than variables, the problem has at least one degree of difficulty, and it is possible to find only a range of values. The degree of difficulty of an equation or system of equations equals the number of terms in the equation(s) to be minimized *minus* number of variables in the equation *minus* 1.

Geometric programming can be used to minimize any polynomial in which the coefficients are positive. It is not appropriate for minimizing quadratic or cubic equations that have a negative coefficient.

EXAMPLE 9.3 **A Geometric Programming Problem Containing Three Variables**

Acme Paper Company transports wood shavings to its manufacturing plant for processing into paper. Transportation costs are $75 for each carton shipped. The cartons containing the shavings are made from a heavy paper material that costs the firm $1 per square foot. The firm's managers want to know the size of container that will minimize the total cost of transporting wood shavings. A typical monthly shipment is 2,500 cubic feet of shavings.

Let X, Y, and Z represent the dimensions of the heavy paper cartons. Shipping 2,500 cubic feet of material in such cartons would incur a transport cost of $75(2,500/X \cdot Y \cdot Z)$. Manufacturing the cartons will cost the firm $2XY + 2XZ + 2YZ$. Thus, total transportation costs are

$$TC = 75\left(\frac{2,500}{XYZ}\right) + 2XY + 2XZ + 2YZ.$$

The objective is to find the values of X, Y, and Z that will minimize the total cost equation.

To apply the A-G mean inequality, we must first introduce weights that will change only the appearance of the TC equation, not its value. Thus,

$$TC = w_1\left[75\left(\frac{2,500}{w_1 XYZ}\right)\right] + w_2\left(\frac{2XY}{w_2}\right) + w_3\left(\frac{2XZ}{w_3}\right) + w_3\left(\frac{2YZ}{w_3}\right).$$

The inequality now becomes

$$TC = w_1\left[75\left(\frac{2,500}{w_1 XYZ}\right)\right] + w_2\left(\frac{2XY}{w_2}\right) + w_3\left(\frac{2XZ}{w_3}\right) + w_3\left(\frac{2YZ}{w_3}\right)$$

$$\geq \left[75\left(\frac{2,500}{w_1 XYZ}\right)^{w_1}\left(\frac{2XY}{w_2}\right)^{w_2}\left(\frac{2XZ}{w_3}\right)^{w_3}\left(\frac{2YZ}{w_4}\right)^{w_4}\right]. {}^{1}$$

---

1. Since the terms on the left side of the inequality are to be multiplied by the weights, the terms must also be divided by the weights in order to avoid changing the values of the terms.

We know that the sum of the weights must equal 1:

$$w_1 + w_2 + w_3 + w_4 = 1.$$

Now in order to eliminate X, Y, and Z from the right side of the inequality, the weights must be chosen so that

$$t_1 w_1 + t_2 w_2 + t_3 w_3 + t_4 w_4 = 0,$$

where the t's represent the exponents of the variables X, Y, and Z. Because we have three variables, we will need three equations that equal zero. The equations are

$$-w_1 + w_2 + w_3 \qquad = 0$$

for X,

$$-w_1 + w_2 \qquad\quad + w_4 = 0$$

for Y, and

$$-w_1 \qquad\quad + w_3 + w_4 = 0$$

for Z. We now have four equations and four unknowns. Therefore, we can solve the equations to find unique values for each w:

$$
\begin{aligned}
(1) &\quad w_1 + w_2 + w_3 + w_4 = 1 \\
(2) &\quad -w_1 + w_2 + w_3 \qquad\quad = 0 \\
(3) &\quad -w_1 + w_2 \qquad\quad + w_4 = 0 \\
(4) &\quad -w_1 \qquad\quad + w_3 + w_4 = 0.
\end{aligned}
$$

First, we can solve (2) for w_1 and substitute this value in (1). Thus,

$$(2) \quad w_1 = w_2 + w_3,$$

and

$$
\begin{aligned}
(1) \quad & w_2 + w_3 + w_2 + w_3 + w_4 = 1 \\
& 2w_2 + 2w_3 + w_4 = 1.
\end{aligned}
$$

Now we can solve (3) for w_1 and substitute this value in (1). Thus,

$$(3) \quad w_1 = w_2 + w_4,$$

and

$$
\begin{aligned}
(1) \quad & w_2 + w_4 + w_2 + w_3 + w_4 = 1 \\
& 2w_2 + w_3 + 2w_4 = 1.
\end{aligned}
$$

We can also solve (4) for w_1 and substitute this value in (1). Hence,

$$(4) \quad w_1 = w_3 + w_4,$$

and

$$
\begin{aligned}
(1) \quad & w_3 + w_4 + w_2 + w_3 + w_4 = 1 \\
& w_2 + 2w_3 + 2w_4 = 1.
\end{aligned}
$$

The three equations we have developed may be solved by multiplication and subtraction. The resulting values are:

$$w_1 = 2/5, \ w_2 = 1/5, \ w_3 = 1/5,$$

and

$$w_4 = 1/5.$$

These weights tell us that the first term in the total cost equation will constitute 2/5 of the minimum value of the equation, and the second, third, and fourth terms will each constitute 1/5 of the minimum.

The minimum value of total costs can be determined by solving for the right side of the A-G mean inequality. Thus,

$$(\text{minimum}) \text{ Total costs} = \left[75\left(\frac{2{,}500}{2/5XYZ}\right)\right]^{2/5}\left(\frac{2XY}{1/5}\right)^{1/5}\left(\frac{2XZ}{1/5}\right)^{1/5}\left(\frac{2YZ}{1/5}\right)^{1/5}.$$

The weights we have chosen allow us to eliminate X, Y, and Z, so that

$$(\text{minimum}) \text{ } TC = \left[75\left(\frac{2{,}500}{2/5}\right)\right]^{2/5}\left(\frac{2}{1/5}\right)^{1/5}\left(\frac{2}{1/5}\right)^{1/5}\left(\frac{2}{1/5}\right)^{1/5} = \$738.54.$$

Total cost cannot be less than $738.54. Furthermore, at minimum total cost transport costs will constitute

$$2/5(738.54) = \$295.42,$$

and constructing the cartons will cost

$$1/5(738.54) + 1/5(738.54) + 1/5(738.54) = 147.71 + 147.71 + 147.71$$
$$= \$443.13.$$

Having determined the value of each term in the total cost equation, we can now determine the values of X, Y, and Z that will yield minimum total costs. Thus,

$$75\left(\frac{2{,}500}{XYZ}\right) = 2/5(TC) = 295.42,$$

$$2XY = 1/5(TC) = 147.71,$$
$$2XZ = 1/5(TC) = 147.71,$$

and

$$2YZ = 1/5(TC) = 147.71.$$

Solving these equations simultaneously is done by solving for their natural logarithmic equivalents, which are

$$\ln 75 + \ln 2{,}500 - \ln X - \ln Y - \ln Z = \ln 295.42,$$
$$\ln 2 \qquad\qquad + \ln X + \ln Y \qquad\quad = \ln 147.71,$$
$$\ln 2 \qquad\qquad + \ln X \qquad\quad + \ln Z = \ln 147.71,$$

and

$$\ln 2 + \ln Y + \ln Z = \ln 147.71.$$

Further simplifying, we get:

$$\ln X + \ln Y + \ln Z = 6.45313,$$
$$\ln X + \ln Y \qquad\quad = 4.30210,$$
$$\ln X \qquad\quad + \ln Z = 4.30210,$$

and

$$\ln Y + \ln Z = 4.30210.$$

Finally, solving for the three variables yields: $\ln X = 2.15105$ and $X = e^{2.15105} =$

8.59. Likewise, $Y = 8.59$ and $Z = 8.59$. These are the dimensions of the carton. The minimum value of total cost is again:

$$\text{(minimum) } TC = 75\left(\frac{2{,}500}{8.59^3}\right) + 2(8.59)^2 + 2(8.59)^2 + 2(8.59)^2 = \$738.54.$$

SUMMARY

Linear programming is a technique for choosing the profit-maximizing combination of products or the minimum-cost combination of resources, where production functions are linear and exhibit constant returns to scale. In a profit-maximizing problem the objective function is to maximize the sum of profits associated with each of several products. The constraints define the available resources necessary for producing each item and include a slack variable measuring the quantity of a resource not used in producing any chosen combination of products. Slack variables must have positive signs in order to change a "less than" inequality to an equality.

Graphing a profit-maximizing problem yields a feasible space with corners defined by simultaneous solutions of the constraint equations. The profit-maximizing corner is the one that touches the highest profit function. Total profit is computed by substitution in the objective function. A zero value for a slack variable identifies that resource as a "bottleneck" resource, additional quantities of which would relax one of the constraints on profit.

In a minimum-cost problem, the objective function includes costs of resources that may be combined in various ways. The constraints define the relationship between quantities of resources and a target quantity of output. Constraints include a surplus variable that represents the excess production associated with a particular combination of resources. The surplus variable has a negative sign to change a "greater than" inequality to an equality.

The graph of a minimum-cost problem yields a feasible space, and the objective is to locate the corner that touches the lowest total cost function. Total cost is computed by substitution in the objective function. A zero value for a surplus variable indicates that the target level of output is precisely achieved by that resource combination.

All linear programming problems have a corresponding "dual" that computes the "shadow price" associated with each unit of resource or each unit of product requirement. The shadow price is the contribution of each resource unit (or product requirement) to the objective function. A dual problem is set up by realigning the coefficients from the "primal" problem. The resulting solution indicates the change in the objective function that would result from relaxing one of the constraints.

Geometric programming uses the algebraic-geometric mean inequality to locate the minimum-cost quantities of resources in a production process where the process cannot be modelled by quadratic or cubic equations.

KEY TERMS

linear programming	**slack variable**
inequalities	**bottleneck resource**
constraints	**geometric programming**
objective function	**set-up costs**
shadow price	**algebraic-geometric mean inequality**
dual	**degrees of difficulty**
primal	**storage and insurance costs**

QUESTIONS AND PROBLEMS

1. Plastic Products Company produces bushings and knobs for use in producing lawn furniture. Available equipment for extruding plastic can be adapted to produce either product, but total equipment time is limited to 40 hours per week. Bushings require two hours of machine time per thousand units, and knobs require three hours per thousand units. Both products require chemical materials available in amounts up to 25 tons. Production of one thousand bushings requires 2.5 tons and production of one thousand knobs requires 1.8 tons. In addition, bushings require one hour of slicing time which is limited to 20 hours per week. Profit per thousand units is $31 for bushings and $18 for knobs. Plot the constraints for this production problem and determine the product mix at the feasible corners. Locate the profit-maximizing corner. What are the values of the slack variables at the profit-maximizing corner? Identify the bottle-neck resource(s).

2. Homestyle Bakery produces rolls and cakes for delivery to local restaurants and public institutions. Current contracts require production of at least 55 dozen rolls and 17 dozen cakes per day. Costs per dozen are $.35 and $1.25 respectively. The firm's suppliers require purchase of at least 150 pounds of butter and 300 pounds of flour per day. The two products require these ingredients in the following amounts:

	Butter (lbs. per doz.)	Flour (lbs. per doz.)
Rolls	2	3
Cakes	3	10

Graph the constraints for this problem and determine the values at the relevant corners. Find the cost-minimizing product-mix, and determine the values of the slack variables. What is the significance of the slack variables in this problem?

3. Super-tronics Corporation produces two types of assemblies for use in television receivers and video-tape equipment. Current production relationships

are linear and involve constant returns to scale. Both products use parts that are available in virtually unlimited quantities. Both require average assembly time, processing time, and testing time in the following amounts:

	Television	Video-tape
Assembly	1.5 hours	3.5 hours
Processing	2 hours	2 hours
Testing	3.25 hours	5 hours

Personnel and equipment for performing the three functions are limited such that hours available for production are: 1,000 hours of assembly time, 500 hours of processing time, and 300 hours of testing. Assemblies for television sets sell for $27 and cost $18 to make. Assemblies for video-tape equipment sell for $39 and cost $28. What is the profit-maximizing product mix? Compute the solution algebraically without using a graph.

4. Industrial Belting Company sells belting to manufacturing firms throughout the Mid-West. The firm uses personal selling and advertisements in trade journals to market its product and allocates $30,000 a month to its total marketing budget. A sales presentation is estimated to cost $200 and requires 150 hours of a salesperson's time. The firm has a total of 20,000 hours a month to allocate to marketing. An advertisement costs $150 and requires 50 hours. Sales presentations bring in 600 units of sales and advertisements bring in 750 units. Each unit sells for $10 and has a profit contribution of $2.

   Set up the dual for allocating the firm's marketing budget and determine the shadow prices of sales presentations and advertisements. What is profit at the profit-maximizing solution? Interpret your results.

5. The following diagram is a network of activities performed in a manufacturing process. It is similar to a transportation problem in that a maximum quantity may leave the starting position (S) and a minimum quantity is required at the finish (F). The stages of processing are shown as circles (A, B, C, and D). The costs associated with processing along the various channels are written near the lines connecting the circles. Managers may choose which channel to use in processing in order to minimize costs. Set up the linear programming problem for making this decision and show how your solution can be generalized to solve more complex networking problems.

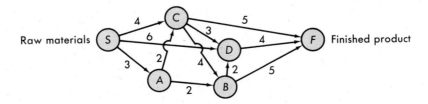

6. Industrial Products Company ships industrial chemicals to manufacturers of paint products. Shipping costs are a total of loading costs, transport costs, and insurance and depend on the volume and number of containers shipped each day. Let X represent the volume of containers in gallons and Y represent the number of containers to be shipped per day. Daily shipping costs are determined by $TC = 9X^3 + 5,000/XY + 8Y$. Use geometric programming to determine the lowest-cost volume and number of containers, as well as the minimum shipping costs per day.

7. Minimize the following total cost equation using geometric programming:

$$TC = 2.5X + \frac{7,500}{X^2}.$$

10

Price Policy and Market Power

To this point, we have considered price a "given": an amount determined by market conditions that are beyond the power of the competitive firm to affect. The role of managers in our discussion until now has been to compare a firm's marginal cost with market price or marginal revenue and determine the profit-maximizing (or loss-minimizing) quantity of output in the short run.

Such conditions are realistic in only a few markets in the United States. Markets for raw agricultural products and certain industrial commodities are examples of markets in which producers have little or no power to set prices. Most markets, however, are less competitive than these. In other markets there are fewer producers, each with control of a particular resource or technology that is unavailable to potential competitors. More importantly, each producer supplies a product that is in some way distinguishable from others in the market. Distinctions among products give the producing firm a degree of control over price.

PRICE AND MARKET STRUCTURE

Price theory focuses on the relationship between a firm's price policy and the structure of the market in which the firm operates. **Market structure** describes the extent and characteristics of competition. The most extreme market structures are **perfect competition** and **monopoly**.

Perfect competition is a market structure characterized by many buyers and sellers, each purchasing or selling so little of the total market as to have no control over price. Perfectly competitive firms sell homogeneous products with many substitutes and have the ability to move fairly easily into or out of the market in response to positive or negative economic profit. Chapter 8 described in detail the results for the economy as a whole when industries are characterized by competition.

Monopoly is a market structure in which one firm sells a unique product that has no close substitutes. In many cases, the monopolistic firm can prevent the movement of other sellers into the market. When the monopolistic firm supplies the entire market, it can set price and the corresponding quantity at which the firm collects economic profit.

Few U.S. firms fall into either of these extreme classifications. Most would fall along a continuum between perfect competition and monopoly. Such firms differ in the amount of competition they face and in the market strategies they use to counter competition. We classify firms in the intermediate range of competition as monopolistic competitors, or oligopolists:

Monopolistic competition is characterized by many small sellers, each supplying a product that is in some way distinguished from other products in the market. The firms' small size relative to the total market often leads to average costs that are higher than minimum. Frequently, monopolistically competitive firms seek to expand their market shares through expenditures for advertising and product differentiation.

A final market structure, **oligopoly**, is characteristic of markets supplied by a relatively small number of firms. Prices are relatively stable in oligopoly, since individual firms are reluctant to risk losing market share through a price increase or reducing economic profits through a price decrease. A dominant firm in an oligopolized industry may act as a "price leader," initiating a price change when demand or cost conditions change significantly. Oligopolistic firms often compete through differing service arrangements with customers and through research and development of new products and processes.

This chapter examines pricing policy in markets generally described as monopolies. Chapter 11 will examine in detail the pricing policies and market strategies in monopolistic competition and oligopoly.

Market Structure and the Demand Curve

Market structure determines the shape of the demand curve for a particular firm. When there are many competing suppliers of identical products, the market equilibrium price is determined by the intersection of market demand and market supply. In this case, the demand curve for an individual competitive firm is a horizontal line at the market equilibrium price. This is because no price cut is necessary to sell an additional quantity, and $p = MR$.

With a constant price, price elasticity of demand is infinitely great over its entire length. That is,

$$\epsilon_p = \frac{\%\Delta Q}{\%\Delta p} = \frac{\%\Delta Q}{0} \approx -\infty.$$

FIGURE 10.1   **Effects of Competition on Demand**

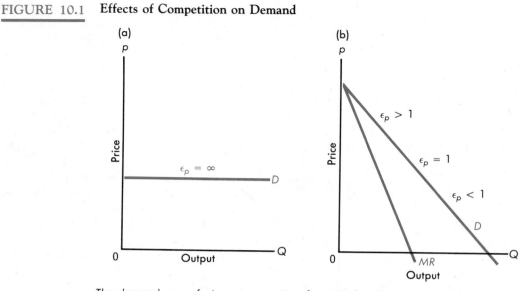

The demand curve facing a competitive firm is infinitely elastic (a). In the absence
of competition, demand curves slope downward and have differing elasticities at
different price levels (b).

In this case, even a very small change in price would bring on an infinite
change in quantity. Thus, the firm in competition has no incentive to change
price and, in effect, no pricing policy.

In general, as the number of suppliers in a particular market becomes
smaller, the demand curve for each individual firm becomes less elastic at
every price level. Price elasticity is lower because of the imperfect substitutability among alternative products. When alternative products differ in some
way from those of other firms, buyers may not adjust their purchases as readily
to price changes. In the extreme case in which a single firm supplies a unique
product, there are no alternative suppliers. The firm faces the entire market
demand curve.

Figure 10.1 shows market demand curves (a) for a firm in perfect competition and (b) for a firm producing a unique product. The horizontal demand
curve in Figure 10.1a is infinitely (or perfectly) elastic at the market equilibrium price. The downward sloping demand curve in Figure 10.1b is less than
perfectly elastic, but note that the absolute value of elasticity differs at every
price. (In Chapter 2 we showed that for any linear demand curve the absolute
value of elasticity is greater than 1 at higher prices, equal to 1 at the precise
midpoint of the curve, and less than 1 at lower prices. We also noted that the
absolute value of elasticity at the current price affects marginal revenue for the
firm and determines the correct price policy for achieving maximum profit.)

Using Price Elasticity of Demand to Set Price

A single supplier of a unique good or service has significant power to set the market price at which the product sells. A monopolistic firm faces a downward-sloping demand curve and can determine the price and corresponding quantity that maximize profit. The price that maximizes profit is determined by marginal revenue and marginal cost.

Remember that marginal revenue is the *change in total revenue* that results from the sale of a single additional unit. Marginal cost is the *change in total cost* that results from the production of an additional unit. The profit-maximizing price is the price at which the addition to the firm's revenue is equal to the addition to the firm's costs.

To illustrate profit-maximization in a monopolistic firm, suppose the firm is producing and selling 50 units of a unique product at a unit price of $6.00. To simplify the explanation at this point, we will assume that marginal and average total costs are constant at $3.00, for unit profit of $3.00 and total weekly profit of

$$\pi = Q(p - ATC) = 50(6.00 - 3.00) = \$150.$$

Is this the firm's maximum profit possible under current market conditions?

The answer depends on elasticity of demand and on marginal revenue at the current market price. Suppose price elasticity at the current price is estimated at $\epsilon_p = 2.4$. That is, a 1-percent change in price will cause a 2.4-percent change in weekly sales (in the opposite direction). We can determine marginal revenue from our estimate of elasticity by using the following formula:

$$\text{Marginal revenue } (MR) = p - \frac{p}{\epsilon_p},$$

where ϵ_p is the absolute value of price elasticity of demand. Note that marginal revenue is always less than price by an amount that depends on elasticity of demand. The greater the elasticity of demand, the smaller the amount that is subtracted from p and the smaller the difference between MR and p. For $\epsilon_p = 1$, the deduction from p would be equal to p, making $MR = 0$. For ϵ_p less than 1, MR is negative. These values are shown in Figure 10.1b.

In our example, marginal revenue is

$$MR = \$6.00 - \frac{6.00}{2.4} = \$3.50.$$

Thus, within the immediate range of sales, a unit change in quantity sold will change total revenue by $3.50. Now compare MR with MC. When $MR = \$3.50 > \$3.00 = MC$, the firm is not maximizing profits. In fact, additional

FIGURE 10.2   **Economic Profit Without Competition**

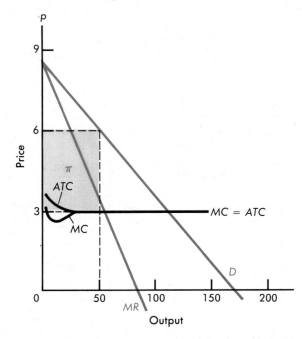

Without competition, price and quantity are determined at the point where MC = MR. Economic profit is the difference between price and average total cost for each unit sold. The firm can increase profit by reducing price and increasing quantity until MR = MC. The resulting area of economic profit will be larger than the area shown here.

units sold each week would add more to total revenue than to total cost, increasing economic profit. To maximize profit, the firm should reduce price and move down the demand curve to a price and quantity where $MR = MC$.

Figure 10.2 is a graph of this market, with volume of sales measured on the horizontal axis and price, average total cost, and marginal cost measured on the vertical axis. Production is occurring at $Q = 50$, with $MR > MC$. Economic profit is represented by the shaded rectangle formed between the demand curve and average total cost at $p = \$6.00$, $ATC = \$3.00$, and $Q = 50$. In order to maximize profits, the firm should reduce MR by reducing price. A price reduction is expected to increase quantity sold by 2.4 percent for each percentage decrease in price.

To illustrate, a 1-percent decrease in price will cause Q to increase by 2.4 percent for total sales of $1.024(50) = 51.2$ units per week. With sales of 51.2, economic profit is

$$\pi = Q(p - ATC) = (51.2)(\$5.94 - 3.00) = \$150.53.$$

FIGURE 10.3   **Maximum Economic Profit Without Competition**

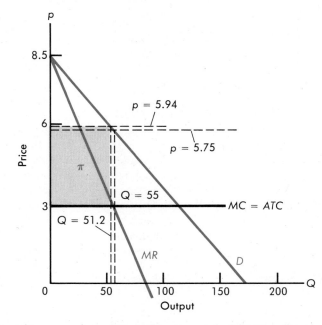

Maximum profit occurs where MC = MR, at a price of $5.75 and a quantity of 55 units. At this level of price and quantity, the economic profit rectangle is largest.

In Figure 10.3, the profit rectangle at $Q = 51.2$, $ATC = \$3.00$, and $p = \$5.94$ is larger than the profit rectangle in Figure 10.2.

Will further price reductions yield additional profit gains? This depends on the relationship between MR and MC. We have assumed that MC is constant and equal to ATC over a certain range of volume. We know that MR depends on price elasticity and that elasticity falls as we move down the demand curve. At some point on the demand curve, elasticity will have fallen so low that the gain from a further price reduction will not be enough to offset the lower price, and the profit rectangle will begin to shrink. In Figure 10.3, maximum profit occurs where $MR = MC$, or $p = \$5.75$ and $Q = 55$. Maximum economic profit for the week would be

$$\pi = Q(p - ATC) = 55(\$5.75 - 3.00) = 316.25 - 165 = \$151.25.$$

Later in this chapter we will examine the pricing decision in more detail and show how the profit-maximizing price and quantity may be determined using differential calculus. First, however, let us look at circumstances in which varying elasticities in various markets may require different price policies for a monopolistic firm.

Price Discrimination

Often, a monopolistic firm produces similar products for sale in different markets. For such a firm, marginal cost is the same regardless of where the product is sold. In certain markets, however, the existence of competing firms supplying acceptable substitutes increases elasticity of demand, so that marginal revenue varies. This characteristic is often true of foreign versus domestic markets and among different regions of the country as well. Differences in elasticity allow the firm to set different prices in the various markets.

Charging different prices in a number of separate markets is called **price discrimination.** Price discrimination is especially common in markets in which an identical service is sold 24 hours a day. Services are different from goods in that they cannot be purchased when price is low and "stored" for use when needed. Neither can they be purchased at low prices and re-sold at higher prices. This means that markets for services can be separated and charged varying prices. In each separate market, price depends on marginal revenue, which depends, in turn, on demand elasticity.

Separation of markets according to time of day is commonly practiced in services such as telephone communications, electric power transmission, and even indoor ice skating. In each of these cases, the firm's productive equipment is operating continuously, meaning that marginal and average costs are roughly the same regardless of the time of day. However, market circumstances differ over any 24-hour period, causing demand elasticity to vary. In fact, demand elasticity is strongly affected by consumers' preferences for the service at various times of the day or night and by the existence of competing firms producing similar services. Differences in demand elasticity may lead to differences in marginal revenue, so that the profit-maximizing price and quantity are different as well.

If consumers can satisfy their needs in alternative ways, they will adjust their purchases readily when prices change. Thus, price elasticity of demand in this case is relatively high, and prices must be set relatively low if customers are to be found. On the other hand, if few alternative sources of the service exist, consumers' responsiveness to price will be low, and price elasticity will be low as well. The profit-maximizing monopoly can set a relatively high price without fear of losing customers.

Consider again the market illustrated in Figure 10.3. As before, assume that marginal and average total costs are constant at $ATC = MC = \$3.00$. We have established the profit-maximizing quantity and price at $Q = 55$ and $p = \$5.75$. Suppose the firm has now moved down the demand curve to the profit-maximizing price and quantity. Suppose also, however, that the product is being sold in separate markets such that $Q_1 = 38$ and $Q_2 = 17$. Elasticity of demand differs in the two markets such that at the current price $\epsilon_1 = 2.2$ and $\epsilon_2 = 1.7$. Note that consumers in the first market are more responsive to price change, perhaps because of the greater availability of substitutes or lower average incomes in that market.

The greater demand elasticity in the first market suggests a stronger responsiveness to price change and a potentially greater addition to total revenue from a price *reduction*. On the other hand, lower demand elasticity in the second market means less consumer response and greater potential gains from a price *increase*.

The same conclusion follows from a comparison of marginal revenue and marginal cost. Differences in elasticity in the two markets indicate differences in marginal revenue:

$$MR_1 = p - \frac{p}{\epsilon_1} = \$5.75 - \frac{5.75}{2.2} = \$3.14,$$

and

$$MR_2 = p - \frac{p}{\epsilon_2} = \$5.75 - \frac{5.75}{1.7} = \$2.37.$$

Compare marginal revenue in the various separate markets with marginal cost. In the first market, where $MR_1 = \$3.14 > \$3.00 = MC$, a price reduction would cause quantity to increase in relatively greater proportion than the price reduction, which, in turn, would cause economic profit to increase. In the second market, where $MR_2 = \$2.37 < \$3.00 = MC$, price should be increased and quantity cut back to increase economic profit.

After implementing these price changes, the profit-maximizing combination of sales is found to be $Q_1 = 39.5$, with $p_1 = \$5.70$, and $Q_2 = 15.5$, with $p_2 = \$5.90$. Economic profit is

$$\pi = Q(p - ATC) = 39.5(5.70 - 3.00) + 15.5(5.90 - 3.00) = \$151.60,$$

an increase of $\$151.60 - \$151.25 = \$0.35$ over profit achieved without price discrimination.

Mark-up Pricing

The previous explanation illustrates an important principle of price policy: that is, the inverse relationship between price elasticity and a firm's power to set price. *The less elastic the demand curve, the greater the firm's market power and the greater its freedom to set price.*

We have seen that a firm's market power may vary over time and geographical location. It is also possible that a single firm's market may vary among *products,* with differing price elasticities of demand for several different items. In such cases, a monopoly may establish **mark-up pricing**: that is, price mark-ups above total cost for each market, depending on price elasticity. Consider the previous example and the formula for computing marginal revenue:

$$MR = p - \frac{p}{\epsilon_p}.$$

Over the range of output with constant average total cost, we know that marginal cost is also constant, so that $MC = ATC$. Since the profit-maximizing output is that at which $MR = MC$, we can re-write the formula for MR as

$$MR = MC = ATC = p - \frac{p}{\epsilon_p},$$

or, rearranging terms,

$$p = ATC \left(\frac{1}{1 - 1/\epsilon_p} \right).$$

The expression in parentheses is the percentage mark-up over average total cost that will produce maximum profit.

Notice the behavior of $(1/1 - 1/\epsilon_p)$ as price elasticity of demand varies. The higher the value of ϵ_p, the closer the denominator of the expression is to 1. Thus, price in such cases is closer to average total cost, and economic profit approaches zero. With a smaller value for ϵ_p the denominator becomes smaller and the value of the entire expression greater. Mark-up over ATC is greater, and economic profit is greater. These results are consistent with our earlier generalizations about the inverse relationship between a firm's pricing power and price elasticity.

BREAK-EVEN ANALYSIS FOR A MONOPOLISTIC FIRM

Possession of market power gives the monopolistic firm a degree of control over price. We have seen that competitive firms face a price determined by industry supply and demand. A competitive firm's demand curve is horizontal, indicating a constant price whatever the firm's own volume of sales.

When a single firm controls a substantial share of the market, however, its own production decisions can affect unit price. In the extreme case in which a single firm controls the entire market, its own production decisions can set unit price. In both cases, the firm's demand curve is not horizontal at the market equilibrium price but slopes downward. The elasticity of demand facing a single firm at any price depends on the extent of the firm's market power.

When the demand curve slopes downward, price is a decreasing function of quantity:

$$p = f(Q).$$

EXAMPLE 10.1 **Mark-up Pricing for a Transportation Firm**

To illustrate mark-up pricing, suppose Dependable Airlines (described in Chapter 6) uses its fixed resources on two commuter routes and charges a price of $0.11 a passenger mile. The presence of a competing airline on the northern commuter route suggests price elasticity of demand at the current price of $\epsilon_N = 4$. The absence of competition on the southern route means that in this case the firm is competing only against ground transportation, and price elasticity of demand is $\epsilon_S = 2$. Average total cost is constant at $ATC = \$0.066$ per passenger mile.

Dependable's managers must first determine the percentage mark-up over average total cost in the two markets that would yield maximum profit. Thus,

$$\text{Mark-up}_N = \left(\frac{1}{(1 - 1/\epsilon_N)}\right) = \left(\frac{1}{(1 - 1/4)}\right) = 1.33,$$

and

$$\text{Mark-up}_S = \left(\frac{1}{(1 - 1/\epsilon_S)}\right) = \left(\frac{1}{(1 - 1/2)}\right) = 2.00.$$

If the firm practices price discrimination, prices in the two markets would be:

$$p_N = ATC(\text{mark-up}_N) = .066(1.33) = \$.088,$$

and

$$p_S = ATC(\text{mark-up}_S) = .066(2.00) = \$.132$$

per passenger mile. The absence of competition in the southern market increases the firm's market power and permits the firm to charge a higher price.

For most purposes, price can be expressed as a linear equation of the form

$$p = a - b(Q),$$

where a is the horizontal intercept of the demand curve and b is the necessary price reduction associated with the sale of each additional unit. Thus,

$$p = \$8.50 - .05(Q)$$

indicates a maximum price of $8.50 at which zero units would be sold and a price reduction of $0.05 for the sale of each additional unit. Figure 10.4a on page 324 is a graph of the price equation

$$p = \$8.50 - .05(Q),$$

which represents the monopolistic firm's demand curve in our example.

Under the conditions in Figure 10.4a, total revenue is

$$TR = (p)(Q) = [\$8.50 - .05(Q)](Q) = \$8.50(Q) - 0.05(Q)^2.$$

FIGURE 10.4   **Economic Profit and Demand for a Monopoly**

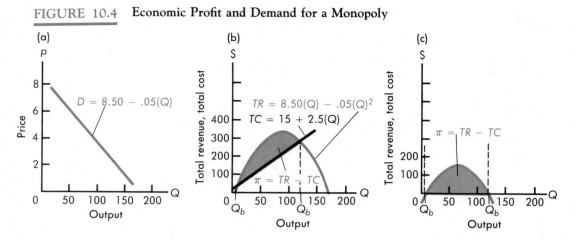

The price equation is the demand curve for a monopoly (a). The break-even point(s) is (are) located by setting TR equal to TC and solving for the value of Q (b). Economic profit is the difference between TR and TC (c).

This equation is graphed in Figure 10.4b. Note that $TR = \$8.50(Q) - 0.05(Q)^2$ is a quadratic equation in which the constant a is zero, and b and c are the parameters of the price equation. A quadratic equation of the form

$$TR = a + b(Q) - c(Q)^2 = 8.50(Q) - 0.05(Q)^2$$

has the shape shown in Figure 10.4b, with $TR = 0$ for $Q = 0$ and increasing TR for values of Q between $Q = 1$ and $Q = 85$. Total revenue increases over the range $1 \leq Q \leq 85$ because price reductions lead to greater percentage increases in quantity. That is, price elasticity of demand is greater than 1. Beyond production of $Q = 85$ units, total revenue declines. This is because price reductions lead to smaller percentage gains in quantity and price elasticity is less than 1. Beyond production of $Q = 170$ units, price falls below zero, causing total revenue to be negative.

A quadratic total revenue function can be used to determine the "break-even" level of output for a firm with market power. This process is similar to that explained in Chapter 6 involving competitive firms. Remember that the break-even quantity is the quantity at which total revenue is equal to total cost:

$$TR = TC,$$

and

$$a + b(Q) - c(Q)^2 = FC + VC(Q).$$

With a cost equation of $TC = FC + AVC(Q) = 15 + 2.5(Q)$, the break-even equation becomes:

$$TR = 8.50(Q_b) - 0.05(Q_b)^2 = 15 + 2.5(Q_b) = TC,$$

or, rearranging terms,

$$-15 + 6(Q_b) - 0.05(Q_b)^2 = 0.$$

Solving for Q_b requires use of the quadratic formula for an equation of the form $a + bQ + cQ^2 = 0$:[1]

$$Q_b = \frac{-b \pm \sqrt{b^2 - 4ac}}{2c}.$$

Substituting the values from our example in the formula yields:

$$Q_b = \frac{-6 \pm \sqrt{36 - 3}}{.1} = \frac{6 \pm 5.74}{.1} = 2.6 \text{ and } 117.45.$$

Note that the use of the quadratic formula yields two positive values for Q_b, indicating two break-even quantities.

A line representing $TC = FC + AVC(Q)$ is also shown in Figure 10.4b. In Figure 10.4, $Q_b = 2.6$ is the point at which TR becomes greater than TC, and $Q = 117.45$ is the point at which TR becomes less than TC. Production of fewer than 2.6 or more than 117.45 units per week would yield negative economic profit. For values of $2.6 \leq Q \leq 117.45$, TR exceeds TC and economic profit is positive.

Locating the Profit-Maximizing Quantity of Output

Economic profit is measured on the graph as the vertical distance between TR and TC at any level of Q. The profit-maximizing firm will seek to produce a level of output for which the vertical distance $TR - TC$ is greatest. In Figure 10.4b, the maximum vertical distance between TR and TC is shown at the level of Q at which the slopes of TR and TC are equal. Since the slopes of the curves are their marginal values, this condition satisfies the maximum-profit condition: $MR = MC$.

The profit-maximizing level of Q can be determined algebraically by writing equations for MR and MC and setting them to equal each other. The equations for MR and MC are the first derivatives of the total revenue and total cost functions, determined through the use of differential calculus (as demonstrated in Appendix 1A). The derivative of $TR = a + b(Q) - c(Q)^2$ is

$$MR = dTR/dQ = b - 2c(Q).$$

---

1. A pocket calculator may also be used for this calculation.

Thus, for

$$TR = a + 8.50(Q) - 0.05(Q)^2,$$

marginal revenue is

$$MR = dTR/dQ = 8.50 - 0.10(Q),$$

which is also the slope of the total revenue function. The slope of the total cost function in Figure 10.4b is constant, since we have assumed constant average variable costs. Thus, for $TC = 15 + 2.5(Q)$, $MC = \$2.50$. The profit-maximizing quantity occurs where $MR = MC$, or

$$2.50 = 8.50 - 0.10(Q)$$
$$= 0.10(Q) = 6.00$$
$$= Q = 60 \text{ units.}$$

Marginal revenue at $Q = 60$ units is

$$MR = 8.50 - 0.10(60) = \$2.50,$$

and marginal cost is also $2.50.

At $Q = 60$, economic profit is determined by substitution of the values we have just found in the profit equation. Thus,

$$\pi = TR - TC = [8.50(60) - 0.05(60)^2] - [15 + 2.50(60)]$$
$$= 510 - 180 - 165 = 165.$$

The economic profit equation is graphed in Figure 10.4c, with maximum profit at $Q = 60$, zero profit at $Q = 2.6$ and $Q = 117.45$, and negative profit outside this range.

Profit-Maximization Through Optimization

The profit-maximizing quantity also can be determined by the process known as optimization. To do this, a manager must first write a profit equation for the relevant cost and revenue conditions. For $TR = 8.50(Q) - 0.05(Q)^2$ and $TC = 15 + 2.50(Q)$, the profit equation is

$$\pi = TR - TC$$
$$= [8.50(Q) - 0.05(Q)^2] - (15 + 2.50(Q))$$
$$= -15 + 6(Q) - 0.05(Q)^2.$$

Note that the profit equation is a quadratic equation. Recall the process for locating the optimum value of a quadratic equation. We must first find the derivative, then set it equal to zero, and solve for the value of the independent variable:

$$\frac{d\pi}{dQ} = 6 - 0.10(Q) = 0$$
$$= Q = 60.$$

Thus, $Q = 60$ is the value of the independent variable at which the economic profit function reaches a peak (or a trough). Now we must find the second derivative of the profit equation to determine whether $Q = 60$ is the maximum or minimum value:

$$\frac{d^2\pi}{dQ^2} = -.1.$$

The negative sign of the second derivative indicates a negative slope for the marginal profit curve. Thus, the value of marginal profit is at first positive, becomes zero where $Q = 60$, and thereafter is negative. These conditions ensure a maximum in the profit function where $Q = 60$.

Break-Even Analysis Using a Quadratic Cost Equation

The previous example was based on the assumption of constant average variable costs. For many production decisions the assumption of constant variable costs is valid, and the simple procedure we have just demonstrated is adequate for locating the break-even quantity of output. In other cases, however, variable costs may behave differently, falling as the quantity of output increases over some range of output and rising as output nears the limited productive capacity of fixed resources. If average variable cost increases with increasing levels of production, it is described by an equation of the form

$$AVC = b + c(Q).$$

If average variable cost decreases with increasing output,

$$AVC = b - c(Q).$$

Total costs then become

$$TC = FC + AVC(Q) = FC + b(Q) + c(Q)^2$$

in the first case and

$$TC = FC + b(Q) - c(Q)^2$$

in the second.

FIGURE 10.5   **Locating Break-Even Points for a Quadratic Cost Function**

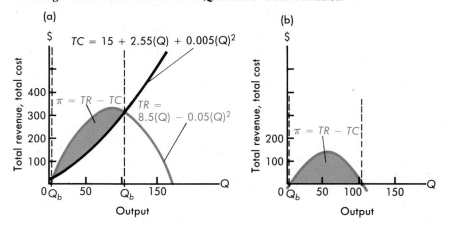

Panel (a) shows the quadratic cost and revenue functions. Economic profit is the difference between TR and TC (b).

The break-even quantity can be determined as before. To illustrate, let us use the same price and total revenue functions. This time, however, we will assume that average variable costs increase with output according to $AVC = 2.5 + .005(Q)$. Unit variable cost is \$2.50 with production of one unit per week and increases \$0.005 with each unit increase in output. Total cost is

$$TC = FC + AVC(Q) = 15 + 2.5(Q) + 0.005(Q)^2.$$

Again, the break-even quantity is the level of Q at which $TR = TC$:

$$TR = 8.50(Q_b) - 0.05(Q_b)^2 = 15 + 2.50(Q_b) + 0.005(Q_b)^2 = TC.$$

Rearranging terms yields:

$$-15 + 6(Q_b) - 0.055(Q_b)^2 = 0,$$

which can be solved by using the quadratic formula:

$$Q_b = \frac{-6 \pm \sqrt{36 - 3.3}}{-.11} = \frac{6 \pm 5.72}{.11} = 2.55 \text{ and } 106.53.$$

Total revenue and total cost for this example are graphed in Figure 10.5a. Note first the curves' typical quadratic shapes. Then note that positive economic profit begins at $Q = 2.55$ units per week, and economic losses occur beyond $Q = 106.53$.

The profit-maximizing level of Q is determined as before by locating the value of Q at which the slopes of TR and TC are equal. The slopes of TR and

TC are marginal revenue and marginal cost respectively, and can be determined using differential calculus. Thus, for $TR = 8.50(Q) - 0.05(Q)^2$, marginal revenue is

$$MR = dTR/dQ = 8.50 - 0.10(Q).$$

Similarly, for $TC = 15 + 2.5(Q) + 0.005(Q)^2$, marginal cost is

$$MC = dTC/dQ = 2.5 + 0.01(Q).$$

Setting *MR* equal to *MC* yields:

$$MR = 8.50 - 0.10(Q) = 2.5 + 0.01(Q) = MC$$

or

$$6 = 0.11(Q) = Q = 54.55.$$

At $Q = 54.55$ units per week, the slopes of *TR* and *TC* are equal, and the (positive) vertical distance between *TR* and *TC* is greatest. Therefore, $Q = 54.55$ is the profit-maximizing quantity of output per week.

Optimization

Again, the profit-maximizing quantity can be determined by optimization. For $TR = 8.50(Q) - 0.05(Q)^2$ and $TC = 15 + 2.5(Q) + 0.005(Q)^2$, economic profit is

$$\pi = TR - TC = [8.50(Q) - 0.05(Q)^2] - (15 + 2.5(Q) + 0.005(Q)^2)$$
$$= -15 + 6(Q) - 0.055(Q)^2.$$

The maximum (or minimum) value occurs where

$$d\pi/dQ = 6 - .11(Q) = 0 \text{ and } Q = 54.55.$$

We know this is a maximum because

$$d^2\pi/dQ^2 = -0.11.$$

Price at the profit-maximizing quantity is determined by substituting the value of *Q* in the price equation:

$$p = 8.50 - 0.05(Q) = 8.50 - 0.05(54.55) = \$5.77.$$

Finally, economic profit is calculated as total revenue less total cost, as shown on Figure 10.5b:

$$\pi = TR - TC = (\$5.77)(54.55) - [15 + 2.5(54.55) + 0.005(54.55)^2]$$
$$= 314.75 - (15 + 136.38 + 14.88) = 314.75 - 166.26 = \$148.50.^2$$

LONG-RUN COST CURVES IN MONOPOLY

The extent of market power in an industry may be influenced by the behavior of long-run cost curves. Remember that a typical long-run average cost curve slopes downward over some range between $Q = 0$ and some other quantity of total output. This is because larger plants enjoy increasing returns to scale from technical, financial, and organizational efficiencies.

Natural Monopolies

A **natural monopoly** is a firm whose long-run average cost curve slopes downward over an exceptionally long range of total output. In such cases, market demand may be too small to justify operation of a plant of optimum scale. A plant of optimum scale would have to spread the cost of its large capital investment over such a relatively small quantity of output that average total cost would be quite high.

These are the circumstances that give rise to natural monopolies. Under these circumstances it is more efficient for one firm to supply the entire market than to encourage competition among a number of smaller firms. Natural monopolies are generally regulated by public commissions to ensure a quantity of output that satisfies market demand at prices that cover full costs, without excessive economic profit.

Artificial Monopolies

In most industries, long-run average cost curves tend to level out over some range of output, so that competing firms can operate plants of various sizes. In many industries the slope of the *LRAC* curve tends to increase for plants designed to produce very large quantities of output. This is because very large plants suffer decreasing returns to scale from technical, financial, and organizational factors. In other words, it becomes increasingly difficult to coordinate operations in larger and larger plants.

---

2. In the first example of this chapter, the profit-maximizing quantity was $Q = 55$. The profit-maximizing quantity was determined by writing a linear equation for price based on points located on the demand curve. Using regression analysis, the price equation was estimated to be $p = 8.50 - 0.05(Q)$. Total revenue was $TR = (p)(Q) = 8.50(Q) - 0.05(Q)^2$, and marginal revenue was $8.50 - 0.10(Q)$. Marginal cost was constant at $MC = \$3.00$. Therefore, the profit-maximizing quantity was determined by:
$$MR = 8.50 - 0.10(Q) = 3.00 = MC,$$
which yielded:
$$5.5 = .10(Q) = Q = 55.$$

Competitive firms cannot operate for long in the upward-sloping portion of the *LRAC* curve. Their costs in this range are greater than necessary, and firms with smaller plants can undercut their prices. Only if a firm establishes an "artificial monopoly" can it continue operating in this range.

Artificial monopolies result from legal restrictions that prevent the entry of new firms into an industry. Legal restrictions include the laws that protect trademarks and patents. Owners of patents are protected from competition for 17 years. Owners of trademarks are protected from competition unless the courts decide the trademark has become a part of everyday language and is no longer exclusive to the original firm. ("Checkers" is an example of a common term that used to be a protected trademark.) Other legal restrictions on competition include legislative acts to exclude competition for purposes other than economic efficiency. Community decisions to limit industrial development and national decisions to coordinate transportation and communication services are examples of this.

Both natural and artificial monopolies tend to dissolve in time. In the case of natural monopolies, the passage of time normally brings growth in market demand. As market demand curves move to the right, new firms can enter the industry and build plants of optimum scale. With market growth, new firms can produce larger quantities of goods and services without paying prohibitively high unit costs for fixed plant and equipment. In the case of artificial monopolies, the passage of time usually removes the legal restrictions on competition. Patents expire, and trademarks are undermined by similar (but not necessarily identical) substitutes. (The proliferation of "designer" jeans provides a recent example of this tendency.) Thus, the tendency over the long run is for industries to move toward the central range of *LRAC*, where average cost is constant at its lowest level. Figure 10.6 illustrates a situation where firms of various sizes operate in long-run competitive equilibrium.

FIGURE 10.6 **Firms of Various Sizes in Long-Run Competitive Equilibrium**

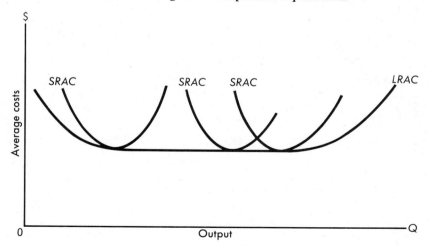

Alternative Pricing Policies for Natural Monopolies

Natural monopolies operate in the downward-sloping portion of the *LRAC* curve in which plants should be built to produce a larger amount than the firm's expected quantity of output and operated at less than the lowest-cost level of operation. Figure 10.7a shows short-run average cost and marginal cost curves for a plant built to produce 1,000 units per production period. However, production is expected to be less than the most efficient quantity, such that average total costs will be greater than the minimum level. For the remainder of this explanation, we will consider only the downward-sloping portion of the *SRAC* curves and the portion of *MC* below *SRAC,* as shown in Figure 10.7b. The horizontal axis in Figure 10.7a has been expanded in Figure 10.7b to make it easier to understand.

Demand and marginal revenue curves for this market also appear in Figure 10.7b. Because the natural monopoly is the only firm in this industry, it faces the entire demand curve in this market. Thus, the downward slope of the demand curve indicates that larger quantities can be sold only at lower prices. Price reductions for larger quantities indicate a downward-sloping marginal revenue curve as well, shown beneath the demand curve in Figure 10.7b and lying midway between the demand curve and the vertical axis.

Three pricing policies are possible for a natural monopoly such as the one in Figure 10.7: **monopoly pricing, average-cost pricing,** and **marginal-cost pricing**.

1. Monopoly pricing would yield maximum economic profit for the natural monopoly, but would involve the smallest quantity of output and the highest

FIGURE 10.7   **Natural Monopoly**

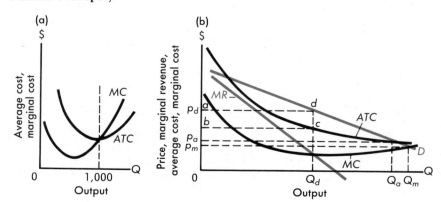

When the expected level of production is less than optimum plant size, the result may be a natural monopoly (a). In natural monopoly, a single firm can satisfy the market at lower average total cost than many small competing firms (b).

price of the three pricing policies. Monopoly pricing is based on the profit-maximizing rule, which states that maximum profit occurs at the point where marginal cost equals marginal revenue. In Figure 10.7b, MC is equal to MR at output of $Q = Q_d$ and price of $p = p_d$. An unregulated natural monopoly would produce at this level and collect economic profit equal to the difference between price and average total cost for each unit produced and sold or:

$$\pi/Q = p - ATC.$$

Total economic profit is represented in Figure 10.7b by rectangle *abcd*, formed beneath the demand curve with a base of $Q = Q_d$ and a height of $\pi/Q = p_d - ATC$.

2. Average-cost pricing would require the natural monopoly to produce and sell a quantity of output at a price that precisely offsets average total cost. Average-cost pricing is generally preferred to monopoly pricing because consumers pay only the full cost of the service, without economic profit. In Figure 10.7b, average total cost is equal to price at quantity $Q = Q_a$ and price $p = p_a$. Quantity is greater and price is lower than when the firm follows a monopoly pricing policy. But since economic profit is zero at $Q = Q_a$, a natural monopoly would not independently decide to implement average-cost pricing. Some form of government regulation would ordinarily be necessary to compel a natural monopoly to increase quantity and reduce price to these levels.

3. Marginal-cost pricing is generally preferred to average-cost pricing because it involves even greater quantity and even lower prices. However, marginal-cost pricing would never occur without government regulation to enforce it. Marginal-cost pricing requires the natural monopoly to produce the quantity of output at which price precisely offsets the *additional* cost associated with the last unit produced. In Figure 10.7b, MC is equal to price at quantity $Q = Q_m$. Note that because MC is less than ATC at $Q = Q_m$, this price does not cover average total cost, and economic profit would be negative. If a natural monopoly is to practice marginal-cost pricing, it generally must receive a subsidy from public funds to cover its full fixed and variable costs.

To summarize, without regulation a natural monopoly would tend to practice monopoly pricing and collect economic profit. Frequently, the first firm in an industry with the largest fixed plant and equipment and the most secure market position would be able to discourage the entry of competing firms and practice monopoly pricing. Under government regulation, a natural monopoly could practice average-cost or marginal-cost pricing, depending on the policy of the public regulatory commission. If production of larger quantities at lower prices is believed to be advantageous to the community as a whole, the commission may decide on marginal cost pricing and agree to finance part of the firm's operating costs with a government subsidy. The U.S. Postal Service and many types of public transportation are examples of this.

EXAMPLE 10.2   Price Discrimination by an Electric Utility

Some natural monopolies are permitted to practice price discrimination. Price discrimination is possible when buyers can be separated according to a particular characteristic and charged varying prices for units of the same service or product. Through price discrimination, a natural monopoly is able to supply a service that would be uneconomical to produce at prices that precisely offset average total cost.

Consider a hypothetical firm in the electric power industry. The fixed costs of generating electric power are so high that the firm must produce a substantial volume of electricity if it is to produce at lowest average total cost. However, homeowners and businesses in areas supplied by the firm's power plant may not use enough power to push average total cost to its lowest level.

Figure A shows the combined demand of business and residential users of electric power, along with the short-run *ATC* curve for producing power. The position of the curves shows that if a single price were charged all customers, no price and quantity would yield sufficient revenue to pay the firm's full costs. Unless the firm were to receive a substantial subsidy from government, it would eventually go out of business.

Now suppose the public regulatory commission allows the power company to charge all of its customers the highest price each buyer would be willing to pay. Charging each individual buyer the price he or she will pay allows the power company to collect all of the revenue shown on the demand curve up to the total quantity produced and sold. Thus, total revenue is represented by the area beneath the demand curve.

Will total revenue be sufficient in this case to cover the firm's costs? To find out, select a quantity of output such as $Q = Q_0$, shown in Figure A. The vertical line

FIGURE A

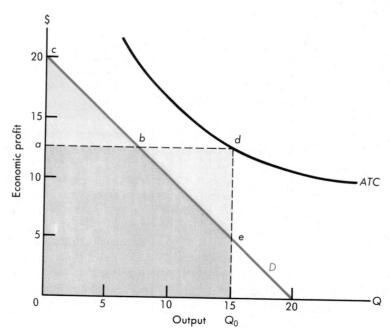

drawn from $Q_0 = 15$ to ATC represents unit cost, and the rectangle formed beneath ATC at $Q = Q_0$ represents total cost. Compare the total cost rectangle at $Q = Q_0$ with the shaded area beneath the demand curve to this quantity. In particular, note that triangle *abc* is precisely equal to triangle *bde*. This means that the space representing total revenue is precisely equal to the rectangle representing total cost at $Q = Q_0$ and that economic profit is zero. For any quantity of output less than $Q = Q_0$ the triangle included in total revenue is smaller than the triangle included in total cost, and our hypothetical power company would experience negative economic profit. For any quantity of output greater than $Q = Q_0$, total revenue would be greater than total cost, and economic profit would be positive.

TRANSFER PRICING IN A VERTICALLY INTEGRATED FIRM

Many U.S. manufacturing firms can be described as **vertically integrated firms**: that is, materials or parts produced by one subsidiary are used as major inputs in the manufacturing process of another. The transfer of component parts among subsidiaries of a single firm involves important pricing decisions. Transfer prices among the integrated subsidiaries should serve to coordinate production of parts and finished products so that profits are maximum for the firm as a whole.

To illustrate transfer pricing, let us consider two different market situations: first, a firm whose subsidiary produces a material or part that is sold in a competitive market and second, a firm whose producing subsidiary enjoys significant market power.

When a subsidiary faces competition, market price reflects the level of total demand and the production costs of the part in the market as a whole. All users of the part will normally choose to buy the quantity at which the additional revenue from its use in production is equal to its price. To maximize profit for the vertically integrated firm, purchasing subsidiaries of the parent firm should follow the same rule, purchasing the quantity that increases total revenue to the purchasing subsidiary by at least as much as the increase in total cost.

Pricing decisions differ, however, if the producing subsidiary is the dominant supplier of the material or part, with power to set different prices for different buyers. Figures 10.8a and 10.8b on page 336 illustrate the pricing decision. In Figure 10.8a, total demand for the part is shown as D and marginal cost of production is MC. An independent, profit-maximizing firm would normally choose to produce the quantity for which marginal revenue from sales is equal to marginal cost. Marginal revenue is shown in Figure 10.8a as MR. Marginal revenue is less than price according to the relationship

$$MR = p - \frac{p}{\epsilon_p}$$

at every point on the demand curve. For a firm with market power, the profit-

FIGURE 10.8   **Transfer Pricing**

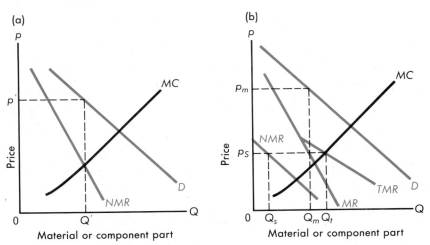

The profit-maximizing price and quantity for an independent firm producing a material or component part is shown in (a). The profit-maximizing price and quantity for a subsidiary of a vertically integrated firm is shown in (b).

maximizing quantity is determined by $MR = MC$ at Q', and the price is shown on the demand curve as p'.

Charging the profit-maximizing price may maximize profits for the producing subsidiary but it may not for the vertically integrated firm as a whole. When other subsidiaries use the material or part, there may be an advantage in setting price below the producing subsidiary's profit-maximizing level. By using the part in further production, another subsidiary may be able to add more to the firm's total profits.

The additional profit to a firm when one subsidiary buys a component part from another and processes it for sale is called **net marginal revenue**. Net marginal revenue is the difference between the additional revenue from sales of the finished product and the cost of purchasing and processing the material or component part. A net marginal revenue curve has been drawn in Figure 10.8a and is labelled *NMR*. When revenues shown on the net marginal revenue curve are added to revenues shown on the marginal revenue curve, the result is a **total marginal revenue curve** (*TMR*) for the vertically integrated firm as a whole.

The profit-maximizing quantity for the vertically integrated firm is the quantity at which $TMR = MC$, shown in Figure 10.8b as Q_t. Of the total quantity, the portion sold to other subsidiaries is Q_s, where the marginal cost of producing the material or part is equal to net marginal revenue from sales of the finished product. The remaining quantity, $Q_t - Q_s = Q_m$, is sold in other markets. At Q_m, marginal revenue from total sales of the component part is equal to marginal cost of total production. Price is set by the demand curve at p_m.

There are several significant differences between Figures 10.8a and 10.8b. In Figure 10.8b, quantity of output is greater. Quantity sold in external markets is less, and price is lower. The actual level of profit for the firm depends on the level of average costs.

SUMMARY

A firm's pricing policy depends on its market power, which depends, in turn, on the structure of the market in which it operates. The extreme market structures are competition and monopoly, but most firms operate in markets described as monopolistically competitive or oligopolistic.

Market structure determines price elasticity of demand which determines a firm's potential mark-up over average total cost. With price discrimination a firm may set a higher price in markets in which demand is less elastic.

With market power, a firm's demand curve slopes downward, and marginal revenue is less than price. Total revenue may be estimated according to a quadratic equation. The break-even quantity of output is that at which total revenue is equal to total cost, as determined through use of the quadratic formula. The profit-maximizing quantity of output can be determined by optimization, using differential calculus.

Natural monopolies occur where optimum scale is too large relative to market demand for competition to survive. Government regulation may be necessary to prevent monopoly pricing. The regulatory commission may permit price discrimination, however, and it may provide for the payment of a subsidy to permit marginal cost pricing. Artificial monopolies result from restrictions on entry to the industry. In the long run, market power tends to dissipate, and markets tend to become more competitive.

In a vertically integrated firm, the pricing decision when a component part produced in one subsidiary is sold to another may differ from pricing decisions when the part is sold only outside the firm. The profit-maximizing price and quantity for the vertically integrated firm is determined at $MC = TMR$, where TMR includes marginal revenue from sale of the component part and sales of the finished good that uses the part in production.

KEY TERMS

price theory	monopoly pricing
market structure	average-cost pricing
perfect competition	marginal-cost pricing
monopolistic competition	vertically integrated firm
price discrimination	net marginal revenue
mark-up pricing	total marginal revenue curve
artificial monopoly	

QUESTIONS AND PROBLEMS

1. Analyze the economic profit position of a firm that sells an average of 3,000 units per month at a price of $175 per unit. Production costs are constant at $100 over a wide range of output. Demand elasticity is estimated to be $\epsilon_p = -2.25$. How would your analysis be affected if average production costs were $125 per unit?

2. Explain the assumptions used by an analyst in writing each of the equations below. Then determine the maximum-profit level of price, output, and economic profit.

$$p = 100 - .5Q$$
$$AVC = 50 + .25Q$$
$$FC = 100.$$

3. Using the information in Question 2, calculate price elasticity at $20 intervals along the demand curve: i.e., $p = 20, 40, 60,$ and 80.

4. Explain the basis on which parking fees in an urban area might be set at different levels throughout the day.

5. Sporting Equipment Company reduced price on its $100 fishing rod to $98 and enjoyed additional sales revenue of $250 on additional monthly sales of 15 units. Calculate price elasticity of demand for this item.

6. Write a price equation for a product that has sales of 50 units a month at $100 per unit with estimated price elasticity of $\epsilon_p = -1.4$.

7. Use the information in Question 6 and assume that total costs are $TC = 500 + (90Q - .6Q^2)$. Determine the price that yields maximum profit. What would monthly profit be?

8. Explain how differences in price elasticity between the subsidiaries of a vertically integrated processing firm and its outside users can increase profits for the firm. What are the consequences of this type of price discrimination for competition in the various markets involved? What circumstances must exist for this strategy to succeed?

9. Compute the profit-maximizing mark-up over ATC for a product with demand elasticity of -1.6.

10. Western Farm Equipment Company sells seed-spreading attachments for tractors at a price of $500 per unit and averages monthly sales of 30 units. Managers estimate price elasticity of demand for the current price at $\epsilon_p = -1.2$. Costs of production include monthly fixed charges of $8,000 and variable costs per unit that increase according to $AVC = 100 + 5Q$, where Q is monthly output. Determine the monthly break-even levels of operation and the price and output for maximum profit. Compare the level of current profit with maximum potential profit and make recommendations for increasing profit.

11

Price and Output Decisions in Oligopoly and Monopolistic Competition

The great richness and diversity of U.S. industry can be better understood by considering the broad continuum between competition and monopoly. The producers of everything from automatic garage door openers to zip-locked storage bags are represented on this continuum. The diversity of firms is exemplified by differences in technical processes, differences in resource requirements and availability, and differences in market demand. It is differences such as these that produce tendencies toward monopoly in some markets and tendencies toward competition in others.

The most interesting aspect of this wide variety of industries, however, is not the industries' inherent differences but their susceptibility to change. Markets that are well served by a particular market structure now may readily change to another market structure in the future.

It is important that managers anticipate and plan for structural changes in their particular industry. Structural changes may result from any of the three types of market changes that have been discussed in this text: *Technical changes* may result from improved production techniques or more widespread information about production processes. *Human or organizational changes* include demographic changes, changes in consumer attitudes or living patterns, and changes in the legal or regulatory environment in which a firm operates. *Economic or financial changes* may involve changes in resource costs or in the availability of financial capital. This chapter will provide examples of each of these types of changes, along with the accompanying changes in market structure.

In order to compensate effectively for those changes, a manager should first understand the fundamental characteristics of his or her industry that distinguish it from other industries and that may provide opportunities for profitable operation. Then, a manager must anticipate the fundamental market changes that might cause a variation in market structure. A manager must always be sensitive to the likely responses to change of other firms in his or her own industry and related industries.

This chapter describes pricing and output decisions in the more typical market structures of the U.S. economy: oligopoly and monopolistic competition. Managers of firms in oligopoly and monopolistic competition must first consider the distinguishing aspects of their own markets (including various aspects of the product and the technical processes involved). Then they will be ready to make decisions based on changes in their markets (including the responses of competing firms to change).

OLIGOPOLY

The degree of interdependence among firms depends strongly on the attributes of their products. Some products are so nearly uniform among suppliers as to be practically identical, a market characteristic of perfect competition. For similar products with high fixed costs of production, however, the actual number of suppliers may be small relative to market demand, and the resulting market structure may more closely resemble a monopoly. When only a few large-scale suppliers are present, the industry's firms may not always compete on the basis of price. Still, each firm will be particularly sensitive to other firms' pricing policies.

These market characteristics are true for many industrial commodities. Industrial materials like raw milk, rubber, steel, chemicals, aluminum, and petroleum are examples of commodities whose attributes are fairly uniform among a relatively few large suppliers. These commodities are produced by what is called **homogeneous oligopoly**. Because their products are easily substitutable, individual supplying firms in homogeneous oligopoly face relatively elastic demand curves. Nevertheless, because there are few firms in such industries, they are not driven by competition to produce at lowest cost and set the lowest price. Figure 11.1 shows graphs of (a) total market demand for products of homogeneous oligopoly and (b) demand for the products of a particular oligopolistic firm.

Firms in homogeneous oligopoly recognize their interdependence and curtail their market behavior to avoid price competition. They seek to expand total market demand for their products as a whole (to shift the industry demand curve to the right), rather than to capture a larger share of a constant market for themselves. Toward this objective, they frequently sponsor institutional advertising, as opposed to advertising for a particular firm. Their trade associations provide product information to all firms and serve to emphasize the firms' interdependence.

FIGURE 11.1 Oligopolistic Demand

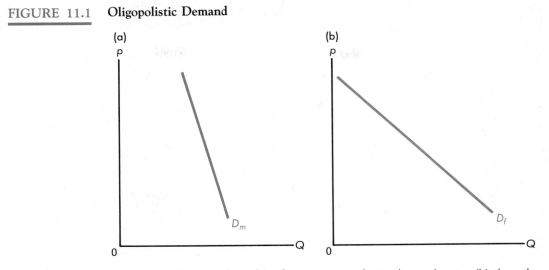

An individual oligopolistic firm faces a more elastic demand curve (b) than the demand curve facing the industry as a whole (a).

Consumer goods oligopolies tend to produce dissimilar products. Certain household appliances, automobiles, tires and long-distance telephone communications are examples of such goods. Because their products are not perfectly substitutable, individual supplying firms in **heterogeneous oligopoly** face less elastic demand curves. Still, the small number of supplying firms generally allows the firms to set prices higher than the competitive market price and collect economic profit.

Firms in heterogeneous oligopoly are more likely to engage in competitive advertising to distinguish their products from others (to shift the individual firm's demand curve to the right and make it less elastic). Advertising is the preferred method of competition in this market situation because it is not easily copied or duplicated by other firms. Each advertising vehicle is in some sense unique and cannot be precisely matched by competing firms in the industry.

Price and Quantity Decisions in Oligopoly: Duopoly

To illustrate pricing policy in oligopoly, we will begin with a special case in which only two similar firms occupy the market. The two firms constitute a **duopoly** and together face the market demand curve in Figure 11.2a on page 342. In our example, the firms recognize their interdependence and tacitly accept market shares equal to one-half the total market. Thus, each firm's demand curve, D_f, shown in Figure 11.2b, is one-half of market demand, D_m. With identical marginal cost curves, profit-maximizing duopolists will set a price of $p = p_d$, where $MC = MR$. Average or unit economic profit for each firm is equal to the difference between p and ATC.

FIGURE 11.2   **Duopolistic Demand and Economic Profit**

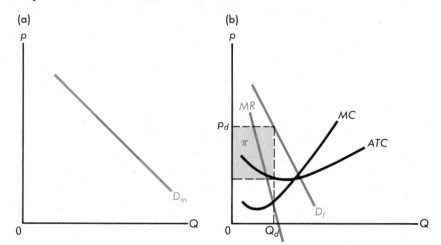

Each duopolistic firm supplies half of the market (a) and collects economic profit equal to the difference between price and average total cost for each unit sold: $\pi = Q_d(p_d - ATC)$.

When duopolists set the profit-maximizing price and quantity, the results for the economy as a whole are similar to those of monopoly. Price is higher and quantity lower than would be true in competition. Moreover, without competition the duopoly firms are neither compelled to produce at the minimum point on their *ATC* curves, nor to construct plants of optimum size.

Duopolies tend to be unstable. This is because positive economic profits eventually attract new firms to the industry. As the number of firms increases, they become less similar and their market shares become more variable. The firms remain strongly interdependent, but their relationships are not as clearly defined as in duopoly. Frequently, the market expands to include a few large firms and a number of small and medium-sized firms. These are the typical characteristics of homogeneous and heterogeneous oligopoly.

The Kinked Demand Curve

In oligopolistic firms, pricing decisions are governed by the expected reactions of other firms in the market. Consider first a typical oligopolistic firm's demand curve in Figure 11.3a. The curve's position and shape depend on the substitutability of the product and the firm's own market share. For a single oligopolistic firm, price (p_m) is determined by the tacit agreement of all firms in the market to accept the given distribution of market shares. Quantity supplied is Q_f.

Agreement on price and market share is achieved through the oligopolistic firms' own recognition of their interdependence. In effect, oligopolistic firms face two different demand curves. A relatively horizontal (or more elastic) de-

FIGURE 11.3   The "Kink" in Oligopolistic Demand

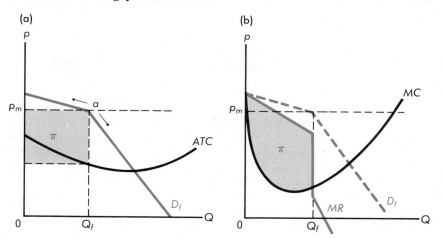

Production at any point other than *a* in panel (a) (the "kink") would result in lower economic profit for the oligopolistic firm (b).

mand curve describes demand if rival firms do not follow price changes. A relatively vertical (or less elastic) demand curve describes demand if rival firms do follow price changes. Oligopolistic firms expect that rival firms will ignore price increases and follow price cuts. This is because a price increase will cause an oligopolistic firm's customers to substitute the products of a rival firm, causing quantity demanded to decrease sharply. A price reduction will not increase quantity demanded significantly, however, since rival firms would cut prices in order to resist the loss in market share caused by maintaining their current price.

Differences in price elasticity of demand are shown in Figure 11.3a by a demand curve with a "kink" at the price tacitly accepted by all of the firms in the industry. The portion of the demand curve above the accepted price has a more horizontal slope reflecting greater elasticity than the portion of demand below the accepted price.

Total revenue for each oligopolistic firm is price times quantity supplied at the tacitly accepted price. Total cost is average total cost times quantity. As long as the firm's *ATC* curve lies beneath the demand curve at the accepted price, the difference between total revenue and total cost is positive, and each oligopolistic firm will collect economic profit. An average total cost curve is also shown in Figure 11.3a, and a rectangle representing economic profit is shown between the demand curve and *ATC*.

Any price other than the tacitly accepted price p_m would result in lower economic profit for each firm. This is apparent from an examination of the marginal revenue curve associated with a demand curve that is "kinked" at price p_m.

Marginal revenue and marginal cost curves are drawn in Figure 11.3b to show that at any price other than p_m, $MR \neq MC$ and the oligopolistic firm would not be maximizing profits. Remember that *MR* and *MC* are the derivatives of a firm's total revenue and total cost functions. The firm's objective is to maximize the difference between *TR* and *TC:* that is, to maximize the value of economic profit $\pi = TR - TC$. Total revenue and total cost are represented in Figure 11.3b by the integrals of *MR* and *MC* which are shown graphically by the areas beneath the respective curves. The difference between these two areas is economic profit, represented by the shaded area in Figure 11.3b. Producing less than Q_f would reduce the shaded area between *MR* and *MC,* causing economic profit to decrease. Producing more than Q_f would also decrease economic profit as can be seen by the negative difference between *MR* and *MC*. Again, economic profit is less than that at the profit-maximizing level of *p* and *Q*.

The kink in an oligopolistic firm's demand curve reflects its tacit acceptance of a given price. When all firms tacitly accept a given price, economic profits may rise or fall with changes in costs of production in the industry as a whole. Thus, the cost curves in Figure 11.3b might shift up or down, causing the space between the curves to vary greatly while market price does not change at all.

Price Leadership

Without competition to compel timely price changes in response to changes in market conditions, oligopolies tend to rely on the pricing decisions of a dominant firm. Typically, the largest or oldest firm in the oligopolized industry is looked upon as a "price leader," responsible for making the initial price change that brings all other firms' prices and quantities in line with changing market conditions. The effect of the new price on economic profits in the industry will depend on the underlying changes in demand and/or costs. The effect on individual firms' market shares will depend on the firms' ability to maintain roughly comparable technological and cost conditions.

Because price competition generally is not an option for oligopolistic firms, other methods of competition may be pursued instead. Research and development of new processes and products is a typical attempt to increase demand, as well as to secure or enhance individual market shares. The four largest pharmaceutical manufacturers in the United States spend between 4 percent and 6 percent of each sales dollar on research, amounting to hundreds of millions of dollars annually. Each firm hopes to develop a "block-buster" drug, a cure for one of man's chronic ailments, and subsequently to enjoy a monopoly in the drug's production. Producers of home computers are constantly developing features they hope will distinguish their model from competing models and help them achieve a secure position in the home computer industry. Such efforts contribute to the technical progress of U.S. industry and enhance our country's international competitiveness as well. The case study that follows describes an oligopolized industry that failed to deal successfully with changes in market conditions.

CASE STUDY 11.1   An Oligopoly (Finally) Faces Up to Change

Since World War II, aluminum has been considered a miracle metal. Produced with bauxite extracted form clay, this lightweight metal conducts heat and electricity well, reflects light and heat, and resists corrosion. It is an important material in building construction and in the production of cans, appliances, and autos.

Recessions in the 1970s and early 1980s greatly affected firms producing durable goods and housing—two of the principal users of aluminum. The market demand curve for aluminum shifted to the left, sales at the tacitly accepted price fell, and economic profits in the industry shrank. Among individual oligopolistic firms, pressure began to build for a price change.

High fixed costs in the aluminum industry have limited the number of producers to three large firms and a scattered assortment of medium-sized firms. (Alcoa, Reynolds, and Kaiser supply about 70 percent of the market, and Alcoa is generally regarded as the price leader.) Declining demand and reduced output for all firms raised average fixed costs and cut into economic profit. In 1974, all of the firms raised their prices by more than 50 percent and cut production severely. Figure A illustrates this change in the market as a whole.

With recovery from recession in 1976, demand for aluminum increased, and prices were raised again by about 20 percent. By 1983, aluminum prices had risen to three times what they were before the 1974 price increase, only to drop again by almost half at the end of the year.

Instability in the market for aluminum has brought serious consequences for producing firms, as well as for the economy as a whole. Declining revenue has pushed smaller producing firms out of the industry and concentrated more of the market in the hands of the giants (who also have not been immune to falling sales). After losing $100 million in 1982 and 1983, Martin Marietta Incorporated sold its aluminum operations to an Australian firm at a 40 percent loss. Atlantic Richfield Incorporated sold its aluminum facilities to Canada's Alcan Aluminum Company. Analysts predict the eventual move of all aluminum production to Canada, Brazil,

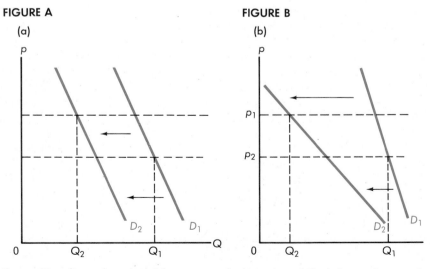

FIGURE A

(a)

FIGURE B

(b)

Competition from abroad and from new substitutes has shifted demand curves for aluminum (a) to the left and made them more elastic (b).

and Australia, where energy costs for producing aluminum are much less than in the United States.

Developments in the aluminum industry demonstrate two important facts about U.S. markets: the inevitability of change and the futility of basing a firm's pricing policy on faulty perceptions of market conditions. Enjoying a market seemingly protected from competition, the oligopolistic firms in the aluminum industry expected demand to remain relatively inelastic, as manufacturing firms and homebuilders satisfied their growing needs for the miracle metal. In the long run, however, no market is truly protected. As aluminum prices rose, substitute materials and imported aluminum began to enter the market as acceptable substitutes for aluminum. In Figure B, market demand for aluminum is shown having shifted to the left and having become more price elastic. Increased competition in the industry has reduced the firms' power to set price and has reduced or eliminated economic profits. (Similar changes confronted U.S. manufacturers of autos during this same period of time.)

The aluminum firms' failure to anticipate and deal with changes in market conditions is not difficult to understand. Their large supply of fixed resources and their tendency to compete in the area of technical superiority compelled them to follow fairly rigid pricing policies and also inhibited each individual firm's efforts to cut costs. The smaller firms are the only ones to have been forced out of the industry so far, but the ultimate result of these policies may be a total collapse of the industry in the United States.

MANAGERIAL THINKING

Draw a graph that shows the effect of a negative shift in demand for aluminum on the "kinked" demand curve of an individual aluminum supplier. How have such changes affected the firm's economic profit rectangle? What is the significance of high fixed costs in your explanation?

Cross Elasticity of Demand: Substitutes

We have seen that a firm's power to set price depends in part on the availability of acceptable substitutes for its product. Within an oligopolized industry, substitutability of products ranges from absolutely perfect (homogeneous oligopoly) to very low (heterogeneous oligopoly). The availability of substitutes within the industry is what keeps price at the level tacitly accepted by the oligopolistic firms. In turn, the availability of substitutes from other industries is what determines the actual level of the accepted price.

This distinction can be measured by calculating a firm's **cross price elasticity of demand**. Recall that cross price elasticity of demand (ϵ_c) is the percentage change in quantity sold of a particular good relative to a percentage change in price of another good:

$$\epsilon_c = \frac{\%\Delta \text{ quantity sold of A}}{\%\Delta \text{ price of B}}$$

Consider first the products of two firms in homogeneous oligopoly. Because their products are essentially identical, they are perfect substitutes. A small percentage change in price by one firm (B) would result in a total shift of buyers to the other firm (A). The value of cross price elasticity in this case is quite high (infinite) and positive. In heterogeneous oligopoly, minor distinctions among products may preclude a total shift of buyers to another supplier. Still, the value of cross price elasticity is also high in this case.

High cross price elasticity of demand gives the oligopoly firms no power *individually* to affect price. The absence of market power for individual firms establishes their interdependence and causes them to rely on a price leader for their pricing decisions.

The cross price elasticity between the products of an oligopolized industry and products of other industries depends on the various attributes of the product. Some goods have absolutely no substitutes in the short run, so that cross price elasticity of demand is very low. Products of the petroleum industry, for example, have no generally accepted substitutes, making it possible for the oligopolized petroleum industry to set prices high without fear of a significant decrease in quantity sold. This result is true only in the short run, however. With the passage of time, high prices for petroleum products will cause buyers to substitute other kinds of products: cotton and silk fabrics for polyester, public transportation and small cars for large cars, and even solar energy and wood-burning stoves for gas furnaces.

The process of developing substitutes has been slow in the petroleum industry because of the existence of much fixed equipment that must be depreciated before new equipment appropriate to the changed market conditions can be acquired. Development of substitutes in the aluminum industry began earlier and has progressed further. While no one material has precisely reproduced the attributes of aluminum, producers of other materials have adapted their products to meet specific needs of particular users: some examples are steel for building construction, car bodies, and appliances, plastics for auto parts, and tin for utensils and containers. In each of these uses, cross price elasticity of demand depends on how close the attributes of the substitute are to the desired qualities of aluminum. Where cross price elasticity is high, aluminum producers face a more elastic demand curve and reduced market power to set price.

Cross Price Elasticity of Demand for Complements

Cross price elasticity of demand also is a useful concept for responding to changes in an industry that is *complementary* to the oligopolized industry. A complementary industry is one that produces a good or service that is used together with that of the industry itself. Among complementary industries, the sign of cross price elasticity is negative:

$$\epsilon_c = \frac{\%\Delta \text{ quantity of A}}{\%\Delta \text{ price of B}} < 0.$$

This is because an increase in the price of the good B reduces the quantity of B sold and reduces buyers' need for its complement, A.

Again, the petroleum industry provides a pertinent example. Because petroleum is complementary to automobile transportation, an increase in the price of gasoline has had the effect of sharply reducing the quantity of autos sold. The results of this relationship for the U.S. auto industry are well-known, particularly to the many managers in the industry who failed to anticipate and plan for the market change (and followed many production workers to the unemployment lines).

Once again, however, it is understandable that U.S. auto manufacturers delayed making the changes necessary for profitable operation in the new market environment. Their large amount of fixed capital and expensive contractual obligations made adjustments slow and difficult. Hence, long-range planning is very important and has been historically difficult to implement in the automobile industry. Moreover, managers of U.S. auto firms are particularly accountable to the demands of their stockholders, who frequently spurn investing in a firm that delivers few dividends today while investments are being made in productive facilities that will only become profitable years in the future.

Multi-Product Decisions

One way to protect against long-run market change for some oligopolistic firms is to expand the firm's product line to include substitutes and complements for its own product. Understanding cross price elasticity can help managers plan a multi-product strategy for dealing with unexpected changes in a variety of markets.

An example of the production of substitutes is the full line of automobiles produced by the major automobile manufacturers. Models appropriate to large or small families, city or country driving, luxury or economy lifestyles, conservative or sporty tastes are available from all major U.S. auto firms. When a firm produces a variety of substitutes, individual product lines can be expanded, cut back, or phased out when market conditions change.

Likewise, when a complementary good strongly affects the oligopolistic firm's own sales, the firm may decide to include it in its product-mix. Producing the complement helps smooth out price fluctuations and stabilizes total production. The complement may even be sold at a loss to increase the market for the firm's primary product. (In retailing, such goods are called "loss leaders.") The Gillette razor company has made profitable use of this principle in its sales of razor blades, shaving creams, and other men's grooming products. The Kodak camera company has acted similarly in the production of film. Diversification among substitutes and complements has other advantages, including the joint use of materials and by-products and joint marketing strategies.

Price and Quantity Decisions for the Multi-Product Firm

The price and quantity decisions of a firm that produces more than one good or service are similar to those of the single-product firm. The decision-making process involves optimization and uses the tools of differential calculus described in Appendix 1A. However, because there is more than one independent variable (good or service to be produced), the profit-maximizing decision requires partial differentiation with respect to each of the separate variables.

To illustrate, consider a firm producing two brands of ice cream: Brand A, a rich, high-fat product suitable for sale in ice cream shops, and Brand B, a lower quality product for sale in school cafeterias. The demand curves for the two brands can be written:

$$p_A = 5 - .03(Q_A)$$

and

$$p_B = 10 - .04(Q_B),$$

where Q represents thousands of gallons per week. Thus, the firm's total revenue function is:

$$TR = p_A(Q_A) + p_B(Q_B) = 5(Q_A) - .03(Q_A)^2 + 10(Q_B) - .04(Q_B)^2.$$

Average variable costs associated with the two brands are

$$AVC_A = 3 + .01(Q_A) \text{ and } AVC_B = 2 + .02(Q_B).$$

With weekly fixed costs of $100, the firm's total cost function is

$$
\begin{aligned}
TC &= FC + AVC_A(Q_A) + AVC_B(Q_B) \\
&= 100 + 30(Q_A) + .01(Q_A)^2 + 2(Q_B) + .02(Q_B)^2.
\end{aligned}
$$

The firm's economic profit function is

$$
\begin{aligned}
\pi &= TR - Tc \\
&= [5(Q_A) - .03(Q_A)^2 + 10(Q_B) - .04(Q_B)^2] - \\
&\quad [100 + 3(Q_A) + .01(Q_A)^2 + 2(Q_B) + .02(Q_B)^2] \\
&= -100 + 2(Q_A) - .04(Q_A)^2 + 8(Q_B) - .06(Q_B)^2.
\end{aligned}
$$

The profit-maximizing quantity of the two brands is that at which the partial derivatives of the economic profit function with respect to each of the brands is equal to zero. Moreover, to ensure a maximum-profit condition, the second partial derivatives of the profit function must be negative.

The partial derivatives of the economic profit function are

$$\partial\pi/\partial Q_A = 2 - .08(Q_A)$$

and

$$\partial\pi/\partial Q_B = 8 - .12(Q_B).$$

Setting the partial derivatives equal to zero and solving yields:

$$2 - .08(Q_A) = 0 \text{ and } Q_A = 25$$

and

$$8 - .12(Q_B) = 0 \text{ and } Q_B = 66.7.$$

The second partial derivatives of the profit function are

$$\partial^2\pi/\partial Q_A{}^2 = -.08$$

and

$$\partial^2\pi/\partial Q_B{}^2 = -.12,$$

ensuring a maximum in the profit function. Thus, the optimum level of production per week is 25,000 gallons of Brand A and 66,665 gallons of Brand B.

The actual level of economic profit also depends on the price of the products. Returning to the equations for demand, we find the firm's prices to be $p_A = 5 - .03(25) = 4.25$ and $p_B = 10 - .04(66.67) = 7.33$. Economic profit is determined by substituting these values in the economic profit function:

$$\pi = -100 + 2(25) - .04(25)^2 + 8(66.67) - .06(66.67)^2$$
$$= 191.67 = \$191,670.$$

Joint Products

The profit-maximizing decision differs slightly when a firm's products must be produced in some constant proportion. We call such products **joint products** because of the interrelationships in their production. Some examples of goods and services produced jointly are steaks and hamburger, gasoline and fuel oil, and freight transportation moving in different directions. The proportions these products represent in a firm's total production remain roughly constant regardless of the total quantities produced.

Suppose a firm's joint products face the following demand curves:

$$p_A = 100 - 15(Q_A)$$

and

$$p_B = 200 - 25(Q_B),$$

where the Q represents thousands of units of the two products sold per day. Suppose also that because of interrelationships in production, the quantity of A produced will always be roughly three times the quantity of B. When products are interrelated in production, it may not be possible to separate their costs. The cost function must be written for the simultaneous production of the two products. Under these conditions, a cost function might be written:

$$TC = 50 + 110(Q) + 0.8(Q)^2,$$

where quantity Q refers to the combination of three units of A and one unit of B.

The total revenue function must also consider the products in combination. When a single combination Q includes three units of A and one unit of B, the revenue from the sale of a single combination is determined by

$$
\begin{aligned}
p_Q &= [3(p_A)] + (p_B) \\
&= 3[100 - 15(Q)] + [200 - 25(Q)] = 500 - 70(Q).
\end{aligned}
$$

We use the value Q because we are considering the sale of entire combinations, including three units of A and one unit of B. This means that total revenue from the sale of combinations of A and B is

$$TR = p_Q(Q) = 500(Q) - 70(Q)^2.$$

Economic profit from the sale of entire combinations is

$$
\begin{aligned}
\pi = TR - TC &= [500\,(Q) - 70(Q)^2] - [50 + 110(Q) + 0.8\,(Q)^2] \\
&= -50 + 390(Q) - 70.8(Q)^2.
\end{aligned}
$$

To determine the profit-maximizing level of output, take the derivative of the profit function with respect to Q, set it equal to zero, and solve for Q:

$$d\pi/dQ = 390 - 141.6(Q) = 0 \text{ and } Q = 2.754.$$

The second derivative of the profit function is

$$d^2\,\pi/dQ^2 = -141.6,$$

ensuring a maximum. Thus, the quantity of Q is 2.754 thousand units per day, making the quantities of A and B 8,263 and 2,754 respectively.

The result of the analysis is a particular quantity of joint products to be produced in combination. However, because of the difference in the products' demand curves, the selling price necessary to sell these quantities may be too low for maximum profit. To ensure maximum profit, it is necessary to calculate marginal revenue for each product. If marginal revenue for either of the products is negative at the optimum quantity, selling that quantity would have the effect of reducing profit.

Total revenue associated with each of the joint products is

$$TR_A = p_A(Q_A) = 100(Q_A) - 15(Q_A)^2$$

and

$$TR_B = p_B(Q_B) = 200(Q_B) - 25(Q_B)^2.$$

The products' marginal revenues are

$$MR_A = dTR_A/dQ_A = 100 - 30(Q_A)$$

and

$$MR_B = dTR_B/dQ_B = 200 - 50(Q_B).$$

For $Q_A = 8.263$ and $Q_B = 2.754$, marginal revenues are

$$MR_A = 100 - 30(8.263) = -147.89$$

and

$$MR_B = 100 - 40(2.754) = 62.30.$$

Therefore, actually selling three units of A for each unit of B would result in negative marginal revenue. The firm should sell only the quantity of A for which MR_A is positive and dispose of the remainder in a manner that keeps it out of the market.

To determine the maximum quantity of A that should be sold, locate the quantity where MR_A passes through the origin and becomes negative. Setting MR_A equal to zero and solving yields:

$$MR_A = 100 - 30(Q_A) = 3.333.$$

Thus, the firm can sell 3,333 units of A without reducing economic profit. The price of the 3,333 units is determined by substituting this value in the demand equation:

$$p_A = 100 - 15(Q_A) = 100 - 15(3.333) = 50.$$

The firm should sell 3.333 thousand units of A at a price of $50 per thousand. The remaining $8.263 - 3.333 = 4.930$ thousand units should be kept off the market and disposed of.[1]

---

1. The analysis assumes that costs of disposal are zero.

The selling price of B is determined similarly:

$$p_B = 200 - 25(Q_B) = 200 - 25(2.754) = 131.15.$$

Economic profit is determined by calculating the difference between total revenue and total costs when the optimum combination of A and B is produced and the profit-maximizing quantities of A and B taken separately are sold. Thus,

$$\begin{aligned} \pi = TR - TC &= p_A(Q_A) + p_B(Q_B) - TC \\ &= [50(3.333) + 131.15(2.754)] - [50 + 110(2.754) + 0.8(2.754)^2] \\ &= 527.84 - 359.01 = 168.83 = \$168,830. \end{aligned}$$

This is the firm's maximum profit per day.

MONOPOLISTIC COMPETITION

We have seen that certain markets adapt slowly to change because of their relatively large fixed resource requirements. In time, however, change may push homogeneous and heterogeneous oligopolies closer to a monopoly structure (as weak firms are forced out of the industry) or closer to competition (as economic profits encourage the entry of new firms).

Other kinds of markets respond so easily to change that there can be even greater variation. Such markets are usually referred to as **monopolistic competition**, and consist of a large number of small firms, each producing a product that is in some way distinguished from its competitors. Thus, each firm enjoys a degree of market power in its own market segment that depends on the perceived uniqueness of its product and the strength of consumer preferences for its product. Monopolistic competition is possible in markets where investment in necessary fixed resources is relatively small. It is especially common in consumer goods markets in which minor product differentiation and advertising can render demand curves less elastic than in competition. Figure 11.4 on page 354 compares firm demand curves in competition and monopolistic competition.

Because monopolistically competitive firms face downward sloping demand curves, they may collect short-run economic profits. Acting as a monopolist in a protected market, the monopolistic competitor sets price where $MR = MC$ and collects economic profit equal to the difference between price and average total cost for each unit sold.

Profits in monopolistically competitive markets are extremely unstable. The existence of economic profit and the relatively small capital investment required encourage the entry of new firms producing similar, but not identical, products. As new substitute products come on the market, current producers experience a leftward shift of their demand curves and a decrease in economic

FIGURE 11.4   Demand in Competition and Monopolistic Competition

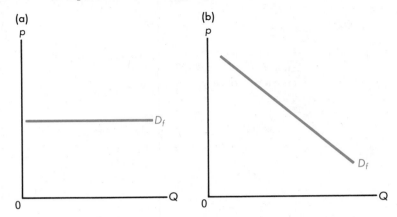

Firm demand in competition is shown in (a). Firm demand in monopolistic competition is shown in (b).

profits. Indeed, as long as any monopolistically competitive firm continues to
collect economic profit, new firms may be expected to enter the market, and
prices, quantities, and the size distribution of firms will come more closely to
resemble competition.

The response of monopolistic competitors to the passage of time is shown
in Figures ll.5a, ll.5b, and ll.5c. Economic profit is shown as the shaded rectangle, which grows smaller with time as new firms offer acceptable substitutes
in the market. Increased substitutability is shown also by the changing slope of
the demand curve. Can you explain why this is so?

FIGURE 11.5   Economic Profit in Monopolistic Competition

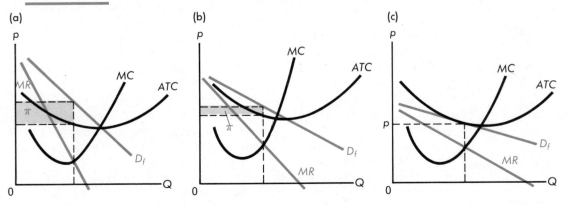

Over time, the existence of economic profit attracts rival firms to the market (a). The existence of acceptable
substitutes makes demand curves for individual monopolistic competitors more elastic (b) and eventually
eliminates economic profit (c).

The passage of time may produce another interesting phenomenon. While product differences initially help establish a firm's market power, such differences may be eroded by market growth. New entrants may strive to duplicate product attributes that have appealed to buyers and enhanced sales growth. Few new firms jeopardize their potential market by featuring an untried, untested variation of a known success. The possible result is greater uniformity in the various products and often in the advertising used to promote them, as well. As the products become more nearly identical, the industry assumes more of the characteristics of competition.

The chief remaining difference between monopolistic competition and competition at this point is the heavy reliance on advertising. As the products become more similar, advertising may not be used to highlight real product differences but to relate certain positive images to particular products. Emphasis on product image rather than on product substance, may become so widespread that each firm's advertising is completely offset by that of the other firms.

Advertising

Advertising policy frequently has a different objective from that of price policy. A firm's price policy is used to exploit elasticity of demand—that is, to move along the demand curve in order to achieve higher economic profit. In contrast, advertising is frequently used to *change* demand elasticity—to shift the entire demand curve upward to achieve greater total sales at constant (or rising) prices. Thus, the objective of advertising is to provide reasons other than low price for purchasing a product.

Advertising generally is expected to increase sales in some direct proportion to advertising expenditures. In general, advertising may cause sales to increase at an increasing, constant, or decreasing rate per dollar of advertising expenditure. The behavior of sales growth in this case is similar to the behavior of total product when additional quantities of a variable resource are added to fixed resources: that is, either increasing marginal product, constant marginal product, or decreasing marginal product. Finally, most products experience a "saturation" level at which additional advertising expenditures yield little or no increase in total sales. Beyond this level of advertising expenditures, the marginal product of advertising may be negative.

The relationship between sales and advertising expenditures can be measured in terms of **advertising elasticity of demand**. Advertising elasticity of demand (ϵ_A) is the percentage change in quantity sold associated with a percentage change in advertising expenditures. Thus,

$$\epsilon_A = \frac{\%\Delta Q}{\%\Delta A} = \frac{(Q_2 - Q_1/[1/2(Q_2 + Q_1)]}{(A_2 - A_1)/[1/2(A_2 + A_1)]},$$

where A represents successive quantities of advertising expenditures.

CASE STUDY 11.2   **Estimating the Effects of Advertising Expenditures**

A regression model can be useful for projecting the effect of advertising on a firm's sales. Nariman K. Dhalla and Sonia Yuspeh used regression analysis to build a regression model of soft drink sales. They began with a series of related assumptions:

1. That consumer attitudes basically depend on advertising expenditures, expressed algebraically as $ATT = f(AE)$.

2. That consumer buying intentions in any period depend on consumer attitudes, expressed as $INT = f(ATT)$.

3. That brand share in a future period depends on consumer intentions in the preceding period, expressed as $BS = f(INT_{t-1})$.

Then the researchers collected data from panels of consumers, advertising agencies, and studies that track consumer behavior over periods of time. The complete regression equations used were set up as follows. For consumer attitudes (ATT) concerning ingredients, nutrition and taste:

$$ATT = f(AE, WM, BS_{t-1})$$
$$= -3.49 + 1.05(AE) + 1.50(WM) + 0.88(BS_{t-1}).$$

For consumer intentions (INT) to purchase the product in the next period:

$$INT = f(ATT, HP)$$
$$= 5.13 + .74(ATT) - 0.44(HP).$$

And, for brand share:

$$BS = f(INT_{t-1}, RP, AC)$$
$$= 129.57 + 1.03(INT_{t-1}) - 0.94(RP) - 0.9(AC).$$

As for the independent variables used in the equations, AE represented advertising expenditures on the brand in millions of dollars, WM represented word of mouth (percentage of subjects who talked about the product with friends or family), BS_{t-1} represented brand share in the previous time period, HP represented the percentage of subjects that regarded the brand as high-priced, INT_{t-1} represented consumer intentions in the preceding time period, RP represented the ratio of the brand price to the average price of competing firms, and AC represented advertising expenditures of major competitors in millions of dollars.

The researchers found that 80 percent of the advertising took effect almost immediately, and 20 percent took effect in the following quarter. Therefore, they adjusted the firm's advertising expenditures (AE) to account for the lagged effect.

At the time of the research, the firm was supplying 12.2 percent of the market. Managers wanted to know the effect on market share of maintaining the current price and increasing advertising expenditures from \$3.3 million to \$3.55 million. Including the lagged effect of advertising expenditures yielded an advertising expenditures variable of $AE = .8(3.55) + .2(3.3) = 3.5$. Other variables were estimated on the basis of past trends and expert opinion. Thus, $WM = 6.5$ percent, $HP = 11.6$ percent, $RP = 105.5$, and $AC = 37.4$.

Substituting the estimated values of the independent variables in the regression equations yields the following:

$$ATT_{t-1} = -3.49 + 1.05(3.5) + 1.5(6.5) + 0.88(12.2) = 20.67,$$
$$INT_{t+1} = 5.13 + 0.74(20.67) - 0.44(11.6) = 15.32,$$

and

$$BS_{t+2} = 129.57 + 1.03(15.32) - 0.94(105.5) - 0.9(37.4) = 12.52.$$

If the independent variables behave as predicted in the next quarter, two quarters hence the firm's market share should rise to 12.52 percent. Managers must decide if the additional 0.32 percent market share is sufficient to justify the additional advertising expenditure of $250,000 in the coming quarter.

Source: Nariman K. Dhalla and Sonia Yuspeh, "Forget the Product Life Cycle Concept,"*Harvard Business Review*, January/February 1976, pp. 102–112.

EXAMPLE 11.1   **A Microeconomic Model of Advertising Expenditures in Monopolistic Competition**

Decisions regarding the appropriate level of advertising expenditures should be based on the same profit-maximizing rule we used in determining appropriate quantities of other variable resources. That is, continue to employ additional units of advertising until the marginal revenue of the last unit sold through advertising is equal to the marginal cost of the advertising. Estimates of advertising elasticity can be used to project sales gains and marginal revenue from additional advertising, so that profit-maximizing comparisons can be made.

In general, it is assumed that the marginal product of advertising decreases with each additional unit of advertising employed. Since marginal revenue from advertising diminishes, we would expect to find increasing marginal cost—additional quantities sold because of advertising expenditures are increasingly costly in terms of those expenditures. Managers must decide the quantity of advertising at which the marginal cost of additional advertising is equal to the marginal revenue from additional sales.

To illustrate the advertising decision, suppose the XYZ Corporation is planning an advertising campaign whose goal is a rightward shift of the firm's demand curve and an increase in quantity sold. Researchers have estimated that the increase in quantity sold depends on the duration of the promotional campaign. In fact, for any target market, the proportion of the market that will respond to the advertising campaign increases according to the following formula:

$$\text{Percent of market} = (1 - e^{-.02t}),$$

where t is the number of days in the campaign and e is the base of natural logs and is equal to 2.72. Thus, a 30-day promotional campaign would be expected to increase sales to $1 - 2.72^{-.02(30)} = .45 = 45$ percent of the market. A 60-day campaign would increase sales to $1 - 2.72^{-.02(60)} = .70 = 70$ percent of the market. Note that doubling the length of the campaign will not double market share, in keeping with our assumption of diminishing marginal product for advertising.

Figure A is a graph of the expression $1 - e^{-0.02t}$, with $t =$ time in days measured along the horizontal axis and the percentage of the market sold measured along the vertical axis. As t increases, the proportion of the market sold also increases—rapidly at first and then more slowly as the firm's market share approaches 100 percent. The decision to move upward on the path shown in Figure A would depend on the cost of additional days of the campaign relative to the revenue gains from selling to the corresponding additional proportion of the market.

Managers must decide the correct value of t (duration of the advertising campaign) for achieving maximum profits. The cost of the campaign includes fixed start-up costs of $2,500 and variable costs of $2,000 each day the campaign continues:

$$TC_A = FC + VC(t) = 2,500 + 2,000(t).$$

FIGURE A

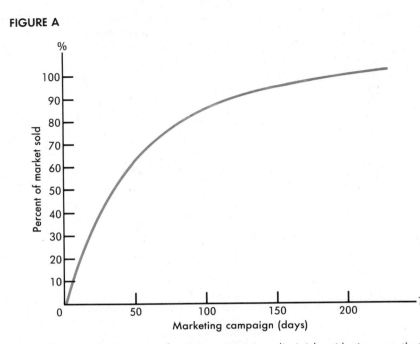

Gains from continuing an advertising campaign diminish with time, so that the proportion of the market sold approaches but does not reach 100 percent.

The target population is a market of $Q = 100,000$ buyers, and each additional buyer will add revenue of $2. Thus, total revenue can be estimated by

$$TR = \$2[100,000(1 - e^{-.02t})].$$

The profit-maximizing duration of the advertising campaign is the value of t at which the marginal cost of the campaign is equal to its marginal revenue, both calculated with respect to time. The marginal values of the cost and revenue equations are determined through calculus. Maximum profit occurs where marginal cost and marginal revenue (expressed as the derivatives of total cost and total revenue with respect to time) are equal. The profit-maximizing equation is:

$$e^{.02t} = \left(\frac{VC}{(MR)\,(Q)\,(.02)}\right),$$

or

$$\left(\frac{2,000}{(2)\,(100,000)\,(.02)}\right) = 1/2.$$

To solve for t, take the natural logs of both sides of the equation, set them equal to each other, and solve for the value of t. Thus,

$$\text{Natural log of } e^{0.02t} = -.02t,$$

and

$$\text{Natural log of } 1/2 = -.69315.$$

The profit-maximizing value of t is that at which $-.02t = -.69315$, so that $t = 35$ days.

One should note an interesting point in this analysis. This is that once the campaign has begun the start-up costs of the campaign are irrelevant to the policy decision. Only the daily costs should be considered in determining the profit-maximizing amount of advertising.

Source: Arthur Meidap, "Deterministic Techniques and Their Marketing Uses," *Management Decisions*, 1981, vol. 19, no. 4/5, pp. 13–35.

EXAMPLE 11.2

Planning Advertising Through Linear Programming[1]

Targetting a firm's advertising precisely to its intended audience can help reduce advertising expenditures and increase effectiveness. The wide variety of advertising media and the complexities of target markets make for a range of possibilities that can be analyzed more effectively through the use of linear programming.

Remember that a linear programming problem consists of an objective function and a set of inequalities that constitute constraints. The variables in an advertising problem are the available advertising media. Managers want to determine the quantity of each medium that maximizes (or minimizes) the value of the objective function.

Frequently the objective function is to maximize the number of total exposures (E) when the expected exposures associated with each advertising medium is known. Thus,

$$(\text{maximize}) \ E = a_1X_1 + a_2X_2 + a_3X_3 \ldots + a_nX_n,$$

where each X represents a particular medium and each a represents the expected numbers of exposures associated with a particular medium. The constraints include a budget constraint:

$$b_1X_1 + b_2X_2 + b_3X_3 \ldots + b_nX_n \leq B,$$

where each b represents the cost associated with a particular vehicle and B is the total advertising budget. Other constraints are used to define certain policy decisions. Thus,

$$X_1 \geq 8$$

means that advertising vehicle X_1 must be used at least 8 times. Similarly,

$$X_2 \leq 10$$

means that X_2 cannot be used more than 10 times. This constraint is used to prevent a particularly effective advertising medium from "running away" with the program: that is, absorbing all of the advertising budget. Finally,

$$b_1X_1 + b_2X_2 \leq .5(B)$$

limits expenditures on X_1 and X_2 to half the total advertising budget.

To illustrate the linear programming decision in this case, let us assume that a firm has established an advertising budget of $100,000. Radio and television commercials cost $5,000 and $8,000 respectively and are expected to yield 10,000 and 30,000 exposures respectively. Management has decided to spend no more than half the advertising budget on radio and wants to use at least 5 radio commercials and no more than 8 television commercials. The problem here is

$$(\text{maximize}) \ \text{Exposures} = E = 10X_1 + 30X_2,$$

1. For an example of research using linear programming see Frank M. Bass and Ronald T. Lonsdale, "An Exploration of LP in Media Selection," *Journal of Marketing Research*, May 1966, vol. 3, pp. 179–88.

FIGURE A

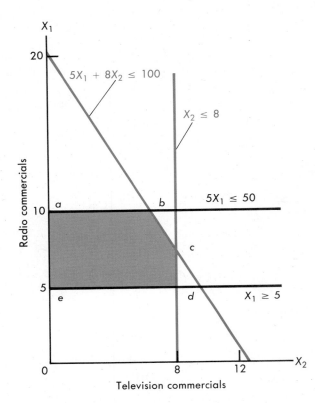

Television commercials

subject to

$$5X_1 + 8X_2 \leq 100,$$
$$5X_1 \qquad \leq 50,$$
$$X_1 \qquad \geq 5,$$

and

$$X_2 \leq 8.$$

These constraints have been graphed in Figure A and the corners have been labelled a, b, c, d, and e.

Corner	X_1	X_2	E (thousands)
a	10	0	100
b	10	6.25	287.5
c	7.2	8	312 *
d	5	8	290
e	5	0	50

Remember that inequalities identify an area within which the solution to the problem may fall and within which the values of the slack variables are positive. The optimum solution lies at one of the corners of the feasible area. The problem is to identify the corner that maximizes the objective function. The procedure is to solve equations simultaneously in order to identify the value of the variables at the corners and calculate the value of the objective function. This has been done, and the results are displayed in the table on page 360.

The optimum solution occurs at corner c, which utilizes 7.2 radio commercials and 8 television commercials. The expected number of total exposures is 312,000.

Advertising elasticity of demand is difficult to measure, since some advertising methods require a long period of time to become effective in increasing sales. Also, other trends in the external environment may affect sales and distort the actual effects of advertising. An example of this type of distortion may be produced by the reaction of competitors to a firm's own advertising campaign. Still, an effort should be made to measure the historical relationship between advertising expenditures and sales and to conduct market experiments on the effects of advertising in representative market segments.

The case study that follows illustrates an attempt to estimate the effect of advertising expenditures on past sales as a means of predicting the effect of a proposed advertising campaign.

POSITIONING

Some firms in monopolistic competition avoid competitive pressures by **positioning** their products in one or more markets. An example of this is toothpaste manufacturers that produce one product that appeals to children and others that are marketed to appeal to consumers who want to guard against bad breath or tooth decay. Manufacturers of breakfast cereals supply products for health-food consumers, finicky children, and weight-conscious adults. Even barber shops feature different kinds of service. They can be regarded as beauty parlors, unisex salons, or convenient hair cut stops for busy executives. By positioning itself in a single market, a firm reduces the number of potential competitors and makes its demand curve less elastic. The expected result is greater pricing freedom and greater potential for economic profit.

The case study that follows illustrates a number of concepts discussed in this text, including:

1. the inevitability of change, resulting from technical progress, legal and environmental developments in the market, and the opening of economic and financial opportunities to new entrepreneurs;
2. the effect of such changes on the structure of the market in which the firm operates, with fundamental consequences for the size distribution of firms;

CASE STUDY 11.3   Changing Market Structures in Telephone Communications

Until January 1982, American Telephone and Telegraph Company was considered a natural monopoly in U. S. telephone communications. Local public service commissions regulated service and fees in order to guarantee a satisfactory return on investment for AT&T stockholders and to prevent economic profits. The schedule of fees was set to permit "cross subsidization," with earnings from long-distance service used to keep the price of local service below full costs.

Pressure began to build for competition in the industry, and in 1982 AT&T divested itself of local operating companies. The communications industry came to include: 7 regulated local service operating companies, a long-distance market dominated by AT&T but including a number of other medium-sized firms, many diverse firms producing telecommunications equipment, including AT&T Technologies (formerly Western Electric) and AT&T Information Systems, and telecommunications research dominated by what is now called AT&T Bell Laboratories. The opportunity to earn large economic profits has attracted foreign firms as well as new U.S. firms into the various communications markets.

Competition has been difficult for the smaller firms, some of which have merged or have been acquired, while others have left the industry. Even the larger firms have been experiencing sharply rising costs and have reported major losses and employee lay-offs. The only significant successes attributable to the new competitive conditions have occurred in firms that were able to position themselves in well-defined market segments.

Independent producers of residential telephone equipment expected huge sales after divestiture. However, many households have continued to lease phones from local firms or buy AT&T equipment. Others have bought lower-priced equipment produced by foreign manufacturers.

In local service markets, suppliers of private branch exchange (or PBX) service have been allowed to compete with AT&T since 1968, but slowing growth in the PBX market and more vigorous marketing efforts by the newly independent Bell operating companies have reduced PBX profits and now threaten the existence of many of the existing firms. (It is estimated that forty firms now occupy a PBX market that can sustain fewer than ten.) Not all of the PBX firms will be able to make the new investments necessary to provide the latest data transmission services.

In long-distance markets, new competitors now have "equal access" with AT&T to local telephone networks. Before divestiture, customers of firms such as MCI were required to dial a numerical code to tie into their long-distance system, but the costs and prices of these firms were low. With equal access, these new firms now experience the same access costs as AT&T and can no longer offer consumers a significant price advantage. Price competition and slowing market growth are shrinking economic profits for such long-distance firms.

When the telephone communications industry finally adjusts to competition, there most likely will be examples of a variety of market structures within the industry. Firms in each particular type of communications market will utilize price and output policies and marketing techniques to maximize profits. For now, natural monopolies of local telephone service continue to be regulated by public service commissions. The seven Bell operating companies provide cost information to the regulatory commissions and must request their approval of rate changes. A minimum of institutional advertising is typically undertaken by these firms, and marketing techniques are used primarily to gain public support in the companies' negotiations with the regulatory commissions.

Long-distance markets are now open to communications firms with the capacity to finance the cost of tapping into existing systems. All firms have equal access to local telephone networks at a price determined by the local companies and their regulatory commissions. As the costs of the long-distance firms become more nearly equal, price competition is likely to be avoided, and firms will resort to advertising and service distinctions to increase their own sales.

Production of communications equipment will probably become more and more segmented, with firms and groups of firms positioning themselves in clearly defined market areas. Some of these markets may be too small or too capital-intensive for healthy competition, enabling small natural monpolies to continue to operate profitably for some time to come.

MANAGERIAL THINKING

How would you characterize each of the following telecommunications markets in terms of market structure: local telephone service, telephone equipment, long-distance telephone service, and telecommunications research?

---

3. the relationship between substitutability among products and elasticity of demand, and, in turn, the relationship between elasticity of demand and market power;
4. the relationship between the structure of the industry and competitive strategies (including positioning).

As you read Case Study 11.3, keep in mind the characteristics of competition, monopoly (including natural monopoly), oligopoly, and monopolistic competition. Consider the changes in the telecommunications industry over the past several years and, in particular, how the microeconomic theory of price and market structure can be applied to this industry. Then examine current developments in telecommunications and make some projections about the future course of this market.

SUMMARY

Most U.S. firms can be classified as oligopolistic or monopolistically competitive. Because of the small number of firms in oligopoly, the firms are interdependent in their pricing policies. Demand curves for firms in homogeneous oligopoly tend to be more elastic than demand curves for firms in heterogeneous oligopoly. For the economy as a whole, the results of pricing decisions in duopoly are similar to those of monopoly.

Demand curves for firms in oligopoly are kinked at the tacitly agreed market price, with relatively elastic demand above the kink and relatively inelastic demand below. Differences in elasticity are a result of the differing responses of other firms to a firm's pricing decision. Price tends to remain at the level of the kink until a price leader initiates a response to a change in market conditions. Failure of an oligopolistic industry to adjust to market changes can result in economic losses and even collapse of oligopolistic firms.

Cross price elasticity of demand is a way to measure the substitutability among products of an oligopolistic industry and between products of an oligopolistic industry and products of other industries. Oligopolistic firms may improve stability of sales by producing complements and/or substitutes for their primary product. Pricing decisions in a multi-product firm should take into consideration the marginal revenues of the various products taken separately. For joint products, only the quantity of a product that has positive marginal revenue should be sold.

Monopolistically competitive industries tend to be unstable because of the large number of firms and the potential for economic profit when products are differentiated. Advertising is a way of achieving product differentiation and of increasing demand. Advertising should be conducted only to the point at which the marginal revenue resulting from the expected added sales is equal to the marginal cost of the advertising. Many monopolistically competitive firms practice "positioning" to define their markets more precisely and increase their market power.

KEY TERMS

homogeneous oligopoly   joint products
heterogeneous oligopoly   advertising elasticity of demand
duopoly   positioning
cross price elasticity of demand

QUESTIONS AND PROBLEMS

1. Explain the expected results of institutional advertising for demand curves in homogeneous oligopoly. What are the objectives in terms of price elasticity of demand (a) for products of the industry as a whole, and (b) for products of individual firms?

2. Answer Question 1 with respect to advertising in heterogeneous oligopoly.

3. Explain the basis for the statement that duopolies are unstable. What is the likely progress of economic events in a duopolized industry?

4. Quality Chemical Company is an oligopoly firm producing 300 pounds of a certain chemical per week at a price of $7.50 and constant average total cost of $3.50. Managers estimate that price elasticity of demand is -2.2 for prices immediately above the market price and -1.8 for prices immediately below. Estimate the firm's economic profit at various price levels and demonstrate the basis for the firm's acceptance of the current price. Show your conclusions graphically.

5. Using the information in Question 4, determine the firm's mark-up over costs and estimate price elasticity of demand in the industry as a whole.

6. Refer again to the information in Question 4. Suppose production costs have risen by 20 percent so that the individual oligopoly firms' profits fall

to $300(7.50 - 4.20) = \$990$ per week. Describe the likely course of events leading to a price change. What will the new price be?

7. Quality Chemical Company produces two chemicals jointly with estimated short-run demand curves of $p_A = 22 - .02(Q_A)$ and $p_B = 35 - .0125(Q_B)$. The chemicals must be produced in a ratio of 1 to 2: that is, 2 units of B must be produced for each unit of A that is produced. The average variable cost of producing a combination that calls for producing one unit of A and two units of B is estimated according to $AVC = 5 + .008(Q)$. Daily fixed costs are \$100. Determine the profit-maximizing price and quantity of the two chemicals per day. Then check whether the marginal revenues associated with both quantities are positive.

8. Explain the basis for the differences in price elasticity of demand in monopolistic competition and competition. How does price elasticity of demand differ among individual monopolistically competitive firms? What is the expected effect of advertising in this market situation? Illustrate your answers graphically.

9. Neighborhood Electronics Company sells video cassettes in a monopolistically competitive market at a constant price of $p = \$12.50$. The number of cassettes sold per week is determined by advertising expenditures according to the equation $Q = 1.15(A^{.7})$. Current advertising expenditures are \$135 per week. A new promotional campaign has been proposed that would cost an additional \$75 per week. Should the firm undertake the advertising campaign? Explain your answer.

10. Find the profit-maximizing price and quantity for a monopolistically competitive firm whose advertising cost per month is $AD = 575 + .10(Q)$. The firm's average variable costs are $AVC = 15 + .01(Q)$, and its fixed costs are $FC = 1,000$. The demand curve for the firm is $p = 115 - .005(Q)$.

11. Dairy Products Company estimates monthly sales as a function of advertising expenditures according to

$$Q = a + b(AD) - c(AD)^2 = 25 + 5(AD) - .2(AD^2),$$

where AD is thousands of dollars of advertising expenditures per month. Currently, monthly advertising expenditures are \$3,500, but the firm's managers are considering a new campaign that would increase advertising expenditures to \$7,500. Assume production costs are constant and decide whether to undertake the new campaign.

12. Use the information in Question 11 to calculate advertising elasticity of demand at the current level and projected level of advertising expenditures.

12

Evaluating Investment Proposals

Most firms go through decision-making processes similar to the ones we have described in this text. A firm's managers must first estimate product demand, accounting for macroeconomic conditions that may affect future sales. Then managers must decide a level of total production for the short run, using available fixed resources and adding variable resources until marginal revenue from sales of the product will equal marginal cost: $MR = MC$. If marginal revenue equals marginal cost at a price greater than average total cost, the firm will collect economic profit. However, in the short-run, production may be carried on at a loss as long as market price exceeds average variable cost.

In the long run, a firm may respond to economic profit by expanding productive capacity. Capacity also can be reduced as contracts expire, if the firm is experiencing short-run losses (that are expected to continue). The actual size or scale of plant to be built in the long run depends on estimates of returns to scale in the industry and on projections of market demand. These kinds of decisions are the primary responsibility of the firm's managers.

In this chapter we will look more closely at long-run production planning. In particular, we will be concerned with decisions to add productive capacity. A firm's long-run investment strategy is similar to that of an individual. Individual investors select from a range of investment opportunities to increase their own real income and wealth. These may include homes, businesses, government securities, and corporate stocks and bonds. Individual investors compare the expected gains associated with each investment property and choose a combination of assets that satisfies their income and security goals. Individual

CASE STUDY 12.1   Sears Shifts Gears

For more than 100 years Sears, Roebuck and Company has been a trusted American institution—sort of like baseball and apple pie. Isolated farm families have shopped using Sears' venerable mail-order catalogue, and city-dwellers have counted on Sears for everything from sneakers to radial tires. In the suburbs, Sears stores have been "anchor" stores around which busy new shopping centers are built.

Even established institutions like Sears have to cope with change, however. In recent decades, changes in the economic environment have forced Sears' managers to plan new long-run strategies, to explore new kinds of businesses, to enter new markets, and to adopt new marketing techniques. Adopting new strategies is risky. It means giving up tried-and-true methods and forging into the unknown. For Sears' managers it meant using scientific decision-making processes: that is, defining the problem, stating the firm's objectives, analyzing and deciding among alternative strategies, and implementing and evaluating the chosen course of action. At all stages of the process, managers had to be sensitive to new developments that might have affected the results of their decision and called for still newer strategies in the future.

Initially, an important source of change for Sears was prosperity. Over the years, rising prosperity turned many of Sears' regular customers away from the store's staple items to the more expensive and more fashionable items sold by other retailers. Lately, many young families have turned to popular new discount stores for their basic household needs. Sales growth has slowed, and Sears has scaled down operations in many of its major stores. Falling profits in retailing prompted managers to search for new investment opportunities.

The first major change in Sears' strategy was a move into the insurance industry in the 1930s. By 1980, Sears' Allstate subsidiary had become the nation's second largest property and casualty insurance company. Then, Sears purchased a mortgage insurance company and a California savings and loan association with 95 branch offices. The business of finance was especially appropriate for Sears. With 24 million charge customers and regular inflows of sales revenue, Sears had a substantial advantage over other financial institutions in collecting and investing the small savings of many families.

Other changes in the economic environment also were opening new opportunities for Sears. For the last half-century, financial institutions in the United States have operated under government regulation. Laws passed in the 1930s limited the kinds of financial services a particular business is allowed to provide: *Banks* could offer checking accounts and commercial loans. *Savings and loan associations* could offer savings accounts and home mortgages. *Investment banks* could sell stocks, bonds, and money market fund shares. *Insurance companies* could sell insurance policies.

Government regulation had the effect of separating financial markets and eliminating competition among the various kinds of financial institutions. Regulation ensured satisfactory profits to some institutions that might not have survived in a competitive environment.

By the late 1970s, however, some financial institutions were demanding greater freedom to compete. They wanted freedom to accept a wider variety of savings funds and to use their funds for a wider variety of financial services. The public also began to favor de-regulation of financial services, in order to encourage greater efficiency in the flow of investment funds. Finally, in 1980 Congress passed a new law changing government regulation to allow many financial institutions to supply a variety of financial services.

Sears' managers saw these changes in government regulation as an opportunity to extend their operations in the financial sector. Sears' retail stores around the country already performed many financial services. However, since Sears has never been a typical financial institution, it has not been subject to regulation. Moreover, Sears' 2,300 stores and their thousands of employees could be quickly adapted to provide a wider range of financial services. In effect, resources used in activities that had been experiencing slow profit growth or even loss could be re-allocated toward activities with greater potential for economic profit.

Sears' strategy thus involved a shift to a more diversified portfolio of investment properties, including financial services and retailing firms. In 1981, Sears purchased Coldwell Banker and Company and Dean Witter Reynolds Organization Incorporated, the nation's largest real-estate brokerage firm and the fifth largest securities company respectively. Together with its other holdings, the new acquisitions started Sears along the road to becoming the largest financial services company in the nation.

As you read this chapter, think about the process of deciding the allocation of investment resources. Consider how each new investment property will affect the firm's profits and what risks are associated with each new investment property. In Chapter 13, we will then consider the essential question of how new investment properties should be financed.

investors realize that changing economic conditions may alter the attractiveness of various investments, so they re-evaluate their investment "portfolio" often.

Business managers are concerned about increasing the income and wealth of the firm. Like individual investors, they face a wide range of possible investments including buildings, equipment, other business firms, and securities. The managers' objective is to select a portfolio of assets that satisfies the firm's long-run goals.

To illustrate planning for the long run, we will first look at a case study of a familiar business firm. Then we will analyze the processes by which managers make the kinds of investment decisions illustrated in the case study.

CASH FLOW AND PROFIT

The quantity of a firm's new capital investment depends in part on its contribution to the firm's **cash flow**. Cash flow is defined as the difference between receipts and cash expenditures over a certain accounting period. Cash flow differs from profit in that profit involves some non-cash items. To illustrate this difference, let us consider the income and expense statement in Table 12.1 associated with a proposed investment in a hypothetical retail store.

Gross profit for the month is the expected difference between total revenue from sales and total production costs. From gross profit, Small Town Store must pay certain operating costs, including administrative expenses and interest. Production and operating costs are sometimes called **out-of-pocket costs** since they are often cash outlays in the current period. In contrast, **depreciation** is a non-cash expense. It represents the gradual wearing out of buildings and equipment used in production and is an allocation of revenues to an account for eventual replacement. For Small Town Store, monthly charges of $8,000 are made to a depreciation account.

TABLE 12.1   Income and Expense Statement for One Month (Anticipated)

Sales revenue for the month		$75,000
Less cost of goods sold		37,000
Gross profit		38,000
Less operating expenses:		
Administrative costs	$15,000	
Interest paid on debt	4,000	
Depreciation expense	8,000	
		$27,000
Net profit before taxes		11,000
Less federal income taxes (46%)		5,060
Net profit after taxes		$ 5,940

The remaining **net profit** after paying out-of-pocket costs and setting aside an allowance for depreciation will be the taxable income from the investment in Small Town Store. We have applied a tax rate of 46 percent to Small Town Store's taxable income for taxes of $.46 \times \$11,000 = \$5,060$. Net profit after taxes of $5,940 will be available for distribution to the firm's stockholders/owners. The portion of net profit after taxes that is not paid to stockholders/owners will be held in the firm as **retained earnings.** Together with the depreciation account, retained earnings will be available to the firm's managers for making new investment expenditures or for lending at interest until needed.

For many investment decisions, net profit after taxes is not appropriate for evaluating investment proposals. The reason is that net profit after taxes understates the actual quantity of funds available for use by the firm's managers and stockholders/owners. In fact, the sum of depreciation allowance plus net profit after taxes is the more appropriate figure for judging this type of investment's performance. Depreciation plus net profit after taxes is investors' *net cash flow* from this investment.

In examples of investment decisions, we will use net cash flow as the basis for evaluating investment proposals. We will also include interest expense paid for funds borrowed to finance the investment, since the ability to pay interest charges is an important criterion for evaluating an investment.[1] Under these circumstances, the appropriate figure for evaluating Small Town Store's performance is expected monthly cash flow plus interest expense on the funds used to purchase the investment: net profit after taxes + depreciation + interest expense = $5,940 + 8,000 + 4,000 = \$17,940$ = net cash flow.

---

1. To add interest expense to cash flow is equivalent to *not* deducting interest expense when computing net profit. Not deducting interest expense is appropriate because we want to determine the income earned from an investment in excess of operating expenses, that is available for paying interest on the purchase price.

THE TIME VALUE OF MONEY

Our example of investment analysis looked at an investment's performance over only one month. Most investment proposals involve a decision to purchase a property to be operated over a number of years. Operating the property will entail certain costs and will generate sales revenues each year. Finally, the property may be sold, either to another investor, as scrap, or as trade-in on new replacement property. A firm's managers must evaluate each proposed acquisition to determine whether expected future cash flows are large enough to justify the necessary current expenditure. Furthermore, managers must determine whether the return on a proposed investment is at least as great as the return that could be earned by using the firm's funds in some other way.

To answer this question, managers must understand a fundamental principle of finance: the **time value** of money. The time value of money is critical in decisions in which a cost is paid in the current period with the expectation that a return payment will be received in the future. We are all familiar with the current cost of acquiring a savings account in a commercial bank. It is the $100 or so we choose to deposit in the current period. The payment to be received in the future depends on two factors: the **interest** return the bank has agreed to pay for the use of our funds and the **time** we are willing to wait before receiving our future payment.

With an annual interest return of 6 percent, for example, in one year a $100 deposit will be worth ($100)(1.06) = $106. Stated algebraically,

$$(C)\ (1\ +\ r)\ =\ (F).$$

where C represents current deposit, r represents rate of interest, and F represents future value after one year. If we agree to leave the deposit to earn interest the second year, we will finally receive ($100)(1.06)(1.06) = $112.36. Interest of 6 percent is earned on $100 in each of the two years and in the second year 6 percent is also earned on the *interest earned* in the first year and left on deposit. Stated algebraically,

$$C(1\ +\ r)(1\ +\ r)\ =\ (F).$$

If the deposit is left to accumulate interest a third year, a third interest factor $(1\ +\ r)$ would be included. In general, we may say that

$$(C)(1\ +\ r)^t\ =\ (F)$$

after t years. Thus, our deposit left to accumulate interest at 6 percent for ten years would finally pay $100(1.06)^{10} = $179.08.

Earning interest on interest is called **compounding**. Compounding interest at 6 percent on our original deposit earns a total payment greater than the sum of 6 percent interest earned in each of ten years taken separately. Each year, the value of our deposit increases by more than the previous year's increase.

FIGURE 12.1 Future Value of an Investment

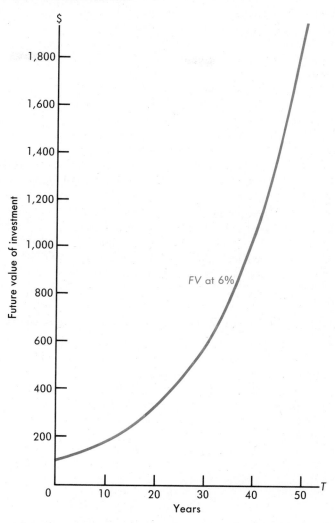

The curve describing the future value of a deposit left to accumulate interest slopes upward with an increasing slope. This is a result of compounding: earning interest on interest.

Figure 12.1 is a graph of the future value of a $100 deposit left indefinitely to earn interest at 6 percent. The curve originates at $100 on the vertical axis, where time (t) = 0. Since each year's gain is 6 percent of the previous year's accumulated total, the curve has an increasing slope. Curves drawn for higher interest earnings would rise more steeply than the curve in Figure 12.1, and those drawn for lower interest earnings would rise less steeply.

The equation above can be rearranged to show the current deposit that would be required if we want to receive a particular amount at a given date in the future. Thus,

$$C(1 + r)^t = F$$

can be re-written as

$$C = \frac{F}{(1+r)^t}.$$

To receive $100 after five years, the necessary current deposit would be $C = 100/(1.06)^5 = \$74.73$. Compounding interest on interest would enable the original deposit to grow by more than the sum of five separate years of 6 percent of $74.73. When the rate of compounding is known, the necessary current deposit for any desired future return can be computed in this way.

Figure 12.2 is a graph showing the deposit in the current period that would be necessary for the depositor to receive $100 in some future period. The graph assumes that the initial deposit is left to accumulate interest at 6 percent for t

FIGURE 12.2   **Present Value of an Expected Future Payment**

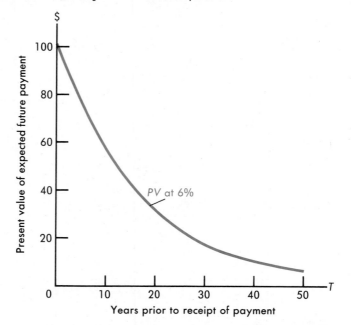

The curve describing the present value of a future payment slopes downward with a decreasing slope. This is a result of discounting, that is, money received in the future is worth less than money held in the present.

$= 1, 2, 3 \ldots n$ time periods. If the deposit is left for $t = 1$ time period, the initial deposit is \$94.34 since $1.06 \times \$94.34 = \$100$. If the deposit is left for $t = 2$ time periods, the necessary deposit is only \$89.00, since $(1.06)^2 \times \$89.00 = \$100$. The decreasing slope of the graph in Figure 12.2 is the reverse of the curve in Figure 12.1 and demonstrates the effects of discounting.

Discounting is the reverse of compounding. Recall that to compound is to *increase* the value of a future payment according to the rate of return and the number of time periods in the future before payment is to be received. To discount is to *reduce* the value of a current outlay by the rate of return and the number of time periods in the future payment is to be received. Curves drawn to illustrate higher rates of discount would fall more steeply than the curve in Figure 12.2, and curves drawn for lower rates of discount would fall less steeply.

This discussion illustrates the fact that money has a time-related value. Money used for gain over a number of years ultimately has a greater final value (computed by the equation $C(1 + r)^t = F$). On the other hand, money to be received in the future has less current value (computed by the equation $C = F/(1 + r)^t$). For investment decisions in which a current expenditure is made, expected future cash flows must be great enough to satisfy the equation $C(1 + r)^t = F$. In other words, expected cash flows must be great enough to offset the current sacrifice expressed by $C = F/(1 + r)^t$.

THE INTERNAL RATE OF RETURN

When the investment return equation is rearranged as in the previous section, it becomes useful for comparing a firm's current investment outlay with expected future cash flows. We have shown that in the case of a bank deposit, the current outlay (C) and interest return (r) are known and the equation is brought into balance by solving for future value (F) after a certain period of time (t). In the case of business investment outlays, the rate of return (r) may not be known. The current cost of the investment will be known, however, and future cash flows can be estimated on the basis of projected sales revenue, production and operating costs, and taxes. Then the equation can be brought into balance by solving for r.

The value of r associated with an investment purchased for C today and yielding cash flows of F in the future is called the **internal rate of return**. We know from our previous example that an investment costing \$74.73 in the current period and paying \$100 at the end of the fifth period has an internal rate of return of 6 percent, since $\$74.73 = \$100/(1.06)^5$.

Most business investments yield returns over several years, such that the investment return equation becomes:

$$C = \frac{F_1}{(1 + r)^1} + \frac{F_2}{(1 + r)^2} + \frac{F_3}{(1 + r)^3} + \cdots + \frac{F_n}{(1 + r)^n},$$

or

$$C = \sum_{t=1}^{n} \frac{F_t}{(1 + r)^t}$$

where F_t is the future cash flow expected in period t.

     This equation can be rearranged so that

$$-C + \sum_{t=1}^{n} \frac{F_t}{(1 + r)^t} = 0.$$

Solving such an equation for r identifies the internal rate of return for an investment that produces income over a number of years. To illustrate, suppose purchase of data processing equipment for $100 thousand in the current year yields expected cash flows of $45 thousand, $35 thousand, and $25 thousand in the next three years. Cash flow in the fourth year plus the scrap value of the equipment is $15 thousand. Thus,

$$-100 + \frac{45}{(1 + r)^1} + \frac{35}{+ (1 + r)^2} + \frac{25}{(1 + r)^3} + \frac{15}{(1 + r)^4} = 0.$$

Solving for r yields $r \approx .09.$[2] Thus, the internal rate of return on this investment is about 9 percent.

THE MARGINAL EFFICIENCY OF INVESTMENT

A firm normally has several investment proposals to be analyzed as described above. In each case, the current cost of each investment property would be known, and future cash flows could be estimated on the basis of managers' assumptions about sales revenues, production costs, operating costs, and taxes. Equations like the ones in the previous section would be solved for r. The result would be a schedule of projected internal rates of return such as the one in Table 12.2.

TABLE 12.2

Proposed investment	Current cost	Internal rate of return
Data-processing equipment	$100,000	9%
Truck	75,000	2%
Fork lift	80,000	7%
Drilling machine	150,000	5%

---

2. Solving for r requires trial and error and may be simplified by the use of a computer program.

FIGURE 12.3   Marginal Efficiency of Investment

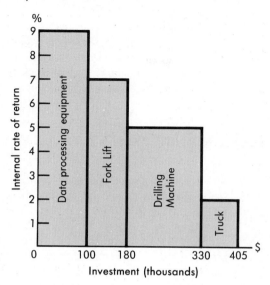

The graph of a firm's marginal efficiency of investment schedule is its demand curve for investments.

This schedule is called a **marginal efficiency of investment** (MEI) schedule and is useful for making investment decisions.

The MEI schedule is, in effect, a firm's demand curve for investments. Figure 12.3 is the graph of a firm's investment demand curve showing the internal rate of return associated with the investment proposals listed in Table 12.2. Projects are arranged in descending order, from the $100,000 investment yielding 9 percent to the $75,000 investment yielding only 2 percent.

By comparing the firm's own investment demand curve with the *cost* of investment funds, a manager chooses projects that yield the greatest return relative to cost. The cost of investment funds is relevant for two reasons. If the firm must borrow for making the proposed investment, it is important that the internal rate of return be at least sufficient to cover the cost of borrowing: $r \geq c$. Cost of borrowing would include the interest and administrative costs of handling the loan. The cost of borrowing is relevant even if the firm has its own internal funds for use. Even with internal funds available, it is important that the funds be used in the most productive way. Unless the proposed investment yields a return equal to or greater than current borrowing costs, the firm should lend its own funds for the highest return.

With an interest cost of 8 percent, for example, a firm should invest its own internal funds only in the first project whose rate of return will be above the cost of borrowing. In our example, this would be the data processing equipment, since $r = 9 > 8 = c$. Any excess internal funds should be loaned out for 8 percent, rather than invested in projects or equipment that yield returns of only 5 percent or 7 percent.

This principle can be stated as follows:

Capital investment should be undertaken only if the internal rate of return is at least as great as the current cost of acquiring investment funds.

In the next chapter, we will look more closely at the costs of investment funds and at the process of financing an investment expenditure.

PRESENT VALUE AND NET PRESENT VALUE

The investment return equation can be used in another way in making investment decisions. Again, let us consider the proposed investment having a current outlay of $100,000 and and an estimated future stream of cash flows amounting to $45,000, $35,000, $25,000, and $15,000. Additionally, let us suppose that the firm has other investment opportunities that would yield a return of $r = 8$ percent. Other investment opportunities might include projects within the firm, purchase of other business properties, or purchase of government securities or high-grade corporate bonds. In each of these circumstances, 8 percent is the firm's **opportunity cost** of capital. Opportunity cost is the value of the opportunity the firm must give up if it is to make the proposed investment.

To illustrate, let us compute values for our previous equation,

$$C = \sum \frac{F_t}{(1 + r)^t},$$

using $r = 8$ percent for the firm's opportunity cost of capital: Now the expression becomes an inequality:

$$100 \neq \frac{45}{1.08} + \frac{35}{(1.08)^2} + \frac{25}{(1.08)^3} + \frac{15}{(1.08)^4}.$$

The value to the left of the inequality sign is the current outlay for the investment, C. The value to the right is the expected stream of future cash flows (F_t), *discounted* according to the firm's opportunity cost of capital.

When an expected stream of cash flows is discounted in this way, its value is called the **present value** of a future income stream. Thus, the expression becomes: $C \neq PV$ = present value of a future income stream. The present value of the income stream above is:

$$PV = \frac{\$45}{1.08} + \frac{35}{(1.08)^2} + \frac{25}{(1.08)^3} + \frac{15}{(1.08)^4}$$
$$= \$41.46 + 30.01 + 19.85 + 11.03 = \$102,550.$$

Compare the present value of future cash flows with the current outlay for the investment. Thus,

$$C \neq PV$$

and $100,000 < 102,550$. With a current outlay less than the present value of future cash flows, we would say that this investment has positive **net present value**. Net present value is the difference between the investment's current outlay and its present value:

$$\text{Net present value} = NPV = -C + PV.$$

The net present value of this investment is $NPV = -\$100,000 + 102,550 = \$2,550$. With $NPV > 0$, a firm would normally choose to make the proposed investment. With $NPV < 0$, future cash flows discounted according to the firm's opportunity cost of capital are too low to justify making the investment.

Net present value varies inversely with an investment's current outlay and directly with future cash flows. NPV is also affected strongly by the magnitude of r and t. A high rate of discount r reduces present value and, therefore, reduces net present value. A high rate of discount implies a high opportunity cost in terms of the profitability of alternative investments. Present value is reduced also if there is a long time t before revenues are to be received.

COMPARING INTERNAL RATE OF RETURN AND NET PRESENT VALUE

If the internal rate of return method and the net present value method use the same formula for evaluating investments, are they of equal value to the decision maker? In fact, both procedures would give "buy" signals to decision makers considering the data processing equipment in our example. This is shown is Table 12.3.

For many investment proposals, the results according to internal rate of return are identical to those of net present value. Still, most analysts prefer the **net present value** method for evaluating investment proposals. The reason for this has to do with the timing and uses of cash flows.

TABLE 12.3

Internal rate of return
$r = 9\% =$ internal rate of return on data processing equipment
$c = 8\% =$ opportunity cost of capital
$r > c$. Therefore, purchase.

Net present value
$NPV = -100 + 102.55 = \$2,550$
$NPV > 0$. Therefore, purchase.

EXAMPLE 12.1   Calculating Depreciation Expense

Depreciation refers to the fact that equipment used in production gradually wears out and must be replaced. Thus, some portion of the cost of capital equipment is a true cost of production and should be included in a firm's financial reporting. An allowance for depreciation is deducted from net income from operations before arriving at taxable income.

Since revenues set aside for depreciation are not subject to tax, there is an incentive to use the largest amount allowed for this purpose. Congress has established rules governing permissible methods of depreciation, some of which are described below.

STRAIGHT-LINE DEPRECIATION

The simplest method of computing depreciation involves the assumption that equipment wears out at a steady rate. This means that equipment expected to last ten years loses one-tenth of its value each year. For example, suppose a milling machine costs $1,250,000 and is expected to be sold as scrap for $50,000 after ten years. The machine's **depreciable value** is its initial cost less scrap value: $1,250,000 − $50,000 = $1,200,000. Depreciation expense for each of the years the machine is operated is 1,200,000/10 = 120,000. Each year, the machine's **book value** is its initial cost less depreciation allowance through that year. Thus, book value declines each year by the amount of the year's depreciation expense. At the end of the machine's life, book value is equal to scrap value. Another way of saying this is that total depreciation expense plus scrap value is equal to the purchase price: 10($120,000) + $50,000 = $1,250,000.

Note that the use of **straight-line depreciation** results in an equal yearly deduction over the life of the equipment. Taxes in each year are reduced by the year's depreciation expense times the tax rate. For a firm paying income tax at the 46-percent tax rate, the tax savings each year is $120,000 × .46 = $55,200. This is the amount by which taxes will be reduced each year. Reducing taxable income by the amount of depreciation helps ensure that the firm will not be taxed on nonexistent profit.

Computations of net present value and internal rate of return require estimates of cash flow during the years an investment is in use. Since funds set aside for depreciation are received by the firm, these funds should be included in cash flow. The total amount of a firm's cash flow is then available for accomplishing the firm's objectives. One disadvantage of straight-line depreciation is the fact that equal allowances for depreciation are deducted in each year of operation. Most firms would prefer greater tax deductions in early years. For such firms, methods of computing depreciation that delay the payment of taxes are more desirable.

DOUBLE DECLINING BALANCE DEPRECIATION

As an incentive to increased capital investment, Congress has given its approval to the use of accelerated depreciation. Accelerated depreciation involves higher depreciation expenses in early years and lower depreciation expenses later in the life of equipment. The result is to reduce taxable income and, therefore, reduce taxes in early years, making funds available for use by the firm. In later years, allowable depreciation expenses will be lower and taxes will be higher.

Consider again the equipment in our previous example. Under **double declining balance depreciation**, the firm may allocate a certain fraction of the equipment's value each year, as long as the cumulative total of depreciation does not exceed the investment's depreciable value. The permitted fraction is double the fraction used in the straight-line method of computing depreciation. Thus, for the first year of operation, the depreciation expense is

$$(2 \times .10)(\$1,250,000) = \$250,000.$$

The larger allocation to depreciation reduces taxable income by more than twice that allowable under the straight-line method and reduces current taxes by a comparable amount. Net profit after taxes is thus greater. Furthermore, depreciation of $250,000 is included in cash flow for computing net present value. This results in increased early net cash flows and increased NPV for the investment.

In the second year, double declining balance allows the firm to deduct the permitted fraction of the remaining undepreciated value of the equipment:

$$(2 \times .10)(\$1,250,000 - \$250,000) = \$200,000.$$

The tax advantage is less than in the first year, and the addition to net cash flow is smaller. Still, the allowance for depreciation is greater than under the straight-line method.

If the firm continues to deduct a fraction of the remaining undepreciated value of the equipment each year under the double declining balance method, total depreciation expense will *never* reach the full value of the equipment! At some point, the firm should convert to the straight-line method in order to use the full depreciation advantage permitted. The decision regarding the appropriate method of computing depreciation for an upcoming year should be made before the end of the previous year. To calculate available depreciation under the straight-line method, the analyst should first compute the undepreciated value of the equipment, deduct its scrap value, then divide by the remaining years of life. The straight-line figure should then be compared with the figure for double declining balance and the larger of the two should be selected. Once conversion to the straight-line method takes place, depreciation expense is constant for the remaining life, and the sum of depreciation expense is the depreciable value of the equipment.

One procedure for computing depreciation is shown in Table A.

TABLE A

	(1)	(2) Depreciation expense: DDB	(3) Undepreciated value (end of year)	(4) Years remaining (end of year)	(5) Depreciation expense: SL [(3) − 50,000] ÷ (4)
Year 1	.2(1,250,000)	= $250,000	$1,000,000	9	$125,000
Year 2	.2(1,000,000)	= 200,000	800,000	8	$105,555.56
Year 3	.2(800,000)	= 160,000	640,000	7	93,750
Year 4	.2(640,000)	= 128,000	512,000	6	84,285.71
Year 5	.2(512,000)	= 102,400	409,600	5	77,000
Year 6	.2(409,600)	= 81,920	327,680	4	71,920
Year 7	.2(327,680)	= 65,536	262,144	3	69,420
Year 8	.2(262,144)	= 52,428.8	209,715.2	2	70,714.67
Year 9	.2(209,715.2)	= 41,943.04	167,772.16	1	79,857.6
Year 10	.2(167,772.16)	= 33,554.432			117,772.16
		$1,115,782.272			

Columns (1) and (2) show computation of depreciation allowance for ten years under the double declining balance method. Note that the sum of depreciation expense (Column (2)) is less than the depreciable value of the equipment. Columns (3) and (5) give alternative computations for depreciation using the straight-line method. In this case, the remaining undepreciated value of the equipment after each year is first reduced by the scrap value of $50,000 and then divided by the remaining years of life to arrive at depreciation expense for the next year. Thus, the first value shown in Column (5) is the appropriate depreciation expense for the second year under the straight-line method.

Compare depreciation expense computed using the double declining balance method with the straight-line alternative for each year. Note that for years one through six the double declining balance method permits a higher deduction for depreciation and, therefore, lower taxes and larger cash flow. In year seven, the straight-line method gives a greater amount. Tax laws permit a change to the straight-line method when this method provides greater depreciation expense. The firm in this example would deduct the amounts shown in Table B as depreciation expense.

TABLE B

Year 1	$ 250,000
Year 2	200,000
Year 3	160,000
Year 4	128,000
Year 5	102,400
Year 6	81,920
Year 7	69,420
Year 8	69,420
Year 9	69,420
Year 10	69,420
Total	$1,200,000

The results of this procedure are larger cash flows and lower taxes in early years and the complete use of allowable depreciation expense.

SUM OF THE YEARS' DIGITS DEPRECIATION

Finally, the sum of the years' digits method of computing depreciation has some advantages. Under **sum of the years' digits depreciation**, the firm deducts a declining fraction of the equipment's depreciable value each year. The denominator of this fraction is determined by adding the number of the years the equipment is to be used. For the equipment described in our example, the denominator would be

$$1 + 2 + 3 + 4 + 5 + 6 + 7 + 8 + 9 + 10 = 55.$$

The numerator is the number of years remaining in the life of the equipment, making the appropriate fractions in this case: 10/55, 9/55, 8/55, 7/55, 6/55, 5/55, 4/55, 3/55, 2/55, and 1/55. The result of sum of the years' digits is to deduct smaller amounts each year, achieving a total equal to the equipment's depreciable value as shown in Table C.

TABLE C

Year 1	$ 218,181.82
Year 2	196,363.64
Year 3	174,545.45
Year 4	152,727,27
Year 5	130,909.09
Year 6	109,090.91
Year 7	87,272.73
Year 8	65,454.55
Year 9	43,636.36
Year 10	21,818.18
Total	$1,200,000.00

Since the sum of the years' digits method yields a smaller depreciation figure for the first year than the double declining balance method would, the latter method is usually preferred.

A Final Note
Regardless of the depreciation method used, the amount of taxes due on an investment will be the same. The only advantage in choosing among various methods is being able to choose *when* taxes are paid. Postponing taxes gives business firms an incentive to invest in productive equipment. Productive equipment benefits the community as a whole by increasing production possibilities and providing jobs.

MANAGERIAL THINKING

1. The tax law of 1981 established an Accelerated Cost Recovery System (ACRS) that significantly changed depreciation rules for many firms. Under ACRS, the allowable period for depreciating buildings and equipment was reduced and salvage value was eliminated as a consideration in determining depreciation. What is the effect of ACRS on business profits? What is the effect of ACRS on incentives to purchase new investments?
2. Sure-Value Tools is considering purchase of a polishing machine for producing industrial dies. The machine is expected to be used for five years and then re-sold for $5,000. Its purchase price is $150,000. Management projects operating costs and revenues from the use of the machine as shown in Table D. The firm pays taxes at the 46-percent rate and has a 12-percent opportunity cost of capital. Determine the machine's net present value, using the preferred method(s) of depreciation.

TABLE D	Revenues	Operating costs
Year 1	300,000	230,000
Year 2	400,000	250,000
Year 3	450,000	300,000
Year 4	400,000	300,000
Year 5	400,000	350,000

Under the internal rate of return method, an investment that yields $r = 9$ percent might be acceptable to a firm for which the opportunity cost of capital is $c = 8$ percent. However, $r = 9$ percent implies that cash received early in the project life is reinvested and continues to earn 9 percent over the remaining life of the project. Many firms would not have additional projects for reinvestment at that rate, making a value of $r = 9$ percent inappropriate for the investment decision.

The net present value method uses the firm's own opportunity cost of capital for discounting future revenues: $r = 8$ percent above. Therefore, it assumes a reinvestment yield of only that rate. Presumably, many other projects would be available yielding that lower rate, making the value $r = 8$ percent appropriate for the investment decision.

EVALUATING THE EFFECTS OF INFLATION ON INVESTMENTS

Inflation affects the cash flows of many investment proposals. Adjusting cash flows for inflation can help avoid incorrect investment decisions. Economists distinguish between *nominal* and *real* dollar values. **Nominal values** are stated in terms of dollars of the current year, and **real values** are stated in dollars of constant purchasing power. A nominal value can be converted to a real value by *deflating*, or dividing by a price index:

$$\text{Real value} = \frac{\text{Nominal value}}{\text{Price index}}$$

A price index reflects the ratio between current prices and prices of a base year. Thus, a price index of 1.05 in Year 1 indicates a price increase of 5 percent over Year 0. The real value of $100 in Year 1 in terms of constant dollars of Year 0 is determined as follows:

$$\text{Real value} = \frac{\$100}{1.05} = \$95.24.$$

Because of 5-percent inflation, the real value of $100 is reduced by almost $5 after one year.

If inflation of 5 percent persists in year 2, the real value of $100 is

$$\text{Real value} = \frac{\$100}{(1.05)^2} = \frac{\$100}{1.1025} = \$90.70.$$

Including a second inflation factor in the price index has the effect of increasing the price index to account for a second year of 5-percent inflation. The result is to reduce the real value of $100 during the second year as well.

Failing to account for inflation in an investment decision may overstate the net present value of an investment or overstate its internal rate of return. Recall the investment proposal for data processing equipment described previously. Suppose cash flows from operating the equipment are expected to increase because of inflation at the rate of 5 percent a year. The investment return equation now becomes:

$$-C + \sum \frac{F_t}{(1 + r)^t} = 0$$

$$= 100 + \frac{45,000(1.05)}{(1 + r)} + \frac{35,000(1.05)^2}{(1 + r)^2} + \frac{25,000(1.05)^3}{(1 + r)^3} + \frac{15,000(1.05)^4}{(1 + r)^4} = 0$$

$$= 100 + \frac{47,250}{(1 + r)} + \frac{38,590}{(1 + r)^2} + \frac{28,940}{(1 + r)^3} + \frac{18,230}{(1 + r)^4} = 0,$$

and $r \approx 14$ percent.

The second investment contributes more to the firm's total profit. Unless alternative investments have the same initial outlay, their rankings according to profitability indexes will differ from those according to net present value (and contribution to total profit).

Average Rate of Return

These and other disadvantages apply to another method of evaluating investment proposals: the average rate of return. **Average rate of return** (r_a) is the average economic profit from the investment relative to its purchase price. Expressed algebraically,

$$r_a = \frac{\pi/n}{C},$$

where π is the total of all economic profit over n years and C is the initial outlay. Some analysts use cash flow (F) instead of economic profit for calculating average rate of return. The result is a superior measure, since it takes into consideration the amount of cash actually available for use by the firm. Even so, the average rate of return ignores the timing of cash flows, making it a less satisfactory method of evaluation than those we have described above.

Pay-Back Period

Investments may also be evaluated in terms of the number of years that elapse before the initial expenditure can be recovered. An investment of $100 that yields cash flows of $45,000, $35,000, $25,000, and $15,000 in each of the next four years recovers the initial investment after:

$$
\begin{array}{ll}
45 & \text{1 year} \\
35 & \text{1 year} \\
\underline{20} \div 25 = & \underline{.8 \text{ year}} \\
100 & 2.8 \text{ years.}
\end{array}
$$

Unlike the average rate of return method, the payback period does consider the timing of cash flows. Note that if the timing of cash flows were reversed, the payback period for this investment would be longer:

$$
\begin{array}{ll}
15 & \text{1 year} \\
25 & \text{1 year} \\
35 & \text{1 year} \\
\underline{25} \div 45 = & \underline{.55 \text{ year}} \\
100 & 3.55 \text{ years.}
\end{array}
$$

One disadvantage of the payback period in evaluating investments is that cash received after the payback period is not considered. Thus, the payback

EXAMPLE 12.2   **Using Present Value Tables**

Computing the present value of an investment can be simplified by the use of tables. Consider an investment that is expected to yield cash flows of $100,000, $95,000, $75,000, $0, and $80,000 over five future years. We know that the investment's present value is

$$PV = \frac{\$100,000}{(1 + r)^1} + \frac{95,000}{(1 + r)^2} + \frac{75,000}{(1 + r)^3} + \frac{0}{(1 + r)^4} + \frac{80,000}{(1 + r)^5}.$$

With $r = 11$ percent, present value is

$$PV = 100,000\left(\frac{1}{1.11}\right) + 95,000\left(\frac{1}{1.11^2}\right) + 75,000\left(\frac{1}{1.11^3}\right)$$
$$+ 0\left(\frac{1}{1.11^4}\right) + 80,000\left(\frac{1}{1.11^5}\right).$$

The values in parentheses in these equations can be called **discount factors**. A discount factor is the factor by which a future cash flow must be multiplied to yield its value in the present. The discount factors in the above example have the following values: $(1/1.11) = .9009$, $(1/1.11^2) = .81162$, $(1/1.11^3 = .72119$, $(1/1.11^4) = .65873$, and $(1/1.11^5) = .59345$. Multiplying $100,000, 95,000, 75,000, 0, and 80,000 by the appropriate discount factor and summing the results yields the investment's present value:

$$PV = \$90,090 + \$79,540 + 54,840 + 0 + \$47,480 = \$271,950.$$

Discount factors are provided in tables in many textbooks and reference books used by financial planners. A portion of such a table is presented in Table A. This

TABLE A   Discount factors: $\dfrac{1}{(1 + r)^t}$

	$r = 8\%$	$r = 9\%$	$r = 10\%$	$r = 11\%$	$r = 12\%$	$r = 13\%$	$r = 14\%$	$r = 15\%$
$t = 1$	.92593	.91743	.90909	.90090	.89286	.88496	.87719	.86957
$t = 2$	.85734	.84168	.82645	.81162	.79719	.78315	.78967	.75614
$t = 3$	.79383	.77218	.75131	.73119	.71178	.69305	.67497	.65752
$t = 4$	.73503	.70845	.68301	.65873	.63552	.61332	.59208	.57175
$t = 5$	.68058	.64993	.62092	.59345	.56743	.54276	.51937	.49718
$t = 6$	.63017	.59627	.56447	.53464	.50663	.48032	.45559	.43233
$t = 7$	.59349	.54703	.51316	.48166	.45235	.42506	.39964	.37594
$t = 8$	.54027	.50187	.46651	.43393	.40388	.37616	.35056	.32690
$t = 9$	.50025	.46043	.42410	.39092	.36061	.33288	.30751	.28426
$t = 10$	.46319	.42241	.38554	.35218	.32197	.29459	.26974	.24718
$t = 11$	.42888	.38753	.35049	.31728	.28748	.26070	.23662	.21494
$t = 12$	.39711	.35553	.31863	.28584	.25667	.23071	.20756	.18691
$t = 13$	.36770	.32618	.28966	.25751	.22917	.20416	.18207	.16253
$t = 14$	.34046	.29925	.26333	.23199	.20462	.18068	.15971	.14133
$t = 15$	.31524	.27454	.23939	.20900	.18270	.15989	.14010	.12289
$t = 16$	.29189	.25187	.21763	.18829	.16312	.14150	.12289	.10686
$t = 17$	.27027	.23107	.19784	.16963	.14564	.12522	.10780	.09293
$t = 18$	.25025	.21199	.17986	.15282	.13004	.11081	.09456	.08080
$t = 19$	.23171	.19449	.16351	.13768	.11611	.09806	.08295	.07026
$t = 20$	.21455	.17843	.14864	.12403	.10367	.08678	.07276	.06110

table shows discount factors for cash received up to ten years in the future for values of r ranging from 8 percent to 15 percent.

You will notice that the discount factors in the table are all less than one. In fact, all discount factors are less than one. The effect of this is to make present value less than the sum of future cash flows. Notice also that discount factors for cash flows far in the future are smaller than those for cash to be received soon. This makes their present value lower as well. Finally, notice that discount factors are smaller for higher values of r. A high r value signifies a high opportunity cost for funds paid out today on the expectation of gains in the future.

To use the discount factor table, find the appropriate discount factor for corresponding values of r and t and multiply the expected future cash flow. For r = 8 percent, for instance, the investment in our most recent example would have a present value of

$$\$100,000(.92593) + \$95,000(.85734) + \$75,000(.79383) + 0(.73503) + \\ \$80,000(.68058) = \$287,720,$$

which is higher than the PV = $271,950 at r = 11 percent.

EQUAL CASH FLOWS

Computing present value is even simpler if cash flows are expected to be equal in future years. Consider an investment that is expected to yield $115,000 in each of the next five years. Its present value is

$$PV = \$115,000\left(\frac{1}{1.11}\right) + \$115,000\left(\frac{1}{1.11^2}\right) + \$115,000\left(\frac{1}{1.11^3}\right)$$
$$+ \$115,000\left(\frac{1}{1.11^4}\right) + \$115,000\left(\frac{1}{1.11^5}\right)$$
$$= \$115,000\left(\frac{1}{1.11} + \frac{1}{1.11^2} + \frac{1}{1.11^3} + \frac{1}{1.11^4} + \frac{1}{1.11^5}\right)$$
$$= \$115,000(.9009 + .81162 + .72119 + .65873 + .59345)$$
$$= \$115,000(3.69589)$$
$$= \$425,030.$$

Thus, the investment's present value is future cash flow multiplied by the sum of the appropriate discount factors.

Note that although cash is to be received for five years, the discount factor for computing present value is less than five. This is because the individual discount factors for each of the five years are less than one. The longer the period of time for which cash is received, however, the greater the sum of the discount factors and the greater the investment's present value. Again, the greater the value of r, the lower the discount factor, since the opportunity cost of the investment is high.

Table B is a portion of a table listing discount factors for equal receipts over a number of years. Values in Table B are the sums of values appearing in Table A.

Suppose an investment is expected to yield $115,000 for each of the next five years and then $65,000 for the next five. Its present value is

$$PV = \$115,000\left(\frac{1}{1.11} + \frac{1}{1.11^2} + \frac{1}{1.11^3} + \frac{1}{1.11^4} + \frac{1}{1.11^5}\right)$$
$$+ \$65,000\left(\frac{1}{1.11^6} + \frac{1}{1.11^7} + \frac{1}{1.11^8} + \frac{1}{1.11^9} + \frac{1}{1.11^{10}}\right)$$

$$= \$115,000(3.6959) + \$65,000(5.8892 - 3.6959) = \$567,590.$$

Can you suggest a method of using Tables A and B to compute present value when payments are received semi-annually for three years and the opportunity cost of capital is 16 percent?) Use the discount factor for r = 8 percent and t = 6.)

TABLE B

$$\text{Discount factors: } \Sigma \, \frac{1}{(1 + r)^t}$$

	r = 8%	r = 9%	r = 10%	r = 11%	r = 12%	r = 13%	r = 14%	r = 15%
t = 1	.9259	9.174	.9091	.9009	.8929	.8850	.8772	.8696
t = 2	1.7833	1.7591	1.7355	1.7125	1.6901	1.6681	1.6467	1.6257
t = 3	2.5771	2.5313	2.4868	2.4437	2.4018	2.3612	2.3216	2.2832
t = 4	3.3121	3.2397	3.1699	3.1024	3.0373	2.9745	2.9137	2.8550
t = 5	3.9927	3.8896	3.7908	3.6959	3.6048	3.5172	3.4331	3.3522
t = 6	4.6229	4.4859	4.3553	4.2305	4.1114	3.9976	3.8887	3.7845
t = 7	5.2064	5.0329	4.8684	4.7122	4.5638	4.4226	4.2883	4.1604
t = 8	5.7466	5.5348	5.3349	5.1461	4.9676	4.7988	4.6389	4.4873
t = 9	6.2469	5.9852	5.7590	5.5370	5.3282	5.1317	4.9464	4.7716
t = 10	6.7101	6.4176	6.1446	5.8892	5.6502	5.4262	5.2161	5.0188
t = 11	7.1389	6.8052	6.4951	6.2065	5.9377	5.6859	5.4527	5.2337
t = 12	7.5361	7.1607	6.8137	6.4924	6.1944	5.9165	5.6603	5.4206
t = 13	7.9038	7.4869	7.1034	6.7499	6.4235	6.1218	5.8424	5.5831
t = 14	8.2442	7.7861	7.3667	6.9819	6.6282	6.3025	6.0021	5.7245
t = 15	8.5595	8.0607	7.6061	7.1909	6.8109	6.4624	6.1422	5.8474
t = 16	8.8514	8.3125	7.8237	7.3792	6.9740	6.6039	6.2651	5.9542
t = 17	9.1216	8.5436	8.0215	7.5488	7.1196	6.7291	6.3729	6.0472
t = 18	9.3719	8.7556	8.2014	7.7016	7.2497	6.8399	6.4674	6.1280
t = 19	9.6036	8.9501	8.3649	7.8393	7.3658	6.9380	6.5504	6.1982
t = 20	9.8181	9.1285	8.5136	7.9633	7.4694	7.0248	6.6231	6.2593

MANAGERIAL THINKING

1. Suppose you are offered an annuity that will pay $1,000 a year for the next 20 years at a current price of $7,963.33. What is the implicit discount rate (value of r) used for determining the current price?
2. Calculate the implicit value of r for a 10-year annuity that pays $1,000 a year and costs $6,275.

---

method does not allow potential investors to distinguish among investments that continue to yield income beyond the payback period. This feature may not be a problem for certain types of investments such as high risk investments that are expected to pay off quickly and then be abandoned. However, this method understates the value of the large majority of investments undertaken by most firms.

A second disadvantage of the payback method is that it contains no explicit recognition of the time value of money.

PRESENT VALUE OF AN INFINITE INCOME STREAM

Some investments are expected to yield income continuously for so many years that ordinary present value computations would become impossible. Land is an example of a resource that continues to yield income to the current owner over an indefinite period. Eventually, land may be sold to another investor at a price that represents its future earning power. This makes the present value of the land equal to expected earnings over an infinite number of years in the future. Rights to many other resources also may be held in perpetuity, so that their value reflects the sum of expected earnings forever.

Fortunately, procedures exist for computing the present value of an investment that is expected to yield income forever. Note that it is not necessary for the original owner to hold the investment forever, since its resale price represents all future income. The present value formula for an infinite period of time is

$$PV = \frac{F}{r},$$

where F represents future cash flows and r represents rate of return (both determined at annual, quarterly, or monthly rates). The investor would compare PV with the purchase price in order to determine net present value:

$$NPV = -C + PV,$$

where C represents purchase price. Positive NPV would generally indicate a positive investment decision.

The formula can be rearranged for computing internal rate of return when initial cost and future cash flows are known: $r = F/C$. In order to use either formula, it is necessary to assume equal cash flows. However, the formula can be adapted to allow for income growth or decline, as we will now demonstrate.

Let us assume that fishing rights in a certain area can be purchased for $1.5 million. The contract extends indefinitely and can be sold at any time for its present value at the time of sale. Cash flows are estimated at $150,000 annually for the indefinite future. The opportunity cost of capital is 10 percent. The present value of an infinite income stream with these characteristics is $PV = \$150,000/.10 = \$1,500,000$. With present value equal to purchase price,

$$NPV = -C + PV = -1.5 + 1.5 = 0,$$

an investor would be indifferent as to whether the purchase should be carried out. In a competitive market, this is the expected result, since all potential investors would compute present value similarly and push the price to a level consistent with expected earnings. Only if purchase price is greater or less than the present value of earnings is there a definite "buy" or "no buy" signal to investors.

Now suppose that cash flows are expected to increase annually at a rate of about 1 percent. The source of increased earnings may be technical improvements in processing equipment, higher prices for seafood products, or a number of cost-saving developments. Earnings growth affects present value computations so that

$$PV = \frac{F}{r - g}.^5$$

In our example,

$$PV = \frac{150,000}{.10 - .01} = \$1,666,666.67.$$

Net present value is

$$NPV = -C + PV = -1.5 + 1.67 = \$166,666.67.$$

Positive net present value from growth would indicate a "buy" decision in this case.

Internal rate of return is also affected by growth according to

$$r = \frac{F}{C} + \left(g\right) = \frac{150,000}{1,500,000} + .01 = .11 = 11 \text{ percent.}$$

With internal rate of return greater than the opportunity cost of capital, the decision again is to invest.

For many investment properties, the expectation may be for a decrease in earnings such that $g < 0$. Higher material costs or a deteriorating market for the finished good or service are some possible causes of this. A 1-percent decrease in cash flows would reduce present value to

$$PV = \frac{F}{r - g} = \frac{150,000}{.10 + .01} = \$1,363,636.36$$

and internal rate of return to $r = \frac{F}{C} + (g) = \frac{150,000}{1,500,000} - .01 = .09 = 9$ percent. If all potential investors have the same expectations with respect to future cash flows, competition would push purchase price to a level consistent with the investment's present value.

ANOTHER LOOK AT SEARS

Coping with change is an important function of managers. Many technical, human, and financial changes call for long-run strategies involving investments. Investments comprise purchases of productive equipment, other business firms, or shares of investment properties. Choosing among investment

---

5. This formula only works if $r > g$.

proposals requires comparisons of projected earnings over the life of the investment.

For a giant enterprise like Sears, a fundamental change in the direction of its investments is a major undertaking. In making such a change Sears managers most likely obtained revenue and cost data from a variety of alternative investment proposals. By comparing net present value, internal rate of return, and other indices of profitability, managers in all likelihood established priorities and laid out a strategy for Sears' long-run growth. On the basis of available evidence and informed judgment about future business conditions, the chosen strategy would be expected to yield maximum opportunities for profit.

CASE STUDY 12.2   Choosing Between Investments with Economic Lives of Varying Lengths

The economic life of an investment may be unrelated to its actual productive life. Economic life depends on the behavior of operating costs as a piece of equipment ages and on advances in technology that reduce the operating costs of replacement equipment. For each year equipment is held, a firm experiences increasing *operating costs* from deterioration and increasing *opportunity costs* from the failure to utilize the most up-to-date equipment. At some point in the life of a piece of equipment its total annual costs rise above the cost of using replacement equipment. This is the point that defines the economic life of an investment.

Frequently, a firm must decide among various kinds of equipment with economic lives of varying lengths. Managers must compute the *present value of the costs* of each piece of equipment and choose the equipment with the *lowest present value of costs.*

The first step in this investment decision is to establish a time frame for comparing costs. The appropriate time frame is the smallest common multiple of the economic lives of each piece of equipment. If, for example, a firm must choose between fork lifts with economic lives of 4 and 6 years, the smallest common multiple is 12. Thus, the appropriate time frame for comparing costs is 12 years.

To illustrate the process, let us analyze the costs of one fork lift with an economic life of 4 years. Its purchase price is $11,300 and its scrap value after 4 years is $3,000. The costs of operating the equipment can be broken down into three categories:

1. Basic operating costs.
2. Additional costs due to aging of equipment.
3. Reductions in costs due to technological improvements when old equipment is replaced by new equipment.

The following table shows all the costs associated with operating the equipment for twelve years.

	Initial purchase				First replacement				Second replacement				Final scrap
Year	0	1	2	3	4	5	6	7	8	9	10	11	12
(1)	−11.3				−11.3				−11.3				
					+ 3.				+ 3.				+3.
					− 8.3				− 8.3				
(2)		−2	−2	−2	−2	−2	−2	−2	−2	−2	−2	−2	−2
(3)			− .9	−1.8	− 2.7		− .9	−1.8	− 2.7		− .9	−1.8	−2.7
(4)						+ .4	+ .4	+ .4	+ .4	+ .8	+ .8	+ .8	+ .8
(5)	−11.3	−2	−2.9	−3.8	−13.	−1.6	−2.5	−3.4	−12.6	−1.2	−2.1	−3.	− .9

The first row in the table includes purchase price less scrap value for each of three purchases of the fork lift over a twelve year period. Row (2) shows basic operating costs, estimated in this example to be $2,000 a year. Row (3) includes expected cost increases due to deterioration of the equipment. Managers estimate that deterioration causes costs to rise by $900 for each year a fork lift is operated. Row (4) shows the reduction in operating costs due to technological improvements incorporated in new equipment. Managers estimate that technological improvements reduce the cost of operating fork lifts $100 a year. Therefore, replacement at four year intervals would result in cost reductions of $400 and $800 annually. Row (5) is the total cost associated with purchasing this equipment and operating it (or replacement equipment) for twelve years. These are the values that should appear in the present value equation:

$$PV = -C + \sum_{t=1}^{12} \frac{(Cost)_t}{(1 + r)^t}.$$

If the firm requires a return of $r = 10$ percent on its investment, the present value of costs would be:

$$PV_c = -11,300 - \frac{2,000}{1.10} - \frac{2,900}{1.10^2} - \frac{3,800}{1.10^3} - \frac{13,000}{1.10^4} - \frac{1,600}{1.10^5} - \frac{2,500}{1.10^6}$$

$$- \frac{3,400}{1.10^7} - \frac{12,600}{1,10^8} - \frac{1,200}{1.10^9} - \frac{2,100}{1.10^{10}} - \frac{3,000}{1.10^{11}} - \frac{900}{1.10^{12}} = -39,930.$$

Thus, the present value of costs for purchasing and operating this fork lift is $-39,930$. A similar procedure should be employed for evaluating other investments, and the one with the lowest present value of costs should then be chosen.

MANAGERIAL THINKING

Assume that basic operating costs increase through inflation at the rate of 5 percent annually and that the purchase price of new equipment increases at a 4-percent rate. Show how these changes would affect the present value of costs of this equipment.

Source: Gary W. Emery, "Some Guidelines for Evaluating Capital Investment Alternatives with Unequal Lives," *Financial Management*, Spring 1982, vol. 11, no. 1, pp. 14–19.

By 1984, Sears' managers were pleased with the results of their new investment strategy. The year-to-year gain in net income for 1984 was more than 50 percent. Sears had become a kind of "holding company": an organization consisting of several operating units, including retailing, investment banking, insurance, real estate, and world trade. Company executives met frequently for further strategic planning.

Financing a firm's chosen investment strategy is the subject of the next chapter: acquiring the funds to implement managers' plan for long-run growth. Then in chapter 14 we will look at the risks associated with long-run investment strategy.

SUMMARY

In the long run, the quantity of all resources can be varied, including capital resources that are considered fixed in the short run. The present value of a proposed new capital investment is the sum of all future cash flows, discounted according to the distance in the future they are to be received and the firm's required rate of return on investments. Cash flow includes net profit after taxes, depreciation allowances, and interest on funds borrowed to purchase the investment.

The marginal efficiency of investment (*MEI*) is the internal rate of return on the investment when its discounted present value is equal to its current outlay. The firm's *MEI* schedule constitutes its demand curve for investment. Managers compare an investment's internal rate of return with current interest rates to decide whether an investment should be purchased. This is true whether or not funds must be borrowed for making the purchase.

The profitability index is the ratio of the present value of an investment to its initial cost. Net present value is the difference between the present value of an investment and its initial outlay. Net present value is generally preferred for distinguishing among proposed investments because it assumes that cash flows continue to earn interest at the firm's opportunity cost of capital. To correct for expected inflation, it is appropriate to deflate cash flows through the use of a price index.

Present value tables are useful for making calculations involving the time value of money.

U.S. tax laws permit various methods of depreciation that vary the timing of a firm's tax payments but not their actual amount.

KEY TERMS

cash flow	present value
gross profit	net present value
depreciation	depreciable value
net profit	book value
retained earnings	straight-line depreciation
time value	double declining balance depreciation
interest	sum of the years' digits depreciation
compounding	nominal value
discounting	real value
rate of return	profitability index
marginal efficiency of	average rate of return
investment schedule	discount factors
opportunity cost	

QUESTIONS AND PROBLEMS

1. Explain the basis for including depreciation allowance in cash flow for calculating the net present value of an investment.

2. Determine the future value of a $100 bank deposit that earns 10 percent interest over a period of 7 years.

3. What amount must be deposited today at 10 percent interest if a depositor is to receive $100 in 7 years?

4. Demonstrate the difference between *discounting* and *compounding*.

5. Discuss the disadvantages of using the internal rate of return method for evaluating investments versus the net present value method.

6. Portside Seafood Company purchases salmon on July 1, stores it throughout the summer and fall at a cost of one-tenth its purchase price per month, then re-sells it on February 1 for double its original cost. Portside's cost of capital is 12 percent a year. What is its profitability index on this operation? Assume storage cost is paid at the end of each month.

7. Southern California Packing Company is planning to install electricity co-generating equipment for an initial cost of $15 million. The equipment will reduce the firm's purchase of electric power and enable it to sell power to the area's public utility. Additional cash flows for the next ten years are estimated as follows:

> Years 1 through 3 $1.7 million per year
> Years 4 through 6   2.1 million per year
> Years 7 through 10   4.3 million per year

Given a cost of capital of 11 percent, determine the net present value of the equipment.

8. Seabed Mining Corporation is considering purchasing a lease for ocean mining southeast of Hawaii. The cost of developing seabed mining technology and beginning operations is about $1 billion. Each site is expected to yield several tons of ore per year, including 45,000 tons of nickel, 39,000 tons of copper, and 750,000 tons of manganese. Production can continue for ten years under the proposed contract, with annual fees of $10 million plus a production charge of 5 percent of the value of production. Annual production costs are expected to be $100 million, and ore prices are expected to be as follows: nickel, $3.50 per pound; copper, $.75 per pound, and manganese, $68.00 per ton. The firm's cost of capital is 8 percent. What is the net present value of this project? Assume a 40-percent tax rate.

9. The BioChem Corporation is considering a research project that would cost $1 million initially and $1 million for each of the next five years. How-

ever, after the initial development period, annual revenues of $650,000 are expected forever. The firm's cost of capital is 9 percent. Should the project be undertaken?

10. Refer again to the information in Question 9. Suppose earnings are expected to increase 1 percent each year. Should the investment be undertaken?

11. Calhoun Paper Company must meet new environmental standards or pay a fine of $10,000 each month. The cost of leasing anti-pollution equipment is $115,000 a year. The firm's after tax cost of capital is 7 percent. Which course should the firm follow? (Assume interest is compounded annually.)

12. Omega Products Incorporated is considering an investment with initial cost of $7.5 million and resale value of $1.9 million after five years. Expected cash flows over the 5 years are $1.3 million, $1.8 million, $2.7 million, $5.1 million, and $6.3 million. Omega's after-tax cost of capital is 9 percent. Evaluate the investment in terms of NPV, Profitability Index, internal rate of return, payback period, and average rate of return. Explain the relative advantages and disadvantages of each of the procedures.

13. Arnaud's Bakery is investigating energy conservation equipment that can be leased for an annual outlay of $9,500. The equipment is expected to reduce energy costs by $800 a month per year. Arnaud's after tax cost of capital is 7 percent. Should the equipment be leased? (Assume interest is compounded annually.)

14. Best Computer Company wants to enter the market for personal computers. Front-end costs for beginning production would be $5,000. Market analysts project sales of 25,000 units annually at a price of $1,000 per unit. Best's low price is expected to increase its market share, however, such that sales will increase by 5 percent annually. Total production costs are expected to begin at $1,200 per unit in the first year and decline by 10 percent each year. The current "generation" of personal computers is expected to be salable for only 6 years. What is the internal rate of return on this proposal?

15. Zero-coupon securities do not pay any annual interest. Instead, they are sold at a deep discount from face value. Zebco Manufacturing Company has an opportunity to purchase a small trucking firm with an internal rate of return of 9 percent or $1,000 deep discount bonds due in 10 years for a price of $400. Use the tables in this chapter to help you choose between these investments.

16. Quality Bakery Products Company requires 10 vans to make local deliveries. The vans can be purchased for $20,000 each and are depreciated (straight-line) over a five year period. Resale value after 5 years is estimated at $5,000 each. A contract trucking company has offered to handle the firm's deliveries at a charge of $50,000 a year, to be paid at the begin-

ning of each year. Entering the proposed agreement would relieve the bakery of insurance and operating costs on the vans, estimated at $8,000 a year. The firm's cost of capital is 8 percent and it pays taxes at the 40-percent rate. What would be the firm's wisest decision concerning its deliveries?

17. Suppose the price index is expected to rise by varying amounts during the years an investment is expected to be operated. How will this affect calculations of net present value?

18. Suppose tax laws allow a firm to deduct larger depreciation allowances from taxable income in the early years of its equipment's life and smaller amounts later on. How will this affect the equipment's net present value?

13

Financing Investment Projects: The Cost of Capital

Investment in productive capital is the means by which business firms expand their capacity or reduce the unit cost of producing goods and services. It is the means by which an economic system as a whole ensures growth in living standards for its people. New buildings and equipment raise worker productivity and increase real incomes.

Deciding on long-run investment strategy is a major responsibility of business managers. It is especially important because of the occurrence of *opportunity costs*. Given a firm's limited resources for investment, every investment actually undertaken means another investment opportunity lost. The preceding chapter demonstrated procedures for evaluating and ranking investment proposals according to their projected internal rates of return. Ranking investments enables managers to establish priorities for investment policy and choose investments with the greatest expectation of gain relative to opportunity costs. For the economic system as a whole, ranking investments according to their projected rate of return ensures that the limited supply of business and personal savings will be allocated toward the most productive investment projects.

This chapter will explore the other side of the investment decision: the costs associated with a firm's investment program. We will use the cost of capital first to determine the cut-off point beyond which the opportunity cost of acquiring funds for additional investment would exceed the projected rate of return. Then we will examine the process by which a firm may accumulate investment funds internally through retained earnings and allowances for depreciation.

CASE STUDY 13.1   Ensuring an Adequate Supply of Electric Power

Few Americans alive today have ever had to worry about the supply of electric power. We flick the switch and the light comes on—or the can opener opens, or the hedge clipper clips. However, ensuring an adequate supply of electricity for the future depends on continued investment in electric generating plants—plants for converting oil, coal, or uranium to usable electric power.

For decades, demand for electric power has been increasing about 7 percent annually as more Americans use more electricity for doing more things. More than three-fourths of electricity in the United States is produced by investor-owned utilities. These, in turn, are responsible for one-fifth of all new industrial construction in the nation each year.

During the 1970s the rising cost of imported oil forced electric utilities to begin replacing their oil-using equipment with equipment powered by coal or nuclear materials. At the same time, rising interest rates and rising construction costs were making new construction prohibitively expensive. Adding to the industry's problems were environmental regulations that would require hundreds of millions of dollars worth of new equipment and reduce the amount of usable energy that could be produced.

Public utility commissions in the individual states regulate the rates local electric utilities can charge their customers. Public regulatory commissions in many states refused to approve adequate rate increases during the 1970s, and consumers responded to higher prices by cutting back their use of electric power. Industry revenues grew more slowly than costs, and investment funds became dangerously low.

Electric power industry analysts estimate industry financial needs at one-half trillion dollars over the next 15 years. Only about 40 percent of construction costs are normally paid from industry profits, so electric utilities will be forced into financial markets to acquire investment funds of about $25 billion a year. Borrowing will be expensive. Interest costs on borrowed funds are strongly influenced by *ratings* established by Moody's and Standard and Poor's investment services. To determine a firm's rating, the investment services look at the value of its productive capital and its potential profitability, both of which have been unfavorable for electric utilities in recent years.

The issue of new corporate stock also is not practical for electric power firms. For many firms, outstanding stock is now selling at about half its book value. (Book value is the difference between what a firm owns and what it owes, divided by the number of shares of stock outstanding). To sell additional shares at half a stock's book value would drastically weaken a firm's financial position.[1] Furthermore, paying dividends on past stock issues already absorbs an average of three-fourths of utility earnings, reducing the amount of internal funds available for investment in new facilities.

The electric power industry seems to be trapped in a vicious cycle. Rising production costs make higher prices necessary, but higher prices reduce purchases of - electricity and force each user to pay a larger share of the costs of electric-generating equipment. The result is to reduce volume of production further and push average production costs up again. Moreover, without profits for re-investment, the industry is unable to replace inefficient equipment, and the threat of a cutback in electric power production is imminent.

MANAGERIAL THINKING

How would you describe the production function in electric power generation? What does the production function reveal about marginal product and average total cost?

---

1. Each new share of stock sold would yield fewer dollars for investment while increasing the number of shares on which dividends would have to be paid.

How would you characterize the "structure" of the electric power industry? Your answers to these questions should provide the basis for a discussion of the reasons for government regulation in the electric power industry. Discuss also the typical consequences of regulation for the industry's long-range health and for the availability of electric power for American consumers.

To understand the problem of financing new investment, it will be helpful to look at the recent experience of a vital sector of the U.S. economy: the electric power industry. As you read the case study that follows, consider the factors that determine an electric power company's internal rate of return on new productive investment. Then ask yourself: What are the sources of funds for financing the appropriate level of new investment? How should the firm's managers balance the projected internal rate of return on new investment against the cost of acquiring investment funds?

THE MARKET FOR INVESTMENT CAPITAL

The preceding chapter demonstrated several processes by which managers may evaluate a firm's alternative investment proposals. These are summarized here:

1. Internal rate of return: r such that

$$C = \Sigma \frac{F_t}{(1 + r)^t}.$$

The internal rate of return is the discount rate that equates the current outlay for investment with the present value of future cash flows. Alternatively, the internal rate of return is the return over costs of an investment, measured in terms of a stream of cash flows over a projected period in the future.

2. Net present value:

$$NPV = -C + PV = -C + \Sigma \frac{F_t}{(1 + r)^t}.$$

Net present value is the difference between the current outlay for an investment and the present value of future cash flows from the investment, discounted at the opportunity cost of capital.

3. Profitability index:

$$PI = \frac{PV}{C} = \frac{\Sigma F_t/(1+r)^t}{C}.$$

The profitability index is the ratio of present value to the initial outlay for an investment.

4. Average rate of return:

$$r_a = \frac{\Sigma \pi / n}{C}.$$

Average rate of return is the ratio of average annual economic profit from an investment to its initial cost.

Each of these analytical tools uses or produces a value r that is a measure of the value of the investment. In methods 1 and 4 a value of r is calculated on the basis of other known and/or estimated values for current outlay and future cash flows. In methods 2 and 3 a value of r is chosen and included in the calculations to yield another value. This distinction is most important, as we will see.

First consider methods 1 and 4 in which r is the result of certain calculations. In these cases, r is the *yield* of the investment, the annual return over the costs of acquiring and operating an investment. Deciding whether to purchase the investment will depend on the relationship between its yield, r, and the opportunity cost of funds used to acquire it. In methods 2 and 3, on the other hand, the investment decision depends directly on the discount rate, r, used to solve the equation. In general, the value of r used in the equation depends on opportunity costs: that is, the expected yield on alternative uses of the firm's funds.

In summary, the value of r determined in 1 and 4 defines a firm's *demand* for investment capital, and the value of r used in 2 and 3 depends on the *supply* of investment funds available to the firm. The following sections will examine demand for and supply of investment capital in detail.

Demand for Investment Capital: The Marginal Efficiency of Investment

The internal rate of return or *yield* of an investment project is also called the **marginal efficiency of investment**. For a particular firm, ranking investment proposals according to projected yield produces a marginal efficiency of investment schedule. Graphing the marginal efficiency of investment schedule produces the firm's demand curve for investment capital. An investment demand curve slopes downward from left to right, since higher-yielding investment proposals will normally have priority over lower-yielding investment proposals. Points on a firm's investment demand curve indicate the quantity of investment that will be undertaken at various prices, or costs of capital.

The marginal efficiency of investment curve of Chapter 12 has been redrawn as a firm's investment demand curve in Figure 13.1. The actual quantity of investment for a firm depends on the cost of acquiring investment funds.

FIGURE 13.1   Marginal Efficiency of Investment

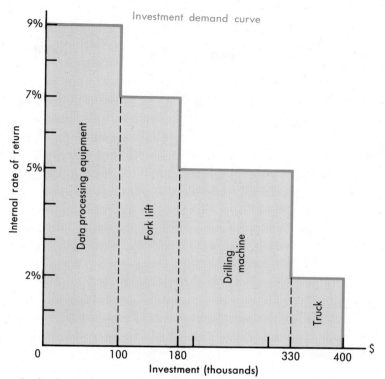

The graph of a firm's marginal efficiency of investment schedule is its demand curve for investments.

Supply of Investment Funds: The Cost of Capital

Investment funds may be acquired from internal or external sources. The costs of various sources differ and determine the supply curve of investment funds: that is, the quantities available at various prices. Finally, equilibrium in financial markets determines the price and quantity of funds actually acquired for new investment.

The Cost of Retained Earnings and Depreciation Allowances

The most common internal source of funds for financing long-term investment projects is retained earnings and depreciation allowances. The cost of these internal funds depends on alternative investment opportunities available to the firm. If other borrowers are willing to pay interest of, say, 8 percent for the use of a firm's own funds, the cost of using them internally is $i = 8$ percent.

FIGURE 13.2   **True Cost of Capital**

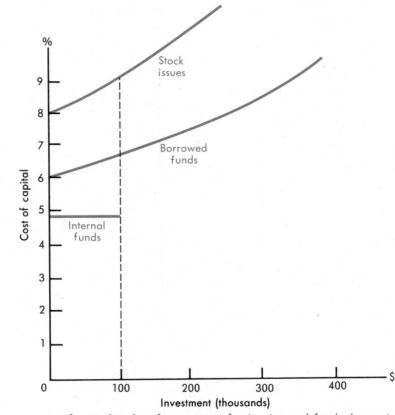

The true cost of capital is the after-tax cost of using internal funds, borrowing, or issuing new stock.

It would be foolish to use funds for internal investment projects yielding a rate of return less than $r = 8$ percent.

Frequently, the interest income from lending outside the firm is less than the firm's own borrowing costs. This is because administrative costs of processing a loan are included in the firm's borrowing charge. Thus, the opportunity cost of lending a firm's own funds can be shown as

$$i_l < i_b,$$

where i_l is the cost of lending and i_b is the cost of borrowing. In addition, the interest earned on loaned funds is subject to income tax. This means that the after-tax return from lending internal funds is

$$i_{AT} = (1 - T)i_l,$$

where T is the firm's corporate tax rate. This is the opportunity cost of using the firm's internal funds for investment.

Figure 13.2 illustrates the various sources of investment funds, beginning with the lowest-cost source of funds, retained earnings and depreciation allowances. The supply of internal funds is shown as \$100,000 and the cost is $i_{AT} = (1 - .40)8$ percent $= 4.8$ percent.

The Cost of Borrowed Funds

When internal funds are not adequate for investment, a firm may have to borrow. The interest cost of borrowing is a deductible business expense, so that the full interest payment would overstate the firm's actual cost. The after-tax cost of borrowing is $i_{AT} = (1 - T)i_b$. With $i_b = 10$ percent and $T = .40$, for instance, the after-tax cost of borrowing is $i_{AT} = (.60)10$ percent $= 6$ percent.

Because interest charges are tax deductible, borrowing is an attractive source of investment funds for many business firms. Too much borrowing, however, may endanger the firm's long-run economic health. This is because interest and principal payments must be made regularly on borrowed funds. In periods of reduced earnings, a firm may be unable to meet its obligations and may be forced into a financial crisis or even bankruptcy. These dangers must be weighed against the tax advantages when deciding on the firm's preferred source of investment funds.

Figure 13.2 shows the supply of borrowed funds beginning at $i_{AT} = 6$ percent and rising as more funds are borrowed. Potential lenders normally require higher interest payments to offset the higher risks associated with larger and more frequent borrowing.

The Cost of New Stock Issues

New stock issues are another external source of funds for which there are advantages and disadvantages. One advantage is that, except in the case of preferred stock, the firm is not required to pay dividends. In fact, some stockholders prefer a low level of dividend income for the sake of their own income tax liabilities. In such cases, a firm may be able to retain earnings over a number of years for use in expanding capital investment. One disadvantage of stock issues is that dividends paid are not deductible for tax purposes, so that the after-tax cost to the firm includes the full amount of dividends. Furthermore, since dividends are paid from taxed income and are received by stockholders as taxable income, dividends are actually taxed twice.

The cost of capital acquired through issues of **preferred stock** is straightforward. It is the annual dividend payment specified in the stock certificate.

Thus, preferred stock issued for $100 a share and having a dividend payment of $8 annually involves a cost of capital equal to

$$d_p = \frac{\text{dividend}}{\text{price of preferred stock}} = \frac{D}{P} = \frac{\$8}{\$100} = 8 \text{ percent.}$$

Preferred stock dividends must be paid on schedule if income is available for distribution, but management may withhold preferred stock dividends in years of sharply reduced earnings. This makes preferred stock an appropriate source of investment capital for many firms.

The cost of funds acquired through issues of **common stock** has two parts: the amount of dividends paid and current additions to retained earnings held for reinvestment within the firm. Together, these elements constitute a cost of capital equal to

$$d_c = \frac{\text{dividends paid plus retained earnings}}{\text{price of common stock}} = \frac{D + RE}{P}.$$

The cost of capital acquired through issue of common stock must be high enough to include reasonable dividends paid out and expected future earnings from reinvestment of current retained earnings. Otherwise, the market value of shares of stock will fall.[1] Managers must decide on the allocation of income between dividends and retained earnings for reinvestment that will ensure a sufficient price for the firm's stock and a continued market for new stock issues.

Since dividend payments are made from after-tax income, the cost of investment capital acquired through stock issue is often greater than the cost of borrowed funds. Moreover, the cost of additional stock issues tends to rise, since more outstanding stock means smaller shares of earnings for individual stockholders. Figure 13.2 shows the rising cost of capital acquired through new stock issues. The rising cost of capital from stock issues may limit the quantity of funds actually acquired for investment purposes through issues of new stock.

THE INVESTMENT DECISION

The cost-of-capital curves in Figure 13.2 have been combined in Figure 13.3 to form a supply curve of investment capital. The supply curve begins with the lowest-cost source of capital, internal funds, and rises discontinuously when internal funds are exhausted and the firm begins to borrow. The second break

---

1. The required rate of return on a share of common stock is similar to that on a piece of real investment. The rate of return is the value of r for which

$$P = \Sigma [D/(1+r)^t] + [P_t/(1+r)^t],$$

where P is the initial stock price, D represents a stream of future dividends, and P_t is the final selling price of the stock. All payments are discounted according to the time t in the future when they are to be received. Market price P_t is the discounted value of the expected future stream of earnings after resale to another buyer.

FIGURE 13.3 **Internal Rate of Return**

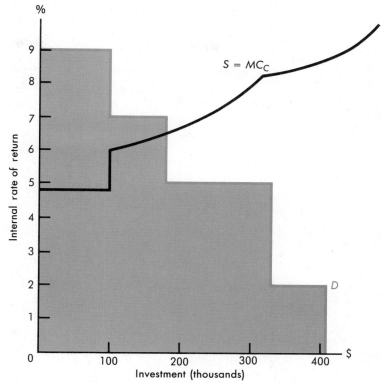

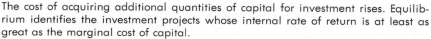

The cost of acquiring additional quantities of capital for investment rises. Equilibrium identifies the investment projects whose internal rate of return is at least as great as the marginal cost of capital.

in the supply curve occurs when the cost of additional borrowed funds rises above the cost of a new stock issue. Thus, the supply curve represents the *marginal cost* of successive quantities of investment funds: Supply = MC_c.

The investment demand curve in Figure 13.3 is based on the marginal efficiency of capital, r, for alternative investment proposals. The intersection of demand and supply determines the equilibrium quantity of investment and the marginal cost of funds at the equilibrium quantity. The equilibrium quantity identifies the projects whose internal rate of return is at least as great as the marginal cost of capital.

The marginal cost of investment funds is high enough to compensate lenders and holders of preferred and common stock for the use of their funds. Proposed investment projects with an internal rate of return greater than the marginal cost of capital should be undertaken. Funds for these projects should be acquired from the lowest-cost sources. In Figure 13.3, a total of $180,000 will be invested in the purchase of the data-processing equipment and the fork lift. One-hundred thousand dollars of the funds will be acquired through internal sources, and $80,000 will be acquired through borrowing. The remaining projects in Figure 13.3 are expected to earn less than the marginal cost of financing them and are not undertaken.

The Weighted Cost of Capital

The marginal cost of investment funds identifies the total quantity of investment and the specific investment proposals that should be undertaken. Once the investment decision is made, the firm may determine the average cost of its total investment program. The average cost of capital is a weighted average of all a firm's capital costs.

Suppose a firm faces the following annual after-tax costs of investment funds:

1. Retained earnings and depreciation: $i_{AT} = (1-T)i_l = (1-.4)8\% = 4.8$ percent.
2. Borrowed funds: $i_{AT} = (1-T)i_b = (1-.4)10\% = 6$ percent.
3. Preferred stock issue: $d_p = D/P = \$8/100 = 8$ percent.
4. Common stock issue: $d_c = (D + RE)/P = (\$5 + 5)/100 = 10$ percent.

The average cost of the firm's investment program depends on the portion of total investment funds acquired in each way. The average cost is the sum of the separate capital costs, weighted by the relevant portion of total funds. For example, for the first $100,000 needed for investment, a firm would normally choose to acquire the funds in the cheapest way, i.e., through retained earnings and depreciation allowances. Its cost of capital would be $1.00(4.8\%) = 4.8$ percent.

Borrowing a second $100,000 for additional investment would incur capital costs of 6 percent. The firm would have a total of $100,000 + $100,000 = $200,000 for making investments. The average cost of acquiring $200,000, half through borrowing and half through internal sources, would be:

Weighted cost of capital $= .50(4.8\%) + .50(6\%) = 5.4$ percent.

Increasing the firm's borrowing for additional investment might aggravate liquidity problems during periods of slow income growth. Therefore, the decision might be to finance the next $100,000 in investment through the issue of preferred stock. The total cost of acquiring $300,000 for investment would be:

Weighted cost of capital $= .33(4.8\%) + .33(6\%) + .33(8\%) = 6.36$ percent.

An issue of common stock might be appropriate for acquiring the fourth $100,000, so that the cost of acquiring $400,000 for investment becomes:

Weighted cost of capital $= .25(4.8\%) + .25(6\%) + .25(8\%) + .25(10\%) = 7.2$ percent.

CASE STUDY 13.2   Choosing a Financing Strategy

Most business firms seek a balance between the use of debt and stock issues for financing investments. They want a "debt/equity ratio" that achieves the tax advantages of borrowing along with the financial safety of stockholder financing. The desired debt/equity ratio differs among industries and among firms. Within a single firm, the actual debt/equity ratio will tend to fluctuate above and below the desired ratio. Because of the initial administrative costs, both borrowings and stock issues occur infrequently and for large amounts, pushing the actual ratio sharply in one direction or the other.

Most firms also seek a balance between short-term and long-term debt. Short-term debt is often necessary for financing current production. However, short-term debt must be repaid on time or re-financed, possibly at higher interest rates. Therefore, long-term debt is generally more desirable, especially for major investment projects. Principal and interest payments on long-term debt can be planned and budgeted rather far in advance.

Researcher Paul Marsh studied financing activity in 748 firms in the United Kingdom between the years 1959 and 1970. He recognized that firms would consider the tax advantages and the possibility of bankruptcy or financial distress in determining their financing plans. He also expected to find that long-term debt issues are highly correlated with firm size and that firms would attempt to "match maturities" of their assets and liabilities: that is, to incur long-term and short-term debt in proportion to their holdings of long-term and short-term assets. He also expected that uncertainty about future inflation rates would cause firms to avoid long-term debt with fixed interest rates and use more short-term or variable rate borrowings.

Marsh used regression analysis to estimate the relationship between a number of independent variables and the proportion of firms that finance new investment through stock issues. The independent variables he used were:

1. Estimates of the historical deviation of debt from desired debt/equity ratios.

2. Estimates of historical deviation of short-term debt from desired ratios of short-term debt to total debt.

3. The absolute level of desired ratios as influenced by company size, risk, and holdings of fixed assets.

4. Current market conditions, including forecasts of debt and equity issues and the return on stocks in the past year.

Results confirmed that stock issues are heavily influenced by market conditions, especially the recent history of security prices. Moreover, firms appeared to decide their financing strategy on the basis of desired long- and short-term ratios. The level of the desired ratios depended on firm size (larger firms issued more debt), risk (firms involving more risk issued more equity), and holdings of fixed assets (firms with greater asset holdings issued more debt).

The regression parameters were used to predict the financing strategy of 110 additional companies over the period 1971–1974.[1] The model's predictions were correct in 71 percent of the cases.

MANAGERIAL THINKING

Explain the significance of recent security prices for a firm's decision to issue new stocks. Why are firm size, risk, and holdings of fixed assets significant determinants of financing decisions?

Source: Paul Marsh, "The Choice Between Equity and Debt: An Empirical Study," *Journal of Finance*, March 1982, vol. 37, no. 1, pp. 121–142.

---

1. The values of the firms' independent variables were substituted in the regression equation and the estimated coefficients applied to compute the value of the dependent variable, stock issues.

In general, we may conclude that the weighted cost of capital is

$$\text{Weighted cost of capital} = (c) = \sum_{i=0}^{n} c_i p_i,$$

where the c_i represents the separate costs of different sources, and the p_i represents the portion of total investment funds represented by each source.

Notice that changing the composition of capital as we have demonstrated has the effect of increasing the firm's average cost of capital as larger quantities are acquired. Small quantities of investment funds can be acquired at lower cost than larger quantities. The case study that follows describes how many firms make the financing decision for their investment program.

USING INTERNAL FUNDS FOR INVESTMENT

We have thus far discussed various sources of investment funds and described various procedures for evaluating investments. We assumed that some funds would accumulate within the firm for investment purposes, in particular, the depreciation account and retained earnings. In the sections that follow, we will consider the following three procedures for allocating internal funds for investment purposes:

1. Calculations to determine the necessary contributions to a sinking fund for making a large lump-sum payment at some future date;
2. Calculations to determine the final value of regular equal payments after a particular period of time; and
3. Calculations to determine the regular payments of interest and principal on a mortgage.

Each of these procedures uses a modified version of the present value techniques described in Chapter 12. In each case, internal funds are set aside in the current period and accumulate toward the achievement of a long-range investment purpose.

Sinking Funds

Many firms want to set aside internal funds regularly for eventual modernization or expansion of productive capacity. A firm might also need to accumulate funds to pay off a large bank loan or redeem its own bonds at maturity. In any case, the investment decision might be to contribute equal amounts to a **sinking fund** at the end of each year. The fund would earn interest until some definite date in the future when the total would satisfy the firm's spending goal. Ordinarily, the necessary amount needed in the future (F), the interest rate to be earned (i),[2] and the number of years (t) before making the planned expenditure would be known. The regular annual payment required to meet the firm's goal would be determined according to the following formula:

$$\text{Present payment} = (P) = F \left[\frac{i}{(1+i)^t - 1} \right].$$

To illustrate, let us consider a firm's proposed expansion five years in the future for which an estimated \$300,000 will be required. Estimated after-tax interest earnings are 9 percent annually, making the necessary present payments

$$P = \$300,000 \left[\frac{.09}{1.09^5 - 1} \right] = \$300,000(.17) = \$50,127.74.$$

The sum of all payments after five years is

$$
\begin{array}{ll}
\$50,127.74 \times (1.09)^4 = & \$70,759.40 \\
50,127.74 \times (1.09)^3 = & 64,916.88 \\
50,127.74 \times (1.09)^2 = & 59,556.77 \\
50,127.74 \times (1.09) = & 54,639.24 \\
50,127.74 & \underline{50,127.74} \\
& \$300,000.02.
\end{array}
$$

The first year's contribution would earn interest at $i = 9$ percent for four years, the second would earn interest for three years, and so forth. The last payment made at the end of the last year earns no interest. The total of all payments, including compounded interest, should be sufficient to make the purchase.

The value in parentheses can be called the "sinking fund" factor. In this example the sinking fund factor is $.17 \approx 1/6$. This indicates that contributing one-sixth of the necessary expenditure to the sinking fund for each of five years will be sufficient to finance the purchase. The higher the interest rate and the greater the number of payments to be made, the smaller the sinking fund factor and the smaller the annual contributions. If payments are to be made over ten years and are to earn 10 percent, for example, required annual contributions are only

$$\left[\frac{i}{(1+i)^t - 1} \right] = \left[\frac{.10}{(1.10)^{10} - 1} \right] = .06 \approx \frac{1}{17}$$

of the desired final amount. Sinking fund factors are available in tables[3] for

2. Since interest earned is subject to income tax, the full value of i may not be appropriate for the computations in this section. With interest earnings of $i = 15$ percent, after-tax earnings are $i(1-T)$, or with $T = .40$, $i_{AT} = .15(.60) = .09 = 9$ percent.

3. These are similar to tables of discount factors used in Chapter 12.

various values of i and t. Using the sinking fund factor for computing regular payments simplifies the process considerably. Many pocket calculators also perform this function.

The sinking fund formula also can be adapted to calculate monthly contributions with interest compounded monthly. For monthly compounding, the exponent becomes ($12t$) and the interest rate for the month becomes ($i/12$). An example of more frequent contributions to sinking funds is the fund for meeting quarterly tax obligations. Quarterly tax payments require business firms to pay a large lump sum every three months. Short-term investments can be made each month to accumulate to the estimated tax bill. With interest earnings of 12 percent compounded monthly, for example, satisfying a $100,000 quarterly tax bill would require three monthly contributions of

$$P = \$100,000 \left[\frac{.12/12}{1.01^3 - 1} \right] = \$100,000(.33002) = \$33,002.21.$$

The sinking fund factor in this example is less than one-third, since the first two payments accumulate interest earnings before the tax bill is due.

Equal Contributions Each Year

The sinking fund formula can be rearranged and adapted to determine the final value of a series of equal payments that earn interest up to some known date in the future. An example of this is a firm's depreciation account for replacing depreciated equipment. We have seen that most firms set aside regular depreciation allowances for use when worn-out equipment must be replaced. Each annual payment earns interest over a period one year shorter than the previous year's payment. The final value of the depreciation account is

$$F = P \left[\frac{(1+i)^t - 1}{i} \right].$$

According to the formula, $100 deposited at 8 percent interest for each of two years is worth

$$100 \left[\frac{1.08^2 - 1}{.08} \right] = \$208$$

at the end of the second year (since the second $100 payment earns no interest).

Most payment schedules cover longer periods of time. To illustrate, suppose a firm purchases equipment for $2,150,000 which it expects to operate for ten years. At the end of the period, the equipment will no longer be usable and will have zero scrap value. The straight-line method for computing depreciation permits the firm to allocate one-tenth of the equipment's depreciable value, or $215,000, to a depreciation account in each of the ten years the equipment is used. The annual payments would accumulate interest and finally be worth

$$F = \$215,000 \left[\frac{1.08^{10} - 1}{.08} \right] = \$215,000(14.49) = \$3,114,610.93.$$

If the price of replacement equipment has risen no more than 3.8 percent annually over the period, the sum of $3,114,610.93 should be sufficient to replace the equipment.

The value in brackets in this expression is called the **equal payments factor**. In this example, the equal payments factor is 14.49. This value means that after ten annual payments the depreciation account will be worth more than fourteen times the annual contributions. Note that the equal payments factor is the reciprocal of the sinking fund factor for the same values of i and t. The higher the interest rate and the greater the number of annual payments, the larger is the equal payments factor and the greater the final value. Tables are also available for determining equal payments factors.

As before, monthly contributions over a period of several years may be left to accumulate interest compounded monthly making the final value

$$F = P \left[\frac{(1+i/12)^{12t} - 1}{i/12} \right].$$

After five years, depreciation allowances of $120 deposited each month would be worth

$$F = \$120 \left[\frac{1.0083^{60} - 1}{.0083} \right] = \$120(77.4371) = \$9,292.45$$

if interest of 10 percent is compounded monthly. The equal payments factor tells us that after sixty months of equal payments the fund would be worth more than 77 times the monthly payment.

Annual Payments on a Mortgage

Many investments are purchased through a mortgage loan extending over many years. Payments in this case are **amortized**: that is, they include interest and a portion of the principal. Again, it is possible to change the formula to determine the necessary annual payments on a mortgage that extends over a known period of time. This formula is

$$P = F \left[\frac{i}{1 - (1 + i)^{-t}} \right],$$

where t is the number of years of the mortgage. A mortgage of $50,000 at 12 percent interest over 25 years requires annual payments of $P = \$50,000$ [.12/1 − .0588] = $50,000(.13) = $6,375. The amount paid over the life of the mortgage is $6,375 × 25 = $159,374.96, of which $50,000 represents the principal of the loan and $109,374.96 is interest on the balance remaining after each payment.

The value in parentheses in this case can be called the "mortgage payment" factor. In this example, the mortgage payment factor is .13 ≈ 1/8. Although 25 payments are made, each payment is equal to one-eighth of the loan obligation. This high fraction is a result of the large amount of interest owed on funds borrowed for many years.

Most mortgage payments are made monthly, so the applicable formula is generally

$$P = F \left[\frac{i/12}{1 - (1 + i/12)^{-12t}} \right].$$

Monthly payments on the $50,000 mortgage we just discussed would amount to

$$P = \$50,000 \left[\frac{.01}{1 - (1.01)^{-300}} \right] = \$50,000 \left(\frac{.01}{.95} \right) = \$526.61.$$

After making 300 monthly payments the total amount paid on the mortgage will be $526.61 × 300 = $157,983.62, of which $107.983.62 is interest. The total amount paid as interest is less for monthly payments, since the principal amount owed is being diminished each month instead of annually.

Note that the first monthly payment of $526.61 includes interest on $50,000 plus a portion of the principal: $\frac{1}{12}(12\%)(\$50,000)$ + principal payment = $500 + $26.61 = $526.61. Since interest is paid on such a large amount, interest comprises the greater part of the monthly payment. Reducing the principal of the loan by $26.61 in the first month means that the second month's payment will include interest and principal payment of $\frac{1}{12}(12\%)(\$50,000 - \$26.61)$ + principal payment = $499.73 + $26.88 = $526.61. The smaller interest payment allows a larger payment on the principal balance.

All of the calculations we have just discussed, as well as present value calculations, can be simplified through the use of tables that provide the value of the factor in parentheses for a large number of possible formulas. The analyst can select the appropriate factor from the table and multiply as indicated to compute the desired value.

A SUMMARY

Even the most carefully planned investment strategies will fall short of expectations unless they are financed in the most economical way. We have described three sources of investment funds, along with the advantages and disadvantages of each. We also demonstrated the analytical procedure that underlies a firm's choice of investment funds. We touched on the difficulties of financing when internal funds are scarce, borrowing costs are high, and new stock sales unfeasible. (Remember that we associated all of these problems with the electric power industry in the United States.)

The next chapter will explore the risks and uncertainties of investment strategies in more detail. In particular, we will look at the ways risk and uncertainty can be incorporated into a firm's calculations of the cost of capital.

CASE STUDY 13.3   **Varying Pension Fund Contributions to Minimize Costs**

Many business firms establish pension funds to provide for employees' retirement. Frequently, contributions from both the employer and the employee are combined and invested. The total of contributions plus investment earnings is then available for distribution to beneficiaries of the fund. Such pension funds are described as "funded" pension plans. (Alternatively, current contributions may be paid out directly to beneficiaries on a pay-as-you-go basis. These funds are described as "unfunded.")

One objective of a manager is to establish a pension-fund financing plan that will achieve the lowest after-tax net present value of contributions without jeopardizing the firm's capacity to pay its pension-fund obligations.

Contributions to a funded pension plan can follow any of the following patterns:
1. Contributions can be set to *increase* relative to the firm's total payroll.
2. Contributions can be set as a *constant* percentage of the firm's payroll.
3. Contributions can be set to *decrease* relative to the firm's total payroll.

Whatever the pattern of contributions, the sum of contributions plus investment income must equal the sum of future benefit payments plus expenses associated with administering the fund.

The first step in deciding the pension fund plan is to determine the necessary contributions for satisfying the firm's pension obligations. Table A is a simple illustration of pension-fund planning. Column (1) lists expected payroll (in thousands of dollars) for the next five years. Column (2) lists *increasing* percentages of payroll that are to be paid to the pension fund. Column (4) lists *constant* percentages, and Column (6) lists *decreasing* percentages. Columns (3), (5), and (7) show computation of the value of the pension fund after each year's contribution and accumulated interest income are added.[1] Percentage contributions are arranged so as to ensure that the fund's value at the end of five years is $2,256,670.

Which pattern of contributions is the most cost effective? That is, which pattern accomplishes the firm's pension fund objective at lowest cost? To answer this question, it is necessary to compare the after-tax cost of pension-fund contributions. The after-tax cost of contributions is $C(1 - T)$, where C is the cash contribution for the year and T is the firm's tax rate. The after-tax cost of the three plans for $T = .40$ is shown in Table B.

Discounting the after-tax contributions according to the firm's after-tax cost of capital determines the present value of pension-fund costs. Table C indicates the present value of all three pension fund plans using opportunity costs of capital of r = 3, 6, 8, 9, and 10, after taxes.

The data in Table C have two significant characteristics. As expected, the higher the firm's opportunity cost of capital, the higher the rate of discount on future contributions to the pension fund whatever the pattern of contributions. Therefore, the present value of pension costs is lower when capital costs are higher. The second characteristic has to do with the pattern of pension-fund contributions. If the firm's

---

1. The after-tax return on invested funds is 8 percent.

TABLE A

	(1)	(2)	(3)	
		Increasing		
	Payroll	% contribution		
	(thousands of	to pension	Year's	
Year	dollars)	fund	contribution*	Fund value at end of year
1	2,000	5	100	100
2	3,000	7	210	310 + .08(100) = 318
3	4,000	9	360	678 + .08(318) = 703.44
4	5,000	12	600	1,303.44 + .08(703.44) = 1,359.72
5	6,000	13.14	788.17	2,147.89 + .08(1,359.72) = 2,256.67

(4)	(5)	
Constant		
% contribution		
to pension	Year's	
fund	contribution*	Fund value at end of year
10	200	200
10	300	500 + .08(200) = 516
10	400	916 + .08(516) = 957.28
10	500	1,457.28 + .08(957.28) = 1,533.86
10	600	2,133.86 + .08(1,533.86) = 2,256.67

(6)	(7)	
Decreasing		
% contribution		
to pension	Year's	
fund	contribution*	Fund value at end of year
15	300	300
12	360	660 + .08(300) = 684
10	400	1,084 + .08(684) = 1,138.72
9	450	1,588.72 + .08(1,138.72) = 1,679.82
7.37	442.46	2,122.28 + .08(1,679.82) = 2,256.67

*Contributions are made at the end of each year.

after-tax cost of capital is the same as the projected after-tax rate of return on invested funds, the present value of contributions is identical for all three pension-funding plans.[2] If the cost of capital is less than the projected rate of return, the lowest-cost pattern of funding is the one in which contributions constitute a decreasing percentage of payroll. This is because of the lower projected yield on alternative uses of the firm's funds. If the cost of capital is greater than the projected rate of return, the lowest-cost pattern of pension fund contributions is the one in which

2. The slight difference in Table C is a result of rounding.

TABLE B

Year	Increasing percentage plan	Constant percentage plan	Decreasing percentage plan
1	60	120	180
2	126	180	216
3	216	240	240
4	360	300	270
5	472.90	360	266.40

TABLE C

After-tax cost of capital	Increasing percentage plan	Constant percentage plan	Decreasing percentage plan
3%	1,106.82	1,082.89	1,067.68
6%	992.40	981.56	976.49
8%	924.94	921.47	922.14
9%	893.55	893.42	396.68
10%	863.62	866.60	872.29

FIGURE A

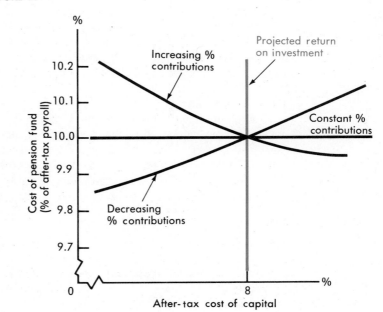

contributions constitute an increasing fraction of payroll. In this case, the firm's high capital costs would force managers to defer necessary contributions as long as possible, while still achieving the fund's objective in the fifth year.

These relationships are shown in Figure A. The curves in Figure A represent the relationship between after-tax cost of capital for the firm and pension-fund costs when costs are measured as a percentage of the firm's after-tax payroll. The curve representing *constant* contributions reveals *constant* percentage cost of 10 percent. The curve representing *increasing* contributions reveals decreasing costs with higher costs of capital. The curve representing *decreasing* contributions reveals increasing costs as costs of capital increase.

Once the firm has determined its cost of capital, it is easy to choose the lowest-cost pension-fund plan. With cost of capital of 5 percent, for example, the decreasing-contribution plan would be most cost-effective. For cost of capital of 12 percent, the increasing-contributions plan would be most cost effective. If the firm's cost of capital is equal to the projected rate of return on invested funds, the cost of the three plans is equal and the firm would have no preference among the investment plans.

Source: Andre E. deMontigny, "Total Pension Cost Control: True Cost vs. Contributions," *Financial Executive,* November 1979, pp. 47–52.

SUMMARY

Business managers typically rank investments according to their projected internal rate of return. Then they allocate the lowest-cost funds toward investments with the highest internal rate of return, or yield. The cost of a firm's retained earnings and depreciation allowances is the after-tax interest rate that might have been earned. The cost of borrowed funds is the after-tax interest rate paid. The cost of preferred stock is the guaranteed dividend relative to the stock's selling price. The cost of common stock is projected dividends plus retained earnings relative to the stock's selling price. Dividends are paid from after-tax income, which has the effect of raising the cost of funds obtained through stock issues.

A firm's weighted cost of capital is the cost of each source of funds weighted by the portion of total funds acquired through each source. Firms typically seek a certain balance between the use of borrowing and stock issues on the one hand, and long-term and short-term borrowing on the other.

When internal funds are used to purchase an investment, a firm may set up a sinking fund or arrange to acquire a mortgage loan.

KEY TERMS

marginal efficiency of investment   sinking fund
preferred stock   equal payments factor
common stock   amortization

QUESTIONS AND PROBLEMS

1. Explain the difference between the values of r in each of the four procedures for evaluating investments. Why is it possible to characterize some of the variables as affecting investment demand and others as dependent on the supply of investment funds?

2. Mother's Home-Style Soups is planning an expansion into new sales territory. The expansion will require $1 million in investment funds. Because of Home-Style's poor credit rating, borrowing costs are 18 percent. Additional preferred stock may be sold for a guaranteed dividend of 12 percent, and common stock may be issued with expected dividend payments of 5 percent. Home-Style intends to retain additional earnings equal to common stock dividends. The firm's corporate tax rate is 40 percent. Assume that Home-Style finances the expansion equally through the three sources of investment capital and determine its weighted cost of capital.

3. Discuss the rationale for including retained earnings in computing the cost of capital acquired through issue of common stock. Why must managers be concerned about using retained earnings profitably?

4. Dependable Electronics Company owns buildings and equipment worth $3.5 million and $7.5 million, respectively. The firm's depreciation account is calculated by the straight-line method. That is, equal depreciation allowances are set aside for each year of the life of the property. The buildings and equipment are expected to last 10 and 5 years, respectively. Determine the value of Dependable's depreciation funds after five years if interest is compounded annually.

5. Refer again to the investment decision described in Figure 13.3 and determine the firm's weighted cost of capital.

6. Better Mousetraps Inc. is planning a $2.5 million increase in plant capacity five years from now. The firm expects to retain earnings throughout the coming year and in the future until the proposed date of expansion. The sinking fund will be invested for an after-tax return of 7 percent. Calculate the necessary level of retained earnings each year and verify that the ultimate value of the sinking fund will be sufficient for the firm's plans.

7. Telephonics Inc. is purchasing a warehouse for $3.5 million with annual payments amortized over 5 years at 12 percent. Determine the firm's annual payment. Then calculate the portion of each year's payment that can be deducted as interest expense from the firm's taxable income.

8. Mavis Auto Parts Company plans to establish a sinking fund toward the purchase of a $25,000 truck. The firm will set aside $500 a month for three years. What is the necessary after-tax interest rate for satisfying the firm's objective?

9. Under the circumstances described in Problem 8, how long will Mavis

Auto Parts Company have to set aside payments if the firm is to acquire a $50,000 truck?

10. Construct a table of mortgage payment factors over the range $0 < i < 4$ percent at .5 percent intervals and $15 < 12t < 35$ months at intervals of five months. Use your table to compare the total payments on a $100,000 loan at 12 percent for 35 months and one at 18 percent for 15 months. What are the advantages and disadvantages of both choices?

Planning for Uncertain Outcomes

Until now we have examined investment decisions as if future economic conditions could be predicted with a fair degree of certainty. Quantity of output and price for determining a firm's sales revenue, production and operating costs, and even the length of time an investment could be expected to be usable have to this point been treated as fairly predictable quantities. Such information is not actually available, of course. Even so, policy makers must estimate with some precision the variables that affect long-run plans. Economic profit or loss from an investment decision may depend on the accuracy of their estimates.

In this chapter we will describe methods by which risk and uncertainty about future economic conditions can be incorporated into managerial decision making.[1] Dealing with uncertain outcomes requires the use of the mathematics of **probability**. The use of probability enables planners to weight their estimates of future economic variables according to their confidence in the estimates' reliability.

We will begin this chapter with a case study involving a business firm's strategic response to expected changes in market conditions. Then we will demonstrate procedures for calculating and using probabilities. We will show how weighting possible future events by their probabilities permits comparisons of alternative strategies and selection of the alternative most likely to satisfy a firm's goals.

---

1. Risk and uncertainty have precise definitions in managerial economics. We will define these concepts fully later in this discussion.

CASE STUDY 14.1   Kaiser Aluminum Deals with Risk and Uncertainty

Producers of industrial commodities are especially subject to risk and uncertainty. Markets for steel, lumber, aluminum, and cement, for example, are strongly affected by consumer spending for finished goods and services. When consumers cut back purchases of autos, homes, and appliances, manufacturers cut back purchases of industrial materials and equipment, and governments cut back public works expenditures. Prices of industrial commodities tumble, while producing firms' fixed costs of extracting and processing remain high. Increasingly, international competition in such markets cuts into domestic sales and eliminates profitable markets abroad.

The recession of 1981–1982 brought economic losses to many firms producing industrial commodities. Furthermore, the growth trend of demand for industrial commodities is expected to slow over the coming decade. Many suppliers of industrial commodities will need to develop new strategies to deal with the risks and uncertainties of a decade of slow growth. One example of such a supplier is Kaiser Aluminum and Chemical Corporation.

Henry J. Kaiser's mammoth enterprise once produced ships, autos, steel, cement, and aluminum. But over the years since World War II, the firm gradually cut back its unprofitable operations to concentrate on basic industrial commodities with an emphasis on aluminum. Production of aluminum is energy-intensive, with almost half of total costs represented by energy costs. Production is centered in the northwestern and southeastern states where cheap energy has generally been available from hydroelectric power. In recent years, however, this source of energy has reached its capacity, with the result that energy costs have risen. Also, production of nuclear energy has proved to be more costly than expected. Producers of aluminum have been caught between falling commodity prices and rising energy and labor costs. To make matters worse, industrial demand for aluminum is projected for growth of only 3.4 percent annually during the 1980s, down from 8 percent annual growth in the 1960s.

Kaiser was slow to respond to the recession of 1981–1982, continuing to operate its plants near capacity and accumulating inventories worth almost a billion dollars. Kaiser's failure to cut prices drove many of the firm's customers to competing suppliers and caused losses of more than $100 million in 1982. Eventually, however, managers acted to cut labor and production costs at Kaiser's major aluminum manufacturing plants. Plans to modernize or expand other plants were abandoned. Plant engineers were instructed to develop energy-saving procedures, with the goal of cutting unit costs of production. Agreements with Kaiser's union were expected to help cut labor costs, and the number of Kaiser's salaried staff was cut by 25 percent.

For the remainder of the decade, Kaiser's managers have decided on a two-part strategy for dealing with expected slow growth in demand:

1. The non-aluminum portions of Kaiser's business will be expanded from one-third to one-half the corporation's total business.

2. Aluminum operations will focus more explicitly on high-profit aluminum products.

As part of the new strategy, Kaiser's managers allocated a large portion of the firm's investment capital to Kaiser's refractory, industrial chemical, and agricultural chemical divisions. An additional $40 million has been invested in oil exploration and development, with the goal of cutting the cost of energy used to process aluminum. Other investments will be made to modernize aluminum plants for producing more profitable fabricated products and specialty aluminum.

What are Kaiser's risks in the future? The market for industrial commodities will continue to be affected by short-run cycles in consumer spending. But with Kaiser's more diversified operations, managers hope "to be able to slide across the middle of the downturns." In the long run, Kaiser's prosperity depends on healthy economc growth for the economy as a whole. Prosperity in aluminum production depends on consumer purchases of automobiles. Prosperity in production of agricultural chemicals depends on growth in farm production. Prosperity in production of materials used in making steel depends on substantial growth in business and government investment. There is one especially hopeful note in Kaiser's forecast. Kaiser's managers believe that the recession of 1981–1982 wiped out substantial aluminum-producing capacity, leaving opportunities for surviving firms to increase their market share.

As you read this chapter, think about the role of managers in business planning. Managers must evaluate the risks associated with various business strategies and choose the alternative that comes closest to satisfying the firm's goals. As you read, also consider the uncertainties associated with changes in the market for the firm's products, with increasing foreign competition, and with faltering resource supplies. Visualize the process of decision making as a kind of tree, in which the branches represent alternative choices, and movement along the branches represents a carefully planned strategic course. Choosing the appropriate series of alternatives depends strongly on managers' understanding of future trends over a wide range of economic and political developments.

Source: "Kaiser: Narrowing Its Aluminum Lines As It Broadens Its Sweep In Chemicals," *Business Week,* August 30, 1982, pp. 81–84.

RISK VERSUS UNCERTAINTY

Most of a firm's decisions are made without perfect knowledge of future economic conditions. Future production costs and sales revenues may differ from forecasted levels, such that profits may be greater than or less than expected. Advances in technical knowledge may render obsolete carefully planned investment projects. Changes in consumer spending patterns may effectively destroy years of costly product development.

Economists distinguish between two circumstances of imperfect knowledge: risk and uncertainty.

Risk is a condition in which various possible future events can be defined. If a firm has conducted similar operations in the past, it will have encountered various circumstances involving risk before. The firm's own experience can provide evidence of the frequency of particular events in the past and thus allow managers to assign probabilities to their occurrence in the future. These are the important characteristics of risk: that possible future events can be defined, and that probabilities can be assigned to their occurrence.

Uncertainty differs from risk in that managers have no clear basis for assigning probabilities. Lacking historical evidence, decision makers may assign probabilities on the basis of subjective judgment alone. Needless to say, different analysts might assign different probabilities to the same possible event.

The distinction between risk and uncertainty is important for several reasons. Circumstances involving risk can be insured against and the costs of insurance can then be included in total costs of production. For example, if past experience indicates that machine break-down normally adds 10 percent to the unit cost of processing a product, this cost can be added to average production costs in making production plans. Then, when break-downs actually occur, there will be little or no unexpected reduction in economic profit for the year.

Other circumstances involving risk may not occur often enough in a single firm for probabilities to be assigned. Fires and other natural disasters are examples of such events. Still, these events do occur often enough in the economy as a whole for insurance companies to assign them probabilities. If past experience indicates that fires destroy a certain percentage of productive assets each year, policy-holders will be charged a premium that covers the expected risk of loss. Including the firm's annual insurance premium in its costs of production spreads this risk over every unit of output and ensures that economic profit will not be unexpectedly affected by a major disaster.

Allowance for risk means that production costs take into consideration the expected occurrence of various events. Because uncertainty deals with less well defined future events, it is more difficult to include uncertainty in costs. Uncertain events may yield substantial gains in profit or substantial losses for a firm. In fact, many economists associate economic profit with how well a firm responds to uncertainty. Thus, *positive* economic profit is the reward for basing policy on the correct uncertain event, and *negative* economic profit (or loss) is the penalty for basing policy on the incorrect uncertain event. Decision makers whose judgment is correct gain, and others lose.

The sections that follow describe analytical tools for incorporating risk in decisions on business strategy. After a thorough examination of risk, we will look at procedures for dealing with uncertainty.

RISK

Risk can be illustrated by diagrams like the ones in Figure 14.1. These diagrams illustrate chance events involving risk that may confront managers of firms producing aluminum. The circle at the left of each figure signifies risk, and the branches indicate possible future events. Panel (a) of Figure 14.1 illustrates future growth trends in industrial demand for aluminum: exceptionally high growth in demand, moderate growth in demand, or decline in demand. Panel (b) illustrates possible changes in energy charges for producing aluminum: a 25-percent annual increase, a 20-percent annual increase, a 15-percent annual increase, and so forth. Panel (c) illustrates possible competition in the production of specialty aluminum products: either vigorous competition from abroad or no competition from abroad.

The probabilities associated with each branch are derived from the experience and subjective judgment of the analyst. Note that the sum of all probabilities associated with a single chance event must equal 1.00.

FIGURE 14.1   **Probability Diagrams**

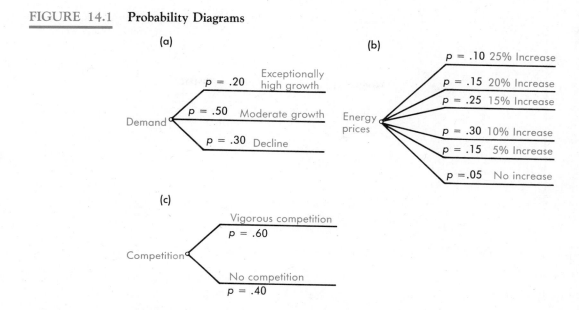

(a)

(b)

Demand

$p = .20$ Exceptionally high growth

$p = .50$ Moderate growth

$p = .30$ Decline

Energy prices

$p = .10$ 25% Increase

$p = .15$ 20% Increase

$p = .25$ 15% Increase

$p = .30$ 10% Increase

$p = .15$ 5% Increase

$p = .05$ No increase

(c)

Competition

Vigorous competition
$p = .60$

No competition
$p = .40$

Computing and Using Expected Value

Since business decisions must be made without perfect knowledge, estimating and using probabilities is important for deciding business strategy. This is especially true of situations in which two or more future events are *mutually exclusive*: that is, occurrence of one future event precludes occurrence of any other. Expected-value techniques enable decision makers to incorporate probabilities in their analyses for choosing among alternative strategies.

In general, the expected value of a strategy is the weighted sum of the values of all possible future events, where the weights are the probabilities assigned to each event. The sum of the probabilities must equal one, but the value of particular events with positive probabilities may be zero. Thus, the (*ev*) equals the sum of the value of particular events times the probability of their occurrence, or

$$ev = \sum x_i p_i.$$

To illustrate, let us suppose a car rental firm is considering two strategies for increasing profits in an urban area. Strategy A includes increased local advertising and expanded sales offices in the central business district. The profitability of Strategy A depends on possible future events regarding decisions of the local government. Specifically, there is a risk that local government may raise tax rates on business properties. Favorable tax treatment would mean an internal rate of return of 15 percent, but a property tax increase would reduce the internal rate of return to 9.5 percent. Managers have assessed the probability

FIGURE 14.2   **Decision Trees**

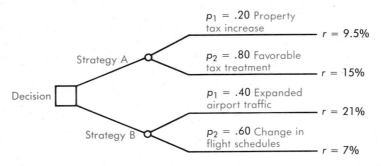

of a property tax increase at about $p_1 = .20$, making the expected value of return for Strategy A:

$$ev(r_A) = \sum r_i p_i = (9.5\%)(.20) + (15\%)(.80) = 13.9 \text{ percent.}$$

Strategy B includes heavy nationwide advertising and substantial increase of airport car-rental facilities. The profitability of Strategy B depends on possible future events regarding the behavior of airline traffic at the airport. If intercity air traffic expands as predicted, the internal rate of return should be 21 percent. Managers estimate the probability of expanded traffic at $p_1 = .40$. If airline routes are revised to eliminate this airport from major flight schedules, however, the internal rate of return for Strategy B is projected at only 7 percent. With these two possible future events, the expected value of return for Strategy B is:

$$ev(r_B) = \sum r_i p_i = (21\%)(.40) + (7\%)(.60) = 12.6 \text{ percent.}$$

Compare the expected value of return for the two strategies. Note that expected-value techniques favor selection of Strategy A over Strategy B. Although the potential for profit is greater with B, the high risk of reduced traffic at the airport makes A the preferred choice.

Figure 14.2 illustrates the strategic decision in the form of a decision tree. The box at the left represents the decision between Strategies A and B, shown by the branches to the right. The expected value of return for the two strategies depends on the risks associated with the events that follow.

Using Probability Distributions

Planning business strategy is an important function of managers in any firm. A firm's survival may depend on correctly assessing the probabilities associated with future events. Needless to say, assessing probabilities is not an exact science. Often, past experience is the only guide to future probabilities.

For example, a mining company may experience periods of high-cost production, such that ore costs are $25 per ton produced. During other periods, however, costs per ton are only $18. If high-cost periods occur about half the time, the expected value of costs, including risk, can be estimated as the sum of the unit costs (c_t) multiplied by the frequency of occurrence (p_t), or

$$ev(\text{costs}) = \sum c_t p_t = (\$25)(.50) + (\$18)(.50) = \$21.50.$$

In this example, the frequency with which an event occurred in the past is used as a measure of its probability in the future. Note that the sum of all frequencies (or probabilities) must equal 1.00.

The events in the previous example can be illustrated graphically by plotting the observed values along the horizontal axis and the probability of their occurrence along the vertical axis. Figure 14.3 shows the probabilities associated with unit costs of $18 and $25. The probability distribution of Figure 14.3 is a straight line, since the same probability is associated with both events.

Most probability distributions are not straight lines. Most show that there is greater probability that some events will occur than there is that others will occur. Suppose a mining company experienced unit costs of $35 during six months of the last year, $42 in three months, and $30 in the remaining three months. Using this information, the expected value of unit costs for the coming year can be calculated as follows:

$$ev(\text{costs}) = (\$35)(.50) + (\$42)(.25) + (\$30)(.25) = \$35.50.$$

The probability distribution for this case is shown in Figure 14.4 on page 426. It is higher in the center to indicate that there is a greater probability that unit costs will occur in the mid-range of the distribution. Other examples of frequency distributions are shown in Figure 14.5 on page 426.

The frequency distributions we have shown thus far are *discrete*: that is,

FIGURE 14.3   Values and Probabilities of Events

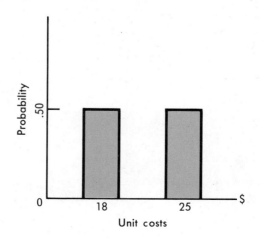

Unit costs

FIGURE 14.4   A Probability Distribution

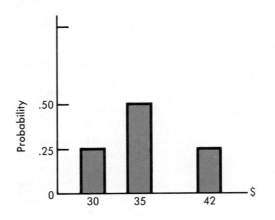

the probabilities involved are associated with a certain number of discrete, or distinct, events. Other kinds of probability distributions may be *continuous*: that is, the probabilities involved are associated with an infinite number of events. The mining company discussed previously, for example, may have unit production costs of $35.01, $35.02, $35.03, and so forth. A continuous probability distribution can be represented by a curve such as the one in Figure 14.6.

In Figure 14.6, the probability associated with unit costs of exactly $35.00 is infinitely small. In this case, instead of associating probabilities with single, discrete events, probabilities are associated with a range of events. The proba-

FIGURE 14.5   Various Probability Distributions

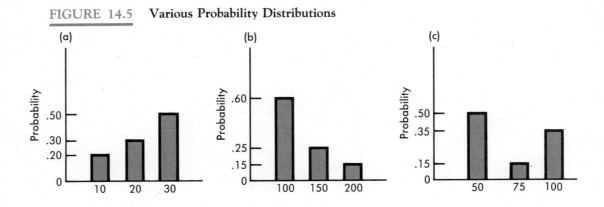

FIGURE 14.6   **A Continuous Probability Distribution**

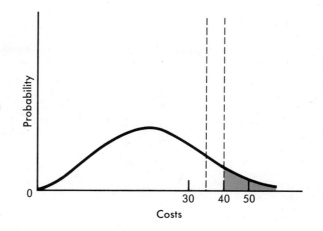

bility of costs between $35.00 and $40.00, for instance, is represented by the area under the curve between $35.00 and $40.00 on the horizontal axis. In general, the firm would be concerned about unit costs of greater than, say, $40.00, as indicated by the shaded area in Figure 14.6.

When decisions are based on the expected value of costs, risk is built into the analytical process. The effect on profit of a particular decision depends on the validity of the probabilities used for predictive purposes. If production costs are actually nearer the upper limit of the range in Figure 14.6, profit will be less than expected. The reverse is also true. However, over a period of several years, above-normal production costs in some years may be offset by below-normal costs in others. The result is a profit level over time that correctly reflects the firm's productivity.

EXAMPLE 14.1   **Assessing Probabilities by Using the Normal Distribution**

One probability distribution often used in business decisions is a **normal distribution.** A normal distribution is a bell-shaped curve, centered on the expected value of the distribution and approaching the horizontal axis on both sides of expected value. Maximum probability is associated with values near the expected value of the distribution, and decreasing probability is associated with values farther to the left and right of expected value. The probability associated with any single value along the horizontal axis is infinitessimally small. But the probability associated with a range of values can be estimated as the area under the probability distribution within that range.

Figures A and B show two normal distributions describing internal rates of return on investment projects. Both normal distributions are centered on an expected value of $r = 10$ percent. For both distributions, the probability of $r < 10$ percent is $p = .50$ and the probability of $r > 10$ percent is $p = .50$. Thus, the areas to the left and right of expected value each constitute one-half of the total area under the curve. The probability of $10 < r < 12$ percent is shown by the shaded areas on both

FIGURE A

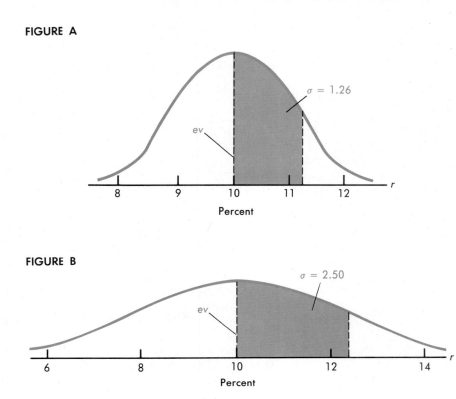

FIGURE B

curves. Determining the value of the shaded areas requires the use of two simple statistical measures: the *expected value* of the distribution and the *standard deviation*.

Expected value is the weighted sum of all past observations, where the weights are the frequencies associated with the observations. For the following set of observations, the expected value of return is calculated as shown.

TABLE A

Period	r
1	10%
2	8
3	12
4	10
5	10
6	12
7	10
8	8
9	10
10	10

$$ev(r) = \sum r_i p_i = (10\%)(.6) + (8\%)(.2) + (12\%)(.2) = 10 \text{ percent.}$$

The standard deviation (σ) of the distribution is a measure of the average dispersion of observations around the expected value. Average dispersion is calculated by squaring the difference between each observation and expected value, averaging the squared differences, and taking the square root of the average.[1] Thus,

$$\sigma = \sqrt{\frac{\sum(ev - x_i)^2}{n}},$$

where x represents the values of the observations and n is the number of observations. For the previous observations, the standard deviation is calculated as shown:

TABLE B

Period	r	$ev - x_i$	$(ev - x_i)^2$
1	10	0	0
2	8	2	4
3	12	-2	4
4	10	0	0
5	10	0	0
6	12	-2	4
7	10	0	0
8	8	2	4
9	10	0	0
10	10	0	0

$$\sigma = \sqrt{\frac{\sum(ev - x_i)^2}{n}} = \sqrt{\frac{16}{10}} =$$

$$\sqrt{1.6} = 1.26.$$

The standard deviation reveals an important characteristic of any normal distribution. This is that two-thirds or 67 percent of all observations fall within one standard deviation of the expected value. For the preceding observations, two-thirds or 67 percent of the r's fall within $ev \pm \sigma$, or $10 \pm 1.26 = 8.74$ and 11.26. If the observations of the distribution are valid as a description of this market, we can expect r to fall between 8.74 percent and 11.26 percent two-thirds or 67 percent of the time.

In addition, 95 percent of the observations of a normal distribution fall within *two* standard deviations of expected value, and 99 percent fall within *three* standard deviations. Thus, 95 percent of the time r will be between 7.48 percent and 12.52 percent, and 99 percent of the time r will be between 6.22 percent and 13.78 percent.

Figure A graphically represents the preceding observations, with $ev = 10$ and $\sigma = 1.26$. Figure B shows another set of observations for which $\sigma = 2.5$. Because the dispersion of observations is greater in Figure B, the curve extends over a longer range on the horizontal axis, with greater probabilities associated with values far distant from expected value than was true in Figure A. Still, 67 percent of the observations fall within one standard deviation, 95 percent fall within two standard deviations, and 99 percent fall within three standard deviations (although the ranges are wider in this case).

Probabilities associated with other ranges of a normal distribution are obtained from tables such as Table A. This table shows the area under the bell-shaped curve between the expected value and any number of standard deviations from $\sigma = 0$ to $\sigma = 2$. To illustrate the use of the table, suppose managers want to assess the

---

1. Unless the differences are squared, positive differences above expected value would be equal to negative differences below expected value, and the sum of the differences would be zero.

probability of r falling between expected value r = 10 percent and r = 8 percent. First note that the space between r = 10 and r = 8 is (10 − 8)/1.26 = 1.59 standard deviations. Then look for the area associated with σ = 1.59 in the table. The table reveals that the area of the space 1.59 standard deviations from the expected value is p = .44408. This is the probability of 8 percent < r < 10 percent. In general, the probability of any range of values is determined by

$$\frac{(ev - x)}{\sigma} = \text{Number of standard deviations from expected value.}$$

TABLE C

σ	0.00	0.01	0.03	0.05	0.07	0.09
0.0	.00000	.00399	.01197	.01994	.02790	.03586
0.1	.03983	.04380	.05172	.05962	.06749	.07535
0.3	.11791	.12172	.12930	.13683	.14431	.15173
0.5	.19146	.19497	.20194	.20884	.21566	.22240
0.7	.25804	.26115	.26730	.27337	.27935	.28524
0.9	.31594	.31859	.32381	.32894	.33398	.33891
1.1	.36433	.36650	.37076	.37493	.37900	.38298
1.3	.40320	.40490	.40824	.41149	.41466	.41774
1.5	.43319	.43448	.43699	.43943	.44179	.44408
1.7	.45543	.45637	.45818	.45994	.46164	.46327
1.9	.47128	.47193	.47320	.47441	.47558	.47670
2.0	.47725	.47778	.47882	.47982	.48077	.48169

What is the probability of r being less than 8 percent? Remember that the entire area to the left of expected value is .50. Therefore, the probability of r < 8 percent is p = .50 − .44408 = .05592.

What is the probability of r being between 8 percent and 11 percent? We know that r = 8 lies 1.59 standard deviations to the left of expected value. We can see that r = 11 lies (ev − x)/σ = (10 − 11)/1.26 = .79 standard deviations to the right of expected value. The combined probability associated with this range is the sum of the separate probabilities: .44808 + .28524 = .73332. Thus, p = .73332.

Finally, what is the probability of r being between 11 percent and 12 percent? We know that r = 11 percent lies .79 standard deviations to the right of expected value. We can see that r = 12 percent lies (ev − x)/σ = (10 − 12)/1.26 = 1.59 standard deviations to the right of expected value. The probability of r falling between these values on the horizontal axis is the difference between their probabilities: .44808 − .28524 = .16284. Thus, p = .16284.

In general, decision makers will be concerned with achieving certain goals such as a rate of return no less than, say, 9 percent, unit costs no greater than, say, $25, or economic profit no less than, say, $1,000. Since the goal is an upper or lower limit on some value, the appropriate probability is that associated with "at least" some value or "at most" some value. When probabilities are used to evaluate alternative strategies, the resulting decision should satisfy the goal. If, through the chosen strategy, the rate of return should actually be greater than 9 percent, unit costs lower than $25, or profits greater than $1,000, this is generally no cause for displeasure with the decision-making tool!

MANAGERIAL THINKING

Over the last 25 years a manufacturing firm has experienced the following internal rates of return on a certain type of equipment leased for periods of one year. Calculate the probability that the rate of return for next year will be at least 15 percent.

Year	r	Year	r
1	10%	13	11%
2	8.5	14	11.5
3	7.5	15	14
4	12	16	15.5
5	13	17	14.5
6	14	18	15.5
7	12.5	19	13.5
8	14	20	12
9	11.5	21	12.5
10	12.5	22	11
11	11	23	10.5
12	10.5	24	9
		25	12.5

CONDITIONAL PROBABILITY

Some business strategies involve a series of events in which the probability of each successive event is dependent on what has happened before. In such cases, it is said that the second event is *conditional* on the previous occurrence of the first. For example, a mining firm may have the option of purchasing exploration rights for five years in either of two areas, A or B. Available financial resources are limited, making it necessary to choose between the two sites for development. After analyzing ore samples from both areas, the firm's geologist estimates a .60 probability of superior ore in Area A and a .70 probability of superior ore in Area B. If Area A is mined and yields superior ore, it may be necessary to expand transportation facilities to meet exceptionally high demand, a probability of $p = .80$. If Area B is mined and the ore is inferior, it may be necessary to install new smelting equipment. A probability of $p = .25$ has been assigned to this event.

The series of events following the above decision can be described in terms of a decision tree, the branches of which represent all possible future events. In Figure 14.7 on page 432, the tree begins at the left with a square denoting the decision. The upper branch describes possible future events following a decision to mine Area A. The lower branch describes possible future events

FIGURE 14.7   **Conditional Probability**

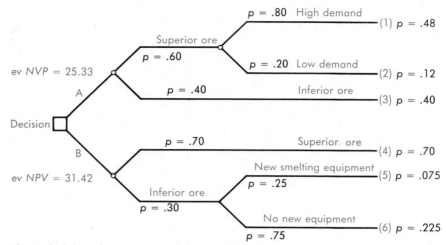

The probability of a sequence of events is the product of their individual probabilities.

following a decision to mine Area B. The circles on the tree indicate a chance event. On the upper branch, the series of possible chance events is:

1. superior ore and high demand
2. superior ore and low demand
3. inferior ore.

Possible chance events following a decision to mine Area B can be described similarly:

4. superior ore
5. inferior ore and new smelting equipment
6. inferior ore and no new investment required.

Conditional probability is the probability that a second event will occur, given that the first event has occurred. Thus, the probability of the series of events marked (1) is the probability of superior ore ($p = .60$) and high demand ($p = .80$). The probability that two events will occur is the product of their separate probabilities. Thus, the probability of the series of events at (1) is:

$$(.60)(.80) = .48.$$

Thus, probability of $p = .48$ has been assigned to the branch representing the series of events at (1) in Figure 14.7. Likewise, the probabilities associated with the remaining series of events are shown on the appropriate branches in Figure 14.7. Note that the sum of the probabilities of the three series of events associated with mining Area A equals 1.00, as does the sum of the probabilities associated with mining Area B.

Once probabilites have been assigned to all possible series of events, decision makers can compute the expected value of alternative strategies and make the decision indicated by the box at the left in Figure 14.7. Various measures such as internal rate of return and net present value might be used for evaluating the two alternatives.

Let us suppose that net present value is to be calculated for each branch in our example. The following equations list projected cash flows for each of the next five years for each of the series of events we have described. All figures are in thousands of dollars and the firm's after-tax cost of capital is 8 percent. The initial investment for mining either A or B is $75,000. Positive cash flows are expected in most years. Expenditures for additional transport facilities and for new smelting equipment are shown as negative amounts in the years they are expected to occur.

$$(1) \; NPV = -\$75 + \frac{30}{1.08} + \frac{-30 + 33}{1.08^2} + \frac{35}{1.08^3} + \frac{40}{1.08^4} + \frac{35}{1.08^5}$$
$$= \$36.36.$$

$$(2) \; NPV = -\$75 + \frac{25}{1.08} + \frac{28}{1.08^2} + \frac{27}{1.08^3} + \frac{26}{1.08^4} + \frac{20}{1.08^5}$$
$$= \$26.31.$$

$$(3) \; NPV = -\$75 + \frac{22}{1.08} + \frac{25}{1.08^2} + \frac{24}{1.08^3} + \frac{22}{1.08^4} + \frac{20}{1.08^5}$$
$$= \$15.64.$$

$$(4) \; NPV = -\$75 + \frac{30}{1.08} + \frac{33}{1.08^2} + \frac{35}{1.08^3} + \frac{40}{1.08^4} + \frac{35}{1.08^5}$$
$$= \$62.08.$$

$$(5) \; NPV = -\$75 + \frac{28}{1.08} + \frac{-10 + 25}{1.08^2} + \frac{-10 + 30}{1.08^3} + \frac{-10 + 29}{1.08^4}$$
$$+ \frac{-10 + 28}{1.08^5} = \$5.88.$$

$$(6) \; NPV = -\$75 + \frac{28}{1.08} + \frac{25}{1.08^2} + \frac{30}{1.08^3} + \frac{29}{1.08^4} + \frac{28}{1.08^5}$$
$$= \$36.55.$$

The expected value of NPV from a decision to mine both Areas A and B is the weighted sum of NPVs associated with all possible series of chance events, using as weights the probabilities taken from the appropriate branch in Figure 14.7. Thus,

$$ev(NPV) \text{ for Area A} = (\$36.36)(.48) + (\$26.31)(.12)$$
$$+ (\$15.64)(.40) = \$26.87$$
$$ev(NPV) \text{ for Area B} = (\$62.08)(.70) +$$
$$(\$5.88)(.075) + (\$36.55)(.225) = \$52.12.$$

Area B has the greater expected value of net present value, making this the preferred area for development.

Again, note that the actual *NPV* of this strategy will probably not be exactly $52,120. The probability of discounted cash flows yielding precisely $52,120 is close to zero. In fact, *NPV* may be as great as $62,080 or as low as $5,880, as shown in Table 14.1. The expected value of net present value is not a prediction of earnings. It is used only for decision-making purposes when it is desirable to incorporate risk in the selection process.

DECISION TREES

Often, managers must make a decision currently on the basis of a possible result of a second decision to be made in the future. For example, a chemical processing firm currently may have the opportunity to purchase either of two machines to be operated for the next five years. The higher-priced machine is expected to have lower operating costs, and the lower-priced machine may have to be overhauled after three years. If not overhauled, it may break down and become unusable. The higher-priced machine uses a particular imported raw material that may rise in price over the life of the equipment. The firm's after-tax cost of capital is 8 percent.

The expected cash flows for both machines are shown in Table 14.1. The rows indicate initial cost and cash flow under various technical and market conditions. Figures are in thousands of dollars.

Since this situation involves a series of decisions and since more than one possible chance event may result from each decision, the problem must be represented by a decision tree, the branches of which are the various possible series of events. A decision tree is represented in Figure 14.8. The first decision to be made is shown by the box labeled 1. A decision to purchase Machine A (the higher-priced machine) will move the firm along one of the paths in the upper branch of the tree. A decision to purchase Machine B will move the firm

TABLE 14.1

	Cost	Cash flows				
		Year 1	Year 2	Year 3	Year 4	Year 5
Machine A:	$55		.			
Current material prices		$18	$17	$16	$15	$14 (1)
Increased material prices		$16	15	14	13	12 (2)
Machine B:	$50					
With overhaul		$15	16	15	$-15+16$	15 (3)
Without overhaul and with break-down		$15	16	15	12	0 (4)
Without overhaul and without break-down		$15	16	15	12	11 (5)

FIGURE 14.8   Choice of Alternative Equipment

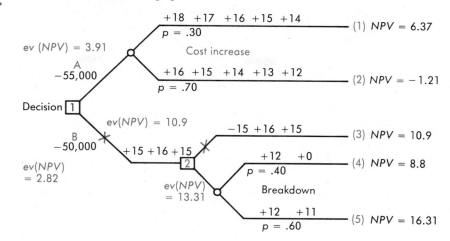

along the lower branch until it reaches the box labeled 2, when another decision must be made. The circles on the decision tree represent points at which circumstances involving risk, such as a change in cost for an essential raw material or possible equipment failure, are possible.

Analysis of circumstances involving risk requires the use of probabilities. In the case of materials costs, the firm's purchasing agent believes there is a $p = .70$ chance of a cost increase. We have assigned probabilities of $p = .30$ and $p = .70$ to the events of no cost increase and cost increase, respectively. The equipment engineer estimates the probability of a break-down if equipment is not overhauled at $p = .40$. Probabilities of $p = .40$ and $p = .60$ have been assigned to the events of break-down and no break-down.

Note that there are five possible series of events facing the firm:

1. Purchase A and no cost increase.
2. Purchase A and a cost increase.
3. Purchase B and overhaul.
4. Purchase B, no overhaul, and break-down.
5. Purchase B, no overhaul, and no break-down.

The branches of the decision tree in Figure 14.8 have been numbered to correspond with these possible series of events.

To solve this problem, it is necessary to look first at the last decision to be made: box number 2, to overhaul or not to overhaul. The firm's engineers have estimated that without overhaul there is a $p = .40$ chance the equipment will break down and be unusable in the fifth year. The values of the two series of events following Box 2 are calculated according to present value techniques and weighted according to their probabilities. The net present value of Branch 3 beyond Box 2 is

$$NPV(3) = \frac{-\$15 + \$16}{1.08^4} + \frac{\$15}{1.08^5} = \$10.9.$$

This is the expected value of a decision to overhaul, including the cost to overhaul ($15) and the revenues from continued operation in the fourth and fifth years ($16 and $15). The net present value of Branch 4 beyond Box 2 is

$$NPV(4) = \frac{\$12}{1.08^4} + \frac{0}{1.08^5} = \$8.2,$$

since the equipment is unusable in the last year. The NPV of Branch 5 is

$$NPV(5) = \frac{\$12}{1.08^4} + \frac{\$11}{1.08^5} = \$16.31.$$

For making the decision at Box 2, it is necessary to consider the probabilities associated with the circumstances at 4 and 5. The expected net present value following a decision not to overhaul is the weighted sum of the separate net present values for each branch:

$$ev(NPV) = (\$8.8)(.40) + (\$16.31)(.60) = \$13.31.$$

Since the event described on Branch 3 has a $p = 1.00$ probability,

$$ev(NPV) = (\$10.9)(1.00) = \$10.9.$$

Compare the expected value of net present value of Branch 3, $ev(NPV) = \$10.9$ with Branches 4 and 5, $ev(NPV) = \$13.31$. On the basis of this comparison, we would conclude that the future decision would be not to overhaul. Although a breakdown would eliminate all revenues the fifth year, the risk of a break-down is small enough to make this the preferred decision.

The data used for making this decision have been added to the decision tree in Figure 14.8. Branch 3 has been crossed out to indicate that this alternative has been eliminated from consideration. The expected value of Branches 4 and 5 has been entered in the space representing the decision not to overhaul.

Now we must move back to the decision at Box 1. If Machine A is purchased, the net present value of cash flows at Branches 1 and 2 would be:

$$1. \ NPV = -\$55 + \frac{18}{1.08} + \frac{17}{1.08^2} + \frac{16}{1.08^3} + \frac{15}{1.08^4} + \frac{14}{1.08^5} = \$9.50,$$

and

$$2. \ NPV = -\$55 + \frac{16}{1.08} + \frac{15}{1.08^2} + \frac{14}{1.08^3} + \frac{13}{1.08^4} + \frac{12}{1.08^5} = -\$1.51.$$

The value of the decision to purchase A is the expected value of net present value. The weights represent the probability of no cost increase and a cost increase:

$$ev(NPV) = (\$9.50)(.30) + (-\$1.51)(.70) = \$3.91.$$

This value has been entered in the space representing the decision to purchase A.

If Machine B is purchased, the net present value would be based on the assumption that the decision will ultimately be not to overhaul the machine. Thus, the relevant value is that of Branches 4 and 5:

$$
\begin{aligned}
4., 5. \ NPV = \ & -\$50 + \frac{15}{1.08} + \frac{16}{1.08^2} + \frac{15}{1.08^3} + .4\left[\frac{12}{1.08^4} + \frac{0}{1.08^5}\right] \\
& + .6\left[\frac{12}{1.08^4} + \frac{11}{1.08^5}\right] = \$2.82.
\end{aligned}
$$

(The last two terms were calculated previously and used for deciding not to overhaul.) This value has been entered in the space representing possible chance events following a decision to purchase B. Now the analyst can compare the expected value of net present value associated with alternative strategies and conclude, in this case, to purchase Machine A. If revenue and cost estimates are correct and if probabilities have been estimated correctly, this decision should yield the greater discounted net cash flow for the firm.

Decision trees can be made as simple or as complex as the situations they describe. They can be expanded to include any number of sequential decisions and a wide range of possible chance events. To solve a problem using decision trees, the analyst must follow these steps.

1. Begin with the most remote decision. Compute the net present value (*NPV*) of all series of events that might follow this decision.
2. Compute the expected value of *NPV* associated with each alternative by multiplying the *NPV*s of all possible series of events by their probabilities and adding.
3. Select the alternative with the greater expected value of *NPV*, and disregard the less preferred alternative(s).
4. Move to a less remote decision and compute the *NPV* of all possible series of events that might follow this decision. Assume that the farthest decision is made as indicated in step 3.
5. Compute the expected value of *NPV* associated with each alternative at this point by weighting the *NPV*s with their probabilities and adding.
6. Select the alternative with the greater expected value of *NPV* and disregard all others.
7. Continue with progressively less remote decisions, following steps 4, 5, and 6 until the current decision can be made. Then disregard the less preferred alternative(s) and implement the decision.

EXAMPLE 14.2   Using a Decision Tree to Plan Investment

California vineyards normally produce about 1.8 million tons of wine grapes annually, but unseasonably cold and rainy weather reduced yields in 1980 by about 4 percent. A strike by farm workers added to industry problems. Delay in processing grapes can cause a change in sugar content, reducing their quality and causing their price to fall. The wine market has also been undergoing restructuring, with consumer tastes changing to favor white wines over red. Between 1975 and 1980, white wine sales almost doubled as a percent of total sales, while red wine sales lost more than 20 percent of market share. Many wine producers subsequently have attempted to expand and diversify operations to protect against risk.

The hypothetical Sun Garden Wine Company is considering investment in new vineyards for producing white wine. The initial outlay for the purchase would be $5 million. Future cash flows will depend on growing conditions in the area and on labor relations with farm workers. With the possibility of deteriorating labor relations after the current three-year contract expires, Sun Garden will probably have to install significant quantities of mechanized equipment for reducing its work force. The cost of the equipment is expected to be $2.7 million.

If Sun Garden does not purchase the additional grape-growing acreage, existing vineyards will have to be replanted for producing white wines. This entails a year's wait before a new grape crop can be harvested. The initial cost of replanting will be $1.3 million with negative cash flow until the new crop can be taken to market. Following the third year of production, cash flows are expected to increase 2 percent annually for an indefinite period of time. Sun Garden requires a return on capital of 8 percent after taxes.

FIGURE A

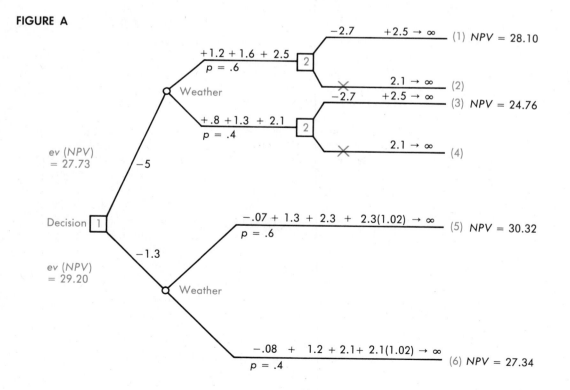

The alternatives facing Sun Garden have been diagrammed in Figure A. They are:

1. purchase property followed by good weather and purchase of labor-saving equipment;
2. purchase property followed by good weather and no additional investment;
3. purchase property followed by poor weather and purchase of labor-saving equipment;
4. purchase property followed by poor weather and no additional investment;
5. do not purchase property and good weather conditions;
6. do not purchase property and poor weather conditions.

National weather service predictions for good grape-growing weather conditions have been given a probability of $p = .60$.

First evaluate NPV for the boxes numbered 2. If labor-saving equipment is purchased, outlay of $2.7 million and cash flow of $2.5 million would occur in year 4. Then, cash flows would increase 2 percent each year indefinitely. Thus, NPV beyond Box 2 is determined by the formula for the present value of an infinite income stream:

$$NPV = -C + \frac{F}{r-g} = -\$2.7 + \frac{\$2.5}{.08-.02} = \$38.97 \text{ million.}$$

The NPV of a decision not to purchase the labor-saving equipment is $NPV = \$2.1/(.08 - .02) = \$35.00$ million. Since a strategy to purchase has the greater NPV, disregard branches 2 and 3 beyond Box 2.

The next step is to compute expected value of NPV associated with purchase of additional acreage as shown here:

Branch 1: $NPV = -\$5 + \$1.2(.92593) + \$1.6(.85734)$
$+ \$2.5(.79383) + \$38.97(.73503)$
$= -\$5 + \$1.11 + \$1.37$
$+ \$1.98 + \$28.64 = \$28.10$ million.

Branch 3: $NPV = -\$5 + \$.8(.92593)$
$+ \$1.3(85734) + \$2.1(.79383) + \$38.97(.73503)$
$= -\$5 + \$.74 + \$1.11 + \$1.67$
$+ \$28.64 = \$27.17$ million.

The expected net present value is the weighted sum of the NPVs for Branches 1 and 3:

$$ev(NPV) = .6(\$28.10) + .4(\$27.17) = \$27.73 \text{ million.}$$

Now enter $27.73 along the upper tier of the decision tree.

The lower tier of the decision tree experiences an initial cash outlay followed by negative cash flow in year 1. Years 2 and 3 experience positive cash flows, and cash flows are expected to grow 2 percent annually thereafter. Net present values associated with retention of existing acreage and replanting are:

Branch 5: $NPV = -\$1.3 - \$.07(.92593) + \$1.3(.85734) + \$2.3(.79383)$
$+ \dfrac{\$2.3(1.02)}{.08-.02}[.73503]$
$= -\$1.3 - .0648 + \$1.1145 + \$1.8258 + \$28.7397$
$= \$30.32$ million.

Branch 6: $NPV = -\$1.3 - \$.08(.92593) + \$1.2(.85734)$
$+ \$2.1(.79383) + \dfrac{\$2.1(1.02)}{.08-.02}[.73503]$
$= -\$1.3 - \$.0741 + \$1.0288 + \$1.667$
$+ \$26.24 = \$27.56$ million.

The expected value of net present value is:

$$ev(NPV) = .6(\$30.32) + .4(\$27.56) = \$29.22 \text{ million.}$$

Now enter $29.22 along the lower tier of the decision tree.

On the basis of expected technical and market circumstances, Sun Garden should retain existing acreage and replant for producing white grapes. Once the decision is implemented, frequent reevaluations should be conducted to consider new circumstances and new opportunities for investment.

ADJUSTING THE DISCOUNT FACTOR FOR RISK

To this point, we have adjusted for risk through the use of probabilities. Risk can be incorporated in project selection in another way, however, by altering the rate of discount r used for computing net present value. If a firm's base cost of capital is $r = 8$ percent, for example, projects with a higher level of risk might require a discount rate of $r = 10$ percent or even 12 percent. If NPV is greater than zero using a *risk-adjusted* discount rate, then the project should be accepted. To illustrate, suppose two projects involve projected cash flows as shown. Discounted at the base cost of capital $r = 8$ percent, their NPVs are:

$$\text{Project I: } NPV = -\$50 + \frac{\$20}{1.08} + \frac{\$30}{(1.08)^2} + \frac{\$40}{(1.08)^3} + \frac{\$50}{(1.08)^4}$$
$$= \$62.74.$$
$$\text{Project II: } NPV = -\$15 + \frac{\$12}{1.08} + \frac{\$18}{(1.08)^2} + \frac{\$24}{(1.08)^3} + \frac{\$30}{(1.08)^4}$$
$$= \$52.65.$$

By this measure, Project I is the preferred alternative. However, if the risk associated with revenues and costs is substantially greater for Project I, the appropriate risk-adjusted discount rate might be as much as $r = 12$ percent, and NPV becomes:

$$\text{Project I: } NPV = -\$50 + \frac{\$20}{1.12} + \frac{\$30}{(1.12)^2} + \frac{\$40}{(1.12)^3} + \frac{\$50}{(1.12)^4}$$
$$= \$52.02.$$

Adjusting for risk reduces the expected value of Project I and suggests that Project II should be selected. The lower risk associated with cash flows from Project II indicates higher expected net present value.

The case studies that follow illustrate other ways by which firms might incorporate risk in decisions involving the discount rate for evaluating investment proposals.

CASE STUDY 14.2 Varying Capital Costs Within a Single Firm

The cost of capital may vary within a single firm according to the characteristics of particular units. *Low-risk* divisions with dependable cash flows may be assigned a lower capital cost than activities involving more risk. Similarly, divisions in a *high-growth* phase of development may be assigned a lower capital cost than divisions in a mature phase with little future growth potential. Determining the precise cost of capital depends on the combination of risk and growth potential embodied in a particular division.

One way to account for risk is to consider the portion of division expenditures to be financed through debt and stock issues. Low-risk divisions can normally be financed largely through debt, allowing the firm to enjoy the tax advantages of debt financing. A "debt/equity" ratio of 4 to 1, for example, signifies $4 of debt for each $1 of new stock issue and is appropriate for low-risk divisions. A debt/equity ratio of 1 to 2 is appropriate for activities involving more risk. Activities with a high level of risk may require 100-percent equity financing, for a debt/equity ratio of 0 to 1.

One way to account for growth potential is to consider the market price of stock in the industry in which a division operates. A division in a high-growth industry may enjoy a high stock price relative to current earnings. A "price/earnings" ratio of 12, for example, suggests that stockholders are willing to pay a high price for expected future earnings growth. A "price/earnings" ratio of only 5 suggests that the industry has reached maturity, and stockholders require relatively high earnings for each dollar of stock price. The reciprocal of the price/earnings ratio is the cost of an issue of capital stock. Thus, for the high-growth division we have just discussed, the cost of a stock issue is $1/12 = 8.33$ percent, and for the division in a mature industry the cost of a stock issue is $1/5 = 20$ percent.

The combined effect of risk and growth potential can be shown in a chart such as the one shown in Table A. Degree of risk is measured along the horizontal axis in terms of the debt/equity ratio of a particular division. Degree of risk ranges from below normal, with a high debt/equity ratio of $4/1 = 80$ percent/20 percent, to

TABLE A

	Degree of risk (debt/equity)		
	Below normal (80/20)	Normal (33/67)	Above normal (0/100)
Growth potential high (P/E = 12)	Assumptions: 80% debt @ 6.5% 20% equity @ 8.3% Cost of Capital: 6.9%	Assumptions: 33% debt @ 6.5% 67% equity @ 8.3% Cost of Capital: 7.7%	Assumptions: No debt 100% equity @ 8.3% Cost of Capital: 8.3%
Medium (P/E = 8)	Assumptions: 80% debt @ 6.5% 20% equity @ 12.5% Cost of Capital: 7.7%	Base Case Assumptions: 33% debt @ 6.5% 67% equity @ 12.5% Cost of Capital: 10.5%	Assumptions: No debt 100% equity @ 12.5% Cost of Capital: 12.5%
Low (P/E = 5)	Assumptions: 80% debt @ 6.5% 20% equity @ 20% Cost of Capital: 9.2%	Assumptions: 33% debt @ 6.5% 67% equity @ 20% Cost of Capital: 15.5%	Assumptions: No debt 100% equity @ 20% Cost of Capital: 20%

above normal, with a low debt/equity ratio of 0/100 percent. Growth potential is measured along the vertical axis in terms of the price/earnings ratio of new stock issues in the relevant industry. High-growth industries experience higher stock prices (and lower capital costs) than low-growth industries. The cells in the chart compute the weighted cost of capital for various combinations of debt and equity and various stock prices. Thus, with a high growth potential and below-normal risk, the weighted cost of capital is:

$$k = .80(6.5\%) + .20(8.3\%) = 6.9 \text{ percent.}$$

(The cost of debt is the after-tax cost of borrowing. For the firm shown in Figure A, the tax rate is $T = .46$ and $i_b = 12\%$, so that $i_{AT} = (1 - T)i_b = (.54)(12\%) = 6.5$ percent.)

Notice that the weighted cost of capital increases with increases in risk (decreases in the debt/earnings ratio) and with declines in growth potential (decreases in the price/earnings ratio). For a high-risk, low-growth division, the weighted cost of capital is 20 percent. For the "base case" the weighted cost of capital is 10.5 percent.

Managers of any firm should adjust the values in this type of chart to reflect their assessment of the appropriate debt/equity mix and costs of capital for each of the divisions within the firm. Using the appropriate weighted cost of capital should ensure that more of the firm's capital resources will be allocated toward growing business units and away from mature business units.

Source: Allen H. Seed, III, "Structuring Capital Spending Hurdle Rates," *Financial Executive*, February 1982, pp. 20–28.

CASE STUDY 14.3 Adjusting the Rate of Discount for a Multi-Divisional Firm

Another procedure for varying the rate of discount within a firm is one employed by Fuqua Industries, Inc. Fuqua Industries is a multi-market firm engaged in manufacturing, distributing, and servicing in a wide range of different industries: recreation products and services, farm and home products, transportation, petroleum, and other products. Its twenty-two divisions handle products as diverse as broadcasting and yogurt. Some of Fuqua's markets involve considerably more risk than others. For Fuqua, using a single discount rate to evaluate investment proposals would likely result in non-optimal investment decisions. Therefore, Fuqua's managers developed a procedure for assessing risk in the various divisions and adjusting the discount rate to reflect differences in risk.

The procedure involves calculating a separate risk index for each division. The risk index is then applied to the firm's base cost of capital to determine the appropriate discount rate for that division. Two measures of risk are used to determine the risk index:

1. *Objective risk* is a measure of actual profit performance of the division relative to previous years and relative to managers' forecasts.

2. *Subjective risk* is the managers' assessment of the level of risk in the industry in which the division operates.

The value of objective risk is based on profit variability over a five year period. Five levels of profit performance are ranked. Table A lists the average variability of profit compared to previous years and compared to budget projections.

Fuqua's mobile home division had *low-to-medium* profit variability in the year-to-year comparison and *low* variability relative to managers' forecasts. Therefore, the division was given a rank of 2 in the first category and a rank of 1 in the second. The measure of objective risk is a weighted average of the division's two rankings. Managers assigned weights of 25 percent and 75 percent to the two

TABLE A

Rank	Actual to previous year	Actual to managers' forecasts
1 (low)	−5% to +10%	−3% to +5%
2	−10% to +20%	−5% to +10%
3 (medium)	15% to +40%	−10% to +20%
4	20% to +60%	−15% to +30%
5 (high)	25% to +70%	−20% to +40%

rankings on the basis of their judgment about the significance of the two profit comparisons. Weights of 25 percent and 75 percent yield objective risk of 2(.25) + 1(.75) = 1.25 for Fuqua's mobile home division.

The value of subjective risk is based on the managers' judgment of the division's performance in the following characteristics:

Consumer base dispersion   Market position
Operational flexibility   Management
Loss of asset value   Brand distinction
Cyclical business   Unionization
Seasonal business   Environmental impact
Government involvement   Availability of resources
Changes in technology   Backlogs

Each of the characteristics was given a value from 1 (low-risk) to 5 (high-risk). The total was then divided by the number of characteristics to yield a measure of subjective risk. For Fuqua's mobile home division, subjective risk is 37.66/14 = 2.69.

The risk class for Fuqua's mobile home division is an average of the measures of objective and subjective risk:

$$\text{Risk class} = \frac{\text{objective risk} + \text{subjective risk}}{2} = \frac{1.25 + 2.69}{2} = 1.97.$$

TABLE B

Risk class	Risk index[1]	Weighted cost of capital
1	.90	10.8 percent
2	.97	11.6
3	1.05	12.6
4	1.10	13.2
5	1.20	14.4

1. The risk index may be determined through subjective judgment. Fuqua determines the risk index by substituting in a formula for the cost of equity capital and then applying a debt/equity ratio of 1/1. The formula for the cost of equity capital is $c_e = i_f + b(i_s - i_f)$, where i_f is the risk-free rate of interest, i_s is an average of returns on all stocks in the market, and b is "beta," a measure of the variability of the returns on stock in this industry relative to returns in the equity market as a whole. The value of "beta" for the mobile home industry is $b = 1.9$. Using typical assumptions for the other values in the equation, the risk index is 1.19. Similar risk indexes were calculated for each line of Fuqua's business until a range of risk indexes was established. The range represents the cost of capital for various types of firms relative to the cost of capital for Fuqua.

The figure 1.97 ≈ 2 identifies the risk class of Fuqua's mobile home division.

Fuqua's managers have defined five risk classes and assigned a risk index to each class. The risk index for each division is then multiplied by the firm's base cost of capital to determine its discount rate. With a base capital cost of 12 percent, the mobile home division would be assigned a discount rate of .97(12 percent) = 11.6 percent. See Table B for the discount rates associated with other risk classes.

This procedure allows considerable flexibility for managers to use subjective judgment in assigning capital costs. However, the fact that the process is highly structured ensures that relevant information is considered and the risk factor is valid for the particular division.

MANAGERIAL THINKING

What do the weights 25 percent and 75 percent for comparisons of profit variability suggest about this firm's decision-making processes? What circumstances might mandate a different selection of weights?

Source: Benton E. Gup and Samuel W. Norwood, "Divisional Cost of Capital: A Practical Approach," *Financial Management*, Spring 1982, vol. 11, no. 1, pp. 20–24.

UNCERTAINTY

Adjusting for uncertainty is less precise than adjusting for risk. Remember that risk involves circumstances for which past experience provides a measure of frequency, or probability, of occurrence in the future. Uncertainty requires greater exercise of subjective judgment, with a wider range of analytical procedures and greater lee-way for managers to express their own preferences and attitudes.

To illustrate decision making under uncertainty, let us suppose that a firm is considering purchase of new materials-handling equipment. Three different models are available, each of which would be appropriate for particular future business conditions. Managers have collected estimates of operating costs, revenues, depreciation allowances, and scrap value under various possible future conditions (including changes in energy costs, introduction of new technologies, trends in demand, and so forth). Using these estimates, managers have calculated net present value for Machines A, B, and C for each of three possible future business environments, X, Y, and Z. The *NPV*s for these possible situations are shown in Table 14.2.

TABLE 14.2

Machines	Future business environments			NPV using bayesian rule	Maximin solution	Maximax solution	Hurwicz Optimistic	Hurwicz Pessimistic
	X	Y	Z					
A	65	45	−10	26.67	−10	65*	35*	12.50
B	40	5	25	23.33	5*	40	26	13.20*
C	40	−15	60	28.33*	−15	60	30	7.50

Lacking precise probabilities for weighting *NPV*s, managers may compare the three machines by using equal probabilities. Assigning equal probabilities to all future conditions is an example of **Bayesian analysis**. The expected value of *NPV* using Bayesian analysis is also shown in Table 14.2. The asterisk marks Machine C as the preferred choice under Bayesian analysis.

Another approach to uncertainty would allow managers to avoid the least desirable results following their decision. This technique is called the **maximin rule** and involves selection of the "least bad" alternative. For the three machines above, A and C involve possible negative *NPV*s of 10 and 15, respectively. Under the worst possible future business environment, Machine B has positive *NPV* of 5, indicating the "least bad" alternative. The maximin rule would call for selection of Machine B, as indicated in Table 14.2.

A more positive solution to this decision problem focuses on the "best best" alternative. This technique is called the **maximax rule**. For the three machines in our example, B and C involve under the best business conditions *NPV*s of 40 and 60, respectively. With a best *NPV* of as high as 65, Machine A is the maximax choice, as shown in Table 14.2.

Hurwicz' rule permits a sort of compromise between the "least bad" and the "best best" alternative. Under Hurwicz' rule, the maximin and the maximax values are weighted according to managers' attitudes toward risk and their degree of optimism regarding future business conditions. Managers who are only slightly concerned about risk and who expect future business conditions to be fairly good may employ weights of, say, .40 and .60 to the maximin and maximax values. Thus, Machine A might be weighted as follows:

$$.40(-10) + .60(65) = 35.$$

More pessimistic managers with greater concern about the future might weight the values .70 and .30. Thus,

$$.70(-10) + .30(65) = 12.50.$$

Hurwicz' estimates for both of these conditions are also shown in Table 14.2.

Finally, the **Savage decision rule** allows managers to select the alternative that would minimize their "regrets" from choosing the incorrect alternative in whatever future business environment should occur. The Savage rule is also called the "minimax regret rule" and requires computation of "regrets" associated with each alternative. A regret table is shown in Table 14.3 on page 446. Values in the regret table are the difference between the *NPV*s for a particular choice and the best possible *NPV* that might have occurred with another choice, given that a particular business environment ultimately occurs.

Note that for alternatives that represent the best possible choice for a particular future business environment, the values in the regret table are zero.

Under the Savage decision rule, managers would choose the alternative for which the maximum regret is lowest. In our example, choosing Machine B would involve regret of only 35 in the worst of future business conditions. If Z actually occurs and Machine B experiences *NPV* of 25, this is only 35 less

TABLE 14.3

Machines	Future business environment			Regrets			Maximum regret
	X	Y	Z	X	Y	Z	
A	65	25	−10	0	0	70	70
B	40	5	25	25	20	35	35*
C	40	−15	60	25	40	0	40

than the maximum possible *NPV* under the conditions in *Z*. In any other future business environment, *NPV* of machine B is even closer to the maximum that could occur.

None of the decision rules for conditions of uncertainty is likely to be completely satisfactory in solving every management problem. Each has particular advantages for particular users. In many cases, the disadvantage of imprecision is offset by the advantage of allowing subjective judgment to influence the analysis. The chief advantage, however, is that each of these tools requires managers to assemble available information into a well-structured framework, to evaluate alternatives in terms of their contributions to the firm's objectives, and to recognize the uncertainties associated with the choosen strategy.

SUMMARY

Risk and uncertainty make it impossible to predict correctly the costs and revenues associated with any long-term investment. Risk can be included in an investment decision through the use of probabilities. A strategy's expected value is the sum of projected future values, each weighted by the probability of its occurrence. Probabilities may be based on historical experience. When historical data follow the form of a normal distribution, probabilities can be obtained from tables measuring areas beneath a normal curve.

Conditional probability is associated with a series of future events, each of which is conditional on the previous occurrence of another event. Conditional probability is illustrated through the use of decision trees. When using a decision tree, it is appropriate first to calculate the net present value of all possible events following the most distant decision. Then calculate the expected value of net present value for each alternative decision. Select the alternative with the greatest expected value of net present value and incorporate that value when making the nearer decisions.

Another way to include risk in investment decisions is to adjust the discount factor for risk.

Uncertainty differs from risk in that past experience provides no objective information for assigning probabilities for the occurrence of future events. Bayesian analysis assigns equal probabilities to all future events. The Maximin Rule selects the "least bad" alternative. The Maximax Rule selects the "best

best'' alternative. Hurwicz' Rule allows managers to weight the maximin and maximax values according to their attitudes toward risk and their relative optimism toward the future. The Savage Rule selects the alternative that minimizes ''regrets'' from choosing the incorrect alternative.

KEY TERMS

probability	Bayesian analysis
risk	maximin rule
uncertainty	maximax rule
normal distribution	Hurwicz' rule
expected value	Savage decision rule

QUESTIONS AND PROBLEMS

1. Draw a continuous probability distribution showing the greatest probability associated with values 10–20, zero probability of values less than zero, and diminishing probability associated with values up to 100.

2. Classify each of the following circumstances under the heading of risk or uncertainty.
   a. Major crop failure.
   b. Changes in consumer tastes.
   c. Scarcity of essential material.
   d. Discovery of a new process.
   e. Obsolescence of a major piece of equipment.

3. What is the relationship between each of the circumstances in Question 2 and economic profit or loss?

4. Tempo Electronics is considering purchase of equipment for which the internal rate of return is estimated at 9.4 percent. However, a technological innovation is expected to occur during the equipment's life that would reduce internal rate of return to 7.8 percent. A probability of .65 has been assigned to this event. The firm's after-tax cost of capital is 8 percent. Should the investment be made?

5. Market researchers have assigned a probability of .50 to the event that Tempo's sales will be at least $45 million for the next seven years and then will grow at an annual rate of 5 percent indefinitely. Show how this information can aid management in planning investments, loan applications, and so forth.

6. Dakota Products is considering expansion into a new territory that offers a .50 probability of profitable sales. After the first year, if sales are less than expected, Dakota may decide to conduct an extended marketing campaign

at an initial cost of $20 million with a .60 probability of success. A decision tree and cash flow table are shown for Dakota. Dakota's after-tax cost of capital is 9 percent. What is the expected net present value of the proposed expansion?

	Current year	Year 1	Year 2	Year 3 to infinity
Branch (1)	− $35	+ $15	+ $21	+ $21 with annual growth of .05
Branch (2)	− 35	+ 8	− 20	+ 18 with annual growth of .05
Branch (3)	− 35	+ 8	− 20	+ 13 with annual growth of .05
Branch (4)	− 35	+ 8	+ 12	+ 12 with annual growth of .04

First place the figures for cash flow on the appropriate branches of the decision tree. Then determine net present value.

7. Better Electronics purchases transistors for which useful life is normally distributed with expected value of 1,000 hours and the standard deviation is 135. What is the probability that transistors will have useful life of less than 850 hours?

8. Calculate the expected value and standard deviation of the following distribution. Then judge whether or not the distribution has the characteristics of a normal distribution. Explain your answer.

5	16	12
13	10	8
7	8	7
4	3	15
9	11	10
12	9	11

9. If a recession occurs next year, the probability of default on trade credit is .75. Without a recession, the probability of default is .40. Suppose the probability of a recession is .30. Determine the probability of default.

15

Government and Business

Accompanying the phenomenal development of U.S. industry has come an increasing role for government in the nation's economic life. Government policies and programs strongly influence the production and distribution of goods and services and necessitate compatible policies in business firms. Understanding the source and intent of government's influence and its likely future direction can help a firm's managers plan business strategies more effectively.

In this chapter we will examine three types of circumstances in which government regulation has appeared to be necessary for achieving certain economic and social goals. We will begin our discussion with a short review of decision making in completely free markets. Then we will contrast the expected results of free market decision making with actual results and show how government intervention has influenced these results.

FREE MARKETS AND THE GOALS OF REGULATION

Free markets yield substantial advantages to society in terms of economic *efficiency*. Economic efficiency can be defined as achieving the greatest possible production of goods and services with the lowest cost or expenditure of scarce resources. In free markets, producers and consumers make their decisions at the market's margin, balancing the expected benefits from additional goods and services against their costs and choosing only those kinds of production whose benefits exceed their costs. The expected result of free market decisions is maximum efficiency.

A market model is a good illustration of how this balancing occurs. Look at Figure 15.1a, which shows demand and supply for a particular good or service. The demand curve reflects the **marginal utility** associated with purchases of the item and the willingness of consumers to allocate portions of their budgets toward acquiring it. The supply curve reflects the **marginal costs** associated with producing the item and the willingness of producers to sell at a comparable price. The equilibrium level of production in the short run for this item is that at which the marginal utility of the item is just sufficient to justify its marginal cost. In addition, in long-run competitive equilibrium, the following results are also true:

1. Price is just sufficient to pay average total cost at the minimum level possible using current technology and available materials.
2. Plants are built at the optimum size for achieving increasing returns to scale and avoiding decreasing returns to scale.
3. The number of competing firms producing any good or service is that at which the entire market can be satisfied at optimum scale.

All of these conditions are reflected in the market model and the model of the individual firm shown in Figure 15.1b. Equilibrium in the market ensures a level of production at which the additional benefits from the final unit of production are precisely offset by the additional costs.

Imagine that all of the nation's markets could be combined into one large model that reflects these same circumstances. This is shown graphically in Figure 15.2. Total demand for all goods and services is shown as a downward sloping curve measuring the additional benefits of every type of production. Additional costs are shown as an upward sloping curve. In the total market model, the efficient equilibrium for the entire nation would occur at the level

FIGURE 15.1   **A Perfectly Competitive Market**

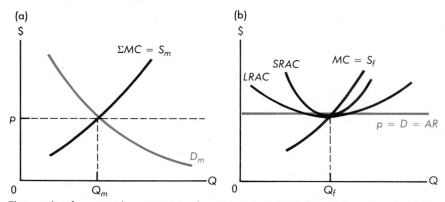

The market for a good or service is shown in (a). A firm's level of production of the good or service is shown in (b). A perfectly competitive market allocates resources efficiently, producing the maximum quantity of output at the minimum cost.

FIGURE 15.2   Free Market Benefits

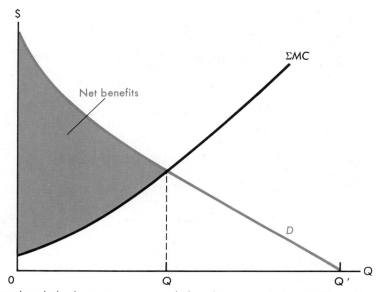

Free markets help the economy as a whole achieve maximum total benefits at the minimum cost in terms of productive resources. Net benefits are at a maximum.

of total production at which additional benefits are equal to additional costs, labelled as Q in Figure 15.2.

At the efficient equilibrium, the nation's available resources are allocated toward production of only those goods and services that yield comparable benefits. Furthermore, at equilibrium the nation as a whole enjoys the maximum quantity of total benefits possible with available resources and technology. Benefits for the nation are shown as the area under the total demand curve up to any level of total production. Total costs are represented by the area under the total supply curve. The amount of total benefits that is greater than total costs is **net benefits**, represented by the shaded area between the two curves. Maximum net benefits for the nation occur at the level of efficient equilibrium, Q. Beyond the efficient equilibrium level, additional costs exceed additional benefits, and net benefits are reduced by the amount represented by the area between the curves.

Given these relationships, an appropriate objective of government policy might be to encourage the kind of market behavior that would ensure efficient results. In fact, government's role in the economy may be seen as an attempt to correct deviations from the most efficient market behavior, that is, to push production toward the level achieved at Q in Figure 15.2. In many instances, government intervention is successful in promoting efficiency. In others, government intervention may add to distortions and create greater inefficiency.

Whatever the outcome of government intervention, it is helpful to understand its source and intent.

The following sections will examine the role of government in dealing with three types of inefficiency in the actual level of production. We will consider first the use of market power by individual firms in holding production below the level of efficient equilibrium, then the influence of third parties in pushing production above the level of efficient equilibrium, and finally the existence of external costs that make locating and achieving efficient equilibrium especially difficult.

PRODUCTION AT LEVELS LESS THAN EFFICIENT EQUILIBRIUM

We have stated that efficient equilibrium for the economy as a whole occurs at the level at which additional benefits from current production are equal to additional costs. This is also the level of maximum net benefits. Perfectly competitive markets can achieve this ideal result, as individual firms seek profits by producing larger quantities at lower costs. The result is different when competition is weak. In the absence of competition, firms tend to produce less than the equilibrium quantity and set price higher than marginal cost and minimum average cost. Under imperfect competition, firms may continue to collect economic profits without the fear of losing their market to competitors.

Inefficiency in the allocation of productive resources means that society fails to receive maximum possible benefits at minimum cost. The earliest forms of government regulation were developed to counteract the inefficiencies caused by imperfect competition in industry.

Regulating Imperfect Competition: Monopoly

The earliest drive toward achieving market power in the United Sates occurred in the late 1800s when giant new industries were developing in the northeastern states. In particular, the steel and railroad industries required enormous investments in productive capital, making large firms necessary for efficient production. Individual steel-producing and rail transport firms combined and cooperated in order to divide markets, set prices and provide for further expansion. Small competitors were absorbed or driven out of business by selective price cutting, enabling the giants to control most markets. Subsequently, market dominance enabled powerful firms to limit production and set prices above the equilibrium level. In terms of Figure 15.2, total production tended to be less than the efficient quantity represented at Q.

This strategy for reducing competition is called **horizontal integration**. Horizontal integration involves a combination of firms that produce the same good or service. In the late 1800s, it occurred in the meat packing, sugar, and petroleum industries as well as in steel production and rail transportation. As the practice of horizontal integration spread in U.S. industries, consumers and other industries suffered the effects of reduced production and higher prices. Political pressure began to build for legislation limiting the spread of market power in industry. The result of this pressure was the Sherman Antitrust Act, passed by Congress in 1890. The Sherman Act forbade any combination of firms or conspiracy to restrain trade, thus making illegal the growth of market power through horizontal merger.

The Sherman Act was first invoked in the early 1900s to prevent the merger of the Northern Pacific and Great Northern Railroads. In 1911, prosecution under the Sherman Act required the American Tobacco Company and the Standard Oil Company to dissolve into smaller companies. However, U.S. Steel, another giant, was allowed to maintain its 60 percent market share because, according to the Supreme Court, simply being big was no offense as long as the firm did not engage in unfair market behavior to exploit its market power. Little else was accomplished in reducing market power until 1945, when Alcoa Aluminum Company was forced to dissolve into smaller companies. Although the firm had achieved its large size through legitimate behavior, its size alone was the basis for the Supreme Court's decision.

Regulating Imperfect Competition: Natural Monopoly

During the late 1800s, Congress also passed legislation affecting **natural monopolies**. Recall that a natural monopoly is an industry in which optimum scale is greater than the size of the market. Under these conditions, competition is inefficient, and a single firm can satisfy the entire market at lowest cost. However, a single firm also would have the power to set the monopoly price and output without fear of pressure from competitors. The transportation industries and public utilities were the major examples of natural monopolies. Legislation passed in 1887 established the Interstate Commerce Commission to regulate railroad pricing and output and to hold railroad profits to a level consistent with competition.

Note the intent of government regulation in these cases. Both types of legislation were passed to correct levels of production lower than and prices higher than the efficient level shown in Figure 15.2. The Sherman Act was intended to enforce a competitive structure in industries that tended toward monopoly. The Interstate Commerce Act forced natural monopolies to behave like competitors. Both laws have been successful in some ways and inadequate in others.

Regulating Monopoly Conduct

Prosecution under the Sherman Act has been difficult and irregular, depending strongly on priorities established by the federal administration in office at a particular time. One problem has been the law's vagueness, which prohibits overt monopoly *structure* but is not very specific about the kinds of monopoly *behavior* that can be prosecuted. Firms have found ways to *behave* like monopolies, achieving substantial market power without actually violating the law. Furthermore, around the turn of the century vertical integration, a new strategy for achieving market power, became more widespread. **Vertical integration** is the combination of firms involving various stages of producing a finished good or service. Combining all of a firm's suppliers and intermediate producers into a single firm reduces costs and enables the expanded firm to drive smaller competitors out of business. The resulting market power enables the vertically integrated firm to behave as a monopoly when making output and pricing decisions.

Concern about the spread of such monopolistic behavior led to the passage of the Clayton Antitrust Act in 1914. The Clayton Act forbids the following monopolistic business practices:

Tying contracts that require a buyer of certain of a firm's products to purchase its full line of products. Tying contracts eliminate competition from other producers.

Price discrimination in which firms set lower prices in areas where the firm faces competition and higher prices elsewhere. Price discrimination can eliminate competitors and eventually raise prices.

Interlocking directorates in which individuals serve on the boards of directors of several firms. Interlocking directorates enable individuals to control the operations of competing firms as if they were a single monopoly.

Stock ownership in competing companies. Again, stock ownership in competing companies enables stockholders to coordinate price and output decisions as if the competing companies were a single firm.

At the same time, the Federal Trade Commission was established to investigate charges of unfair competition and file suit against firms found to be in violation of the law. The Clayton Act was expanded in 1950 with the addition of the Celler-Kefauver Amendment. While the original law had prohibited stock ownership in competing firms, it had not prohibited outright acquisition of competing firms. The 1950 amendment forbids acquisitions that might "lessen competition, or tend to create a monopoly."

Resale Price Maintenance Laws

During the 1930s a different remedy for market power in industry appeared to be necessary. The Great Depression had brought falling sales, price cutting, and negative economic profits in many industries. Bankruptcies increased, and Congress looked for ways to protect weak business firms from collapse. The result was a series of "price maintenance" laws that forbid giant firms from using price discounts to undersell their smaller competitors. The Robinson-Patman Act of 1936 forbids wholesale discounts to large purchasers when the resulting advantage would tend to create a monopoly. The Miller-Tydings Act of 1937 permitted manufacturers to set retail prices on their products. While the intent of these laws was to protect competition, the actual result was often to prolong inefficient operations among small retail establishments.

In 1975 the Miller-Tydings Act was repealed, making resale price maintenance agreements illegal under the Sherman Act. Some states still permit the practice on intrastate sales, however.

Recent Problems with Antitrust Legislation

In all of these actions, the intent of government intervention was to strengthen competition in order to move the economy toward the efficient level of production, Q, shown in Figure 15.2. While government regulation has not always been successful, the objectives of these early forms of government intervention were more clear-cut than those of more recent forms. In recent years, regulation of monopolistic structure and behavior has had to correct a third business strategy for reducing competition: conglomerate mergers. **Conglomerate mergers** are combinations of firms in unrelated industries.

High economic profits during the 1960s enabled many large firms to acquire smaller firms outside their own industries, resulting in a type of merger not specifically prohibited by existing antitrust laws. Expanding firms expected that the advancing technology of information would enable management to organize large amounts of productive resources in several firms more effectively to produce increasing profits. Many of the conglomerates did not live up to their promoters' enthusiastic projections, however. Managing a highly diverse enterprise proved to be more difficult than expected, and enormous profits failed to materialize. Still, critics worried that substantial concentrations of economic power in conglomerates might ultimately be misused to achieve political advantages. Current antitrust laws and enforcement agencies are poorly equipped for controlling the economic effects of conglomerate mergers.

Current antitrust laws also are poorly equipped for dealing with the problem of parallel behavior. **Parallel behavior** refers to similar pricing and output decisions among different firms even when there is no overt agreement not to compete. After many years in business, managers of many firms can anticipate the pricing and output behavior of other firms and set their own policies to maximize industry profits. The judicial system so far has been reluctant to attack the problem of parallel behavior.

Current federal policy toward monopoly can be briefly summarized as follows. Where market power does not yet exist, the Justice Department has sought to prevent horizontal and vertical mergers in an effort to slow the growth of monopolistic structure in industry. The Antitrust Improvements Act of 1976 requires that large enterprises give written notice to the Federal Trade Commission and to the Antitrust Division of the Justice Department before any planned acquisition. Firms must then wait a specified time to see if there is any objection to the proposed merger.

Changes in Regulatory Policy: Natural Monopolies

Government's role in the economy has evolved over the last century along with changing consumer and producer markets and changing technology. Such changes continue to take place because of the constant need to evaluate and adapt government policy to new circumstances. One of the most significant changes occurring in the 1980s has to do with government policy toward natural monopolies, particularly in the transportation industry.

Regulation of the nation's railways began with the Interstate Commerce Commission Act in the late 1880s and was extended to the airline and trucking industries in the early 1900s. In general, these regulations attempted to protect small firms from dominance by the market giants. Through control of transport rates and routes, regulatory commissions attempted to preserve a share of the market for small firms. Control over rates ensured that prices could not be set high enough to include monopoly profits nor low enough to destroy competing firms. Control over routes made possible a guaranteed market for small firms even when their costs were higher than their competitors'. A successful regulatory policy guaranteed a degree of competition in industries typically described as natural monopolies.

Changes in the economic climate of the 1970s appeared to call for changes in government regulatory policy. Rising energy costs and slower productivity growth made achieving increasing returns to scale critical in many industries. Protecting small firms from dominance by more efficient giants seemed inefficient for the nation as a whole, particularly in view of declining real growth, deteriorating international competitiveness, and stagnating real incomes in the United States. In response to these new circumstances, regulatory commissions began to relax the rules that many believed were responsible for reduced efficiency in industry.

In 1978 Congress passed the Airline Deregulation Act formally restoring competition in airline pricing and route selection. The immediate results included price wars among competing airlines, reduced profits for most firms, and the reduction or elimination of service on many air routes. Still, there was a general feeling that increased competition would ultimately benefit consumers and improve efficiency in the production of air transportation. The railroad industry joined the airlines in pressing for greater freedom to set prices and routes, partly to redress what they considered to be inequities between railroad and trucking regulation. Congress began considering trucking deregulation and in 1980 passed legislation to phase out regulatory control of trucking rates and routes.

How will the new policies affect the level of total production in the nation's economy? Will freer competition move production more closely to the efficient equilibrium represented by Q on Figure 15.2? Or will removal of regulatory restraints result finally in greater market dominance by industrial giants, with reduced production and higher prices? The answer is not clear. However, the Sherman and Clayton Acts remain to prohibit monopoly structure and behavior, and the tremendous expansion of national and international markets has

CASE STUDY 15.1   **Deregulation in the Trucking Industry**

Of the total amount spent each year on newly produced goods and services, about $400 billion is spend for the actual physical distribution of the products. This figure amounts to almost one-seventh of gross national product. Such a large expenditure of the nation's resources necessitates close attention to efficiency to make sure that adequate transportation services are provided at the lowest possible cost.

Until 1980, trucking in the United States was regulated by the Interstate Commerce Commission (ICC). One effect of ICC regulation was to hold freight shipping rates above the true competitive level in order to protect small, inefficient trucking firms. In addition, contract truckers were limited in the number of corporate customers they could serve.

Soon after deregulation of the trucking industry, recession hit the U.S. economy. Freight shipping rates fell an average of 20 to 40 percent for many trucking firms. Profits for 1981 averaged only 1 percent of trucking revenues, down from 3.4 percent in 1978. Return on stockholders' equity fell to 4.5 percent, down from 16.9 percent in 1976. Within two years, an estimated 183 trucking firms went out of business, and another 21 declared bankruptcy. Analysts estimated that an additional 30 firms were on the brink of failure. The American Truckers Association petitioned Congress to bring back regulation.

In spite of the recession, the total number of trucking firms increased from 17,083 in 1979 to 22,270 in 1981. Most of the new firms were small, non-unionized firms with low labor costs that provided a competitive edge.

Generally, when the economy begins to recover from recession, trucking is one of the first industries to experience increasing sales. This is because when recovery occurs manufacturers and retailers rush to replenish inventories depleted during the recession. Wall Street analysts project a 15-percent increase in freight handled over the next year. With further cuts in labor costs, that could mean a substantial increase in industry profits.

MANAGERIAL THINKING

Compare and contrast the deregulatory experience of trucking with that of the airline industry (Case Studies 6.1 and 8.1). What aspects of the response to deregulation in each industry have increased efficiency? Are there also aspects that have reduced efficiency?

Source: Thomas G. Donlan, "Turning the Corner: Trucking Industry Gears Up for Recovery," *Barron's*, September 6, 1982.

reduced the number of industries that can be classified as natural monopolies. Larger markets make it possible for a larger number of firms of optimum size to operate efficiently. Finally, many of the regulated giants now compete across industry lines with other giants.

PRODUCTION AT LEVELS GREATER THAN EFFICIENT EQUILIBRIUM

In the preceding sections of this chapter we described market circumstances in which production and pricing tend toward a level to the left of the level of maximum efficiency, shown in Figure 15.2 as Q. Different circumstances, however, may occasionally push production beyond the efficient equilibrium represented at Q, causing the additional benefits from current production to be less than the additional costs. In this case, too many resources are allocated to current production, and net benefits are lower than the maximum possible with available resources and technology.

Such a result can not last under perfect market conditions. Buyers do not demand and producers do not supply items for which marginal utility is less than marginal cost. This situation is possible only if the price of the good or service is paid by some individual or some institution other than the buyer and if the cost of producing it is of no concern to the seller. In the United States, the health care industry is the most typical example of this type of market situation.

The consumption of health care services in the United States is normally financed through third parties in the form of public or private insurance. The decision to purchase health services is governed by concerns other than purely market considerations and is generally made by a physician or by hospital personnel. For both of these reasons, there is no direct link between an individual consumer's decision to purchase health care and the price of the service. Under such circumstances, demand ceases to be a function of price and instead becomes a function of the availability of the service. In the extreme case, demand for a service might be pushed as far as any positive utility is produced at all; that is, to the level of production at Q' in Figure 15.2.

Supply is likewise less a function of cost than of available technology. Since costs will be paid by insurers, producing firms are not restricted by market conditions from expanding their capacity to perform all types of medical services. Although many health care services require very large scale for efficient operation, small firms purchase the equipment and hire the personnel to perform them. The resulting duplication of services and other disincentives to cost-cutting keep health care costs higher and production greater than would be true under competition.

These kinds of inefficiency have created substantial cost increases in the health care industry. The share of gross national product allocated to medical care rose from 4.5 percent in 1950 to more than 9 percent in 1980. Expenditures for hospital care, physicians' and dentists' fees, drugs, nursing home care, and other medical services in 1980 totaled more than $200 billion.

Government Intervention in the Health Care Industry

During the early 1900s, public pressure began to build for legislation requiring health insurance to be supplied for the general public. In part to avoid new legislation, the American Hospital Association and the American Medical Association took steps to establish Blue Cross and Blue Shield to provide voluntary insurance coverage for the general public. Even so, by 1950 only 51 percent of the population had hospital insurance, 36 percent had surgical insurance, and 14 percent had insurance for nonsurgical services performed by physicians in hospitals. The percentage of coverage was even lower for individuals over age 65, a portion of the population that tends to have substantial medical expenses and below average income.

In 1960, Congress passed the Kerr-Mills Act which increased medical assistance funds for the elderly, and in 1965 the Medicare program was established to cover most hospital expenses and 80 percent of physicians' fees[1] for all individuals over age 65. The program is financed by payroll taxes, premiums paid by enrollees, and the general revenue of the federal government. At the same time, Congress established the Medicaid program for welfare recipients and other medically needy persons. This program set standards for the kinds of care individual states must offer.

By 1980 most of the U.S. population was covered by public or private health insurance, which paid more than 90 percent of hospital costs and 66 percent of physicians' fees. The results have been improved health care and better preventive medicine for many of the nation's 23 million poor and 25 million elderly. Life expectancy has risen sharply and death rates fallen since 1965.

There are still problems, however. Since states set their own standards for Medicaid, only about two-thirds of the poor are covered. Two-parent families, single people, and childless couples frequently do not qualify for aid. For the estimated 5 to 8 percent of the public not covered by any health program at all, catastrophic medical expenses can be devastating.

An Evaluation

Government policy toward health care was designed with humanitarian objectives: that is, to improve the health of the population as a whole and to distribute the costs of health care among all sectors of the population. In promoting these humanitarian goals, however, U.S. policy has tended to reduce efficiency in the production and distribution of health care services.

The influence of third parties in the health care industry has pushed production beyond the level of maximum efficiency and pushed costs above the level of minimum costs. When the Medicare and Medicaid programs were initiated, their costs were estimated at about $4.3 billion for 1965. By 1981, actual costs were more than $53 billion for the year. Deciding whether production of health care services is efficient depends on measurement of resulting benefits to consumers—clearly an impossible task. However, there is general agreement that the absence of market forces in the health care industry has contributed to excessive capacity and higher costs, with resulting inefficiency in the allocation of resources.

The public's dissatisfaction with the results of existing programs has led to demands for reform. Some proposals would increase the level of government

---

1. Enrollment for physicians' insurance is voluntary.

intervention in the health care sector by setting legal limits on increases in hospital revenues or by including national health insurance in the public health program. Other proposals emphasize market decision making in the production and distribution of health services. An efficient health policy would include free or low-cost health care for the poor in addition to incentives to seek the lowest-cost source of care. A more market-oriented approach to the production and distribution of health services would help ensure that the additional benefits from the service are indeed equal to the additional costs.

THE PROBLEM OF EXTERNALITIES

Maintaining production for the nation as a whole at the level of maximum efficiency is complicated by another problem. In free markets, efficient decision making depends on direct links between benefits and costs for each individual consumer and producer. For production to be efficient, the costs of benefits received should be paid by every market participant. Achieving this result is fairly simple in less highly developed economies than our own, since an individual's consumption is tied directly to his or her own production. It is more difficult, however, at high levels of industrial and agricultural technology in which many costs are spread over wider geographic areas and even cover a longer period of time than is perceived by individuals at the time they consume benefits. Under such circumstances, measuring an individual consumer's benefits and allocating costs according to his or her level of consumption may no longer be possible.

Costs that extend beyond the individual consumer or business firm are called **external costs** or **social costs**. These include such things as water and air pollution, soil erosion, and the hazards created by the disposal of toxic waste. Such costs are difficult to identify precisely and even more difficult to measure, making it nearly impossible to determine the efficient level of production. Production may be carried on for extended periods of time under conditions in which net benefits for the community are not the maximum quantity with available resources and technology.

This problem can be illustrated with a little algebra. Efficient production occurs where marginal benefits are equal to marginal costs:

$$MB = MC$$

and

$$\frac{MB}{MC} = 1.$$

At lower levels of production,

$$\frac{MB}{MC} > 1,$$

and society is sacrificing benefits that are possible using its available resources. At higher levels,

$$\frac{MB}{MC} < 1,$$

and the use of scarce resources is excessive. Including the external costs of production changes the efficient benefit/cost ratio to

$$\frac{MB}{MC + MC_s} = 1,$$

where MC_s represents social costs. Defining efficient production requires a summation of MC_s, discounted according to when in the future they occur and weighted by the probability of their occurrence. Without clear information on quantities, discount rates, probabilities, and so forth, each analyst may measure the ratio differently and propose different levels of production.

Figure 15.3 illustrates this dilemma. According to Figure 15.3, adding MC_s to the cost curve shifts the level of efficient production to Q''. However, other measures of social costs could identify efficient production at any other point along the axis. Various special interest groups might be expected to understate certain costs and overstate others in order to justify projects favorable to that particular group.

FIGURE 15.3   **External Costs**

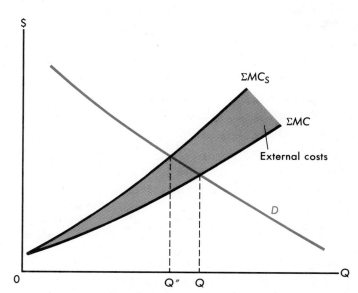

Adding external costs to costs of production complicates the process of selecting efficient equilibrium for the economy.

Ambiguity in measuring external costs has often led to policies that are ineffective or counterproductive. In such cases, production is continued beyond the point at which additional benefits are equal to additional costs. Some obvious examples of this problem come to mind.

1. Expelling industrial waste into lakes and rivers has destroyed wildlife habitats and endangered public health.
2. Some toxic chemicals and by-products of industrial processes have caused serious health problems for workers and may cause genetic mutations in future generations.
3. Industrial and residential development has infringed on wilderness areas, forever altering oxygen and water cycles and worsening the problems of air pollution and soil erosion.
4. Finally, and perhaps most frightening, expulsion of chemical wastes into the atmosphere may portend unforeseeable and life-threatening climatic and environmental changes for the planet as a whole.

Costs such as these are imposed on persons far beyond the reach of current production. With no link between costs and benefits, the tendency is to ignore the social costs and expand production to the level at which only private costs are covered. Look again at Figure 15.3. At the level of production determined by the free market, external costs may be borne inequitably by certain individuals, neighborhoods, and even other nations who receive no current benefits at all.

Regulation of Production Standards

Widespread public awareness of the problem of social costs has come about only recently. Important legislation was passed in 1965 and in the 1970s setting production standards in particular industries and establishing agencies to enforce the standards. Some examples include the following.

Air pollution regulation. The Clean Air Act and its amendments authorize the Environmental Protection Agency to define air quality standards and establish emissions standards to achieve them. Auto emissions standards have been a major focus of the law. In 1977, the EPA was ordered to set sulfur standards for coal burned as an energy source in industry.

Water pollution regulation. The Federal Water Pollution Control Act requires that industrial discharges into surface water be controlled by the best available technology. The aim is to protect wildlife, to provide for recreation, and by 1985 to eliminate all discharges of pollutants into navigable waterways. Federal funds were allocated to local governments for pollution control.

Toxic substances regulation. The Toxic Substances Control Act of 1976 requires manufacturers to prove that a chemical is safe before it is introduced into the market. Strict enforcement of the standard would bring many industries to a virtual standstill; so the EPA was ordered to set standards for only the most dangerous chemicals. The Resource Conservation and Recovery Act ordered the EPA to set standards for disposal of toxic wastes. However, the difficulty of defining a safe level of wastes and the costs of achieving a safe level have made strict enforcement infeasible.

Occupational safety and health regulation. The Occupational Safety and Health Act of 1970 requires that workplaces be free from recognized hazards that pose immediate or long-range danger to workers' health. Initially, about 7,000 standards were adopted by the Occupational Safety and Health Administration, many having little relation to health or safety. Without clear priorities, the agency has had little success in dealing with the serious problems of safety at work.

Highway safety regulation. The National Traffic and Motor Vehicle Safety Act of 1966 established the National Highway Transportation Safety Administration to set safety standards for automobiles. In 1978 the agency was ordered to set fuel economy standards as well. Enforcement in this case has been relatively simple, since many of the mandated standards would have been undertaken independently by the industry in response to market forces. Furthermore, the agency is required to deal with only a few firms, and the standards are relatively easy to measure.

Consumer product regulation. The Consumer Product Safety Commission was established in 1972 to balance the benefits and costs of new products and ban those found to be hazardous. In general, its effects have been hampered by industry opposition and legal suits.

Critics of regulation have pointed to some serious problems with these approaches toward controlling external costs:

1. Many of the production standards have been poorly defined, leaving substantial decision making responsibility in the hands of the various enforcement agencies.
2. Funding has frequently been inadequate for hiring expert personnel with the necessary experience to evaluate individual situations and make decisions affecting a variety of technical disciplines.
3. As a result of (2), rigid rules have been established to deal with only the most easily perceived and easily corrected external costs. Many of the standards have had only lax enforcement.
4. The inevitable problems associated with beginning work in a complex and unfamiliar area have generated hostility, frustrating legal delays, and a general lack of cooperation in working toward the solution of technical problems.

Some Recommendations

Whereas some positive results have come from the types of social regulation discussed above, legislation to improve environmental quality, worker health and safety, and consumer protection has been largely unsuccessful. Critics complain that the apparent objective of the regulatory agencies has been to

CASE STUDY 15.2   The Costs of Regulation

Economist Murray L. Weidenbaum, former Chairman of the Council of Economic Advisers under President Reagan, is a student of regulation and the costs regulation imposes on the economy. He has divided the costs of regulation into three categories:

1. the direct costs of administering regulatory agencies;
2. the indirect costs of compliance by the private sector;
3. the induced costs in terms of the nation's long-range productivity.

Let us take a closer look at each of these categories of costs.

DIRECT COSTS

In 1980, the combined budgets of the federal regulatory agencies totaled more than $6 billion. This was a substantial increase over the $0.9 billion spent on regulation in 1970. Newer forms of social regulation involving job safety, energy, the environment, and consumer health and safety comprised 83 percent of the 1980 regulatory budget.

INDIRECT COSTS

The indirect costs of complying with government regulation are more difficult to measure, however. These include the costs of automobile safety equipment, pollution-control equipment, and clerical personnel to handle government forms and questionnaires. Including such costs in the prices of finished goods and services produces a kind of "hidden tax" on consumers, which Weidenbaum estimates at about $20 for each dollar appropriated for regulation by Congress. Table A shows the direct and indirect costs of regulation in the major areas of regulation.

TABLE A

Area	Administrative cost	Compliance cost	Total cost
Consumer safety and health	1,516	5,094	6,610
Job safety and work conditions	483	4,015	4,498
Energy and environment	612	7,760	8,372
Financial regulation	104	1,118	1,222
Industry-specific regulation[1]	484	19,919	20,403
Paperwork	included in other categories	25,000	25,000
Total	3,199	62,906	66,105

1. Includes the Interstate Commerce Commission, the International Trade Commission, the Civil Aeronautics Board, the Federal Communications Commission, the National Railroad Commission, the Commodity Futures Trade Commission, the Federal Maritime Commission, and the Renegotiation Board.

INDUCED COSTS

Even more difficult to measure are the long-run effects on production that result from government regulation. Critics contend that regulation forces firms to allocate excessive portions of their budgets to mandated equipment rather than to investments in new product research and development. The costs of compliance push small firms out of many markets, leaving the way open to monopolization by giants. Finally, regulation may stifle new investment and entrepreneurial behavior in general. Weidenbaum does not attempt to measure these costs but recommends that the regulatory agencies consider them when making decisions based on regulatory policy.

ANOTHER VIEW

Weidenbaum's conclusions have been challenged by William K. Tabb, Associate Professor of Economics at Queens College CUNY. According to Tabb, the 20 to 1 multiplier Weidenbaum used in computing compliance costs conceals a wide variation of actual costs in different industries. For example, compliance with ICC regulations requires a 2,000 to 1 multiplier, and compliance with EPA regulations requires only a 12 to 1 multiplier. Actual compliance costs for the nation as a whole depend on the current regulatory mix. Moreover, most of the total costs are attributed to long-standing economic regulation, not, as Weidenbaum implies, to recent social legislation. Also, automobile safety and energy-conservation improvements should have been undertaken initially by the firms in response to market circumstances. And, finally, the cost assigned to paperwork in Weidenbaum's study is inordinately high, according to Tabb, since much of the paperwork would probably have been necessary without regulation. Social regulation, says Tabb, requires very little paperwork.

Most importantly, Professor Tabb is critical of Weidenbaum's failure to measure the benefits of regulation. The important consideration is not cost alone, he says, but *net benefits*—the difference between total benefits received and total costs incurred. Reduced health problems caused by the effects of the Clean Air Act may have yielded net benefits of as much as $21.4 billion in 1978. Net benefits in water purity, worker safety, drug regulation, and consumer safety and protection were estimated at $28.2 billion in the same year. These benefits, says Tabb, are substantially greater than the costs attributed to social regulation. In addition, he says, there are undoubtedly other external benefits—to the United States and to other nations—whose value is impossible to measure.

Source: Murray L. Weidenbaum, "The High Cost of Government Regulation," *Challenge*, November/December 1979, pp. 32–39.
William K. Tabb, "Government Regulation: Two Sides to the Story," *Challenge*, November/December 1980, pp. 40–48.

eliminate social costs entirely, that is, to reduce production to a level at which no external costs occur. A more suitable objective, they say, would be to conduct benefit-cost analyses to determine the level of production at which $MB/(MC + MC_s) = 1$. Quantifying external costs is difficult and controversial, however, and includes many risks and contradictions. Still, it must be attempted, and then the industries involved should be encouraged to conform to established standards.

Many of the recommendations for achieving compliance would rely on the use of market incentives rather than on coercive rules. For example, one proposal would set fines for discharging wastes in excess of some standard; firms would be expected to seek new technology for reducing wastes in order to escape the fine. A second proposal would call for the issue of pollution "licenses" to all firms, with the understanding that the licenses could be bought and sold among firms; the expected result would be a transfer of licenses to firms where pollution control would be especially costly, with other firms taking steps to eliminate pollution entirely. Finally, another proposal would tie employee health and safety insurance premiums directly to the incidence of accidents or disease; firms would take care to ensure safe working conditions so as to avoid high insurance costs.

Market-oriented incentives like these would encourage firms to seek solutions to complex environmental problems, rather than to evade nuisance regulations. Moreover, placing much of the responsibility on individual business firms relieves government bureaucrats of the necessity to mandate preventive measures or to design corrective technology.

SUMMARY

Much government intervention in markets has as its objective moving total production in the nation to the level of maximum efficiency, where the marginal benefits of production are equal to the marginal costs and net benefits are greatest. When there is market power in industry, total production may be held below the level of maximum efficiency. Legislation to moderate the effects of horizontal and vertical integration includes the Sherman Antitrust Act, the Interstate Commerce Act, the Clayton Antitrust Act, and the Celler-Kefauver Amendment. In recent decades, the judicial system has examined the problems associated with resale price maintenance, conglomerate mergers, and parallel behavior. In the 1970s, regulatory policy in the United States began to allow more competition in industries traditionally considered natural monopolies.

In the U.S. health sector, production may have been pushed beyond the level of maximum efficiency, causing marginal benefits to be less than marginal costs. This is in part because of the influence of third parties in health care markets. A major third party is the federal government, which is involved through its funding of the Medicare and Medicaid programs. There is great concern about the rising costs of health services. As a result, proposals to impose more market-oriented procedures in the health sector have been made.

The efficient level of total production is difficult to identify because of social costs that destroy the link between benefits and costs for individual consumers and are impossible to measure. Various pieces of legislation to set production standards in most industries were passed in the 1970s. Enforcing the legislation has been difficult and costly, and current proposals call for more market-oriented approaches to achieve environmental objectives.

KEY TERMS

marginal utility	conglomerate mergers
marginal costs	parallel behavior
net benefits	external costs
horizontal integration	social costs
vertical integration	

QUESTIONS AND PROBLEMS

1. List the efficiency characteristics of long-run competitive equilibrium that may be missing when competition is imperfect.

2. What is the rationale behind the shape of the curves in Figure 15.2?

3. Distinguish between horizontal and vertical integration and give examples of each. How can horizontally and vertically integrated firms achieve profitable advantages over their competitors?

4. What actions are prohibited by each of the major pieces of antitrust legislation? Discuss the features that weaken the effectiveness of each. What current business practices achieve a degree of market power outside the jurisdiction of current laws?

5. What are the advantages and disadvantages of conglomerate integration from the point of view of the firm and of the economy as a whole?

6. Distinguish between monopoly and natural monopoly and discuss the effects of each in terms of economic efficiency.

7. What characteristics of health care tend to move the health care industry outside the free market and reduce efficiency? Discuss current proposals for reforming the nation's health care industry in terms of efficiency of resource allocation, equity in the distribution of services, and economic incentives. What problems may be associated with each proposal?

8. What characteristics of resource use give rise to the problem of external or social costs? Identify local examples of external costs. How might such costs be measured?

9. Identify recent attempts to deal with the problem of social costs. What have been the weakness of these approaches?

10. What information is necessary for evaluating government policies toward business?

16

Production Decisions in Not-For-Profit Firms

Our economic system is described as a ''market system.'' Buyers and sellers come together in markets and agree on prices and terms of exchange. A fundamental characteristic of exchange in markets is that both buyers and sellers must be satisfied with the results of the exchange.

Before the full development of markets, exchange was not as systematic or efficient. Within primitive tribes, goods and services were shared on the basis of tradition or acknowledged need. Even with the early growth of markets, certain goods and services continued to be provided through non-market sources; religious rituals and cultural events are examples. In addition, certain kinds of entertainment were made available to all members of the community without charge. In the United States and most other modern nations, education and health services were eventually added to the list of services provided free or for prices below their costs of production.

These activities remain the major examples of goods and services produced for consumption by the community as a whole. The costs of production of these goods and services are met through non-market means. Because this kind of production is not intended to earn a profit, it is not subject to many of the conventional analyses described in this text. Nevertheless, because these producers are subject to the same resource limitations as other firms, most seek to accomplish their objectives efficiently. Toward this objective, many of the analytical tools described in this text are indeed applicable.

COLLECTIVE GOODS AND SERVICES

Certain goods and services are classified as "collective" goods and services because they can be used by the community as a whole. The earliest examples of such goods and services in the United States were roads and other transport facilities such as bridges, piers, lighthouses, and improved river channels for barge traffic. Governments provided such facilities through tax revenues. Public education was another collective service provided by government, and health and recreation facilities were added when the collective wealth of the community permitted.

Collective goods and services have a particular characteristic that is not true of other goods and services. Goods or services produced for individual use can be provided *exclusively* to consumers who are willing to pay the price of their use. When goods or services are provided to all citizens by government, however, it is not generally possible to exclude citizens of the jurisdiction from their use. (The captain of a ship cannot be prevented from seeing a lighthouse.) Thus, the distinguishing characteristic of collective goods and services is their "non-exclusivity."

Exclusivity versus **non-exclusivity** has a significant effect on the production and use of certain products. When a product is non-exclusive in consumption, consumers tend to use more than they might otherwise use and to avoid, insofar as possible, paying its price. (This is the reason public radio stations campaign so relentlessly for donations with so little apparent success.) Those who consume a collective good or service without paying for it are often referred to as "free riders." As a result of "free riders," producers of collective goods and services are plagued by shortages, excess demand, and insufficient revenues.

Demand for Collective Goods and Services

Collective goods and services today continue to be supplied primarily by governments. In addition, however, some of these products are now supplied by private firms. In fact, in certain types of production, private for-profit and not-for-profit firms compete with government for consumers' demand. The basis for production by private firms is illustrated in Figure 16.1 on page 470. Figure 16.1 represents a hypothetical community of five citizens whose demand for a particular collective service is based on the marginal utility the citizens expect to gain from its use. The five citizens' demand curves indicate their willingness to pay a certain price for particular quantities of health care, for example.[1]

---

1. See Burton A. Weisbrod, "Toward a Theory of the Voluntary Non-Profit Sector in a Three-Sector Economy," *Altruism, Morality, and Economic Theory,* ed. Edmond S. Phelps (New York: Russell Sage Foundation, 1975).

FIGURE 16.1   **Demand for a Collective Good or Service**

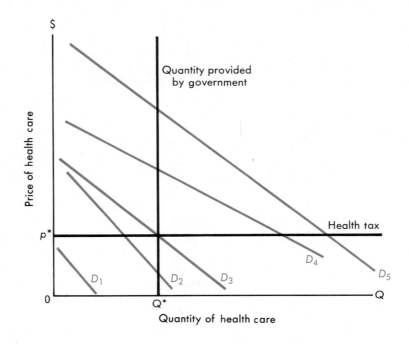

The local government is willing to provide tax-supported health care up to some quantity and price appearing on the demand curve of the median (or middle) citizen (citizen number 3 in our example). Thus, the quantity Q^* will be made available to all citizens at no charge. The price of that quantity, p^*, will constitute a health tax, which will be collected from all the citizens in this jurisdiction regardless of the quantity of health care they actually use.

Notice that at Q^* and p^*, citizens 1 and 2 will be more than satisfied with the available quantity of health care. In fact, citizens 1 and 2 will receive a total quantity of health care for which their marginal utility is less than the tax they pay. (Citizens 1 and 2 may eventually use their influence to try to reduce the quantity of health care provided from their tax revenues, but that is a subject for another text.) Notice also that citizens 4 and 5 would be willing to pay over and above the amount of their present health-care tax bill for access to a larger quantity of health services.

Consumer Surplus and the Entry of Private Firms

Differences in demand among consumers lead to differences in "consumer surplus." **Consumer surplus** is the total utility consumers gain from consumption of a good or service *less* the total cost they pay. Look again at Figure 16.1.

For consumer 3, the total utility from consuming health care is represented by the entire space under that consumer's demand curve up to the actual quantity consumed at Q^*. The total cost paid is the area under the price line p^* up to Q^*. Therefore, consumer 3's consumer surplus is the area of the space under his or her demand curve to the left of Q^* and above p^*. Consumers whose expected marginal utility from health care is greater (so that their demand curves lie farther to the right) will enjoy greater consumer surplus than consumers with lower expected marginal utility. (Note that citizen 1 in our example has negative consumer surplus.)

Whenever some members of a potential market are unsatisfied with the current quantity of production, there exists unexploited consumer surplus, shown as the areas between their demand curves and price to the right of Q^*. In such cases, there are opportunities for other suppliers to move into the market. "For-profit" firms may be expected to supply specialized service for those consumers who are willing to pay the full cost of individualized health care. "Not-for-profit" firms may provide low-cost health care and depend on voluntary contributions or some type of public subsidy to help pay their costs. The price of the collective good or service set by private firms will determine the distribution of consumer surplus: that is, the portion captured by the supplying firm and the portion retained by the consumer.

For-profit and not-for-profit firms can both reduce the "free rider problem" and gain a degree of exclusivity for their customers. In the case of for-profit firms, exclusive consumption of the product is assured consumers who will pay the full costs of production, including economic profit. In the case of not-for-profit firms, a degree of exclusivity is assured consumers who pay a certain price for the product. However, since price is (by definition) less than full production costs in not-for-profit firms, consumers may be asked to make voluntary contributions to production. Often, consumers who are willing to make voluntary contributions are assured a greater degree of exclusivity. This is the reason consumers who purchase season tickets for symphony concerts are assured preferred seating, while contributors may be offered the additional opportunity to attend special commemorative concerts not open to the general public.

Equilibrium in the Market for Collective Goods and Services

The ultimate equilibrium condition in the production of collective goods and services may include:

1. public goods or services provided by government and financed through tax revenues,
2. ordinary private goods or services provided by for-profit firms at market prices, and
3. imperfect substitutes for both of these categories provided by not-for-profit firms at prices generally below full costs.

Examples of the three types of service are public police protection provided for all citizens free of charge, private security systems for citizens who pay full costs of the service, and neighborhood watch organizations for members who pay a membership fee and possibly donate their time or money as well. Other examples are public libraries available to all citizens of a jurisdiction, books and periodicals purchased at market prices and held in private collections, and university research libraries frequently limited to use by enrolled students. In all of these cases, there are alternative versions of the basic good or service that are suitable for production by government or by a variety of for-profit and not-for-profit firms.

Income Elasticity of Demand and Demand for Collective Goods

The division of production of collective goods and services between government and private for-profit and not-for-profit firms may depend on the level of income in the community and on income elasticity of demand. With high income elasticity, rising consumer incomes will cause demand curves to shift to the right, increasing unexploited consumer surplus and encouraging the entry of private firms.

With an increase in private suppliers of a good or service, consumers can obtain increased *control* over the product's quality and improved assurance of its *availability*. More private suppliers also make possible more heterogeneous production that will satisfy a wider variety of consumers' preferences. In fact, in any community, the greater the variety of consumer preferences, the more production we would expect to find in private firms and the less production we would expect to find in the government sector. In the health-care industry, for example, we find hospital services (measured by expenditures) provided in the following proportions in the United States:

22 percent provided by government;

5 percent provided by private for-profit firms; and

73 percent provided by private not-for-profit firms.

Private health-care firms tend to specialize in particular kinds of health services, while public and not-for-profit firms provide more comprehensive types of health care. This division of production enables U.S. citizens to satisfy a wide range of health-care preferences.

SOME COMPARISONS BETWEEN FOR-PROFIT AND NOT-FOR-PROFIT FIRMS

Many of the assumptions we have employed for analyzing production in for-profit firms in this text are not appropriate for analyzing not-for-profit firms. The most obvious is the assumption of profit-maximizing as the firm's objective. Although we have recognized the validity of other objectives—sales maximization, growth, technical supremacy—none of these objectives is really consistent with the goals of not-for-profit firms.

Analysis of not-for-profit firms differs in an even more fundamental way than this, however. Microeconomic analysis depends fundamentally on measurements to achieve *efficiency* in the allocation of productive resources:

1. Managers must be able to measure the value of resources and their marginal products when they are used in various production functions. Although these measurements may not be precise, they are essential for deciding efficient technologies and projecting costs of production.
2. Managers must also be able to evaluate consumers' marginal utilities and estimate demand curves in particular markets. Understanding the values buyers place on particular goods and services enables the firm to plan efficient production and set prices.
3. Finally, managers must be able to put together all of their measurements of costs, total output, and price to project the rate of return on investments in productive assets. Decisions based on these final measurements determine the firm's capacity to satisfy consumers' demands efficiently and ensure sufficient revenues for efficient operation in the long run.

Not-for-profit firms are similar to for-profit firms in only one of these measurement questions. In general, not-for-profit firms compete with for-profit firms in the same markets for productive resources. Prices of productive resources are determined through the demand of all firms in the market for the limited supplies of a particular resource. If both for-profit and not-for-profit firms use the same production technology, we would expect their costs of production to be the same. Beyond this similarity, a fundamental difference separates for-profit and not-for-profit firms: that is, the inability of not-for-profit firms to measure the value of output.

In certain not-for-profit firms, this difference is even more fundamental in that they are unable even to *define* output. For example, what is the output of a public library? Is it the number of visitors to the library, the number of books checked out, its hours of operation, or the percentage of local population it reaches? Even less precise than this, what is the output of the U.S. Postal Service? Is it the amount of mail delivered, the distance traveled by the mail, the number of homes and businesses served, the number of advertising circulars delivered, or the number of mail orders solicited? When it is impossible to define a firm's product, measuring its value is equally impossible.

One further complication of the analysis of not-for-profit firms is that much of their productive activity is not expected to yield a return until far in the future. The public libarary may help prepare young readers for productive careers in adulthood, at which time their higher tax payments may return to the government to finance increased library services. The postal service may help establish the networks among markets that make possible large-scale production at lower costs and that yield higher profits to tax-paying firms at some time in the future. Measles vaccinations dispensed by public health nurses may eventually eliminate this disease, resulting in future reductions in time lost from work and reductions in birth defects.

The problem facing the not-for-profit firm is to project and evaluate future benefits resulting from production and choose a rate of discount that reflects the community's preference for benefits today over benefits in the future. Whenever the net present value of a service is positive, investments may be made in its production. Such projections are difficult enough for the for-profit firm to make, but they are virtually impossible for the not-for-profit firm. Therefore, microeconomic analysis cannot always ensure efficiency in production for not-for-profit firms.

The Consequences

When goods and services are exchanged in markets, consumers select combinations in which marginal utility per dollar of purchase price is equal for all purchases:

$$MU_a/p_a = MU_b/p_b \ldots = MU_z/p_z.$$

This result is described as efficient because it results in maximum total utility within the individual consumer's budget. Prices and quantities of goods and services are determined at the level at which marginal revenue is equal to marginal cost: $MR = MC$. Moreover, in long run competitive equilibrium, the entry and exit of firms into a particular industry pushes market price toward equality with long-run average cost:

$$MR = MC = p = \text{Minimum } LRAC.$$

This result is efficient because it guarantees that the community's productive resources are allocated according to the priorities of consumers in the community as a whole. The central force for bringing about these efficient results is market price.

With collective goods and services, however, there is no well-established pricing mechanism to ensure efficient results. Without such prices, consumers have no way to express their subjective preferences. (They may be completely unaware of such preferences, having become so accustomed to the availability of collective goods and services from non-market sources that they can't imagine life without them.)

Without prices and marginal revenues, not-for-profit firms have difficulty deciding the most efficient quantity of output. To make matters worse, many not-for-profit firms produce such a heterogeneous "bundle" of goods and services that the problem of deciding prices and quantities is complicated even further. Finally, not-for-profit firms differ widely among themselves both in the goods or services they produce and in the priorities they place on alternative types of production.

COST EFFECTIVENESS THROUGH LINEAR PROGRAMMING

Given these fundamental gaps in information regarding not-for-profit firms, it is appropriate to identify certain tools of analysis that can be used to accomplish the firm's goals efficiently. Most not-for-profit firms can be expected to establish measurable goals such as number of season tickets sold, number of vaccinations administered, or number of passengers carried. An institution's goals reflect the firm's expected types of output and, thus, the firm's priorities. A library that stresses hours of operation as a measurement of output, for example, has fundamentally different priorities from one that stresses the number of new acquisitions.

On the basis of the firm's goals, it is possible to use some of the tools of managerial economics to decide productive strategy: more specifically, to choose the most efficient quantities of resources for achieving acknowledged goals.

Achieving efficient production involves analysis of the "cost-effectiveness" of production. Cost-effectiveness analysis determines the lowest-cost combination of resources for producing a desired quantity of output. Cost-effectiveness ensures the maximum utility to the community (in terms of total production of goods and services) with the least expenditure of scarce resources.

When production has the characteristics of a linear production function, linear programming is particularly well-suited for cost-effectiveness problems. The goal of the not-for-profit firm is the desired level of production, and the firm's objective function is to minimize the costs associated with achieving the goal. Thus, the linear programming model identifies the most efficient combination of resources for achieving the firm's production goals.

To illustrate cost-effectiveness analysis, let us consider an educational institution supported by students' tuition fees plus a tax-financed subsidy from government. The institution serves three kinds of students: on-campus students, off-campus students, and executive education students. The goal of the institution is to serve at least 8,000 on-campus students, at least 5,000 off-campus students, and at least 1,200 executive education students. More students in each category may be served, but the amounts we have given are the minimum accepted quantities.

The different categories of students can be served through various combinations of professional faculty and electronic transmission equipment (videotape recorders, live video broadcasts, computer terminals, and so forth). For example, on-campus students can be served by professional faculty in the ratio of 40 students per faculty member, while off-campus students would require instruction in the ratio of 10 students per faculty member. On the other hand, on-campus students can be served efficiently by electronic instructional units in the ratio of 10 students to one unit, and off-campus students can use this equipment in the ratio of 50 to one.

In a cost-effectiveness problem, the constraint inequalities define the relationships between resource requirements and the minimum acceptable quantity of output in each of the product categories. The axes or variables represent quantities of particular resources. Thus, the resource constraint describing on-campus education would be:

$$40(Y) + 10(X) \geq 8,000 \text{ on-campus students,}$$

where Y represents quantity of professional faculty and X represents quantity of electronic instructional units. The constraint inequality tells us that 8,000 on-campus students could be served by 200 professional faculty or 800 electronic instructional units, or any combination of the two resources between these extremes on a linear path described by the graph of this inequality.

Similarly, the resource constraints for off-campus and executive education students would be:

$$10(Y) + 50(X) \geq 5,000 \text{ off-campus students,}$$

and

$$3(Y) + 4(X) \geq 1,200 \text{ executive education students.}$$

As is true in other cost-minimizing problems, the technology of production governs the relationship between productive resources and the desired quantity of output.

FIGURE 16.2   **Constraints in a Cost-Minimization Problem**

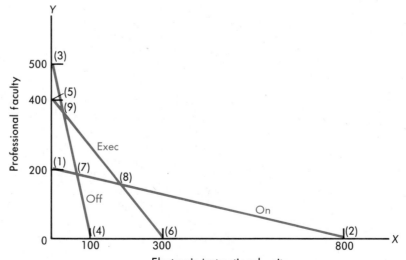

The feasible solutions in the cost-minimization problem are (3), (9), (8), and (2). With prices of $p_F = \$40,000$ and $p_E = \$100,000$, the lowest cost solution is (9). If the price of electronic instructional units should fall to $p_E = \$50,000$, the lowest cost solution would change to (8).

Figure 16.2 is a graph of the constraint equations. The feasible space lies to the right of all the constraints, where all quantities are at least as great as the institution's goals.

The cost function is the objective function in the cost-minimization problem. With the annual prices of faculty and electronic units fixed at $p_F = \$40,000$ and $p_E = \$100,000$, the objective function is written

Minimize $(TC) = \$40,000(Y) + \$100,000(X)$.

Linear programming enables us to identify the combination of faculty and electronic equipment that serves the desired numbers of students at the lowest cost. Thus, linear programming locates the point in the feasible space that achieves the institution's goals most efficiently.

The Solution

To solve our problem, we must first re-write the constraint inequalities to include surplus variables. Remember that a cost-minimization problem requires negative values for the surplus variables in order to change the expression from an inequality to an equality. The constraint equations are:

$$40(Y) + 10(X) - S_{on} = 8,000 \text{ on-campus students,}$$
$$10(Y) + 50(X) - S_{off} = 5,000 \text{ off-campus students,}$$

and

$$3(Y) + 4(X) - S_{ex} = 1,200 \text{ executive education students.}$$

Now, we must set up a table listing all possible values of the variables, given that for any solution at least two variables will be equal to zero. This is shown in Table 16.1.

TABLE 16.1

	Y	X	S_{on}	S_{off}	S_{ex}	
(1)	200	0	0	3,000	600	
(2)	0	800	0	−35,000	−2,000	*
(3)	500	0	−12,000	0	−300	*
(4)	0	100	7,000	0	800	
(5)	400	0	−8,000	1,000	0	
(6)	0	300	5,000	−10,000	0	
(7)	184.21	63.16	0	0	394.73	
(8)	153.85	184.62	0	−5,769.5	0	*
(9)	363.64	27.27	−6,818.33	0	0	*

Solutions (1) through (6) were computed by solving each constraint equation separately setting first X and then Y equal to zero and the appropriate surplus variables equal to zero. Thus, solutions (1) through (6) represent intersections with either the horizontal or vertical axis, as shown in Figure 16.2. The values of the remaining two surplus variables in (1) through (6) were determined by substituting the previously determined values of X and Y in the remaining two constraint equations and solving for the appropriate surplus variables.

For solution (1), using the on-campus constraint with $X = 0$ and $S_{on} = 0$,

$$40(Y) + 10(0) - 0 = 8,000,$$

and $Y = 200$. Substituting these values in the off-campus constraint yields:

$$10(200) - 50(0) - S_{off} = 5,000,$$

and $S_{off} = 3,000$. Substituting these values in the executive education constraint yields:

$$3(200) - 4(0) - S_{ex} = 1,200$$

and $S_{ex} = 600$.

Solutions (7), (8), and (9) were computed by taking the constraint equations in pairs, setting the surplus variables equal to zero, and solving the two constraint equations simultaneously. Once values of X and Y were determined, their values were substituted in the remaining constraint equation and the surplus variable was determined.

For solution (7), using the on-campus and off-campus constraints,

$$40(Y) + 10(X) - 0 = 8,000,$$

and,

$$10(Y) + 50(X) - 0 = 5,000,$$

yields values of $X = 63.16$ and $Y = 184.21$.

Substituting these values in the executive education constraint yields:

$$3(184.21) + 4(63.16) - S_{ex} = 1,200$$

and $S_{ex} = 394.73$.

For $X = 63.16$ and $Y = 184.21$, the executive education constraint tells us that $3(184.21) + 4(63.16) = 805.27$ executive education students would be served. This is $1,200 - 805.27 = 394.73$ less than the institution's goal, indicating that solution (7) is not a feasible solution. We also know this because the sign of the surplus variable (S_{ex}) is positive. In fact, if any of the surplus variables associated with a particular solution is a positive number, the solution lies outside the feasible space. (A positive surplus variable indicates the constraint is under-fulfilled.)

In this example, the feasible solutions are (2), (3), (8), and (9), denoted by an asterisk in the solutions table. The next step in finding our solution would be to compute the value of the objective function at each solution and select the minimum value. Total costs associated with solutions (2), (3), (8), and (9) are determined by the substitution of our previous values in the total cost equations:

(2) $TC = \$40,000(0) + \$100,000(800) = \$80,000,000,$
(3) $TC = \$40,000(500) + \$100,000(0) = \$20,000,000,$
(8) $TC = \$40,000(153.85) + \$100,000(184.62) = \$24,616,000,$

and

(9) $TC = \$40,000(363.64) + \$100,000(27.27) = \$17,272,600.$

The most efficient resource combination for achieving the institution's goals is shown in solution (9). With 363.64 faculty units and 27.27 electronic units, the institution will produce the desired numbers of off-campus and executive education students, and 6,818 "surplus" on-campus students.

A Change in Resource Price

Now let us suppose a technological advance occurs that reduces the price of electronic instructional units to $50,000 per year. The new prices yield the following values for total costs:

(2) $TC = \$40,000(0) + \$50,000(800) = \$40,000,000,$
(3) $TC = \$40,000(500) + \$50,000(0) = \$20,000,000,$
(8) $TC = \$40,000(153.85) + \$50,000(184.62) = \$15,385,000,$

and

(9) $TC = \$40,000(363.64) + \$50,000(27.27) = \$15,909,100.$

The price change has the effect of making solution (8) more cost-effective. With 153.85 faculty units and 184.62 electronic units, the institution will produce the desired number of on-campus and executive education students and 5,769.5 "surplus" off-campus students. Furthermore, the total cost of the instructional program has been reduced from $17,272,600 to $15,385,100 annually.

OPTIMIZATION TO MINIMIZE THE PUBLIC SUBSIDY

Cost-effectiveness analysis is not entirely satisfactory in analyzing the production decisions of not-for-profit firms. The reason is that cost-effectiveness analysis assumes that measurable goals will actually be achieved. This result is not always assured, since shortfalls in revenues may force adjustments in production goals.

Certain not-for-profit institutions provide services to citizens of the local community at prices that are below costs of production. The objective in such cases is to encourage maximum consumption of a service that is expected to yield external economies to the community as a whole. Often, producers of the service experience increasing returns to scale, such that a larger volume of service can be produced at lower average total cost.

Under these conditions total revenue from sales may be insufficient to pay total costs, and a subsidy may be required. Government pays this subsidy as a means of ensuring certain advantages to the community that should result from broad participation. Some examples of government-subsidized services are:

1. Low-cost higher education, which is expected to raise the level of skills and ultimately the tax-paying capacity of the local workforce.
2. Cultural or recreational services, which help bring emotional and physical well-being to community members and help attract new job-producing industry to an area.
3. Mass transit, which reduces the use of private automobiles (with their accompanying congestion and environmental damage) and makes employment possible for otherwise immobile workers.

One characteristic of these kinds of activities is increasing returns to scale. All of these activities require heavy investment in plant and equipment or in specially trained personnel. Once the initial investment is made, however, it is generally possible to satisfy higher and higher demand for the service at lower average cost. While revenue from sales will never be expected to cover full costs, producing a larger volume will reduce the difference between price and average total cost and may reduce the necessary subsidy from public sources. Thus, increasing participation in the service achieves more of the advantages expected from its use while reducing the necessary public expenditure for the service.

A Sample Problem

To illustrate production decisions in which a public subsidy is required, let us look at a hypothetical mass transit system located in a congested urban area. Significant investment must be made to bring the transit system into operation, but variable costs associated with providing the service are relatively low. Because fixed costs per unit of service fall sharply as service increases, average total costs decline over a wide range of output. In cases such as this, average total cost may be considerably greater than price for a small volume, but the difference between price and average total cost diminishes as volume increases.

One goal of the mass transit system might be to provide the quantity of service at the corresponding price that minimizes the deficit to be funded through public subsidy. The problem is a typical optimization problem except that instead of identifying the *profit-maximizing* levels of p and Q, the goal is to identify the *loss-minimizing* levels.

Let us assume that surveys of ridership in similar communities have produced the following estimate of demand for any 24-hour period:

$$p = 100 - .4(Q),$$

where p is price in cents and Q is number of riders in thousands. This is a typical linear demand curve, showing that larger quantities will be purchased only if price is reduced.

For $p = 100 - .4(Q)$, total revenue is determined by

$$TR = p(Q) = 100(Q) - 0.4(Q^2).$$

Total revenue increases with quantity of service along the segment of the demand curve where percentage increase in quantity is greater than percentage decrease in price (that is, where demand is elastic). At some level of service, further price reductions would result in smaller percentage increases in quantity (demand is inelastic), and total revenue would fall.

The cost functions facing the transit firm are also typical of cost functions for many collective goods and services. The large initial capital investment makes fixed costs high, but variable costs are relatively low. Managers have estimated average variable costs according to the following quadratic cost equation:

$$AVC = 172 - 1.5(Q) + .005(Q^2),$$

where AVC is cost in cents, and Q is number of riders per day in thousands.[2]

This is a typical saucer-shaped cost function that reaches its minimum where the derivative of the function is equal to zero (and the second derivative is positive). Thus, $dAVC/dQ = -1.5 + .01(Q) = 0$, and $Q = 150,000$ riders per day represents the level of plant operation that minimizes unit variable costs.

The demand and average variable cost equations are graphed in Figure 16.3 on page 482. Fixed costs of $20,000 per day were divided by Q and added to AVC to yield the curve labeled ATC. The equation for total cost is:

$$TC = FC + Q(AVC) = 2,000 + 172(Q) - 1.5(Q^2) + .005(Q^3).$$

(Because Q is measured in thousands and costs are measured in cents in this equation, fixed costs of $20,000 have been converted to dimensions consistent with the other variables in the equation.)

---

2. Both the demand and cost equations were estimated through the regression techniques explained in Chapter 3.

FIGURE 16.3   Demand and Average Variable Cost

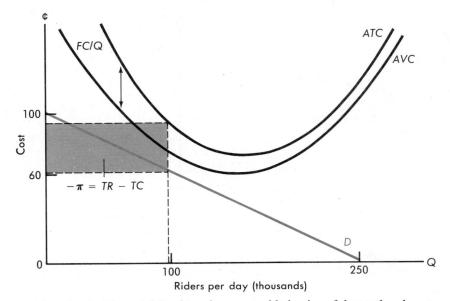

Riders per day (thousands)

Note that in Figure 16.3, given the assumed behavior of demand and costs, no single price would be sufficient to cover average total costs, so that the transit firm will always operate at a loss:

Economic loss $(-\pi) = TC - TR > 0$.

The loss will have to be offset by a subsidy from public funds.

Deciding Quantity and Price

The objective of the transit firm in this example is to set the price at which the difference between total cost and total revenue is at a minimum. To determine the loss-minimizing quantity and price, first write an equation for economic loss:

$$-\pi = TC - TR = [2,000 + 172(Q) - 1.5(Q^2) + .005(Q^3)]$$
$$- [100(Q) - .4(Q^2)]$$
$$= 2,000 + 72(Q) - 1.1(Q^2) + .005(Q^3).$$

Economic loss is minimized where $d\pi/dQ = 0$. Thus,

$$\frac{d\pi}{dQ} = 72 - 2.2(Q) + .015(Q^2).$$

Use of the quadratic formula (or a pocket calculator) reveals the following values for Q: $Q = 49.3$ and $Q = 97.37$. These are the values of Q where $d\pi/dQ$ becomes more horizontal. The minimum of the function occurs where $d\pi^2/d^2Q$ is positive. Substituting the values for Q in the second derivative yields:

$$-2.2 + .03(Q) = -2.2 + .03(49.3) = -.72 < 0,$$

and

$$-2.2 + .03(Q) = -2.2 + .03(97.37) = +.72 > 0.$$

The positive second derivative tells us that minimum economic loss occurs where $Q = 97.37$.[3] The corresponding price for $Q = 97.37$ is determined by substitution in the demand equation:

$$p = 100 - .4(97.37) = 61.05 = \text{approximately 60 cents.}$$

Economic loss at $Q = 97.37$ and $p = 61.05$ is represented in Figure 16.3 by the shaded rectangle formed between ATC and the demand curve. Average or unit economic loss is shown as the dashed line between $p = 61.05$ measured on the demand curve at $Q = 97.37$ and $ATC = 93.89$ and is equal to 32.84 cents per rider. Total economic loss per day is

$$-\pi = TC - TR = 9,142.07 - 5,944.44 = 3,197.63,$$

which equals \$31,976.30 per day when converted to appropriate dimensions for this problem. This is the smallest economic loss rectangle possible with current demand and cost conditions.

The behavior of TC and TR can easily be seen in Figure 16.4a on page 484, which uses the same horizontal axis as Figure 16.3. TR reaches a peak at $Q = 125$, the point at which elasticity of demand is equal to one. Total variable cost rises slowly at first as volume of service approaches the level of minimum average variable cost. The constant fixed cost of \$20,000 per day has been added to total variable cost. Economic loss is represented by the vertical distance between TC and TR. This distance is greatest where $Q = 49.3$ and least where $Q = 97.37$. Beyond $Q = 97.37$, the TC and TR curves diverge sharply and economic loss increases. Economic loss is graphed separately in Figure 16.4b.

---

3. Obviously, economic loss is lowest where $Q = 0$ and increases beyond $= 97.35$. The use of differential calculus identifies the "local" maximum or minimum and is appropriate for solutions with values of Q other than 0.

FIGURE 16.4   Total Revenue and Total Cost

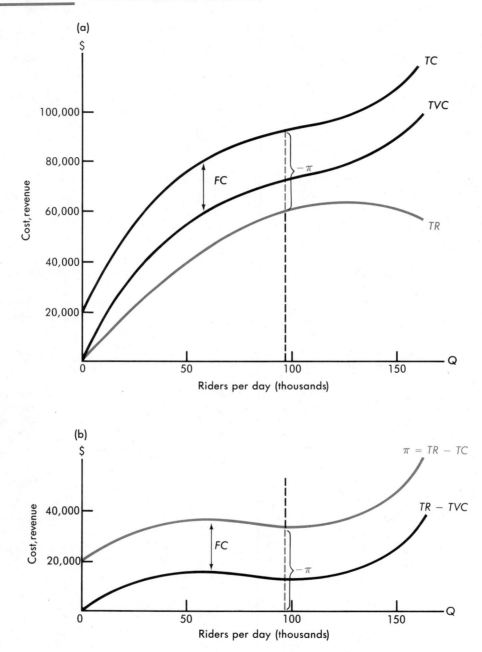

Increasing Demand to Reduce Economic Loss

A not-for-profit firm might decide to undertake certain promotional activities with the aim of increasing demand and reducing economic loss. The significant variables in the decision would be the cost of the promotional campaign and the expected reduction in economic loss.

A change in demand is shown in Figure 16.5. In Figure 16.5, the demand curve has shifted to the right to include 50,000 more passengers at each price level. The equation for the new demand curve is

$$p = 120 - .4(Q).$$

With the increase in demand, more passengers can be served at a smaller economic loss per passenger, as indicated by the smaller distance between ATC and the demand curve in Figure 16.5. The loss-minimizing quantity of service occurs where $Q = 117,050$ passengers, at a price of $p = 120 - .4(117.05) = 73.18 =$ approximately 75 cents. Total revenue is

$$TR = 120(Q) - .4(Q^2) = \$85,657.20 \text{ per day},$$

and total cost is

$$TC = 2,000 + 172(Q) - 1.5(Q^2) + .005(Q^3) = \$95,998.80,$$

FIGURE 16.5   **An Increase in Demand**

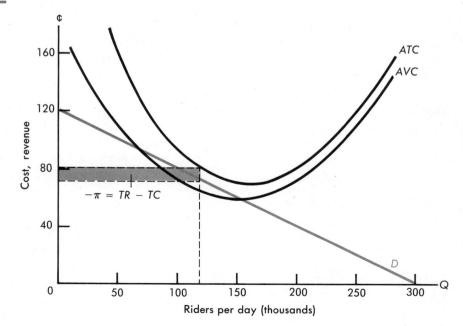

for economic loss of \$10,341.60 per day. This represents an improvement of \$31,976.30 − \$10,341.60 = \$21,634.70 per day, and a loss of less than 9 cents per rider. Moreover, the benefits to the community associated with the reduction in traffic congestion and environmental pollution presumably are greater with increased public participation in the transit service.

Still, managers will compare the expected gain from the reduced subsidy over some future period of time with the cost of the promotional campaign. If future campaigns could shift demand even further to the right, it is conceivable that economic loss might be reduced to zero. In fact, with 160,000 riders per day and a price of only 72.5 cents per rider, the transit system would be operating at maximum efficiency and without a public subsidy. Look at the *ATC* curve in Figure 16.5 to verify this result.

RETURNS TO SCALE AND THE NOT-FOR-PROFIT FIRM

The preceding sections revealed an important characteristic of production in firms producing collective goods and services. Many such firms require substantial initial investment in plant, equipment, and specialized personnel, causing fixed costs for any period of time to be relatively high. Variable costs of production are low relative to fixed costs and low relative to the variable costs of producing comparable goods and services in private firms. Under these conditions, we would expect the firms producing collective goods and services to enjoy increasing returns to scale.

Increasing returns to scale in the production of collective goods and services may justify efforts on the part of not-for-profit firms to expand their markets and increase their level of service to the community. By providing larger quantities of desired goods or services at decreasing average total costs, not-for-profit firms increase the total utility enjoyed by the community as a whole.

Sources of Increasing (and Decreasing) Returns to Scale

Increasing returns to scale typically result from the intensive use of physical facilities such as laboratories, conference rooms, and equipment. In educational institutions, increasing returns to scale are associated with increasing the ratio of students to teachers. In universities that conduct research, there are further opportunities for increasing returns to scale when an increased number of specialists in a particular area stimulates the generation of ideas relevant to the research activity. Larger educational institutions also have the advantage of larger administrative staffs, with specialized functions appropriate to the institution's objectives. Large medical institutions enjoy all these returns to scale in addition to the advantages associated with a larger professional staff with more diverse medical specializations.

We might summarize the sources of increasing returns to scale in the production of collective goods and services under the following headings:

1. *Standardization of procedures.* When a large volume of similar work is to be accomplished, it is generally possible to simplify and standardize certain procedures in such a way that the administrative costs associated with each are reduced. There may be offsetting decreasing returns to scale at some level of production, however, if standardization results in a decrease in attention to detail and a deterioration in quality of work.

2. *Opportunities for diversification.* Large-scale production makes investments in a more diverse productive capacity possible in terms of both material and human resources. Some analysts refer to opportunities for diversification in not-for-profit firms as "economies of scope." At some level of diversification, however, a not-for-profit firm may become unwieldy and difficult to manage efficiently, causing it to experience decreasing returns.

3. *Development of and investment in new technology.* The impetus for development of and investment in new technology is similar to that for other investments: the initial costs and the risks associated with innovative investment can more readily be justified if the investment is to be used intensively. Large-scale institutions can spread the costs and risks over more units of service, possibly causing average or unit costs to be lower for large-scale institutions than for small-scale institutions.

4. *Specialization in administrative functions.* The administrative staff of a large-scale not-for-profit institution can include persons with specialized skills appropriate for assisting professional staff in the performance of their duties. The result may be increased output among the most costly personnel, with correspondingly reduced average costs. Again, at some level an institution risks the onset of decreasing returns from further specialization. Decreasing returns occur when personnel become so specialized that it becomes increasingly difficult for managers to coordinate job functions, causing resource productivity to decline.

5. *Removal of competition in fund-raising activities.* Whether a not-for-profit institution is supported through a government subsidy or through private contributions, it faces the problem of a limited source of funding. Applying a concentrated fund to a substantial volume of needed goods or services appears more efficient to many contributors than using separate funds for a wider range of services. By reducing the number of persons required to solicit, budget, and administer funds, a large-scale not-for-profit institution increases the portion of available funds that can be used for actual provision of the service. Again, there may be decreasing returns associated with institutions that reach such a large scale that contributors lose the personal satisfaction associated with supporting smaller, more immediate causes.

MAXIMIZING OUTPUT WITH A BUDGET CONSTRAINT

One further microeconomic model may be useful for analyzing production in a not-for-profit firm. This is the model that maximizes output with a budget constraint (explained in Chapter 7). (The same results can be achieved through simple algebra or through the use of a LaGrangian multiplier.)

Consider a health clinic that charges fees below costs of production and receives a fixed subsidy from the local government. The clinic seeks to maximize the total number of patients treated within this fixed budget constraint. Assume that production requires the use of professional (P) and nonprofessional (N) medical personnel: physicians and nurses, on the one hand, and paramedics and medical technicians, on the other. The daily cost of personnel is $p_P = 300$ and $p_N = 100$. The total cost per day of operating the clinic is

$$TC = P(p_p) + N(p_N),$$

where N and P are quantities of professional and non-professional personnel employed.

The production function for the clinic is estimated to behave according to a multiplicative function of the form

$$TP = a(P^b)(N^c)$$

where TP is the number of patients served per day, P and N are the quantities of professional and non-professional personnel employed, and the exponents b and c are the elasticities of production of the respective personnel variables.

Managers have estimated the parameters of the production function in such a way that

$$TP = 3.2 \ (P^{.45}) \ (N^{.63}).[4]$$

Currently, the clinic employs $P = 35$ and $N = 55$ personnel and serves an average of

$$TP = 3.2 \ (35^{.45}) \ (55^{.63}) = 197.88 \text{ patients per day.}$$

Total costs per day are

$$TC = 35(300) + 55(100) = \$16,000,$$

which is the budget constraint imposed by the clinic's total fees plus the regular appropriation from the local government.

---

4. Note that the sum of the exponents indicates that the clinic is operating in the range of increasing returns to scale.

The clinic's managers want to ensure that resources are used most efficiently: that is, that the maximum number of patients is served within the budget constraint. Managers are prepared to vary the numbers of professional and non-professional personnel if the result will be to increase the number of patients served within the clinic's fixed budget. To achieve maximum efficiency in production, the marginal product per dollar for all resources must be equal. Stated differently, the marginal products of the resources employed must be proportional to their respective marginal costs:

$$MP_P/MP_N = p_P/p_N.$$

The marginal products of the two resources are determined by taking the partial derivatives of the production function with respect to each of the variable resources. Thus, the marginal product of professional personnel is

$$MP_P = \partial TP/\partial P = .45[3.2(P^{.45-1})(N^{.63})]$$

and the marginal product of non-professional personnel is

$$MP_N = \partial TP/\partial N = .63[3.2(P^{.45})(N^{.63-1})].$$

The ratio of marginal products is

$$\frac{MP_P}{MP_N} = \frac{.45[3.2(P^{.45-1})(N^{.63})]}{.63[3.2(P^{.45})(N^{.63-1})]},$$

which reduces to

$$\frac{MP_P}{MP_N} = \frac{.45(N)}{.63(P)}.$$

The ratio of prices is

$$\frac{p_P}{p_N} = \frac{300}{100} = \frac{3}{1}.$$

Maximum output occurs where the ratio of marginal products is equal to the price ratio:

$$\frac{.45(N)}{.63(P)} = \frac{3}{1}.$$

This result can be interpreted as follows: Because the price of professional resources is three times the price of non-professional resources, their marginal products must also be in the ratio of three to one. The most efficient quantities of P and N are determined jointly where their marginal products achieve this ratio.

Solving, we find that

$$\frac{.45(N)}{.63(P)} = \frac{3}{1}$$

indicates that

$$45(N) = 189 \ (P),$$

so that $N = 4.2(P)$. That is, for most efficient production the quantity of non-professional personnel should be 4.2 times the quantity of professional personnel.

The actual quantities of resources employed are limited by the fixed budget appropriation of $TC = \$16,000$ per day. This means that total employment is

$$TC = \$16,000 = P(\$300) + [4.2(P)](\$100)$$

and

$$720(P) = \$16,000,$$

so that $P = 22.22$ and $N = 4.2(22.22) = 93.33$. With these resources, the number of patients served is

$$TP = 3.2(22.22^{.45})(93.33^{.63}) = 225.07,$$

for an increase of 14 percent per day within the current budget.

Note that by increasing the resource with the greater elasticity of production and the lower price, the clinic is able to increase its contribution to total utility in the community.

The model used here is appropriate for a wide range of managerial decisions that involve a cost constraint. It is useful for production functions of the linear, quadratic, or cubic form, as well as for multiplicative production functions. In each case, the procedure is to take the deriviative of the total product function with respect to the separate resource variables and set the ratio of marginal products equal to the ratio of prices:

$$\frac{MP_A}{MP_B} = \frac{p_A}{p_B}.$$

Once the most efficient proportion of resource quantities is determined, it is a simple matter to substitute this value in the cost function and compute the most efficient quantities.

THE ECONOMIC IMPACT OF NOT-FOR-PROFIT FIRMS

This chapter has described the role of not-for-profit firms in terms of their production of collective goods and services and their contributions to external economies in the community as a whole. External economies include the benefits associated with improved health and education, availability of cultural and recreational facilities, and opportunities for employment in a wider variety of business firms. Although external economies cannot be precisely measured, it *is* possible to estimate the economic impact of not-for-profit firms in terms of the expenditures they generate that are received by for-profit firms in the area. The economic impact of not-for-profit firms includes both the expenditures made by such firms and expenditures made by persons associated with the firms themselves.

Any expenditure sets in motion a chain of additional expenditures that enrich numerous recipients all along the chain. A purchase of a load of a bread, for instance, enriches first the grocer, the baker, the miller, and the farmer. Then each of these recipients re-spends some portion of the initial receipt, so that other retailers, wholesalers, and manufacturers also receive increases in income. Economists define the total change in income that results from a single dollar of new expenditure as the ''multiplier effect.'' The larger the rate of re-spending in the community, the larger the multiplier and the greater the change in income that results from each initial dollar of expenditure.

Not-for-profit firms are responsible for various kinds of expenditures. The most obvious are their outright payments to suppliers of productive resources. In order to produce a collective good or service, not-for-profit firms must hire workers, own or rent a building, purchase utilities and supplies, and arrange for advertisement. Then these resource suppliers spend their incomes according to their individual preferences. In the process of re-spending their incomes, resource owners stimulate other kinds of economic activity.

The second kind of expenditure associated with not-for-profit firms is less obvious. The second kind of expenditure is related to patrons or users of the good or service produced by the not-for-profit firm. Expenditures made in association with the use of the collective good or service stimulate additional economic activity in the same way as other expenditures.

Consider the expenditures of visitors to an art exhibit, for example. Such a visit would normally involve, first, a purchase of gasoline, a bus or train ticket, or a taxi ride, and possibly hotel accommodations if the visitors live out-of-town. The visit might also involve a parking fee and possibly the purchase of souvenirs. Finally, a typical excursion to an art exhibit might also involve the purchase of a meal. All of these expenditures would increase other incomes in the community and stimulate additional spending.

Measuring the multiple effect of expenditures is difficult and imprecise. Nevertheless, some information can be gained by surveying a representative sample of visitors to a particular event. Questionnaires can be administered to determine whether visitors are local or out-of-town, their expected expenditures, and other general characteristics. Then the responses of the sample can be summarized and the results extrapolated to the group as a whole.

The next step in measuring the multiple effect is to estimate the portion of initial expenditures that remains in the community in the form of continued spending in the local economy. Such estimates are available from input-output studies tracing the flows of resources (and corresponding payments) through an economy. Researchers[5] at the 1977 Barnum Festival in Bridgeport, Connecticut, estimated that $.56 of every initial dollar of expenditure was re-spent in the local area. Further, $.56 of each dollar received as income was re-spent again. The researchers concluded that roughly 56 percent of receipts continued to circulate in the local economy.

The local multiplier is determined by the following formula: Local multi-

$$\text{plier} = \frac{1}{(1 - \text{rate of respending})} = \frac{1}{(1 - .56)} = 2.26.$$

Thus, each dollar initially spent in the area was estimated to yield $2.26 in local income. The $2.26 is the sum of

the initial $1.00
plus $.56 that is re-spent on the first round,
plus .56($.56) = $.31 re-spent on the second round,
plus .56($.31) = $.17 re-spent on the third round,
and so forth, until the amount respent is very small.

For the Barnum Festival, estimated expenditures from out-of-town visitors were as follows:

Food	$159,686
Shopping	82,076
Parking	1,850
Other entertainment	81,594
Gasoline	77,952
Lodging	41,558
Total	$444,716

With a multiplier effect of 2.26, the visitors' expenditures would have stimulated total economic activity amounting to $444,716 × 2.26 = $1,005,058. If expenditures of local residents are also included in the analysis (since without the festival local residents may have traveled to events outside the area), the economic impact increased to more than $2 million.

CONCLUSION

This chapter has provided examples of instances in which microeconomic analysis can be used for strategic planning in not-for-profit firms. We have reviewed such concepts as:

5. Lawrence S. Davidson and William A. Schaffer, "The Impact of the Barnum Festival," 1977, The Barnum Festival.

1. *demand,* including income elasticity of demand, the equal marginal utility principle that underlies consumer choices, and changes in demand;
2. *efficient resource allocation,* including fixed and variable costs, the techniques of optimization and linear programming, elasticity of production, and output maximization with a budget constraint;
3. *long-run strategic planning,* including increasing and decreasing returns to scale, external economies and diseconomies, and net present value.

We have extended our applications of microeconomic analysis to include these new concepts: consumer surplus, cost-effectiveness, economic impact, and multiplier effects. You may recognize further opportunities to use the tools you have learned to aid decision-making in firms such as the ones we have discussed in this chapter and in a range of firms spanning the broad spectrum of production in the U.S. economy.

This has been the objective of this text: to acquaint the student with useful procedures for analyzing the economic environment, evaluating alternative courses of action, and selecting a strategy that most nearly satisfies the firm's goals.

We have emphasized that the tools of managerial economics are only aids to complement the good judgment of the manager. They are procedures for organizing information in a systematic, goal-oriented way. They are not substitutes for creative thinking. In fact, they may prompt the decision maker to continue seeking additional information so that he or she may find a decision-making model that more nearly resembles the actual problem situation.

CASE STUDY 16.1 Corporate Contributions

Private corporations encounter two kinds of public pressure with respect to philanthropic contributions. On the one hand, federal tax policy encourages corporate giving by allowing firms to deduct a certain amount of corporate gifts from taxable income. Moreover, in recent years public sentiment has moved more sharply to encourage increased local, private responsibility for providing services that were formerly the responsibility of government. On the other hand, corporate contributions to particular institutions have been criticized for the occasional accompanying corporate pressure with respect to the institution's policy decisions.

Any level of corporate contributions at all is in a sense contrary to microeconomic theory. The goal of profit maximization would prohibit a firm from diverting resources from whatever is determined to be their most efficient use. Any diversion at all reduces measured productivity and yields a net loss to owners-stockholders, workers, customers, and the community at large. Nevertheless, it is recognized that no institution is committed to exclusively economic objectives, and that in actual fact activities supported by private philanthropy may be the source of external economies accruing to the corporation itself (in the form of a healthier, better educated, more socially conscious work force).

Professors Ferdinand K. Levy and Gloria M. Shatto have examined the relationship between corporate giving and significant variables describing corporations' philanthropic capacity. The regression analysis used 1971 corporate tax returns and estimated the functional relationship between rates of change in corporate contributions and net investment, net income, and advertising expenditures. The estimated regression equation was[1]

$$C = -3.092 + .0824(I) + .0265(Y) + .0636(A),$$

where C is the log of change in corporate contributions, I is the log of total net investment, Y is the log of total net income, and A is the log of total net advertising expenditures, each expressed in thousands of dollars for each industry. The coefficient of determination was $R^2 = .76$, suggesting that the regression equation explains 76 percent of changes in the rate of corporate contributions.

Of the three independent variables, the variable most closely correlated with corporate giving was found to be advertising. This result suggests that corporate giving is perceived as a way of attracting public attention, particularly in industries in which firms depend on favorable public sentiment in appeals before regulatory commissions.

Researchers Levy and Shatto pursued the question of corporate giving further in examining the relationship between contributions and tax rates. The regression equation in this case was

$$C = -.398 + .00726(t) + .00897(Y) + .0259(D),$$

where C is growth in average contributions for the year, t is average tax rate, Y is aggregate income before taxes for all corporations, and D is aggregate dividends for the year. (All monetary values are expressed in thousands of dollars.) The dividend variable was included because dividends are related to net income in the same way as philanthropic contributions. In fact, dividends are shown to be highly correlated with corporate giving for the year. The coefficient of determination for this equation was $R^2 = .948$.

Finally, the researchers recognized that in many corporations, philanthropic contributions are expected to confer certain benefits to managers. For instance, if managers are rewarded for corporate contributions by appointments to boards of directors, contributions may be regarded as a "preferred expense." Under these assumptions, the regression equation was estimated to be

$$\Delta C = .00193 + .0111(\Delta Y),$$

where ΔC is the deviation of corporate contributions from an expected 6 percent growth in corporate philanthropy, and ΔY is the deviation of corporate income from expected 5 percent growth. The coefficient of determination for this equation was $R^2 = .247$, giving considerable support to the preferential nature of corporate contributions.

---

1. Note that this equation is the linear form of a multiplicative equation $C = a(I^b)(Y^c)(A^d)$, where C is change in contributions; I, Y, and A are the actual values of the above variables; the exponents b, c, and d are the coefficients in the linear equation above; and a is the anti-log (10^a) of $a = -3.092$ above.

Source: Ferdinand K. Levy and Gloria M. Shatto, "Corporate Contributions," *Public Choice*, vol. 33, issue 1, pp. 19–28.

SUMMARY

Collective goods and services are non-exclusive goods and services that can be consumed by "free riders." Production can be carried out by a government enterprise, a private for-profit firm, or a not-for-profit firm. Achieving efficiency in allocation of resources is difficult in not-for-profit firms because of the difficulty of measuring the value of marginal product, consumers' marginal utility, and rate of return on new investments. Moreover, many of the benefits from production in not-for-profit firms may occur at some time in the distant future.

A not-for-profit firm may use linear programming analysis to achieve cost-effectiveness in the production of specific quantities of output. The firm may use optimization to locate the minimum cost level of operation, at which the necessary public subsidy is also at a minimum. Finally, the firm may use calculus and the LaGrangian multiplier to maximize output within a budget constraint.

Many not-for-profit firms benefit from increasing returns to scale, as well as from the opportunities for diversification that come with increasing scale. The economy as a whole may benefit from the economic impact that results from the higher spending associated with a not-for-profit firm.

KEY TERMS

exclusivity
non-exclusivity
consumer surplus

QUESTIONS AND PROBLEMS

1. Cite examples of collective goods and services that are produced in several versions by government, by for-profit firms, and by not-for-profit firms. Explain the differences in exclusivity for the three classes of products.

2. What incentives may explain the willingness of some consumers to make contributions (over and above price) to obtain a certain collective good or service? What disincentives may also be present?

3. List all the significant reasons you can think of for difficulty in analyzing production in not-for-profit firms.

4. A not-for-profit speech school provides instruction in English as a second language to immigrants to the United States. The school offers courses designed for (a) adults, (b) children, and (c) handicapped persons. Instruction consists of audio-visual laboratory instruction and classroom recitation. Adult instruction requires 10 hours of laboratory time and 4 of class-

room time per day. Children require 2 hours of laboratory time or 8 of classroom time. Handicapped persons require 5 hours of laboratory time and 6 hours of classroom time. The costs of laboratory and classroom time are p_L = $4.50 and p_C = $5.50. The school must serve at least 500 adults, 400 children, and 600 handicapped persons. Set up a linear programming problem and determine the lowest-cost combination of resources for achieving the school's goal.

5. a. In a cost-minimizing linear programming problem, what values are measured on the axes?
   b. What information is contained in the constraints?
   c. What is the significance of the intersection of a constraint with an axis?
   d. What sign should the surplus variable have and why?
   e. How is a change in resource price typically shown on a graph of a linear programming problem?

6. Describe the external economies that may be expected to accompany production of particular collective goods and services and that may justify payment of a tax-supported subsidy.

7. A theater group performs regularly in a major metropolitan area. Revenues include ticket sales and a tax-financed subsidy from the local government. Each production added to the group's repertoire requires substantial initial costs, including the services of a playwright, producer, and director and stage settings, props, and lighting equipment. Total fixed costs for each new production amount to $10,000,000. Once this amount is provided, the additional costs associated with repeat performances are relatively low, including theater rental, performers' wages, and ticketing facilities for each performance. Average variable costs are estimated according to $AVC =$ 13,000 − 10(Q) + .002(Q^2), where Q represents total number of spectators at all performances and all values are in cents. Thus, the theater group's total cost equation is estimated as TC = 1,000,000 + 13,000(Q) − 10(Q^2) + .002(Q^3). Demand for tickets behaves typically, such that numerous performances to serve wider audiences are possible only if ticket price is reduced. Estimates of demand yield p = 1,000 − .1(Q), again with Q representing number of spectators and price measured in cents. Thus, the total revenue function is TR = 1,000(Q) − .1(Q^2). Revenues are expected to be less than costs, and the group's economic loss is covered by a public subsidy. Determine the total number of spectators for any production (including repeat performances) that would result in minimum economic loss.

8. Refer again to the information in Problem 7. With Q = 2,500, determine ticket price and economic loss associated with a single production.

9. Refer again to the information in Problem 7. Determine the number of spectators at which marginal costs of additional spectators begins to rise. What is the marginal cost associated with 2,500 spectators?

10. A not-for-profit transit company has a fixed budget of $50,000 per week and seeks to serve the maximum number of riders. The firm uses two types of vehicles and estimates its production function according to $TP = .9A^{.8}B^{.75}$, where A and B represent hours of use of the two types. Hourly costs of operating the vehicles are $p_A = \$10.00$ and $p_B = \$12.50$. Calculate the quantities of A and B for serving the maximum number of riders efficiently.

11. Refer again to the information in Problem 10. Using the most efficient hours of the two types of vehicles, calculate the number of riders served.

12. Refer to Problem 10 and assume a technological change increases the elasticity of production of A by 10 percent without changing its price. Determine the new quantities and total product.

13. Write a clear explanation of each of the following concepts:
    a. Non-exclusivity and the "free rider problem."
    b. Efficiency in the allocation of resources.
    c. The economic impact of not-for-profit firms.
    d. Consumer surplus and the growth of private schools.

17

Managerial Economics and the Theory of Location

A great twentieth century economist, Joseph A. Schumpeter, had a theory about how economic systems grow and develop. He coined the phrase "creative destruction" to describe how new, technically advanced activities replace old, inefficient ones and move regions or nations forward to higher and higher plateaus of development. An important part of "creative destruction" is the movement that takes place when business firms abandon old locations for new sites that offer advantages such as lower costs, superior resource supplies, and improved access to markets.

This chapter will examine the location decisions of business firms in detail, applying some of the analytical tools we have learned in earlier chapters. We will find that many of the familiar concepts involving consumer demand, short- and long-run costs, capital investment, and risk and uncertainty are also applicable to location decisions.

We will begin the chapter with a description of recent locational trends in the United States and continue with an analysis of some of the factors that have contributed to these trends. Finally, we will qualify our conclusions with some observations about current locational attitudes and policies.

THE THEORY OF LOCATION

As you read the theoretical explanations that follow, consider carefully the factors that enter into locational decisions and think about how they have influ-

CASE STUDY 17.1   **The Rise of the Sunbelt**

Throughout history the growth and decline of various regions and nations has been a major source of conflict, occasionally leading to outright warfare. This was true in the United States in the 1860s, when the growth of the industrial Northeast jeopardized the economic institutions of the Southeast. In the 1970s, the situation appeared to be reversed. To some analysts, the growth of the Southeast seemed to be draining the economic vitality of the Northeast.

During the 1970s, population growth in the "Sunbelt" (including the Southeastern and Southwestern states) exceeded that of the "Snowbelt" (the Northeastern and Great Lakes states) by as much as six times. Many factors contributed to the population shift:

1. *Labor costs* were lower in the Sunbelt, particularly in rural areas. Labor unions were not as active in the Sunbelt, which include most of the nation's 21 right-to-work states.[1] Moreover, the advance of automation and accompanying increases in labor productivity reduced the need for highly skilled workers such as those located in the Snowbelt. Energy costs were also lower in the Sunbelt.

2. *Social attitudes and local government policies* in the Sunbelt favored growth. In contrast, citizens of the Snowbelt had begun to resist further industrial growth that threatened additional environmental damage. Furthermore, the movement of industry from older regions had reduced the tax base of many of these areas, providing less tax revenue for maintaining their vital infrastructure, including roads, schools, and other public services.

3. A general *shift of economic activity* out of manufacturing and into services made location near raw materials and highly developed transportation facilities less necessary than in previous decades. Two-thirds of the nation's private sector work force is now employed in the production of services.

4. All these factors contributed to *growing per capita incomes* in the Sunbelt, enlarging markets and increasing profitability. Increased profitability attracted capital inflows from Snowbelt investors and further enhanced the advantages enjoyed in the Sunbelt. New investment made possible more advanced technology and accelerated the momentum for movement South.

5. *Policies of the federal government* favored the Sunbelt, both through public investment in irrigation projects, dams, roads, and canals, and through federal expenditures for military bases. In addition, the federal tax law that permits deduction of interest on home mortgages from taxable income encouraged new home buyers to move to newly opened areas in the Sunbelt and hurt residents of older urban areas (who tend to be renters) in the Snowbelt. On the average, citizens of the Snowbelt states send more in tax revenues to Washington than they receive in federal programs, while citizens of the Sunbelt receive more than they send.

The shift to the Sunbelt has caused some concern about a tendency toward "polarization" in regional economic development. Polarization occurs when **poles of growth** experience advantages that accelerate their growth tendencies and **poles of decline** experience the opposite. (Their most productive workers move away, their profits are invested elsewhere, and their tax bases thus erode further.)

Extreme differences in income and wealth raise difficult federal policy questions. Some policy makers have recommended modifying policies of the federal government to treat regions of the country in a more uniform way and possibly to use some of the tax revenues collected in the Sunbelt to subsidize new economic activity in the stagnant Snowbelt.

---

1. Right-to-work states have laws forbidding union shop. Union shop is the requirement to join the union once a worker accepts employment in a unionized firm.

MANAGERIAL THINKING

1. Can you name other policies of federal, state, and local governments that have influenced regional economic development in the ways described here?
2. What are the advantages and disadvantages of "neutral" governmental policies?
3. Are there parallels between the circumstances described here and tendencies for certain industries to re-locate abroad?

enced recent trends in the United States. At the end of this chapter we will return to the issue of general locational trends and suggest some possible modifications in the trends for the future.

The theory of the location of a business firm is complicated by a number of interrelationships that make simple step-by-step analysis impossible. Therefore, you will note a number of instances when we seem to be repeating concepts discussed earlier. When we have completed the chapter, we will appear to have returned full circle to some of the simplest concepts developed initially.

We will undertake the complex problem of location theory under four main headings:

First, we will examine the effect of *increasing returns to scale* on the location of economic activity. We will find that exploiting increasing returns to scale requires large markets and that large markets require transportation facilities. Business firms are faced with a *trade-off* between the lower production costs associated with increasing returns to scale and the higher transportation costs associated with serving a larger market.

Second, we will examine transportation costs in detail. We will note a second *trade-off* facing business firms: that is, the trade-off between transporting material inputs to a manufacturing site and transporting the finished product to buyers. We will also be interested in the relationship between the prices of transport services and competition in transportation markets.

Third, we will consider the additional complication of resource cost differentials among locations. When resource costs differ, there are additional *trade-offs* involving plant location near various resource markets.

Finally, we will summarize the various aspects of location decisions in terms of the actual distribution of economic activity and in terms of locational trends among productive activities.

SCALE ECONOMIES AND LOCATION

Any location decision must first take into consideration the potential market. Market potential includes all factors that affect demand, including the number of buyers, their incomes and preferences, and the prices and availability of all goods. In addition, market potential includes the distance of buyers from the point of production of the finished good.

The market potential of a particular location can be expressed algebraically as

$$MP = \sum \frac{M_i}{d_{Oi}},$$

where M_i is determined by multiplying the population of neighboring areas by real per capita income in the area, and d_{Oi} is the distance between each neighboring area and the central location. In the United States as a whole, market potential is highest in the region between New York, Boston, Chicago, and Washington, D.C., and lowest in the Pacific Northwest. For individual regions of the country, market potential is greatest around state capitals, river and sea ports, and other large cities.

A firm's location in an area of high market potential raises the possibility of large-scale production, with the accompanying advantages of technical and financial returns to scale. Still, the cost savings from increasing returns to scale must be weighed against the higher cost of transporting large quantities of output to a wider market.

Figure 17.1a illustrates the problem of choosing optimum or minimum-cost scale. Average costs are measured on the vertical axis, and quantity of output is measured on the horizontal axis. The curve labelled $LATC$ shows the average total cost of production associated with plants built to produce various quantities of output per production period. Minimum-cost scale occurs with production of Q_o units.

Selling any quantity of output involves the cost of transporting the product to the relevant market. Average or unit transport costs are shown in Figure

FIGURE 17.1   Optimum Scale

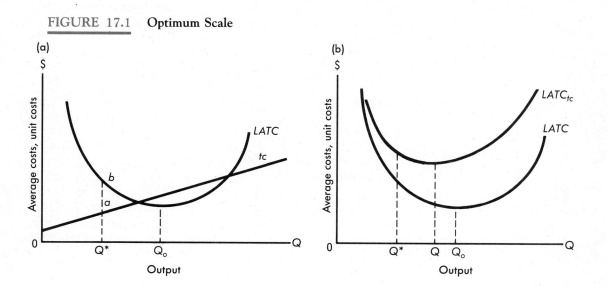

17.1a by the line labelled *tc*. Transport costs start at some positive amount that depends on the initial handling and loading requirements of the product, whatever the distance it is to be carried. Then transport costs increase as distance to the market increases. Thus, serving a wider market requires higher transport costs for each unit of product sold.

When rising transport costs are added to long-run average total costs, the result is $LRAC_{tc}$, as shown in Figure 17.1b. In Figure 17.1b the average cost of producing and delivering to market some quantity OQ^* is the sum of production costs, Q^*b, and transport costs, Q^*a. Note that the effect of adding transport costs is to shift $LRAC$ upward by larger and larger amounts as quantity increases. In practical terms, the result is to reduce the level of minimum-cost scale from Q_o to Q^*. Thus, the addition of transport costs may prevent firms from taking advantage of technical and financial returns to scale.

The extent of the upward shift of $LRAC$ (and the reduction of minimum-cost scale) depends on market potential. For regions with high market potential, a sufficient market may be accessible in the immediate area, causing lower costs, as shown in Figure 17.1b. The more horizontal the transport cost line, the smaller the upward shift in $LRAC$ and the more nearly plant design may approach minimum-cost scale. Of course, this is the reason large-scale factories are frequently located near large cities.

Once plant location is selected and the scale decision made, the firm is operating under short-run conditions, with price and output decisions that depend on short-run costs. Short-run average costs include the average cost of transporting the total quantity of output to buyers in the relevant market. Individual firms must calculate short-run average total cost (ATC) associated with the fixed plant and add transport cost (tc) to determine ATC_{tc}. The profit-maximizing quantity of output is that at which marginal revenue or price is equal to marginal cost. Economic profit per unit is the difference between price and average total cost, where average total cost includes transport cost. Total profit is:

$$\pi = Q(p - ATC_{tc}).$$

External Economies and Agglomeration

Profitable locations tend to attract new, large-scale firms seeking the advantages of increasing returns to scale and low transportation costs. Clusters of firms are the basis for external economies, which may combine to shift long-run average costs curves downward. External economies result from the development of activities that supply low-cost resource inputs to a dominant industry or that use its primary product or by-product. The lower costs of communication and transportation in a densely populated area encourage new firms to provide specialized functions for existing firms. Each new activity spurs multiple responses throughout the area, and "agglomeration" increases.

Agglomeration is the concentration in one area of a variety of related economic activities. Agglomeration takes place through backward and forward "linkages." **Backward linkages** are relationships with firms that supply resource inputs or component parts to an existing firm. **Forward linkages** are relationships with firms that buy a firm's own product. Backward and forward linkages provide the opportunities for the external economies associated with a region's economic growth and development.

The garment district in New York City is an example of an agglomeration of related activities within a single urban area. Small-scale manufacturers supply accessories to large-scale apparel producers. Advertising firms provide specialized marketing services, and financial institutions specialize in short-term commercial credit.

Silicon Valley in California, Route 128 in Massachusetts, and the Research Triangle in North Carolina are examples of agglomerations of "high tech" production and research activities. In each of these areas, an infrastructure appropriate to the dominant industry has developed, both through public and private investments in production facilities, transportation and communications and job training.

In each area, however, there may also be some optimum level of agglomeration above which further economic development may produce external *diseconomies*. External diseconomies are the result of increasing demand for limited supplies of particular resources. They have the effect of shifting an industry *LRAC* curve upward. External diseconomies may be the reason certain urban areas in the United States have been losing population to "satellite" centers of economic activity in the suburbs. Ultimately, bands of urban economic activity may develop that connect large urban areas such as the "BosWash" band that connects Boston and Washington, D.C.

Scale Economies and Competition

Regions with high market potential may be expected to include a number of competing firms, each serving a portion of the concentrated market. Figure 17.2a on page 504 shows *LRAC* curves for plants located at A and B and supplying the market that extends between them along the horizontal axis. (Measurements along the horizontal axis are read from left to right from A and from right to left from B.) For buyers arranged along the axis from A to Q^*, average production and transport costs are lowest from plant A. For buyers from B to Q^*, production and transport costs are lowest from plant B. Thus, the two producing firms divide the market equally at Q^*.

Figure 17.2b illustrates the effect of differences in production costs for the two firms. If technical or financial advantages or advantages associated with transportation costs enable the firm producing at A to produce at lower long-run average cost, the effect is to shift this firm's $LRAC_{tc}$ downward, so that minimum-cost scale is greater than for the firm producing at B. Furthermore,

FIGURE 17.2   Location and Competition

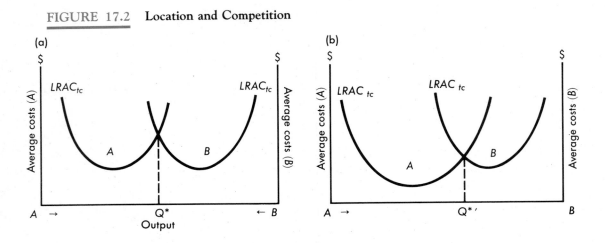

lower average total cost enables the firm at A to serve a larger portion of the market than the firm at B, as shown by the shift of Q^* to $Q^{*\prime}$.

With a larger volume of sales, the firm producing at A can be expected to exploit additional technical or financial economies in order to enjoy further reductions in costs. In addition, the larger volume of sales at A may justify investments in in-house transportation facilities, allowing possible additional savings in transport costs. Managers of both firms should be alert to these possibilities, in order to avoid losing the market to more vigorous competition.

External Economies and Alternative Technologies

We have noted that external economies and diseconomies have the effect of decreasing or increasing resource costs as demand for those resources increases. The result of differential resource costs is to alter costs of production along locations and to alter minimum-cost plant design. To understand the various possibilities, look at Figure 17.3a. Figure 17.3a is drawn with the assumption that production requires certain quantities of two resource inputs, capital and labor, measured along the vertical and horizontal axes. The straight line is an isocost line, showing the quantities of capital (Q_K) and labor (Q_L) that can be purchased with a fixed budget, given the prices of the two resources in location A. The steep slope of the isocost line indicates the relatively higher price of the resource on the horizontal axis:

$$\text{Slope} = \frac{p_L}{p_K}.$$

The relatively low price of capital in location A means that larger quantities of capital resources can be purchased with the firm's fixed budget as defined by

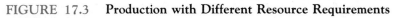

FIGURE 17.3   **Production with Different Resource Requirements**

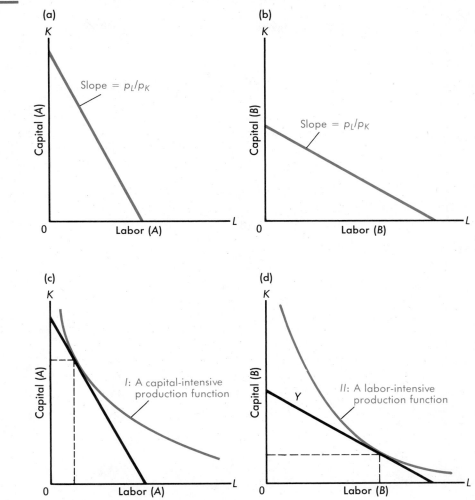

the isocost line. The reason for lower capital prices might be the greater supply of business savings for investment in that location.

Figure 17.3b shows an isocost line for the same budget in another location (*B*). At location *B*, the price of labor is substantially lower than the price of capital, as indicated by the more horizontal isocost line. The reason for the lower price of labor might be the relative scarcity of employment opportunities at this location.

In many manufacturing processes, a firm may choose among production functions with different resource requirements. The use of various combinations of resources to produce a particular quantity of output is illustrated through the use of isoquants. Different resource combinations are represented by points comprising the relevant isoquants. The slope of an isoquant reflects the resources' marginal rate of technical substitution in a particular production function. The marginal rate of technical substitution associated with any isoquant is the ratio of the marginal products of the two resources:

$$\text{Slope} = MRTS_{KL} = \frac{MP_L}{MP_K},$$

when the resource on the horizontal axis provides the ratio's numerator. The slope of an isoquant is relatively steep when the marginal product of labor, MP_L, is relatively high. (In this case, a large quantity of capital is required to replace a given quantity of labor.) A more horizontal isoquant indicates relatively high MP_K.

The isoquants drawn in Figures 17.3c and 17.3d represent production functions with (I) a high marginal product of capital (c) and (II) a high marginal product of labor (d). Isoquants that have a steep slope such as the curve in (d) represent production functions that utilize more labor than more horizontal isoquants such as the one in (c). Figure 17.3c thus illustrates the more capital-intensive production function, and Figure 17.3d illustrates the more labor-intensive production function.

When alternative isoquants are combined with isocost lines for particular locations, it is possible to identify the most efficient technology for producing a particular item. Look first at the capital-intensive isoquant labelled I in Figure 17.3c. It can easily be seen that a capital-intensive production function should be used at location A. The most efficient quantities of labor and capital are determined at X, the point of tangency, the slope of the isocost line is equal to the slope of the isoquant:

$$\frac{p_L}{p_K} = \frac{MP_L}{MP_K}.$$

This is the lowest-cost combination of L and K for producing the quantity I in a plant located at A. The labor-intensive technology should be employed at location B, however with quantities of capital and labor indicated by the point of tangency at Y.

The Marginal Efficiency of Investment and the Cost of Capital

Labor or capital intensity may have implications for a region's long-run economic growth and development. Regional differences in resource costs are a result of differences in the demand for or supply of particular resources. Recall from Chapter 12 that the demand for capital is a firm's marginal efficiency of investment (MEI) schedule, where MEI is the expected rate of return associated with a variety of investment projects. When risk is incorporated in the MEI schedule, the result is to reduce the expected rate of return and shift the firm's demand curve for capital downward.

In general, a change of location involves significant risk. A firm may have incomplete information regarding resource costs and quality in a new location, appropriate labor skills may be undeveloped, and the new market may be untested. The higher level of risk would call for a significant downward shift in *MEI*. At the same time, the supply of capital may be lower in a less developed location. The relative scarcity of capital may be the result of low profits in local industry and a sparse influx of capital from outside the region.

In Figure 17.4, downward shifts in *MEI* and in the supply of capital yield a smaller quantity of investment, indicating tendencies toward low capital intensity. (The effect of the downward shifts on the cost of capital would depend on the relative magnitude of the shifts in *MEI* and supply.)

The effect of low capital intensity may be to worsen trends of polarization among regions. If a region's profits are not invested locally in capital resources,

FIGURE 17.4   **Marginal Efficiency of Investment**

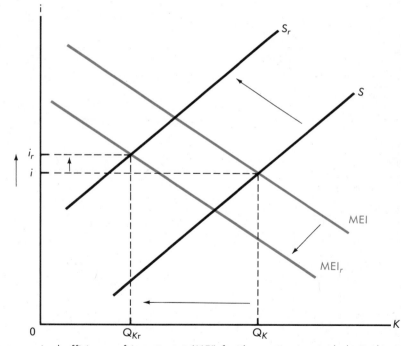

The marginal efficiency of investment (*MEI*) for the nation as a whole is shown as *MEI*. For regions with investment potential involving risk, marginal efficiency of investment is lower, as shown by line *MEI$_r$*. The lower expected rate of return requires a lower market rate of interest if investment projects are to be undertaken. However, if the region also lacks sufficient savings for investment, the regional supply of capital may shift from *S* to *S$_r$*. The equilibrium rate of interest in the region will rise from *i* to *i$_r$*, and the level of investment will fall from *Q$_K$* to *Q$_{Kr}$*.

the region will be unable to exploit advances in technology. Its firms will be increasingly unable to compete with firms in other regions, and profits may decline further. Slow growth in industrial capacity will reduce the area's tax base and its capacity to construct and maintain an infrastructure capable of attracting new kinds of economic activity. Most of us know of towns whose dependence on a single labor-intensive industry has made the town vulnerable to these kinds of change.

TRANSPORTATION COSTS

The location of economic activity is also complicated by variations in transport costs. Transport costs vary with the characteristics of the product being transported and the characteristics of the firms supplying transportation services. Some products require special transport facilities because they are heavy or bulky. Others require special handling because they are perishable or fragile. These special characteristics increase the handling costs associated with particular types of freight at the point of origin and the point of delivery.

Handling costs can also be described as "terminal costs" and include the costs of all the resources used at the beginning and ending points of transport. Terminal costs are classified as *fixed costs* because they are associated with all freight, regardless of the distance it is carried. Fixed transportation costs are distinguished from *variable costs,* which are primarily energy costs that vary with the distance a product is carried. Figure 17.5a is a typical graph of transport costs per unit of weight of freight, showing the vertical sum of fixed and variable costs associated with transporting freight over varying distances.

FIGURE 17.5 **Transport Costs**

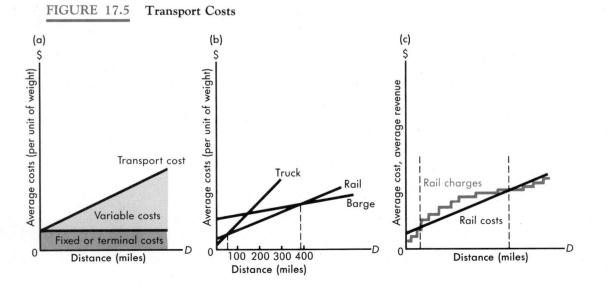

The relationship between fixed and variable costs varies for different means of transportation. Inland water transport, for example, requires high fixed costs because of the costs of maintaining navigable waterways and providing port facilities for loading and unloading freight. Rail transport has lower fixed costs, and truck transport has the lowest fixed costs of all. Variable costs rise fairly quickly in truck transport, however, and relatively slowly for inland water transport.

Differences in fixed and variable costs affect the choice of means of transportation for moving goods over varying distances. Figure 17.5b illustrates the differences. Again, cost per unit of weight of freight is measured on the vertical axis and distance is measured on the horizontal axis. Because of low fixed costs, truck transport is most efficient for short distances of up to about 50 miles. Rail transport is most efficient for intermediate distances of between 50 and 400 miles. Inland water transport is most efficient for distances of greater than about 400 miles. This is because rail and water transport require fewer terminal facilities en route, with fewer requirements for cargo to be transferred from one means of transportation to another.

The transport cost lines in Figure 17.5b are somewhat unrealistic because of the difficulty of precisely relating variable transport costs to the distance freight is moved. Most transportation firms set transport charges on the basis of zones, so that the transport cost line, instead of rising with a constant slope, rises in increments as the freight being shipped moves through zones farther and farther from its origin. Zones are established according to the number of shippers in the area and the kinds of freight being carried. The increments generally become more horizontal with greater distance as a means of encouraging long hauls, which are easier for transportation firms to handle.

The transport cost lines in Figure 17.5b are also unrealistic because of variations in competitive pressures along various transport routes. A particular transportation firm may set its rates below costs along portions of a route where it faces competition from another means of transportation and above costs where it faces no competition.

Consider the cost of rail transport, shown again as the black line on Figure 17.5c. Because rail transport faces competition from trucks for distances of up to 50 miles, rail charges may be set below actual costs for very short distances. The same is true for distances of above 400 miles, in which railroads must compete against inland water transport. Losses from below-cost charges along these route segments may be offset by above-cost charges along route segments where rail transport faces no competition.

Price Discrimination in Transportation Charges

Competition between various means of transportation may give rise to price discrimination. In general, price discrimination leads to higher rates where *demand* for transportation is inelastic and lower rates where *supply* of transportation is inelastic.

Elasticity of transportation *demand* depends on the urgency of need for transportation services, whatever the cost to acquire the service. Urgency of need depends on the availability of substitutes and the portion of the total cost of the product paid for transportation. In general, the higher the value of the freight, the lower the portion of total costs represented by transport costs and the more willing shippers are to accept a particular transport charge. We would describe their demand for transportation as inelastic. We would also expect a price-discriminating transportation firm to set a relatively high transport rate on freight that has a high value relative to transportation costs.

Shippers of lightweight, bulky freight would also tend to have inelastic demand for transport, since they are often unable to establish their own "in-house" transportation system. We would expect a price-discriminating transport firm to set relatively high transport rates for shippers of light, bulky freight. Shippers of compact, high-value freight generally have more transport options (including "in-house" transportation systems). Therefore, their demand for transportation is elastic, and their transport charges tend to be low.

Elasticity of transportation *supply* depends on the transportation firm's ability to withhold their service if the market price is regarded as too low. One circumstance in which the service cannot possibly be withheld is the "back haul." After delivering a particular type of freight, vehicles must return to the freight's origin to pick up the next shipment. Other goods can be carried on the back haul at little or no additional cost to the transportation firm, so that any payment by a back-haul shipper represents a net gain. Thus, the supply of transport service on the back haul is inelastic. We would expect a price discriminating transport firm to set relatively low rates on a typical back haul.

These kinds of price discrimination influenced the early growth and development of the Northeastern region of the United States relative to the Southern states. In the Northeastern states, navigable waterways connect the major population centers, making for vigorous competition among means of transportation and a tendency toward low transport rates on Northern manufactured goods. Manufactured goods also benefited from low back-haul rates. Shipments of bulky raw cotton from Southern plantations to textile mills in the North left transport vehicles empty for the return South. Relatively low transport rates on high-value manufactured goods yielded high profits in manufacturing in the Northeast and slowed the development of competing manufacturing industries in the South.

Another form of price discrimination involves the distinction between full carload and less-than-carload shipments. Because of the difficulty of handling the latter, the transport charge for such shipments is generally higher.

TRANSPORT CHARGES AND INDUSTRIAL LOCATION

In this section we will reconsider what we have learned about transport costs in order to draw some conclusions regarding industrial location.

Most economic activities fundamentally involve two operations: *assembling* material inputs for production and *distributing* finished output to buyers.

Transportation facilities may be necessary for either or both of these operations. Thus, two kinds of transport costs are generally added to production costs to arrive at the average total cost of the product.

Transport costs are graphed in Figure 17.6a, where the two vertical axes are drawn from A, the location of the material input, and B, the location of the market for the finished product. The horizontal axis represents distance in miles between A and B. Manufacturing plants may be built at any point along the distance AB. Manufacturing at X, for example, would require transporting the material from A to X for a transport cost read from the line labelled M_{tc}. Then transporting the finished product from X to B would require a transport cost read from the line labelled P_{tc}. Total transport cost associated with manufacture at X is the sum of the separate transport costs, shown by the curve labelled $M_{tc} + P_{tc}$.

Note that minimum transport costs occur at either A or B, where the firm avoids transporting either the material, on the one hand, or the finished product, on the other. Any location other than A or B would involve higher than necessary transport costs. Locations beyond A or B would be uneconomic as well, since either the material or the finished product would have to be carried even farther than the distance AB. The cost curves extend beyond the two vertical axes of the graph to illustrate this point.

Figure 17.6a suggests that, in general, manufacturing operations will be carried on where total transportation costs are lowest, either at the source of material inputs or at the market. If transporting the material costs more than transporting the product, manufacturing plants will tend to locate at the material source. Higher transport costs for the finished product would indicate the reverse, as is true in Figure 17.6a. This is the reason steel manufacture tends to locate near sources of iron ore, and brewers tend to locate near consumer markets (a primary ingredient in beer is water).

FIGURE 17.6 **Transport Costs and Location**

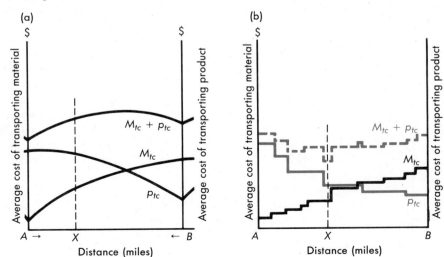

Location at the source of materials or at the market identifies production as either "materials-oriented" or "market-oriented." **Materials-oriented production** generally involves bulky or heavy materials, materials that are fragile or perishable, or materials that lose substantial weight in processing. High terminal or moving costs of such materials generally encourage location near their source.

Market-oriented products are those that acquire substantial weight or value in processing, that become fragile or perishable, or that use a cheap, widely available resource in the final stage of processing. It has been estimated that approximately one-fourth of total production in the United States is materials-oriented and one-half is market-oriented.

When both material and product transport costs rise in increments, manufacturing may be carried on at an intermediate point. In Figure 17.6b, the sum of material and product transport costs has been computed as before. However, because incremental charges in transport costs are irregular, a location between A and B is preferable to location at either of the extremes. Typically, the lowest transport costs occur at the juncture between the various means of transportation appropriate for transporting either the material or the finished product. This is due to the tendency for transport rates to increase sharply when it is necessary to transfer freight from one means of transportation to another. This is the reason for the location of many manufacturing plants at sea ports or river ports where materials can be unloaded from barges for processing and then re-loaded onto rail or truck transport for delivery to final buyers.

When production can be carried on independently of materials or markets, the industry is frequently described as **footloose**. About one-fourth of U.S. industries are estimated to be footloose.

Locational Decisions with More Than One Resource Input

Locational decisions become more complicated when more than one resource is used in production. The problem facing a firm then becomes one of selecting the location at which the cost of transporting all resources is at a minimum.

To illustrate the location decision in this case, consider the use of two resource inputs M and L, certain quantities of which are necessary for producing a single unit of product N. In Figure 17.7a, the vertical axes represent transport costs per unit of weight of the two resources, and the horizontal axis represents locational space. The sources of the two resources are shown at M and L along the horizontal space. The curves in Figure 17.7a are called **space-cost curves** and represent the costs of transporting the two resources to various locations along the horizontal axis for processing into the finished product. The space-cost curves reach their lowest points at the sources of the two resources, and transport costs raise their prices at delivery as distance from the source increases. In fact, resource L has a higher cost at its source than resource M and higher transport costs as well.

The cost of transporting both M and L is determined by adding their space-cost curves vertically, such that their sum is the space-cost curve SC_{ML}. Thus,

FIGURE 17.7   Space-Cost Curves

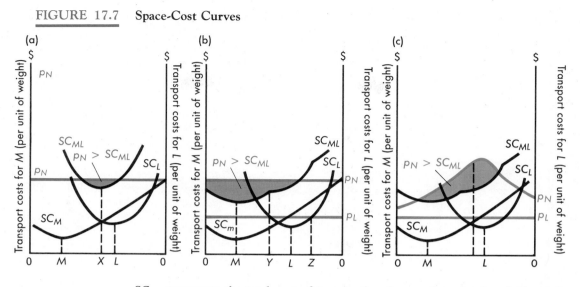

SC_{ML} represents the total cost of transporting the number of units of M and L required per unit of finished product. With a constant market price P_N for the finished product, the location with the lowest transport cost per unit of product is that at which the difference between P_N and SC_{ML} is greatest. In Figure 17.7a, transport costs per unit are less than price at any location over the range indicated by the shaded area. However, the higher cost of L and its higher transport costs indicate a minimum-cost location closer to resource L at point X.

Now consider Figure 17.6b. Assume that resource L is a type of highly skilled labor located in a particular region or locale, as shown at L. Resource M is a composite unit of all other material resources that are available at lowest cost at M. Furthermore, assume that technical developments occur in the industry causing a change in the type of labor required. Specifically, assume that the development of new technology makes it possible to utilize less skilled workers who are now available over a wider portion of the area being considered for production. The price of widely available, unskilled labor is shown in Figure 17.7c at a constant price of p_L.

When the option of less-skilled workers is included in the location model, the space-cost curve must be changed to incorporate this option. The new space-cost curve SC_{ML}, includes the addition of a constant labor cost to the materials cost up to the point where the cost of the initial labor is lower, that is, at point Y. Between Y and Z, the space-cost curve includes the lower cost of skilled workers at their source, L. The result of this change is to broaden the geographic area over which transport costs per unit of output are lower than the product's unit selling price. Whereas location was formerly limited to the central urban area around X in Figure 17.7a, broader labor options have now extended location possibilities to the wider area shown in Figure 17.7b. The greatest difference between product price and total transport costs occurs at M where the cost of transporting the material is lowest.

EXAMPLE 17.1   **Space Cost Curves and Government Policy**

Frequently, state and local governments undertake policies designed to influence the location of economic activity. In general, the objective of such policies is to discourage additional congestion in a central urban area and to encourage economic development in an outlying area that may lack some of the natural attractions of the urban location. It is expected that once economic development begins, a certain momentum will build up, causing the distribution of economic activity to become more balanced throughout the region as a whole.

Policies of this sort may take the form of taxes and subsidies. Taxes to discourage congestion in one location may provide the revenue to finance subsidies for encouraging development in another. The effect of taxes and subsidies is to alter a firm's space-cost curve in the way the governmental unit intended.

The space-cost curve (SC) in Figure A illustrates this effect. In the absence of government policy, the firm's lowest cost location is Z, where the difference between price and total transportation cost per unit of output is greatest. Any location within the area *AD* would be profitable. A tax imposed on economic activity in the central location, however, would shift upward a segment of the space cost curve to SC_t, where average transport cost would exceed price. This location would no longer be profitable, and firms would be expected to locate manufacturing plants elsewhere. On the other hand, a subsidy paid to producers outside the urban area would shift another segment of the space cost curve downward to SC_s, causing production to become profitable in this area.

MANAGERIAL THINKING

1. How have taxes and subsidies been influential in the economic development of the Sunbelt?

FIGURE A

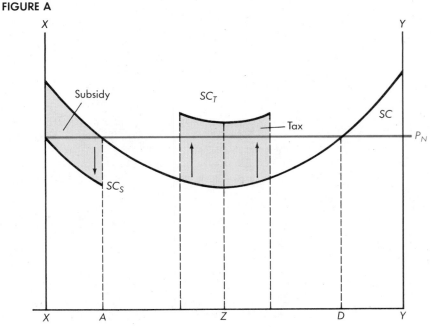

2. What environmental regulations have had similar effects on industrial location?
3. How might the model described in this example be adopted to illustrate policies designed to encourage movement of industry *into* an urban area?

Source: Harry W. Richardson, *Regional Economics*, (New York: Praeger Publishers, 1972).

This analysis explains the shift of textile production from the New England states to the South in the nineteenth century. Prior to the shift, raw cotton was shipped to the Northeast for the production of textiles by skilled workers. As new technology developed, however, it became more economical to use widely available unskilled Southern labor near the source of the raw material.

A further refinement of this model is possible. We have to this point assumed that buyers are evenly spaced over the market causing price to remain constant over the entire space shown on our graph. Let us now change that assumption to allow for the possibility of a more concentrated market in the urban area around L. With more buyers in the area, we would expect demand for the product to increase and equilibrium price to rise. Thus, the product price line p_N may change from a straight line to a curve that rises in the area around the urban center. In Figure 17.7c, the effect is to change the possible range of production in favor of the urban center. In fact, in Figure 17.7c the difference between product price and total transport costs shifts closer to the urban center at X.

THE SPATIAL DISTRIBUTION OF ECONOMIC ACTIVITY

In this section we will utilize what we have learned about location decisions in order to make some generalizations about the distribution of economic activity across geographic space.

One primary generalization that can be made is that similar kinds of economic activity tend to cluster in certain areas. Finance and commerce tend to cluster in large urban areas, and manufacturing and agriculture tend to cluster outside a city's central business district. Location trends also tend to accelerate as the long-run growth of particular kinds of economic activity supports the development of new backward and forward linkages which, in turn, encourage further concentrations of the particular economic activity.

At any point in time, a particular firm may be expected to earn a certain economic return that differs from economic profit in the industry as a whole as a result of its location. For a firm, economic return is the difference between total revenue from sales and total costs associated with its location. In any area, industries with higher economic return will tend to displace those with lower economic return, so that particular industries come to dominate particular areas.

Figure 17.8 illustrates the distribution of economic activity around a central market area. The vertical axis in Figure 17.8a measures economic return,

FIGURE 17.8   **Typical Distribution of Economic Activity Around a Market**

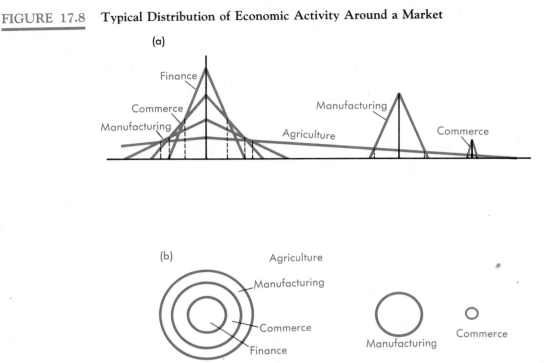

and the horizontal axis measures distance from the central market. Since potential sales extend in all directions from the market center, the various lines for different types of activity actually represent cones having a height of π_{max} that represents economic return to that activity over the entire relevant area. Note that commercial activity occupies a wide band around the center financial core, as shown by the circle in Figure 17.8b. This panel represents an overhead view of the area shown in Figure 17.8a. Manufacturing occupies a slimmer band farther out from the central financial core. Agriculture yields sufficient economic return only in locations far from the market center.

Note that the various activities arrange themselves around the central market in a series of concentric circles. Most large urban areas exhibit locational patterns of this kind. Figure 17.8 illustrates economic return over a broad region capable of supporting more than one market having varying locational patterns. Particular features of each market help determine the economic return associated with particular activities and lead to further concentrations of that activity.

CASE STUDY 17.2   **Locational Trends: A Recap**

The Snowbelt-to-Sunbelt economic shift that seemed so inexorable in the 1970s may have encountered some resistance in the 1980s, a resistance originating in the unpredictable nature of human beings. The savings many business firms expected to enjoy as a result of locational changes were frequently not sufficient to sever the ties many employees felt to their native regions. While more than 3 million people moved to the Sunbelt during the 1970s, mobility has slowed considerably in the 1980s, and many firms are looking for new ways to improve profitability in their home locations.

Probably the most significant factor in recent immobility has been the growth of two-career families. More than half of all married women now hold jobs. In addition, these are increasingly career-oriented positions, as opposed to short-term jobs. Another factor is the increasing emphasis on "quality of life"—recreational activities and community involvement that strengthen a region's hold on its citizens. Moreover, the population's rising average age nationwide is reducing opportunities for job advancement, and high moving costs and inflated home prices have reduced the incentives for lateral moves. Unemployment benefits and regulations prohibiting plant closings may also have slowed worker mobility.

A new trend may now be replacing the previous massive population shift. Industrial activity may be becoming more de-centralized, with more smaller manufacturing facilities located in growing suburbs and small towns near workers' homes. Such facilities can be linked electronically through modern communications networks to command centers in urban areas.

The implications of these developments are significant for managerial policy makers. As the possibility of locational change diminishes, firms may have to work out their problems locally by doing things such as increasing investment in the local work force to improve its productivity, installing modern communications and transportation facilities to improve efficiency, and increasing awareness of market trends that will call for further adjustments. Managers may also want to explore the area of "corporate culture," that is, the many subtle ways employees can be encouraged to feel like participants in a worthwhile activity that transcends their personal lives outside the work environment.

SUMMARY

Locational decisions contribute to the economic growth and development of regions and nations. All such decisions involve trade-offs between returns to scale in production and transportation costs, between transportation of material resources and finished products, and between the transportation costs of various material resources to a single manufacturing site. Market potential analysis helps establish the appropriate weight for a particular manufacturing site.

Areas of market concentration provide backward and forward linkages, but excessive concentration may result in external diseconomies. Local resource endowments affect resource prices and the appropriate technologies for particular locations.

Transportation costs vary with various production techniques and various means of transportation. These costs include fixed terminal and handling costs and costs that vary with distance. Some transportation firms practice price discrimination based on price elasticity of demand and supply. A particular industry may be classified as materials-oriented, market-oriented, or footloose.

For a particular industry, the lowest-cost location depends on prices and relative ubiquity of resources and market potential. However, governments may influence locational decisions through the use of taxes and subsidies.

KEY TERMS

poles of growth   materials-oriented production
poles of decline   market-oriented production
agglomeration   footloose production
backward linkages   space-cost curves
forward linkages

QUESTIONS AND PROBLEMS

1. Discuss the cost advantages and disadvantages associated with industrial locations within various regions of the nation, particularly with respect to: heavy manufacturing, "high-tech" production, agriculture and forest products, and tourism.

2. What specific external economies and diseconomies are associated with the following industrial locations: insurance in Hartford, Connecticut; chemicals in Galveston, Texas; recreation in Aspen, Colorado; carpets in Dalton, Georgia.

3. Distinguish between regional specialization and "polarization." What are the expected advantages and disadvantages of each.

4. Compute the market potential of locations A and B below. Which location appears to be more appropriate for the location of a large-scale manufacturing enterprise?

Industrial location			Markets		
	A	B		X	Y
Distance from X	8	5	Population	500,000	750,000
Distance from Y	3	10	Real per capita income	12,500	8,000

5. Explain the statement that transport costs reduce the level of minimum-cost scale. Illustrate your explanation graphically. How does high market potential affect your result?

6. Consider the following production functions:

$$TP_1 = 1.1L^{.8}K^{.4}$$

and

$$TP_2 = 1.1L^{.4}K^{.8}.$$

Resource prices differ in two proposed plant locations, A and B, in the following manner: $p_{LA} = 5$, $p_{KA} = 8$, $p_{LB} = 8$, and $p_{KB} = 5$. The budget for each location is $1,000. Identify the labor- and capital-intensive technologies, then calculate the most efficient quantities of the two resources at the two locations.

7. Refer once again to the information in Problem 6. Determine total product at each of the two locations and decide the appropriate technology for each.

8. Zero Defects Widget Company calculates its marginal efficiency of investment as the rate of return, r, necessary to equate the investment's purchase price with discounted cash flows over its lifetime:

$$C = \sum \frac{\text{cash flows}}{1 + r}.$$

Show how the introduction of risk in the *MEI* formula has the effect of reducing the marginal efficiency of investment.

9. Refer once more to the information in Question 8. Explain how the introduction of risk is likely to affect the flow of capital investment into capital-poor locations.

10. a. Discuss the bases for price discrimination in transportation when a railroad and a trucking company compete for freight over a particular route.
    b. How will the means of transportation and transport charges be expected to differ for: coal, cotton cloth, baked goods, calculators, and apparel. Explain your answers.

11. What considerations determine location for each of the following types of economic activity: materials-oriented, market-oriented, and footloose.

12. Illustrate graphically the effects of taxes and subsidies intended to influence the location of economic activity. How have such policies affected the relative growth of Sunbelt and Snowbelt states?

18

Topics in International Business

American business is becoming increasingly international. By 1980, international trade consumed almost 10 percent of gross national product, up from 4 percent only a decade before. Increasing international trade reflects the growing **interdependence** of the global economy, both in terms of dependence on resources and equipment for use in production and in terms of markets for finished consumer goods and services. Rising productivity and incomes around the world have had the effect of increasing demand for a wider variety of the world's products.

International trade is based on the principle of **comparative advantage**. Comparative advantage arises from differences in resource endowments that encourage specialization in the production of certain goods and services. A nation with relatively large endowments of skilled labor, for example, would be expected to specialize in production of skilled labor-intensive goods and services. Japan's specialization in consumer electronics is an example of this. We say that Japan has comparative advantage in production of consumer electronics. Similarly, a land-rich nation such as Argentina has comparative advantage in land-intensive types of production such as livestock. The United States is capital-rich and specializes in production of capital-intensive goods such as aircraft. Global specialization and exchange according to comparative advantage increases technical efficiency and pushes prices toward the minimum level consistent with full costs of production.

The United States enjoyed significant trade advantages during its early stages of economic development. The most obvious of these were the *geo-*

graphic advantages consisting of a varied land and climate that provided many minerals and forest products cheaply and permitted a wide range of agricultural production. In addition, the large U.S. market yielded advantages in terms of *increasing returns to scale* and allowed business firms to shift economic profits from one type of economic activity into capital investment in another. Both of these advantages contributed to a third type of advantage, *technological advance*. Low-cost raw materials and large-scale production encouraged the use of manufacturing profits for research and development, further improving the international competitiveness of U.S. manufacturing industry.

Since World War II, some of our nation's former trade advantages have slipped away. Many strategic resources are now more limited in supply, and others are available only from other countries. Many of our agricultural products face import restrictions in other nations. Cooperative trade agreements in other parts of the world have created large, integrated markets comparable in wealth and size to the United States. Finally, the spread of technology to other nations—partly through the activities of multinational corporations and partly through natural processes—has reduced our nation's technical advantages.

The narrowing of international differences has made U.S. firms more vulnerable to price competition from other nations. Unless U.S. products can gain distinction through higher quality, improved innovation, and more reliable service, U.S. manufacturers stand to lose markets to lower-cost manufacturers abroad. The result of our declining exports relative to our necessary imports has been slower growth in production for U.S. firms, slower growth of income for the nation as a whole, and a gradual transfer of wealth abroad. Avoiding these unpleasant results in the future will require close attention to fundamental trends, scientific analysis of alternative business strategies, and precise implementation of technical and managerial decisions.

The preceding chapters in this text have demonstrated strategic decision making as it applies both to domestic and foreign operations. This chapter will concentrate on aspects of markets and production that apply only to international activities. We will begin with a discussion of exchange rates and the consequences of variability in exchange rates for international trade and international financial relations. We will demonstrate processes by which firms adjust their practices to increase profits and reduce risks from exchange rate movements. Then we will consider the advantages and disadvantages of direct investment abroad and the business practices associated with direct foreign investment.

EXCHANGE RATES

The primary economic relationship among nations is through trade. Many aspects of international trade are similar to those of domestic sales. One aspect that is different, however, has to do with the fact that international trade requires the use of international currencies. Changes in the relative prices of international currencies can affect opportunities for trade.

The price of one currency in terms of another is called its **exchange rate**. Thus, the exchange rate for dollars can be expressed as:

$1 = 2 DM, $1 = .4 £, $1 = 250 Y, $1 = 50 pesos.

Exchange rates are determined in foreign exchange markets by the intersection of currency demand and currency supply curves.

Figure 18.1 illustrates a typical foreign exchange market in which U.S. dollars are sold for German deutsche marks (DMs). The demand curve in Figure 18.1 shows the quantities of dollars that will be demanded at various DM prices. Demand for dollars results from the desire of people worldwide to acquire dollars for purchasing U.S. goods and services, investing in U.S. industry, or participating in U.S. financial markets. The demand curve slopes downward because at lower prices more people will normally want to acquire more dollars for these purposes.

The supply curve in Figure 18.1 shows the quantities of dollars that will be offered for sale at various DM prices. The supply of dollars results from foreign sales of goods and services to U.S. citizens, U.S. purchases of foreign investments, and the participation of U.S. citizens in financial markets in other nations. Persons who have acquired dollars in any of these ways may decide to hold them as part of their own wealth, or they may offer them to others for

FIGURE 18.1   **The Equilibrium Exchange Rate**

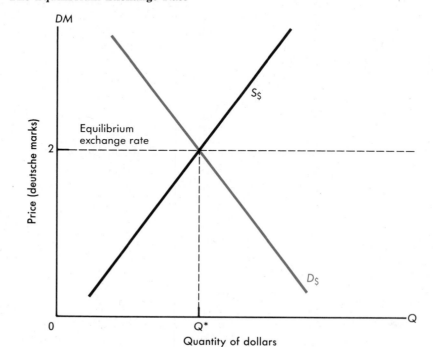

Quantity of dollars

immediate use. A currency supply curve slopes upward because at higher prices more holders of dollars would normally be willing to supply them to other users.

The intersection of currency demand and supply determines the exchange rate of dollars and the equilibrium quantity that will be traded. At any exchange rate above the equilibrium level, the supply of dollars would exceed demand. At any rate below the equilibrium level, demand would exceed supply. In either case, the plans and expectations of currency traders would not be satisfied. The exchange rate would be bid up or down until demand and supply are equal.

For any exchange market like the one in Figure 18.1, there is a corresponding one in which the relationship between the two currencies is reversed. The market that corresponds to Figure 18.1 is the one in which DMs are sold for dollars. The equilibrium exchange rate would also be reversed. Thus, a dollar exchange rate of $1 = 2 DM corresponds to a DM exchange rate of 1 DM = $.50. (To determine the DM exchange rate divide both sides of the dollar exchange rate by the coefficient of DM.)

With a dollar exchange rate of $1 = 2 DM, U.S. consumers and business firms can determine the dollar price of German products. A German automobile priced at 10,000 DM, for instance, would sell for $5,000. (To determine the dollar price, multiply both sides of the DM exchange rate by 10,000.) Similarly, German consumers and business firms would calculate the DM price of a $1,000,000 U.S. aircraft as 2,000,000 DM. (Multiply both sides of the dollar exchange rate by 1,000,000.) When currency exchange rates are known and are relatively constant, consumers and investors around the world can arrange their purchases at known prices in terms of their domestic currencies.

Changes in Exchange Rates

Shifts in currency demand or supply have the effect of changing the exchange rate, which, in turn, influences the ability and willingness of consumers and business firms to participate in trade. Changes in currency demand and supply are often associated with changing economic conditions in the affected countries. A sharply rising price level in one nation, for example, causes a decrease in *quantity demanded* for that nation's exports. The result is likely to be a decrease in *demand* for the nation's currency and a decrease in its exchange rate. A decrease in a currency's exchange rate is called **depreciation**.

The reason for currency depreciation is illustrated in Figure 18.2. In Figure 18.2, domestic inflation has raised the prices of U.S. goods relative to foreign goods and caused buyers to move into other markets. As a result, the demand for dollars has fallen, shown in Figure 18.2 as a leftward shift of the currency demand curve. At every price on the new demand curve, foreign buyers are willing to purchase fewer dollars. Similarly, rising U.S. prices cause more U.S. citizens to purchase goods abroad. This means that more dollars will be offered in currency exchange markets in exchange for other currencies. The increased supply of dollars in foreign exchange markets is shown as a rightward

FIGURE 18.2   Disequilibrium in Currency Exchange

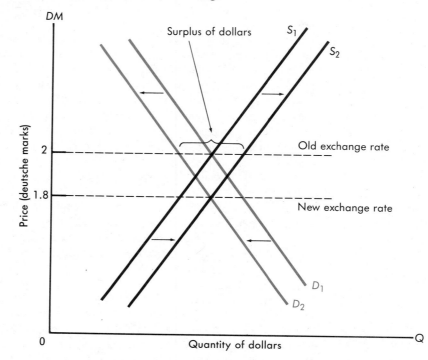

shift of the currency supply curve. At every price on the new supply curve, holders of dollars offer more dollars for exchange in foreign exchange markets.

The decrease in currency demand and increase in supply create disequilibrium in currency exchange markets and disequilibrium in the "balance of trade." When more dollars flow out through trade than in, we say the balance of trade has turned negative for the United States. Correcting disequilibrium in currency markets requires a change in exchange rates, with corresponding changes in the balance of trade.

Refer again to Figure 18.2. Following shifts in demand and supply, the supply of dollars exceeds demand at the current exchange rate, such that there is a surplus of dollars in currency exchange markets. The exchange rate thus begins to fall. As the exchange rate falls, foreign buyers move down the new demand curve and acquire more (cheaper) dollars for purchasing U.S. goods, investing in the U.S. industry, or participating in U.S. financial markets. Foreign holders of dollars move down the new supply curve and offer fewer (cheaper) dollars for exchange. The exchange rate continues to fall until currency demand and supply are again equal. In Figure 18.2, the new equilibrium exchange rate for dollars is $1 = 1.8 DM.

Movement down the demand and supply curves to the lower exchange rate takes place through increased sales of U.S. exports and reduced U.S. purchases of foreign imports. To understand this, note the corresponding changes in the prices of traded goods. For $1 = 1.8$ DM, the DM price of the U.S. aircraft mentioned above would fall to $(1.8 \text{ DM})(1,000,000) = 1,800,000$ DM, while the dollar price of the German auto would rise to $(\$.566)(10,000) = \$5,600$. Thus, the lower exchange rate would tend to stimulate sales of U.S. goods and reduce U.S. purchases of foreign goods. Exports and imports would again come into balance.

To summarize, rapidly rising prices in a nation generally lead to a negative trade balance. However, the resulting depreciation in the currency's exchange rate stimulates a higher level of sales abroad and a lower level of purchases from abroad, bringing international accounts back into balance.

Exchange Rates and Price Elasticity of Demand for Traded Goods

We have shown how changes in currency supply and demand cause changes in exchange rates and may cause changes in the flow of currencies in trade. The effect of a decrease in the currency exchange rate on the equilibrium quantity exchanged depends on the magnitude of the shifts in currency demand and supply. With roughly equal shifts in the curves, as shown in Figure 18.2, the equilibrium quantity changes hardly at all, and the total level of trade remains relatively constant. However, if buyers of U.S. exports are more sensitive to rising prices of U.S. goods than are U.S. buyers of foreign imports, the leftward shift in currency demand will be greater than the rightward shift in currency supply. The result will be a decrease in the equilibrium quantity of dollars used in trade. U.S. manufacturing firms will thus suffer a loss of foreign markets.

The magnitude of demand and supply shifts also determines the magnitude of the decrease in the exchange rate. In general, the greater the responsiveness of consumers to price changes for traded goods, the greater the shift in currency supply and demand curves.

The responsiveness of consumers to changes in currency exchange rates depends on price elasticity of demand for traded goods and services. Remember that currency demand results from the desire of consumers to purchase goods and services produced in the issuing nation. Rising prices for U.S. goods and services would normally cause a decrease in the quantities demanded—and a leftward shift in the currency demand curve. The magnitude of the shift in currency demand depends on price elasticity of demand for U.S. goods and services. If global demand for a nation's exports is relatively price elastic, the shift in currency demand will be quite large. Demand is relatively price elastic when there are acceptable substitutes available from other nations. In this case, consumers may choose to buy or not, depending on the price of the good. On the other hand, if global demand is relatively inelastic, the currency demand curve will shift relatively little. Consumers in this case must continue to buy in relatively constant quantities regardless of price.

Price elasticity of demand for traded goods also affects shifts in currency supply. Remember that the currency supply curve results from sales of foreign goods and services to the issuing nation—in this example, to the United States. Relatively lower prices for goods produced elsewhere would normally cause an increase in purchases of imports and a rightward shift in the currency supply curve. If U.S. demand for imported goods and services is relatively price elastic, the shift in currency supply will be large. Demand is relatively price elastic when foreign imports are easily substituted for goods available in the domestic economy. On the other hand, if demand for imports is relatively price inelastic, the currency supply curve will shift hardly at all.

Wide shifts in currency demand and supply lead to wide swings in exchange rates, with the potential for wide fluctuations in the total level of trade. All of these tendencies are associated with high price elasticity for traded goods. A nation's trade is particularly subject to high price elasticity if its exports must compete against acceptable substitutes in other nations or if its imports are easily substitutable for domestically produced goods.

These characteristics are true of many manufacturing nations and many developing nations dependent on primitive agriculture. They are less true of industrial nations producing high technology equipment and of nations producing a specialized industrial commodity or agricultural product. Aircraft, bauxite, and coffee are examples of the latter.

Income Elasticity of Demand for Traded Goods

While emphasizing the trade effects of price elasticity of demand, we should not ignore the effects of income elasticity. Changes in income growth also have the effect of shifting demand for traded goods, with a corresponding shift in currency demand and supply curves. Widespread recession, with decreases in consumer incomes around the world, can cause a sharp drop in demand for exports of certain manufactured goods, particularly luxury items and capital equipment. For the producing nation, a leftward shift in currency demand can cause a drop in the currency exchange rate, making foreign purchases more costly. The total level of trade in such cases will tend to fall, spreading the decline in sales to other nations and aggravating the recession.

Currency Appreciation

A decrease in a nation's exchange rate implies a corresponding increase in another's. Thus, currency **depreciation** in the U.S. must be accompanied by currency **appreciation** among certain of our trading partners. The behavior of particular currencies relative to the U.S. dollar depends on shifts in particular supply and demand curves and, more fundamentally, on price and income elasticity of demand for particular traded goods.

Recent Behavior of Exchange Rates

Changes in exchange rates influence the relationship between a nation's exports and imports. During 1977–1978, the value of the U.S. dollar fell 20 to 30 percent against the German mark and the Japanese yen. The immediate result was an increase in the outflow of U.S. currency, as importers required larger dollar amounts to pay for foreign goods and services ordered previously. The longer-term result was more favorable to the United States, however. As the dollar price of foreign goods increased, U.S. consumers reduced their purchases of imports. Foreigners acquired more cheap dollars for purchasing U.S. exports, and the outflow of dollars was reversed.[1]

Between 1980 and the middle of 1982 the situation changed again. Contractionary economic policy in the United States had resulted in slower monetary growth, lower price inflation, and slower income growth. The exchange value of the dollar rose by as much as 50 percent against the currency of some of our trading partners. The higher exchange rate encouraged U.S. consumers to import more foreign goods (move up the dollar supply curve) and foreign buyers to purchase fewer U.S. exports (move up the dollar demand curve). The result was an increase in the outflow of dollars.

Further dollar appreciation continued through 1984, with increased competition from foreign producers for U.S. manufacturers. Exports declined by $35 billion and imports increased by about one-third. The result was a substantial increase in the outflow of U.S. dolllars. The decline in exports threatened to reduce total production, employment, and income in the United States.

EXCHANGE RATES AND FINANCIAL MARKETS

Thus far we have emphasized the effect of exchange rate changes on a nation's level of trade. However, changes in currency exchange rates also affect participation in a nation's financial markets.

Borrowers enter financial markets to acquire funds at the lowest interest charge. Lenders enter the market to supply funds for the highest interest income. Using foreign funds for borrowing or lending requires consideration of exchange rate movement. In general, borrowers seek to borrow currencies that are expected to decrease in value so that their loans can be repaid with a smaller expenditure of domestic currency. Lenders seek to lend currencies that are expected to increase in value so that the value of their loan will increase along with the currency. The result of these contrary tendencies is relatively higher interest charges in markets for depreciating currencies and relatively lower interest charges in markets for appreciating currencies. The movement in interest rates roughly offsets the expected change in exchange rates.

---

1. Economists refer to the lagged response of exports and imports as the J-effect. The first result of a change in exchange rates is a sharper movement of currency flows away from balance. Then, as new orders are made or cancelled, currency flows tend toward balance.

CASE STUDY 18.1   **Exchange Rates and Pass-Through Pricing**

When the dollar's exchange rate rises, U.S. importers pay out fewer dollars for each foreign purchase. If importers reduce their own prices to U.S. consumers, we say that the full amount of the dollar's appreciation is "passed through." If foreign goods are priced in dollars, however, a rise in the dollar's value has no effect on import prices, and there is no "pass through."

Frequently, an increase in the dollar's value leads some foreign exporters to increase prices in terms of their own currency in order to capture some of the gain from the dollar's rise. Others who price their goods in dollars may reduce their dollar price in order to remain competitive with U.S. manufacturers. We would call such policies "partial pass-throughs" since not all the gain from the dollar's appreciation is enjoyed by U.S. consumers.

Whether or not exchange rate changes are passed on to consumers depends on characteristics of the market. If demand for imported goods is relatively price elastic and marginal costs are relatively constant, pass-throughs tend to be greater. By reducing price, the U.S. importer can increase sales and gain market share, while discouraging the growth of domestic competition. These circumstances are frequently true of differentiated consumer goods like apparel, wine, and certain household items.

If demand is relatively inelastic or marginal costs are increasing, there may be no pass-through. These conditions are true of markets in which the United States has a major share and in which products are relatively homogeneous: agricultural commodities and minerals are examples of such markets. For such goods, world prices are determined in world markets, so that changes in exchange rates have little effect in a single market. Often, these goods are specialized, with few substitutes, causing price changes to have little effect on sales. In addition, long-term contracts govern the prices of many of these items.

A rise in the dollar's exchange rate also affects U.S. exporters. Exporters may try to offset the higher cost of their product by reducing the dollar price to foreign buyers. A reduction in the dollar price is more likely in foreign markets in which demand is relatively price elastic or in which there is strong competition. These circumstances are true of the markets for computers, office machines and many manufactured goods. Reducing the dollar price of exports reduces profit per unit but may protect against a decline in volume and a drop in total profit. When foreign demand is relatively inelastic, exporters may safely maintain dollar prices even in the face of an increase in the dollar's value. These circumstances are true of goods such as oil and gas drilling equipment as well as farm machinery, since exports make up only a small part of a firm's total sales.

The Federal Reserve Bank of New York reports that pass-throughs on U.S. imports constitute almost two-thirds of the change in the dollar's value and pass-throughs on exports about one-third. Stated differently, decreases in import prices offset about 6 of each 10 percentage points of increase in the dollar's value, splitting the gain from currency appreciation about 60/40 between U.S. consumers ad U.S. business profits. Similarly, decreases in export prices split the gain from currency appreciation between foreign consumers and U.S. business profits about 40/60.

Taken as a whole, U.S. imports and exports tend to be relatively price elastic: $e_X = -1.6$, and $e_M = -1.3$. If the value of the dollar increases by 10 percent, import prices tend to fall about 6 percent and the volume of imports tends to rise about 10 percent. For the same dollar increase, export prices tend to rise about 4 percent and volume tends to decline about 5 percent.

MANAGERIAL THINKING

1 Discuss the basis for a lagged response of consumers to changes in currency exchange rates. What is the likely result of such lags?

2 What are the likely macroeconomic results of the 20-percent appreciation of the dollar that occurred in the first two years of the 1980s in terms of trade balance, domestic employment and prices, per capita incomes, and economic growth?

Source: Robert A. Feldman, "Dollar Appreciation, Foreign Trade, and the U.S. Economy," *Federal Reserve Bank of New York Quarterly Review,* Summer 1982, pp. 1–9.

To illustrate, suppose the exchange rate for DMs is 1 DM = $.50 and the rate is expected to decline by 20 percent to 1 DM = $.40. Suppose also that the exchange rate for pounds is 1£ = $2.50 and that the rate is expected to rise by 20 percent to 1£ = $3.00. In addition, interest charges in both nations are i = 10 percent. Now suppose that a U.S. business firm wants to borrow the equivalent of $100,000. What is the lowest-cost source of the funds?

One option would be to borrow deutsche marks at the current exchange rate and convert them to dollars. The necessary quantity of DMs would be:

$$\frac{\$100,000}{\$.50} = 200,000 \text{ DM}.$$

After using the funds for one year, the firm would need to repay

$$1.10(200,000 \text{ DM}) = 220,000 \text{ DM}$$

at the end of the year. To acquire 220,000 DMs at the new exchange rate would require 220,000 DM($.40) = $88,000. In this case, a 20-percent drop in the currency's value would more than offset the interest charge, making it possible to repay the loan with fewer dollars than the amount of dollars borrowed.

Borrowing pounds would have a different result. To obtain $100,000, it would be necessary to borrow:

$$\frac{\$100,000}{\$2.50} = 40,000£$$

and convert them to (40,000£)($2.50) = $100,000. At the end of the year the loan would be repaid with

$$1.10(40,000£) = 44,000£.$$

Acquiring 44,000£ at the new exchange rate would require

$$(44,000£)(\$3.00) = \$132,000.$$

In this case a 20-percent increase in the currency's exchange rate combines with the 10-percent interest charge to increase the cost of borrowing.

CASE STUDY 18.2   Borrowing Foreign Currencies

The decision as to whether a firm finances investment projects with domestic or foreign funds depends on the cost of borrowing in the various currencies. The cost of borrowing foreign currencies includes not only the regularly scheduled interest payments but also changes in the currency's value. If a foreign currency rises in value, making regular interest payments will become increasingly costly, as will repaying the face value of the loan at maturity. Managers must compare the total cost of borrowing under the various alternatives and select the alternative with the lowest cost.

To illustrate, suppose ABT Corporation is planning a $50 million capital investment in West Germany. The funds can be acquired in any of the following ways:

1. An issue of dollar bonds with an 11-percent annual interest coupon and issuing costs equal to 2.5 percent of the bond's dollar value.

2. A deutsche mark (DM) bond with an 8-percent annual interest coupon issued at 99-percent discount and with issuing costs equal to 2.5 percent of the dollar value.

3. A Swiss franc (SF) bond with a 4.5-percent annual interest coupon issued at par value and with issuing costs equal to 2.5 percent of the dollar value.

Notice that each of the foreign loans would achieve a lower interest cost of domestic borrowing. Still, managers must also consider the possibility of rising currency values, which might cause interest and principal payments actually to cost more in terms of domestic currency paid out.

The following tables show the costs of borrowing in domestic and foreign currencies. Look first at Table A. A $1,000 bond at 11-percent interest requires annual

TABLE A

(1) Year	(2) Interest payment	(3) After-tax interest cost	(4) Annual issuing cost	(5) Annual tax saving	(6) After-tax cost of dollar bond
1	$110	$59.40	$2.50	$1.15	$58.25
2	110	59.40	2.50	1.15	58.25
3	110	59.40	2.50	1.15	58.25
4	110	59.40	2.50	1.15	58.25
5	110	59.40	2.50	1.15	58.25
6	110	59.40	2.50	1.15	58.25
7	110	59.40	2.50	1.15	58.25
8	110	59.40	2.50	1.15	58.25
9	110	59.40	2.50	1.15	58.25
10	110	59.40	2.50	1.15	58.25

Proceeds: $1,000 − 25 = $975

$$975 = \frac{58.25}{(1 + r)} + \frac{58.25}{(1 + r)^2} + \frac{58.25}{(1 + r)^3} + \frac{58.25}{(1 + r)^4} + \frac{58.25}{(1 + r)^5} + \frac{58.25}{(1 + r)^6}$$
$$+ \frac{58.25}{(1 + r)^7} + \frac{58.25}{(1 + r)^8} + \frac{58.25}{(1 + r)^9} + \frac{1,058.25}{(1 + r)^{10}},$$

where $r = .0617$. Therefore, $i_{AT} = 6.17$ percent.

interest payments of $110, as shown in Column (2). However, because interest payments are tax deductible, the after tax cost of borrowing is only $i_b(1 - t) = $110(1 - .46) = 59.40.

The proceeds of a $1,000 bond are the face value less issuing costs:

$$\text{Proceeds} = \$1,000 - .025(\$1,000) = \$975.$$

The issuing cost of $.025(\$1,000) = \$25$ is a tax deductible expense that can be distributed equally over the ten years of the bond's life. Thus, annual issuing costs are $\$25/10 = \$2.50$. Annual issuing expenses of $2.50 reduce the firm's taxable income and its tax bill by $t(\$2.50) = .46(\$2.50) = \$1.15$. Thus, the annual after tax cost of the bond is $\$59.40 - \$1.15 = \$58.25$.

These values have been included in the equation shown in Table A. Solving this equation for r produces the rate of discount that equates the proceeds from a $1,000 bond issue with the present value of annual cash flows where the final payment includes repayment of the face value of $1,000. The discount rate is $r = 6.17$ percent. This is the after-tax cost of borrowing through the issue of dollar bonds.

Tables B and C show computation of the after-tax cost of borrowing through the issue of bonds denominated in deutsche marks (DMs) and Swiss francs (SFs). International borrowing requires considerations of currency exchange rates. An exchange rate is the cost of DMs or SFs in terms of U.S. dollars. Tables B and C show initial exchange rates of $p_{DM} = \$.5701$ and $p_{SF} = \$.6232$. Managers' projections of exchange rates are shown in Column (2) of Tables B and C. The value of the DM is expected to rise at between 4.0 percent and 4.3 percent per year over the life of the bond, and the SF is expected to rise between 6.4 percent and 6.8 percent.

With an initial exchange rate of $p_{DM} = \$.5701$, the face value of a 1,000 DM bond would be $Q_{DM}(p_{DM}) = 1,000 \text{ DM}(\$.5701) = \$570.10$. If a 1,000 DM bond is

TABLE B

(1)	(2)	(3)	(4)	(5)	(6)	(7)
				Interest	Tax saving from	
	Exchange	DM	$	after-	discount and	After tax
Year	rate	interest	interest	tax	issuing expenses	cost
1	.5937	80DM	$47.50	$25.65	$.92	$24.72
2	.6185	80	49.42	26.72	.92	25.80
3	.6437	80	51.50	27.81	.92	26.89
4	.6696	80	53.57	28.93	.92	28.01
5	.6979	80	55.83	30.15	.92	29.23
6		80	58.11	31.38	.92	30.46
7	.7569	80	60.55	32.70	.92	31.78
8	.7883	80	63.06	34.05	.92	33.13
9	.8201	80	65.61	35.43	.92	34.51
10	.8542	80	68.34	36.90	.92	35.98

Proceeds = 965 DM = $550.15.   Initial exchange rate: DM = $.5701.

$$550.15 = \frac{24.72}{(1 + r)} + \frac{25.80}{(1 + r)^2} + \frac{26.89}{(1 + r)^3} + \frac{28.01}{(1 + r)^4} + \frac{29.23}{(1 + r)^5} + \frac{30.46}{(1 + r)^6}$$
$$+ \frac{31.78}{(1 + r)^7} + \frac{33.13}{(1 + r)^8} + \frac{34.51}{(1 + r)^9} + \frac{35.98 + 854.20 - 130.69}{(1 + r)^{10}},$$

where $r = .0755$. Therefore, the after-tax cost of issuing deutsche mark bonds is 7.55 percent.

TABLE C

(1)	(2)	(3)	(4)	(5)	(6)	(7)
	Exchange	SF	$	Interest	Tax savings from discount and	After-tax
Year	rate	interest	interest	after-tax	issuing expenses	cost
1	.6680	45SF	$30.06	$16.23	$.72	$15.51
2	.7124	45	32.06	17.31	.72	16.59
3	.7593	45	34.17	18.45	.72	17.73
4	.8079	45	36.36	19.63	.72	18.91
5	.8618	45	38.78	20.94	.72	20.22
6	.9188	45	41.35	22.33	.72	21.61
7	.9811	45	44.15	23.84	.72	23.12
8	1.0463	45	47.08	25.43	.72	24.71
9	1.1157	45	50.21	27.11	.72	26.39
10	1.1909	45	53.59	28.94	.72	28.21

Proceeds = 975, SF = $607.62.   Initial exchange rate: P_{SF} = $.6232.

$$607.62 = \frac{15.51}{(1+r)} + \frac{16.59}{(1+r)^2} + \frac{17.73}{(1+r)^3} + \frac{18.91}{(1+r)^4} + \frac{20.22}{(1+r)^5} + \frac{21.61}{(1+r)^6}$$
$$+ \frac{23.12}{(1+r)^7} + \frac{24.71}{(1+r)^8} + \frac{26.39}{(1+r)^9} + \frac{28.21 + 1,190.90 - 261.14}{(1+r)^{10}},$$

where r = .0718. Therefore, the after-tax cost of issuing Swiss franc bonds is 7.18 percent.

---

sold at a 99-percent discount and with a 2.5-percent issuing charge, the proceeds from the sale of the bond would be [.99(1,000 DM) − .025(1,000 DM)]($.5701) = $550.15. Annual interest charges of 8 percent would amount to 80 DM. The equivalent interest cost in dollars is determined by the exchange rate each year interest is paid. Thus, the first year's interest cost is $Q_{DM}(p_{DM})$ = 80 DM($.5937) = $47.50. Interest payments on a bond are tax deductible. Therefore, the after-tax cost of interest payments is determined by multiplying Column (4) by $(1 - t)$: $i_b(1 - t)$, as shown in Column (5) of Table B.

The initial costs of the bond are the discount below face value and the issuing costs. With discounted sale at 99 percent and issuing charges of 2.5 percent of face value, initial costs are 10 DM + 25 DM = 35 DM or, in dollar terms, 35 DM(.5701) = $19.95. Dividing initial charges of $19.95 over the ten years of the bond yields $19.95/10 = $2.00 annual expense. Since these charges are also tax deductible, they result in tax savings of .46($2.00) = $.92 for each year of the bond's life. Total annual charges after taxes are shown in Column (7).

After-tax charges are substituted in the formula shown in Table B for computing r, the rate of discount that equates the initial proceeds from the bond with the costs over its ten-year life. The cost of the bond in the tenth year includes interest due and repayment of the face value of 1,000DM. With an exchange rate of DM = $.8542, payment of the face value requires $854.20. The difference between the initial proceeds from the bond and the payment of face value at maturity is considered a loss (or a gain) for tax purposes. Therefore, the difference ($854.20 − $550.15 = $284.10) can be deducted from taxable income for a tax savings of .46($284.10) = $130.69. Thus, the net cost of the bond in the tenth year is $35.98 + $854.20 − $130.69 = $759.49. Solving the equation for r yields an after-tax cost for deutsche mark bonds of 7.55 percent.

Compare the cost of borrowing under each of the alternatives that have been presented. Even though the interest charge on the dollar loan is greater, changes in currency values increase the cost of borrowing through both of the foreign sources. Because deutsche marks and Swiss francs are expected to increase in value, the cost of paying interest and principal would be greater.

MANAGERIAL THINKING

1 Assume that in the previous example the Swiss franc will increase at the rate of 5 percent per year. This will require a change in Columns (2), (4), (5), and (7) of Table C. Now compute the rate of discount that equates the after-tax cost of issuing Swiss franc bonds with the proceeds. (Hint: Determine first whether the rate of discount will increase or decrease. Then try several values until the discounted value is equal to the initial proceeds of $607.62.)

2 What adjustments in international finance would you expect to take place that would affect the interest rates and exchange rates in the three nations represented in this Case Study? Explain your answer.

Source: William R. Folks, Jr. and Ramesh Advani, "Raising Funds with Foreign Currency," *Financial Executive*, February 1980, pp. 44–49.

EXAMPLE 18.1   Hedging and Arbitrage in Foreign Exchange Markets

Most foreign trade is conducted through the use of credit. Frequently, an importer arranges with his bank for a letter of credit to be paid to the exporter when the goods are delivered to an authorized shipper. In other cases, a currency draft may be drawn by the exporter against the bank account of the importer. When the importer signs the draft, it becomes an **acceptance** and is returned to the exporter to be held until due or sold to a bank at a discount.

Between the time an order is placed and the time payment is due, the value of currencies may change. Traders protect themselves against changes in currency values by "hedging." Hedging involves the purchase or sale of foreign currencies to be delivered in the future. An importer who will need foreign currency to pay for goods expected in ninety days in the future can purchase a "forward" contract for the necessary amount. In the meantime, exporters who will receive foreign currencies in ninety days in payment for goods shipped currently will be selling "forward" contracts. The advantage of forward contracts for both importers and exporters is the reduction of risk associated with changes in currency values between the time an order is placed and the time payment is due.

The price of a "forward" contract is roughly equal to the current price of the foreign currency plus or minus the difference in interest rates in the two countries. A forward contract for a foreign currency sells for a lower price (at "discount") if interest rates in the foreign country are higher than in the United States. A forward contract for a foreign currency sells for a higher price (at a "premium") if interest rates in the United States are higher than in the foreign country.

Whether a forward contract sells at a discount or for a premium depends on arbitrage. **Arbitrage** is the simultaneous purchase and sale of equivalent currencies for a profit. To make this clearer, suppose the current or "spot" price of English pounds is $2.50 and the ninety-day forward price is $2.45. The difference between the spot and the forward price is the **implied interest differential:**

$$\text{Implied interest differential} = \frac{2.50 - 2.45}{2.50} = \frac{.05}{2.50} = .02$$

which equals 2 percent for ninety days or 8 percent annually.[1] If the **actual interest rate differential** is 10 percent annually, or 2.5 percent for ninety days, an arbitrageur would borrow dollars in the United States and use them to purchase pounds at the spot price for lending in Great Britain. The gain on the transaction would be the ½-percent interest earned above the cost of borrowing. At the same time, the arbitrageur would protect against a change in exchange rates by selling forward pounds. For each pound loaned the arbitrageur expects to receive an additional 2.5 percent. Selling 2.5 percent additional pounds forward for a price that is 2 percent less than the spot cost of pounds yields an additional gain of ½ percent.

As arbitrageurs buy spot pounds and sell forward pounds, the effect is to raise the price of spot pounds and reduce the price of forward pounds. Arbitrage will continue until the relationship between spot and forward pounds correctly reflects the interest rate differential in the two financial markets.

This adjustment can be shown algebraically by expressing the relationship between forward and spot price as a ratio:

$$\frac{r_f}{r_s} = \frac{2.45}{2.50}.$$

Interest rates can also be expressed as a ratio:

$$\frac{1 + i_{US}}{1 + i_{GB}} = \frac{1.10}{1.20}.$$

The ratios can then be compared.

$$\frac{r_f}{r_s} = \frac{2.45}{2.50} \neq \frac{1.10}{1.20} = \frac{1 + i_{US}}{1 + i_{GB}},$$

and $.98 > .92$. If the forward/spot ratio is higher than the interest rate ratio, there are gains to be made from selling pounds forward. An arbitrageur would borrow dollars to purchase pounds for lending and eventual forward sale. Arbitrage transactions would have the effect of increasing the spot price and reducing the forward price, pushing the ratio $r_f/r_s = .98$ down toward the level of the interest rate ratio.

Other adjustments also would be occurring in financial markets. Increased borrowing in the United States and lending in Britain would raise U.S. interest rates and lower those in Britain, pushing the interest rate ratio $(1 + i_{US})/(1 + i_{GB}) = .92$ up toward the level of the forward/spot ratio.

MANAGERIAL THINKING

Describe the adjustments that would take place if the forward/spot ratio should be less than the interest rate ratio.

---

1. In other words, interest rates in Britain are 8 percent higher than interest rates in the United States. The forward rate on 90-day pounds includes an 8 percent discount.

Klaus Friedrich, *International Economics: Concepts and Issues*, (New York: McGraw-Hill Book Company, 1974).

Typically, more borrowers would enter financial markets in the first nation, putting upward pressure on interest rates and eventually on the currency's exchange rate as well. Borrowers would leave financial markets in the second nation, putting downward pressure on interest and exchange rates. The final result would be a combination of interest and exchange rates that correctly reflects the marginal efficiency of investment, the supply of investment funds, and the level of currency risk in each country.

DIRECT FOREIGN INVESTMENT

Typically, the first relationship between a firm and foreign consumers and business firms is through trade. We have seen that international trade affects and is affected by the exchange rate for international currencies. Exchange rates—and expected future exchange rates—also influence participation in international financial markets. In general, funds for lending tend to flow into nations whose exchange rates are expected to rise, and borrowing is done in currencies whose exchange rates are expected to fall.

All of these factors also influence a third type of relationship between a business firm in one nation and consumers and business firms in another: that is, direct investment. **Foreign direct investment** is the purchase of productive facilities in another country.

Direct investment in a foreign country has various advantages. Production abroad is a way of avoiding import tariffs or quotas on sales to the affected country. Production abroad may make use of plentiful resource supplies in particular parts of the world, adapt techniques of production to resource capabilities, or adapt product design to the requirements of particular markets.

On the other hand, foreign direct investment is subject to risks over and above the risks of operating in the domestic economy. Some of the risks of foreign investment result from inherent differences in economic circumstances among various nations. For example, differences in resource supplies affect resource prices differently. Differences in the stage of economic development of a nation affect the supply of skilled and unskilled labor and their wage rates. Differences in inflation rates affect currency exchange rates and the value of earnings when they are repatriated to the parent country.

Some of the risks associated with direct foreign investment result from policies of the foreign government. Governmental risks can be classified under the following headings.

Tariffs

A tariff is a tax on a material or a good as it passes over a national border. **Import tariffs** frequently have the intent to protect local producers of the taxed material or good or to encourage domestic production. Import tariffs have the effect of raising the price of necessary materials or parts used in production. An increase in the costs of production can impair a firm's competitiveness in world markets. **Export tariffs** have the intent of discouraging foreign sales in order to maintain a sufficient supply of finished goods—and low prices—in the producing country. Export tariffs have the effect of raising the prices of finished goods sold abroad and damaging a firm's international competitiveness.

The cost to the foreign investor of import and export tariffs depends on price elasticities: price elasticity of supply of the material or component part the firm buys and price elasticity of demand for the finished good the firm sells. Costs are greatest if supply is inelastic and global demand is elastic. (Can you explain why?)

Restrictions on Repatriation of Earnings

Some governments place restrictions on the quantity of earnings a foreign firm can repatriate to its home country. Restrictions on repatriation of earnings have several objectives, including conservation of the host nation's limited supplies of foreign exchange and increasing the host nation's net benefits from foreign investment. A government may place an absolute ceiling on repatriation of earnings, forcing foreign investors to re-invest accumulated earnings in the local economy. Repatriated earnings also may be taxed or may be subject to less favorable currency exchange rates. The cost of such restrictions to the foreign investor depends on the opportunity cost of capital. If other investment opportunities promise lower yields than the net yield of foreign investment after restrictions, foreign investment should continue to be profitable.

Expropriation

Expropriation is probably the most feared government policy toward foreign investment. Expropriation is the seizure of foreign-owned assets. Governments have the legal right to expropriate properties, along with an obligation to compensate the owners for the properties that have been seized. Occasionally, governments exercise the right but ignore the obligation. This has been particularly true of revolutionary governments in recent decades. The most frequently expropriated properties have been those involved in extractive industries, agriculture, and public utilities. The cost of expropriation to the foreign investor depends on what point in the life of the investment expropriation takes place. An investment that has served long years may have already returned sufficient yield to justify the initial outlay.

Government policies that are unfavorable to foreign investment also impose costs on the host economy. By increasing risks, governments may discourage foreign investment and forfeit the advantages of spreading technology and economic growth. A decrease in foreign investment may have the effect of reducing access to foreign markets, reducing the inflow of technical skills, and reducing the inflow of managerial talent. A government should weigh the expected gains from such policies against these costs before taking action.

Measuring the Risk of Direct Foreign Investment

The effect on foreign investment of the risks we have discussed depends on their predictability. If managers can assign probabilities to possible future events, their costs can be built into the investment decision. The net yield of

TABLE 18.1

Import tariff	Probability
(p_1) 50 percent tariff on imported raw material	.30
(p_2) 30 percent tariff on imported raw material	.50
(p_3) no tariff on imported raw material	.20

Restrictions on repatriation of earnings	Probability
(p_4) No repatriation allowed	.25
(p_5) Ceiling equal to 10 percent of stockholders' equity	.60
(p_6) No restrictions on repatriation	.15

Labor supply and wage rates	Probability
(p_7) Extreme shortage with 10 percent increase in wage rates	.25
(p_8) Moderate shortage with 5 percent increase in wage rates	.45
(p_9) No labor shortage	.30

the investment after all costs, including risk, must be sufficient to justify the initial outlay. To illustrate, suppose managers estimate the probabilities associated with possible future events as shown in Table 18.1.

Under the circumstances in Table 18.1, managers can estimate the probability of a wide range of future events. Thus, the probability of a 50-percent import tariff, total restrictions on repatriation of earnings, and an extreme labor shortage is:

$$(p_1)(p_4)(p_7) = (.30)(.25)(.25) = .0188.$$

A less restrictive policy on repatriation would change the probability of this event to:

$$(p_1)(p_5)(p_7) = (.30)(.60)(.25) = .045.$$

The probabilities associated with all possible events would be determined similarly. The sum of all probabilities would be 1.00.

After assigning probabilities to future events, managers should calculate the net present value of the foreign investment under each set of circumstances. Cash flows under the least favorable circumstances described above would be reduced by the effects of a 50-percent import tariff on necessary materials and a 10-percent annual increase in wage rates. Earnings would accumulate abroad, earning whatever interest rate is possible on re-invested earnings in the local economy. The discounted value of future cash flows and earnings from re-investment would constitute the *NPV* of investment under conditions least favorable to the firm.

The *NPV* of the investment under all other sets of circumstances could be determined similarly. Finally, the expected value of *NPV* of the foreign investment is the weighted sum of all *NPV*s, when the weights are the probabilities assigned to each event:

$$(ev)\ NPV = (p_{1,4,7})(NPV_{1,4,7}) + (p_{1,5,7})(NPV_{1,5,7}) \ldots (p_n)(NPV_n).$$

A comparison of the (*ev*)*NPV* of a particular foreign investment with the (*ev*) *NPV* of other alternatives would permit the selection of the optimum strategy.

Another procedure for including risk in the foreign investment decision would be to adjust the discount factor for risk. Increasing the discount factor has the effect of reducing the present value of earnings received late in the life of an investment. At the same time, a larger discount factor increases the relative size of costs incurred early in the investment's life. The combined effect is to reduce a project's *NPV* and to make it less competitive with other alternatives available to the firm.

Managers may adopt a wide range of procedures for adjusting the discount rate, from simple increases to increases based on precise classifications of circumstances involving risk and appropriate risk indices or weights. Managers may also calculate a "threshold" discount rate, above which a particular foreign investment becomes competitive with other investment alternatives.

Transfer Pricing in a Multinational Firm

Decisions concerning transfer pricing are an important concern of managers of multinational firms. Fundamental decisions about transfer pricing are based on considerations of market demand (discussed in detail in Appendix 10A). In general, a firm should set a competitive price where the global market for the material or part is competitive and should use price discrimination where the firm enjoys a monopoly. With a monopoly price for users outside the firm and a lower price for the firm's subsidiaries, the firm maximizes profits for the enterprise as a whole.

A multinational firm must take other factors into account, however. Pricing according to simple profit-maximizing rules may reduce the firm's total profits after taxes in the various nations in which the firm operates. The objectives of a firm's pricing policy will vary according to circumstances within the various nations.

One objective of transfer pricing might be to shift profits to a low-tax country in order to reduce the firm's total tax bill. In this case, the transfer price would be adjusted downward for sales to subsidiaries in low-tax countries.

Another objective might be to reduce import tariffs paid by the processing subsidiaries. Transfer price would be adjusted downward in order to reduce the value on which a tariff must be paid. Another objective might be to transfer profits from a nation that restricts repatriation of earnings. Transfer prices would be adjusted upward for sales to processing subsidiaries in such a nation. Finally, another objective might be to discourage competition in later stages of processing the material or part. Transfer and market prices in this case would be adjusted upward to concentrate profits in markets where the subsidiary enjoys monopoly power and reduce profits for rival firms using the material or part in the production of other goods.

Many of these objectives may be contradictory, so that managers must establish priorities and set transfer prices accordingly. Some firms establish

CASE STUDY 18.3   Using Foreign Earnings Profitably

Many U.S. firms earn as much on their foreign operations as they do in the United States. When the exchange rates on foreign currencies change, the firm's income may fluctuate widely, regardless of the actual level of sales in the foreign nation. The significance of foreign earnings for a firm's economic health makes it necessary for many firms to establish a foreign currency trading department.

The Coca Cola Company does business in 145 countries, earning nearly two-thirds of total earnings from foreign operations. In the early 1980s, the head of Coke's foreign currency trading department was Sam Ayoub, a native Egyptian with substantial experience in international economics and politics. Ayoub made Coke's financial plans on the basis of expected changes in currency values. For example, during 1981 he believed that the German mark was undervalued against the U.S. dollar and would eventually rise. Therefore, he held $30 million of Coke's earnings in marks. The mark did rise 8.6 percent against the dollar, and Coke gained $2.6 million when the earnings were finally converted to dollars.

In 1982, Ayoub expected the Mexican peso to be devalued and recommended a 30-percent increase in Coke's borrowings in Mexico. As predicted, the peso fell to one-fourth of its former value relative to the dollar, making it possible to pay back the Mexican loan with fewer dollars.

Ayoub's strategy in Chile was different because of Chile's restrictions on repatriation of earnings. He recommended spending excess Chilean earnings on construction, equipment, and real estate in Chile. The result was to minimize losses on currency trading and to earn a return on local investment.

A firm's international borrowing and lending must be settled at the end of each year and the results must be reported for tax purposes. This makes it especially necessary to have current information on economic and political developments in other countries where the firm may have financial interests.

MANAGERIAL THINKING

Explain how the use of probabilities can help managers of foreign currency determine the optimum level of borrowing and lending in other nations.

Source: Jody Long, "By Trusting Intuition, Educated Guesses, Coke Capitalizes on Exchange-Rate Shifts," *The Wall Street Journal*, September 3, 1982.

"tax havens" in low-tax countries. A "tax haven" may play no part in actual production or distribution, but may act solely to collect profits. However, if more than 30 percent of a "tax haven's" profits result from purchases from or sales to a single firm, these profits may be subject to U.S. taxes.

THE STRUCTURE OF A MULTINATIONAL ENTERPRISE

When a firm makes a decision to invest directly in productive facilities abroad, managers must decide the appropriate structure of the enterprise. The structure of a foreign enterprise depends on *legal* considerations in the parent country and on the *technical* characteristics of the operation itself.

The principal legal considerations in the structure decision involve taxation. Taxation of foreign earnings depends largely on the degree to which the accounts of the foreign enterprise are consolidated with those of the parent country. In general, the accounts of a *branch* are fully consolidated with those of the parent so that earnings are taxed in the parent country. In contrast, the accounts of a *subsidiary* may not be taxed in the home country until they are actually repatriated to the parent firm.

Structure is also influenced by technical characteristics. When technical aspects of production are closely interdependent, there is greater need for close coordination between the parent firm and the foreign enterprise. This is particularly true of operations involving products or by-products used in successive stages of production within the firm. Subsequently, close coordination depends on a well-developed communication system. When communication among various units is poor, there is a greater tendency toward separation of operations. Decision making moves closer to production, and individual units may operate relatively independently.

A firm's foreign and domestic operations may be coordinated according to functions, products, or geographic areas.

Functional coordination would centralize decision making in activities such as marketing, finance, and product development or research in the parent firm. All marketing decisions, for example, would be made at the home office and then carried out by branches or subsidiaries around the world.

Functional coordination is less common than **product coordination,** however, since technical similarities among products make for more efficient decision making along product lines. Product lines would be organized as "profit centers," with incentive systems to encourage more efficient performance in the individual operating units. Management along product lines permits more flexible response to frequent changes in market conditions around the world. Enterprises that are organized along product lines may also subdivide decision making along functional lines.

Enterprises with far-flung operations and difficult channels of communication may be organized according to **geographical coordination.** Area managers can concentrate on all decisions involving production throughout well-defined areas such as Latin America, Europe, Southeast Asia, and so forth. They would make decisions to shut down low-profit operations, exploit new market opportunities, and arrange production to take advantage of increasing returns to scale. Decentralized decision making along area lines has various advantages. Often, the opportunity to deal with problems locally encourages more effective performance. It adds flexibility to a firm's operations and avoids costly delays from imperfect communications.

Financial Structure for a Multinational Enterprise

A foreign venture can be financed in either of two ways: through sale of stock or through borrowing from the parent company. Borrowing from the parent company has various advantages. Interest on a loan is a business expense, deducted from foreign earnings before taxes are paid. The parent company thus reduces foreign tax payments and avoids the risks of foreign restrictions on repatriation of earnings.

EXAMPLE 18.2   Choosing Technology for a Foreign Enterprise

Foreign investment decisions involve a choice regarding the appropriate technology for the investment enterprise. Most production processes can be carried on in a variety of ways, depending on the availability of particular resources and the level of technological development of the area involved. Figure A illustrates the choice between technologies *I* and *II*. The graph's axes represent quantities of capital and labor used in production. The curves are isoquants representing (*I*) capital-intensive and (*II*) labor-intensive technologies for producing one hundred units of output during a particular period of time. Isoquants for producing larger quantities would be drawn higher and to the right of the isoquants in Figure A. Isoquants for capital-intensive technologies would be drawn in increments closer to the capital axis, and isoquants for labor-intensive technologies would be drawn in increments closer to the labor axis.

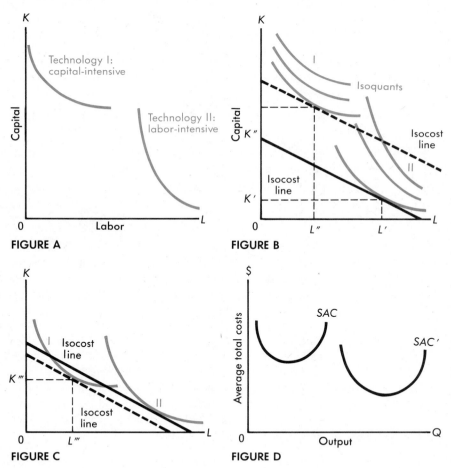

Choice of technologies would depend on the relative prices of capital and labor. If the price of labor is relatively low, isocost lines will be more horizontal, as shown in Figure B. A firm would choose the technology represented by the lowest isocost line tangent to the isoquant. Thus, production using technology *II* would use *OK'* units of capital and *OL'* units of labor. This is the lowest total cost. Using technology

I at existing prices would require *OK″* units of capital and *OL″* units of labor for higher total costs.

Improvements in either technology might call for a different decision. Figure C illustrates an improvement in the capital-intensive technology causing the isoquant for producing one hundred units to appear nearer the origin. With the improved technology, the lowest-cost production technology is technology *I*, using *OK‴* units of capital and only *OL‴* units of labor. Over time, we might expect all the variables in the decision to change: labor and capital costs, as well as available technologies for production. Managers must project the probable effects of such changes and consider them when choosing the appropriate technology.

Another important variable that is subject to change over time is market size. The size of the market affects decisions as to plant size and opportunities for returns to scale. Labor-intensive technologies are generally associated with small-scale production, where the ratio of labor to capital resources is high. Fixed costs are low relative to variable costs. Capital-intensive technologies are associated with larger scale production, with relatively small quantities of labor resources and relatively higher fixed costs.

Now consider Figure D. Figure D shows short-run average cost curves for small-scale and large-scale production. Early in a product's life, a small market would normally call for small-scale production. Unit costs of production would be rather high, even at the lowest-cost level of plant operation. Later in a product's life, however, a growing market may permit larger-scale, lower-cost production, as shown by SAC′.

Scale economies do not necessarily dictate the use of more capital-intensive technologies. In fact, small-scale production may involve the same ratio of labor and capital as large-scale production. The critical consideration is the flexibility of the technology in substituting capital for labor.

Loans may also be extended through generous credit terms on supplies furnished the foreign subsidiary by the parent or by government institutions. The Export-Import Bank is a source of trade credit for U.S. exports. The Agency for International Development (AID) provides loans of working capital in local currencies, and the International Bank for Reconstruction and Development (World Bank) provides long-term loans for high-priority operations in developing countries. Regional Development Banks throughout the world also provide loans for projects judged to be beneficial to the local economy. Finally, the International Finance Corporation (IFC) in the United States and the Overseas Private Investment Corporation (OPIC) provide equity capital and insurance for private enterprises operating abroad.

The parent company can acquire funds for lending from domestic financial markets or from financial markets abroad. Beginning in the early 1960s, many international holders of U.S. dollars began leaving their funds on deposit in European banks. For such banks, dollar deposits became a valuable source of loanable funds, often known as "Eurodollars." Eventually, European banks and banks around the world came to hold deposits in many foreign currencies, giving rise to a "Eurocurrency" market for borrowers of financial capital. Many large European financial institutions issue "Eurobonds" to attract foreign currencies, lending the proceeds to multinational corporations at rates generally above the most favorable rates available in U.S. markets.

SUMMARY

The growing interdependence of international economies is reflected by the expansion of global trade and investment. International economic relations depend on comparative advantage in production and on exchange rates between national currencies. Changes in a currency's demand or supply can cause it to appreciate or depreciate and, ultimately, can cause changes in the flows of imports and exports. The magnitude of the change in a nation's balance of trade depends on price and income elasticities of demand for traded goods and on the nation's fundamental macroeconomic policies.

International financial relationships depend on interest rates and on expected changes in currency values. Borrowers tend to borrow depreciating currencies, pushing the interest rates for these currencies up. Lenders tend to lend appreciating currencies, pushing the interest rates for these currencies down. Arbitrageurs deal in forward contracts and help adjust forward and spot prices to current interest rates.

Direct foreign investment is subject to risks associated with tariffs, restrictions on repatriation of earnings, and expropriation. A multinational firm may be structured on the basis of legal considerations or technical considerations, including managerial functions or products. The technology of a foreign manufacturing subsidiary depends on relative costs of resources.

KEY TERMS

interdependence	direct foreign investment
comparative advantage	import tariffs
exchange rate	export tariffs
depreciation	repatriation restriction
appreciation	expropriation
acceptance	functional coordination
arbitrage	product coordination
implied interest differential	geographical coordination
actual interest differential	

QUESTIONS AND PROBLEMS

1. Use the following exchange rates to compute the maximum price in foreign currencies you would pay for each of the listed items. Explain your answer.

   $1 = £.67, $1 = 8 Francs, $1 = 153 pesos, $1 = 240 Yen.

   a. An English sweater.
   b. A bottle of wine in a Paris cafe.
   c. A night at a seaside resort in Acapulco.
   d. A steak dinner in a restaurant in Tokyo.

2. Translate each of the dollar exchange rates in Problem 1 into exchange rates for the foreign currency.

3. The exchange rates in Problem 1 were quoted from the Foreign Exchange table in an issue of the *Wall Street Journal* from April 1983. Consult a recent issue to determine current exchange rates and report on the percentage change of each currency relative to the dollar. What are the implications of your findings with respect to U.S. trade, employment, and price inflation?

4. Which of the following U.S. imports are likely to experience relatively large pass-throughs when the dollar's exchange rate rises? Explain your answer.

    luxury foreign cars   tin
    shirts made in Hong Kong   camera lenses

5. Which of the following U.S. exports are likely to experience relatively large pass-throughs when the dollar's exchange rate rises? Explain your answer.

    specialized agricultural equipment   soybeans
    office machines   aircraft
    wheat

6. Assume the spot rate for Yen is $1Y = \$.004184$ and the 180-day forward rate is $1Y = \$.00425$. Interest rates are 11 percent in the United States and 10 percent in Japan. Describe the arbitrage adjustments that would take place between the two countries.

7. a. Explain the relationship between a nation's trade flows and supply and demand for the nation's currency in foreign exchange markets.
   b. How is the "balance of trade" reflected on a graph of a nation's foreign exchange market?
   c. What is the relationship between elasticity of demand for a nation's exports and demand for the nation's currency?
   d. What is the relationship between elasticity of demand for a nation's imports and supply of the nation's currency?

8. Suppose Alpha experiences substantially greater price inflation than other nations with which it trades. What is the likely effect on borrowing and lending in Alpha's currency? How will trends in borrowing and lending affect Alpha's interest rates? Illustrate your answer graphically.

9. A U.S. importer of cameras plans to buy a 90-day forward contract for a foreign currency as a hedge against changes in its exchange rate. What would the importer have to pay for German marks if the current exchange rate is $1 DM = \$0.48$ and interest rates are $i_{US} = 9$ percent and $i_G = 5$ percent?

10. Suppose you are considering investing in a textile mill in a foreign country. Explain the statement that the cost to you, the investor, of import and export tariffs in that country are greatest if the supply of material inputs is inelastic and global demand for the finished product is elastic.

11. Suppose you are considering investing in a textile mill in a foreign country. Explain the statement that the cost to you, the investor, of foreign restrictions on repatriation of earnings depends on the opportunity cost of capital.

Solutions to Selected Exercises

Chapter 1

4. $TR = 50(Q)$, $TC = 600 + 3(700) + 20(Q) = 2,700 + 20Q$, $\pi = 50(Q) - [2,700 + 20(Q)] = 30(Q) - 2,700$. If the firm is to cover all its costs, the value of Q must be such that $TR = TC$. Therefore, $50Q = 2,700 + 20Q$ and $Q = 90$.

5. $\pi = 30(120) - 2,700 = 900$.

6. $\pi = 50(Q) - [2,800 + 15(20) + 20(Q)] = 30 Q - 3,100$. After five months: $\pi = 50Q - 2,200 - 20Q = 30Q - 2,200$.

9. Currently, costs are represented by the equation $TC = 4,500 + 150 Q$ where Q represents ton-miles of service monthly. With $Q = 3,700$, $TC = 559,500$. Alternative (1) would increase costs to $TC = 3,500 + 175(3,700) = 651,000$. Alternative (2) would reduce costs to $TC = 4,750 + 125(3,700) = 467,250$. Without other information about the firm's objectives, alternative (2) should be chosen.

Appendix 1A

1. Economic profit $= \pi = TR - TC = 8(Q) - [50 - 6(Q) + 0.5(Q)^2] = -50 + 14(Q) - 0.5(Q)^2$. Marginal profit $= d\pi/dQ = 14 - 1(Q)$, and $Q = 14$. The firm should produce 1,400 gallons a day for maximum profit.

2. Economic profit on 1,200 gallons is $\pi = -50 + 14(12) - 0.5(12)^2 = 46 = \$4,600$. Economic profit on 1,000 gallons is $\pi = -50 + 14(10) - 0.5(10)^2 = 40 = \$4,000$. Therefore, economic profit on 1,000 through 1,200 gallons is $\$46 - \$40 = 6 = \$600$.

3. With $TC = [75(Q)^{1/4} + 120$, marginal cost is $MC = \frac{1}{4}[(75Q)]^{-3/4}$. The second derivative is

$$\frac{d^2TC}{dQ^2} = -.1875[75(Q)]^{-7/4}.$$

The negative sign of the second derivative indicates a negative slope for marginal cost (and implies that total cost is increasing).

4. For $MC = f(t) = 500 + 20(t) - 2.4(t)^2$, total costs can be represented by the integral:

$$TC = \int f(t)\, dt = 500(t) + 10(t)^2 - 0.8(t)^3.$$

At the end of five years, total costs will have been: $500(5) + 10(5)^2 - 0.8(5)^3 = 2,500 + 250 - 100 = \$2,650$. Dividing total costs of $2,650 over five years yields an annual charge of $530.

5. Total costs are $TC = Q[2.50 + .003(Q)]$.
Total Revenue is $5.98(Q)$.
Economic profit is $\pi = TR - TC = -500 + 3.48(Q) - .003(Q)^2$.
To determine the level of Q at which the economic profit equation is equal to zero, apply the quadratic formula:

$$Q = \frac{-b \pm \sqrt{b^2 - 4ac}}{2c} = \frac{-3.48 \pm \sqrt{12.11 - 6}}{-.006}$$

$$= 168.03 \text{ and } 991.97.$$

Therefore, the lowest number of meals for achieving economic profit is 169.

6. Economic profit is maximum when the derivative of the profit function is equal to zero and the second derivative is negative. Therefore, $d\pi/dQ = 3.48 - .006(Q) = 0$ and $Q = 580$ (with $d^2\pi/dQ^2 = -.006$) indicates a maximum at $Q = 580$.
Also, by setting $MR = MC$, we find $5.98 = 2.50 + .006(Q)$, and $Q = 580$.

11.

$$TR = 7.5[5(N) - .1(N)^2] = 37.5(N) - .75(N)^2,$$
$$TC = 6.75[5(N) - .1(N)^2] = 33.75(N) - .675(N)^2,$$
$$MR = 37.5 - 1.5(N)$$

and

$$MC = 33.75 - 1.35(N).$$

Maximum profit occurs where $MR = MC$. Therefore, $37.5 - 1.5(N) = 33.75 - 1.35(N)$, and $N = 25 = 25,000$. Zero profit would occur where $TR = TC$. Therefore, $37.5(N) - .75(N)^2 = 33.75(N) - .675 (N)^2$, and $N = 50 = 50,000$.

Chapter 2

1. The consumer would achieve greater marginal utility per dollar of expenditure by increasing consumption of good *a*, causing its marginal utility to fall, and reducing consumption of good *b*, causing its marginal utility to rise. The result would be greater total utility per dollar of expenditure.

2. The decreasing slope of an indifference curve reveals that fewer quantities of a good held in smaller quantities will be given up for larger quantities of a good held in larger quantities. At the point of tangency with a budget line, the consumer's willingness to give up one good for another is precisely equal to their relative prices.

3. Indifference curves representing higher levels of utility will lie closer to the axis representing superior goods, since greater utility is gained through smaller additional quantities of such goods. As a result, the consumer's income expansion path will curve toward the axis of the superior good.

4. When the price of bus tickets increases, bus riders will experience a reduction in real income. As a result, they may have to reduce their use of other forms of transportation (taxi rides) and resort to more bus rides.

5. Cardinal theories of demand require measurement of utility, and ordinal theories require only that items be ranked according to utility.

7. In the place of utility, total utility, and marginal utility of particular goods, a business firm would consider productivity, total product, and marginal utility of a particular resource. The purchase decision would depend on $MP_a/p_a = MP_b/p_b \ldots = MP_z/p_z$, where the items are resources.

8. Proportions of goods depend on price ratios. Quantities depend on the total budget available for spending.

11. Other possible combinations are: 9 meals and 16.2 gallons, 6 meals and 21 gallons, 10 meals and 15 gallons. Drawing a demand curve for meals would require information about the behavior of *MU* as quantities increase. An increase in the consumer's budget would move the consumer to a higher indifference curve, with a possible change in the proportions of the two goods.

16. For many consumers, HMOs will serve as substitutes for medical services. Therefore, their demand for medical services will decrease, causing their demand curves to shift to the left.

Chapter 3

1. Since price elasticity is percentage change in quantity divided by percentage change in price,

$$\epsilon_p = \frac{-.06}{(177.9 - 118.1)/[\frac{1}{2}(177.9 + 118.1)]} = -.15.$$

10. Using a pocket calculator with linear regression, the equation is $Q = 112.3 - 14p$. The values for price elasticity are $-.47$, $-.41$, $-.33$ and $-.32$, but elasticity is likely to increase in the long run. Since the absolute value of elasticity at current prices is less than one, revenue is not being maximized and a price increase might be expected. Maximum total revenue occurs where

$$\frac{dTR}{dp} = 112.3 - 28p = 0.$$

Thus, $p = 4.01$ and $Q = 112.3 - 14(4.01) = 56.15$.

11. ϵ_p for alcoholic beverages $= .59, .63, 1.72, .39, .43$. ϵ_p for tobacco $.43$, $.46, .41, 0, -.15$. The Engel curve slopes upward for alcoholic beverages and downward for tobacco.

12. The regression equation is $Q = 19.98 - 2.19(p)$. Total revenue is $TR = Q(p) = 19.98\,(p) - 2.19(p)^2$. The maximum occurs where the derivative of the function is equal to zero and the second derivative is negative. The derivative is $dTR/dp = 19.98 - 4.38(p) = 0$ and $p = 4.56$. The second derivative is $d^2TR/dp^2 = -4.38$. Therefore, total revenue reaches a maximum where $p = \$4.56$ and $Q = 19.98 - 2.19(4.56) = 9.99$.

13. Determine the value of p at which $Q = 0$. Substituting, $0 = 19.98 - 2.19(p)$, and $p = \$9.12$.

14.

$$\epsilon_c = \frac{(112.8 - 111)/\frac{1}{2}(112.8 + 111)}{(127.2 - 132.8)/\frac{1}{2}(127.2 + 132.8)} = -.37.$$

The negative result indicates the items are substitutes.

15. Before the ad: $\epsilon_p = b\left(\dfrac{P}{Q}\right) = -5\left(\dfrac{5}{30}\right) = -.83.$

After the ad: $\epsilon_p = -2\left(\dfrac{5}{65}\right) = -.154.$

The ad did have the effect of reducing price elasticity. Also, the change in the constant from 55 to 75 indicates a rightward shift of the demand curve. Sales would be zero where $Q = 75 - 2(p) = 0$. Therefore, $p = \$37.50$.

16. The normal equations are:

$$67.4 = 13a + 48b + 26c,$$
$$229.05 = 48a + 207.48b + 99c,$$

and

$$149.3 = 26 + 99b + 60c.$$

The demand equation is: $Q = 4.09 - .86(p) + 2.13(Y)$. Price elasticities are: For A, $\epsilon_p = -2.15$. For B, $\epsilon_p = -1.08$. For C, $\epsilon_p = -.70$. Income elasticities are: For A, $\epsilon_Y = 1.078$. For B, $\epsilon_Y = 1.07$. For C, $\epsilon_Y = 1.03$.

Chapter 4

12. Annual sales are 985, so that average monthly sales are 82.08. The seasonal factors are:

$$\frac{50}{82.08} = .61, .67, .73, .91, 1.04, 1.10, 1.10, 1.22,$$

$$1.22, .98, 1.22, 1.22.$$

Since January sales are typically $.61(\frac{1}{12})$ of annual sales, annual sales should be $65/.61(\frac{1}{12}) = 1{,}278{,}690$.

Chapter 5

2. a. $MP_L = 3$ and $MP_M = 7$, $AP_L = 3 + 7M/L$, and $AP_M = 3L/M + 7$.
   b. $MP_L = 2 - 1.6L$; $AP_L = 4/L + 2 - .8L$.
   c. $MP_L = 7$ and $MP_M = 2 + 10M - .3M^2$, $AP_L = 7 + (2M + 5M^2 - .1M^3)/L$ and $AP_M = 7L/M + 2 + 5M - .1M^2$.

3. a. $AP_L = 17$; $AP_M = 8.5$
   b. $MP_L = -6$; $AP_L = -1.2$.
   c. $MP_M = 72$; $AP_L = 91$, $AP_M = 45.5$.

Marginal products are constant and average products vary with quantities.

The marginal product of labor is below average product (and negative) at this quantity and pulling average product down.

Both resources' marginal products are below average product and pulling average product down.

8.

$$50,000 = 3.9L^{.82}(750)^{.5}$$
$$= 50,000(.0094) = L^{.82} = (468.14 = L^{.82})^{1/.82}$$

and $L = 1,805.32$.

10. Opportunity costs per chick increase as follows: $(3,500 - 3,000)/1,000 = .5$, $(3,000 - 1,500)/2,000 = .75$, $(1,500 - 600)/1,000 = .9$, and $(600 - 0)/400 = 1.5$. Opportunity costs increase because the proportion of variable to fixed resources for producing either product changes from an efficient proportion to a less efficient proportion. Possible production of both products might be increased by increasing the quantity of certain fixed resources.

11. Maximum revenue occurs with production of 600 eggs and 4,000 chicks. Producing the last 400 chicks would involve opportunity costs of 1.5 eggs per chick. Since the price of chicks is $7¢/5¢ = 1.4$ times the price of eggs, the gain is not worth the opportunity cost.

12. The marginal product of the ninth worker is expected to be 3 tons. If a ninth worker is employed, average product per worker will drop from 4.63 tons to 4.44 tons. Marginal product is below average product and is pulling the average down. This is the typical behavior of average and marginal product when variable resources are employed beyond the most efficient proportion relative to fixed capital.

13. With $L = 4.9$, total production is $Q = 99.94$. With $L = 5$, total production is $Q = 102.5$. Therefore, the marginal product of one hundred additional labor hours per week is $102.5 - 99.94 = 2.56$. Average product at current employment is $99.94/4.9 = 20.4$ per thousand labor hours or 2.04 per hundred labor hours. Since marginal product is above average product, average product must be rising. Values for plotting the curve are: $L = 2.5$, $Q = 37.19$; $L = 3$, $Q = 49.5$; $L = 3.5$, $Q = 62.56$; $L = 4$, $Q = 76$; $L = 4.5$, $Q = 89.44$; $L = 5$, $Q = 102.5$; $L = 5.5$, $Q = 114.81$; $L = 6$, $Q = 126$; $L = 6.5$, $Q = 135.69$. Marginal product values are: 23.63, 25.50, 26.63, 27.00, 26.63, 25.50, 23.63, 21.00, 15.66. Marginal product reaches a peak and is constant at $Q = 4,000$ hours and then begins to decline. The firm would employ at least 4,000 hours. Employing fewer hours would sacrifice the greater additional production possible with a larger quantity of labor. Employment would typically occur in the range of falling marginal product. An equation for average product is $Q/L = 3 + 6L - .5L^2$.

14. The exponent $-.093$ indicates that total production decreases by .093 percent for each one-percent increase in p. Therefore, a 40-percent increase in p should reduce potential production by $40 \times .093 = 3.7$ percent.

Chapter 6

2. Unit profit changed from $12.40 - 8.50 = 3.90$ to $15.50 - 11.50 = 4.00$. The increase in unit profit is a result of applying the smaller percentage increase (25 percent) to a larger base (price), so that the absolute change in price is greater than the change in cost.

3. The $8.54 cost figure probably does not include the implicit cost of using the producers' own land. The result is to understate costs and overstate profit.

4. The break-even quantity is that at which savings from the equipment are equal to its costs. With average production costs of $9.75, savings are $11.50 - 9.75 = 1.75 per gallon. The break-even quantity is $4,000/1.75 = 2,286$ gallons.

5. The unit contribution to fixed costs is $(p - AVC) = 15.50 - 9.75 = 5.75$. Total annual contribution is $Q(p - AVC) = 700(5.75) = 4,025$. The equipment pays for itself in $32,000/4,025 \approx 8$ years.

6. Profit without pre-heater $= TR - TC = 700(15.50) - 700(11.50) = 10,850 - 8,050 = 2,800$. Profit with pre-heater $= TR - TC = 700(15.50) - 700[11.50 - .15(.75)11.50] - 600 = 10,850 - 7,144 - 600 = 3,106$.

7. This is a break-even problem where Q is distance in miles, $FC = 1.30$, and $AVC = .17$. The break-even distance is the one at which $.35(Q) = 1.30 + .17(Q)$. Therefore $Q_b = 7.22$ miles. The degree of operating leverage with respect to distance is

$$\frac{Q(p - AVC)}{Q(p - AVC) - FC} = \frac{9(.18)}{9(.18) - 1.30} = \frac{1.62}{.32} = 5 \text{ percent.}$$

8. With production of $1.20(1,350) = 1,620$ units per hour, total costs are $1,620(50.00 - 7.50) = 68,850$. With fixed cost of $2,000, average variable cost is $(68,850 - 2,000)/1,620 = 41.27. If the average variable cost of $41.27 is 5 percent higher than minimum, minimum average variable cost is $41.27/1.05 = 39.30. This is the firm's shut-down price.

9. This is a break-even problem where Q is acres cultivated, $FC = \$575$, and $AVC = \$5.3$. The break-even number of acres is that at which $TR = TC$ or $Q(110 \times 5.25) = 575,000 + 5.3Q$ and $Q_b = 1,005$.

10. Economic profit or loss $= TR - TC = 1,005(110)(5) - 575,000 - 1,005(5.3) = -\$27,576.50$.

11. With yield per acre of $1.20(110) = 132$, economic profit is $TR - TC = 1,005(132)(5) - 575,000 - 1,005(5.3) = \$82,973.50$.

12. This is a break-even problem with variable costs and varying revenues. Q is number of hours, FC is \$575 and AVC is \$415 for the first eight hours and $1.2(415) = \$498$ for greater than eight hours. First determine whether revenues exceed costs at the level of Q where costs change: $TR = 8(535) = 4,280$ and $TC = 575 + 8(415) = \$3,895$. With $TR > TC$, the break-even number of hours occurs before $Q = 8$. Solving for the break-even quantity yields: $Q(535) = 575 + Q(415)$ and $Q_b = 4.79$.

13. For 8 hours of operation, revenues and costs are $TR = 8(535) = \$4,280$ and $TC = 575 + 8(415) = \$3,895$ for profit of $TR - TC = \$385$. Beyond $Q = 8$, revenues increase more slowly and costs increase more rapidly. The second break-even point is the one at which $TR = TC$ or $4,280 + 450(Q - 8) = 3,895 + 498(Q - 8)$ and $Q_b = 16$ hours.

14. a. Total costs must be $\$705,000 + 115,000 = \$820,000$, making variable costs $\$820,000 - 250,000 = \$570,000$ per month. With average variable costs of $VC/Q = \$570,000/94 = \$6,063.83$, this is the lowest price that is acceptable.
    b. With revenues of \$705,000 on output of 94 units, price must be $\$705,000/94 = \$7,500$. Although the firm is experiencing losses, the excess of price over average variable cost ($\$7,500 - 6,063.83 = \$1,436.17$) can be applied to monthly fixed charges to minimize loss.
    c. Estimated revenue following the marketing campaign would be $TR = (Q)(p) = 131(\$7,500) = \$982,500$. Costs would be $FC + Q(AVC) = \$250,000 + 50,000 + 131(6,063.83) = \$1,094,361.73$, for losses of \$111,861.73 a month, which is lower than current losses.
    d. With total costs of \$1,094,361.73 on 131 units, price would have to rise to $\$1,094,361.73/131 = \$8,353.91$.

15. a. AVC figures are: 35.5, 35.45, 36.25, 37.69, 39.64, and 42. MC figures are 35, 45, 55, 65, and 75. Equations for AVC and MC are: $AVC = 21.14 + 1.33Q$ and $MC = -75 + 10Q$. ATC figures are: 60.5, 58.18, 57.08, 56.92, 57.5, and 58.67.
    b. AVC for producing 18 units is $AVC = 21.14 + 1.33(18) = 45.14$. Total cost is $TC = FC + Q(AVC) = 250 + 18(45.14) = 1,062.52$. An equation for total cost is $TC = 250 + 21.14Q + 1.33Q^2$. This is a quadratic production function.
    c. Total cost rises at an increasing rate. Average variable cost is saucer-shaped, and marginal cost intersects average variable cost at its lowest

point. Average total cost is saucer-shaped, and reaches a minimum at Q = 13.

d. The profit-maximizing quantity is that at which $MC = MR = p$. With $p = 65$, the profit-maximizing quantity is $Q = 14$. Economic profit is π = $TR - TC = (p)(Q) - TC = 910 - 805 = 105$.

e. Price of \$55 is lower than average total cost at its lowest point. The firm will experience losses. However, because $p = 55$ is greater than average variable costs, the firm should continue to produce, moving down its MC curve to $Q = 13$. If losses persist beyond the time when fixed contracts expire, this operation should be discontinued.

16. At the current level of sales, average price is \$21.67/112 = \$.1935 million and average variable cost is $(21.67 - .43 - .08)/112 = \$.1889$ million. The initial break-even quantity is that at which $Q(.1935) = .43 + (Q)(.1889)$ and $Q_b = 93.5$ units. After the loan, the break-even quantity is determined by $Q(.1935) = .43 + .031 + (Q)(.1889)$ and $Q_b = 100.2$ units. Economic profit is reduced by \$.031 million each month. The elasticity of profit changes from

$$\frac{Q(p - AVC)}{Q(p - AVC) - FC} = \frac{112(.0046)}{112(.0046) - .43} = 6.05 \text{ percent}$$

to

$$\frac{112(.0046)}{112(.0046) - .461} = 9.51 \text{ percent.}$$

Higher fixed costs increase the elasticity of profit—the relative change in profit associated with changes in sales—although the absolute amount of profit is lower.

17.

(1) $Q_b = \dfrac{FC + (Q)(AVC_1 - AVC_2)}{p - AVC_2} = \dfrac{9,890 + 1,000(-3)}{5}$

= 6,890/5 = 1,378 units.

(2) $Q = (Q)(p) - [FC + AVC_1(Q^*) + AVC_2(Q - Q^*)]$

= 143,450 - [9,890 + 87,000 + 510(90)] = 660.

(3) DOL = (percentage change in profit)/(percentage change in sales).

Increasing sales by 1 percent increases profit by 15.1 times the profit contribution of additional units: 1 percent of 1,510 = 15.1. Additional profit is 15.1(95 - 90) = 75.5. Since 75.5 = 11.44 percent of 660, DOL = 11.44. Because projected sales may be off by plus or minus some percentage, it is helpful to know the possible effect on profit.

18. \$5m + \$3.50 (miles) = \$7.50 (miles) and $(miles_b)$ = 1.25 million. \$20m + \$2.00 (miles) = \$7.50 (miles) and $(miles_b)$ = 3.64 million.

19. With economic profit of $1,000, profit per unit is $0.0175. Producing the fittings would raise average fixed cost by $3,500/57,000 = $0.0614 and reduce variable cost by $0.20, a net change in average total cost of .0614 − .20 = −.1386. Profit per unit would increase to .0175 + .1386 = .1561, for total economic profit of $8,897.70 and a margin of profit of 8,897.70/8,500 = 1.0468. Currently, the firm's break-even quantity may be determined by

$$MOP = \frac{Q - Q_b}{Q_b}$$

so that

$$.20 = \frac{57,000 - Q_b}{Q_b}.$$

Thus, 1.20 Q_b = 57,000 and Q_b = 47,500. If the fittings are purchased, the break-even quantity is determined by $MOP = \dfrac{Q - Q_b}{Q_b}$ so that 1.0468 $= \dfrac{57,000 - Q_b}{Q_b}$ and Q_b = 27,848.35.

20. The firm's required 5-percent profit margin means that a price of $7.90 must be 105 percent of costs. Then, the portion of unit price applied to costs would be 7.9/1.05 = 7.52. Using this value in break-even analysis yields:

$$Q = \frac{FC}{P - VC} = \frac{84}{7.52 - 3.7} = 21.97,$$

which is 44 percent of the total market.

Chapter 7

4. a. For Q = 100, L = 1, K = 32.67; L = 2, K = 32; L = 3, K = 31.33; L = 4, K = 30.67; and L = 5, K = 30. For Q = 200, L = 1, K = 66; L = 2, K = 65.33; L = 3, K = 64.67; L = 4, K = 64; and L = 5, K = 63.33.
   b. For Q = 100, L = 1, K = 26.83; L = 2, K = 20.67; L = 3, K = 14.83; L = 4, K = 9.33; and L = 5, K = 4.17. For Q = 200, L = 1, K = 60.17; L = 2, K = 54; L = 3, K = 48.17; L = 4, K = 42.67; and L = 5, K = 37.5.

6. Elasticity of production for C_1 is .3. A 1-percent increase in C_1 will yield a 0.3-percent increase in color intensity. Scale effects are indicated by the sum of the exponents. Since the sum is less than one, this process experiences decreasing returns to scale. That is, equal percentage increases in both ingredients will yield a smaller percentage change in color intensity. This is a result of the nature of the chemical process. If C_2 is fixed at 25 units, a one unit increase in C_1 would increase the color rating from 4.08 to 4.16, a marginal product of .08. Under the opposite conditions, the rating increases from 3.88 to 3.98 for a marginal product of .10. This is due to the higher elasticity of production associated with C_2. Average products are:

$$\frac{Y}{C_1} = \frac{.5C_2^{.4}}{C_1^{.7}}$$

and

$$\frac{Y}{C_2} = \frac{.5C_1^{.3}}{C_2^{.6}}.$$

The least-cost combination is the one at which

$$\frac{p_{C_1}}{p_{C_2}} = \frac{MP_{C_1}}{MP_{C_2}} = \frac{bC_2}{cC_1}.$$

Substituting yields: $2 = .3C_2/.4C_1$ and $C_1 = .38C_2$. Substituting this value in the production function yields: $5 = .5(.38C_2)^{.3}(C_2)^{.4}$ and $13.37 = C_2^{.7}$. Solving for C_2: $(13.37 = C_2^{.7})^{1.43}$, and $C_2 = 40.61$ units. Since $C_1 = .38C_2$, $C_1 = 15.43$ units.

7. (1) The isoquant slopes downward from left to right. It is convex to the origin, and it does not touch or intersect the axes.
(2) Between A and B, the slope of the isoquant is $\Delta C_1/\Delta C_2 = (.9 - .8)/(.32 - .35) = .1/-.03 = -3.33$.
(3) To answer this question, we must know the slope of the isoquant at every combination of C_1 and C_2. The slopes are:

A-B	−3.33
B-C	−2.
C-D	−1.33
D-E	−1

The slope of the isoquant is a ratio of the marginal products of the two ingredients, with the ingredient on the horizontal axis as the numerator. The ratio of their prices is $p_2/p_1 = 2.5/1. = 2.5$. Setting $MP_2/MP_1 = p_2/p_1$ identifies B as the most efficient, least-cost combination of ingredients.

(Since the data in the table are discrete rather than continuous, it is not likely that the ratios will be precisely equal.)

(4) The process will probably experience constant returns to scale, since repeated uses of the same formula will continue to produce the same results in terms of output.

8. a. $p_Z/p_G = 13.5/3.5 = 3.86$, and $MP_Z/MP_G = .58G/.1021Z = 5.68\ G/Z$. Thus, the least-cost combination is that at which $3.86 = 5.68\ G/Z$ or $Z = 1.47G$. Substituting in the production function:

$$3.25 = .09(1.47G)^{.58}G^{.1021}$$
$$= .09(1.47)^{.58}G^{.58\ +\ .1021}$$
$$= .09(1.25)G^{.6821}.$$

Solving for G:

$$[28.88 = G^{.6821}]^{1.47},$$

and $G = 138.46$. Substituting in the previous equation and solving for Z: $Z = 1.47\ G = 203.54$.

b. $p_Z/p_G = 13.5/4.5 = 3$

The least-cost combination is that at which $3 = 5.68\ G/Z$ or $Z = 1.89G$. Substituting in the production function:

$$3.25 = .09(1.89G)^{.58}G^{.1021}$$
$$= .09(1.45)G^{.6821}.$$

Solving for G:

$$[24.94 = G^{.6821}]^{1.47}$$

and $G = 111.65$. Substituting in the previous equation and solving for Z: $Z = 1.89(111.65) = 211.02$. The change in relative prices changes the least-cost combination of fuels to increase the use of oil.

9. Total Costs:

a. $TC = (Z)\ (p_z) = (G)(p_G) = 203.54(13.5) + 138.46(3.5) = \$3,232,400$.

b. $211.02(13.5) + 111.65(4.5) = \$3,351,200$.

Economic profit:

a. Economic profit $= TR - TC = 3.25$ billion$(5¢) - 3,232,400 = 162,500,000 - 3,232,400 = \$159,267,600$.

b. 3.25 billion $(5¢) - 3,351,200 = 162,500,000 - 3,351,200 = \$159,148,800$.

10. Lowest-cost production occurs where $MP_C/MP_H = p_C/p_H$ or $.48H/.35C = 3.8/21$ and $.48(H)(21) = (.35C)(3.8)$. The value of H must be $H = .13C$.

With a budget of 750, quantities of H and C are determined by $3.8(C) + 21(.13C) = 750$. Thus, $C = 114.85$ units and $H = .13(114.85) = 14.93$ units. Applying 114.85 degrees centigrade for a period of 14.93 hours would satisfy the budget constraint and produce an amide yield of: $Q = 1.3(114.85)^{.48}(14.93)^{.35} = 32.64$ percent. The isocost line for $TC = 750$ is tangent to the isoquant for $Q = 32.64$, at which point their slopes are equal. Thus, $MP_C/MP_H = p_C/p_H$, and production is most efficient.

11. The ratios of marginal prices and prices are equal where:

$$\frac{50 - .06(C150)}{75 - .10(F40)} = \frac{17.50}{21.90}$$

so that $(F40) = 124.29 + .75(C150)$. Substituting this value in the budget equation yields:

$$17.5(C150) + 21.9[124.29 + .75(C150)] = 3,000$$

and $C150 = 8.20$. $F40 = 124.29 + .75(C150) = 13,044$ pounds.

12. With $MP_N/MP_P = p_N/p_P$, $.75P/.37N = 12.15/13.50$, and $N = 2.25P$. Substituting this value in the budget equation yields: $12.15(2.25P) + 13.50P = 50$, and $p = 1.22$. Therefore, $N = 2.25(1.22) = 2.75$. Total production is $Q = 1.15(2.75)^{.75}(1.22)^{.37} = 264$ bushels.

13. Using the form $Q = aL^bK^c$, the firm's production function is $Q = 66.1L^{.6}K^{.5}$. Lowest-cost production occurs where $MP_L/MP_K = p_L/p_K$. Substitution yields: $.6K/.5L = 7.5/13.5$ and $K = .46L$. With $210 = 66.1(L)^{.6}(.46L)^{.5}$, $L = 4.07$ and $K = 1.87$, for total cost of $55.73 per acre or $55.73/210 = 0.27$ per bushel.

14. $.27C/1.9S = 2.6/7.3$, and $C = 2.51S$. Substituting this value in the production function yields: $10 = S^{.27}(2.51S)^{1.9} = 1.74 = S^{2.17}$ and $S = 1.29$. Therefore, $C = 3.24$.

15. Average total costs are:

With $K = 1$:		With $K = 2$:		With $K = 3$:	
Q	ATC	Q	ATC	Q	ATC
30	166.67	33.5	179.10	38	184.21
35.38	163.93	38.88	174.90	43.38	179.81
40.44	163.20	43.94	172.96	48.44	177.54
45.06	164.23	48.54	173.05	53.06	177.16
49.12	166.94	52.62	174.84	57.12	178.56
52.5	171.43	56	178.57	60.57	181.61
52.02	178.12	58.58	184.36	63.08	187.06
56.74	186.82	60.24	192.56	64.74	194.62
57.36	198.74	60.86	203.75	65.36	205.02

Plant $K = 1$ produces at lowest cost for 45 and 50 units, $K = 2$ produces 55 units at lowest cost, and $K = 3$ produces 60 and 65 units at lowest cost.

16. With $L = 265(3.5) = 927.5$ and $K = 265(5) = 1,325$, total costs are $444,915.75 for the smaller plant and $454,387.02 for the larger plant. The smaller plant should be selected.

Chapter 8

1. $Q_f = 6$, and economic profit $= TR - TC = 6(75) - 400 = 50$.

6. $\epsilon_s = -1.6$. Negative supply elasticity indicates a decreasing cost industry in the long run.

8. $ATC = 500(Q)^b$ for 20 units would be $.6(80) = 500(20)^b$. To solve for b, write the equation in logarithmic terms: $\log 48 = \log 500 + b(\log 20)$ and $-1.02 = b(1.3)$. Therefore, $b = -.78$. The cost equation is $ATC = 500(Q)^{-.78}$.

Chapter 9

1. Constraints:

$$2X_1 + 3X_2 + \quad S_m = 40$$
$$2.5X_1 + 1.8X_2 + S_c = 25$$
$$3X_1 + \qquad\qquad S_s = 20.$$

Objective function: (max) total profit $= 31X_1 + 18X_2$. Corner solutions:

X_1	X_2	TP
6.67	0	206.77
0	13.33	239.94
.77	12.82	254.63
6.67	4.63	290.11*

At the profit-maximizing solution, S_c and S_s are equal to zero. $S_m = 12.77$ indicates that machine time is adequate. The bottle-neck resources are chemicals and slicing time.

2. Constraints:

$$X_1 \qquad\quad - S_r = 55$$
$$X_2 - S_c = 17$$
$$2X_1 + 3\ X_2 - S_b = 150$$
$$3X_1 + 10X_2 - S_f = 300.$$

Objective function: (min) total cost $= .35X_1 + 1.25X_2$. Corner solutions:

X_1	X_2	TC
54.55	13.64	36.14
55	13.33	35.91
43.33	17	36.42

Slack variables: $S_r = 0$, $S_c = 3.67$, $S_b = 0$, $S_f = 0$. All of the butter and flour are used, and production of cakes is 3.67 dozen more than required.

3. Constraints:

$$1.5X_1 + 3.5X_2 + S_a = 1,000$$
$$2X_1 + 1.4X_2 + S_p = 500$$
$$.4X_1 + 1.1X_2 + S_t = 300.$$

Objective: max $TP = (27 - 18)X_1 + (39 - 29)X_2$.

Corner solutions: At each corner, at least two variables will be zero. The corners will occur: at the origin where X_1 and X_2 will be zero; along the axes where X_1 will be zero for each of three constraints and X_2 will be zero for each constraint; where the constraint variable will also be zero; and at three points where the constraint lines intersect and the constraints are zero. The only feasible corners will be those with positive slack variables. Negative slack variables would indicate over-use of the constraint.

Corner solutions:	X_1	X_2	S_a	S_p	S_t	Total profit
Origin	0	0	1,000	500	300	0
Television axis	666.67	0	0	−833.33	33.33	
	250	0	625	0	200	2,250.00
	750	0	−125	−1000	0	
Video-tape axis	0	285.71	0	100	−14.29	
	0	357.14	−250	0	−92.86	
	0	272.73	45.45	118.18	0	3,000.03
Interior solutions	72.04	254.8	0	0	−9.14	
	79.27	243.9	27.44	0	0	3,152.43
	204.37	198.41	0	−186.5	0	

Eliminate the solutions with negative slack variables. Along the axes, these are the solutions with intercepts beyond the minimum, given the particular constraint. In the interior, these are the solutions that over-use certain constrained variables. Total profit for the feasible solutions is shown above. $S_a = 27.44$ at the profit-maximizing product mix indicates slack assembly time and limiting constraints in processing and testing.

4. The dual problem is to minimize total shadow prices: $30,000(p_B) +$

$20,000(p_H)$, where p_B and p_H are shadow prices of the budget and hours available. The constraints are:

personal selling constraint: $\quad 200(p_B) + 150(p_H) \geq 1,200,$

advertising constraint: $\qquad 150(p_B) + 50(p_H) \geq 1,500.$

The constraints specify that the resources must be worth at least the amount of their profit contribution.

The following is the solutions table with S_S and S_A indicating surplus variables for personal selling and advertisements, respectively.

p_B	p_H	S_S	S_A
0	0	$-1,200$	$-1,500$
0	8	0	$-1,100$
0	30	3,300	0
6	0	0	-600
10	0	$-1,000$	0
13.20	-9.60	0	0

Discard solutions with negative surplus variables and look at the remaining solutions. The only viable solution is the one with $p_B = 0$ and $p_H = 30$. The solution with a negative shadow price is unacceptable. A zero shadow price for budget indicates that this constraint is not binding. With a positive shadow price for time, we know that the time constraint is fully used. Also, with $S_A = 0$ we know we are exercising the advertising function fully. With $S_S = 3,300$, we have surplus resources in personal sales. This information enables us to solve the primal problem. Thus, with a time constraint of $150(S) + 50(A) - S_H = 20,000$ and $S_H = 0$ and $S = 0$ the quantity of advertising is $A = 400$. With $A = 400$, total profit is determined by the primal profit equation: $\pi = 1,200(S) + 1,500(A) = 600,000$.

These results suggest that additional hours should be allocated to the marketing function to take advantage of potential profit increases.

5. The objective function is to minimize costs:

$$(\text{min}) \; TC = 4(SC) + 3(SA) + 6(SD) + 5(CF)$$
$$+ \; 3(CD) + 4(CB) + 2(AC) + 2(AB)$$
$$+ \; 2(BD) + 5(BF) + 4(DF),$$

where the parentheses represent quantities processed along the indicated channels.

The constraints are:

$$(SC) + (SD) + (SA) \leq \text{ the quantity of materials}$$
$$\text{available for processing,}$$

$(CF) + (DF) + (BF) \geq$ the required quantity
of finished materials.
$(AC) + (AB) \leq (SA)$
$(CB) + (CD) + (CF) \leq (SC) + (AC)$
$(BD) + (BF) \leq (AB) + (CB)$
$(DF) \leq (BD) + (SD) + (CD)$.

6. The weights must satisfy the following constraints:

$$w_1 + w_2 + w_3 = 1,$$
$$3w_1 - w_2 \qquad = 0,$$

and

$$-w_2 + w_3 = 0.$$

The solutions are $w_1 = \frac{1}{7}$, $w_2 = \frac{3}{7}$, and $w_3 = \frac{3}{7}$. Applying the weights yields:

$$(\min)TC = \left(\frac{9X^3}{1/7}\right)^{1/7}\left(\frac{5,000}{3/7\ XY}\right)^{3/7}\left(\frac{8Y}{3/7}\right)^{3/7},$$

and eliminating the unknowns yields:

$$(\min)TC = \left(\frac{9}{1/7}\right)^{1/7}\left(\frac{5,000}{3/7}\right)^{3/7}\left(\frac{8}{3/7}\right)^{3/7} = \$350.57.$$

With $9X^3 = \frac{1}{7}(350.57) = 50.08$, $5,000/XY = \frac{3}{7}(350.57) = 150.24$, and $8Y = \frac{3}{7}(350.57) = 150.24$. We know that:

$$1n9 + 3(1nX) = 1n50.08,$$
$$1n5,000 - 1nX - 1nY = \ln150.24,$$

and

$$1n8 + 1nY = 1n150.24.$$

Solving: $X = 1.77$ gallons and $Y = 18.82$.

7. The weights for the A-G mean inequality must satisfy:

(1) $w_1 + w_2 = 1$
(2) $w_1 - 2w_2 = 0$.

Substituting (2) into (1) yields: $2w_2 + w_2 = 1$ and $w_2 = 1/2$. Furthermore, $w_1 + 1/3 = 1$ and $w_1 = 2/3$. Now we know that:

$$2/3\left[\frac{2.5X}{2/3}\right] + 1/3\left[\frac{7,500}{1/3X^2}\right] \geq \left[\frac{(2.5X)}{2/3}\right]^{2/3}\left[\frac{(7,500)}{1/3X^2}\right]^{1/3}.$$

Removing the unknowns from the right side of the inequality yields minimum total cost:

$$TC \geq \left[\frac{2.5}{2/3}\right]^{2/3}\left[\frac{7,500}{1/3}\right]^{1/3} = (2.41)(28.23) = 68.14.$$

At minimum total cost, each term in the cost equation comprises a portion of total cost equal to its weight. Therefore,

$$2.5X = 2/3(68.14), \quad \text{and} \quad \frac{7,500}{X^2} = 1/3(68.14).$$

Solving for X yields $X = 18.17$. This is the value of X at which total costs are minimized.

Chapter 10

1. Current profit is $\pi = Q(p - ATC) = 3,000(175 - 100) = \$225,000$ per month. Marginal revenue is $MR = 175 - 175/2.5 = 105$. With such high demand elasticity, the firm could expect substantial sales gains to follow a price reduction. A 1-percent cut in price could cause profit to change to $\pi = (1.025)(3,000)[.99(175) - 100] = \$225,243.75$. A price reduction would cause a movement down the demand curve and a reduction in price elasticity. At some point, further price reductions would yield no change in profit.

If average cost were \$125, price should be raised to maximize profit.

2.

$$TR = 100Q - .5Q^2,$$
$$TC = 100 + 50Q + .25Q^2,$$

and

$$MR = 100 - 1Q = 50 + .5Q = MC.$$

Therefore, the profit-maximizing quantity is $Q = 33.33$. Price is $p = 100 - .5(33.33) = \$83.33$, and profit is

$$
\begin{aligned}
\pi &= TR - TC \\
&= [100(33.33) - .5(33.33)^2] - \\
&\qquad\qquad [100 + 50(33.33) + .25(33.33)^2] \\
&= (3,333 - 555.44) - (100 + 1,666.50 + 277.72) \\
&= 2,777.56 - 2,044.22 = \$733.34.
\end{aligned}
$$

3. Change price by \$1 and note the effect on quantity. With $p = 80$,

$$
\epsilon_1 = \left[\frac{80 - 81}{1/2(80 + 81)}\right] \div \left[\frac{40 - 38}{1/2(40 + 38)}\right] = .2422.
$$

With p = 60,

$$
\epsilon_2 = \left[\frac{60 - 61}{1/2(60 + 61)}\right] \div \left[\frac{80 - 78}{1/2(80 + 78)}\right] = .6529.
$$

With p = 40,

$$
\epsilon_3 = \left[\frac{40 - 41}{1/2(40 + 41)}\right] \div \left[\frac{120 - 118}{1/2(120 + 118)}\right] = 1.4691.
$$

With p = 20,

$$
\epsilon_4 = \left[\frac{20 - 21}{1/2(20 + 21)}\right] \div \left[\frac{160 - 158}{1/2(160 + 158)}\right] = 3.8780.
$$

5. Marginal revenue $= 250/15 = 16.67$. Using $MR = p - p/\epsilon$, $16.67 = 99 - 99/\epsilon$, and $\epsilon = -1.2$.

6. Change price by 1 percent and quantity by 1.4 percent in the opposite direction and use linear regression to write a linear equation.

p	Q
100	50
101	49.3

Thus,
$p = 171.43 - 1.43\ Q$.

7. $TR = 171.43Q - 1.43Q^2$, and $TC = 500 + 90Q - .6Q^2$. Therefore, $MR = 171.43 - 2.86Q$, $MC = 90 - 1.2Q$, and $Q = 49.05$. Substitut-

ing this value in the price equation: $p = 171.43 - 1.43(49.05) = \$101.28$. Profit is $TR - TC = -500 + 81.43Q - .83Q^2 = \$1,497.25$. (Answers may differ slightly because of rounding.)

9.

With mark-up $= \left(\dfrac{1}{1 - 1/\epsilon_p}\right)$,

the profit-maximizing mark-up is

$$\frac{1}{1 - 1/1.6} = 2.67.$$

10. With $\epsilon_p = -1.2$, linear regression yields a demand equation of $p = 916.6667 - 13.8889Q$. With $TR = 916.6667Q - 13.8889Q^2$ and $TC = 8,000 + 100Q + 5Q^2$, the break-even quantities are $Q_1 = 15.00$ and $Q_2 = 28.23$. Maximum profit occurs where $MR = MC$ or $916.6667 - 27.7778Q = 100 + 10Q^2$ and $Q = 21.62$. Current profit is $\$500.00$ and maximum profit is $\$826.76$. Price should be increased to $\$616.37$ to reduce volume and increase monthly profit.

Chapter 11

4. Economic profit at the current market price is $\pi = Q(p - ATC) = 300(7.50 - 3.50) = \$1,200$ per week. Increasing price by 1 percent to $1.01(7.50) = 7.575$ causes quantity demanded to drop to $(1 - .022)(300) = 293.40$ for economic profit of $\pi = Q(p - ATC) = 293.400(7.575 - 3.50) = \$1,195.605$. Reducing price by 1 percent to $.99(7.50) = 7.425$, causes quantity demanded to increase to $(1 + .018)(300) = 305.40$, for economic profit of $305.40(3.925) = 1,198.695$. Therefore, economic profit is greatest at the tacitly accepted market price.

5. Recall the expression

$$p = ATC\left(\frac{1}{1 - 1/\epsilon_p}\right),$$

where the value in parentheses is mark-up over average total cost in markets where there is power to set price. Substituting and solving for

ϵ_p: $7.50 = 3.50[1/(1 - 1/\epsilon_p)]$, $2.14 - 2.14/\epsilon_p = 1$,
       $1.14 = 2.14/\epsilon_p$,

and $\epsilon_p = 1.88$.

6. Price leadership may be expected to bring on a price increase that will retain the same mark-up over costs. Thus,

$$p = 4.20\left(\frac{1}{1 - 1/1.88}\right) = \$8.97.$$

7. Revenue from the sale of one combination is $TR = Q_A[22 - .02(Q_A)] + 2Q_B[35 - .0125(Q_B)] = 92(Q) - .045(Q^2)$. Total costs are $TC = 100 + 5(Q) + .08(Q^2)$. The profit function is $\pi = [92(Q) - .045(Q^2)] - [100 + 5(Q) + .08(Q^2)] = -100 + 87(Q) - .125(Q^2)$. Using optimization to maximize profit, take the derivative of the profit function and set it equal to zero: $d\pi/dQ = 87 - .25(Q) = 0$. Solving: $Q = 348$, so that $Q_A = 348$ and $Q_B = 696$. The second derivative of the profit function is $d^2\pi/dQ^2 = -0.25$, ensuring a maximum. Substituting in the demand functions to determine prices: $p_A = 22 - .02(348) = 15.04$ and $p_B = 35 - .0125(696) = 26.3$. Making sure marginal revenues are positive at these quantities we find: $TR_A = 22(Q_A) - .02(Q_A^2)$ with $dTR_A/dQ_A = 22 - .04(Q_A) = 8.08$ and $TR_B = 70(Q_B) - .025(Q_B^2)$ with $dTR_B/dQ_B = 70 - .05(Q_B) = 35.2$. Since both marginal revenues are positive, these quantities should be sold.

9. Current quantity is $Q = 1.15(135^{.7}) = 35.64$, and total revenue is $TR = p(Q) = 12.50(35.64) = 445.50$. Adding advertising expenditures of \$75 would increase quantity sold to $Q = 1.15(210^{.7}) = 48.56$ units per week for $TR = \$607$. Thus, an additional \$75 of advertising expenditures yields additional sales revenue of $607.00 - 445.50 = \$161.50$. Yes.

10. Total costs are $TC = 1,000 + Q[15 + .01(Q)] + Q[575/Q + .10] = 1,575 + 15.10(Q) + .01(Q^2)$. $MC = dTC/dQ = 15.10 + .02(Q)$. With total revenue of $TR = 115(Q) - .005(Q^2)$, marginal revenue is $MR = dTR/dQ = 115 - .01(Q)$. Setting $MC = MR$ yields $15.10 + .02(Q) = 115 - .01(Q)$, so that $Q = 3,330$ and $p = 98.35$.

11. The additional \$4,000 in monthly advertising expenditures may be expected to render additional sales of $\$51.25 - 40.05 = \$10,200$. Therefore, with marginal revenue greater than marginal cost, the campaign should be undertaken.

12. With expenditures of $(1.01)(3.5)$, sales increase to \$40.18 for a gain of 0.32 percent. With expenditures of $(1.01)(7.5)$, sales increase to \$51.4 for a gain of 0.29 percent. Therefore, advertising elasticity of demand is currently $\epsilon_{A1} = .0032$ and falls to $\epsilon_{A2} = .0029$ with increased advertising expenditures.

Chapter 12

2. $FV = PV(1 + r)^7 = \$100(1.10)^7 = 100(1.95) = \$195$.

6. Let purchase price $= 100$, monthly storage cost $= 10$, and resale price

$= 200$. The present value of cash flows is $PV = -10/1.01 - 10/1.01^2 - 10/1.01^3 - 10/1.01^4 - 10/1.01^5 + 190/1.01^6 = 130.45$. The profitability index is $130.45/100 = 1.3045$.

7. $NPV = -15 + 1.7(2.4437) + 2.1(4.2305 - 2.4437) + 4.3(5.8892 - 4.2305) = -15 + 4.1543 + 3.7523 + 7.1324 = \$39,000$.

8.

Total revenues from sales: $315 + 58.5 + 51$ = 424.5 million a year
Annual lease charges: $10 + .05(424.5)$ = 31.225
Annual production costs: = 100.

Taxable income per year = 293.28
Less taxes at 40 percent = 117.31

Annual cash flow = 175.97
$NPV = -1,000 + 175.97(6.7101)$ = \$180.76 million.

9. $NPV = -1 - 1(3.8896) + (.65/.09)(.64993) = -.195661$. No.

10. $NPV = -1 - 1(3.8896) + [.65/(.09 - .01)](.64993) = .391081$. Yes.

11. The present value of 12 monthly payments of \$10,000 discounted at $r = .07$ is $PV = 10,000(11.558) = \$115,580$. Since the present value of paying the fine exceeds the cost of leasing anti-pollution equipment, the equipment should be purchased.

12. (1) $NPV = -7.5 + 1.3(.91743) + 1.8(.84168) + 2.7(.77218) + 5.1(.70845) + 6.3(.64993) = -7.5 + 12.71 = 5.21$ million.
(2) $PI = 12.71/7.5 = 1.69$.
(3) Internal rate of return $= r \approx .26$.
(4) Payback period $= 1.3 + 1.8 + 2.7 + 1.7 = 7.5$ and $1.7/6.3 = .27$. Therefore, payback period is 3.27 years.
(5) Average rate of return $= r_a = (17.2/5)/7.5 = .46 = 46$ percent.

13. $NPV = -9,500 + 800/(1 + .07/12)^{12} = -9,500 + 800(.9942 + .9884 + .9827 + .9770 + .9713 + .9657 + .9601 + .9545 + .9490 + .9435 + .9380 + .9326) = -9500 + 800(11.56) = -9,500 + 9,245.60 = -254.40$. No.

14. With $r = 8$, the value of the rate of return equation is $-5 - 5(.93) - 2.1(.86) + .772(.79) + .362(.74) + 6.46(.68) + 9.298(.63) = -5. + 4.70 < 0$. Testing for $r = 7\frac{1}{2}$, the rate of return equation is $-5. + 4.95 \approx 0$. Therefore, the rate of return is $r \approx 7\frac{1}{2}$ percent.

15. A ten-year bond selling for \$422.41 would have a return of $r = 9$ percent. Therefore, at \$400, the bonds are a better buy.

16. The contract arrangement requires an initial payment of \$50,000 and additional payments for each of the next four years. However, since the lease payment is tax deductible, it reduces taxes by $.4(50,000)$ for a net annual cost of $(1 - .4)(50,000) = \$30,000$. Therefore, the net present value of the lease is $NPV = -30,000 - 30,000(3.3121) = -\$129,363$. Purchase

of needed vans requires an initial outlay of $200,000. Monthly expenses for insurance and depreciation are $8,000 + ⅕(200,000 − 50,000) = 38,000 for tax savings of .4(38,000) = $15,200. Net annual cost is 38,000 − 15,200 = $22,800. However, since depreciation of $30,000 is positive cash flow, annual cash flow is $−22,800 + 30,000 = $7,200. The net present value of purchase is $NPV = −200,000 + 7,200(3.9927) + 50,000(.68058) = $−137,223.56. Leasing would be the lower-cost alternative.

Chapter 13

2. $.33[.18(1 − .4)] + .33(.12) + .33(.10) = 10.9$ percent.

4. Annual contribution = $.35 million + .15million = $.5 million. $F = .5[(1.12)^5 − 1/.12] = .5(6.35) = $3.18 million.

5. $C = (100/180)(.048) + (80/180)(.06) = .0533 = 5.33$ percent.

6. $P = 2.5[.07/(1.07)^5 − 1] = 2.5(.173891) = $434,726.74. The final value of the sinking fund will be:

$$434,726.74(1.07)^4 = 434,727(1.31) = 569.838.07$$
$$434,726.74(1.07)^3 = 434,727(1.23) = 532,558.94$$
$$434,726.74(1.07)^2 = 434,727(1.14) = 497,718.64$$
$$434,726.74(1.07)\ \ = 434,727(1.07) = 465,157.61$$
$$434,726.74 \qquad\qquad\qquad\quad\ \ = 434,726.74$$
$$\qquad\qquad\qquad\qquad\qquad\qquad\quad \$2,500,000.$$

7. $P = 3.7(.12/1 − 1.12^{-5}) = 3.7(.2774) = 1,026,416$. Interest payments are determined as follows:

	Annual payment	Interest payment	Payment on principal	Remaining principal
Year 1:	1,026,416	.12 × 3.7 = 444,000	1,026,416 − 444,000 = 582,416	3,700,000 − 582,416
				3,117,584
Year 2:	1,026,416	.12 × 3,117,584 = 374,110	1,026,416 − 374,110 = 652,306	3,117,584 − 652,306
				2,465,278
Year 3:	1,026,416	.12 × 2,465,278 = 295,833	1,026,416 − 295,833 = 730,583	2,465,278 − 730,583
				1,734,695
Year 4:	1,026,416	.12 × 1,734,695 = 208,163	1,026,416 − 208,163 = 818,253	1,734,695 − 818,253
				916,442
Year 5:	1,026,416	.12 × 916,442 = 109,973	1,026,416 − 109,973 = 916,442	916,442 − 916.442
				0

8. Rearrange the sinking fund formula to read: $P(1 + i)^n - Fi = P$. Then substitute: $500(1 + i)^{36} - 25,000i = 500$. Now solve by iterations. The interest rate is found to be $i = 1.8$. Therefore, the necessary annual interest return is $1.8(1 - .4) = 3$ percent.

9. Substitute and solve by iterations: $500(1.018)^n - 900 = 500$. The value of n is found to be 58 months.

10.

$n =$	$i = .5$	1	1.5	2	2.5	3
15	.0694	.0721	.0749	.0778	.0808	.0838
20	.0527	.0554	.0582	.0612	.0641	.0672
25	.0427	.0454	.0483	.0512	.0543	.0574
30	.0360	.0387	.0416	.0446	.0478	.0510
35	.0312	.0340	.0369	.0400	.0432	.0465

Chapter 14

4. Estimated value of return $= (.35)(9.4\%) + (.65)(7.8\%) = 8.36$ percent. Yes.

6.

Branch (1): $NPV = -\$35 + 15(.91743) + 21(.84168)$
$$+ \frac{21}{.09 - .05}(.77218) = \$401.83.$$

Branch (2): $NPV = -\$35 + 8(.91743) - 20(.84168)$
$$+ \frac{18}{.09 - .05}(.77218) = \$302.99.$$

Branch (3): $NPV = -\$35 + 8(.91743) - 20(.84168)$
$$+ \frac{13}{.09 - .05}(.77218) = \$206.46.$$

Branch (4): $NPV = -\$35 + 8(.91643) + 12(.84168)$
$$+ \frac{12}{.09 - .04}(.77218) = \$167.76.$$

The expected value of a decision to conduct the marketing campaign is $.6(\$302.99) + .4(206.46) = \$264.38$. Since this is greater than the expected value of a decision not to conduct the campaign ($\$167.76$), the campaign should be conducted. This makes the expected value of net present value for the expansion $evNPV = .5(\$401.83) + .5(264.38) = \$333.10$.

7. $(1,000 - 850)/135 = 1.11$ standard deviations. Probability is $.5000 - .3665 = .1335$.

8. The expected value is 9.44, and the standard deviation is 3.54. If the distribution has the characteristics of a normal distribution, two-thirds of the observations would fall within one standard deviation of expected value. It is true that 12 of the observations fall between 5.90 and 12.98. Moreover, 95 percent or 17 of the observations fall between 2.36 and 16.52.

9. $.30(.75) + .70(.40) = .51$.

Chapter 15

1. When competition is imperfect, price is not forced to the lowest level of average total cost, with plants built of optimum scale in the long run.

2. Diminishing marginal benefits from additional quantities cause the curve measuring benefits to slope downward. Increasing marginal costs from additional production cause the curve measuring costs to slope upward.

3. Horizontal integration applies to firms producing the same good or service. Vertical integration applies to firms that use the products of each other in further production.

5. Conglomerate integration enables a firm to use funds earned in one kind of production for expansion of other kinds of production. There are frequently difficulties in coordinating and controlling production. Also, for the economy as a whole, there are difficulties associated with large concentrations of economic power.

6. Monopolies may be achieved by technical or market advantages that exclude competition. Natural monopolies result from high capital requirements that make production by a single firm more efficient than production by many competing firms.

Chapter 16

4. The resources are $X = $ laboratory hours and $Y = $ classroom hours. The constraints define minimum output goals:

> For adults (A): $10X + 4Y \geq 500$,
> For children (B): $2X + 8Y \geq 400$,

and

For handicapped persons (C): $5X + 6Y \geq 600$.

The solutions table:

	X	Y	S_A	S_B	S_C		TC
(1)	50	0	0	300	350		
(2)	0	125	0	−600	−150	*	687.50
(3)	200	0	−1,500	0	−400	*	900.00
(4)	0	50	300	0	300		
(5)	120	0	−700	160	0		
(6)	0	100	100	−400	0		
(7)	33.33	41.67	0	0	183.33		
(8)	15	87.50	0	−330	0	*	548.75
(9)	85.71	28.57	−471.38	0	0	*	542.83

The school should plan 85.7 hours of laboratory time and 28.6 classroom hours for a total cost of $542.83 per day. With these resources the school will achieve its goals for instructing children and handicapped persons and instruct 240 more adults than required.

7. With $TC = 1,000,000 + 13,000(Q) - 10(Q^2) + .002(Q^3)$ and $TR = 1,000(Q) - .1(Q^2)$, economic profit is $\pi = -1,000,000 - 12,000(Q) + 9.9(Q^2) - .002(Q^3)$. The derivative of the economic profit function is $d\pi/dQ = -12,000 + 19.8(Q) - .006(Q^2)$. The derivative is equal to zero where $Q = 2,500$ and $Q = 800$. Substituting these values in the second derivative identifies the point of maximum economic profit (or minimum economic loss): $d\pi^2/dQ^2 = 19.8 - 0.012(Q)$. With $Q = 2,500$, the value of the second derivative is negative, indicating maximum economic profit.

8. Price is determined by $p = 1,000 - .1(2,500) = 750 = \$7.50$. Economic profit is determined by $\pi = -1,000,000 - 12,000(2,500) + 9.9(2,500^2) - .002 (2,500^3) = -375,000 = \$-3,570$ for each production.

9. With $TC = 1,000,000 + 13,000(Q) - 10(Q^2) + .002(Q^3)$, marginal cost is $MC = 13,000 - 20(Q) + .006(Q^2)$. Marginal cost is lowest where $dMC/dQ = -20 + .012 = 0$ and $d^2MC/dQ^2 > 0$. This is true where $Q = 1,666.67$.

10. With $TR = .9A^{.8}B^{.75}$, the ratio of marginal products is

$$\frac{\partial TP/\partial A}{\partial TP/\partial B} = \frac{.8B}{.75A}.$$

Setting the ratio of marginal products equal to the price ratio yields: $.8B/.75A = 10/12.50$ and $A = 1.33B$. Determining quantities by substitution in the total cost function gives us: $TC = A(p_A) + B(p_B) = (1.33B)(10) + B(12.50) = 50,000$, so that $B = 1,935.5$ and $A = 2,580.6$

11. $TP = .9(2,580.6^{.8})(1,935.5^{.75}) = 140,836$.

12. With $TP = .9A^{.88}B^{.75}$, $.88B/.75A = 10/12.5$, so that $A = 1.47B$. $TC = (1.47B)(10) + B(12.5) = 50,000$, so that $B = 1,840.5$, $A = 2,699.4$, and $TP = 264,518.5$.

Chapter 17

4. Market potential for A is the sum of $(500,000)(12,500)/8 + (750,000)(8,000)/3 = 2,781,250,000$. Market potential for B is $(500,000)(12,500)/5 + (750,000)(8,000)/10 = 1,850,000,000$. Location A has the greater market potential.

6. In A, using TP_1, $MP_L/MP_K = .8K/.4L = 5/8 = p_{LA}/p_{KA}$. Therefore, $6.4K = 2L$ and $L = 3.2K$. Substituting in TC for A: $TC = L(p_{LA}) + K(p_{KA}) = 1,000 = (3.2K)(5) + K(8)$. Therefore $K = 41.67$ and $L = 133.33$. In A, using TP_2, $.4K/.8L = 5/8$, so that $4L = 3.2K$ and $L = .8K$. Substituting in TC: $1,000 = (.8K)(5) + K(8)$, so that $K = 83.33$ and $L = 66.67$. In B, using TP_1: $.8K/.4L = 8/5$, so that $4K = 3.2L$ and $K = .8L$. Substituting this value in TC: $1,000 = L(8) + (.8L)(5)$ so that $L = 83.33$ and $K = 66.67$. In B, using TP_2, $.4K/.8L = 8/5$, so that $2K = 6.4L$ and $K = 3.2L$. Substituting this value in TC: $1,000 = L(8) + (3.2L)(5)$, so that $L = 41.67$ and $K = 133.33$. Now set up a table of quantities.

	TP₁		**TP₂**	
	L	**K**	**L**	**K**
A:	133.33	41.67	66.67	83.33
B:	83.33	66.67	41.67	133.33

TP_1 is shown to be the more labor-intensive and TP_2 the more capital-intensive, as indicated also by the exponents of the two resource variables.

7. With the quantities shown in the solution to Problem 6, total product is found to be:

	TP₁	**TP₂**
A:	245.06	203.05
B:	203.05	245.06

The labor-intensive production function yields higher total product in A, where the price of labor is lower, and the capital-intensive production in B, where the price of capital is lower.

8. Assume the following values for a one-year investment: $100 = 125/(1 + r)$, so that $r = MEI = 25$ percent. Now assume risk of $.90$ associated

with a cash flow of 125. The values in the formula change to $100 = .9(125)/(1 + r)$ so that $100(1 + r) = 112.5$. Solving for these values gives us: $r = MEI = .125 = 12.5$ percent.

Chapter 18

2. $1£ = \$1.49$, 1 Franc $= \$0.13$, 1 peso $= \$0.0065$, and 1 Yen $= \$.004167$

6. With a forward/spot ratio of $.00425/.00418 = 1.02$ and an interest rate ratio of $(1 + i_{US}/2)/(1 + i_Y/2) = 1.0048$, arbitrageurs would borrow dollars and purchase spot yen for lending and eventual forward sale. The gain on the forward transaction would be greater than the interest differential on the loans.

9. The 90-day interest differential is $\frac{4}{4} = 1$ percent. Therefore, the importer would pay $1.01(.48) = .4848 \approx \$0.485$ for forward marks. Higher interest rates in the United States mean that the importer would have to compensate for reserving a quantity of marks whose interest earnings are lower than the dollars used to reserve them.

Index